ALL ■ IN ■ ONE

CompTIA

Linux+™ Certification

EXAM GUIDE

(Exam XK0-004)

Ted Jordan
Sandor Strohmayer

New York Chicago San Francisco
Athens London Madrid Mexico City
Milan New Delhi Singapore Sydney Toronto

CompTIA Linux+™ Certification All-in-One Exam Guide (Exam XK0-004)

1 2 3 4 5 6 7 8 9 LCR 24 23 22 21 20

Library of Congress Control Number: 2019955326

ISBN 978-1-260-45734-6
MHID 1-260-45734-6

Sponsoring Editor
Amy Gray

Editorial Supervisor
Patty Mon

Project Editor
Laura Stone

Acquisitions Coordinators
Claire Yee, Emily Walters

Technical Editor
Kenneth Hess

Copy Editor
Bart Reed

Proofreader
Richard Camp

Indexer
Ted Laux

Production Supervisor
James Kussow

Composition
Cenveo® Publisher Services

Illustration
Cenveo Publisher Services

Art Director, Cover
Jeff Weeks

This book is dedicated to my parents, Gwendolyn and Theodore Jordan, who helped me find my passion for technology and teaching others "how to fish."

—Ted Jordan, MSc, Linux+, CISSP

This book is dedicated to the memory of my parents and grandparents, who let me understand by example how to respect all life, honor the rights of living things, and be the best that I can at any given time.

—Sandor Strohmayer

ABOUT THE AUTHORS

Ted Jordan (MSc, Linux+, CISSP) has over 25 years of UNIX, IRIX, Solaris, and Linux engineering experience. He studied coding and UNIX as a graduate student of the University of California, Berkeley and Kettering University. During Mr. Jordan's engineering career, he performed UNIX coding for General Motors, Silicon Graphics, Fakespace CAVE Virtual Reality, and Sun Microsystems. He is the Founder and President of successful tech startups, Funutation, Inc., and JordanTeam LLC, both providing Linux coding and education. He has taken and passed all Linux+ exams since 2001 and successfully trains hundreds of others to attain their Linux Certification. Follow him on Twitter and YouTube @JordanTeamLearn.

Sandor Strohmayer is a trainer and curriculum developer who has been teaching and writing Linux and UNIX training material for more than 20 years. Mr. Strohmayer began as a hardware and operating system instructor for Sun Microsystems. Since then he has developed and taught UNIX, Linux, and other training programs for schools, corporations, and the military, using study guides and blended learning techniques supplemented with individually paced learning via a learning management system. Mr. Strohmayer also offers study, Linux, and other IT hints on LinkedIn (www.linkedin.com/pub/sandor-strohmayer/4/702/765).

About the Technical and Developmental Editor

Kenneth "Ken" Hess is a practicing senior system administrator and a technology author, blogger, columnist, editor, and podcaster. Ken has written hundreds of technology articles on topics that cover Linux, open source software, Windows, Mac, mobile devices, databases, and cryptocurrencies. He also reviews technology products and is an avid photographer and filmmaker.

CONTENTS AT A GLANCE

CONTENTS

ACKNOWLEDGMENTS

Thank you to my wife, Cheryl, and my children, Theo and Aria, for allowing Daddy to toil, peacefully, in the basement, alone, to complete this work.

Also I would like to thank my Cass Technical High School teachers Mr. Max Green and Mr. Walter Downs, a Tuskegee Airman who felled 6½ enemy aircraft in WWII, for giving me my "serious fun" teaching style.

Dr. David "Doc" Green and Dr. Duane McKeachie of Kettering University showed me how to simplify difficult concepts for students.

Dr. Larry Stark and Dr. Masayoshi Tomizuka of the University of California at Berkeley introduced me to UNIX, which has taken me further than I imagined.

—Ted Jordan

I would like to thank the staff of McGraw-Hill for their belief, patience, kindness, and support.

I would like to thank you, the reader, for having faith in us and allowing us to be a part of your learning experience.

—Sandor Strohmayer

INTRODUCTION

Congratulations on your decision to become CompTIA Linux+ certified! By purchasing this book, you have taken the first step toward earning one of the hottest certifications around. Being CompTIA Linux+ certified provides you with a distinct advantage in today's IT job market. When you obtain your Linux+ certification, you prove to your employer, your coworkers, and yourself that you truly know your stuff with Linux.

The new CompTIA Linux+ exam, XK0-004, is an expanded version of the previous CompTIA Linux+ LX0-103 and LX0-104 exams. In addition to Linux, it covers some DevOps, virtualization, and cloud topics. The Linux portion of the test includes SELinux and other security topics as well as device management firewall and server commands used in a multiserver environment.

The XK0-004 exam is designed for those with at least nine months of administrative experience. The questions are multiple choice. You will also be expected to solve scenario-based questions. This will require a working knowledge of the test topics.

We first need to introduce you to the nuts and bolts of this book and the CompTIA Linux+ certification program. Let's take a look at the following topics:

- Who this book is for
- How to use this book
- How this book is organized
- Special features of the all-in-one certification series
- Becoming a CompTIA certified IT professional is easy
- The CompTIA Linux+ certification exam
- Tips for succeeding on the Linux+ certification exam
- Objective map: Exam LX0-004

Let's begin by discussing who this book is for.

Who This Book Is For

Before you start this book, you need to be aware that we have two primary goals in mind:

- To help you prepare for and pass the Linux+ exam offered by CompTIA
- To provide you with the extra skills and knowledge you need to be successful on the job after you are certified

How to Use This Book

We suggest you use the virtual machine image supplied with the book (see the Appendix for more details). Although it is a large download, the image contains everything you need to study for the test offline. The image is CentOS 7–based, but it also contains Docker images to review the material specifically related to Fedora, openSUSE, and Debian. We have also included an Ubuntu image. Each of these images may be opened by executing the command **fedora**, **opensuse**, **debian**, or **ubuntu**.

Prior to working with the image, make certain you have made a clone. Before experimenting, make a snapshot so if you mess up you can just roll it back. Don't be afraid to trash the image. That is what learning is about.

There are two users on the system: root and student1. To log in as root from the graphical interface, select Unlisted and then use the username root and the password **password**. To log in as student1, select student1 and supply the password **student1**.

We have also provided a directory called */LABS*. This directory contains lab files for specific chapters. Each chapter directory contains a *source* directory and a *work* directory. We suggest you practice with the copy in the *work* directory; if you make a mistake or want to start over, you can easily copy the original lab files from the *source* directory to the *work* directory.

As you are reading, use the Linux image to test what you have read. Read a section and then try the commands in the section. These actions will help you remember the material better and also improve your problem solving skills. If there is an exercise, do each step. Don't just complete the exercise—understand what each step does. Anticipate what your actions will affect and then verify results. If something unexpected happens, try to understand why, and try again. These activities will help you understand the material better. Don't be afraid to experiment.

There are instances in the exercises when we have not supplied all the steps. We are not trying to trick you. We want you to build your assessment skills that you will need on the test and in real life. Always ask, what do I have? What do I need? Don't be afraid to examine pertinent variable or parameter settings as well as related configuration files. If you are having difficulty, some exercises have hints at the end, and check out the videos provided in the online content.

Take your time studying. The object of the test is to certify you know what you are doing, not that you can pass a test. Rome wasn't built in a day. Take the time to prepare. If you can explain concepts, complete the exercises while understanding them, and discriminate why a question's answer is correct whereas other choices are incorrect, you are ready to take the test.

How This Book Is Organized

The CompTIA Linux+ exam objectives, as currently published, are organized by topic. They aren't organized into a logical instructional flow. As you read through this book, you'll quickly notice that we don't address the CompTIA Linux+ objectives in the same order as they are published by CompTIA. All the objectives are covered; however, we've reorganized them such that we start with the most basic Linux concepts first. Then, as we progress through the course, we'll address increasingly more advanced CompTIA Linux+ objectives, building on the skills and knowledge covered in preceding chapters.

The Objective Map that follows this introduction has been constructed to help you cross-reference the official exam objectives from CompTIA with the objectives as they are presented and covered in this book. References have been provided for each objective exactly as CompTIA presents it, and a chapter reference.

Special Features of the All-in-One Certification Series

To make our exam guides more useful and a pleasure to read, we have designed the All-in-One Certification series to include several conventions.

Icons

To alert you to an important bit of advice, a shortcut, or a pitfall, you'll occasionally see Notes, Tips, Cautions, and Exam Tips peppered throughout the text.

NOTE Notes offer nuggets of especially helpful stuff, background explanations, and information. They also define terms occasionally.

TIP Tips provide suggestions and nuances to help you learn to finesse your job. Take a tip from us and read the Tips carefully.

CAUTION When you see a Caution, pay special attention. Cautions appear when you have to make a crucial choice or when you are about to undertake something that may have ramifications you might not immediately anticipate. Read them now so that you don't have regrets later.

EXAM TIP Exam Tips give you special advice or may provide information specifically related to preparing for the exam itself.

End-of-Chapter Reviews and Questions

An important part of this book comes at the end of each chapter, where you will find a brief review of the main points, along with a series of questions followed by the answers to those questions. Each question is in multiple-choice format.

The questions are provided as a study aid to you, the reader and prospective CompTIA Linux+ exam taker. We cannot guarantee that if you answer all of our questions correctly you will absolutely pass the certification exam. But we can guarantee that the questions will provide you with an idea about how ready you are for the exam.

Online Content

This book comes with access to a companion website that includes virtual machine files you can download and use to set up your very own Linux system to practice with. It also includes video clips from the authors demonstrating some of the exercises you'll find within the book's chapters, as well as TotalTester practice exams to prepare you for the real certification exam. Read more about the online content and how to access it in the Appendix.

NOTE Some of the figures in the book were too large to fit the book's format. We have placed those figures online.

The CompTIA Linux+ Certification Exam

Now that you understand how this book is organized, it's time for you to become familiar with the CompTIA Linux+ certification program and the associated exam. Let's review the following topics:

- About the CompTIA Linux+ certification
- Taking the CompTIA Linux+ exam

About the CompTIA Linux+ Certification

The CompTIA Linux+ certification is an excellent program! It is a vendor-neutral certification designed and administered by the Computing Technology Industry Association, affectionately known as CompTIA.

The CompTIA Linux+ certification is considered "vendor neutral" because the exam is not based on one specific vendor's hardware or software. This is somewhat unique in the information technology industry. Many IT certification programs are centered on one particular vendor's hardware or software, such as those from Microsoft, Cisco, SUSE, or Red Hat.

The CompTIA Linux+ certification, on the other hand, is designed to verify your knowledge and skills with the Linux operating system in general, not on any one particular distribution. The following is according to CompTIA:

> *CompTIA Linux+ is a high-stakes, vendor-neutral certification that validates the fundamental knowledge and skills required of junior Linux administrators.... Candidate job roles include junior Linux administrator, junior network administrator, systems administrator, Linux database administrator and web administrator. Companies such as Dell, HP, IBM, Lenovo and Xerox recommend or require CompTIA Linux+.*

CompTIA has published objectives for the exam that define the CompTIA Linux+ certification. These objectives specify what a Linux system administrator should know and be able to do. You can view the CompTIA Linux+ objectives at https://certification.comptia.org/. To be CompTIA Linux+ certified, you have to be able to do the tasks contained in these objectives.

Taking the Linux+ Exam

The Linux+ exam is a timed exam and delivered electronically on a computer. The exam is composed of 90 questions and must be completed within 90 minutes. (A countdown timer is provided in the upper-right corner of the screen.)

NOTE You might actually see fewer than 90 questions on the exam because scenario questions carry more weight. The more scenario questions on the exam, the fewer total questions provided.

The exam interface is fairly straightforward. Items are displayed one at a time on the screen. You are presented with a question along with a series of responses. You mark the appropriate response and then go to the next question. You are allowed to go back to questions that you've marked for review.

Each exam is composed primarily of multiple-choice items. Most of the multiple-choice questions require only one answer; however, some will require the selection of multiple correct responses. If you forget to select one, the exam will warn you that your answer is incomplete.

After you complete the exam, the computer will immediately evaluate it and your score will be printed out. To pass, you need a minimum score of 720 points out of a possible 900. If you do not pass, your score printout will list the objectives where you missed questions. You can use this information to review and prepare yourself to retake the exam.

To make the exam globally available, CompTIA administers the CompTIA Linux+ exam through its testing partner, Pearson VUE (home.pearsonvue.com).

To sign up for the CompTIA Linux+ exam, visit the CompTIA website (store.comptia.org) and purchase an exam voucher. Then visit the Pearson VUE website and locate a testing center near you. Just specify the exam you want to take and your local information. You will then be provided with a list of testing centers near you, as shown in Figure 1.

Then use the Pearson VUE website to schedule the exam and submit the exam voucher. You can also call the test provider directly and schedule the exam over the phone. Be aware that they will need to verify your identity, so be prepared to share your Social Security or National ID number. The test provider will send you a confirmation e-mail listing the time and location of your exam.

On the day of the test, be sure to allow adequate travel time. You never know when you will run into a traffic jam or your car will break down. Try to show up early. If you are taking your exam at a community college, you may have to walk a very long distance to reach the exam.

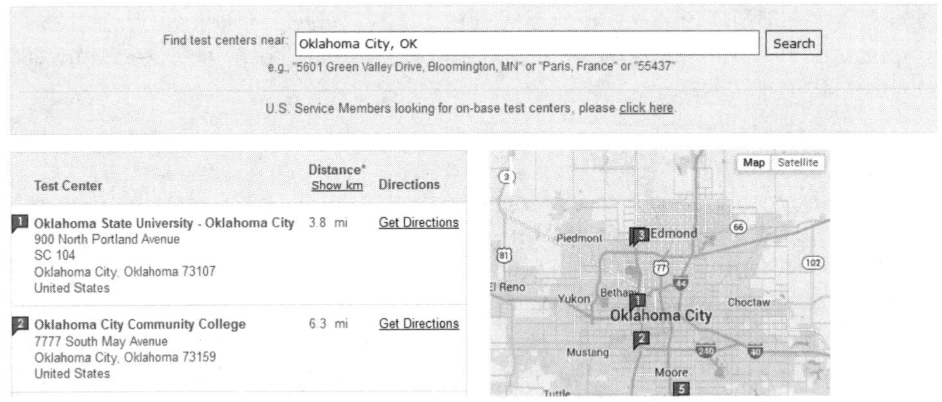

Figure 1 Locating a testing center near you

When you check in at the testing center, you will be required to show *two* forms of original, unexpired identification, at least *one* of which must have your photo on it. The following are acceptable forms of ID:

- Driver's license
- Passport
- Social Security card or National ID card
- Signed credit card
- Common Access Card
- Personal identity verification card
- Military ID card
- NEXUS card
- State-issued ID card

When you check in, you must surrender your phone, tablet, keys, wallet, reference materials, and so on to the test proctor, who will place them in a locker. The center may inspect your eyeglasses for cameras. You are not allowed to take any materials into the exam room, including blank paper. Most testing centers will provide note-taking materials that remain in the room after the exam is completed.

Tips for Succeeding on the CompTIA Linux+ Certification Exam

Over the last decade, we have helped hundreds prepare for a variety of certification exams. As a result, we have learned several tips to help you pass the exam.

The most important things you can do are to thoroughly study and practice. No tip, trick, or strategy can compensate for a lack of study and practice. The goal is to move the information into your long-term memory. Here are some study tips to help you prepare.

Preparing for the Exam

- Set a daily study appointment. Start slow and build. Start with a half hour a day, and work up to an hour session twice a day if possible. (Studying two hours in a row is not productive.). Remember to keep this appointment just as you would any other important appointment. If you miss an appointment don't worry, just don't miss the next one. Don't study more than two one-hour sessions per day.
- If you are studying after work, give yourself a chance to wind down. Try taking a shower and changing clothes. Maybe take a walk or spend some time listening to music. If you are hungry, eat light and healthy. Avoid watching video games or television before you study.
- Your study environment should be well lit and uncluttered. Turn off the telephone. Have everything you need to study within your study environment. Once you sit down to study, stay there.
- Use flashcards and mind maps. These are great study tools. For more information on how flashcards can help, view the information found on the Mnemosyne Project website (https://mnemosyne-proj.org/).
- Good health is important for successful study. Make time to get exercise and rest for best performance. You do not need to go to a gym; try walking after lunch and dinner. Television, video games, and cell phones interfere with study and sleep hours long after you have turned them off.
- Study in manageable chunks. After you have read a section, when possible, use the virtual machine image to validate what you studied. Make flashcards and mind maps to help retain that section's material, and use these tools for future study.
- When you come to a quiz or chapter exam, don't blow through it. Use the opportunity to learn how to evaluate a question. Make certain you understand why the correct answer or answers are correct and the other answers are incorrect.
- When you do the labs, understand what each command does and how and where to test the results. Before you execute a command, determine what settings or configuration files will affect the command. Using this methodology will help you in real life and when breaking down questions. Get into the habit of executing a command and then testing the results.
- Some recommend setting a deadline by scheduling your exam in advance. We can't recommend this strategy for everyone. Scheduling the test can be productive or counterproductive. Setting a 30- or 60-day deadline may put unnecessary pressure on you, especially if you find a chapter that is giving you problems.

We have seen success with the tortoise approach: slow and steady. If you are truly motivated to accomplish your goal, you will. Use your motivation to keep your study appointments. When you are ready to take the test, schedule the exam.

If, however, you are the type of person who thrives under a deadline, go ahead and schedule the exam.

Close to the Exam Date

- Continue to use your flashcards and mind maps to review the material.
- Familiarize yourself with what 60 seconds of time passing feels like. During the test, the worst thing you can do is get stuck on a question. Use a timer to get used to 60-second intervals. When taking the test, if you can't answer a question within 60 seconds, mark the question to return to later.
- Practice evaluating questions. Write down key points or create a simple diagram.
- Pretend you are teaching the material. Try to explain the material in a section. If you can explain it, you know it.
- Use the virtual machine image and apply the knowledge you have learned.

The Night Before Your Exam

- Don't study.
- Place all the paperwork you will need for the exam in one place.
- Get a good night's rest.
- Set your alarm to allow plenty of time in the morning to get ready and go to the testing center.

Taking the Exam

- *Evaluate the question.* Determine what the question is asking. Break out the question into what information is pertinent and what is fluff. Determine how you would solve the problem. Here's an example:

    1. User student1 wants to copy a file in the subdirectory */public/test* to the directory */data*. User student1 does not own either of the parent directories, */public* or */data*, but is a member of the group that is the group owner for all directories. The group has read and execute permissions for all directories. What command will enable student1 to copy the file from */public/test* to */data*?

       To answer the question you must be familiar with which permissions are necessary to copy a file from one directory to another. To copy the file you need execute permissions on the source directory and write and execute permissions on the target directory.

The question tells you that the student1 is a member of the group that has group ownership of all directories and the group has read and execute permissions.

What is missing? student1 cannot write the file to the target directory, */data*, because the group student1 belongs to only has read and execute permissions.

What is required? The group owners need write permissions on directory */data*.

Now you can look for the answer or answers that will apply write permissions to the directory */data*.

- *Visually assess the question*. You can use the writing materials given to you to. As you had practiced earlier, write down key points or create a simple diagram. This might seem like a waste of time, but visual clues can help bring back memory. Your brain stores and relates to data in memory based on context.
- *Read each answer carefully*. Use the information from your assessment to determine if an answer satisfies the question's requirements. Eliminate the obviously incorrect answers first.
- *Make your best choice and move on*. From experience, we know that your first impression is usually the correct one.
- *Don't spend more than 60 seconds on a question*. If you pass 60 seconds, mark it so you may return to it and move on.
- *Your first answer is usually correct*. If you are concerned about a question, mark it for review and return to it later, but your first answer is usually correct.

After you finish the exam, your results will be automatically printed out for you. The report will be embossed with their CompTIA-certified examiner seal by your test proctor to certify the results. Don't lose this report; it is the only hard copy you will have until you receive your certification in the mail.

The report will display your performance on each section of the exam. The CompTIA Linux+ exam is pass/fail. Based on the information available upon publication of this book, if you score 720 or better, you pass!

If you don't pass, you can use the information on your report to identify the areas where you need to study. You can retake the exam immediately if you wish. However, there are two things to keep in mind:

- You have to pay full price for the retake exam (although you can find discount coupons via a quick online search).
- The retake exam probably will not be the same as your first exam.

If you don't pass the second exam, you must wait at least 14 days before taking the exam a third time.

If you fail with a score of 650 or higher, we suggest you study up on the items missed and schedule your retake within a day or two. If you wait any longer than that, your memory will probably go "cold," and you may need to go through the entire preparation process again.

EXAM TIP Avoid TNC failure! CompTIA provides you 28 minutes to read the "Terms and Conditions" (TNC) of the exam. If you do *not* select ACCEPT within that time period, *whether you have finished reading the terms or not,* the screen defaults to "Denied Acceptance of Terms," the exam shuts down, and your test voucher is "burned." No refunds. No voucher reuse. You must spend another $320. Therefore, be sure to read the TNC at the CompTIA website, if desired, before you take the exam.

Objective Map: Exam XK0-004

The following table cross-references the official exam objectives with the chapters where they are covered in this book.

Official Exam Objective	Chapter No.
1.0 Hardware and System Configuration	
1.1 Explain Linux boot process concepts.	11
Boot loaders	11
GRUB	11
GRUB2	11
Boot options	11
UEFI/EFI	11
PXE	11
NFS	11
Boot from ISO	11
Boot from HTTP/FTP	11
File locations	11
/etc/default/grub	11
/etc/grub2.cfg	11
/boot	11
/boot/grub	11
/boot/grub2	11
/boot/efi	11
Boot modules and files	11
Commands	11
mkinitrd	11
dracut	11
grub2-install	11
grub2-mkconfig	11

Official Exam Objective	Chapter No.
initramfs	11
efi files	11
vmlinuz	11
vmlinux	11
Kernel panic	11
1.2 Given a scenario, install, configure, and monitor kernel modules.	10
Commands	10
lsmod	10
insmod	10
modprobe	10
modinfo	10
dmesg	10
rmmod	10
depmod	10
Locations	10
/usr/lib/modules/[kernelversion]	10
/usr/lib/modules	10
/etc/modprobe.conf	10
/etc/modprobe.d/	10
1.3 Given a scenario, configure and verify network connection parameters.	14, 15, 16, 17, 19
Diagnostic tools	14, 15, 16, 19
ping	14, 15, 16, 19
netstat	14, 15, 19
nslookup	14, 19
dig	14, 15, 19
host	14
route	14
ip	14
ethtool	14
ss	14
iwconfig	14
nmcli	14
brctl	15
nmtui	14
Configuration files	14
/etc/sysconfig/network-scripts/	14
/etc/sysconfig/network	14
/etc/hosts	14
/etc/network	14
/etc/nsswitch.conf	14
/etc/resolv.conf	14
/etc/netplan	17

Official Exam Objective	Chapter No.
/etc/sysctl.conf	14
/etc/dhcp/dhclient.conf	14, 19
Bonding	15
Aggregation	15
Active/passive	15
Load balancing	15
1.4 Given a scenario, manage storage in a Linux environment.	5, 7, 8, 19
Basic partitions	8
Raw devices	8
GPT	7, 8
MBR	7, 8
File system hierarchy	5, 7
Real file systems	7
Virtual file systems	7
Relative paths	5
Absolute paths	5
Device mapper	8
LVM	8
mdadm	8
Multipath	7
Tools	7, 8, 19
XFS tools	7, 19
LVM tools	8
EXT tools	7
Commands	7, 8, 19
mdadm	8
fdisk	7, 8
parted	7
mkfs	8
iostat	19
df	7, 19
du	7
mount	7, 8
umount	7, 8
lsblk	7
blkid	7
dumpe2fs	19
resize2fs	8
fsck	7
tune2fs	7
e2label	7

Official Exam Objective	Chapter No.
Location	7, 8
/etc/fstab	7, 8
/etc/crypttab	7
/dev/	7
/dev/mapper	7
/dev/disk/by-	7
id	7
uuid	7
path	7
multipath	7
/etc/mtab	7
/sys/block	7
/proc/partitions	7
/proc/mounts	7
File system types	7
ext3	7
ext4	7
xfs	7
nfs	7
smb	7
cifs	7
ntfs	7
1.5 Compare and contrast cloud and virtualization concepts and technologies.	15, 18
Templates	18
VM	18
OVA	18
OVF	18
JSON	18
YAML	18
Container images	18
Bootstrapping	18
Cloud-init	18
Anaconda	18
Kickstart	18
Storage	18
Thin vs. thick provisioning	18
Persistent volumes	18
Blob	18
Block	18

Official Exam Objective	**Chapter No.**
Network considerations	15
Bridging	15
Overlay networks	15
NAT	14
Local	15
Dual-homed	15
Types of hypervisors	18
Tools	18
libvirt	18
virsh	18
vmm	18
1.6 Given a scenario, configure localization options.	3, 19, 20
File locations	3, 20
/etc/timezone	3, 20
/usr/share/zoneinfo	3, 20
Commands	3, 20
localectl	3, 19
timedatectl	3, 20
date	3, 20
hwclock	3
Environment variables	3, 20
LC_*	3, 20
LC_ALL	3, 20
LANG	3, 20
TZ	3, 20
Character sets	3, 20
UTF-8	3, 20
ASCII	3, 20
Unicode	3, 20
2.0 Systems Operation and Maintenance	
2.1 Given a scenario, conduct software installations, configurations, updates, and removals.	8, 10
Package types	10
.rpm	10
.deb	10
.tar	8
.tgz	8
.gz	8
Installation tools	10
RPM	10
Dpkg	10

Official Exam Objective	**Chapter No.**
APT	10
YUM	10
DNF	10
Zypper	10
Build tools	10
Commands	10
make	10
make install	10
ldd	10
Compilers	10
Shared libraries	10
Repositories	10
Configuration	10
Creation	10
Syncing	10
Locations	10
Acquisition commands	10
wget	10
curl	10
2.2 Given a scenario, manage users and groups.	3, 4, 7, 16
Creation	4
useradd	4
groupadd	4
Modification	4, 16
usermod	4
groupmod	4
passwd	4
chage	16
Deletion	4
userdel	4
groupdel	4
Queries	4
id	4
whoami	4
who	4
w	4
last	4
Quotas	7
User quota	7
Group quota	7

Official Exam Objective	**Chapter No.**
Profiles	3
Bash parameters	3
User entries	3
.bashrc	3
.bash_profile	3
.profile	3
Global entries	3
/etc/bashrc	3
/etc/profile.d/	3
/etc/skel	3
/etc/profile	3
Important files and file contents	4
/etc/passwd	4
/etc/group	4
/etc/shadow	4
2.3 Given a scenario, create, modify, and redirect files.	2, 3, 5, 13, 15, 16
Text editors	2
nano	2
vi	2
File readers	5, 13
grep	5
cat	13
tail	13
head	13
less	13
more	13
Output redirection	3
<	3
>	3
|	3
<<	3
>>	3
2>	3
&>	3
stdin	3
stdout	3
stderr	3
/dev/null	3
/dev/tty	3
xargs	5
tee	3
Here documents	3

Official Exam Objective	Chapter No.
Text processing	3, 5, 13, 16
grep	5
tr	13
echo	3
sort	13
awk	13
sed	13
cut	13
printf	16
egrep	5
wc	13
paste	13
File and directory operations	3, 5, 15
touch	5
mv	5
cp	5
rm	5
scp	15
ls	3
rsync	15
mkdir	5
rmdir	5
ln	5
Symbolic (soft)	5
Hard	5
unlink	5
inodes	5
find	5
locate	5
grep	5
which	5
whereis	5
diff	5
updatedb	5
2.4 Given a scenario, manage services.	3, 7, 9, 11, 14
Systemd management	11
Systemctl	11
Enabled	11
Disabled	11
Start	11
Stop	11
Mask	11

Official Exam Objective	Chapter No.
Restart	11
Status	11
Daemon-reload	11
Systemd-analyze blame	11
Unit files	3, 7, 11, 14
Directory Locations	11
Environment parameters	3
Targets	11
hostnamectl	14
Automount	7
SysVinit	9, 11
chkconfig	11
on	11
off	11
level	11
Runlevels	9, 11
Definitions of 0–6	11
/etc/init.d	11
/etc/rc.d	11
/etc/rc.local	11
/etc/inittab	11
Commands	11
runlevel	11
telinit	11
Service	11
Restart	11
Status	11
Stop	11
Start	11
Reload	11
2.5 Summarize and explain server roles.	14
NTP	14
SSH	14
Web	14
Certificate authority	14
Name server	14
DHCP	14
File servers	14
Authentication server	14
Proxy	14
Logging	14
Containers	14

Official Exam Objective	Chapter No.
VPN	14
Monitoring	14
Database	14
Print server	14
Mail server	14
Load balancer	14
Clustering	14
2.6 Given a scenario, automate and schedule jobs.	9
cron	9
at	9
crontab	9
fg	9
bg	9
&	9
kill	9
Ctrl+c	9
Ctrl+z	9
nohup	9
2.7 Explain the use and operation of Linux devices.	
Types of devices	
Client devices	12
Bluetooth	12
WiFi	12
USB	12
Monitors	12
GPIO	12
Network adapters	12
PCI	12
HBA	12
SATA	12
SCSI	12
Printers	12
Video	12
Audio	12
Monitoring and configuration tools	12
lsdev	12
lsusb	12
lspci	12
lsblk	12
dmesg	12
lpr	12
lpq	12

Official Exam Objective	Chapter No.
abrt	12
CUPS	12
udevadm	12
add	12
reload-rules	12
control	12
trigger	12
File locations	7, 12, 20
/proc	12
/sys	12
/dev	12
/dev/mapper	7
/etc/X11	20
Hot pluggable devices	12
/usr/lib/udev/rules.d (System rules - Lowest priority)	12
/run/udev/rules.d (Volitile Rules)	12
/etc/udev/rules.d (Local Administration - Highest priority)	12
/etc/udev/rules.d	12
2.8 Compare and contrast Linux graphical user interfaces.	3, 20
Servers	3, 20
Wayland	20
X11	3
GUI	20
Gnome	20
Unity	20
Cinnamon	20
MATE	20
KDE	20
Remote desktop	20
VNC	20
XRDP	20
NX	20
Spice	20
Console redirection	20
SSH port forwarding	20
Local	20
Remote	20
X11 forwarding	20
VNC	20
Accessibility	20

Official Exam Objective	Chapter No.
3.0 Security	
3.1 Given a scenario, apply or acquire the appropriate user and/or group permissions and ownership.	6, 9, 16
File and directory permissions	6
Read, write, execute	6
User, group, other	6
SUID	6
Octal notation	6
umask	6
Sticky bit	6
SGID	6
Inheritance	6
Utilities	6
chmod	6
chown	6
chgrp	6
getfacl	6
setfacl	6
ls	6
ulimit	16
chage	16
Context-based permissions	16
SELinux configurations	16
disabled	16
permissive	16
enforcing	16
SELinux policy	16
targeted	16
SELinux tools	16
setenforce	16
getenforce	16
sestatus	16
setsebool	16
getsebool	16
chcon	16
restorecon	16
ls -Z	16
ps -Z	16
AppArmor	16
aa-disable	16
aa-complain	16

Official Exam Objective	Chapter No.
aa-unconfined	16
/etc/apparmor.d/	16
/etc/apparmor.d/tunables	16
Privilege escalation	6, 16
su	6
sudo	6, 16
wheel	6
visudo	16
sudoedit	16
User types	4
Root	4
Standard	4
Service	4
3.2 Given a scenario, configure and implement appropriate access and authentication methods.	15, 16, 19
PAM	16
Password policies	16
LDAP integration	16
User lockouts	16
Required, optional, or sufficient	16
/etc/pam.d/	16
pam_tally2	16
faillock	16
SSH	15
~/.ssh/	15
known_hosts	15
authorized_keys	15
config	15
id_rsa	15
id_rsa.pub	15
User-specific access	15
TCP wrappers	15
/etc/ssh/	15
ssh_config	15
sshd_config	15
SSH-copy-id	15
SSH-keygen	15
SSH-add	15
TTYs	19
/etc/securetty	19
/dev/tty#	19

Official Exam Objective	Chapter No.
PTYs	19
PKI	15
Self-signed	15
Private keys	15
Public keys	15
Hashing	15
Digital signatures	15
Message digest	15
VPN as a client	15
SSL/TLS	15
Transport mode	15
Tunnel mode	15
IPSec	15
DTLS	15
3.3 Summarize security best practices in a Linux environment.	7, 15, 16, 19
Boot security	16
Boot loader Password	16
UEFI/BIOS Password	16
Additional authentication methods	15
Multifactor authentication	16
Tokens	15
Hardware	15
Software	15
OTP	15
Biometrics	16
RADIUS	15
TACACS+	15
LDAP	15
Kerberos	15
kinit	15
klist	15
Importance of disabling root login via SSH	15
Password-less login	15
Enforce use of PKI	15
Chroot jail services	19
No shared IDs	15
Importance of denying hosts	15
Separation of OS data from application data	7
Disk partition to maximize system availability	7
Change default ports	15

Official Exam Objective	Chapter No.
Importance of disabling or uninstalling unused and unsecure services	15
FTP	15
Telnet	15
Finger	15
Sendmail	16
Postfix	16
Importance of enabling SSL/TLS	15
Importance of enabling auditd	16
CVE monitoring	19
Discouraging use of USB devices	12
Disk encryption	7
LUKS	7
Restrict cron access	19
Disable Ctrl+Alt+Del	16
Add banner	19
MOTD	16
3.4 Given a scenario, implement logging services.	16
Key file locations	16
/var/log/secure	16
/var/log/messages	16
/var/log/[application]	16
/var/log/kern.log	16
Log management	16
Third-party agents	16
logrotate	16
/etc/rsyslog.conf	16
journald	16
journalctl	16
lastb	16
3.5 Given a scenario, implement and configure Linux firewalls.	15
Access control lists	15
Source	15
Destination	15
Ports	15
Protocol	15
Logging	15
Stateful vs. stateless	15
Accept	15
Reject	15
Drop	15
Log	15

Official Exam Objective	Chapter No.
Technologies	15
firewalld	15
Zones	15
Run time	15
iptables	15
Persistency	15
Chains	15
ufw	15
/etc/default/ufw	15
/etc/ufw/	15
Netfilter	15
IP forwarding	15
/proc/sys/net/ipv4/ip_forward	15
/proc/sys/net/ipv6/conf/all/forwarding	15
Dynamic rule sets	15
DenyHosts	15
Fail2ban	15
IPset	15
Common application firewall configurations	15
/etc/services	15
Privileged ports	15
3.6 Given a scenario, backup, restore, and compress files.	8, 9, 15
Archive and restore utilities	8
tar	8
cpio	8
dd	8, 9, 15
Compression	8
gzip	8
xz	8
bzip2	8
zip	8
Backup types	8
Incremental	8
Full	8
Snapshot clones	8
Differential	8
Image	8
Off-site/off-system storage	15
SFTP	15
SCP	15
rsync	15

Official Exam Objective	**Chapter No.**
Integrity checks	15
MD5	15
SHA	15
4.0 Linux Troubleshooting and Diagnostics	
4.1 Given a scenario, analyze system properties and remediate accordingly.	7, 8, 14, 15, 19
Network monitoring and configuration	19
Latency	19
Bandwidth	19
Throughput	19
Routing	19
Saturation	19
Packet Drop	19
Timeouts	19
Name resolution	19
Localhost vs. Unix socket	19
Adapters	19
RDMA drivers	19
Interface configurations	19
Commands	15
nmap	15
netstat	15
iftop	19
route	14
iperf	19
tcpdump	15
ipset	15
Wireshark	15
tshark	15
netcat	14
traceroute	14, 19
mtr	14
arp	14
nslookup	14
dig	14
host	14
whois	14
ping	14, 15
nmcli	14
ip	14
tracepath	19

Official Exam Objective	Chapter No.
Storage monitoring and configuration	19
iostat	19
ioping	19
IO scheduling	19
cfq	19
noop	19
deadline	19
du	8
df	8
LVM tools	8
fsck	7
partprobe	7
CPU monitoring and configuration	19
/proc/cpuinfo	19
uptime	19
loadaverage	19
sar	19
sysctl	19
Memory monitoring and configuration	19
swapon	19
swapoff	19
mkswap	19
vmstat	19
Out of memory killer	19
free	15, 19
/proc/meminfo	19
Buffer cache output	19
Lost root password	19
Single User mode	19
4.2 Given a scenario, analyze system processes in order to optimize performance.	9, 14, 15, 19
Process management	9
Process states	9
Zombie	9
Uninterruptible sleep	9
Interruptible sleep	9
Running	9
Priorities	9
Kill signals	9
Commands	9
nice	9
renice	9

Official Exam Objective	Chapter No.
top	9
time	19
ps	9
lsof	14, 15
pgrep	9
pkill	9
PIDs	9
4.3 Given a scenario, analyze and troubleshoot user issues.	3, 6, 7, 19
Permissions	19
File	19
Directory	19
Access	19
Local	19
Remote	19
Authentication	19
Local	19
External	19
Policy violations	19
File creation	
Quotas	7
Storage	19
Inode exhaustion	19
Immutable files	6
Insufficient privileges for authorization	19
SELinux violations	19
Environment and shell issues	3
4.4 Given a scenario, analyze and troubleshoot application and hardware issues.	6, 8, 10, 11, 16, 19
SELinux context violations	16
Storage	8
Degraded Storage	8
Missing devices	8
Missing volumes	8
Missing mount point	8
Performance issues	8
Resource exhaustion	8
Adapters	8
SCSI	8
RAID	8
SATA	8
HBA	12
/sys/class/scsi_host/host#/scan	12

Official Exam Objective	Chapter No.
Storage integrity	8
Bad blocks	8
Firewall	19
Restrictive ACLs	19
Blocked Ports	19
Blocked protocols	19
Permission	6
Ownership	6
Executables	6
Inheritance	6
Service accounts	6
Group memberships	6
Dependencies	11
Patching	11
Update issues	11
Versioning	10
Libraries	10
Environment variables	11
GCC compatibility	11
Repositories	10
Troubleshooting additional hardware issues	19
Memory	19
Printers	19
Video	19
GPU drivers	19
Communications Ports	19
USB	19
Keyboard mapping	19
Hardware or software compatibility issues	19
Commands	19
dmidecode	19
lshw	19
5.0 Automation and Scripting	
5.1 Given a scenario, deploy and execute basic BASH scripts.	3, 6, 9, 13
Shell environments and shell variables	3
PATH	3
Global	3
Local	3
export	3
env	3
set	3

Official Exam Objective	**Chapter No.**
printenv	3
echo	3
#!/bin/bash	13
Sourcing scripts	13
Directory and file permissions	6, 13
chmod	6, 13
Extensions	9
Commenting	3
#	3
File globbing	3
Shell expansions	13
${}	13
$()	13
\` \`	13
Redirection and piping	3
Exit codes	13
stderr	13
stdin	13
stdout	13
Metacharacters	3
Positional parameters	13
Looping constructs	13
while	13
for	13
until	13
Conditional statements	13
if	13
case	13
Escaping characters	3, 13
5.2 Given a scenario, carry out version control using Git.	17
Arguments	17
clone	17
push	17
pull	17
commit	17
merge	17
branch	17
log	17
init	17
config	17

Official Exam Objective	Chapter No.
Files	17
.gitignore	17
.git/	17
5.3 Summarize orchestration processes and concepts.	17
Agent	17
Agentless	17
Procedures	17
Attributes	17
Infrastructure automation	17
Infrastructure as code	17
Inventory	17
Automated configuration management	17
Build automation	17

CHAPTER 1

An Introduction to Linux and a Pre-Assessment Exam

In this chapter, you will learn about

- A brief history of Linux
- Linux operating system structure
- Distributions
- Common Linux implementations

A Brief History of Linux

To understand Linux and its different distributions, you need to understand what was going on in the world of computing when Linus Torvalds began developing the Linux kernel. The 1950s saw the evolution of computers from single-user, single-task systems to batch processing systems.

Batch Processing

Batch processing is the sequential execution of programs. A programmer would submit a program on punch cards or paper tape to a system operator. The system operator would later "run" the job and give the results back to the programmer. Unfortunately, a programming error, typing error, damaged card (or tape), or card out of sequence would cause the program to fail. The programmer would have to repair the difficulty and resubmit the job.

ARPA/DARPA

On October 4, 1957, the Soviet Union launched Sputnik. The launch had many people wondering if the United States was falling behind technically. At that time, the Army, Navy, and Air Force had their own defense development projects. The rivalries between the services were unproductive and wasteful. President Eisenhower asked members of his Science Advisory Committee to meet with Defense Secretary to find a solution to the problem. The scientists' solution was to have a single civilian agency to control research and development and report to the Secretary of Defense.

Six months after the establishment of the Advanced Research Projects Agency (ARPA), NASA was created to separate civilian and military space travel. In 1972, ARPA's name was changed to DARPA (the Defense Advanced Research Projects Agency).

Compatible Time-Sharing System

Batch processing could not keep up with the increasing demand for computer resources. MIT was one of several colleges that began to develop time-sharing systems. Time-sharing allows multiple users to access system resources concurrently through remote terminals. MIT developed an experimental time-sharing system called CTSS (Compatible Time Sharing System). The CTSS project produced the following applications that were later used in UNIX development.

- **RUNOFF** A text formatting and printing utility that was the predecessor of roff, groff, nroff, and troff.
- **RUNCOM (run commands)** One of the first applications for running scripts. The *rc* directories in directory are named after RUNCOM scripts.

MULTICS

In 1964, MIT, General Electric, and Bell Labs began the development of the Multiplexed Information and Computing Service (MULTICS) operating system. Much of the initial funding was provided by DARPA. The goals for MULTICS were as follows:

- Remote terminal use
- Continuous operation
- Wide range of configuration capabilities that could be dynamically varied without changes to the operating system or user method of operation
- A high reliability internal file system
- Selective sharing of specific information among specific users
- Hierarchical structures of information for system administration
- Support for a wide range of applications executing concurrently
- A system that can evolve with changes in technology and user requirements

The project's scope presented many difficulties, and consequently schedule delays. In 1968, ARPA considered removing funding for the project.

Bell Labs had joined the project to obtain a time-sharing system for itself. The company was paying the rent for the GE computer used by the project and the provided personnel. Bell Labs withdrew from the project in April 1969, believing there was a large amount of work to do and not wanting to invest any more resources.

GE sold its computer business to Honeywell in 1970. Honeywell and MIT completed MULTICS and launched the first commercial version in October 1969. MULTICS remained a viable operating system for 25 years.

UNIX

Computer scientists Ken Thompson and Dennis Ritchie of Bell Labs worked on the MULTICS project. After Bell Labs withdrew, Ken Thompson decided he would develop his own operating system based on MULTICS operating principles. The initial version was released in 1970 and was called UNICS, for Uniplexed Information and Computing.

NOTE The UNIX development team consisted of Ken Thompson, Dennis Ritchie, Doug Mcilroy, and Joe Ossanna.

The first two versions of UNICS were written in assembly language. Assembly language is specific to a processor family. Therefore, applications written in assembly language for one processor family had to be rewritten for another processor family.

Dennis Ritchie had developed the compiler programing language C. Compiled languages convert source code to assembly language. This mitigated the need to rewrite the operating system for each new processor family. In 1973, UNICS was rewritten in C and renamed UNIX.

In 1974, AT&T held a monopoly on the U.S. telephone systems. As part of an agreement with the federal government, the company could keep its monopoly but was not allowed to sell software. Since it could not sell UNIX, AT&T licensed UNIX to educational institutions for a small distribution charge. This allowed colleges and universities to obtain the operating system and use it for teaching and development.

In 1982, AT&T was broken up into smaller phone companies. This permitted AT&T to sell software. Thus, UNIX was no longer "free" to educational institutions, which created financial difficulty for many.

MINIX

When Andrew Tanenbaum heard AT&T UNIX Version 7 would no longer be made available for educational institutions, he began to work on MINIX, a microkernel-based, UNIX Version 7–compatible operating system. Initially, the operating system kept crashing, and Tanenbaum was about to terminate the project until one of his students informed him the crash was due to the Intel chip overheating and generating a thermal interrupt.

Tanenbaum fixed the problem, and MINIX was released freely to universities in 1987. Unfortunately, MINIX was copyrighted; therefore, no one was allowed to modify the source code. In 2000, MINIX licensing was changed to a permissive license (BSD). Permissive licensing allows users to modify the source code, but does not require modified source code to be made available to the end user.

The current version of MINIX, MINIX 3, is designed to be used in embedded systems. An embedded system contains an operating system and control program that is used to manage a device.

GNU

On September 27, 1983, Richard Stallman announced the GNU project (GNU stands for GNU is Not UNIX). GNU was to be a free UNIX-like operating system that could be shared, studied, and modified by anyone. At that time, a free (as in cost) and open source version of UNIX did not exist. AT&T no longer provided free versions of UNIX to learning institutions, and Andrew Tanenbaum's MINIX was copyrighted.

In 1985, Stallman founded the Free Software Foundation and, with attorney David Wheeler, created the General Public License (GPL). GPL is also referred to as copyleft. The GPL license dictates that any software or work of art may be modified and distributed freely as long as the modified versions are also distributed without restrictions or cost.

Since no free UNIX kernel existed, the GNU project had to develop one. Initially, the project attempted to modify MIT's TRIX kernel, but later decided to develop the HURD kernel. The HURD kernel was designed to run on top of the Mach microkernel, which had been developed by Carnegie Mellon University. Unfortunately, HURD kernel development and Mach licensing issues delayed the GNU project for many years.

Linus Torvalds

Linus Torvalds entered the University of Helsinki in 1988. At that time, most universities used MINIX to teach UNIX to their students. Torvalds did not like the MINIX terminal emulator and decided to write a better one. As he added functionality to his emulator, he concluded it would be better to create an operating system from scratch.

On September 17, 1991, Torvalds released a development environment called Freax (Free UNIX) under a GPL license. Freax used many of the tools and utilities created by Richard Stallman's GNU project. One of the major design differences was that Torvalds decided to use a monolithic kernel rather than a microkernel. Six months later, the name of the operating system was changed to Linux. Linus then posted the source code and invited other programmers to review, modify, and contribute enhancements. This was the original Linux operating system.

Linus Torvalds holds a registered trademark for the Linux operating system and controls Linux kernel development. When most people talk about Linux, they're usually talking about an operating system with a Linux kernel.

Linux Operating System Structure

An operating system provides a means for users to execute programs on a computer. The Linux operating system consists of multiple functional layers (layered architecture), as detailed in the following list:

- **Hardware layer** Responsible for interacting with system hardware.
- **Kernel** The kernel layer is the core of the operating system. It provides the system with process, memory, and task management. The kernel also connects applications to system hardware. The kernel is divided into the following components:
  - **System Call Interface** The System Call Interface (SCI) provides a connection between user space and kernel space.

- **Process management** Responsible for creating, stopping, and communicating with system processes.
- **Memory management** Responsible for memory allocation, virtual memory, and paging.
- **Virtual File System** Provides an abstraction layer for multiple filesystem types.
- **Network stack** Provides protocols used in network communications.
- **Device drivers** Software used to communicate with hardware.
- **Architecture-dependent code** System code specific to the type of processor.

- **Shell** Application and user environment and interface.
- **Operating system software** Used to manage the operating system.
- **Application software** Editors and other user applications.

Kernel

The kernel layer is the core of the operating system. Most Linux distributions use a monolithic kernel. Some (GNU) use a microkernel.

To understand the difference between a monolithic and microkernel, you must understand the terms *user space* and *kernel space.* Kernel processes execute in memory reserved for kernel processes (kernel space). User processes execute in memory reserved for user applications (user space). Separating user and kernel space protects kernel processes.

Monolithic Kernel

A monolithic kernel executes in kernel space. Monolithic kernels are made up of modules that perform specific functions. These modules may be dynamically loaded or unloaded.

Microkernel

A microkernel uses a small kernel executing in kernel space to manage memory, multitasking, and interprocess communication. Most other kernel functions are built in to "servers" that execute in user space.

Operating System Software

Operating system software is designed to manage system resources and provide a platform for application software. Most operating system software starts as part of the boot process and terminates when the system is shut down.

Application Software

Application software is user-space software (for example, editors and spreadsheets) designed to perform specific tasks. Application software is not required to run the operating system. Application software only executes or terminates when requested by a user or another application.

Distributions

The Linux operating system was created by Linus Torvalds. Linux is also the name of an open source kernel developed by Linus Torvalds.

A Linux distribution is an operating system that contains the Linux kernel and a specific selection of operating system and application software. The selection of software is distribution dependent.

Distribution Differences

Distributions may have technical or philosophical differences. Some distributions are designed to perform a specific function in a specific environment. Others are designed based on the publisher's interpretation and adherence to open source guidelines.

Technical Differences

Technical differences between distributions can include operating system and application software, configuration files, and command differences.

For instance, Red Hat and Debian distributions have the following differences:

- They use different package managers.
- They have different names for and locations to similar configuration files.
- They have differences in some command implementations.

For example, Red Hat currently uses rpm and yum as its package managers, whereas Debian uses dpkg and apt.

NOTE As of RHEL 8, Red Hat uses the DNF package manager.

The generic bash configuration file in Red Hat is */etc/bashrc*, and the generic bash configuration file in Debian is */etc/bash.bashrc*. The useradd command in Red Hat does not have the same functionality as the useradd command in Debian.

Philosophical Differences

Most philosophical differences between distributions are based on their interpretation of open source licensing. For example, Fedora and Debian will only use free and open source software, whereas Red Hat Enterprise allows proprietary (copyrighted) software.

Red Hat

In 1994, Marc Ewing developed his own Linux distribution called Red Hat Linux. In 1995, Bob Young purchased Red Hat Linux and merged his UNIX software distribution company with Marc Ewing's Red Hat company. Red Hat Enterprise is a commercial root distribution using the Linux kernel. Red Hat will provide its source code, but derivatives must remove any reference to Red Hat and components that are sold by Red Hat.

Fedora

Fedora is a root Linux distribution that has a large development community. Fedora uses faster release cycles to provide the latest technology to its users.

The Fedora project is sponsored by Red Hat. Many of the advances developed in Fedora find their way to Red Hat Enterprise.

NOTE Red Hat Enterprise has a separate set of quality control tests from Fedora.

Debian

Debian is a root Linux distribution that was started by Ian Murdock in 1993. Debian's goal was to provide an operating system based on the principles of free software. Debian created the Debian Free Software Guidelines, which are used to determine what software may be included in Debian.

NOTE Initially, Debian provided two distributions: One distribution used the Linux kernel and the other distribution used the FreeBSD kernel. Debian discontinued the FreeBSD distribution.

Linux Derivatives

Derivatives are operating systems derived from a distribution (root distribution) or another derivative. The derivative operating system may focus on a specific task by adding more or less software or a modified kernel.

TIP A great deal of information on distributions and packages associated with distributions can be found at www.distrowatch.com.

The Linux kernel has several root distributions and many derivative distributions. Let's take a look at a few derivatives of both the Red Hat and Debian root distributions.

Red Hat Derivatives

CentOS, openSUSE, and Oracle Unbreakable Linux are examples of Red Hat derivatives.

CentOS CentOS provides a free binary compatible version of Red Hat Enterprise, but contains none of Red Hat Enterprise's proprietary software.

OpenSUSE OpenSUSE uses YaST rather than Anaconda as a setup program, zypper rather than yum as a package management application, and AppArmor (by default) over SELinux for enhanced security.

NOTE It is possible to disable AppArmor in SUSE and install SELinux.

Oracle Linux Oracle Linux is binary-compatible derivative of Red Hat Enterprise Linux. Oracle customers have a choice of a compatible kernel or the Unbreakable Enterprise kernel. The Unbreakable Enterprise kernel is optimized to provide better performance.

Debian Derivatives

Although Debian has multiple derivatives, we are going to briefly look at two: Kali and Ubuntu.

Kali Kali is one of several Debian derivatives used for penetration testing. Kali is an example of creating a derivative for a specific task.

Ubuntu Ubuntu is one of the more popular Debian derivatives. Ubuntu, Linux for human beings, is an example where design philosophy takes precedence. The word *Ubuntu* is defined as a quality that includes the essential human virtues of compassion and humanity. Ubuntu's design philosophy was to make Linux more useable for human beings.

Linux Mint and Xubuntu are examples of Ubuntu derivatives.

Common Linux Implementations

Because Linux is distributed under the GPL, software vendors can customize Linux to operate in a variety of roles, including the following:

- Using Linux on the desktop
- Using Linux on the server
- Using Linux on mobile devices
- Using Linux for virtualization
- Using Linux with cloud computing
- Using embedded Linux

Linux on the Desktop

Linux can be optimized to function extremely well as a desktop system. However, Linux has been somewhat slow to make inroads into this market. As of 2019, Linux had garnered only about 2 percent of the desktop market share, while Windows occupies over 90 percent.

There has been a historical lack of desktop productivity applications available for Linux. Fortunately, many productivity applications are available today that make Linux a viable option for the desktop (for example, LibreOffice).

Many vendors have been working on desktop-oriented Linux distributions that seek to simplify it. They have bundled application suites such as LibreOffice and added an easy-to-use graphical interface. Here are some of the more popular desktop Linux distributions:

- Ubuntu Desktop Edition
- openSUSE
- Fedora Desktop Edition

Linux on the Server

Linux works great as a server. In fact, Linux has experienced widespread acceptance in the server room, much more so than on the desktop. Depending on the services provided, Linux occupies between 40 and 97 percent of the server market share. This is because Linux can assume a variety of server roles, including the following, and perform them extremely well:

- **File and print server** Using the Network File System (NFS), the Common UNIX Printing System (CUPS), or Samba services, system administrators can configure Linux to provide network storage and printing of users' files.
- **Web and database server** Linux has been widely deployed as a web server. In fact, the most popular web service currently used on Linux is the Apache web server combined with MySQL, MariaDB, NoSQL, or PostgreSQL.
- **E-mail server** There are a variety of e-mail services available for Linux that can turn your system into an enterprise-class mail server.
- **Super computer** Linux is the preferred operating system for deploying high-powered super computers.

The widespread popularity of Linux as a server is due to a number of reasons. These include stability, performance, and cost. Red Hat offers the Red Hat Enterprise Linux Server distribution, which has a proven track record as an enterprise-class server. SUSE Linux Enterprise Server (SLES) is also optimized for servers.

Mobile Linux

Linux has nearly taken over the mobile device market in the form of the Android operating system provided by Google, accounting for almost 50 percent of the smartphone market. Android is so popular for the following reasons:

- **Price** It is much cheaper than iOS.
- **Performance** Android performs extremely well on mobile devices.
- **App support** A plethora of apps are available for Android devices.

Linux and Virtualization

Virtualization is an aspect of information technology that is gaining a great deal of momentum in the industry.

Traditionally, one operating system (for example, Linux) is installed on a computer that has full reign over all the resources in the system, including the following:

- RAM
- Processor time
- Storage devices
- Network interfaces

Virtualization offers an alternative deployment model. Virtualization pools multiple operating system instances onto the same computer and allows them to run concurrently. To do this, virtualization uses a mediator called a *hypervisor* to manage access to system resources.

Each operating system instance is installed into a *virtual machine* and functions just like a physical host. This allows multiple platforms, including Windows and Linux, to run at the same time on the same hardware. This is a huge benefit for software developers and testers, making it much easier to test how an application in development performs on different platforms.

Several virtualization platforms are available for Linux, including the following:

- Xen (open source)
- VMware Workstation, Player, ESX, and ESXi (proprietary)
- VirtualBox (open source)
- KVM (open source)

These hypervisors turn the Linux system into a hypervisor that can run virtual machines.

Linux and Cloud Computing

Virtualization is a key component of cloud computing, where the hardware, software, and/or network resources are moved offsite and delivered over a network connection, and even over the Internet.

With cloud computing, a provider on the Internet deploys a new Linux virtual machine at their site. Customers pay fees to access this virtual server through their organization's network connection. The provider assumes all the responsibility of implementing, maintaining, and securing the server. This model is referred to *Infrastructure as a Service (IaaS)*.

In addition to IaaS, there are other cloud computing models, including the following:

- **Software as a Service (SaaS)** Provides access to software and data through the cloud. Examples of SaaS include Gmail, Outlook 365, and Salesforce.
- **Platform as a Service (PaaS)** Provides access to a full solution suite to accomplish a computing task, including networking and storage. An example of PaaS is HTML website hosting.

Many organizations set up Linux and virtualization using a private cloud, offering on-demand computing resources to other users in the organization.

Embedded Linux

One benefit of Linux is that it can be optimized down to a small footprint for IoT (Internet of Things) devices. Linux is ideal for embedding within intelligent devices such as the following:

- Network routers
- Video game systems
- Smart TVs
- Smartphones and tablets

Linux is customized to provide just essential functions, and unnecessary elements are removed. The operating system is finally embedded into flash memory chips within the device.

Chapter Review

This chapter provided you with an overview of the history of the Linux kernel and structure of Linux-based distributions. It also defined the differences between Linux distributions and derivatives and explained why the different distributions exist. Lastly, it described the various environments in which Linux-based distributions may be found. Here are some key takeaways from the chapter:

- Linux is an open source monolithic kernel.
- Linus Torvalds first developed the Linux kernel and Linux operating system in the early 1990s.
- Linux is licensed under the GPL.
- An operating system consists of kernel system software and application software.
- The kernel layer is the core of the operating system and provides process, memory, and task management.
- System software is used to manage system resources.
- Application software is used to perform user tasks.
- A Linux-based distribution contains the Linux kernel (possibly modified) and a selection of operating and application software.
- Linux-based distributions provide a stable environment for embedded systems and desktop, server, and cloud environments.

Pre-Assessment Test

Prior to reading the rest of the chapters of this book, first complete this pre-assessment test to identify key areas to focus on as you study for the CompTIA Linux+ exam.

In this activity, you will be presented with 90 assessment questions that mirror the type you are likely to see on the real exam. The weighting of objective domains used in the real exams is approximated in this activity.

To make this experience as realistic and accurate as possible, you should allocate 90 minutes of uninterrupted time to complete your practice exam. Turn off your phone, computer, TV, and music player and find a comfortable place to work. Set a timer for 90 minutes and then begin this activity. Allowing more than 90 minutes to complete this experience will yield inaccurate results. Be sure to work through all the questions in this activity before checking answers. Again, this pre-assessment should mimic a real testing environment as much as possible. Wait until answering every question before checking the answers.

Once the pre-assessment test is complete, use the "Quick Answer Key" along with the "In-Depth Answer Explanations" sections to evaluate the responses. Keep track of the number of questions answered correctly and compare this number with the table found in the "Analyzing Your Results" section. This table will give you valuable feedback based on the number of correct answers given. Finally, compare the questions missed with the domain maps at the end of this activity to identify areas to focus on as you study.

Ready? Set the timer for 90 minutes and begin!

Questions

1. Which bash configuration files are used for non-login bash shell sessions? (Choose two.)

A. /etc/profile

B. /etc/bashrc

C. ~/.bashrc

D. ~/.profile

E. ~/.bash_profile

2. You need more information on the ls command. Which commands can be used to learn how to use this utility? (Choose two.)

A. ls --help

B. help ls

C. ls -h

D. man ls

3. You've opened the */var/opt/myapp/settings.txt* file in the vi editor. You need to enter new text into the file. Which key should you press to switch into Insert mode from Normal or "Command" mode?

   A. I

   B. A

   C. O

   D. R

4. YAML files used to configure network cards to use DHCP or set up static IP addressing can be found where?

   A. /etc/X11

   B. /etc/yum

   C. /etc/yum.repos.d

   D. /etc/netplan

5. To create a new directory in a user's home directory named MyFiles, you use which of the following commands?

   A. mkdir ~/myfiles

   B. mkdir ~/MyFiles

   C. md ~/myFiles

   D. mkdir ~ MyFiles

6. The sealert utility is used to determine that a user cannot access a file. Which command would aid in troubleshooting by showing access settings?

   A. ls -s

   B. ls -Z

   C. ls -l

   D. restorecon

7. Which vi command-line mode commands can be used to save changes to the current file being edited and close the vi editor? (Choose three.)

   A. ZZ

   B. :wq

   C. :q

   D. :q!

   E. :x

8. You need to change the permissions of a file named widgets.odt such that the file owner can edit the file, but no other users on the system will be allowed to view or modify it. Which command will do this?

   A. chmod 660 widgets.odt

   B. chmod 640 widgets.odt

   C. chmod 777 widgets.odt

   D. chmod 600 widgets.odt

9. You need to change the permissions of a file named projectx.odt such that the file owner can edit the file, users who are members of the group that owns the file can view and edit it, and users who are not owners and don't belong to the owning group cannot view or modify it. Which command will do this?

   A. chmod 660 projectx.odt

   B. chmod 640 projectx.odt

   C. chmod 777 projectx.odt

   D. chmod 644 projectx.odt

10. Which **usermod** command options must be used to add user accounts as members of a secondary group? (Choose two.)

    A. -a

    B. -s

    C. -g

    D. -p

    E. -G

11. Which control structure processes over and over as long as a specified condition evaluates to **false**?

    A. while

    B. until

    C. for

    D. case

12. For designing the implementation of a new Linux server in the company's network, the server will function as an internal file and print server for the organization. Employees will save their work-related files in shared storage locations on the server, and print jobs for shared printers will be managed by the server as well. What services should be included in the specifications? (Choose two.)

    A. Apache

    B. MySQL

C. Samba

D. Telnet

E. Pure-FTP

F. CUPS

13. This process takes over and kills processes that use too much memory because they score too high under this process's monitoring system?

A. BOMB

B. BOM

C. KaBOOM

D. OOM

14. Which tools can be used to check for open network ports? (Choose two.)

A. nmap

B. lsof

C. pwconv

D. ssh

E. cpio

15. To insert a new kernel module into a Linux system that has no dependencies, which tool is best to use to utilize the module?

A. dmesg

B. modinfo

C. insmod

D. depmod

16. Which of the following commands is used to find the domain's mail server?

A. dig

B. ping

C. traceroute

D. route

17. Which command updates every few seconds, displaying the routers that packets use to reach their destination within a GUI?

A. mtr

B. traceroute

C. tracert

D. iftop

18. When local authentication is used on a Linux system, which file contains the passwords for the user accounts?
    A. /etc/passwd
    B. /etc/group
    C. /etc/gshadow
    D. /etc/shadow
19. Consider the following entry from the */etc/passwd* file: algreer:x:1001:100:Albert Greer:/home/algreer:/bin/bash. What user ID (UID) has been assigned to this user account?
    A. algreer
    B. 1001
    C. 100
    D. Albert Greer
20. Consider the following entry from the */etc/shadow* file: kmorgan:$2a$05$KL1DbTBqpSEMiL.2FoI3ue4bdyR.eL6GMKs7MU6.nZl5SCC7/REUS:15043:1:60:7:5::. In how many days will this account be disabled after the user's password has expired?
    A. One day
    B. Seven days
    C. Five days
    D. Null value (never)
21. Which of the following contains files that populate new users' home directories created with useradd?
    A. /etc/login.defs
    B. /etc/default/useradd
    C. /etc/skel
    D. /etc/default/grub
22. You need to create a new account for a user named Ian Mausi on a Linux system and specify a username of imausi, a full name of Ian Mausi, a default shell of /bin/bash, and that a home directory be created. Which command will do this?
    A. useradd -c "Ian Mausi" -m -s "/bin/bash" imausi
    B. useradd -c "Ian Mausi" -m -s "/bin/bash" -u imausi
    C. usermod -c "Ian Mausi" -m -s "/bin/bash" imausi
    D. useradd -c "Ian Mausi" -s "/bin/bash" imausi

23. Which file keeps a list of intentionally untracked files that git should ignore?

A. .gitnot

B. gitnot

C. .gitignore

D. .git

24. Command substitution, which allows a command to run within a command, is performed with which operators?

A. ` `

B. $( )

C. ' '

D. " "

E. ${ }

25. An administrator runs **mount /dev/sdb2 /external** and realizes they have made a mistake because a filesystem was already mounted to /external. What happened to the files that were initially mounted onto /external?

A. The files are destroyed and can only be recovered from backup tape.

B. Linux does not allow for a filesystem to be mounted onto another.

C. The files are temporarily merged with the new filesystem.

D. When the administrator runs **umount /dev/sdb2**, the files will reappear unharmed.

26. A script that requires the end user to enter the name of their supervisor will use which of the following lines to input the user's response into a variable named SUP?

A. read SUP

B. input SUP

C. prompt SUP

D. query SUP

27. When a new user attempts to run a script while in their home directory using the **./runme.sh** command from the shell prompt, they see the following error:

bash: ./runme.sh: Permission denied.

Which resolution will fix this issue?

A. Copy the file to the ~/bin directory.

B. Add the home directory to the PATH environment variable.

C. Enter **chmod u+x runme.sh** at the shell prompt.

D. Change the shebang line of the script to **#!/bin/sh**.

28. Which of the following will make for the fastest restore, and fewest number of tapes to restore, assuming the system fails shortly after the Friday backup completes?
Key: F=Full, I=Incremental, D=Differential.

A. Mon-F1, Tue-D1, Wed-I1, Thu-D2, Fri-F2

B. Mon-F1, Tue-D1, Wed-I1, Thu-D2, Fri-I2

C. Mon-F1, Tue-D1, Wed-D2, Thu-D3, Fri-D4

D. Mon-F1, Tue-I1, Wed-I2, Thu-I3, Fri-I4

29. Which of the following commands can convert a SHELL variable to an ENVIRONMENT variable?

A. env

B. export

C. set

D. chmod

30. Which command would an administrator run to generate a sequence of numbers that starts at 1, increments by 1, and stops at 100? (Choose all that apply.)

A. seq 1 100

B. seq 100

C. seq 1 1 100

D. seq 1-100

31. Which command can uncover a remote user's login name and password when they connect using telnet or ftp?

A. dig

B. nslookup

C. tcpdump

D. ip

32. Which protocols encrypt the network traffic? (Choose two.)

A. SSH

B. FTP

C. Telnet

D. HTTPS

E. Finger

33. Which of the following is *not* a single sign-on system?

A. RADIUS

B. Kerberos

C. TACACS+

D. Circumference

E. LDAP

34. Consider the following IP address: 172.17.8.10/22. Which subnet mask is assigned to this address?

A. 255.255.252.0

B. 255.255.0.0

C. 255.255.255.0

D. 255.255.255.252

35. Which command would assign the ens32 interface an IP address of 172.17.8.1 with a subnet mask of 255.255.0.0 and a broadcast address of 172.17.255.255?

A. ip addr set ens32 172.17.8.1/255.255.0.0 bcast 172.17.255.255

B. ip addr 172.17.8.1/255.255.0.0 broadcast 172.17.255.255 dev ens32

C. ip addr set 172.17.8.1/255.255.0.0 broadcast 172.17.255.255 dev ens32

D. ip addr add 172.17.8.1/255.255.0.0 broadcast 172.17.255.255 dev ens32

36. Which directive in */etc/sysconfig/network/ifcfg-eth0* is used to specify whether the interface is automatically enabled when the system is booted?

A. STARTMODE

B. BOOTPROTO

C. IPADDR

D. USERCONTROL

37. Which system keeps one NIC sleeping and awakens when another NIC fails?

A. Active-passive

B. Active-active

C. Load balancing

D. Aggregation

38. For security reasons, a Linux system should resolve hostnames using the DNS server before trying to resolve them using the */etc/hosts* file. Which file is reconfigured to change the name resolver order?

A. /etc/resolv.conf

B. /etc/sysconfig/network/ifcfg-eth0

C. /etc/nsswitch.conf

D. /etc/sysconfig/services

39. The */etc/sudoers* file on your Linux system is configured by default such that users must supply the root password when using **sudo**. Which commands are *best* used to modify the */etc/sudoers* file? (Choose two.)

A. gedit

B. vi

C. notepad

D. sudoedit

E. visudo

40. Which setting made in the proper file in the */etc/pam.d/* directory tracks login attempts and locks out users after multiple attempts?

A. pam_access.so

B. pam_loginuid.so

C. pam_limits.so

D. pam_tally2.so

41. To secure the sshd service running on a Linux system from hackers, it is decided to configure it to listen for SSH requests on a port other than the default of 22. Which directive in the */etc/ssh/sshd_config* file can do this?

A. Port

B. BindAddress

C. Protocol

D. Tunnel

42. You want to write the **stdout** from the **ps** command to a file named *myprocesses* in the */tmp* directory without overwriting the existing contents of that file. Which command will do this?

A. ps < /tmp/myprocesses

B. ps > /tmp/myprocesses

C. ps <> /tmp/myprocesses

D. ps >> /tmp/myprocesses

43. Which Linux runlevel puts the system in multiuser mode as a network server with a command-line interface?

A. 1

B. 2

C. 3

D. 5

44. An administrator must configure the GRUB2 bootloader such that it will boot the first operating system in the boot menu by default unless an end user manually selects an operating system within the timeout period. Which directive should be set within the */etc/default/grub* configuration file to do this?

   A. GRUB_DEFAULT=0

   B. GRUB_SAVEDDEFAULT=true

   C. GRUB_HIDDEN_TIMEOUT_QUIET=true

   D. GRUB_CMDLINE_LINUX=saved

45. Which commands will switch a Linux system from a graphical environment to a multiuser text-based environment? (Choose two.)

   A. systemctl isolate runlevel3.target

   B. systemctl isolate rescue.target

   C. systemctl isolate multi-user.target

   D. systemctl isolate runlevel5.target

   E. systemctl isolate graphical.target

46. The systems administrator just added a third SATA hard disk drive to the Linux system and needs to create a GPT partition on it. Which command should they use to do this?

   A. fdisk /dev/sdb

   B. fdisk /dev/sdc

   C. fdisk /dev/sd2

   D. fdisk /dev/sd3

47. On a Linux system with 16GB of RAM, two additional SATA hard disks (/dev/sdb and /dev/sdc) are added to the system and a partition is created on each one. The partitions are defined as LVM physical volumes. Which command is run to add both physical volumes to a new volume group named DATA?

   A. lvscan -v

   B. vgcreate DATA /dev/sdb1 /dev/sdc1

   C. pvcreate /dev/sdb1

   D. lvcreate -L 700G -n research DATA

48. Which statements are true about logical volumes? (Choose three.)

   A. Logical volumes may be extended and resized.

   B. Logical volumes and RAID are the same.

   C. Logical volumes can span multiple block devices.

   D. The command lvscan will display a list of logical volumes.

49. A new Linux system was installed about a week ago. Three days ago, an administrative user compiled and installed a new application from source code. Now, the Ethernet interface in the system sporadically goes offline. Which command does the administrator run to see the boot messages generated by the system when it was in a pristine state shortly after being installed?

A. journalctl -b 2

B. logger -p 2

C. journalctl -b

D. journalctl -b -2

50. The following content is listed in which file?

```
# Virtual consoles
tty1
tty2
tty3
```

A. /etc/securetty

B. /dev/tty

C. /etc/yum.conf

D. /etc/ld.so.conf

51. After installing GIT, which two configuration properties must you define before issuing a commit?

A. Username and e-mail address

B. MAC address and project name

C. IP address and MAC address

D. Username and password

52. Which of the following is *not* a Linux Desktop Environment?

A. GNOME

B. VNC

C. Unity

D. Cinnamon

53. You have lost the system's root password. What must you add to the kernel line in the Grub bootloader to change root's password?

A. init=1

B. systemd.unit=rescue.target

C. systemd.unit=emergency.target

D. init=/bin/sh

54. Which of the following allows the network administrator to add a default gateway of 10.5.3.1? (Choose two.)

A. route add gateway 10.5.3.1

B. ip route add default via 10.5.3.1

C. ip route add default 10.5.3.1

D. route add default gw 10.5.3.1

E. route add default 10.5.3.1

55. Consider the following routing table:

```
# netstat-rn
Kernel IP routing table
Destination    Gateway Genmask          Flags MSS Window irtt Iface
192.168.8.0    0.0.0.0 255.255.255.0 U     0   0        0    eth0
```

Given this routing table, why does the following command fail?

```
route add default gw 10.5.3.1
```

A. A default route is already defined.

B. Default routes must defined on static networks only.

C. Because there is no route to 10.5.3.1.

D. The genmask value must be 255.0.0.0.

56. The network administrator modified a configuration file to utilize a tier 1 time server. Since making the change, time updates via NTP are no longer occurring. What most likely has occurred?

A. Port 123 is blocked on the firewall.

B. The network administrator forgot to reboot the system.

C. The network administrator improperly ran the **timedatectl** command.

D. The feature is not available on Red Hat strains of Linux and must be converted to a Debian strain.

57. Which of the following commands can change the time zone on a Linux system?

A. timedatectl

B. date

C. time

D. hwclock

58. Which utility will convert text to audio on a Linux system, allowing blind users to hear what is typed?

 A. qt

 B. daisy

 C. speakeasy

 D. orca

59. Which of the following describes the columns of the */etc/fstab* file best?

 A. Device, mount point, filesystem type, options, fsck order, dump option

 B. Device, mount point, filesystem type, options, dump option, fsck order

 C. Device, mount point, options, filesystem type, dump option, fsck order

 D. Mount point, device, filesystem type, options, dump option, fsck order

60. Which are *not* journaled filesystems? (Choose two.)

 A. Ext2

 B. Ext3

 C. Isofs

 D. XFS

 E. NTFS

61. Which is NOT a method that results in an Ext3 type filesystem?

 A. mke2fs -j /dev/sda2

 B. mkfs.ext3 /dev/sdb3

 C. tune2fs -t ext3 /dev/sdd4

 D. mkfs -t ext3 /dev/sdc7

 E. tune2fs -j /dev/sde8

62. Which command shows who is logged in and which commands they are running?

 A. whoami

 B. whom

 C. who

 D. w

 E. id

63. Which command searches */var/log/wtmp*?

 A. last

 B. lastb

 C. who

 D. whoami

 E. w

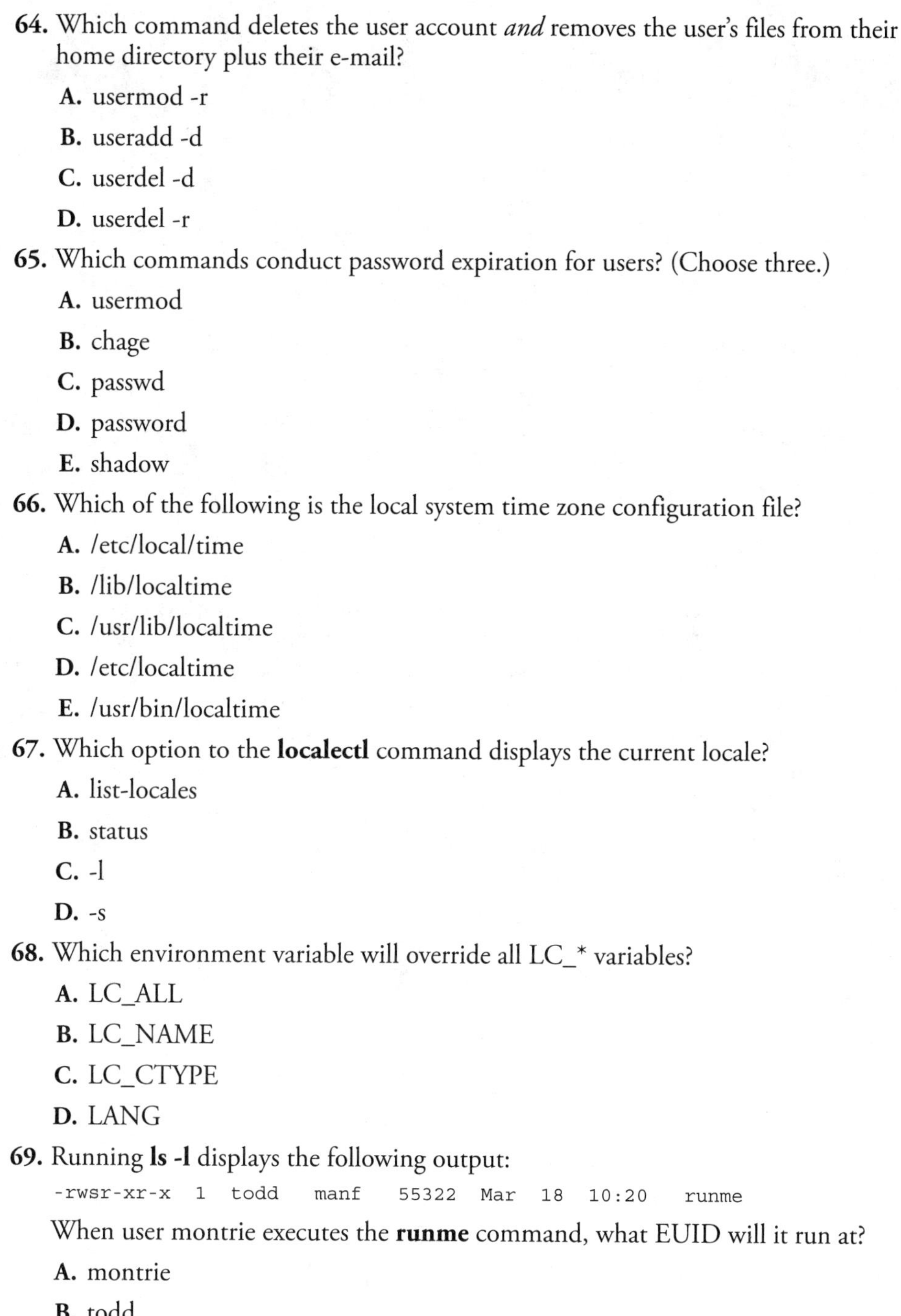

64. Which command deletes the user account *and* removes the user's files from their home directory plus their e-mail?
    A. usermod -r
    B. useradd -d
    C. userdel -d
    D. userdel -r
65. Which commands conduct password expiration for users? (Choose three.)
    A. usermod
    B. chage
    C. passwd
    D. password
    E. shadow
66. Which of the following is the local system time zone configuration file?
    A. /etc/local/time
    B. /lib/localtime
    C. /usr/lib/localtime
    D. /etc/localtime
    E. /usr/bin/localtime
67. Which option to the **localectl** command displays the current locale?
    A. list-locales
    B. status
    C. -l
    D. -s
68. Which environment variable will override all LC_* variables?
    A. LC_ALL
    B. LC_NAME
    C. LC_CTYPE
    D. LANG
69. Running **ls -l** displays the following output:

```
-rwsr-xr-x  1  todd   manf   55322  Mar  18  10:20   runme
```

    When user montrie executes the **runme** command, what EUID will it run at?
    A. montrie
    B. todd
    C. root
    D. manf

70. So that new directories have a default permission of 750, and regular files have a default permission of 640, what must the umask be? (Choose two)

A. 026

B. 0026

C. 027

D. 0027

E. 0036

F. 036

71. User Sue gets an error message that she cannot create a new file because there is no more disk space; however, she is well below her quota use. What is the next command she runs to view total disk space utilization?

A. quota

B. df -i

C. du -sh

D. df -h

72. User John notices that system performance is slowing and suspects that memory shortages are the issue. He cannot add additional memory, so as a quick fix decides to add a swapfile to use as additional swap space. After creating the swapfile and setting up the Linux swap area, he notices no change in performance. What command did he most likely forget to run?

A. swapon

B. swapoff

C. mkswap

D. mount

73. User Quincy discovers that she can get better disk drive performance by converting from **cfq** or **noop** to **deadline**. What command should she run for proper conversion to **deadline**?

A. cat deadline < /sys/block/sda/queue/scheduler

B. cat deadline > /sys/block/sda/queue/scheduler

C. echo deadline > /sys/block/sda/queue/scheduler

D. echo deadline < /sys/block/sda/queue/scheduler

74. User Elimu is working on a bash script. The script contains this **case** statement:

```
case $fruit ________
  orange|tangerine)  echo taste like orange ;;
  *berry)   echo taste like berry ;;
  *)        echo Error: fruit not found ;;
esac
```

Which command should Elimu place into the blank?

A. at

B. in

C. of

D. if

75. User Wade is working on a bash script. The script contains this **for** statement:

```
for fruit in orange apple berry grape
do
    echo this fruit tastes like $fruit
______
```

Which command should Wade place into the blank?

A. end

B. rof

C. od

D. done

76. User Nadia is learning how to examine disk-drive performance and learns to use **iostat**. To monitor performance, she would like to see five outputs, with 10 seconds of difference between them. Which of the following is the best way for her to accomplish this?

A. iostat 5 10

B. iostat 10 5

C. iostat --count 5 --period 10

D. iostat 10

77. User Walter needs to examine the performance of his RAID array. He is learning how to use **mdadm**, but is unsure which option to **mdadm** will show negative issues with the system (for example, disk failures). Which of the following are the best ways for Walter to accomplish this? (Choose three.)

A. mdadm --build

B. mdadm --follow

C. mdadm -F

D. mdadm --monitor

78. Users Landon and Lonnie monitor their virtual machines. One of the applications they use requires telnet, which unfortunately uses the same escape string ^]. Which option to **virsh** allows them to change the escape string to ^[?

A. --debug

B. --chstr

C. --esc

D. --escape

79. System administrators Laeia and Liara work side by side examining accounting results of disk drive performance. Laeia believes that poor performance is related to aging hard drives, and she consults with Liara as to the next steps. Liara knows that exact command to run to check for bad blocks. She recommends which of the following?

   A. blockcheck

   B. badblocks

   C. kill

   D. bbcheck

80. Sorana desires to display memory and swap utilization using the **free** command. Unlike **iostat**, **sar**, and others, **free** does *not* update periodically by default. Which command can she run with **free** to automatically display updates every two seconds, refreshing the screen every time?

   A. period

   B. watch

   C. free

   D. twosec

81. User Ugo decides that he wants new files and directories below the directory work to automatically have the same group permission as work. Which command can Ugo run to do this?

   A. chmod g+s work

   B. chmod +a work

   C. chmod g=w work

   D. chmod g=rw work

82. Zhang is a network administrator that needs to open the firewall to allow web access. Which of the following would do this for her?

   A. firewall-cmd --zone=public --allow=http

   B. firewall-cmd --zone=public --add-service=http

   C. firewall-cmd --zone=public --add-service=web

   D. firewall-cmd --zone=public --add=http

83. Henri is a network administrator who is required to open new ports for NTP and HTTPd. He needs to display the current firewall settings using **iptables**. Which of the following would do this for him?

   A. iptables -d

   B. iptables -s

C. iptables -L

D. iptables -F

84. Petra is a systems administrator working on a Linux system running SysV init. She runs the following as root:

```
# chkconfig --list | grep auditd
auditd 0:off 1:off 2:off 3:off 4:off 5:off 6:off
```

Which of the following would she run to enable **auditd** to start at run state 3 or 5 upon reboot?

A. chkconfig --level 35 auditd start

B. chkconfig --level 35 auditd on

C. chkconfig --level 35 start auditd

D. chkconfig --level 35 on auditd

85. Milos is a storage administrator and notices disk space is running out on one of the logical volumes. Before using **lvextend** to enlarge the volume, what must he do first?

A. Know which volume group device to extend.

B. Reboot the system.

C. Restart the logical volume service.

D. Restart meta-device management.

86. Ushna is a cloud administrator who would like to orchestrate the setup of 500 CentOS Linux servers. Of the tools listed, which is the one she would *not* choose as part of the configuration?

A. Cloud-init

B. Orchestrate

C. Anaconda

D. Kickstart

87. Thanasi, a cloud engineer, is updating files for orchestration. Here is some sample content that he is editing with /bin/vi:

```
yum_repos:
     epel-testing:
        baseurl: http://ftp.wheezy.com/pub/epel/$basesearch
        enable: false
        failovermethod: priority
```

This is most likely what type of file?

A. SAML

B. XML

C. JSON

D. YAML

88. Teliana, a cloud engineer, is updating files for orchestration. Here is some sample content that she is editing with /bin/vi:

```
{
      "firstName": "Maria",
      "lastName": "Bueno",
      "age": 25,
```

This is most likely what type of file?

A. SAML

B. XML

C. JSON

D. YAML

89. Systems administrator Juan has just enabled SELinux and is finding it is very difficult to work. He is just testing the system and does not require it to be fully functional. What should he run that will simply warn of any SELinux offenses?

A. setenforce permissive

B. setenforce enforcing

C. setenforce disabled

D. setenforce warning

90. Systems administrator Katerina is running a foreground job and she would like to stop it temporarily and have it continue later. What key sequence does she run to stop the job?

A. CTRL-C

B. CTRL-Z

C. CTRL-\

D. CTRL-S

Quick Answer Key

1. B, C	**10. A, E**	**19. B**
2. A, D	**11. B**	**20. C**
3. A	**12. C, F**	**21. C**
4. D	**13. D**	**22. A**
5. B	**14. A, B**	**23. C**
6. B	**15. C**	**24. A, B**
7. A, B, E	**16. A**	**25. D**
8. D	**17. A**	**26. A**
9. A	**18. D**	**27. C**

28. A
29. B
30. A, B, C
31. C
32. A, D
33. D
34. A
35. D
36. A
37. A
38. C
39. D, E
40. D
41. A
42. D
43. C
44. A
45. A, C
46. B
47. B
48. A, C, D
49. A
50. A
51. A
52. B
53. D
54. B, D
55. C
56. A
57. A
58. D
59. B
60. A, C
61. C
62. D
63. A
64. D
65. A, B, C
66. D
67. B
68. A
69. B
70. C, D
71. D
72. A
73. C
74. B
75. D
76. B
77. B, C, D
78. D
79. B
80. B
81. A
82. B
83. C
84. B
85. A
86. B
87. D
88. C
89. A
90. D

In-Depth Answer Explanations

1. ☑ **B** and **C** are correct. Both */etc/bashrc* and *~/.bashrc* are used to configure non-login shell sessions, although other files may be used on some distributions.
   ☒ **A, D,** and **E** are incorrect. The */etc/profile*, *~/.profile*, and *~/.bash_profile* files are used to configure login shell sessions. (Domain 2: Systems Operation and Maintenance)

2. ☑ **A** and **D** are correct. ls --help and man ls will display help information for the ls command.
   ☒ **B** and **C** are incorrect. (Domain 5: Automation and Scripting)

3. ☑ **A** is correct. Press the Insert or I key to enter Insert mode in the vi editor.
   ☒ **B, C,** and **D** are incorrect. The A key is used to append text after the cursor. The O key opens a new line below, before allowing for text to be inserted. The R key is used to replace a single character, and the X key is used by the vi editor to delete a single character. (Domain 2: Systems Operation and Maintenance)

4. ☑ **D** is correct. Save a network configuration inside the */etc/netplan/config.yaml* file to automate the configuration at boot time.
   ☒ **A, B,** and **C** are incorrect. The */etc/X11* file is for X-Window GUI setups, and the */etc/yum* and */etc/yum.repos.d* files point to software installation repositories. (Domain 1: Hardware and System Configuration)

5. ☑ **B** is correct. The **mkdir** command is used to create new directories in the filesystem, where ~ stands for the user's home directory (in this case, /home/user/*Myfiles* or *~/MyFiles*).
   ☒ **A, C,** and **D** are incorrect. **A** is incorrect because it uses the wrong case for the directory name. **C** is incorrect because it uses the incorrect command for creating new directories (**md**). **D** is incorrect because it omits the / character after the tilde. (Domain 2: Systems Operation and Maintenance)

6. ☑ **B** is correct. Running **ls -Z** will allow the user to see the current SELinux settings and determine whether or not they need to be changed.
   ☒ **A, C,** and **D** are incorrect. Neither the **ls -s** nor **ls -l** command will list any SELinux file information, instead only showing file sizes and a "long listing," respectively. The **restorecon** command fixes and repairs SELinux labels. (Domain 3: Security)

7. ☑ **A, B,** and **E** are correct. The **ZZ**, **:x**, and **:wq** commands will save any changes to the current file and then close the vi editor.
   ☒ **C** and **D** are incorrect. The **:q** command will close the current file and exit the editor without saving changes. The **:q!** command will discard any changes made to the current file, close it, and then exit the editor. (Domain 2: Systems Operation and Maintenance)

8. ☑ **D** is correct. The **chmod 600 widgets.odt** command grants the owner **rw-** permissions but takes away permissions from all other users.
   ☒ **A, B,** and **C** are incorrect. **A** is incorrect because it allows the file owner to edit the file, but also grants read and write access to the group. **B** is incorrect because it grants the group the read (**r**) permission. **C** is incorrect because it grants the owner, group, and others all permissions to the file. (Domain 3: Security)

9. ☑ **A** is correct. The **chmod 660 projectx.odt** command grants the owner **rw-** permissions, the group **rw-** permissions, and others **---** permissions.
   ☒ **B, C,** and **D** are incorrect. **B** is incorrect because it fails to grant the group the write (**w**) permission. **C** is incorrect because it grants the owner, group, and others all permissions to the file. **D** is incorrect because it fails to grant the group the write (**w**) permission and it grants others read (**r--**) permission to the file. (Domain 3: Security)

10. ☑ **A** and **E** are correct. The **usermod -aG** command adds the users you specify as members of the specified group(s).
    ☒ **B, C,** and **D** are incorrect. The **-s** option is used by the **usermod** command to define the "login shell" that the user will run. The **-g** option assigns the user's *primary* group. The **-p** option changes the password assigned to the user. (Domain 2: Systems Operation and Maintenance)

11. ☑ **B** is correct. An **until** loop runs over and over as long as the condition is **false**. As soon as the condition is **true**, it stops.
☒ **A, C,** and **D** are incorrect. A **while** loop executes over and over until a specified condition is no longer **true**. A **for** loop processes a specific number of times. A **case** statement is not a looping structure. (Domain 5: Automation and Scripting)

12. ☑ **C** and **F** are correct. The Samba service provides file sharing. CUPS is used to manage printing.
☒ **A, B, D,** and **E** are incorrect. The Apache web server is frequently implemented on Linux in conjunction with the MySQL database server to develop web-based applications. Telnet is an older service that was formerly used for remote access. Pure-FTP provides an FTP service. (Domain 2: Systems Operation and Maintenance)

13. ☑ **D** is correct. The Out of Memory Killer watches for processes that use too much memory and selects them for killing when the system has a serious memory shortage.
☒ **A, B,** and **C** are incorrect and are nonexistent Linux tools, but the names sure sound cool :-). (Domain 4: Linux Troubleshooting and Diagnostics)

14. ☑ **A** and **B** are correct. Either **nmap -sT -p 1-1024 10.0.0.*** is used to scan for open ports between 1 and 1024 or **lsof -i** is used to scan for open network ports.
☒ **C, D,** and **E** are incorrect. The **pwconv** command is used to create the */etc/shadow* file from the */etc/passwd* file. The **ssh** command is used to make secure remote login connections. The **cpio** command is used to create tape backups. (Domain 4: Linux Troubleshooting and Diagnostics)

15. ☑ **C** is correct. Use **insmod** to insert a module.
☒ **A, B,** and **D** are incorrect. The **dmesg** program shows hardware found during bootup. The **modinfo** command provides the user info about a module. Finally, the **depmod** command looks for module dependencies and updates the *modules.dep* file. (Domain 1: Hardware and System Configuration)

16. ☑ **A** is correct. A systems administrator could run **dig jordanteam.com MX** and list the location of the mail server.
☒ **B, C,** and **D** are incorrect. The **ping** command is used to test networks, and **traceroute** will list the routers used for a packet to reach its destination. The **route** command is used to define or display the default gateway. (Domain 2: Systems Operation and Maintenance)

17. ☑ **A** is correct. Use the **mtr** command to visualize the routes a packet takes to reach its destination within a GUI.
☒ **B, C,** and **D** are incorrect. The **traceroute** command is similar to **mtr**, but it is entered at the command line and does not operate periodically. The **tracert** command is the same as **traceroute** but works on the Windows operating system. The **iftop** command updates periodically displaying network traffic. (Domain 4: Linux Troubleshooting and Diagnostics)

18. ☑ **D** is correct. The */etc/shadow* file contains the encrypted passwords for user accounts.

☒ **A, B,** and **C** are incorrect. The */etc/passwd* file contains the user accounts and user IDs. The */etc/group* file is used for local group definitions. The */etc/gshadow* file contains passwords for the groups. (Domain 2: Systems Operation and Maintenance)

19. ☑ **B** is correct. The third field in each user entry in */etc/passwd* specifies the user's ID number (UID). In this case, it's 1001.

☒ **A, C,** and **D** are incorrect. **A** is incorrect because it specifies the username. **C** is incorrect because it specifies the group ID (GID) of the user's primary group. **D** is incorrect because it specifies the user's full name. (Domain 2: Systems Operation and Maintenance)

20. ☑ **C** is correct. The seventh field in each record in */etc/shadow* specifies the number of days to wait after a password has expired to disable the account.

☒ **A, B,** and **D** are incorrect. **A** is incorrect because it specifies the minimum number of days (one) required before a password can be changed. **B** is incorrect because it specifies the number of days prior to password expiration before the user will be warned of the pending expiration. **D** is incorrect because it is assigned to the eighth field, which specifies the number of days since January 1, 1970, after which the account will be disabled. (Domain 2: Systems Operation and Maintenance)

21. ☑ **C** is correct. The */etc/skel* directory contains files (usually startup scripts, like .bashrc) that populate a new user's home directory when created with useradd.

☒ **A, B,** and **D** are incorrect. The */etc/default/useradd* file contains defaults used by the useradd utility (for example, user ID and default shell). The */etc/default/grub* file contains booting defaults. The */etc/login.defs* file defines the locations of new user's mail directories and such. (Domain 2: Systems Operation and Maintenance)

22. ☑ **A** is correct. The **useradd -c "Ian Mausi" -m -s "/bin/bash" imausi** command creates a new user account for a user named Ian Mausi with a username of imausi, a full name of Ian Mausi, a default shell of /bin/bash, and a home directory.

☒ **B, C,** and **D** are incorrect. **B** is incorrect because it uses incorrect syntax for the **useradd** command, where **-u** is followed by a user ID number. **C** is incorrect because it uses an incorrect command (**usermod**). **D** is incorrect because it omits the **-m** option, which is required to create a home directory. (Domain 2: Systems Operation and Maintenance)

23. ☑ **C** is correct. The *.gitignore* file keeps a list of files that should be ignored by the **git** command.

☒ **A, B,** and **D** are incorrect. **A** and **B** are incorrect because there are no such files as *.gitnot* and *gitnot*. **D** is incorrect because *.git* is a directory that contains the repository for the project. (Domain 5: Automation and Scripting)

24. ☑ **A** and **B** are correct. Users can use backticks (for example, **echo Today is `date`**) or a dollar sign and parentheses (for example, **echo Today is $(date)**). The output of the **date** command will be the input to the **echo** command.

☒ **C, D,** and **E** are incorrect. The single quotes make all characters *literal.* The double quotes make all characters literal except for \, $, and ` (backtick), with some exceptions, such as !, @, and *, that are outside the scope of the exam. The dollar sign with curly braces are used to dereference a variable. (Domain 5: Automation and Scripting)

25. ☑ **D** is correct. When the administrator runs **umount /dev/sdb2**, the files will reappear unharmed.

☒ **A, B,** and **C** are incorrect. A mount point creates a connection between a directory and a block device. The directory (mount point) is mapped to another block device, so any files stored in the directory are not accessible until the mount point is removed. (Domain 1: Hardware and System Configuration)

26. ☑ **A** is correct. The **read** command is used to pause the script and prompt the user to provide some type of input, which is assigned to the specified variable.

☒ **B, C,** and **D** are incorrect. The **input**, **prompt**, and **query** commands cannot be used to read user input and are distractors. (Domain 5: Automation and Scripting)

27. ☑ **C** is correct. The error shown is caused by not having the execute permission set for the user trying to run the script. The **chmod u+x runme.sh** command will allow the user who owns the file to run it.

☒ **A, B,** and **D** are incorrect. **A** and **B** are incorrect because they resolve path-related problems, which are not an issue in this scenario. **D** is incorrect because it changes the command interpreter to the /bin/sh (Bourne) shell, which is not necessary in this scenario. (Domain 5: Automation and Scripting)

28. ☑ **A** is correct. If the system fails after the backup completes on Friday, the only tape required to fully restore would be F2 (Full backup, Number 2 made on Friday).

☒ **B, C,** and **D** are incorrect. **B** would require three tapes to recover in this order: Full-1, Differential 2, and Incremental 2. **C** would require two tapes to recover in this order: Full 1 and Differential 4. **D** would require all tapes to recover in the order of F1, I1, I2, I3, and I4. (Domain 3: Security)

29. ☑ **B** is correct. Running **export VAR1** will convert VAR1 from a SHELL variable to an ENVIRONMENT variable.

☒ **A, C,** and **D** are incorrect. The **env** command will display all the ENVIRONMENT variables defined. The **set** command will display all the SHELL variables defined. The **chmod** command can change **read**, **write**, and **execute** permissions on files. (Domain 5: Automation and Scripting)

30. ☑ **A, B**, and **C** are correct. The syntax for the sequence command is **seq <first> <increment> <last>**. If <first> or <last> are omitted, they default to 1. The commands **seq 100**, **seq 1 100**, and **seq 1 1 100** would all generate a sequence of numbers staring at 1, incrementing by 1, and stopping a 100.
☒ **D** is incorrect because it uses incorrect syntax for the seq command. (Domain 5: Automation and Scripting)

31. ☑ **C** is correct. The **tcpdump** command monitors network traffic and can display unencrypted login names and passwords.
☒ **A, B,** and **D** are incorrect. The **dig** and **nslookup** commands list the IP addresses that domain names belong to. The **ip** command is used to define and set up network devices. (Domain 4: Linux Troubleshooting and Diagnostics)

32. ☑ **A** and **D** are correct. SSH and HTTPS encrypt traffic traveling along the network.
☒ **B, C,** and **E** are incorrect. FTP, Telnet, and Finger communicate across the network using unencrypted data, and they should be disabled for best security. (Domain 3: Security)

33. ☑ **D** is correct. There is no single sign-on system referred to as Circumference.
☒ **A, B, C,** and **E** are incorrect. All of these are single sign-on systems that allow a user to employ a single digital identity across multiple domains. (Domain 3: Security)

34. ☑ **A** is correct. The /22 prefix length indicates the first two octets of the subnet mask (16 bits) are populated, plus six additional bits in the third octet.
☒ **B, C,** and **D** are incorrect. The prefix length for 255.255.0.0 would be /16. The prefix length for 255.255.255.0 would be /24. The prefix length for 255.255.255.252 would be /30. (Domain 4: Linux Troubleshooting and Diagnostics)

35. ☑ **D** is correct. This command will assign the ens32 interface an IP address of 172.17.8.1, with a subnet mask of 255.255.0.0 and a broadcast address of 172.17.255.255.
☒ **A, B,** and **C** are incorrect because they use incorrect parameters for setting the subnet mask and broadcast address. (Domain 4: Linux Troubleshooting and Diagnostics)

36. ☑ **A** is correct. STARTMODE determines whether the interface is started automatically at system boot or must be manually enabled.
☒ **B, C,** and **D** are incorrect. The BOOTPROTO parameter can be set to a value of STATIC to use static IP address assignments or to DHCP to configure dynamic IP addressing. IPADDR assigns an IP address to the interface but only works if BOOTPROTO is set to STATIC. USERCONTROL determines whether standard user accounts are allowed to manage the interface. (Domain 4: Linux Troubleshooting and Diagnostics)

37. ☑ **A** is correct. Active-passive clusters reserve a passive NIC that becomes active when another NIC fails.

☒ **B, C,** and **D** are incorrect. Active-active clusters systems keep all NICs active and running and are designed primarily for load balancing and load aggregation. Load balancing is used to divide IP traffic between multiple network cards. (Domain 1: Hardware and System Configuration)

38. ☑ **C** is correct. Use */etc/nsswitch.conf* (name service switch) to define the order in which services will be used for name resolution.

☒ **A, B,** and **D** are incorrect. **A** is incorrect because it is used to configure the IP address of the DNS server but does not configure the name service order. **B** is incorrect because it is used to configure IP addressing information but does not contain name resolution information. **D** is incorrect because it is used to configure how services will behave after they are updated. (Domain 1: Hardware and System Configuration)

39. ☑ **D** and **E** are correct. Use **visudo** or **sudoedit /etc/sudoers** to modify the */etc/sudoers* file securely.

☒ **A, B,** and **C** are incorrect. The **gedit** and **vi** commands could be used to edit */etc/sudoers* as root, but are insecure as multiple users may be editing the file simultaneously, causing changes to be lost. The **notepad** command is an editor used with Microsoft Windows. (Domain 3: Security)

40. ☑ **D** is correct. Defining **pam_tally2.so** within proper files under */etc/pam.d/* can lock an account after three improper login attempts, for example.

☒ **A, B,** and **C** are incorrect. Use **pam_access.so** for auditing and logging of access control. Use **pam_loginuid.so** to assist in login auditing as well. Use **pam_limits.so** to take advantage of **ulimit** features. (Domain 3: Security)

41. ☑ **A** is correct. The **Port** directive specifies the port on which the sshd daemon will listen for SSH requests.

☒ **B, C,** and **D** are incorrect. The **BindAddress** directive is used to specify the address on the local machine to be used as the source address of the connection. The **Protocol** directive specifies the protocol versions SSH should support. The **Tunnel** directive is used to set up forwarding between the SSH client and the SSH server. (Domain 3: Security)

42. ☑ **D** is correct. The **ps 4 >> /tmp/myprocesses** command appends the stdout from the **ps** command to a file named *myprocesses* in the */tmp* directory.

☒ **A, B,** and **C** are incorrect. **A** is incorrect because < attempts to use */tmp/myprocesses* as stdin to the **ps** command. **B** is incorrect because > will redirect stdout to the file */tmp/myprocesses* and overwrite any data within the file. **C** is incorrect because, in some versions of bash, <> stands for read-write and would overwrite any data within */tmp/myprocesses*. (Domain 2: Systems Operation and Maintenance)

43. ☑ **C** is correct. Runlevel 3 puts Linux in multiuser mode with networking services enabled. The command-line interface (CLI) is used.
☒ **A, B,** and **D** are incorrect. Runlevel 1 uses a command-line interface and puts the system into single-user mode. Runlevel 2 also uses a command-line interface and runs in multiuser mode; however, the system is set up as a network client. Runlevel 5 runs Linux in multiuser mode with networking services enabled and a graphical user interface. (Domain 2: Systems Operation and Maintenance)

44. ☑ **A** is correct. The **GRUB_DEFAULT=0** directive causes GRUB2 to use the first menu entry by default, regardless of which operating system was selected on the last boot.
☒ **B, C,** and **D** are incorrect. If you set **GRUB_SAVEDDEFAULT** to **true**, then GRUB will automatically select the last selected operating system from the menu as the default operating system to be used on the next boot. This parameter could conflict with the **GRUB_DEFAULT** parameter. Therefore, administrators can use either one, but not both. The **GRUB_HIDDEN_TIMEOUT_QUIET=true** directive causes no countdown timer to be displayed. The **GRUB_CMDLINE_LINUX** directive is used to pass options to the kernel. (Domain 1: Hardware and System Configuration)

45. ☑ **A** and **C** are correct. Both **systemctl isolate runlevel3.target** and **systemctl isolate multi-user.target** are used to switch the system into a text-based, multiuser environment comparable to runlevel 3 on an init-based system.
☒ **B, D,** and **E** are incorrect. To switch to the systemd equivalent of runlevel 5, enter either **systemctl isolate runlevel5.target** or **systemctl isolate graphical .target**. The **systemctl isolate rescue.target** command switches the system to a rescue environment equivalent to runlevel 1. (Domain 2: Systems Operation and Maintenance)

46. ☑ **B** is correct. To create a GPT partition on the third SATA hard disk in a Linux system, first switch to the root user and enter **fdisk /dev/sdc** at the shell prompt.
☒ **A, C,** and **D** are incorrect. **A** is incorrect because the **fdisk /dev/sdb** represents the second SATA hard drive. **C** and **D** are incorrect because they are improper hard-drive representation syntax. (Domain 1: Hardware and System Configuration)

47. ☑ **B** is correct. You use the **vgcreate** command to define a new volume group and assign physical partitions to it (*/dev/sdb1* and */dev/sdc1* in this case). The **vgcreate** command is used after defining the physical volumes with **pvcreate /dev/sdb1 /dev/sdc1**.
☒ **A, C,** and **D** are incorrect. You use the **lvscan** command to view the logical volumes defined on the system. You use the **pvcreate** command to define a partition (or even an entire disk) as an LVM physical volume. The **lvcreate** command defines logical volumes on the system. (Domain 4: Linux Troubleshooting and Diagnostics)

48. ☑ **A, C,** and **D** are correct. Logical volumes may span across multiple blocks and be extended and resized. The command lvscan can be used to display a list of logical volumes.
☒ **B** is incorrect. Logical volumes and RAID are not the same, but it is possible to RAID logical volumes. (Domain 4: Linux Troubleshooting and Diagnostics)

49. ☑ **A** is correct. The **journalctl -b 2** command displays messages created during the second boot event found at the beginning of the journal. This should contain boot messages from the system's pristine state required by the scenario.
☒ **B, C,** and **D** are incorrect. The **journalctl -b -2** command displays system messages that were logged two boot events ago. The **logger** command is used to send test log events to the logging daemon. The **journalctl -b** command displays boot messages that were logged in the most recent boot event. (Domain 3: Security)

50. ☑ **A** is correct. The content shown is from the */etc/securetty* file. This file lists the terminals from which root *can* log in.
☒ **B, C,** and **D** are incorrect. **B** is incorrect because the */dev/tty* file is a character device driver. **C** is incorrect because */etc/yum.conf* is the configuration file for YUM repositories. **D** is incorrect because */etc/ld.so.conf* is the configuration file for the location of dynamically linked libraries. (Domain 3: Security)

51. ☑ **A** is correct. For GIT to work properly, every commit must relate to some username and e-mail address so that all of the co-contributors can keep track of the changes.
☒ **B, C,** and **D** are incorrect and are not required for co-contributor communications. (Domain 5: Automation and Scripting)

52. ☑ **B** is correct. VNC (Virtual Network Computing) is not a Linux Desktop Environment but a utility for remote desktop computer access.
☒ **A, C,** and **D** are incorrect because they are all Linux Desktop Environments providing login screens and varied desktop appearances. GNOME is the default environment for several distributions, including openSUSE and Fedora. Unity is a popular desktop environment for Ubuntu Linux. Cinnamon is the popular on Linux Mint. (Domain 2: Systems Operation and Maintenance)

EXAM TIP Knowledge of default desktop environments is *not* a requirement for the Linux+ exam.

53. ☑ **D** is correct. To change root's password, boot the system and when the GRUB menu appears, hit the ESC key. Press E to edit, and then scroll down to the **linux** line. At the end of the **linux** line, enter **init=/bin/sh**. After pressing CTRL-X, the system will boot into a shell, which does not require a password. Use the password command to change root's password.
☒ **A, B,** and **C** are incorrect. For systemd systems, init=1 is incorrect, although it would enter single-user mode on SysV init systems when entered at the end of the kernel line. systemd.unit=rescue.target and systemd.unit=emergency.target

would enter single-user mode on a systemd system, requesting the root password, and so the administrator would not be able to change the root password. (Domain 4: Linux Troubleshooting and Diagnostics)

54. ☑ **B** and **D** are correct. Either the **route** or **ip** command can be used to add a default gateway.

☒ **A, C,** and **E** are incorrect. They would result in syntax errors because of missing arguments within the commands. (Domain 1: Hardware and System Configuration)

55. ☑ **C** is correct. In order for the gateway to exist, there must be some connection to the router, but the only connection shown is to the 192.168.8.0 network.

☒ **A, B,** and **D** are incorrect. In this case, the issue is there is no connection to the 10.5.3.0 network. (Domain 4: Linux Troubleshooting and Diagnostics)

56. ☑ **A** is correct. When the network administrator converts to a tier 1 time server, that implies the system changes time updates from the intranet (LAN) to now from the Internet (WAN). NTP uses port 123, which now must be opened on the firewall.

☒ **B, C,** and **D** are incorrect because the update can be made without a reboot. Since the administrator modified a configuration file, there is no need to use the **timedatectl** command, and of course NTP is available on all enterprise versions of Red Hat Linux. (Domain 4: Linux Troubleshooting and Diagnostics)

57. ☑ **A** is correct. To change the time zone of the Linux server, run **timedatectl set-timezone "Europe/Lisbon"**, for example. To list the available time zones, run **timedatectl list-timezones**.

☒ **B, C,** and **D** are incorrect. The **date** command will display the current date and time. The **time** command will display how long it takes for a command to run. The **hwclock** command is used to set the computer hardware clock. (Domain 1: Hardware and System Configuration)

58. ☑ **D** is correct. The orca screenreader is a very popular text-to-speech tool for Linux.

☒ **A, B,** and **C** are incorrect because qt is a programming language, daisy is an accessibility braille tool for the blind community, and speakeasy is a voice-to-text utility for varied systems, including Linux. (Domain 3: Security)

59. ☑ **B** is correct. The correct */etc/fsck* column order is as follows: device, mount point, filesystem type, options, dump option, fsck order.

☒ **A, C,** and **D** are incorrect. None of these shows the correct column order. (Domain 1: Hardware and System Configuration)

60. ☑ **A** and **C** are correct. Ext2 and isofs are not journaled filesystems.

☒ **B, D,** and **E** are incorrect and Ext3, XFS, and NTFS are journaled filesystems, which save changes in a buffer so that data loss is minimized in case of a system interruption. (Domain 1: Hardware and System Configuration)

61. ☑ C is correct. The **tune2fs -t ext3 /dev/sdd4** command fails because there is no **-t** option for **tune2fs**.
☒ A, B, D, and E are incorrect because **mke2fs -j /dev/sda2**, **mkfs.ext3 /dev /sdb3**, and **mkfs -t ext3 /dev/sdc7** will create an Ext3-type filesystem on the partition. The **tune2fs -j /dev/sde8** command will convert an Ext2-type filesystem to Ext3 by adding the journal. (Domain 1: Hardware and System Configuration)

62. ☑ D is correct. The **w** command displays who is logged into the system and which processes they are running.
☒ A, B, C, and E are incorrect. The **whoami** and **id** commands show who the user is currently logged in as, but not the processes they are running. The **who** command will display all logged in users, but not the processes they are running. The **whom** command is a distractor and currently does not exist for Linux systems. (Domain 2: Systems Operation and Maintenance)

63. ☑ A is correct. The **last** command searches /var/log/wtmp to display a list of the last logged in users.
☒ B, C, D, and E are incorrect. The **lastb** command searches the */var/log/btmp* file and displays a list of *bad* login attempts. The **who** command searches */var/log/utmp*, when available, and displays a list of currently logged on users. The **whoami** command displays the user's current username, and the **w** command also searches */var/log/utmp* to display who is logged in and which processes they are running. (Domain 2: Systems Operation and Maintenance)

64. ☑ D is correct. Running **userdel -r** will delete the user and the files from their /home directory and their mail spool. Files in other filesystems need to be deleted manually.
☒ A, B, and C are incorrect. The **usermod** and **useradd** commands are not capable of removing users. The **-d** option is not available to **userdel**. (Domain 2: Systems Operation and Maintenance)

65. ☑ A, B, and C are correct. Running **usermod e** allows an administrator to add an expiration date. Running **passwd e** will immediately expire a user's account. The **chage** command stands for "change age" and offers many password expiration features.
☒ D and E are incorrect. The shadow file is a database of password expiration details, and *not* a command. The password command is a distractor and is not available in standard Linux. (Domain 2: Systems Operation and Maintenance)

66. ☑ D is correct. The time zone configuration file is called */etc/localtime*.
☒ A, B, C, and E are incorrect and are all distractors. None of these files exist in standard Linux. (Domain 1: Hardware and System Configuration)

67. ☑ B is correct. Running **localectl status** will display the current locale setting, keymap, keymap layout, and X11 model.
☒ A, C, and D are incorrect. The **-s** and **-l** options are distractors, and are currently not available within **localectl**. Running **localectl list-locales** will list available locales that can be set using **set-locale**. (Domain 1: Hardware and System Configuration)

68. ☑ **A** is correct. Use **LC_ALL** to override the locality variables.
   ☒ **B, C,** and **D** are incorrect. The **LC_NAME** environment variable formats how first and last names appear in different countries. The **LC_CTYPE** environment variable determines how characters are classified. The **LANG** variable specifies the encoding format for all LC variables (LC_*). (Domain 1: Hardware and System Configuration)

69. ☑ **B** is correct. The runme program will run at the effective user ID (EUID) of todd because the SUID bit is set, as shown with the "s" in the permissions **-rwsr-xr-x**; therefore, the command is run at the EUID of the *owner* of the file, not the *user*, which is normally done.
   ☒ **A, C,** and **D** are incorrect. If the SUID bit were not set, runme would run with the montrie user's permissions. When logged in as a standard user, jobs do not normally run with an EUID of root or the group they belong to (in this case, manf). (Domain 3: Security)

70. ☑ **C** and **D** are correct. The default file permissions are 666, and the default directory permissions are 777. The purpose of **umask** is to make files more secure by removing permissions when files are created. 0027 or 027 removes write permission for the group, and read, write, and execute for other.
   ☒ **A, B, E,** and **F** are incorrect. 026 and 0026 would fail because the directory permission results in 751 instead of 750. 0036 and 036 fail because, although the file permission would result to 640, directory permissions would result to 741. (Domain 3: Security)

71. ☑ **D** is correct. When Jeongeun runs **df -h**, she will see that the hard drive is 100 percent full, and that is why she cannot create a new file.
   ☒ **A, B,** and **C** are incorrect. The question implies that she has already run the **quota** command because of not getting any quota errors. The **df -i** command will show inode utilization, not disk space use. Running **du -sh** will only show disk space use in her home directory and below, not the entire system. (Domain 4: Linux Troubleshooting and Diagnostics)

72. ☑ **A** is correct. User John forgot to run **swapon /d/swapfile** to enable the swap area.
   ☒ **B, C,** and **D** are incorrect. The **swapoff** command would disable the swap area. The **mount** command is used to access a filesystem, not swap space. John already ran **mkswap** since the swap area was already set up, as stated in the question. (Domain 4: Linux Troubleshooting and Diagnostics)

73. ☑ **C** is correct. User Quincy would run **echo deadline > /sys/block/sda /queue/scheduler** to update the I/O scheduler from **cfq** or **noop** to **deadline**.
   ☒ **A, B,** and **D** are incorrect because either the **cat** command would attempt to list a file called *deadline* in **A** and **B**, or the **<** means to read from standard input, instead of to write to standard output, as shown in **A** and **D**. (Domain 4: Linux Troubleshooting and Diagnostics)

74. ☑ **B** is correct. User Elimu completes the command as follows for proper completion of the **case** statement:

```
case $fruit in
```

☒ **A, C,** and **D** are incorrect and all would be syntax errors. The **at** command is used to schedule jobs. The **if** command is a decision construct used within scripts. The **of** command is a distractor and not a part of standard Linux. (Domain 5: Automation and Scripting)

75. ☑ **D** is correct. User Wade would complete the statement with the **done** command.

☒ **A, B,** and **C** are incorrect. The **end** and **rof** commands are distractors and not a part of standard Linux. The **od** command provides an "octal dump" representation of a file. (Domain 5: Automation and Scripting)

76. ☑ **B** is correct. User Nadia runs **iostat 10 5** to view CPU and disk drive performance for five counts at 10 second periods.

☒ **A, C,** and **D** are incorrect. Running **iostat 5 10** outputs 10 counts at 5 second intervals, and **iostat 10** outputs performance data every 10 seconds until interrupted with **^C** (CTRL-C). Finally, **iostat --count 5 --period 10** is currently not a feature of **iostat** and results in a syntax error. (Domain 1: Hardware and System Configuration)

77. ☑ **B, C,** and **D** are correct. Walter can run either **mdadm -F**, **mdadm --follow**, or **mdadm --monitor** to "follow" or "monitor" the RAID array as a foreground or background job that notifies system administrators of any RAID issues.

☒ **A** is incorrect as **mdadm --build** creates a legacy RAID array that does not use superblocks. Superblocks are a type of filesystem database that tracks filesystem state and changes. (Domain 1: Hardware and System Configuration)

78. ☑ **D** is correct. Lonnie and Landon run **virsh --escape** ^[to override the default escape sequence that Telnet normally uses, ^].

☒ **A, B,** and **C** are incorrect. Both **--esc** and **--chstr** do not exist and are distractors. The --**debug** option performs up to five levels of logging and accounting for the **virsh** command. (Domain 1: Hardware and System Configuration)

79. ☑ **B** is correct. Laeia and Liara end up running the **badblocks** command to check for bad blocks on the hard drive.

☒ **A, C,** and **D** are incorrect. Both **blockcheck** and **bbcheck** are not presently Linux commands and are distractors. The **kill** command is used to control running processes. (Domain 4: Linux Troubleshooting and Diagnostics)

80. ☑ **B** is correct. Sorana runs the **watch** command. For GIT to work properly, every commit must relate to some username and e-mail address so that all of the co-contributors can keep track of the changes.

☒ **A, C,** and **D** are incorrect. Both **period** and **twosec** are commands that do not exist or are not available with standard Linux. Running **free --count 5 --seconds 2** would give similar results, but it does *not* refresh the screen during each update. (Domain 4: Linux Troubleshooting and Diagnostics)

81. ☑ **A** is correct. User Ugo runs **chmod g+s work** so that files and directories created below the work directory will belong to the same group as the work directory.

☒ **B, C,** and **D** are incorrect as **chmod +a work** will result in a syntax error, and **chmod g=w work** as well as **chmod g=rw work** provide write and read/write privileges to the group, respectively, but new files and directories below the directory will belong to the EGID (effective group ID) of the creating user. (Domain 3: Security)

82. ☑ **B** is correct. Ms. Zhang runs

```
firewall-cmd --zone=public --add-service=http
```

so that users can access her website.

☒ **A, C,** and **D** are incorrect and would give syntax errors because **--allow, =web,** and **add** are improper arguments for **firewall-cmd**. (Domain 3: Security)

83. ☑ **C** is correct. Henri runs **iptables -L** to display the current firewall settings.

☒ **A, B,** and **D** are incorrect. He would use **iptables -s** and **iptables -d** to set up the source and destination port, respectively and would use **iptables -F** to flush (delete) the DNS tables. (Domain 3: Security)

84. ☑ **B** is correct. Petra runs **chkconfig --level 35 auditd on** to enable logging and accounting services for her Linux system.

☒ **A, C,** and **D** are incorrect and would cause syntax errors because **start** is an improper argument and **service** cannot be the last argument. (Domain 2: Systems Operation and Maintenance)

85. ☑ **A** is correct. Milos needs to know which volume group device to extend so that he can then run **lvextend -L+20G /dev/myvg/myvol** to add another 20GB to the /dev/myvg/myvol volume.

☒ **B, C,** and **D** are incorrect because it is not necessary to restart services or reboot the system for extending or growing to take effect. (Domain 4: Linux Troubleshooting and Diagnostics)

86. ☑ **B** is correct. Ushna would not use a tool called Orchestrate because there is no such tool available to her on CentOS Linux.

☒ **A, C,** and **D** are incorrect and are tools that Ushna could use to set up and orchestrate the installation of 500 servers. Anaconda sets up cloud images. Cloud-init makes it easy to configure cloud images, and Kickstart can perform automated operating system installation. (Domain 1: Hardware and System Configuration)

87. ☑ **D** is correct. Thanasi is currently editing a YAML file.

☒ **A, B,** and **C** are incorrect. The file does not represent either a SAML, XML, or JSON file. (Domain 5: Automation and Scripting)

88. ☑ **C** is correct. Teliana is currently editing a JSON file.

☒ **A, B,** and **D** are incorrect. The file does not represent either a SAML, XML, or YAML file. (Domain 5: Automation and Scripting)

89. ☑ **A** is correct. Juan runs the **setenforce permissive** command as root to use SELinux in warning mode only.
☒ **B, C,** and **D** are incorrect. **setenforce enforcing** is the current state Juan is in, and has made the system mostly unfunctional. Running **setenforce disabled** allows Juan to work, but will not load any SELinux policies, so he will not be able to test it. Running **setenforce warning** would result in an error, as the warning option does not exist and is a distractor. (Domain 2: Systems Operation and Maintenance)

90. ☑ **D** is correct. The question asks how to suspend a process running in the foreground. To suspend a process running in the foreground, use the key sequence CTRL-S. To restart the process, press the ENTER key. To suspend a job running in the background, bring it to the foreground using the command **fg% <job_number>** and then press CTRL-Z to suspend the job. To restart the job, execute the command **bg% <job_number>**.
☒ **A, B,** and **C** are incorrect. CTRL-C and CTRL-\ will terminate the current foreground process. CTRL-Z will suspend a background job that has been brought to the foreground. (Domain 2: Systems Operation and Maintenance)

Analyzing Your Results

Now analyze the results! Use this information to identify two things:

- What resources to use to prepare for the exam
- Domains to spend some extra time studying

First, use the following table to determine what tools and resources to use to prepare for the exams:

Number of Answers Correct	Recommended Course of Study
1–25	If this had been the actual Linux+ exam, you most likely would not have passed. Additional study is necessary before taking the real exam. At this level, it is recommended you review each chapter in detail. Set up the Linux virtual machine included with this book and practice completing the tasks covered in this book. Get real-world Linux experience at work, by taking on more Linux assignments, or volunteer at a non-profit and assist them with their Linux projects. Plan on taking the exam about 180 days from now, assuming scores of 85%+ on "fresh" practice exams.
54–72	If this had been the actual Linux+ exam, you likely would not have passed. Additional study and targeted review is recommended. At this level, list each item missed on paper and spend extra time studying the missed topics while going through this book. Set up the Linux virtual machine included with this book and practice completing the tasks covered in this book. You should be ready for the actual exam in 90 days or more, assuming you are scoring 85%+ on "fresh" practice exams.

Number of Answers Correct	Recommended Course of Study
73–90	Congratulations! If this had been the actual Linux+ exam, there is a good chance you would have passed. The authors recommend scheduling the exam for about 14 days from now, to give you time to study and strengthen weaknesses, set up a test environment, and complete most of the Lab Projects in the book. The Linux+ exam is *very* difficult, so use the practice exam simulations and ensure scoring is consistently 85 percent or greater with "fresh" questions.

With the recommendations in the preceding table in mind, you can now use the following table to determine which domains to focus your study efforts on:

Official Exam Domain	Question Number
Hardware and System Configuration	4, 15, 25, 37, 38, 44, 46, 54, 57, 59, 60, 61, 66, 67, 68, 76, 77, 78, 86
Systems Operation and Maintenance	1, 3, 5, 7, 10, 12, 16, 18, 19, 20, 21, 22, 42, 43, 45, 52, 62, 63, 64, 65, 84, 89, 90
Security	6, 8, 9, 28, 32, 33, 39, 40, 41, 49, 50, 58, 69, 70, 81, 82, 83
Linux Troubleshooting and Diagnostics	13, 14, 17, 31, 34, 35, 36, 47, 48, 53, 55, 56, 71, 72, 73, 79, 80, 85
Automation and Scripting	2, 11, 23, 24, 26, 27, 29, 30, 51, 74, 75, 87, 88

CHAPTER 2

Using the vi Text Editor

In this chapter, you will learn about

- The role and function of the vi text editor
- Editing text files in vi
- Editing text files in nano

One of the key skills you will need when working with any Linux system is the ability to use a text editor effectively. Most system-configuration tasks in Linux are completed using a text editor to edit a text file, whether you're configuring the operating system itself or configuring a service running on the system.

The Role and Function of the vi Text Editor

At this point, you may be thinking, "I know how to use text editors on other operating systems. I can use Notepad on Windows. Why are you devoting an entire chapter to text editors in this book?" There are two reasons:

- Knowing how to use a text editor is absolutely critical to being able to manage a Linux system. If you can't use a text editor, you will struggle with the topics presented throughout the rest of this book.
- Linux editors, frankly, are difficult for most new users to learn how to use, especially if you're coming from a Windows background.

There are two versions of vi. The older version is called simply vi. The newer version is called vim, which is short for Vi IMproved. In newer versions of the OS, executing the command **vi** actually executes the command **vim**.

Executing the command **vim** opens Vi IMproved (see Figure 2-1). Depending on your system, executing the command **vi** may open vim in compatible mode.

Each vim installations contain a tutorial. If your system contains the older version of vi, the command **vitutor** will start the tutorial. If your system contains vim, the command **vimtutor** will start the tutorial.

With this in mind, let's discuss how to edit text files in vim.

```
rtracy@openSUSE:~
File  Edit  View  Search  Terminal  Help

                     VIM - Vi IMproved

                      version 7.4.52
                  by Bram Moolenaar et al.
         Vim is open source and freely distributable

                Become a registered Vim user!
        type  :help register<Enter>   for information

        type  :q<Enter>               to exit
        type  :help<Enter>  or  <F1>  for on-line help
        type  :help version7<Enter>   for version info

                                              0,0-1          All
```

Figure 2-1 Using vim

Editing Text Files in vi

The first time you run vim, you'll notice right away that its user interface is very different from what you may be used to with other text editors. To familiarize you with vi, we'll discuss the following topics:

- Opening files in vi
- The vi modes
- Working in command mode
- Working in command-line mode

Opening Files in vi

To open a file from the shell prompt to manipulate in vi, simply enter **vi <filename>** or **vim <filename>**.

NOTE For the remainder of the chapter assume that vi and vim are the same command.

For example, suppose there is a file named *myfile.txt* in your user's home directory. If the file resides in the current directory, you can simply enter **vi myfile.txt** at the shell prompt to load this file into the vi editor. If the file resides in a directory other than the current directory, you then need to include the full path to the file. For example, if your current directory is */tmp* and you need to open the */home/student1/myfile.txt* file in vi, you would enter **vi /home/student1/myfile.txt** at the shell prompt.

It's also possible to create a new text file using vi. To do this, simply enter **vi** followed by the name of the file you wish to create at the shell prompt. If you don't include a path with the filename, the file will be created in the current directory. If you specify a path, the file will be created in that directory.

For example, in Figure 2-2, the current directory is /home/student1 and the command **vi yourfile.txt** has been entered at the shell prompt. Notice that a blank file has been opened in the vi editor interface, as indicated by the "[New File]" text at the bottom of the screen. It's important to note that when you're creating a new file with vi, the file isn't actually created on disk until you save the file. Until then, all the lines of text you enter in the vi interface are saved only in a memory buffer. If you don't save the file, you will lose it!

Now, let's discuss vi modes.

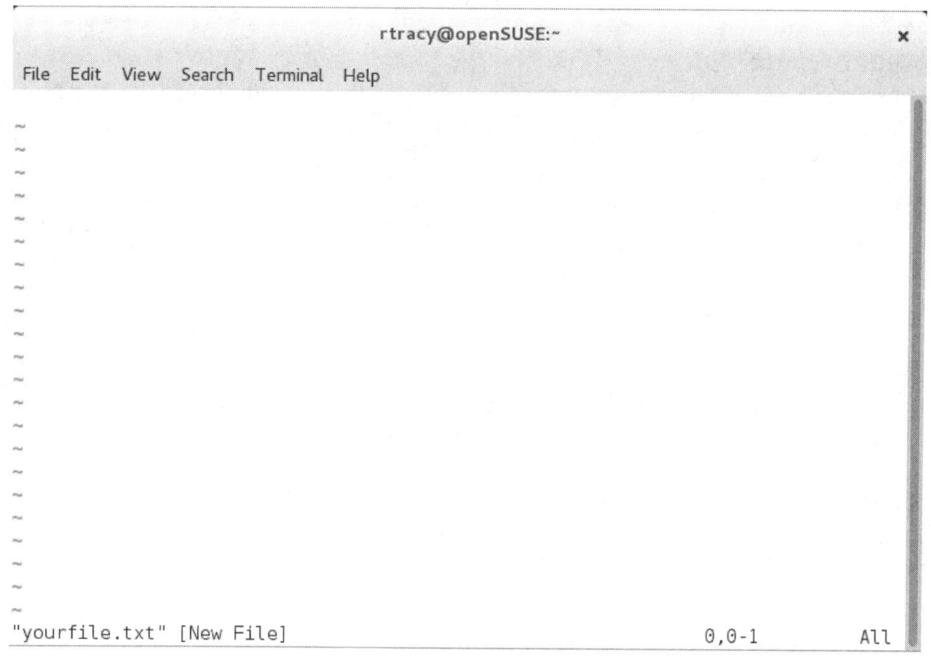

Figure 2-2 Creating a new file with vi

The vi Modes

So far, so good, right? Most of the students we teach vi to can handle opening a file in vi or creating a new file. However, once the file is opened, things start to get a little confusing. That's because vi uses five different operating modes:

- Command mode
- Command-line mode
- Insert
- Append
- Open

You can switch between modes by pressing either ESC : (colon) or the ESC key. For example, let's say you are moving the cursor to the left using ESC l and now want to go into insert mode. You would type ESC **i**.

Command Mode

Pressing the ESC key once places you in command mode. The command mode allows you to issue local editing commands. Local commands would be used to add or modify a character, word, single line, or multiple lines.

Command-Line Mode

Pressing ESC : places you in command-line mode. Commands issued in command-line mode are global commands; they affect the entire document. Examples of global commands are write, search, and search and replace.

NOTE The Linux+ exam refers to "command-line mode" as "lastline" mode.

Insert Mode

Insert mode inserts text to the left of the cursor. ESC **i** (lowercase i) inserts text immediately to the left of the cursor, and ESC **I** (uppercase I) inserts text at the left margin.

Append Mode

Append mode adds text to the right of the cursor. ESC **a** (lowercase a) appends text immediately after the cursor, and ESC **A** (uppercase A) appends text at the end of the current line.

Open Mode

The open mode is used to open a line above or below the current cursor position and places the editor in insert mode and the cursor at the left margin. ESC **o** (lowercase o) opens a line below the current cursor position, and ESC **O** (uppercase O) opens a line above the current cursor position.

Working in Command Mode

Once you have opened a file in vi and entered insert mode, you can edit the text as you would with any other text editor.

Note that on the left side of the screen you see several lines of tildes (~). These characters simply indicate that the corresponding lines do not contain text. After adding lines to the file, you'll see that the tildes disappear one at a time.

Repeating a Command

You can repeat the last command in command mode by pressing the period (.) key. Prior to pressing the period key, you may move the cursor to a new position.

Cursor Movement

You can navigate around to different insertion points in the file by pressing the arrow keys as well as the PAGE UP, PAGE DOWN, HOME, and END keys.

Some additional command-line (ESC <command>) cursor movement commands are shown in the following list. Preceding any command by a number, *n,* repeats the command *n* number of times. For example, the command ESC **2h** will move the cursor two characters to the left.

- **h** Moves the cursor one character to the left
- **l** Moves the cursor one character to the right
- **k** Moves the cursor one character to the line above
- **j** Moves the cursor one character to the line below
- **w** Moves the cursor right to the next word
- **b** Moves the cursor left to the previous word
- **f <c>** Moves the cursor left to the matching character
- **F <c>** Moves the cursor right to the matching character
- **0** Moves the cursor to the beginning of the line
- **^** Moves the cursor to the first printable character on the line
- **$** Moves the cursor to the last character on the line
- ***n*G** Moves the cursor to line *n*
- **gg** Moves the cursor to the first line of the document
- **G** Moves the cursor to the last line of the document
- **H** Moves the cursor to the top of the current screen
- **M** Moves the cursor to the middle of the current screen
- **L** Moves the cursor to the bottom of the current screen

Deleting and Replacing Characters and Words

You can remove text by pressing DELETE or BACKSPACE. Some commands associated with deleting a character, word, or line are shown in the following list:

- **x** Deletes the character in the current cursor position
- **X** Deletes the character to the left of the cursor
- **u** Undoes last edit
- **U** Undoes all edits on the current line
- **r** Replaces the character in the current cursor position
- **R** Enters Replace mode.
- **dw** Deletes a word from the current cursor position to the end of the word

NOTE A word is defined as a string of characters terminated by a delimiter. In a text processing environment, the delimiter is a space, tab, or newline character.

- **D** Deletes the rest of the current line from the cursor position
- **d$** Deletes from the current cursor position to the end of the line
- **p** Puts the deleted text to the right of the cursor
- **P** Puts the deleted text to the left of the cursor
- **dd** Deletes the current line.
- **:d*n*** Command-line command (ESC :) to delete a specific line (*n*)
- **:*n*,*y*d** Command-line command (ESC :) to delete from line *n* to line *y*

Changing a Word or Line

The C or c prefix indicates you are going to change text.

- **cw** vi deletes from the current cursor position until the end of the word and places itself in insert mode.
- **C** Changes from the current cursor position to the end of the line by deleting from the current cursor position to the end of the line and placing vi in insert mode.
- **cc** Changes the line. vi deletes the entire line and places itself in insert mode.

Copying and Moving a Line

To copy a line, you place the line in the buffer, move the cursor, and then put the copied line above or below the current cursor position. Use the yank and put commands to do this.

- **yy** Yanks (copies) the current line into the buffer. Multiple lines may be copied by preceding **yy** with a number. For example, **3yy** will place the current line and the next two lines into the buffer.
- **p** Puts the yanked lines from the buffer in the line below the cursor. If there are multiple lines, it places the lines in the same order.
- **P** Puts the yanked lines from the buffer in the line above the cursor.

To move a line from one place to another, you delete the line, move the cursor, and then put the deleted line above or below the current cursor position. Use the **dd** and put commands to do this.

- **dd** Deletes the current line and places it into the buffer. Multiple lines may be moved by preceding **dd** with a number. For example, **3dd** will place the current line and the next two lines into the buffer.
- **p** Puts the deleted line from the buffer in the line below the cursor. If there are multiple lines, it places the lines in the same order.
- **P** Puts the deleted line from the buffer in the line above the cursor. If there are multiple lines, it places the lines in the same order.

Saving and Exiting

The command **ZZ** is used to save the current document to disk and quit vi. The document must have a filename associated with it.

Working in Command-Line Mode

The command line executes commands that are asserted against the entire document. To enter command-line mode, enter ESC :. This will place your cursor at the bottom of the current screen, as shown in Figure 2-3. You can then enter commands at this prompt to accomplish file-related tasks.

Deleting Text

To delete lines in command-line mode, specify a line number or a range of line numbers followed by the letter *d*.

- **nd** Deletes line *n*
- ***n*,*y*d** Deletes from line *n* to line *y*

Searching for Text

You do not need to preface any of the following with ESC : or the ESC key:

- **/<string>** Forward search. A forward slash (/) followed by a string of characters will search the document from the current cursor position to the bottom of the file for the string. For example, **/test** will search for the string "test" from the current cursor position to the bottom of the document.

Figure 2-3 The vi command-line mode command prompt

- **?<string>** Reverse search. A question mark (?) followed by a string of characters will search the document from the current cursor position to the bottom of the file for the string. For example, **?test** will search for the string "test" from the current cursor position to the top of the document.
- **n** Continue the search in the same direction. Searches for the same string specified by **/<string>** or **?<string>** in the same direction.
- **N** Continue the search in the opposite direction. Searches for the same string specified by **/<string>** or **?<string>** in the opposite direction.

Search and Replace Text

The following are command-line commands that need to be prefaced with ESC **:** (by default, the search begins at the top of the document and goes until the end of the document):

- **:s<string>** Search for the string. To search for the text "test," open the command-line mode (ESC **:**) and enter **:s/test**.
- **:s/<current_string>/<replacement_string>/** Search for a string on the current line and replace the first instance of the string. Given the line "breakfast is our morning break," the command-line command **:s/break/old/** would produce the line "oldfast is our morning break."
- **:s/<current_string>/<replacement_string>g** Search for a string on the current line and replace all instances of the string on the line. Given the line "breakfast is our morning break," the command-line command **:s/break/old/g** would produce the line "oldfast is our morning old."
- **:%s/<current_string>/<replacement_string>/** Search for all instances of the string in the document and replace every instance.

Writing and Quitting a Document

To write the file to disk, enter ESC **:** **w** ENTER. After entering **w** at the command prompt, you'll see a message at the bottom of the screen indicating that the file has been written to disk, as shown in this example:

```
"file.txt" [New] 1L, 28C written                        1,26          All
```

Entering **w <filename>** or **save <filename>** at the command line prompt will write the file to a different filename. You can also enter these other commands at the command-line prompt:

- **exit** Writes the current file to disk and quits vi.
- **wq** Writes the current file to disk and quits vi.
- **q** Quits vi without saving the current file. This can be used only if the file hasn't been changed. If the file has been changed, you must enter **q!** to override the error "No write since last change."

- **w!** Used to override read-only files.
- **e!** Forgets changes since the last write and opens another file for edit.

Syntax Checker

Another helpful feature of the vi editor is that it provides a very useful syntax checker. This feature can be a real lifesaver when you're writing scripts or editing a configuration file. There's nothing more frustrating than having a script or daemon not work because you forgot a semicolon or closing parenthesis somewhere. The syntax checker can be enabled or disabled using the syntax command-line command. Press ESC to enter command mode, and then enter **:syntax on | off**. For example, to enable the syntax checker, you would enter the following:

```
:syntax on
```

When you do, different elements in the script or configuration file are denoted with different colors. If you make a syntax error, the mistake will be highlighted with an alternate color, making it easy for you to spot. An example of using the vi syntax checker while editing a daemon's configuration file is shown in Figure 2-4.

As you can see, vi is a simple yet fairly powerful text editor. The only complaint about vi is that its user interface can be difficult to learn. However, once you've used vi for a while, it will become second nature to you. Therefore, let's spend some time practicing with vi in the following exercise.

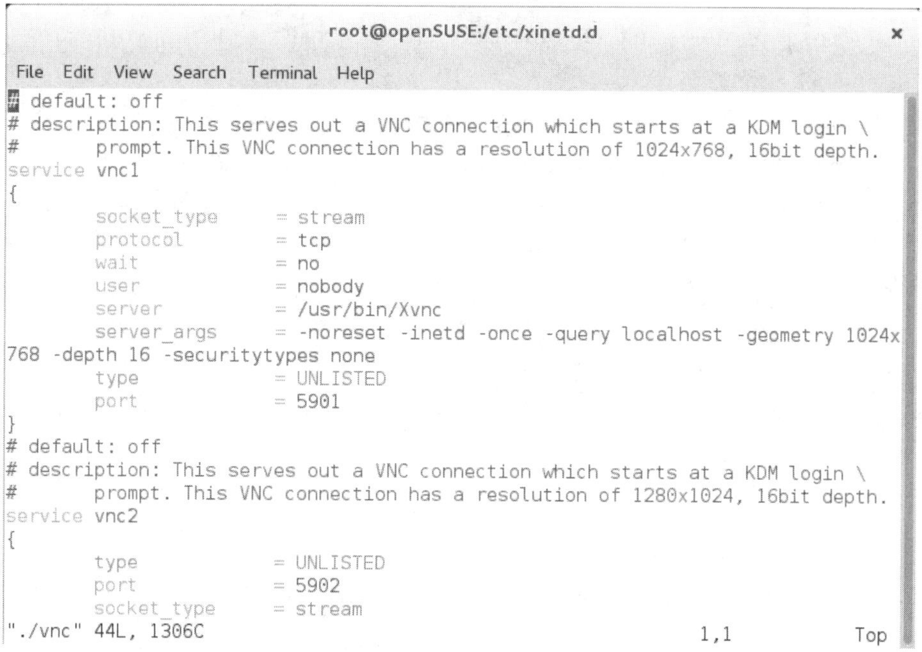

```
root@openSUSE:/etc/xinetd.d
File  Edit  View  Search  Terminal  Help
# default: off
# description: This serves out a VNC connection which starts at a KDM login \
#       prompt. This VNC connection has a resolution of 1024x768, 16bit depth.
service vnc1
{
        socket_type     = stream
        protocol        = tcp
        wait            = no
        user            = nobody
        server          = /usr/bin/Xvnc
        server_args     = -noreset -inetd -once -query localhost -geometry 1024x
768 -depth 16 -securitytypes none
        type            = UNLISTED
        port            = 5901
}
# default: off
# description: This serves out a VNC connection which starts at a KDM login \
#       prompt. This VNC connection has a resolution of 1280x1024, 16bit depth.
service vnc2
{
        type            = UNLISTED
        port            = 5902
        socket_type     = stream
"./vnc" 44L, 1306C                                    1,1           Top
```

Figure 2-4 Using the vi syntax checker

Exercise 2-1: Using the vi Editor

In this exercise, you will practice using the vi editor to create and manipulate text files.

VIDEO Watch the Exercise 2-1 video for a demonstration.

Log on to the virtual machine provided with this course as **student1** (password **student1**) and then follow these steps:

1. Open a terminal.
2. The current directory should be your user's home directory. You may verify this by entering the command **pwd** at the shell prompt. (Typing the command **cd** will always return you to your home directory.)
3. At the shell prompt, enter **vi test.txt**. The vi editor should run with test.txt open as a new file.
4. Press the INSERT key on your keyboard. You should now be in insert mode.
5. Enter the following text in the file:
   ```
   Now is the time for all good men to come to the aide of their country.
   ```
6. Save your file by completing the following steps:
   a. Press ESC to return to command mode.
   b. Enter **:w**. You should see a message indicating that the file was written.
7. Exit vi by entering **:exit**.
8. Reload test.txt in vi by entering **vi test.txt** at the shell prompt.
9. Display the status line by pressing CTRL-G while in command mode.
10. Use the arrow keys to move the cursor to the beginning of the first word in the first line of the file.
11. Search for all occurrences of the letter *a* by completing the following steps:
    a. While in command mode, enter **/a**. The first instance should be highlighted.
    b. Find the next instance of the letter *a* by pressing the n key.
12. While in command mode, use the arrow keys to place the cursor on the first letter of the word *time*.
    a. Delete the word *time* using the command **dw**. Remember, a word is a string terminated by a space, so the string time and the following space will be deleted.
    b. Use the arrow keys to move the cursor to the period at the end of the last line.
13. Exit the file without saving your changes by entering **:q!**.
14. vi provides a user tutorial. The command **vimtutor** will execute a self-paced tutorial for vim. If you have an older system, execute the command **vitutor**.

Editing Text Files in nano

GNU nano is a clone of Digital Equipment's pico editor. It is easier to use than vim as it does not contain command modes and has a context-driven menu displayed at the bottom of the page (see Figure 2-5).

Configuration files

nano uses two configuration files: the system-wide configuration file */etc/nanorc* and the user-specific file *.nanorc* in the user's home directory. The statement set nowrap in either of these files mitigates the need for the -w option.

Command Keys

nano uses both the control key (prefix ^) and a meta key to issue commands.

The meta key is either the ESC or ALT keys and is designated by the prefix M- in the help literature.

The command key sequence ^G (CTRL-G) will open nano's help screen. The command sequence M- / (ESC or ALT-/) will move the cursor to the bottom of the document.

Table 2-1 illustrates some options for opening a file.

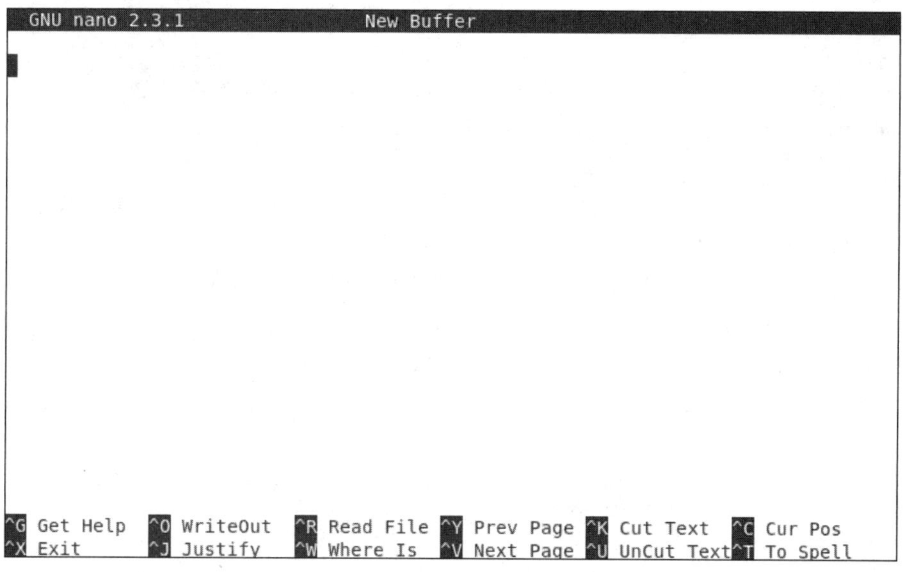

Figure 2-5 The nano editor; note the menu at the bottom.

Table 2-1 nano Open File Options

Option	Description
<file_name>	Open a file with the name <file_name>. If the file does not exist, the file will be created once it is written.
-v <file_name>	Open a file in view (read-only mode)
-w	Prevent line wrapping. This option (enabled by default in /etc/nanorc) is necessary when editing configuration files to prevent entering a CR+LF (Windows) rather than LF (Linux) to designate a new line.

To move the cursor, you can use one of the key sequences specified in Table 2-2. Additional nano documentation may be found at www.nano-editor.org.

Chapter Review

This chapter introduced you to some of the tools used to edit files using vi. You should be able to open a file, modify the contents of the file, and save the file.

It is in your best interest to use a built-in tutorial (vitutor or vimtutor) to practice your vi skills.

Let's look at what you have learned:

- Linux uses text files to store operating system and application-configuration settings.
- The older version of vi was called *vi*, and the newest version is called *vim* (Vi IMproved).
- You can open a file with vi by entering **vi <filename>**. If the file doesn't exist, a new file will be created.
- The vi editor opens in command mode by default.
- To switch to insert mode, press I, S, or INSERT.
- In insert mode, you can directly edit the text of a file.
- Pressing INSERT while in insert mode will cause vi to switch to replace mode.

Table 2-2 nano Key Sequences

Key Sequence	Description
CTRL-F or RIGHT ARROW	Moves the cursor one character to the right
CTRL-B or LEFT ARROW	Move the cursor one character to the left
CTRL-P or UP ARROW	Move the cursor up one line
CTRL-N or DOWN ARROW	Move the cursor down one line.
CTRL-<SPACE>	Move the cursor one word forward
M-<SPACE>	Move the cursor one word back

- To switch back to command mode, press the ESC key.
- **ESC-dw** Deletes the word that comes immediately after the cursor, including the space following the word.
- **ESC-d$** Deletes from the insertion point to the end of the line.
- **ESC-dd** Deletes the entire current line.
- **ESC-p** Inserts deleted text before or below the current cursor location.
- **ESC-P** Inserts deleted text after or above the current cursor location.
- **ESC-u** Undoes the last action.
- **ESC-U** Undoes all changes made on the current line.
- **ESC-D** Deletes the rest of the current line from the cursor position.
- **ESC-yy** Copies the line in which the cursor is located to the buffer.
- **ESC-a** Appends after cursor.
- **ESC-A** Appends after line.
- **ESC-C** Changes to the end of the line.
- **ESC-cc** Changes the whole line.
- **ESC-ZZ** Saves the current file and ends vi.
- **ESC-h** Moves the cursor left one character.
- **ESC-j** Moves the cursor down one line.
- **ESC-k** Moves the cursor up one line.
- **l** Moves the cursor right one character.
- **0** Moves the cursor to the start of the current line.
- From within command mode, you can enter a colon (:) to switch to command-line mode.
- **ESC-:w** Writes the current file to disk.
- **ESC-:exit** Writes the current file to disk and then closes vi.
- **ESC-:wq** Also writes the current file to disk and closes vi.
- **ESC -:q** Closes vi without saving the current file.
- **ESC-:q!** Closes vi without saving the current file, even if the file has been modified.
- **ESC-:w!** Overwrites the current file.
- **ESC-:e!** Forgets changes since the last write.
- Pressing CTRL-G displays a status line at the bottom of the interface.
- Entering **/search <string>** searches from the current cursor position to the bottom of the document for the specified string.
- Entering **?search <string>** searches from the current cursor position to the top of the document for the specified string.

Questions

1. How are operating system and application configuration parameters stored on a Linux system?
   - **A.** In text files
   - **B.** In the Registry
   - **C.** In .ini files
   - **D.** In the system database
2. You are trying to quit a file without saving any new edits since the last time you wrote the file to disk. You receive the error message "No write since last change." Select the answer or answers that correctly describe what has occurred.
   - **A.** This is a bug in vi.
   - **B.** The buffer has been modified without writing the change to disk. Execute ESC : **w!**.
   - **C.** The buffer has been modified without writing the change to disk. Execute ESC : **w** and then ESC : **q**.
   - **D.** The buffer has been modified without writing the change to disk. Execute ESC : **q!**.
3. Your cursor is positioned at line 14 of the document. Which command or commands will bring your cursor to the top of the document? (Choose two.)
   - **A.** ESC :1G
   - **B.** ESC : GG
   - **C.** ESC : gg
   - **D.** ESC: 1g
4. You have a terminal window open on your Linux system, and the current directory is /tmp. You need to use vi to edit a text file named *vnc* in the */etc/xinetd.d* directory on your system. Which of the following commands will do this?
   - **A.** vi vnc
   - **B.** vi /tmp/vnc
   - **C.** vi /etc/xinetd.d/vnc
   - **D.** vi /etc/xinetd.d
5. You have a terminal window open on your Linux system, and the current directory is your user's home directory. You need to create a new file in your home directory named *resources.txt* using vi. Which of the following commands will do this?
   - **A.** vi resources.txt -new
   - **B.** vi resources
   - **C.** vi ~/resources
   - **D.** vi resources.txt

6. Which mode does vi open in by default?
   A. Command-line mode
   B. Insert mode
   C. Command mode
   D. Replace mode
7. After opening a file, you use the arrow keys to move the cursor to the line you want to edit. You try to type, but nothing happens. Why?
   A. The vi editor is in insert mode. You need to switch to command mode.
   B. The vi editor is in command mode. You need to switch to insert mode.
   C. The vi editor is in insert mode. You need to switch to replace mode.
   D. The text file is corrupt.
8. Which keys will switch vi from command mode to insert mode? (Choose two.)
   A. DELETE
   B. ESC
   C. INSERT
   D. S
   E. FI
9. You're using vi to edit a text file in insert mode. Because of the nature of the changes you're making to the file, you need to switch to replace mode. Which of the following keys will do this? (Choose two.)
   A. ESC R
   B. CTRL-X CTRL-R
   C. :
   D. INSERT
10. You're using vi to edit a file in insert mode. You need to switch back to command mode. Which key will do this?
    A. INSERT
    B. :
    C. ESC
    D. BACKSPACE
11. You're using vi to edit a file in command mode. You try to use the BACKSPACE key to delete a word, but nothing happens. What's wrong with the system?
    A. You need to switch to normal mode.
    B. You need to press CTRL-BACKSPACE.
    C. Nothing is wrong. BACKSPACE doesn't work in command mode.
    D. You need to switch to command-line mode.

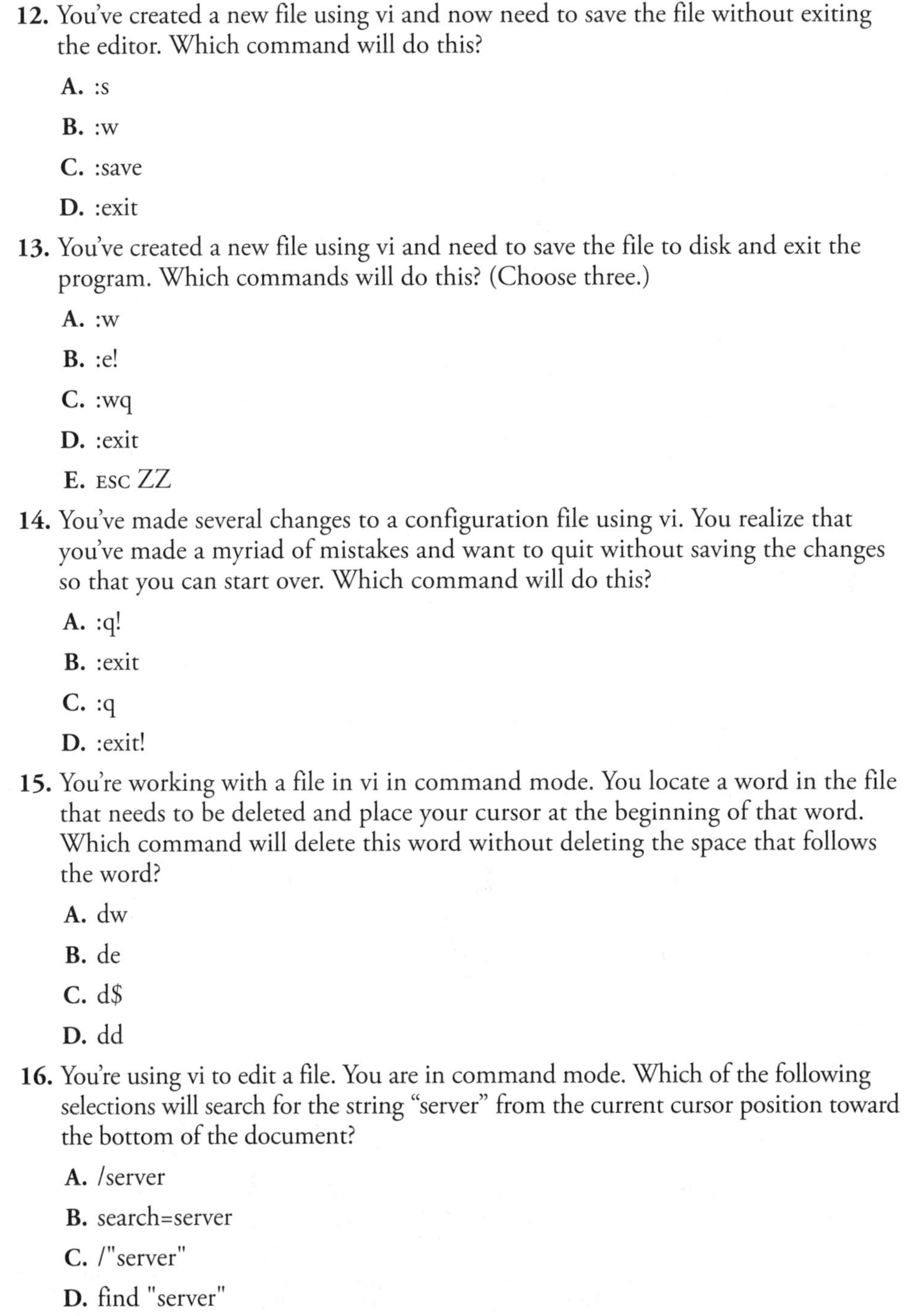

12. You've created a new file using vi and now need to save the file without exiting the editor. Which command will do this?

    A. :s

    B. :w

    C. :save

    D. :exit

13. You've created a new file using vi and need to save the file to disk and exit the program. Which commands will do this? (Choose three.)

    A. :w

    B. :e!

    C. :wq

    D. :exit

    E. ESC ZZ

14. You've made several changes to a configuration file using vi. You realize that you've made a myriad of mistakes and want to quit without saving the changes so that you can start over. Which command will do this?

    A. :q!

    B. :exit

    C. :q

    D. :exit!

15. You're working with a file in vi in command mode. You locate a word in the file that needs to be deleted and place your cursor at the beginning of that word. Which command will delete this word without deleting the space that follows the word?

    A. dw

    B. de

    C. d$

    D. dd

16. You're using vi to edit a file. You are in command mode. Which of the following selections will search for the string "server" from the current cursor position toward the bottom of the document?

    A. /server

    B. search=server

    C. /"server"

    D. find "server"

17. Refer to question 16. You would like to continue searching for the string "server" but want to reverse the search direction. What command would do this?

    A. n

    B. N

    C. ?

    D. /

Answers

1. **A.** Linux uses text files to store configuration parameters for both the operating system and applications or services running on the system.
2. **D.** vi requires you write the contents of the buffer to disk before quitting. You may override any errors by adding ! to the end of the command. Therefore, the command-line command **q!** will quit the file without writing new entries in the buffer to disk.
3. **A, C.** Both ESC **: 1G** and ESC **: gg** will move the cursor to the first line (top) of the document.
4. **C.** Because the file to be loaded doesn't reside in the current directory, you have to provide the full path to the file along with its filename when starting vi.
5. **D.** Because you haven't specified a path, vi will create the file in the current directory, which is what you want.
6. **C.** By default, vi opens in command mode.
7. **B.** The vi editor opens by default in command mode. You must press INSERT to switch to insert mode to start editing the file.
8. **C, D.** Pressing INSERT or S switches vi from command mode to insert mode.
9. **A, D.** Pressing the INSERT key will toggle between insert and replace mode. The key sequence ESC **R** will also place vi in replace mode.
10. **C.** Pressing ESC while in insert mode switches vi to command mode.
11. **C.** The BACKSPACE key doesn't work in command mode. You must first switch to insert or replace mode.
12. **B.** Entering **:w** will write the current memory buffer to disk without exiting the editor.
13. **C, D, E.** Entering **:exit** will cause vi to save the current file and exit the program, as will entering **:wq** or ESC **ZZ**.
14. **A.** Entering **:q!** will exit vi without saving changes to the current file.
15. **B.** Entering **de** in command mode will cause vi to delete the word without deleting the space that follows the word.
16. **A.** Entering **/server** in command mode will search for the expression "server" in the file.
17. **B.** The **N** command will reverse the current search direction.

CHAPTER 3

Working with the Linux Shell

In this chapter, you will learn about

- What a shell is
- Setting a local environment
- Setting time
- Configuring the shell
- Bash configuration files
- Redirection

You may find it helpful to log on to the virtual machine as user student1 (password student1) while reading this chapter.

What Is a Shell?

A *shell* is a program that functions as a user interface, command-line interpreter, and programing (scripting) language. Let's take a brief look at each of these entities.

Users need a way to tell the operating system what tasks it needs to complete, and the operating system needs a way to communicate results to the users. A user interface allows a user to interact with the operating system. Linux provides two types of user interfaces:

- **Command-line interface (CLI)** With the command-line interface, the user communicates with the Linux operating system by typing commands at a command prompt.
- **Graphical user interface (GUI)** In addition to a command-line interface, Linux also offers users an easy-to-use graphical user interface, which allows them to interact with the Linux kernel using a mouse.

Once a command is entered, it must be presented to the operating system for execution. A command-line interpreter reads the user input, analyzes the input, and produces a command that is understood by the operating system.

Rather than you needing to type a list of commands over and over again, most shells provide a method of automating tasks. A *script* is a series of commands stored in a file and executed by a program. You will see an example of using a script to configure the bash shell later in this chapter.

Configuring the Shell

In this section of this chapter, we will discuss shell configuration files. The shell configuration files set up the user environment (*/etc/profile* and *~/.bash_profile*) and regulate how the shell operates (*/etc/bashrc* and *~/.bashrc*).

Processes

A *process* is a single instance of a program that operates in its own memory space. The operating system assigns a unique process ID (PID) each time a program is started. This PID is used to control and track resources assigned to the program.

If you execute the command vim, a process would be created and assigned a PID. If you open another terminal and executed the vim command again, another process would be created and assigned a PID. Executing the command vim again would produce another instance of vim. In this scenario, you would have three unique processes (instances) executing the vim command, as shown in Figure 3-1.

Parent and Child Processes

When you log on a system, you are presented with a default logon shell. This shell is a program (by default, bash) that allows you to execute additional programs.

When you execute a command such as ls, a subshell or child process is created. This means that a copy of the current process (parent) is created and a new instruction set is loaded into the new process (child), as shown in Figure 3-2.

Once the command has executed, the child is killed and control reverts to the parent.

NOTE The term *spawn* is used to describe a parent process creating a child process.

Variables

A *variable* is a memory location that is assigned a name and is used to store data. Variables are used to configure operating environments or to temporarily store program data. When a user logs off or the system is turned off, data stored in these memory locations are lost.

The two types of variables we'll discuss are local and environmental variables.

Local Variables

A local variable only exists in the memory space of the shell in which it is created. This means if you create a variable in a parent process and then create a child process, the variable created in the parent will not be present in the child.

```
student1  7555  3442  0 17:59 pts/1    00:00:00 vim
student1  7567  3336  0 17:59 pts/0    00:00:00 vim
student1  7568  3497  0 17:59 pts/2    00:00:00 vim
```

Figure 3-1 Instances of a process (vim)

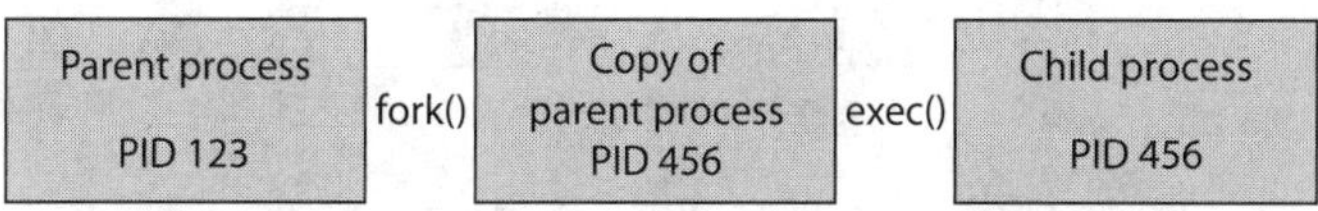

Figure 3-2 Creating a child process

The syntax for creating a local variable is **<variable_name>=<value>**. The command **flower=rose** will create the local variable flower and store the word rose. If you execute the command **flower=daisy**, the contents of the local variable flower will contain the word daisy.

To view the contents of a variable, execute the command **echo $<variable_name>**. The echo command displays a line of text. The dollar sign preceding the variable name is a meta character that replaces the name of the variable with the value stored in the variable. Therefore, if the current value of the variable flower is daisy, the command **echo $flower** would display the output daisy.

The **set** command will display a list of all the variables and functions that exist in the current process. Figure 3-3 displays an edited output of the set command.

Environmental or Global Variables

The variable EDITOR contains the name of the system editor. If no assignment is made, vi is the default. I prefer the nano editor, so I must change the value of the variable EDITOR by executing the command **EDITOR=nano**. This is a local variable. Since local variables only exist in the shell in which they are created, the new value of the variable EDITOR will not be present when a child process is created.

In order to copy a shell variable from the parent process to the child process, you need to assign an export attribute to the variable. When a parent spawns a child process, all variables with this attribute are copied to the child, as illustrated in Figure 3-4.

An environmental (or global) variable is any variable assigned an export attribute. To create a variable and assign an export attribute, execute the command **export <variable_name>=<value>**. For example, the command **export truck=chevy** would create the environmental variable truck and assign it a value of chevy. This variable would be available in the parent process and any child processes. The command **export <variable_name>** will assign an export attribute to an existing variable.

How can you tell if a variable has an export attribute? Unfortunately, the command **echo $<variable name>** will only display the value and not the properties of the variable. The command **env** will display a list of all environmental variables in the current shell. To determine if a specific variable has an export attribute, execute the

```
BASH_ALIASES=()
BASH_ARGC=()
BASH_ARGV=()
BASH_CMDS=()
BASH_COMPLETION_COMPAT_DIR=/etc/bash_completion.d
BASH_LINENO=()
BASH_SOURCE=()
```

Figure 3-3 Edited output of the set command

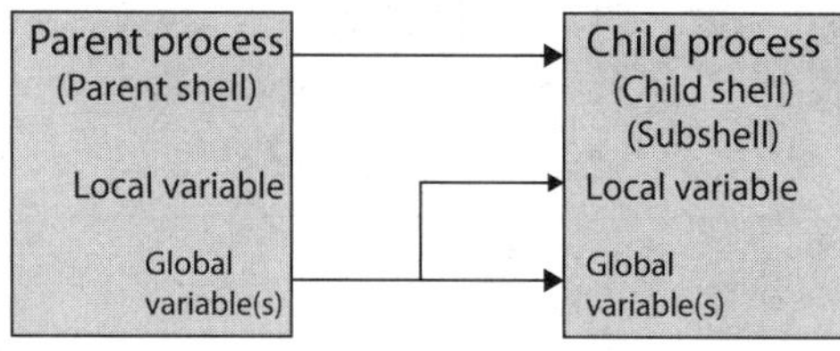

Figure 3-4 Transferring environmental variables from parent to child process

command **env | grep <variable_name>**. If the variable name is displayed, the export attribute has been applied.

The command **declare -p <variable_name>** displays the properties of a variable.

NOTE If you see an x in the properties section of the output, the variable is an environmental variable.

Aliases

An alias is a command shortcut. By default the ls command would display a monochrome output. To colorize the output, you would execute the command **ls --color=auto**. To avoid entering the option each time you execute the ls command, you can create an alias using the following command syntax:

alias <alias_name>='<command>'

The command **alias ls='ls --color=auto'** would create an alias for the command ls. Aliases take precedence over all other command types, so each time you execute the command ls, the command **alias ls --color=auto** will execute.

NOTE An alias will only exist in the shell in which it was created or loaded.

On line 1 of Figure 3-5, you can see the results of creating the **alias ls --color=auto** (although the color may be hard to discern in this black-and-white book; you can download a color version of this figure from the online resources). Executing the alias command (line 5), you can display a list of aliases loaded into memory. Use the grep command to filter out the alias you created.

On line 8, a backslash (\) precedes the ls command. This temporarily negates the alias. Notice the output on line 9 (it is monochrome, although it may be hard to tell in this book).

On line 16, the command **unalias <alias_name>** (**unalias ls**) removes the alias from memory. The output on line 23 is monochrome.

To permanently remove an alias you must remove it from memory (unalias) and, if necessary, remove it from the file from which the alias was loaded.

```
# ls
anaconda-ks.cfg  Documents  initial-setup-ks.cfg  Pictures  Templates  vmware-tools-distrib
Desktop          Downloads  Music                 Public    Videos
#
# alias | grep ls=
alias ls='ls --color=auto'
#
# \ls
anaconda-ks.cfg  Documents  initial-setup-ks.cfg  Pictures  Templates  vmware-tools-distrib
Desktop          Downloads  Music                 Public    Videos
#
# ls
anaconda-ks.cfg  Documents  initial-setup-ks.cfg  Pictures  Templates  vmware-tools-distrib
Desktop          Downloads  Music                 Public    Videos
#
# unalias ls
#
# alias | grep ls=
#
# ls
anaconda-ks.cfg  Documents  initial-setup-ks.cfg  Pictures  Templates  vmware-tools-distrib
Desktop          Downloads  Music                 Public    Videos
```

Figure 3-5 Creating and removing an alias

CAUTION Before creating an alias, you need to make certain the alias name is not used as a keyword. The command **type -a <proposed_alias_name>** will display any commands, aliases, or functions currently using the proposed alias name.

The backslash is a meta character used to negate the special significance of the following character or word. Preceding an alias with a backslash (\ ) forces the command-line interpreter to choose the next command type for the same command name based on the order of precedence. Notice in the following example how the backslash before **$** negates the special significance of the meta character:

```
# echo $SHELL
/bin/bash
echo \$SHELL
echo SHELL
```

To ensure an alias, function, or builtin does not interfere with a command, provide the absolute path to the command. The absolute path to a command takes precedence over aliases, functions, and builtins. To determine the absolute path to a command, execute the command **whereis -b <command_keyword>**.

Setting Up the Local Environment (Locale)

Locale settings are used to set language and country-specific settings (regional settings).

To understand locale settings, you must first understand character encoding.

Character Encoding

A character is a written symbol. A character set is a defined list of characters used for a specific purpose. The English alphabet is a character set that contains 26 letters, 10 digits, and 14 punctuation marks.

Regular expressions uses the left and right brackets to define a character set. For example, [ABC] defines a character set that contains the character list A, B, C.

Characters are stored by assigning a numerical value to the character. The process of assigning a numerical value to a character is called encoding. The stored value is called a code point. An encoding format defines the number of bits used to store a character (code unit) and how the character is stored.

Let's take a brief look at the ASCII and UTF encoding formats.

ASCII

The American Standard Code for Information Interchange (ASCII) character set uses a 7-bit code unit. ASCII supports up to 128 characters (95 printable characters, 32 control codes, and one space character).

Extended ASCII uses an 8-bit code unit and can support 256 characters.

Unicode

The code unit size of encoding formats such as ASCII and EBCDIC are unable to store all the different world characters. Unicode uses variable and fixed encoding formats to provide up to a 32-bit code unit and is capable of storing 1,114,112 different characters.

Unicode defines three encoding formats: UTF-8, UTF-16. and UTF-32 (see Table 3-1).

UTF-8 and UTF-16 use up to 32 bits and variable encoding to store characters. Variable encoding uses the most significant bits of a byte or bytes of the code point to determine how to decode character information. How this decoding is accomplished is beyond the scope of the exam.

UTF-32 uses fixed encoding. This means all 32 bits (4 bytes) are used to store a character.

locale Settings

Locale settings are used to define output formats used by applications.

Table 3-1 Unicode Encoding Formats

Encoding Format	Description
UTF-8	Variable encoding. Uses one, two, three or four bytes to encode a character.
UTF-16	Variable encoding. Uses two or four bytes to encode a character.
UTF-32	Fixed encoding. Uses four bytes to encode a character.

Table 3-2
Locale Categories

Locale Category Variables	Definition
LC_ADDRESS	Address format
LC_COLLATE	How characters are compared and sorted
LC_IDENTIFICATION	Local code
LC_MEASUREMENT	Measure format
LC_MONETARY	Money format
LC_PAPER	Paper sizes
LC_TELEPHONE	Telephone number format

You can set the locale using the LANG variable, LC category variables (Table 3-2), or the variable LC_ALL.

The command **locale -k <locale_category>** will display formatting information for that category. For example, the command **locale -k LC_TELPEHONE** will display the following output:

```
# locale -k LC_TELEPHONE
tel_int_fmt="+%c (%a) %l"
tel_dom_fmt="(%a) %l"
int_select="11"
int_prefix="1"
telephone-codeset="UTF-8"
```

Locale categories are associated with a locale name. The locale name defines formatting for a specific region. Locale names are formatted as follows :

```
<language>_<region>.<encoding_format>@<modifier>
```

The modifier is used to specify use of euro currency (@euro).

An example of a locale name is en_US.UTF-8.

Executing the command **locale -a** or **localectl list-locales** will list available locale names. The command **localectl list-locales | grep en** will display all locale names for the English language.

The command **locale** will display the value of locale categories for our current session, as shown here.

```
#locale
LANG=en_US.UTF-8
LC_CTYPE="en_US.UTF-8"
LC_NUMERIC="en_US.UTF-8"
LC_TIME="en_US.UTF-8"
LC_COLLATE="en_US.UTF-8"
LC_MONETARY="en_US.UTF-8"
LC_MESSAGES="en_US.UTF-8"
LC_PAPER="en_US.UTF-8"
LC_NAME="en_US.UTF-8"
LC_ADDRESS="en_US.UTF-8"
LC_TELEPHONE="en_US.UTF-8"
LC_MEASUREMENT="en_US.UTF-8"
LC_IDENTIFICATION="en_US.UTF-8"
LC_ALL=
```

The variable LANG stores the locale name for the current login session. The following locale name shows that our current session uses the US English character set which is encoded using UTF-8.

```
# echo $LANG
en_US.UTF-8
```

The variable LC_ALL will override all locale category settings and the LANG variable.

localectl

The file */etc/locale.conf* (Debian: */etc/default/locale*) stores system locale and keyboard map settings.

The command **localetcl** is used to view and modify system locale and keyboard settings.

You may make changes to the settings stored in */etc/locale.conf* using the **localectl** command or editing this file manually.

The command **localectl set-locale LANG=<locale_name>** will set the default system locale variable.

The command **localectl set-locale LANG=en_CA.UTF-8** will modify the */etc/locale.conf* file.

The commands **localectl**, or **localectl status** will verify the change to the file.

NOTE If you make any changes to the file */etc/locale.conf* via the localectl command or by manually editing the file, you must source the configuration file to implement the changes immediately.

The command **localectl set-locale <locale_category>=<locale_name>** will also modify the */etc/locale.conf* file.

A user may prefer different locale settings than the system locale settings. These changes may be made temporarily via the command line (**export $<locale variable=<value>**) or permanently by adding the appropriate setting to the *~/.bash_profile* file.

Setting Time

The Linux operating system uses two clocks: the real time (hardware) clock and the system clock.

The real time clock (RTC) is a battery-powered circuit that maintains time even when system power is removed.

The system clock is the operating system clock. During the boot process, the system clock is set to the same value as the hardware clock. From that moment until the time the operating system is terminated, the system clock is maintained by the kernel. The system clock reports time using Coordinated Universal Time (UTC) and depends on individual processes to change UTC into local time.

TIP UTC is a time standard and is also referred to as Zulu time.

date

The date command is primarily used for reporting information from and managing the system clock.

The date command, shown next, will display the day, month, time (24-hour clock), time zone, and year.

```
# date
Thu Nov  6 23:02:00 EST 2014
```

The **date -u** command will display the date in Coordinated Universal Time (UTC), as shown next

```
Mon Jun 27 13:14:01 UTC 2016
```

The **date -s** command is used to set the current date using this format:

"Day Month Date Time Time-Zone Year"

The time uses a 24-hour clock and is formatted as

HH:MM:SS

You can see the **date -s** command in action here.

```
# date
Wed Jun 22 14:56:06 EDT 2016
#
# date -s "Mon June 27 09:00:00 EDT 2016"
Mon Jun 27 09:00:00 EDT 2016
#
# date
Mon Jun 27 09:00:03 EDT 2016
```

/etc/timezone and /usr/share/zoneinfo

The files */etc/timezone* and */usr/share/zoneinfo* are used to configure the system's timezone.

/usr/share/zoneinfo

The directory */usr/share/zoneinfo* contains binary data files for worldwide time zones. We will use this data to set a default system-wide time or user time zone.

tzselect

The **tzselect** command is used to determine the absolute path to a specific time zone.

For our example we would like to determine the data file for the US Pacific time zone.

The initial menu, shown here, asks you to select the continent or ocean of the required time zone.

```
# tzselect
Please identify a location so that time zone rules can be set correctly
.
Please select a continent or ocean.
 1) Africa
 2) Americas
 3) Antarctica
 4) Arctic Ocean
 5) Asia
 6) Atlantic Ocean
 7) Australia
 8) Europe
 9) Indian Ocean
10) Pacific Ocean
11) none - I want to specify the time zone using the Posix TZ format.
#? █
```

We will then select the following menu numbers:

- **2** Americas
- **49** United States
- **21** Pacific.

Lines 3 and four of the output displayed here show that we have found the data file for the United States Pacific time zone.

```
 1 The following information has been given:
 2
 3         United States
 4         Pacific
 5
 6 Therefore TZ='America/Los_Angeles' will be used.
 7 Local time is now:      Sun Aug 18 18:35:14 PDT 2019.
 8 Universal Time is now:  Mon Aug 19 01:35:14 UTC 2019.
 9
10 Is the above information OK?
11 1) Yes
12 2) No
13 #?
```

Line 6 shows us we must set the value of the variable TZ to */usr/shareinfo America/ Los_Angeles* to set the default time zone to United States Pacific.

Setting the time zone for a specific user To set the time zone for a specific user, add the line **TZ=/usr/shareinfo/America/Los_Angeles** to *~/.bash_profile*. Next append the export line with **TZ.**

A user can temporarily change their time zone by executing the command **export TZ=<path_to_binary>**. For example:

export TZ=/usr/share/zoneinfo/America/Los_Angeles

Changing system wide time zone The commands **date**, **date +%Z**, **ls -l /etc/localtime** and **timedatectl** will display the current system time zone.

To reset the system wide time zone create a you must first remove the current symbolic link to */etc/localtime* by executing the command **unlink /etc/localtime** or **\rm /etc/localtime.**

Once this is done, create another symbolic link using the command **ln s /usr/share/zoneinfo/<path_to binary>**. For example:

ln -s /usr/share/zoneinfo/America/Los_Angeles /etc/localtime

hwclock

The **hwclock** command is used to manage the RTC. The commands **hwclock**, **hwclock -r**, and **hwclock -- show** (Figure 3-14) display the current hardware clock time in local time.

```
# hwclock
Tue 13 Aug 2019 10:39:04 AM EDT  -1.043752 seconds
#
#
# hwclock -r
Tue 13 Aug 2019 10:39:10 AM EDT  -1.042820 seconds
#
#
# hwclock --show
Tue 13 Aug 2019 10:39:19 AM EDT  -1.043072 seconds
```

The output to the right displays the time offset. Applying the offset to the displayed time will produce the actual time.

NOTE The output will always be displayed in local time.

hwclock --set --date

The command **hwclock --set --date "dd mm yyyy HH:MM"** will set the hardware clock to the date, month, year, hour, and minute.

You may use the option **--utc** or **--localtime** to set the time to UTC or local time. The default is local time.

hwclock -s

The commands **hwclock -s** or **hwclock --hctosys** (hardware clock to system clock) will set the system time using the hardware clock and set the time zone to the current value of the TZ variable.

hwclock -w

The commands **hwclock -w** or **hwclock --systohc** will set the system clock to the same time as the hardware clock.

timedatectl

The **timedatectl** or **timedatectl status** commands are used to view and manage system hardware clocks. Executing the command timedatectl will produce the output shown here.

```
1 # timedatectl
2        Local time: Sun 2019-08-18 20:17:49 PDT
3    Universal time: Mon 2019-08-19 03:17:49 UTC
4          RTC time: Mon 2019-08-19 03:17:49
5         Time zone: America/Los_Angeles (PDT, -0700)
6       NTP enabled: yes
7 NTP synchronized: yes
8  RTC in local TZ: no
9        DST active: yes
10  Last DST change: DST began at
11                   Sun 2019-03-10 01:59:59 PST
12                   Sun 2019-03-10 03:00:00 PDT
13  Next DST change: DST ends (the clock jumps one hour backwards) at
14                   Sun 2019-11-03 01:59:59 PDT
15                   Sun 2019-11-03 01:00:00 PST
```

Lines 2–3 show the operating system time in both local and UTC and local time.

Line 4 displays the time stored in the hardware clock

Line 5 displays the system wide time zone.

Line 6 and 7 tell us NTP is enabled and the hardware clock is being synchronized with an NTP server (this occurs every 11 minutes).

Lines 9–11 show that daylight savings time (DST) is enabled, and the daylight savings time will be applied in both Pacific Standard Time (PST) and Pacific Daylight Time (PDT).

System Clock Commands

Next we'll look at commands to manage system clock settings.

timedatectl list-timezones The command **timedatectl list-timezones** will display a list of time zone data files in */usr/share/info*.

timedatectl set-timezone The command **timedatectl set-timezone "<time zone>"** will immediately change the system-wide time zone.

For example, the command **timedatectl set-timezone "America/New_York"** will immediately change the system-wide time zone to Eastern time. The command will update the symbolic link between */etc/localtime* and */usr/share/zoneinfo*.

This command may also be used to change the real time clock from local time to UTC using the command **timedatectl set-timezone UTC**.

Setting system time and date

If automatic time synchronization (for example, NTP) is enabled, the following commands will not work.

The command **timedatectl set-time 'HH:MM:SS'** (hours:minutes:seconds) will set the system time.

To change the system date, execute the command **timedatectl set-time 'YYYY-MM-DD'** (year, month, day).

The command **timedatectl set-time 'YYYY-MM_DD HH:MM'** will change both the system time and date.

Changing the Real Time Clock

You can use the **timedatectl** command to change the real time clock to store the time as local time or UTC.

The command **timedatectl set-local-rtc 1** will set the real time clock to local time.

The command **timedatectl set-local-rtc 0** will set the real time clock to UTC.

To test the change, execute the **timedatectl | grep local** command.

Bash Configuration Files

In the previous section, you learned how to manage variables, shell options, and aliases via the command line and how to change the system's locale and time settings.

Variables, aliases, and shell option settings executed on the command line are stored in the current process's memory space. These settings disappear when the shell in which they are defined is terminated.

Configuration files define settings that will be persistent after a user logs off or the system is rebooted.

The bash configuration files are:

- */etc/profile*
- */etc/bashrc*
- *~/.bash_profile*
- *~/.bashrc*
- *~/.bash.logout*

The files */etc/profile* and */etc/bashrc* are system (global) configuration files that are applied to all applicable users. Files located in the user's home directory (*~/<user_name>*) contain user-specific configuration information. Settings in these files override the */etc* configuration file settings.

The configuration files */etc/profile* and *~/.bash_profile* contain a series of commands used to configure the user's working environment. The configuration files */etc/bashrc* and *~/.bashrc* are used to configure how the bash shell executes.

/etc/profile

The file */etc/profile* is a generic file only read when a user logs on to the system or executes a command that forces a logon (such as **su -**).

When a login shell is run, the bash shell program searches for configuration files in the following order:

1. *~/.bash_profile*
2. *~/.bash_login*
3. *~/.profile*

Once one of those configuration files is found the remaining files are ignored. This file is used to set up the environment for any user whose default shell is either the bourne, korn, or bash shell. The file */etc/profile* is read when a user logs on.

In */etc/profile* you will find the following:

- **HOSTNAME** The HOSTNAME variable is set to the system's DNS name.
- **HISTCONTROL** History environmental variable that determines if bash will store command lines that begin with spaces or are duplicates.
- **HISTSIZE** History environmental variable that shows the number of commands stored by the history facility in memory.
- **umask** The value of umask determines what permissions will be denied when a file is created.

/etc/bashrc

The letters *rc* stand for "run command." rc (run command) files contain startup configuration information that determines how an application will operate. Other rc files may exist in the user's home directory to configure application attributes for that user. Here are some examples of run command files:

- **~/.toprc** Configures how the top command operates
- **~/.exrc** Configures how vi operates

The file */etc/bashrc* contains commands that affect how the bash shell runs for all users whose default shell is bash. This file is read when called by a command found in *~/.bashrc*. This configuration file contains system-wide configuration elements such as

- Aliases
- Functions
- Shell configuration options
- PS1 prompt configuration

~/.bash_profile

The file *~/.bash_profile* is read after the file */etc/profile* only when the user logs on to the system and if a user's default shell is bash. The file *.bash_profile* is used to customize the bash environment for a user. The file contains variables used to configure the user's working environment (such as time zone, locale, and editor).

Let's assume user student2 would rather use nano as their default editor. In this case, the statement **EDITOR=nano** would be included in their .bash_profile.

NOTE If you want a variable assignment to be removed permanently, you must remove the assignment from the configuration file and from memory. You would issue the command **unset <variable_name>** and then delete the statement that creates the variable in the configuration file (*/etc/profile* or *~/.bash_profile*).

~/.bashrc

The file *~/.bashrc* is found in the user's home directory and is used to customize how the bash shell runs. The *~/.bashrc* file contains aliases, functions or shell parameters. *~/.bashrc* is executed each time a process is started. This file would contain user specific:

- Aliases
- Functions
- Shell configuration options
- PS1 prompt configuration

CAUTION ~.bashrc is read each time a process is open. If you want to permanently remove an alias, shell option, or function, you must remove it from memory and, if applicable, remove the configuration statement from ~/.bashrc.

/etc/profile.d

The files in the directory */etc/profile.d* contain configuration information for specific programs and are read automatically during the login process.

The file */etc/profile* (for bourne, korn, and bash users) contains a statement that reads all the files in */etc/profile.d* with a suffix of .sh (for example, vim.sh). The file *csh.login* (for C shell users) contains a statement that reads all the files in */etc/profile.d* with the suffix .csh (for example, *vim.csh*).

The source Command

Configuration changes are not active until they are stored in memory. To place changes in memory, you must execute the commands in the configuration file. The command **source <filename>** or **. <filename>** will execute the commands in a configuration file.

The file *~/.bash_profile* is only read when the user logs on. Changes to a user's *.bash_profile* would not be read until the user's next logon. The source command **source ~/.bash_profile** or **. ~/.bash_profile** would make those configuration changes available immediately.

Exercise 3-1: Working with Variables, Parameters, and Aliases

In Exercise 3-1, you will practice creating and removing variables, aliases, and shell options as well as editing shell configuration files. But first, we would like to emphasize something you will find useful in your career. When you execute a command, be sure to test the results. For example, if you are asked to open a child shell, you should follow this procedure:

1. Verify the process ID (PID) of the current shell using the **ps** or **ps -f** command.
2. Create the child process (bash).
3. Verify you are in a child shell by executing the **ps -f** command and then look for a PID whose parent process (PPID) is the same as you verified in step 1.

With that in mind, log on as user student1 (password: student1) on the virtual machine provided with the book and then follow these steps:

1. Right-click the Desktop and select Open Terminal. This will open a text terminal (pseudo-terminal).
2. Execute the **ps** command to display a list of processes executing on the current terminal. Notice the process bash. Also notice the process ID associated with the command bash in the PID column. This is your current shell.
3. Execute the **bash** command.
4. Execute the command **ps -f**. Look at the second instance of bash and its process ID. Now look at the parent process ID (PPID). The PPID is the process number of the shell that spawned the current shell (child). The second instance of bash is the child shell.
5. Type the **exit** command. This terminates the current shell and returns you to the parent shell.
6. Execute the **ps** command. Notice the PID.
7. Create the local variable **flower** and assign it the value **rose** by executing the **flower=rose** command.
8. Execute the command **echo $flower** to see if the variable has been created. Type the **set** command to see all local variables and the **set | grep flower** command to view the local variable flower.
9. Create the variable **nut** and assign it the value **almond**. Test to see if the variable has been created.

10. Open a child shell by executing the command **bash** and test to ensure you have created a child shell.
11. Determine if the variables **flower** and **nut** are present in the child shell.
12. Return to the parent shell.
13. Add an export attribute to the variable flower by executing the command **export flower**.
14. Open a child process by executing the command **bash**. Use the commands **echo $flower** and **echo $nut** to determine if either the variable flower or nut exists in the child process. Explain the results.
15. Return to the parent shell by executing the command **exit**.
16. Create an environmental variable called **fruit** and assign it the value **apple** by executing the command **export fruit=apple**. Test to determine the following:
    - The variable has been created and is a local variable in the current shell. To do this, type the command **echo $fruit** or **set | grep fruit**.
    - The variable has been assigned an export attribute. To do this, use the command **env | grep fruit**.
17. To view the status of all shell parameters, execute the command **set -o**.
18. Type the command **set -o | grep allexport** to view the status of the shell parameter allexport.
19. Type the command **set -o allexport**. This will turn on the bash parameter, which automatically applies an export attribute to all newly created variables.
20. Verify the allexport parameter has been turned on by executing the command **set -o | grep allexport**.
21. Create the variable **truck** and assign it the value **chevy**. Execute the command **env | grep truck** determine if the variable has been assigned an export attribute.
22. Turn off allexport by executing the command **set +o allexport** and verify the shell parameter has been turned off.
23. Create the alias **ldetc**, which will execute the command **ls -ld /etc**, by executing the command **alias ldetc='ls -ld /etc'**.
24. Type the command **alias** to verify the alias ldetc has been created. You could also type the command **alias | grep ldetc**.
25. Type the command **ldetc**.
26. An alias only exists in the shell in which it is created. To test this, open a child shell and perform the following procedure:
    a. Execute the **ps** command to determine what the PID of the current shell is.
    b. Execute the **bash** command to open a new shell.

   c. Execute the command **ps -f** to verify a child shell has opened by making certain the PPID of the current shell is the process ID discovered in step a.
   d. Determine if the alias created in step 23 exists by trying to execute **ldetc**. Alternatively, you could execute the command **alias, alias ldetc**, or **alias grep | ldetc** to list the aliases in memory.

27. Return to the parent shell by exiting the current process (**exit**).
28. Remove the alias ldetc by executing the command **unalias ldetc**. Use the command **alias**, **alias ldetc**, or **alias | grep ldetc** to verify the alias has been removed from memory.
29. Use vi to add **set -o noclobber** to the last line of the file *~/.bashrc* and then save the file. The shell option noclobber does not allow a user to redirect the standard output (>) to an existing file.
30. Execute the command **set -o | grep noclobber**. Is noclobber turned on or off? Why?
31. Start a child process by executing the command **bash**.
32. Determine if the shell option noclobber is turned on or off. Why?
33. Return to the parent process. Execute the command **source ~/.bashrc**. Is noclobber turned on or off? Why?

VIDEO Watch the Exercise 3-1 video for a demonstration of this exercise.

Answers to Exercise 3-1

Answer to step 29 vi ~/.bashrc

Answer to step 30 noclobber will be turned off. After you edit a configuration file, the changes must be read into memory.

Answer to step 32 noclobber is turned on. The file *~/.bashrc* is read each time a process is opened; therefore, changes were read into memory.

Answer to step 33 .bashrc is read when a child shell is created or a source command is issued. When you made the first change to .bashrc in the parent shell, you did not source .bashrc, so noclobber was off in the parent shell. When you opened a child shell (step 31), .bashrc was read; therefore, noclobber was turned on in the child shell. When you returned to the parent shell, noclobber is turned off. The command **source ~/.bashrc** executes each line in ~/.bashrc (including **set -o noclobber**). This command turns noclobber on in the current shell.

Redirection

When a user executes a command, user input is received via the standard input device (stdin). The default stdin device is the keyboard. All output, except error messages, is sent to the standard output device (stdout). The default stdout device is the console (monitor).

Error messages are output to the standard error device (stderr). The default stderr device is the console (monitor).

Redirection permits a user to alter the stdin, stdout, or stderr device or file.

File Descriptors

A file descriptor is a reference (also called a handle) used by the kernel to access a file. A file descriptor table is created for all process. This table tracks all files opened by the process. A unique index number (file descriptor number) is assigned to a file when it is opened by a process.

When a process is created, the file descriptor numbers 0, 1, and 2 are reserved for the stdin, stdout, and stderr devices, respectively:

- **fd0** Standard input device (stdin).
- **fd1** Standard output device (stdout).
- **fd2** Standard error device (stderr).
- **fd255** The bash file descriptor 255 keeps track of controlling terminal information.

Terminal devices

Terminal devices may be represented by /dev/pts/#, /dev/tty, /dev/console, or /dev/ttyS. To view the device path to the current terminal execute the command **tty**.

/dev/pts/#

A pseudo terminal is a dynamically created virtual terminal that consists of a master and slave combination.

A pseudo terminal device name is pts/# The # represents the logical unit number of the slave (pts/0).

NOTE Remember the name of the device

The master device is connected to a terminal emulator (such as xterm) that provides terminal services, and the slave is connected to the application. The kernel provides bidirectional communication between the master and the slave.

Pseudo terminals are used in the GUI environment and network logins such as ssh, telnet, rlogin, and terminals accessed using the screen application.

NOTE A terminal emulator is a software application that provides a "monitor" and keyboard.

/dev/tty

Linux provides for 62 virtual text terminals (tty1 through tty63). Naming conventions for these terminals are either /dev/tty# or /dev/vc/#.

/dev/tty and /dev/tty0 are attached to the current process.

NOTE The exam refers to /dev/tty0 or /dev/tty1 as the terminal device name. Remember that the */dev* directory is used to provide a path to a device. More accurate names for these devices would be tty0 and tty1.

/dev/ttyS refers to the system's serial ports.

console

A console can refer to the primary physical monitor or a virtual device.

The kernel outputs kernel messages to the console device, **printk()**.

The console device is the primary physical monitor during boot.

You may specify a single or multiple virtual console devices on the kernel command line by adding the directive **console=<device>, <device_options>**.

Adding **console=/dev/tty1 console=/dev/tty0** on the kernel command line will cause kernel messages to be printed on tty1 and the current terminal device (/dev/tty0). The last console device specified on the kernel command line is /dev/console.

/dev/null

/dev/null is a zero-byte character device that is created each time the system boots. Data written to /dev/null is discarded immediately.

/dev/null is used to prevent stdout and stderr messages from being written to tty0.

stdin

User input is received through the standard input device. The default standard input device is the console keyboard, which is assigned the file descriptor number 0; therefore, the device name is fd0. Here are some other key points to keep in mind about stdin:

- The control operators < and << are used to choose an alternate standard input device.
- The command **cat < /etc/hosts** instructs cat to take its input from the file */etc/hosts* rather than the keyboard. (This is the same as executing the command **cat /etc/hosts**.)
- Another form of input redirection is the heredoc, or here document. The heredoc reads each input line from the current source (file) until it reaches the limit word.
- All the lines read up to that point are used as the standard input for a command.

The following example creates a here document named heredoc. Line 1 instructs the grep command to search through the input source for a string specified by the first argument of the command line until it sees the limit word EOF. The input source begins on line 2.

```
1. grep $1 << EOF
2. Alexandre Dumas
3. Paulo Coelho
4. Don Miguel Ruiz
5. EOF
6. Charles Dickens
```

Executing the command **heredoc Dumas**, as shown in Figure 3-6, will search line 2 through line 5 for the string "Dumas". Once the grep command finds the string, it will print the line it is found on to the standard output device. Notice the error message "line 6: Charles: command not found." The operator >> will only search up until the limit word, EOF, which is specified on line 1 and found on line 5. Since heredoc is a script, bash will try and execute the command Charles (the shell considers Dickens as an argument to the command Charles). Since the command Charles does not exist, the error message is displayed.

Executing the command **heredoc Dickens** would not produce an output since the string Dickens occurs after the limit word EOF.

stdout

The output of a successful command is directed to the standard output device, stdout. The default standard output device is the /dev/console (unless otherwise assigned at boot time, the console device is the current terminal), and the default file descriptor number for the standard output device is 1. Unless otherwise assigned at boot time, the console device (/dev/console) is the current terminal. Therefore, the device name is fd1. Here are some other key points to keep in mind about stdout:

- The greater-than (>) and double greater-than (>>) symbols are control operators used to choose an alternate stdout device.
- The > symbol will create a file if one does not exist and overwrite the file if one does exist.
- The command **ls -ld /etc /user > filea** will take the output and either create or overwrite *filea* with the contents of the output. This command may also be written **ls -ld /etc /user 1> filea**. **ls -ld /etc /user 1> filea.**

NOTE The shell parameter noclobber will not allow the > redirection to overwrite an existing file. The command **set -o | grep noclobber** will verify if noclobber is set. The command **set +o noclobber** will turn the parameter off.

```
# bash ./heredoc Dumas
Alexandre Dumas
./heredoc: line 6: Charles: command not found
```

Figure 3-6 Heredoc example

- The command **ls -ld /etc /user >> filea** will create or append *filea* with the contents of the output. This command may also be written **ls -ld /etc /usr 1>> filea**.

stderr

Error messages are output to the standard error device, stderr. The default standard error device is /dev/console. The default file descriptor number for the standard error device is 2. Therefore, the device name is fd2. The control operators 2> and 2 >> are used to choose an alternate standard error file or device. The 2> symbol will create a file if one does not exist and overwrite the file if one does exist. The 2>> symbol will create a file if one does not exist and append the file if one does exist.

The command **ls -ld /etc /roses 2> errorfile** will attempt to list the properties of the directories */etc* and */roses*. The directory */roses* does not exist. Since the */etc* directory exists, its properties will be displayed on the standard output device. Since the directory *rose* does not exist, it will produce an error message. The 2> control operator will redirect the error message to the file *errorfile*.

Combining stdout and stderr

The control operators > and 2> may be combined to send both outputs to the same file or device. The control operators 2>&1 redirect the standard error to the same location as the standard output. Here's how this works:

- The control operator 2> designates that you are altering the data stream for error messages.
- The & character is a Boolean AND.
- The 1 is the file descriptor number for the standard output device.

The command **ls -ld /etc /roses 2>&1 errorfile** will write the standard output and standard error to the file *errorfile*.

The control operators 1>&2 redirect the standard output to the same location as the standard error. Here's how it works:

- The 1> control operator redirects the standard output.
- The & is a Boolean AND.
- The 2 is the file descriptor number for the standard error data stream.

The command **ls -ld /etc /roses 1>&2 errorfile** will write the standard output and standard error to the file *errorfile*. The control operator >& redirects both the standard error and standard output to the same file. The command **ls -ld /etc /roses >& errorfile** will write the properties of the */etc* directory and the error message to the file *errorfile*.

Pipe

A pipe is a method of connecting the stdout of one process to the stdin of another process. There are two types of pipes: named and unnamed.

A named pipe is a file that facilitates interprocess communication. A named pipe takes output from one process and places it in a file. Another process removes the information from the file. The mknod and mkfifo commands create a named pipe file. Deleting the file removes the named pipe.

An unnamed pipe is used on the command line (**<commanda> | <commandb>**). An unnamed pipe uses the standard output from the command to the left of the pipe symbol (|) as the stdin to the command to the right of the pipe symbol. In order to do this, a temporary file is created. When the command is completed, the temporary file is removed.

To understand how an unnamed pipe works, we will use a fictitious temporary file called *pipetemp*. The command **cat file1 | cat > filea** redirects the stdout of the command **cat file1** to be the input of the command **cat > filea**. The left part of the pipe executes **cat file1 > pipetemp** and then the right side of the pipe executes the command **cat pipetemp > filea.**

The **tee** command displays the output of a command to the console device and redirects the output to a file or device. The command **cat /etc/hosts | tee filea** will display the contents of */etc/hosts* on the console device and write the contents of the file to *filea.*

Exercise 3-2: Redirection

In Exercise 3-2, you will perform the following tasks:

- Determine what your login shell is.
- Create local and environmental values.
- Determine your process ID and parent process ID.
- Change shell options.
- Create aliases.

VIDEO Watch the Exercise 3-2 video for a demonstration.

Log on as user student1 (password: student1) on the virtual machine provided with the book and then follow these steps:

1. Execute the **cd** command.
2. Type the **pwd** command. The output should display /home/student1.
3. Create the directory *redir* by executing the command **mkdir redir.**
4. Execute the command **cd redir.**

5. Execute the command **pwd**. The output should display /home/student/redir.
6. Use the command **cat /etc/hosts > filea** to read the contents of the file */etc/hosts* and place the output in *filea*.
7. Read the contents of the file */etc/default/useradd* and output the contents to *fileb*.
8. Use the **cat** command to view the contents of *filea* and *fileb*.
9. Redirect the output of the command **ls -ld /etc** to *filea* by executing the command **ls -ld /etc > filea**. What happened to the original contents of *filea*?
10. Append the output of the command **ls -ld /etc** to *fileb* by executing the command **ls -ld /etc/ >> fileb**.
11. Redirect the standard output of the command **ls -ld /etc /roses** to *filea* and the standard error to *fileb* by executing the command **ls -ld /etc /roses > filea 2 >fileb**.
12. Execute the command **ls -ld /etc /roses**. Redirect the standard output to *fileb* and append the standard error to *filea*.
13. Execute the command **ls -ld /etc /roses** using three methods to redirect both the standard output and stderr to *file3*.
14. Redirect the output of the command **cat /etc/hosts** to *file4* and display the contents on the console device using the command **cat /etc/hosts | tee file4**.
15. What does the command **cat < /etc/hosts > file5** do?
16. Execute the command **echo hello > /dev/tty2**.
17. Switch to a text terminal by using the key sequence CTRL-ALT-F2. Notice the output on the terminal.
18. Return to the graphics environment by using the key sequence ALT-F1.

NOTE This lab omits some steps. This was intentional. We want you to be able to troubleshoot issues. If you find a lab step is not working, make certain no other conditions exist to prevent a command from executing properly. If you have difficulty, look at the answer section that follows.

Answers to Exercise 3-2

Answer to step 9 If you tried to execute the command **ls -ld /etc > filea** you would receive the error **bash: filea: cannot overwrite existing file**. The shell parameter noclobber is preventing you from overwriting an existing file. Executing the command **set +o noclobber** will turn noclobber off and allow you to redirect the output to an existing file.

Answer to step 12 Use the command **ls -ld /etc /roses >> fileb 2> filea**.

Answer to step 13 The three methods are **ls -ld /etc /roses >& file3**, **ls -ld /etc /roses > file3 2>&1**, and **ls -ld /etc /roses 2> file3 1>&2**.

Answer to step 15 The command **cat < /etc/hosts > file5** uses the file */etc/hosts* as the input to the cat command and outputs the results to *file5*.

Chapter Review

This chapter introduced the bash shell. We covered what a shell is and how to use various facilities to customize the user's environment and the shell's operating parameters. Here are some important points to note:

- The shell is a user interface, command-line interpreter, and programming language.
- A process is a single instance of a program.
- A parent process can spawn child processes.
- Variables are used to store data.
- Local variables only exist in the process in which they were created.
- Environmental variables are copied from the parent process to the child process.
- Shell options are used to configure how a shell operates.
- When programs start, they may use configuration files to configure how they operate.
- The bash shell has four configuration files: */etc/profile*, */etc/bashrc*, *~/.bash_profile*, and *~/.bashrc*.
- */etc/profile* and *~/.bash_profile* are read when a user logs on or executes a command that requires a logon.
- *~/.bashrc* is read each time a new process is started.
- The source command is used to read changes in configuration files into memory.
- Redirection permits a user to alter the stdin, stdout, or stderr device or file.

Questions

1. Which of the following functions are associated with bash shell distributions? (Select all that apply.)
   A. Command-line interpreter
   B. User interface
   C. Programing language
   D. System-wide editor
2. Which of the following statements concerning a local variable are true?
   A. The variable will be copied when a new process is spawned.
   B. The variable will not be copied when a new process is spawned.
   C. The variable name must be in capital letters.
   D. The variable name must be in lowercase letters.

3. What does the set command do?
   A. Displays a list of shell options and their status
   B. Displays a list of environmental variables
   C. Displays a list of local variables
4. User student1 has logged on and discovered a user-specific variable assignment is causing a problem. Select all actions student1 must complete to permanently resolve the problem.
   A. Remove the variable assignment from ~/.bashrc.
   B. Remove the variable assignment from *~/.bash_profile*.
   C. Remove the variable from memory.
   D. Remove the variable assignment from */etc/profile*.
5. A user creates the environmental variable test in their logon shell. They then execute the command **bash**. Executing the command **env | grep test** verifies the variable is present in the child process. The user executes the command **unset test**. Which of the following statements is true?
   A. The variable test is removed from the parent and child processes.
   B. The variable test is removed from the child process and the child process is exited.
   C. The variable is removed from the child process.
   D. The variable is removed from the child process and becomes a local variable in the parent process.
6. Select all commands that create an environmental variable in the bash shell.
   A. export <variable_name> = value
   B. setenv <variable_name>
   C. export <variable_name>=value
   D. <variable_name>=<value>;export <variable_name>
7. Which commands are associated with local variables?
   A. export <variable_name> = value
   B. <variable_name>=<value>
   C. env
   D. set
8. Which commands are associated with environmental variables? (Select all that apply.)
   A. export <variable_name> = value.
   B. export <variable_name>
   C. <variable_name>=<value>

D. env

E. set

9. User student1 executes the command history and sees a list of commands, but realizes the bash shell is no longer storing command history. Select all the conditions that would cause the problem.

   A. The file *~/.bash_history* does not exist.

   B. The shell history option has been turned off.

   C. The history command is missing.

   D. Someone has executed the command **history -c** to remove command history entries from memory.

10. What would you do to fix the problem stated in question 9? (Select all that apply.)

    A. Determine the current condition of the history option.

    B. Determine if */etc/bashrc* has a statement that turns history off.

    C. Determine if *~/.bashrc* has a statement that turns history off.

    D. As a remedial action, turn the history option on.

11. You find when executing the command rm, it actually executes the alias rm, which is equal to **rm -i**. Without removing the alias from memory, what command or commands would offer a way around the issue? (Select all that apply.)

    A. unalias rm

    B. /rm

    C. \rm

    D. /usr/bin/rm

12. A user wants to redirect the standard output of a command to a file without overwriting the contents of the file. Which redirection operators should be applied?

    A. >

    B. 2>

    C. >>

    D. 2>>

13. Which of the following will redirect the standard input and standard output to the same file? (Select all that apply.)

    A. >&

    B. 1>&2

    C. 2>&1

    D. >

    E. 2 <

14. Assume the directory */fred* does not exist and the files *error1* and *error2* contain content. What will the command **ls –ld /etc /fred > error1 2>> error2** do? (Select all that apply.)

   A. Overwrite the content of the file *error1*.

   B. Overwrite the content of the file *error2*.

   C. Append file *error1*.

   D. Append file *error2*.

15. Refer to question 14. Which file will contain the error messages?

   A. *error1*

   B. *error2*

   C. None of the above

   D. Both *error1* and *error2*

16. The file *error1* exists in the current directory, but when a user attempts to redirect the output of a command to the file, they receive the message "cannot overwrite an existing file." What is the cause of and fix to this problem?

   A. noglob is turned on and it must be turned off using **set -o noglob**.

   B. noglob is turned on and it must be turned off using **set +o noglob**.

   C. noclobber is turned on and it must be turned off using **set -o noclobber**.

   D. noclobber is turned on and it must be turned off using **set +o noclobber**.

17. Where is the system console set?

   A. /root/.bash_profile

   B. Boot kernel command line

   C. /etc/systemd/system/default.target

   D. /etc/profile

18. Which device name represents the terminal connected to the current process?

   A. /dev/null

   B. /dev/pts/0

   C. /dev/tty0

   D. /dev/console

19. Which locale variable will override all locale category settings?

   A. LANG

   B. LOCALE

   C. LC

   D. LC_ALL

20. What must you do if you modify settings in the file */etc/locale.conf* using the **localectl** command?
    - **A.** Reboot the system
    - **B.** Execute the command **source /etc/locale.conf**
    - **C.** Reload systemd
    - **D.** Execute the command **localectl**
21. Which commands will display system clock information? (Select all that apply.)
    - **A.** date
    - **B.** hwclock
    - **C.** timedatectl
    - **D.** localectl
22. Where are time zone data files stored?
    - **A.** /etc/locale
    - **B.** /etc/local
    - **C.** /usr/share/zoneinfo
    - **D.** /usr/lib/time
23. Which commands will display the current system time zone? (Select all that apply.)
    - **A.** timedatectl
    - **B.** date
    - **C.** ls -l /etc/localtime
    - **D.** date +%Z

Answers

1. **A, B, C.** The bash shell is a user interface, command-line interpreter, and programming language.
2. **B.** The variable will not be copied when a new process is spawned.
3. **C.** The set command displays a list of local variables.
4. **B, C.** The question states that user student1 is logged on to the system Therefore, to remove the problem immediately, student1 must remove the variable from memory. *~/.bash_profile* contains user environment statements. In order to prevent the variable from being created the next time the user logs on, the variable assignment must be removed from *~/.bash_profile.*
5. **C.** Each process executes in its own memory space. Any actions in a child process will not affect the parent process. Therefore, removing a variable from a child process will not affect the variable in the parent process.

6. **C, D.** The command **export <variable_name>=<value>** will create an environmental variable. The command **<variable_name>=<value>; export <variable_name>** uses a compound command to create and then export the variable.

7. **B, D.** The command **<variable_name>=<value>** will create a local variable. The set command will display a list of all local variables.

8. **A, B, D.** The command **export <variable_name>=<value>** will create an environmental variable, and the command **export <variable_name>** will assign an export attribute to an existing variable. The **env** command will display a list of all variables in the current shell that have been assigned an export attribute.

9. **B.** The history option is turned off. The file *~/.bash_history* is only populated when the user logs off or the number of commands stored in memory exceed the number specified in the variable HISTSIZE. If the file *~/.bash_history* is missing, the current command history would still be visible. The command **history -c** would remove history commands from memory, but would not prevent the addition of new commands.

10. **A, B, C, D.** Use the **set -o | grep history** to determine if the option has been turned off. For a remedial fix, turn the option on by executing the command **set -o history**. Then discover if the option was turned off in any configuration file. If the option was turned off in */etc/bashrc*, making a change there would affect all users. It would be more prudent to turn the option on in *~/.bashrc*. If you do not see any statement that turns history off in in */etc/bashrc*, check *~/.bashrc*.

11. **C, D.** The backslash (\) negates the special meeting of a character; when placed in front of an aliased command, it negates the alias. You could also supply the absolute path to the command. The absolute path to a command takes precedence over aliases, functions, and builtins.

12. **C.** The > and >> symbols redirect the stdout of a file. The >> symbol will create a file if one does not exist and append to an existing file if it does exist, so it is the best choice for this scenario. The > symbol will create a file if it does not exist, but will or overwrite the file if it does exist. The 2> operator redirects the standard error and would overwrite the file. 2>> would redirect the standard error and append the file.

13. **A, B, C.** The operator >& redirects both the standard output and the standard error to the same file. The operator 1>&2 redirects the standard output and ANDs the standard error to the same file. The operator 2>&1 redirects the standard error and ANDs the standard output.

14. **A.** The > operator will create a file or overwrite the content of a file. The operator >> will create a file or append the file.

15. **B.** The operator 2> redirects the standard error. In question 14, the operator 2>> appends error messages to file error2.

16. **D.** The bash option noclobber prevents redirecting the standard output to an existing file. The command **set +o noclobber** will turn the option off.
17. **B.** A system console or multiple console devices are defined in the boot loader's kernel command line.
18. **C.** The device name /dev/tty0 represents the terminal connected to the current process.
19. **D.** The LC_ALL variable will override all local category variables and the LANG variable.
20. **B.** Anytime you modify */etc/locale.conf*—either by the **localect** command or manually—you must read the new configuration into memory by executing the command **source /etc/locale.conf**.
21. **A, C.** The commands **date** and **timedatectl** will display the system clock (operating system clock) information.
22. **C.** The directory */usr/share/zoneinfo* contains time zone data files
23. **A, B, C, D.** The output of each of these commands will display the current system time zone.

CHAPTER 4

Managing Linux Users and Groups

In this chapter, you will learn about

- Linux users and groups
- Creating and managing Linux user accounts

Linux is a multiuser operating system, so you need a method of restricting users' access to only those resources they should have permission to access. This chapter introduces Linux users and groups.

Understanding Linux Users and Groups

Linux uses a method called Discretionary Access Control (DAC) to permit or restrict access to an object (resource) based on the user and group identities associated with the user accessing the resource and the permissions granted to that user ID or group ID by the resource.

NOTE Linux supports a more granular permission structure called Mandatory Access Control (MAC). These permissions are controlled by either SELinux or AppArmor, which are covered in Chapter 16.

Linux User Accounts

A user is a person or service that requires access to system resources. A user account is a method of providing or restricting access to system resources.

User IDs

Linux implements user ID ranges to organize users.

User IDs 0–99 Administrative users 0–99 are added to the operating system during the installation process. According to the Linux Standard Base (LSB) Core Specification, user accounts within this range are created by the operating system and may not be created by an application (such as useradd).

root The user root is a privileged Linux account. Privileged accounts are granted greater access and management capabilities over nonprivileged user accounts. The user root has access to all files and commands and full control of the operating system, including the ability to bypass the operating system or application restrictions. Any user assigned the user ID 0 has root privileges.

NOTE Linux does not restrict the number of users who share a user ID. It is possible to assign the user ID 0 to multiple users, but not advisable.

Many companies choose to prevent local root logon on by restricting terminal access (/etc/securetty).

You should not allow the user root to have remote access to your system. Some services such as NFS prevent root access by default. Others require you to edit configuration files. For example, you may prevent root from logon via ssh by setting the value of the directive PermitRootLogin in the file */etc/ssh/sshd_config* to **no**.

Access to root privileges either via the user ID 0 or the group wheel user root should be limited. sudo should be used for users who require access to a few privileged commands.

NOTE The group wheel is a sudo group definition that gives a user access to all commands.

System Account System accounts are nonprivileged accounts created by a system administrator or application and assigned user IDs within the range specified by the variables SYS_UID_MIN and SYS_UID_MAX in */etc/login.defs*.

System accounts may be assigned to applications or services and are sometimes used to restrict access to configuration or data files. System accounts are not able to log on to the system, do not require a password, do not have password aging applied, and do not have home directories.

NOTE We discuss passwords and password aging later in the chapter.

A system account is created by executing the command **useradd -r <user_name>**. The command will automatically assign the new account a user ID in the range specified by SYS_UID_MIN and SYS_UID_MAX. It will also make the appropriate password and password aging entries in */etc/shadow*.

User Account A user account provides nonprivileged access to system resources. User account ID ranges are specified by the variables UID_MIN and UID_MAX in */etc/login.defs*.

A Linux service (an application that is running in the background, such as abrt) may be assigned a *user account*. The user account ID for a service will be in the range 0–99 or between the values set by SYS_UID_MIN and SYS_UID_MAX in */etc/login.defs*.

The CompTIA exam objective uses the term *service account*. They are referring to an application executing in the background that has been assigned a user account ID.

NOTE There are many services that are not assigned a user account.

Where Linux User Account Information Is Stored

For our purposes, we're going to focus on how Linux stores user configuration files on the local system. This option stores user and group information in the following files in the file system:

- **/etc/passwd** Contains user account information
- **/etc/shadow** Contains user password and password aging information
- **/etc/group** Contains a list of groups and their members
- **/etc/skel** A directory that contains files automatically copied to a user's home directory when the user is created

etc/passwd The file */etc/passwd* is an example of a flat file database. Each line of the file contains a unique user record. Each record contains seven fields. A colon (:) is used as a delimiter (data boundary) to separate the fields.

The following example illustrates the fields found in an */etc/passwd* user record:

```
User_Name:Password:UID:GID:Comment:Home_Directory:Default_Shell
root: :0:0:root:/root:/bin/bash
student1: :0:0:Student1:/home/student1:/bin/bash
```

- **User Name** The username is a unique word used to identify a user who has access to the system. The username is supplied by the administrator creating the account.
- **Password** When UNIX was first developed, the user's password was stored in this field. Unfortunately the */etc/passwd* file's permissions allowed everyone to read the file, so it was easy to hijack a user's password. Passwords are now stored in the file */etc/shadow*. When shadow passwords are not implemented, passwords are stored in */etc/passwd*.
- **UID** The Linux kernel identifies a user by their user ID, not their username. A user ID is a numerical identifier assigned each user and mapped to their username. Each user ID should be unique. However, although it is not a secure practice, you can map multiple usernames to the same user ID.

- **gid** The gid field contains the group ID number of the user's primary group. When a user creates a file, their primary group ID is assigned as the file's group owner.

TIP The term gid is associated with a user's primary group id, and the term GID represents secondary groups. We discuss secondary groups later in the book.

- **Comment** By default, this field contains the user's full name. You may change the information that appears in this field when adding or modifying the user account.
- **Home_Directory** This field contains the absolute path to the user's home directory.
- **Default_Shell** Some accounts (system accounts) do not require a login shell. You will find these accounts have either **/sbin/nologin** or **/bin/false** in this field. Both prevent login. **/bin/false** immediately exits the login process. **/sbin/nologin** will display the message found in */etc/nologin* and exit the login process.

/etc/shadow Shadow utilities were implemented to fix security issues. In order to accommodate the new shadow utilities, the files */etc/shadow* and */etc/gshadow* were added, along with the commands gpasswd, pwconv, pwunconv, pwck, and grpck.

The */etc/shadow* file is a flat file database which stores user password and password aging information. Each record in */etc/passwd* should have a corresponding record in */etc/shadow*. The format for a record in this file is as follows:

```
Username:Password:Last_Modified:Min_Days:Max_Days:Days_Warn:Disabled_Days:Expire
```

Here's an example:

```
# grep ^student1 /etc/shadow student1:$2a$05$KL1DbTBqpSEMiL.2FoI3ue4bdyR
.eL6CC7REUS:15043:0:99999:7:::
```

Here's what each of these fields contains:

- **Username** This is the user's login name.
- **Password** This field stores the user's password in encrypted format.

If the account is a user account and this field only contains two exclamation points (Figure 4-1), an account password has never been assigned.

Refer to Figure 4-2 and notice the string 6. The characters between the first two dollar signs (6 in this example) indicate the encryption algorithm used to create the password. The default algorithm is assigned in */etc/login.defs*.

Figure 4-1
No password assigned

```
# grep ^student2 /etc/shadow
student2:!!:17951:0:99999:7:::
```

```
student2:!!$6$4nmscQwe$yPvdTP/lmGkyWELEBbODHiCLCdZ69hBnQyrId1BcXzKMPpckniyyq3YiX
kbx29AcK0UoCBIeOFI8BpYX1mp8P.:17951:0:99999:7:::
```

Figure 4-2 Account locked by passwd -l

To prevent a user from logging on, you can lock the account using the commands **passwd -l <user_name>** or **usermod -L <user_name>**. If the account has been locked by the command **passwd -l**, the password field will be prefaced by double exclamation marks (Figure 4-2). If the password has been locked using the command **usermod -L**, the password field will be prefaced by a single exclamation mark (!<encrypted_password>). You may also see this if the account has expired.

If a user account has an asterisk (*) in the password field, the account is disabled (Figure 4-3). An account is automatically disabled if it has been *x* amount of days after the password expired. The default number of days is specified by the variable INACTIVE in */etc/default/useradd*. The inactive days for a specific user may be set using the command **passwd -i <number_of_days>** or **chage -I <number_of_days>**. If a user account is disabled, you must remove the asterisk from the password field in */etc/shadow*. User accounts in the ID range 1–99 that do not require a password will display an asterisk in this field.

You can force a user to change their password when they log on next by expiring the account using the command **passwd -e <username>** or setting the last change date to 0 using the command **chage -d 0 <username>**.

- **Last_Modified** This field displays the number of days since January 1, 1970, that the password was last changed. This number is used to calculate password aging dates.

  To change the last modified date for a user, execute the following command:
  chage -d <YYYY-MM-DD> <username>
- **Min_Days** This field displays the minimum number of days required before a password can be changed. The default value is specified in */etc/login.defs*.

  To change the minimum number of days for a user, execute the command
  chage -m <number_of_days> <username>
  or
  passwd -n <number_of_days> <username>
- **Max_Days** This field displays the maximum number of days before a password expires. The default value is specified in */etc/login.defs*.

  To change the maximum number of days for a user, execute the command
  chage -M <number_of_days> <username>
  or
  passwd -x <number_of_days> <username>

```
# grep ^student2 /etc/shadow
student2:*:17951:0:99999:7:::
```

Figure 4-3 Disabled account

- **Warn Days** This field displays the number of days prior to password expiration the user will be warned of the pending expiration. The default value is specified in */etc/login.defs*.

  To change the number of days before warning a user, execute the command
  chage -W <number_of_days> <username>
  or
  passwd -w <number_of_days> <username>

- **Inactive** This field displays the number of days after password expiration the user account will be disabled. The purpose of this field is to prevent open accounts that are not being used.

  During the period between password expiration and the number of inactive days being exceeded, the user may still log on but will be forced to change their password. After the number of inactive days is exceeded, the account is disabled and will require an administrator to remediate the situation.

  The default inactive value is specified in */etc/default/useradd*. If the value of this variable is set to 0, the account is disabled the same time the password expires. If the value of the variable is -1, the inactive function is disabled. If the variable is set to a value of *n,* the account will be disabled *n* days after the password expires.

  To change the default value of the variable INACTIVE (*/etc/default/useradd*) execute the following command:
  useradd -Df <number_of_days>

  To change the inactive days for a user, execute the command
  chage -I <number_of_days> <username>
  or
  passwd -i <number_of_days> <username>

- **Expire** This field displays the number of days since January 1, 1970, after which the account will be disabled.

  To change the account expiration date for a single user, execute the following command:
  chage -E <YYYY-MM-DD> <username>

pwconv and pwunconv

To verify */etc/passwd* and */etc/shadow* contain matching records, use the command pwconv. This command checks all user records in */etc/passwd* and determines if there is a corresponding record in */etc/shadow*. If a user record in */etc/shadow* is required but does not exist, pwconv will create the record in */etc/shadow* using default settings. Next, pwconv will compare the user records in */etc/shadow* and determine if there is a corresponding record in */etc/passwd*. If a record exists in */etc/shadow* but a corresponding record does not exist in */etc/passwd*, the record will be deleted in */etc/shadow*.

pwunconv will move all passwords stored in the second field of */etc/shadow* into the second field of */etc/passwd* and then remove the file */etc/shadow*. This can be useful. The default aging dates defined in */etc/login.defs* are not conducive to a secure environment. One of the problems is the password max days is too long, and a user may change their password back immediately after changing it (PASS_MIN_DAYS). Create better aging using the following settings:

- MAX_DAYS 30
- WARN_DAYS 7
- MIN_DAYS 22

Executing the command pwunconv will move all passwords stored in the second field of */etc/shadow* into the second field of */etc/passwd* and then remove the file */etc/shadow*. Next, execute the command pwconv. This will rebuild */etc/shadow* using the default values in */etc/login.defs*.

NOTE The file */pam.d/passwd* enables you to configure password complexity, password history (prevent reuse of previous passwords), what to do when a log-in is incorrect, and other user management elements.

Real and Effective User and Group IDs

When a user logs on to a system, they are assigned the user ID stored in their */etc/passwd* record. This user ID is called their real user ID, or RUID.

Both the **w** and **who** commands will display the real user ID of a logged-on user, what process they are executing, and what device the process is executing from. An effective user ID (EUID) is the user ID that determines access to resources (Figure 4-4).

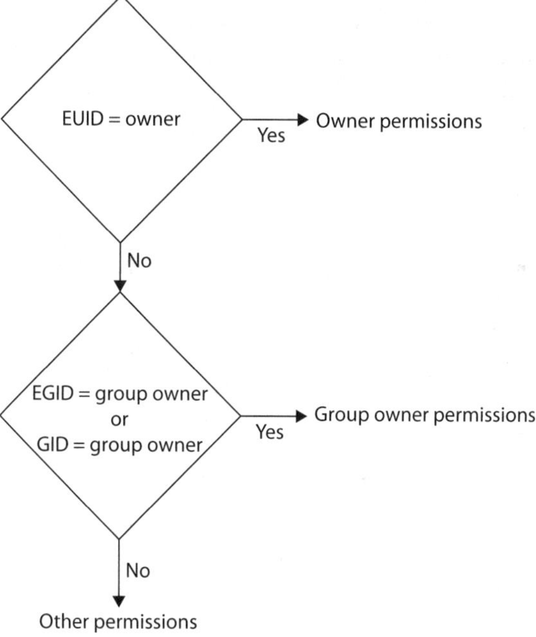

Figure 4-4 Permissions based on EUID and EGID

When you log on, your real user ID and effective user ID are the same.

The **su** (substitute user) command allows a user to assume the privileges of another user by changing their effective user and group ID. Non-root users must know the password of the user they are changing to.

There are two formats for the su command: **su <username>** and **su - <username>**. The command **su <username>** will change the current user's UID, primary group ID, and home directory. The command **su - <username>** will log in as the user. This will change the current user's UID, primary group ID, and home directory as well as read all of the user's configuration files. The **su -** command is useful if you want to test a user problem using the user's environment.

Whenever you execute the **su** or **su -** commands your effective user id (EUID) and effective group ID (EGID) change. To view the current user's effective user ID, execute the command **whoami** or **id**.

The id command will display the current user's effective user ID, effective group ID, and the user's secondary groups. The command **id <username>** will display the user ID, primary group ID, and secondary groups for the user specified by the argument <username>.

Figure 4-5 displays the relationships between RUID and EUID.

We are logged on as user root (UID 0). The tty command on line 1 shows that we are using the pseudo-terminal /dev/pts/0.

On line 4 we execute the **w** command to display our real user ID. Line 8 shows user root (UID 0) executing a process on */dev/pts/0.*

We verify our EUID is the same as our RUID by executing the ID command on line 10.

On line 13 we execute the command **su student1**. This will change our effective user ID to user student1 (UID 1000).

When we execute the command w and review line 15, we see that our real user name is root (UID 0). When we execute the commands whoami (line 21) and id (line 24), however, we see our effective user ID is 1000.

```
 1 # tty
 2 /dev/pts/0
 3 #
 4 # w
 5  00:49:25 up 3 min,  2 users,  load average: 0.83, 1.04, 0.48
 6 USER     TTY      FROM             LOGIN@   IDLE   JCPU   PCPU WHAT
 7 root     :0       :0               00:47   ?xdm?  31.02s  0.32s /usr/libexec/gnome-session-binary --session gnome-classic
 8 root     pts/0    :0               00:48    5.00s  0.09s  0.05s w
 9 #
10 # id
11 uid=0(root) gid=0(root) groups=0(root) context=unconfined_u:unconfined_r:unconfined_t:s0-s0:c0.c1023
12 #
13 # su student1
14 #
15 # w
16  00:51:15 up 5 min,  2 users,  load average: 0.13, 0.72, 0.43
17 USER     TTY      FROM             LOGIN@   IDLE   JCPU   PCPU WHAT
18 root     :0       :0               00:47   ?xdm?  34.22s  0.32s /usr/libexec/gnome-session-binary --session gnome-classic
19 root     pts/0    :0               00:48    3.00s  0.11s  0.00s w
20 #
21 # whoami
22 student1
23 #
24 # id
25 uid=1000(student1) gid=1000(student1) groups=1000(student1) context=unconfined_u:unconfined_r:unconfined_t:s0-s0:c0.c1023
26 #
27 # useradd fred
28 bash: /usr/sbin/useradd: Permission denied
```

Figure 4-5 Real and effective user IDs

Notice when we try to execute the command useradd on line 27, we cannot. Even though we are logged on as root (who should be able to execute the command useradd), our effective user ID is 1000 (student1), and student1 does not have permissions to execute the useradd command.

Creating and Managing User Accounts from the Command Line

Next we review how to create and manage user accounts.

useradd

The useradd utility is used to add users to the Linux system. The useradd command obtains default values from */etc/default/useradd* and */etc/login.defs*. The directory */etc/skel* is used to populate the new user's home directory.

/etc/default/useradd

The directory */etc/default* is used to specify default variable settings. The file */etc/default/useradd* contains default variable used by the command useradd. To view the values set in */etc/default/useradd*, execute the command **useradd -D**:

```
# useradd -D
GROUP=100
HOME=/home
INACTIVE=-1
EXPIRE=
SHELL=/bin/bash
SKEL=/etc/skel
CREATE_MAIL_SPOOL=yes
```

You can change the value of most of the variables in */etc/default/useradd* by executing the command **useradd -D*x***. See Table 4-1 for available options.

GROUP The GROUP variable defines the default group ID. There are several considerations to note:

Option	Definition
-Dg <group_id>	Sets the default primary group
-Db <directory>	Sets the default absolute path to the location of the home directory
-Df <number_of_days>	Sets the default number of days after a password expires for the account to become inactive -1 disables inactivity -0 sets the account to be inactive upon expiration Any other number sets that number of days after the password expires until the account is disabled
-De <YYYY-MM-DD>	Sets the default expiration date
-Ds <shell>	Sets the default absolute path to the default shell

Table 4-1 Changing default entries in */etc/default/useradd*

User Private Group (UPG) is a mechanism that creates a private group for each user when a user is created. The variable USERGROUPS_ENAB in */etc/login.defs* controls the implementation of UPG. If this variable is set to yes, a user group with the same name as the user is created.

If the USERGROUPS_ENAB variable is set to no or the -n option is used (**useradd -n <user_name>**) the default group in */etc/default/useradd* is the user's primary group.

You may select a specific group for a user. Use the -g option followed by an existing group number or group name (for example, **useradd -g 1001 student2**). The group must exist.

HOME The HOME variable stores the location of the base directory used when a new user is created. For example, if you were to create a new user student2 and the base directory is */home*, the new user's home directory would be */home/student2*. The **useradd -d <directory>** command (for example, **useradd -d /home/fred fred**) is used to specify the absolute path to the location of the user's home directory.

To create the home directory, the variable CREATE_HOME in the file */etc/login.defs* must be set to yes. To create the directory for a user via the command line, you must use the -m option (for example, **useradd -d /home/fred -m fred**).

INACTIVE Inactive days are the days a user has not logged on to the system. The purpose of the INACTIVE field is to prevent open accounts that are not being used from remaining open.

The INACTIVE variable sets the number of days after a password expires that the user account will be disabled. If this variable is set to 0, the account is disabled when the password expires. If the value of the variable is -1, the inactive function is disabled.

If the variable is set to a value of *n*, the account will be disabled *n* days after the password expires. If the number of days past password expiration is less than the value of *n*, the user may still log on but will be forced to change their password. The account is disabled when the number of days specified by *n* is exceeded. A system administrator is required to remediate a disabled account.

To change the default value, execute the command **useradd -Df <number_of_days>**.

EXPIRE This field is used to specify an account expiration date that's applied to all users created. For example, expiration dates are normally assigned to contract employees.

To change the default value, execute the command **useradd -De <YYYYMMDD>**.

SHELL This field specifies the absolute path to the default logon shell. A list of available shells may be obtained by executing the command **cat /etc/shells** or **chsh -l**.

To change the default value, execute the command **useradd -Db <logon_shell>**.

SKEL The SKEL variable defines the skeleton directory. This directory contains all the files that will be copied to a user's home directory when a user is created.

To change the default value of the variable SKEL in */etc/default/useradd*, execute the command **useradd -Dk <directory_name>**. We discuss the directory */etc/skel* in more depth later in this chapter.

CREATE_MAIL_SPOOL The file */etc/login.defs* defines the location of a user's mailbox. The variable CREATE_MAIL_SPOOL determines whether the user's mail file or directory will be created when the user is created.

To change this variable you must edit */etc/default/useradd.*

/etc/login.defs

The settings in the file */etc/login.defs* are used when a user is created.

NOTE Be sure to understand the difference between settings in */etc/login.defs* and configurations found in */etc/pam.d/passwd*. The settings in */etc/login.defs* only affect shadow utilities. The settings in */etc/pam.d/passwd* affect a specific command. For example, the file */etc/login.defs* specifies a minimum length for a user password. The PAM file that affects the passwd command, */etc/pam.d/passwd*, may also have a configuration setting for password length. */etc/pam.d/passwd* will override the password length defined in */etc/login.defs*.

Location of User Mail The following entries specify where the user's mail will be stored. In the first example, notice the uncommented line that begins with MAIL_DIR. This indicates the user's mail will be located in the directory */var/spool/mail.* The value of the variable CREATE_MAIL_SPOOL in */etc/default/useradd* will determine if the file will be created when the user is added.

```
#QMAIL_DIR          Maildir
MAIL_DIR            /var/spool/mail
#MAIL_FILE          .mail
```

The following values set the password aging defaults and the minimum password length. If the password length is set differently in */etc/pam.d/passwd*, the password length setting is ignored.

```
PASS_MAX_DAYS       99999        Max Days
PASS_MIN_DAYS       0            Min Days
PASS_MIN_LENGTH     5
PASS_WARN_AGE       7            Warn Days
```

NOTE The default aging settings are a security risk. It is advisable to change the default min, max, and warn days in */etc/login.defs* and the inactive variable in */etc/default/useradd.* The following settings would be more secure:

PASS_MAX_DAYS 45
PASS_MIN_DAYS 37
PASS_MIN_LENGTH 7
PASS_WARN_AGE 7

User ID Ranges The next entries specify a range of user IDs and group IDs:

```
UID_MIN              1000
UID_MAX             60000
SYS_UID_MIN           201
SYS_UID_MAX           999
GID_MIN              1000
GID_MAX             60000
SYS_GID_MIN           201
SYS_GID_MAX           999
```

USERDEL_CMD This is the command executed when deleting a user. Notice this line is commented out.

```
USERDEL_CMD        /usr/sbin/userdel_local
```

CREATE_HOME The CREATE_HOME directory determines if a user's home directory will be created when a user is added.

```
CREATE_HOME        yes
```

UMASK The UMASK variable assigns the umask value that will be applied when creating the user's home directory. A value of 077 will create a home directory with the permission 700.

```
UMASK        077
```

This entry turns on Universal Private Group:

```
USERGROUPS_ENAB    yes
```

If USERGROUPS_ENAB is no, the -U option will create a group with the same name as the user name.
This entry sets the password encryption method:

```
ENCRYPT_METHOD            SHA512
```

/etc/skel

The */etc/skel* directory is the default directory that contains the files and directories copied to a new user's home directory. You may modify the files in this directory if you want all new users to have specific files or settings.

You may also create skeleton directory for users with similar needs. Let us assume you have a specific group that requires specific settings in *~/.bash_profile* and *~/.bashr*, and have certain scripts available. Create a directory named */etc/skel_<group_name>*. Next copy all the files in */etc/skel* to that directory and edit the appropriate configuration files or add any additional files you want in the group's home directory.

When adding a user for that group, use the option -k <skel_directory> (for example, **useradd -k /etc/skel_<group_name> <user_name>**).

useradd Options

You can use the following useradd options:

- **-c** User comment field. Place the comments between double quotes (for example, -c "Computer Lab"). Make certain your comment does not contain any personal information.
- **-e** Specifies the date when the user account will be disabled (**-e YYYY-MM-DD**).
- **-f** Inactive. Specifies the number of days to wait after password expiration before disabling the account.
- **-g** Specifies the user's primary group
- **-n** Override the USERGROUP_ENAB variable in */etc/login.defs* and use the default group specified in the variable group in the file */etc/default/useradd.*
- **-G** Specifies additional groups (secondary groups) that the user is to be made a member of. You may enter a comma-delimited list of group names or group IDs.
- **-d** Defines the location of the home directory. The default home directory is a sub directory of the base home directory specified by the variable HOME in */etc/default/useradd.* If the variable HOME is equal to /home and the new user is equal to student2, the default home directory for user student2 would be */home/student2.*
  Use the **-d <absolute_path_to_home_directory>** command to specify a different location for a user's home directory.
- **-m** Create (make) the home directory. This option is not necessary if the variable CREATE_HOME in */etc/login.defs* is yes.
- **-r** Specifies that the user being created is a system user. The system user ID will be in the range specified by SYS_UID_MIN and SYS_UID_MAX in */etc/login.def.*
  A user created with the -r option will not be able to log on, have a home directory, or have any password aging settings.
- **-s** Specifies the absolute path to the default shell for the user.
- **-u** The useradd command will automatically assign a user ID. The -u option allows an administrator to manually specify a user ID. If the user already exists you will receive an error message.

Any required settings not specified on the command line are supplied by */etc/login.defs* and */etc/default/useradd.*

passwd The passwd utility allows the user to change their password and allows a system administrator to manage password aging.

Password aging defines how long a password maximum number of days a password may exist before it must be changed (max days).

Password aging also specifies the number of days a user will be warned before the password must be changed (warn days).

Min days defines the number of days a user must wait before changing their password. This was designed to prevent a user from changing their password and then changing back to the previous one.

A user can change their own password by executing the command **passwd**. Password construction is managed by PAM (*/etc/pam.d/passwd*). While entering the new password, nothing will appear on the terminal.

```
# passwd lmorgan
New password:
Retype new password:
passwd: password updated successfully
```

A system administrator may change a user's password by executing the command **passwd <username>**. Other passwd options that may be used by the system administrator include the following:

- **-l** This option locks the user account but does not remove the current password. The encrypted password of an account locked using passwd -l will have two exclamation points (!!) preceding the password.
- **-u** Unlocks a user's account.
- **-d** Removes a user's password. This leaves the user account open, which is not recommended.
- **-n** Sets the minimum number of days (MIN_DAYS) required before a password can be changed.
- **-x** Sets the maximum number of days (MAX_DAYS) before a password must be changed.
- **-w** Sets the number of days prior to password expiration (WARN_DAYS) when the user will be warned of the pending expiration.
- **-i** Sets the number of inactive days to wait after a password has expired before disabling the account.
- **-S** Displays password aging information. Password aging information may also be displayed by executing the **chage -l <username>** command.

chage The chage (change aging) command allows you to view or change a user's password aging information.

The command **chage -l** will display the current user's aging information. As a system administrator, the command **chage -l <username>** will display password aging for a specific user. This is a beneficial troubleshooting tool if a user cannot logon.

Let's look at some other system administrator chage options:

- **-d YYYY-MM-DD** Changes a user's last change date.
- **-m** Sets the minimum number of days (MIN_DAYS) required before a password can be changed.

- **-M** Sets the maximum number of days (MAX_DAYS) before a password must be changed.
- **-W** Sets the number of days prior to password expiration (WARN_DAYS) when the user will be warned of the pending expiration.
- **-I** Sets inactive (the number of days to wait after a password has expired to disable the account).
- **-E YYYY-MM-DD** Sets the account expiration date.

A system administrator may also use the command **chage <username>** to change a user's password aging information. This command opens a text-based user interface (TUI) that will step through each aging parameter, display the current value, and allow the value to be changed (see Figure 4-6).

usermod The usermod command is used to modify an existing user account. The options for usermod are likewise similar to those used by useradd, with a few noted changes:

- **-G <group_name |group_id>** This option removes all of the user's current secondary groups and replaces them with the group or comma-delimited list of groups.
- **-aG <group_name |group_id>** To avoid overwriting existing secondary, groups preface the -G with -a (append).
- **-l** Changes the username (logon name).
  Once you change the username, you must change the location of the home directory and create the home directory.
  - **-d** Location of the user's home directory.
    Suppose you are modifying the username of student2 to user2. You want user2's home directory to be /home/user2. You must specify the location of the new home directory by using the option **-d /home/user2**.
  - **-m** This option moves (renames) the current user's home directory to the new user's name.
    If you view the inode number of the home directories before and after the username is modified, you will see the inode numbers are the same.

The following command will rename user student2 to user2: **usermod -l user2 -d /home/user2 -m student2**.

```
# chage student2
Changing the aging information for student2
Enter the new value, or press ENTER for the default

        Minimum Password Age [0]: █
```

Figure 4-6 chage TUI

userdel The userdel command is used to remove a user account. The command **userdel <username>** will only remove a user's record from */etc/passwd* and */etc/shadow*.

To remove the user's home directory, cron jobs, at jobs, and mail, execute the command **userdel -r <username>**.

NOTE If you do not use the -r option with the userdel command, you must manually delete a user's home directory, cron jobs, at jobs, and mail.

Neither **userdel** nor **userdel -r** will remove any groups from */etc/group*.

You'll practice managing users in Exercise 4-1.

Exercise 4-1: Managing User Accounts from the Command Line

In this exercise, you will practice creating and modifying user accounts from the shell prompt of your Linux system. You can perform this exercise using the virtual machine that comes with this book.

VIDEO Please watch the Exercise 4-1 video for a demonstration on how to perform this task.

Complete the following steps:

1. Boot your Linux system and log in as the **root** user with a password of **password**.
2. Open a terminal session.
3. Execute the commands **who**, **whoami**, **id**, **echo $HOME**, and **echo $PATH**.
4. Open a second terminal and execute the command **su student1**.
5. Execute the commands **who**, **whoami**, **id**, **echo $HOME**, and **echo $PATH**. What has changed?
6. Open a third terminal and execute the command **su - student1**.
7. Execute the commands **who**, **whoami**, **id**, **echo $HOME**, and **echo $PATH**. Compare the difference in outputs in all three terminals. What are the differences? Why?
8. Close the second and third terminals by typing the command **exit** twice. In the first terminal, type the **clear** command.
9. Create the user student2 by executing the **useradd student2** command.
10. Use the command **grep ^student2 /etc/passwd /etc/shadow /etc/group /etc/gshadow** to view the changes made to these files. Remember the settings in */etc/default/useradd* and */etc/login.defs*? Execute the command **ls -l /var/spool/mail** to determine if user2's mail file was created.
11. Execute the command **passwd student2**. Use the password **student2**.

12. Execute the command **grep ^student2 /etc/shadow**. Look at the password field. What has changed?
13. Use the key sequence CTRL-ALT-F2 to open a text terminal. Log in as user student2.
14. To determine your real user ID, execute the **who** command.
15. Use the key sequence ALT-F3 to open another text terminal.
16. Log in as root, execute the command **passwd -l student2**, and then execute the command **grep ^student2 /etc/shadow**. What does the change in the password field indicate?
17. Use ALT-F2 to return to the previous text terminal. Execute the **clear** command. Notice that even though you have prevented student2 from logging in, student2 can still execute commands.
18. Type the **exit** command to log out and then try to log back in as student2. Notice you cannot log in because the account is locked.
19. Use the key sequence ALT-F3 to change to the terminal where you are logged in as root.
20. Execute the **su - student2** command.
21. Verify your effective user ID using the **whoami** command. Then execute **id** so you can see the difference in output between the two commands. If you execute the **who** command, you will see your real user ID is root.
22. Try to execute the command **passwd -u student2**. Why does the command fail?
23. Execute the commands **exit** and **whoami**. Now execute the **passwd -u student2** command.
24. Go back to the second text terminal (ALT-F2) and try to log on as student2.
25. As student2, view your password aging by executing the commands **passwd -S** and **chage -l student2**. Notice only root can execute the **passwd** command.
26. Return to the GUI by entering the key sequence ALT-F1.
27. Type **chage student2**. The text user interface will open. Change **inactive** to **0**. What will that do? Use the command **grep ^student2 /etc/shadow** to view the changes.
28. Use the command **chage -m 37 -M 45 -W 7 -I 14 student2** to change the min days (37), max days (45), warn days (7), and inactive (14) for user student2. Now view the changes by executing the **grep ^student2 /etc/shadow** command.
29. Create the user student3. This user's default group should be the group specified in */etc/default/useradd* or */etc/login.defs*. Use the command **id student3** to make certain student3's primary group is 1003 because */etc/login.defs* defines USERGROUPS_ENAB=yes.

30. Add the group student1 as a secondary group for student3 by executing the command **usermod -G student1 student3**. Type the **groups student3** command. This will display what groups student3 is a member of.
31. Add the group 100 (users) as a secondary group for student3 using the command **usermod -G 100 student3** and then type the command **groups student3**. Notice that the group student1 is no longer a secondary group. Using the -G option overwrote all the existing secondary groups. Execute the command **usermod -aG student1 student3** and then execute the command **groups student3**. The -a "appends" the group to the secondary group list.
32. Delete user student2 using the command **userdel student2**. Then execute the **grep ^student2 /etc/passwd /etc/shadow; ls -l /var/spool/mail/student2** command. Notice that student2's records in */etc/passwd* and */etc/shadow* have been removed, but student2's mail file remains.
33. Delete user student3 using the command **userdel -r student3**. Execute the **grep ^student3 /etc/passwd /etc/shadow; ls -l /var/spool/mail/student3** command. Notice student3's records in */etc/passwd* and */etc/shadow* have been removed as well as student3's mail file in */var/spool/mail*.

Now that you know how to manage users, we need to discuss how to manage groups. Let's do that next.

Linux Groups

Linux uses groups to provide common access to a system resource for multiple users. In this part of the chapter, we're going to discuss how Linux groups work and how to manage groups from the command line.

How Linux Groups Work

Assume you have a resource that all of the company's tech writers need to access. By creating a group called tech_writers and making tech_writers the group owner of the resource, you can assign the necessary access permissions to the resource for the group.

Group information is stored in the */etc/group* and */etc/gshadow* files. The *gshadow* file is part of shadow utilities.

The */etc/group* file is a flat-file database that contains four fields:

```
Group:Password:GID:Users
#getent root student1

root:x:0:
users:x:1000:
```

- **Group** Specifies the name of the group. In the example, the name of the group is "video."
- **Password** Specifies the group password, if shadow passwording is not enabled and one is assigned. If shadow passwording is enabled, the group password would be stored in */etc/gshadow*.

- **GID** Specifies the group ID (GID) number of the group.
- **Users** Lists the members who are secondary members of the group. Some distributions use an additional group file to store group passwords.

If shadow passwording is enabled, the file */etc/gshadow* will contain the group password and contain an additional field for storing group administrators, as shown next. A group administrator may add or remove users from the group, change the group password, remove the group password, and enable or disable the **newgrp** command for that group.

```
Group_Name:Password:Group_Admins:Group_Members
```

With this in mind, let's review how you can manage your groups with command-line tools.

Managing Groups from the Command Line

As with users, groups can also be managed with either command-line or graphical tools. For example, both YaST and User Manager can be used to create, modify, and delete groups, as well as user accounts, on your Linux system.

However, for the reasons specified earlier, we're going to focus on managing groups from the shell prompt in this chapter. We will review the following tools:

- groupadd
- gpasswd
- groupmod
- groupdel

Let's begin by looking at groupadd.

groupadd As you can probably guess from its name, the groupadd utility is used to add groups to your Linux system. The syntax for using groupadd at the shell prompt is relatively simple. Just enter **groupadd *options groupname***. For example, if you wanted to add a group named dbusers, you would enter **groupadd dbusers** at the shell prompt.

When using groupadd, you can use the following options:

- **-g** Specifies a GID for the new group. As with users, it is not necessary to specify a group ID, as the system will automatically assign one.
- **-r** Specifies that the group being created is a system group.

gpasswd The gpasswd command is used to manage the files */etc/group* and */etc/gshadow*. This command may be executed by a system administrator or a group administrator.

To assign a group administrator, a system administrator or group administrator should execute the **gpasswd -A <username>** command.

A system or group administrator may use any of the following gpasswd options:

- **-a <username>** Add a user to the group.
- **-d <username>** Delete a user from the group.
- **-r** Remove the group password.

groupmod The groupmod command is used to modify group information using the following options:

- **-g** Change the group's GID number.
- **-n** Change the group name.

groupdel If, for some reason, you need to delete an existing group from the system, you can do so using the groupdel command at the shell prompt. For example, to delete the dbusers group, you would enter **groupdel dbusers**.

Before deleting a group, make certain the users' access to files and directories is not compromised.

You'll practice managing groups in Exercise 4-2.

Exercise 4-2: Managing Groups from the Command Line

In this exercise, you will practice creating and modifying groups from the shell prompt of your Linux system. You can perform this exercise using the virtual machine that comes with this book.

VIDEO Please watch the Exercise 4-2 video for a demonstration on how to perform this task.

Suppose your company is putting together a new research and development team that will be using your Linux system. You need to create a new group for users who will be members of this team. To do this, complete the following steps:

1. Log on to the system as the user root.
2. Create a new group named **research** by executing the **groupadd research** command.
3. Add the group research as a secondary group of student1 by executing the command **usermod -aG research student1**.
4. View the members of the research group by executing the command **getent group research**.
5. View all the secondary groups student1 is a member of by executing the command **grep student1 /etc/group**.
6. View all the groups student1 belongs to by executing the **groups student1** command.
7. Delete the group research by executing the **groupdel research** command. Verify the group has been removed by executing the **grep research /etc/group** command.

Chapter Review

In this chapter, we reviewed the user configuration files, how to use user and group management commands and configuration files, as well as how to temporarily change user and group IDs. Here are some key takeaways from this chapter:

- To authenticate to a system, a user must supply a username and password.
- User home directories are created in /home by default.
- The root user's home directory is /root.
- Every Linux user account should have a unique user ID (UID) number assigned to it.
- The root user's UID is 0.
- The starting UID for standard users is 1000 on some distributions and 500 on others.
- You may use the su command to temporarily switch your user ID, primary group ID, and home directory.
- You can temporarily log on as another use by executing the **su - <username>** command.
- You can use the id command to view a user's effective user ID.
- You can use many different authentication methods with a Linux system.
- With local authentication, user accounts are stored in */etc/passwd* and */etc/shadow*.
- The */etc/passwd* file stores user account information.
- The */etc/shadow* file stores encrypted passwords and password aging information.
- You can use the pwconv utility to verify that */etc/passwd* and */etc/shadow* are synchronized.
- You can use the useradd utility to add users to a Linux system.
- When used without any options, useradd uses system defaults defined in */etc/default/useradd* and */etc/login.defs* to create user accounts.
- You can use the passwd utility to set a user's password.
- The commands **passwd -S** and **chage -l <username>** may be used to check password aging for a user account.
- You can use the usermod utility to modify an existing user account.
- You can use the userdel utility to delete an existing user account.
- By default, userdel will not remove a user's home directory, cron and at jobs, and mail unless you specify the -r option with the command.
- Group accounts are stored in */etc/group*.
- */etc/gshadow* is the shadow utility file for groups.

- You may make a user a group administrator by executing the command **gpasswd -A <username>**.
- You use the groupadd utility to add a new group to your system.
- You use the usermod utility to add or remove users to or from an existing group.
- You use the groupdel utility to delete an existing group.

Questions

1. Which file or files contain generic (global) user configuration files for a user with /bin/bash as their default shell? (Choose two.)

   A. /etc/passwd

   B. /etc/profile

   C. ~/.bash_profile

   D. /etc/group

   E. /etc/bashrc

   F. ~/.bashrc

2. A user has a primary group and may be a member of more than one secondary group. Which file would you look in to find a user's secondary groups.

   A. /etc/passwd

   B. /etc/profile

   C. ~/.bash_profile

   D. /etc/group

3. Which entry or entries in an */etc/passwd* record will prevent a user from logging on to the system? (Choose two.)

   A. /bin/bash

   B. /bin/false

   C. /sbin/nologin

   D. /bin/nologin

4. Which entry in an */etc/shadow* record's password field will indicate a user password has not been set for that user.

   A. !!

   B. NP

   C. LK

   D. !

5. A user cannot log on. Their password field in */etc/shadow* contains !!<encrypted_password>. What action would fix this problem? (Choose two.)
   - **A.** The user should change their password.
   - **B.** An administrator should execute the command **passwd -u <user_name>**.
   - **C.** An administrator should execute the command **chage -u <user_name>**.
   - **D.** An administrator should execute the command **usermod -U <user_name>**.
6. Which file contains the default password aging values used when adding a user?
   - **A.** /etc/default/useradd
   - **B.** /etc/login.defs
   - **C.** /etc/skel
   - **D.** /etc/profile
7. You are adding a user. The value stored in the variable USERGROUPS_ENAB in */etc/login.defs* is yes. You do not wish to create a new group, but want the user's primary group to be the same as the value (100) stored in the GROUP variable in */etc/default/useradd*. Which of the following commands would accomplish this? (Choose two.)
   - **A.** Create the user and then execute the command **usermod -g <username>**.
   - **B.** useradd -n <username>
   - **C.** useradd -G 100 <username>
   - **D.** useradd -g 100 <username>
8. A user cannot log on. You wish to view the password aging information for that user. What command would you execute? (Choose two.)
   - **A.** chage -S <username>
   - **B.** passwd -S <username>
   - **C.** chage -l <username>
   - **D.** passwd -l <username>
9. Which configuration file influences the permissions of the user's home directory when creating a user?
   - **A.** /etc/default/useradd
   - **B.** /etc/login.defs
   - **C.** /etc/skel
   - **D.** /etc/profile

10. You want the default editor for all new users to be nano. Which file would you edit?
    A. /etc/default/useradd
    B. /etc/login.defs
    C. /etc/profile
    D. /etc/skel/.bash_profile
11. A user's password expired five days ago. The value of inactive is 14. What can the user do?
    A. Nothing, the account has been disabled.
    B. Log on normally.
    C. Log on, but be ready to change their password.
    D. Contact the system administrator to reset the account.
12. A user's password expired five days ago. The value of inactive is 0. What can the user do?
    A. Nothing, the account has been disabled.
    B. Log on normally.
    C. Log on, but be ready to change their password.
    D. Contact the system administrator to reset the account.
13. A user with a user ID of 3 has an asterisk in their password field in */etc/shadow*. What does this indicate?
    A. The account has been disabled.
    B. This is a system account and does not require a password.
    C. This is a system application account and does not require a password.
    D. This a system account that can only be called by root and does not require a password.
14. The command **wc -l <filename>** will count the number of lines in a file. You execute the commands **wc -l /etc/passwd** and **wc -l /etc/shadow**. You find you have an extra record (line) in */etc/shadow*. What command will fix this?
    A. pwconv
    B. pwck
    C. pwunconv
    D. groupdel

15. You are changing the logon name for user student1 to student3. What is the appropriate command?
    - **A.** usermod -l student1 student3
    - **B.** usermod -l student3 student1
    - **C.** usermod -l student3 -d /home/student3 student1
    - **D.** usermod -l student3 -d /home/student3 -m student1
16. What command will only delete the user record for student3 in */etc/passwd* and */etc/shadow*?
    - **A.** userdel -r student3
    - **B.** userdel student3
    - **C.** rm student3
    - **D.** rm -r student3
17. You have removed the user records for student3 in */etc/passwd* and */etc/shadow* but did not remove the home directory, cron jobs, at jobs, and mail associated with student3. What command will do this?
    - **A.** userdel -r student3
    - **B.** userdel -rf student2
    - **C.** The files must be removed manually.
    - **D.** \rm -r /home/student3
18. What file would you view to determine if user student1 was the administrator for group lab1?
    - **A.** /etc/group
    - **B.** /etc/gshadow
    - **C.** /etc/shadow
    - **D.** /etc/passwd
19. You are logged in as student1. You execute the command **su student2**. What command or commands will display who you have logged on to the system as? (Choose two.)
    - **A.** id
    - **B.** who
    - **C.** w
    - **D.** whoami
20. What command would only display your effective user ID?
    - **A.** id
    - **B.** who
    - **C.** w
    - **D.** whoami

Answers

1. **B, E.** */etc/profile* and */etc/bashrc* are generic (global) configuration files applied to all users whose default shell is the Bash shell. */etc/profile* would also be read for users whose default shell is the Bourne or Korn shell.
2. **D.** The file */etc/group* would contain a user's secondary group information. A user's primary group information would be stored in */etc/passwd*.
3. **B, C.** */bin/false* and */sbin/nologin* will prevent a user from logging on.
4. **A.** If the password field of a user account in the file */etc/shadow* only contains two exclamation points, a password has never been set.
5. **B, D.** The two exclamation points preceding the password indicate the account has been locked by the command **passwd -l**. The commands **passwd -u** or **usermod -U** will unlock the account.
6. **B.** /etc/login.defs.
7. **B, D.** The command **useradd -n** negates the setting in */etc/login.defs* and would force the default in */etc/default/useradd* to be used. The command **usermod -g 100** would set the primary group ID to 100. Although answer A would work, the question species the administrator does not wish to create a new group. The command **useradd <username>** would create a new group.
8. **B, C.** The commands **chage -l <username>** and **passwd -S <username>** would display the password aging for a user.
9. **B.** The UMASK variable in */etc/login.defs* would influence the permissions on the user's home directory.
10. **D.** Editing the file */etc/skel/.bash_profile* would cause any changes to the file to be propagated to new users.
11. **C.** The user may log on, but will be forced to change their password.
12. **D.** An inactive value of 0 automatically disables the account when the password expires, so there is nothing the user can do to fix the problem. A system administrator will have to manually remove the asterisk from the password field in */etc/shadow*.
13. **B.** The user ID indicates this is a system service account that does not require a password.
14. **A.** The pwconv command will fix this issue; the pwconv command compares the user records in */etc/shadow* and */etc/passwd*. If a record exists in */etc/shadow* but a corresponding record does not exist in */etc/passwd*, the pwconv commands deletes the record in */etc/shadow*. The pwunconv command removes */etc/shadow* and places existing passwords in */etc/passwd*. The pwck command checks for the validity of the entries in */etc/passwd*. The groupdel command deletes an existing group from the system.

15. **D.** When modifying a username, you must specify the location of the user's home directory (**-d <home_directory>**) and move the contents from the old username's directory to the new username's home directory (**-m**).
16. **B.** To remove a user record from */etc/passwd* and */etc/shadow*, use the **userdel <username>** command.
17. **C.** The files must be removed manually.
18. **B.** The command **grep ^lab1 /etc/gshadow** can be used to display administrator information for the group lab1.
19. **B, C.** The commands who and w will display the users RUID or who they logged in as. The commands id (A) and whoami (D) will display their effective user id.
20. **D.** Either the who or w command will display real user IDs. Although the id command would display your effective user ID, the question specifically asked for only your effective user ID, so the most correct answer is D.

CHAPTER 5

Managing Linux Files and Directories

In this chapter, you will learn about

- The Filesystem Hierarchy Standard (FHS)
- Managing Linux files
- Finding files in the Linux filesystem
- Commands and precedence
- Finding content within files

In this chapter, you get to know the Linux filesystem, including the hierarchical structure of the Linux filesystem and Linux file types. Then you will work with files and directories. Let's begin by discussing the role of the filesystem.

Understanding Filesystem Hierarchy Standard (FHS)

Linux stores data on physical hard disks, which in many cases are subdivided into partitions. Storing data on a partition requires a method for managing how the data is stored and retrieved. A filesystem controls how data is managed on a hard disk. Figure 5-1 shows one hard disk with three partitions. Each partition has a filesystem on which data is stored. What data is stored in on a disk or partition and what filesystems are used to manage the data are determined as part of the system design process.

The logical location of a directory has no relationship to where the data is physically stored. A hierarchy is a method of organizing objects based on some classification. The Filesystem Hierarchy Standard (FHS) defines a suggested logical location of directories and files on Linux (and UNIX) distributions. These definitions include what should be contained in specific directories and files. An example of this structure can be found in Figure 5-2. Currently, FHS is maintained by the Linux Foundation (https://refspecs.linuxfoundation.org/fhs.shtml).

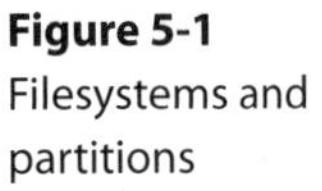

Figure 5-1 Filesystems and partitions

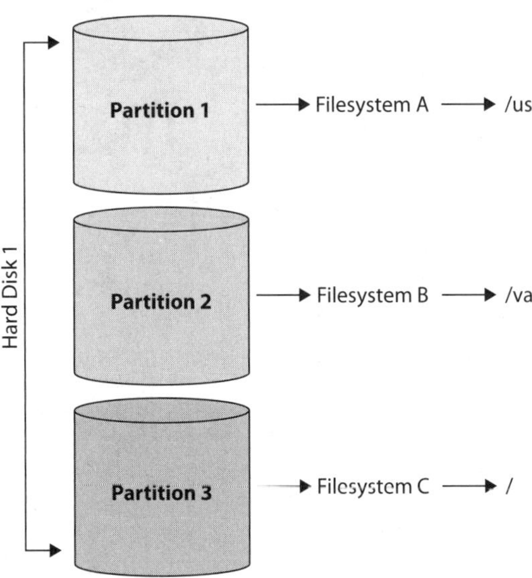

Let's review the purpose of some of these directories:

- **/bin** This directory is linked to */usr/bin*. */usr/bin* contains user commands.
- **/boot** This directory contains files required to boot your system.
- **/dev** This directory contains special files used to represent the various hardware devices installed in the system.
- **/etc** This directory contains global configuration files.
- **/lib** This directory contains system library files. Kernel modules are stored in /lib/modules.
- **/mnt** This directory is intended to be a temporary mount point.
- **/media** This directory is intended to contain subdirectories used as mount points for removable media.
- **/opt** This directory is the suggested location for third-party applications.
- **/sbin** This directory contains system binaries used by root or other system administrators for booting, restoring, or repairing the operating system.

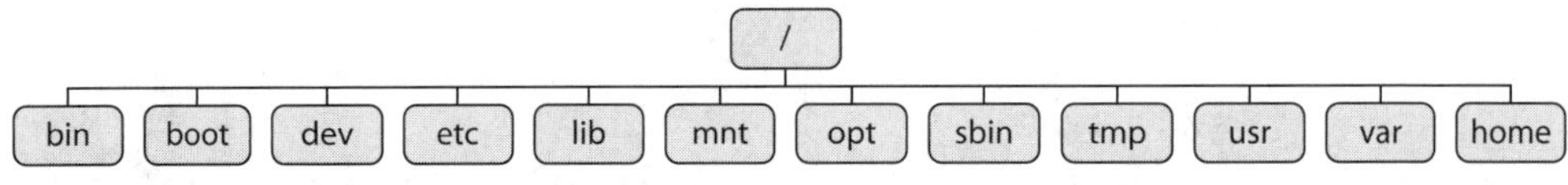

Figure 5-2 Directory structure

- **/tmp** This directory contains temporary files created by user applications.
- **/usr** This directory contains user system files.
- **/var** This directory contains variable data, including your system log files.
- **/home** This directory contains home directories for user accounts.
- **/root** This is the user root's home directory.
- **/run** The */run* directory contains system information gathered from boot time forward. This directory is cleared at the start of the boot process.
- **/srv** This directory contains data for services (HTTP and FTP) running on the server.
- **/sys** This directory provides device, driver, and some kernel information.
- **/proc** */proc* is a dynamic memory-based directory that contains process and other system (CPU, DMA, and IRQ) information. When viewing */proc*, you will see a number of directories identified by a number rather than a name, as shown in Figure 5-3. These numbers correspond to the process ID (PID) of running processes. The */proc* directory contain statistics for these processes.

  You will also see a list of files, and these files also contain statistical information. Some of the files contain a list of available filesystems, loaded kernel modules, and mounted partitions.

  /proc also contains a special directory called */sys*. This directory contains a list of kernel operating parameters. An administrator can temporarily change these settings for testing purposes.

```
# ls /proc
1     1409  2316  2916  3573  45    4753  4951  buddyinfo    misc
10    1410  2318  2921  3581  4514  4757  4968  bus          modules
1092  1432  2324  2964  3584  4516  4758  4982  cgroups      mounts
1095  1434  2326  2965  3585  4526  4761  4984  cmdline      mpt
11    1435  2329  2966  3824  4528  4763  5     consoles     mtrr
1103  1436  2330  2967  3826  4532  4768  5037  cpuinfo      net
1104  1437  2334  2970  3921  4535  4775  5038  crypto       pagetypeinfo
1105  1438  2337  2981  3922  4539  4777  5098  devices      partitions
1107  1439  2341  2982  3997  4543  4779  5108  diskstats    sched_debug
1108  1440  2350  2983  4015  4558  4781  5137  dma          schedstat
1109  1491  2391  2984  4027  4572  4783  5147  driver       scsi
1112  15    2393  2990  4090  4577  4796  5153  execdomains  self
1113  1515  24    2996  41    4583  4798  5154  fb           slabinfo
1114  1525  2773  2997  4149  4609  4806  60    filesystems  softirqs
1116  16    2816  3     4151  4664  4808  6215  fs           stat
1117  17    2817  30    4166  4668  4809  6329  interrupts   swaps
1265  18    2830  3000  42    4672  4810  6711  iomem        sys
13    19    2831  3027  4237  4675  4814  6768  ioports      sysrq-trigger
1368  2     2832  3031  4283  4685  4818  6822  irq          sysvipc
1369  20    2833  3032  43    4686  4822  6853  kallsyms     timer_list
1386  2091  2834  3034  4303  4695  4847  6967  kcore        timer_stats
1391  21    2835  3050  4308  47    4868  6975  keys         tty
```

Figure 5-3 A sample view of /proc

Navigating the Filesystem

As you work with the Linux filesystem from the shell prompt, one of the most common tasks you will perform is moving around among the different directories on your storage devices. Your Linux system provides the following shell commands that you can use to do this:

- pwd
- cd

pwd

The pwd (print working directory) command displays the absolute path of the current directory on the terminal. The absolute path to a file is the path from the root (/) directory. Figure 5-4 displays the absolute path to *file2* as */dir1/file2*. An absolute path will always begin with /.

To display your current directory, execute the command **pwd**. Here's an example:

```
$ pwd
/home/student1
```

cd

The cd (change directory) command is used to change from your current working directory to another directory. When specifying a directory, you may use the absolute or relative path. The relative path specifies the path to a directory from the current directory. In Figure 5-5, our current working directory is *dira*. The relative path to *fileb* is *dirb/fileb*.

The absolute path to *fileb* is */dira/dirb/fileb*. To change our directory to the directory that contains *fileb* (*dirb*), we could execute the command **cd dirb** or **cd /dira/dirb**.

Executing the command **cd** without an argument will change your current working directory to your home directory. Executing the command **cd ~** will also change your current working directory to your home directory. Executing the command **cd ~<username>** will change your current working directory to the home directory of

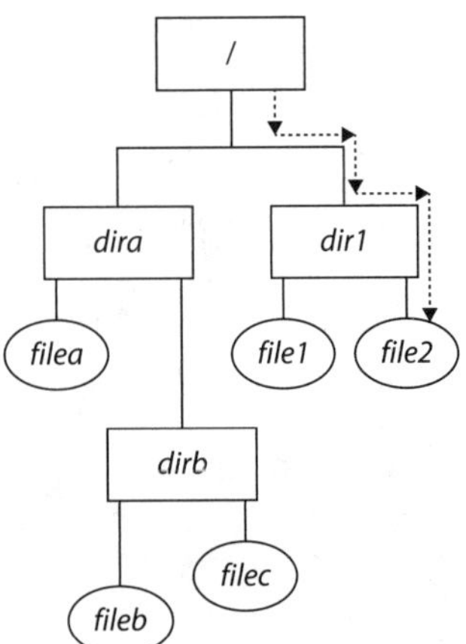

Figure 5-4 Absolute path

Figure 5-5 Relative path

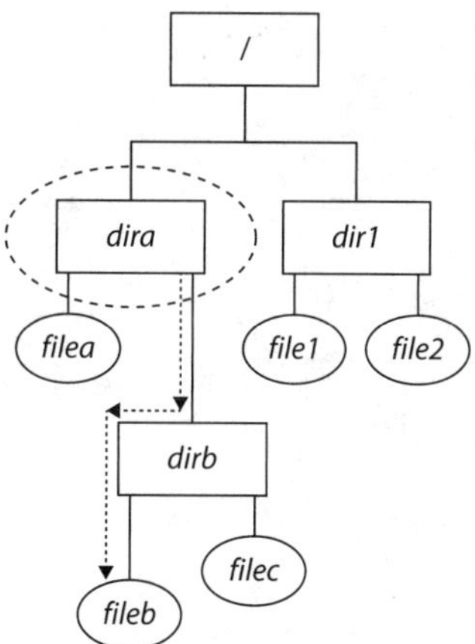

the user specified by the argument <username> as long as you have permissions to enter that home directory. The command **cd ~student1** will change your current working directory to user student1's home directory, */home/student1*. Finally, executing the command **cd ..** will change your current working directory to the parent directory.

Viewing Directory Contents

The ls command will show a list of filenames and directories stored in the current directory. Here's an example:

```
# ls
bin       Documents  Music     Public       Templates  test.txt  words
Desktop   Downloads  Pictures  public_html  test2.txt  Videos    yourfile.txt
```

If you provide an absolute path to a directory, ls will display the contents of the directory, as shown here:

```
# ls /var/log
acpid       cups          mail            ntp                Xorg.0.log.old
apparmor    faillog       mail.err        pk_backend_zypp    YaST2
audit       firewall      mail.info       pm-powersave.log   zypp
boot.log    gdm           mail.warn       samba              zypper.log
boot.msg    krb5          messages        warn
boot.omsg   lastlog       NetworkManager  wtmp
ConsoleKit  localmessages news            Xorg.0.log
```

When working with ls, you can use a variety of options to customize how it works. Here are some of these options:

- **-a** Displays all files, including hidden files. Hidden filenames are prefixed with a period. Many configuration files are hidden files. The thinking was that if nonprivileged users could not easily see these files, they would not inadvertently change them.

In the following example, the **ls -a** command has been issued in the */home/student1* directory:

```
$ ls -a
.               .esd_auth           .inputrc              test2.txt
..              .fontconfig         .local                test.txt
.bash_history   .fonts              .mozilla              .themes
.bashrc         .gconf              Music                 .thumbnails
bin             .gconfd             .nautilus             Videos
.cache          .gnome2             Pictures              .viminfo
.config         .gnome2_private     .profile              .vimrc
.dbus           .gstreamer-0.10     Public                words
Desktop         .gtk-bookmarks      public_html           .xim.template
.dmrc           .gvfs               .pulse                .xinitrc.template
Documents       .hplip              .pulse-cookie         .xsession-errors
Downloads       .ICEauthority       .recently-used.xbel   .xsession-errors.old
.emacs          .icons              Templates             yourfile.txt
```

If you are providing the filename of a hidden file (for example, **ls -l .exrc**), the -a option is not necessary.

- **-l** Displays a long listing of the directory contents. The long listing displays the file's name and properties. You can use it to see the filenames, ownership, permissions, modification dates, and sizes. An example is shown here:

```
$ ls -l
total 56
drwxr-xr-x 2 student1 users 4096 2011-01-19 10:41 bin
drwxr-xr-x 2 student1 users 4096 2011-01-19 10:42 Desktop
drwxr-xr-x 2 student1 users 4096 2011-01-19 10:42 Documents
drwxr-xr-x 2 student1 users 4096 2011-01-19 10:42 Downloads
drwxr-xr-x 2 student1 users 4096 2011-01-19 10:42 Music
drwxr-xr-x 2 student1 users 4096 2011-01-19 10:42 Pictures
drwxr-xr-x 2 student1 users 4096 2011-01-19 10:42 Public
drwxr-xr-x 2 student1 users 4096 2011-01-19 10:41 public_html
drwxr-xr-x 2 student1 users 4096 2011-01-19 10:42 Templates
-rw-r--r-- 1 student1 users   37 2011-01-20 11:04 test2.txt
-rw-r--r-- 1 student1 users  182 2011-01-21 11:48 test.txt
drwxr-xr-x 2 student1 users 4096 2011-01-19 10:42 Videos
-rw-r--r-- 1 student1 users   23 2011-01-20 11:32 words
-rw-r--r-- 1 student1 users  121 2011-01-21 11:46 yourfile.txt
```

- **-R** Displays directory contents recursively; that is, it displays the contents of the current directory as well as the contents of all subdirectories. Depending on the number of entries in the directory, you may want to append **| more** after using this option. This will cause the more utility to pause and display one page at a time.

Let's practice navigating the filesystem in Exercise 5-1.

Exercise 5-1: Navigating the Filesystem

In this exercise, you practice using shell commands to navigate the Linux filesystem. For this exercise, you must be logged on to the virtual machine provided with the book as user root (password **password**). Follow these steps:

1. Open a terminal session.
2. Assuming you have just logged on, what should be your current working directory? Use the **pwd** command to verify your current working directory. If you are not in your current working directory, execute the **cd** command to return you to your home directory. Test the results with the **pwd** command.
3. You would like to change your current working directory to user student1's home directory. How many commands could you execute to do this?
   - cd ~student1
   - cd /home/student1
4. Execute the command **ls** and then the command **ls -a**. What is the difference in the output? Why?
5. Execute the commands in step 4 again, but this time display the file's properties (**-l**).
6. Use an absolute path to change your current working directory to the *pam.d* subdirectory in */etc*. Once you have executed the command **cd /etc/pam.d**, verify you are in the correct directory.
7. Move up to the parent directory by executing the command **cd ..** and verify you are in the */etc/ directory.*
8. Return to your home directory and again verify you are in the correct directory.

VIDEO Please watch the Exercise 5-1 video for a demonstration on how to perform this task.

Answer to Exercise 5-1

Step 4 If you execute the command cd, you will return to your home directory. Your home directory contains many configuration files and directories, which you will not see if you execute the command ls, but you will see if you execute the command ls -a.

Managing Linux Files

Everything in Linux is referenced by a file. Even a directory is a file. We will now investigate the types of Linux files and how to manage them.

Linux files consist of a filename, inode, and data block(s). Figure 5-6 shows an example of an ASCII file. When a file is created, it is given a name by the user or application and assigned a unique inode number (index number) by the filesystem. The operating system uses the inode number, not the filename, to access the file and its information.

Filenames

A file is container that stores data. Each file has a filename. A Linux filename may contain up to 255 characters, but must not contain a space, forward slash, or null character. A filename may contain metacharacters (file1*), but this is not advisable.

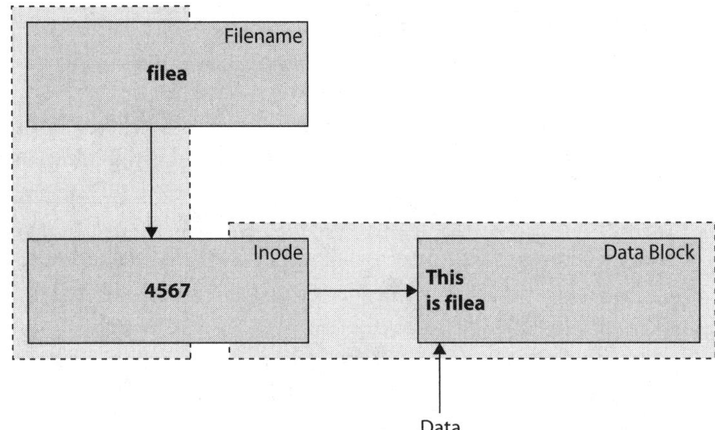

Figure 5-6 Structure of a text file

The Linux operating system does not use extensions (for example, mfc70.dll) to indicate the type of file. Each file (except plain text files) contains a signature called a magic number. This magic number indicates the type of file.

NOTE The CompTIA exam requires you to know the term *extension*. An extension is a suffix at the end of a file that indicates the file type. Linux uses a file's magic number, not the suffix, to determine the type of file, so we will use the more appropriate term for this operating system suffix.

Linux requires the application accessing a file to understand what to do with the data in the file. That said, some applications will apply their own suffix to their files.

By default, LibreOffice stores files using Open Document Format and uses Open Document filenames to distinguish its files. For example, the suffix .odt indicates a text file, .ods a spreadsheet, and .odp a presentation document.

You can apply multiple suffixes on a filenames to make searching for files easier. The filename *fstab.12232019.abc* could indicate that this is a copy of the file */etc/fstab* made on December 23, 2019, by a user with the initials abc.

To make your life easier if you are sharing files among multiple operating systems, make certain your filenames follow the rules for all operating systems. For example, if you create the files *version1.txt* and *Version1.txt* on a Linux system in the same directory, Linux will treat them as separate files. If you want the content of those two files shared with a Windows system, however, you might run into issues because Windows is not case-sensitive.

Types of Files Used by Linux

Linux file types indicate what sort of data is stored in the data block. Table 5-1 details some of these file types.

File Type	Description
Regular file ASCII file	Store text data. This data could be a document or database.
Symbolic link	Stores a pointer to another file. When this file is accessed, the file indicated by the stored pointer is read.
Directory	A directory contains a list of the files stored in it and their inodes.
Named pipe	A named pipe is used to move data from one running process on the system to another. Data can only move in one direction through a named pipe.
Character device	Represents a device that transfers data one character at a time.
Block device	Represents a device that transfers data a block at a time.
Sockets	A socket is a method of communication between two processes on the same or different machines. The four types of sockets are stream, datagram, raw, and sequenced.

Table 5-1 Linux File Types

Creating New Files

Creating a new file can be accomplished by executing the touch command. Assuming *filea* does not exist, the command **touch filea** will create an empty file (0 bytes) named *filea*.

```
$ touch filea
$ ls -l filea
-rw-r--r-- 1 student1 users 0 2011-02-01 11:36 filea
```

There are three file timestamps—access, modification, and change—which are part of a file's metadata. The access timestamp is updated, by default, each time the file contents are read. The modification timestamp is updated each time the contents are changed. The change timestamp is updated whenever the file's metadata (for example, ownership or permissions) is changed. The touch command may be used to modify timestamps. If a file exists, you can change its modification time by executing the command **touch <filename>**.

Symbolic and Hard Links

A link is a method of referring to data stored in another file. This allows us to change the data in one file (original) and have that change reflected in all files that reference the original file.

Prior to discussing links, however, we must look at how files are stored on most filesystems.

A file's metadata is stored in an inode (index node). This data structure contains a file's ownership, permissions, timestamp, and data block information. When a file is created, it is assigned an inode number from a list of available inode numbers in the filesystem. When a user enters a filename, the operating system looks for the inode number associated with that filename. Access to the file is based on the information stored in the file's inode.

For our discussion, we will use the term *source* to indicate the original file and the term *target* to indicate the file we are creating.

Hard Link

A hard link is an entry in the data block of a directory that associates the file's name with the file's inode (see Figure 5-7).

We can create additional hard links to existing files within the same filesystem. Figure 5-8 shows the relationship between the filename inode and data block of two files sharing a common inode.

Figure 5-7 Directory data block

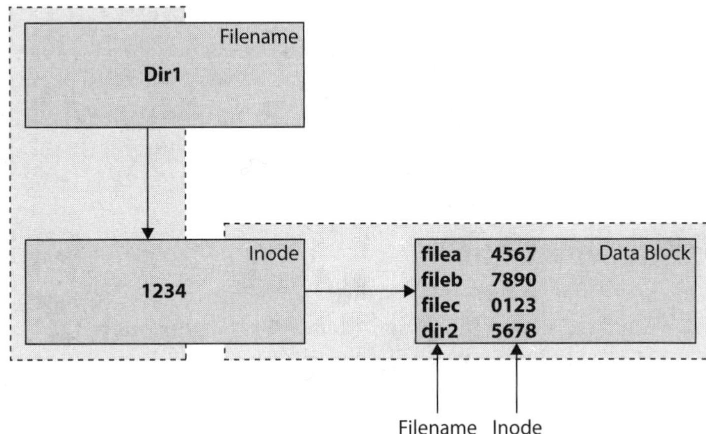

Figure 5-8 Structure hard link

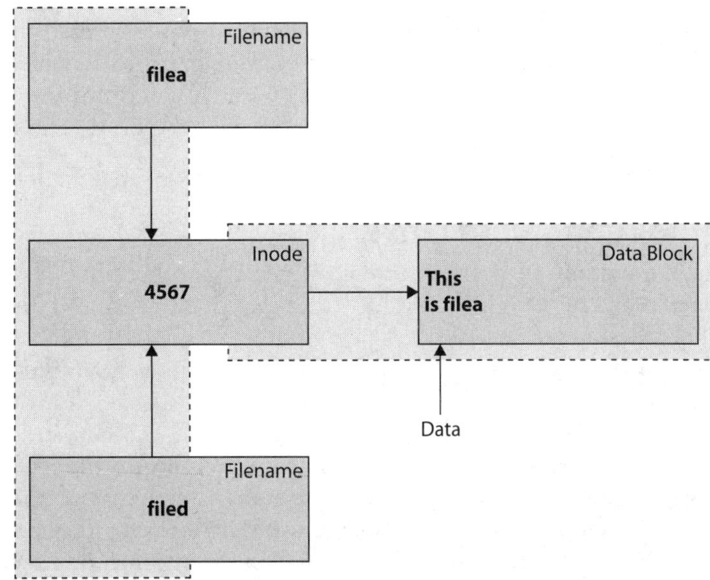

Figure 5-9
Creating hard links

```
# touch hardlink1
#
# ls -il hardlink1
1077977 -rw-r--r--. (1) root root 0 Mar 12 11:36 hardlink1
#
# ln hardlink1 hardlink2
#
# ls -il hardlink[12]
1077977 -rw-r--r--. (2) root root 0 Mar 12 11:36 hardlink1
1077977 -rw-r--r--. (2) root root 0 Mar 12 11:36 hardlink2
#
# \rm hardlink1
#
# ls -il hardlink[12]
1077977 -rw-r--r--. (1) root root 0 Mar 12 11:36 hardlink2
```

To create a hard link, we execute the command **ln <source_file> <target_file>**. In Figure 5-9, we create the file *hardlink1* (**touch hardlink1**). The **ls -il hardlink1** command will display the inode and other properties of the file *hardlink1*. Notice the circled number. This indicates the number of files sharing this file's inode number.

The second command, **ln hardlink1 hardlink2**, creates a hard link between files *hardlink1* and *hardlink2*. Notice the output of the command **ls -il hardlink[12]**. Both filenames are associated with the same inode (1077977). Since the inode contains a pointer to the file's data, when either file is accessed, the same data will be displayed. Also notice how many files now share the inode number 1077977.

In the last command, we remove the file *hardlink1* using the command **\rm hardlink1**. The file *hardlink2* can still access its data because its filename is still associated with inode 1077977. You may also use the unlink command (**unlink hardlink1**). Remember, no disk space is recovered until the number of files sharing the inode's number becomes 0 (zero).

Symbolic Link

A symbolic link (also called a soft link) references a file in the same or another filesystem. Unlike the hard link, each symbolic link file has its own inode, but the data block of the file contains the path to the file it is linked to (see Figure 5-10).

In Figure 5-11, notice a source file called *symlink1* that is populated with the text "this is a symbolic link source file."

We then create two symbolic links, *symlink2* and *symlink3*, using the command **ln -s <source_file> <target_file>**. Notice the output of the **ls -il** command. Each file has its own inode.

Look at the output of the command **ls -il symlink[1-3]**. Remember *symlink1* is our source file and *symlink2* and *symlink3* are the symbolic links.

Notice the file type and properties of *symlink2* and *symlink3*. The lowercase **l** indicates the file is a symbolic link, and the permissions rwxrwxrwx grant all permissions to all users when accessing the file. Also notice the filename has an arrow pointing to the file it is linked to.

Permissions to a symbolic link are based on the file it is linked to. Look at the output of the command **ls -ilL symlink[1-3]**. The -L option references the permissions on the source file. The actual permissions granted a user accessing *symlink2* and *symlink3* are rw-r--r--.

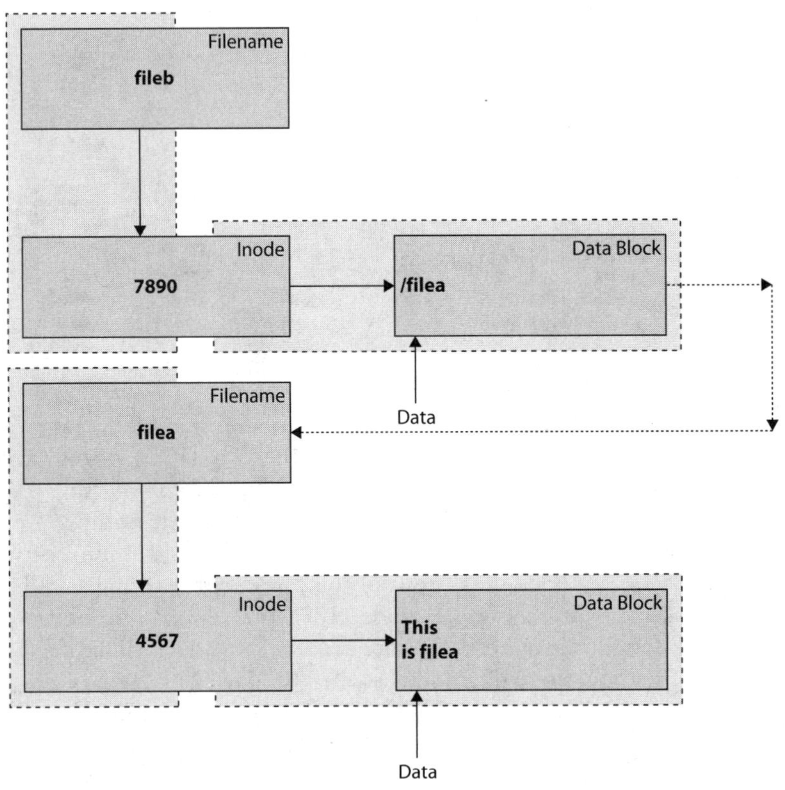

Figure 5-10 Symbolic link

Figure 5-11 Symbolic links (1)

```
# ls -il symlink1
1077940 -rw-r--r--. 1 root root 36 Mar 12 11:58 symlink1
#
# cat symlink1
this is a symbolic link source file
#
# ln -s symlink1 symlink2
# ln -s symlink1 symlink3
#
# ls -il symlink[1-3]
1077940 -rw-r--r--. 1 root root 36 Mar 12 11:58 symlink1
1077983 lrwxrwxrwx. 1 root root  8 Mar 12 12:13 symlink2 -> symlink1
1077023 lrwxrwxrwx. 1 root root  8 Mar 12 12:13 symlink3 -> symlink1
#
# ls -ilL symlink[1-3]
1077940 -rw-r--r--. 1 root root 36 Mar 12 11:58 symlink1
1077940 -rw-r--r--. 1 root root 36 Mar 12 11:58 symlink2
1077940 -rw-r--r--. 1 root root 36 Mar 12 11:58 symlink3
#
# cat symlink2
this is a symbolic link source file
#
# cat symlink3
this is a symbolic link source file
```

Figure 5-12 Symbolic links (2)

```
# file symlink[1-3]
symlink1: ASCII text
symlink2: symbolic link to `symlink1'
symlink3: symbolic link to `symlink1'
#
# \rm symlink3
#
# ls -il symlink[1-3]
1077940 -rw-r--r--. 1 root root 36 Mar 12 11:58 symlink1
1077983 lrwxrwxrwx. 1 root root  8 Mar 12 12:13 symlink2 -> symlink1
#
# cat symlink2
this is a symbolic link source file
#
# \rm symlink1
#
# ls -il symlink[1-3]
1077983 lrwxrwxrwx. 1 root root 8 Mar 12 12:13 symlink2 ->
#
# cat symlink2
cat: symlink2: No such file or directory
```

You can also use readlink (**readlink symlink2**) to determine what file a symbolic link is linked to.

In Figure 5-12, we see that *symlink1* is an ASCII text file and that *symlink2* and *symlink3* are symbolic links linked to *symlink1*.

You can remove a symbolic link by executing the command **rm <target_link_file_name>** or **unlink <target_link_file_name>**.

Removing *symlink3* with the command **\rm symlink3** (or **unlink symlink3**) has no effect other than the loss of the symbolic link. When we remove the source file, *symlink1*, by executing the command **\rm symlink1**, however, the path to the link stored in file *symlink2*'s data block no longer exists, so the file is not found.

Hard links point to a number; soft links point to a name.

Creating New Directories

The mkdir (make directory) command is used to create a directory. Here, the command **mkdir MyDir** has been executed in student1's home directory:

```
$ cd
$ mkdir MyDir
$ ls
bin        Downloads  Pictures     Templates  Videos
Desktop    Music      Public       test2.txt  words
Documents  MyDir      public_html  test.txt   yourfile.txt
```

You may use an absolute or relative path to create a directory somewhere other than the current directory. For example, if you wanted to create a new directory named backup in the */tmp* directory, you would enter **mkdir /tmp/backup** at the shell prompt.

The **mkdir -p** command creates a directory tree. The command **mkdir -p ~/temp/backups/daily** creates the *temp* directory, then creates the subdirectory *backup*, and finally creates the subdirectory *daily*.

Table 5-2 File Type Codes

File Type Code	Description
-	ASCII
l	Symbolic link
d	Directory
p	Named pipe
c	Character device
b	Block device
s	Socket

Determining the File Content

The first character of the output of the **ls -l** command is a code that indicates the file type, as shown in Table 5-2.

If you look at lines 1 through 3 in Figure 5-13, you can see each file is an ASCII file. This information tells you nothing about the content of the files.

When most files are created, the first several bytes of the file contain the file signature (also called the magic numbers), which indicates content stored in the file.

The file command compares the file's magic numbers with databases of file signatures contained in */usr/share/misc/magic*, */usr/share/misc/magic.mgc*, and */etc/magic* to determine the file type.

Figure 5-14 displays sample outputs of the file command. Notice how the file command provides a description of the content of the file.

```
1 -ro-r--r--. 1 root root  2316 Jan 25 17:25 /etc/passwd
2 -rw-r--r-- root 8018 Mar 12 10:38 testfile1.odt
3 -rwsr-xr-x. 1 root root 27832 Jun 10  2014 /usr/bin/passwd
```

Figure 5-13 ASCII file type

```
# file /etc/passwd
/etc/passwd: ASCII text
#
# file testfile1.odt
testfile1.odt: OpenDocument Text
#
# file /usr/bin/passwd
/usr/bin/passwd: setuid ELF 64-bit LSB shared object, x86-64, version 1 (SYSV), dy
namically linked (uses shared libs), for GNU/Linux 2.6.32, BuildID[sha1]=1e5735bf7
b317e60bcb907f1989951f6abd50e8d, stripped
```

Figure 5-14 The file command

Viewing File Contents

There will be many occasions when you simply want to quickly view a text file onscreen and don't need or want to load up a text editor. Linux provides you with a variety of command-line tools you can use to do this, including the following:

- **cat** The cat command is used to display ASCII text. The command **cat *filename*** will display the specified text file onscreen. For example, if you needed to view the contents of */etc/passwd*, execute the command **cat /etc/passwd**.
- **less** The less command is called a pager. It may be used to manage how text is displayed and how the cursor is moved with a file. The less command automatically pauses a long text file one page at a time. You can use the SPACEBAR, PAGE UP, PAGE DOWN, and ARROW keys to navigate around the output.
- **head** By default, the head command displays the first 10 lines of a file. The command **head -*n*** will display the first *n* number of lines of a file.
- **tail** The tail command is used to display the last 10 of lines of a text file onscreen. The command **tail -*n*** will display the last *n* lines of a file. The tail command is particularly useful when displaying a log file onscreen. When viewing a log file, you usually only need to see the end of the file. You probably don't care about log entries made several days or weeks ago. You can use tail to see just the last few log entries added to the end of the file.

  The tail command also includes the -f option, which is very useful. This option is used to monitor input to a file. As new content is added to the end of the file, the new lines will be displayed onscreen. In Figure 5-15, the **tail -f /var/log/messages** command has been issued to monitor the file for new entries.

```
openSUSE:/ # tail -f /var/log/messages
2014-10-28T19:38:44.586183-06:00 linux ifup[4070]: eno16777736 DHCP6 continues in backg
round
2014-10-28T19:38:44.607193-06:00 linux ifup-dhcp[4159]:     eno16777736 DHCP6 continues
 in background
2014-10-28T19:38:45.186547-06:00 linux systemd[1]: Started ifup managed network interfa
ce eno16777736.
2014-10-28T19:38:45.296665-06:00 linux network[3638]: ..done..doneSetting up service ne
twork  . . . . . . . . . . . . . ...done
2014-10-28T19:38:45.307283-06:00 linux systemd[1]: Started LSB: Configure network inter
faces and set up routing.
2014-10-28T19:45:01.078673-06:00 linux /usr/sbin/cron[5915]: pam_unix(crond:session): s
ession opened for user root by (uid=0)
2014-10-28T19:45:01.140646-06:00 linux systemd[1]: Starting Session 30 of user root.
2014-10-28T19:45:01.145664-06:00 linux systemd[1]: Started Session 30 of user root.
2014-10-28T19:45:01.450926-06:00 linux /USR/SBIN/CRON[5915]: pam_unix(crond:session): s
ession closed for user root
2014-10-28T19:51:50.678645-06:00 linux gdm-password]: gkr-pam: unlocked login keyring
█
```

Figure 5-15 Using tail with the -f option to monitor a log file

Deleting Files

There will be times when you need to delete an existing file from the Linux filesystem. To delete a file, you must have execute permissions on the file, write and execute permissions on the directory the file is located in, and execute permissions on any parent directories.

To delete a file, simply enter **rm <filename>**. In the following example, the *myfile.txt* file is deleted using the rm command:

```
$ rm myfile.txt
$
```

In many distributions, the rm command is aliased to **rm -i**. The -i option requires user confirmation prior to deleting a file.

Copying and Moving Files

In addition to creating and deleting files in the Linux filesystem, you can also copy or move them. To copy or move a file, you must have read permissions to the file, execute permissions to the directory the file is located in, execute permissions to any parent directories, and write and execute permissions to the target directory.

cp

The cp (copy) command makes a duplicate of a file. The command **cp <source> <target>** is used to copy a file. For example, **cp file1 file2** would make a duplicate of *file1* named *file2*. The ownership of a copied file is changed to the user who copied the file. For example, if user root copied a file owned by student1, the copied file would be owned by user root.

Multiple files may be copied as long as the target is a directory (for example, **cp file1 file2 dira**).

The cp option -i prevents a user from copying a file to an existing file. In many systems, the alias **cp='cp-i'** is a default. The recursive option, -R or -r, is used to repeat the copy command until all files, directories, and subdirectories are copied to the target directory.

mv

The mv command is used to rename a file or directory when the source and target files are in the same filesystem. For example, to rename *mvtest1* to *mvtest2*, you would execute the command **mv mvtest1 mvtest2**. Notice the inode numbers in Figure 5-16. This seems to indicate that the filename-to-inode reference has changed.

If the source and target files are not in the same filesystem, the mv command copies the source to the new location and then deletes the original. The -R option executes the mv command recursively.

Figure 5-16 The mv command

```
# ls -il mvtest1
1072491 -rw-r--r--. 1 root root 0 Mar 13 11:48 mvtest1
#
# mv mvtest1 mvtest2
#
# ls -il mvtest[12]
1072491 -rw-r--r--. 1 root root 0 Mar 13 11:48 mvtest2
```

Exercise 5-2: Managing Files and Directories

In Exercise 5-2, you will practice creating and viewing the properties of files and directories and moving between directories.

VIDEO Please watch the Exercise 5-2 video for a demonstration on how to perform this task.

For this exercise, you must be logged on to the virtual machine provided with the book as user student1 (password **student1**). Then follow these steps:

1. Open a terminal session.
2. Verify that you are in student1's home directory. If not, change your current working directory to user student1's home directory.
3. Execute the **touch touchtest**; **alias rm='rm -i'** command.
4. Create the subdirectory *cars* relative to your home directory by executing the **mkdir cars** command.
5. Verify the directory has been created by executing the command **ls -ld cars**.
6. Execute the **ls -lR cars** command. Notice there are no subdirectories.
7. Execute the **rmdir cars** command.
8. Execute the **ls -ld cars** command. Notice the directory has been removed.
9. Create the subdirectory *pastry* relative to your home directory by executing the **mkdir pastry** command.
10. Verify the directory has been created by executing the **ls -ld pastry** command.
11. Execute the **ls -lR pastry** command. Notice there are no subdirectories.
12. Execute the **mkdir -p pastry/pies/cakes** command.
13. Execute the command **ls -lR pastry** to view the new subdirectories.
14. Try to use the **rmdir pastry** command to remove the *pastry* directory. Why did this command not work?
15. Execute the **\rm -r pastry** command. Did the directories delete?
16. Using vi, create the file filea with the content "This is filea."
    a. Start vi by executing the **vi filea** command.
    b. Place vi in insert mode by pressing ESC **i**.
    c. Type "This is filea."
    d. Save the file and exit vi by pressing ESC **ZZ**.
    e. Type the command **ls filea** to verify the file has been created.
    f. Type **cat filea** to verify the contents of the file.

17. Create a symbolic link where the source file is *filea* and the target file is *fileb* by executing the **ln -s filea fileb** command.
18. Test the results of the preceding command by executing the **ls -il file[ab]** command. Notice the file types. *filea* is an ASCII file, and *fileb* is a symbolic link. Look at the inode numbers of the files. Are they the same or different? Why?
19. Execute the command **cat filea; cat fileb** to view the content of the files. Was the output what you expected?
20. Create a hard link where filea is the source and filec is the target by executing the **ln filea filec** command.
21. Execute the command **cat filea; cat fileb; cat filec** to view the contents of the files.
22. Test the results of the command executed in step 6 by executing the command **ls -il file[a-c]**. Look at the properties of *filea* and *filec*. Notice the files have the same inode and the number of files sharing the inode is 2. Why?
23. Remove *filea* by executing the **\rm filea** command.
24. Execute the command **ls -l file[a-c]** and examine the output. Notice the number of files sharing the inode in filec and notice the broken link of *fileb*.
25. Use the vi command to create a new filea with the content "This is new filea."
26. Execute the **ls -il file[a-c]** command. Notice the symbolic link is no longer broken. Why?
27. Execute the command **cat filea; cat fileb; cat filec**. Is the output what you expected?
28. Execute the commands **ls -l fileb** and **file fileb**.
29. Execute the command **ls /var/lib/mlocate/mlocate.db** and **file /var/lib/mlocate/ mlocate.db**.
30. Execute the **ls -il touchtest** command. Notice the timestamp. Execute the command **touch touchtest** and view the timestamp again.
31. Use the **touch** command to create the file cpytest.
32. Execute the command **ls -l cpytest**. Notice the file is owned by the user student1.
33. Execute the command **su -** and press the ENTER key. When asked for root's password, enter **password**.
34. Execute the **id** or **whoami** command to ensure your effective user ID is 0.
35. Execute the command **cp ~student1/cpytest .** (the period after the filename cpytest means "current directory"). This command will copy the file *cpytest* from student1's home directory to root's home directory.
36. Execute the command **ls -l cpytest**. Notice that root owns the file.
37. Type the command **exit**.
38. Execute the command **touch cpytest2** and verify the file was created.
39. Execute the command **alias | grep cp**. You should see the alias **cp='cp -i'**. If it is not there, execute the **alias cp='cp -i'** command.

40. Execute the **cp cpytest2 cpytest** command. You should receive an error because the -i option will not allow you to overwrite an existing file. Try the command again by negating the alias (**\cp cpytest2 cpytest**).
41. Execute the **ls -il cpytest2** command. Notice (write down) the inode number.
42. Execute the **mv cpytest2 mvtest1** command.
43. The command **ls -il copytest2 mvtest1** will verify the name of cpytest2 has been changed to mvtest1, but the inode has stayed the same.
44. Change your effective user ID to user root by executing the su command and entering the appropriate password.
45. Execute the **mv ~student1/mvtest1 /etc** command.
46. Execute the commands **ls -il ~student1/mvtest1** and **ls -il /etc/mvtest1**. Notice the file no longer exists in student1's home directory, and the inode number has changed. In the virtual machine supplied with this book, */etc* is on a different filesystem than */home*, so the mv command copied the file to the new filesystem and deleted the file in */home/student1*.

Finding Files in the Linux Filesystem

Linux includes utilities you can use to search for files in the filesystem. In this part of the chapter, you'll learn the following commands:

- find
- xargs
- locate
- whereis
- which
- type

Using find

The find utility is a fantastic tool that you can use to search for files. find's access permissions are limited to those available to the user executing the command. find searches by default are recursive, but can be limited using the mindepth and maxdepth options (both options are beyond the scope of this text).

To use find, simply enter **find <root_directory> <expression>** at the shell prompt. The <root_directory> argument defines the search start point. You can specify multiple root directories. If you do not enter a root directory, the current working directory is the start point.

The expression defines what you are searching for. If you want to use metacharacters in your expression (for example, *) the expression must be enclosed in quotes.

File Type	Description
-name	Name of file (for example, **-name filea**).
-type	**-f** Regular file (ASCII) **-d** Directory **-l** Symbolic link **-p** Named pipe
-inum <number>	File with a specific inode number (for example, **-inum 10977**).
-user	Owner of file (for example, **-user student1**).
-group	Group owner (for example, **-group admin**).
-perm	**-perm 644** finds files with the permissions 644. **-perm -644** finds files with the permissions 644 or greater (655).
-readable	Has read permissions for the user executing the command.
-writeable	Has write permissions for the user executing the command.
-executable	Has execute permissions for the user executing the command.

Table 5-3 Find Expressions

Table 5-3 illustrates some of the single-word expressions, but there are many others. (Refer to the man pages for more information.)

The size expression will search for a file based on its size. The size of the file may be specified as follows:

- **b** Blocks (512-byte block)
- **c** Bytes
- **w** Word (2 bytes)
- **k** Kilobytes
- **M** Megabytes
- **G** Gigabytes

The command **find -size 5M** will find files that are exactly 5MB. The command **find -size +5M** will find files larger than 5MB. You may also use the command **find -size +5M -size -10M** to find a file that is smaller than 10MB but greater than 5MB.

You can combine expressions using Boolean operators:

- **-a** and
- **<space>** and
- **-o** or
- **-not** not
- **!** not

For example, the command **find -name test -user student1** or **find -name test -a -user student1** will find all files with the name of *test* owned by student 1. The command **find -name test -o -user student1** will find all files with the name of *test* or files that are owned by student1. The command **find -name test ! -user student1** will find all files with the name of *test* and not owned by student1.

You may also execute a command on the results of the find command. The two expressions -exec and -ok take the standard output from the find expression and make it the standard input to the specified command. When find executes a command, it disregards any defined aliases.

- **-exec** Executes the command to the right without asking for confirmation
- **-ok** Executes the command to the right, but requires user confirmation

The command **find /var/log -name "*.log -exec ls l {} \;** will find all the files in */var/log* with the name <name>.log and then automatically execute the command **ls -l**. The command **find /var/log -name "*.log -ok ls l {} \;** will find all the files in */var/log* with the name <name>.log and then require user confirmation before executing the command **ls -l**.

NOTE The curly braces (**{ }**) are used as a placeholder for the standard output of the find command. This standard output becomes the standard input of the command executed by **-exec** or **-ok**.

Using xargs

xargs is used to read whitespace-delimited input and execute a command on each input. A whitespace delimiter is a nonprintable character that takes up space. Examples of whitespace characters are <space>, <tab>, <new_line>.

In the example shown in Figure 5-17, we take the space-delimited output of the echo command and use it to create files. Remember, the pipe takes the standard output of the command on the left and makes it the standard input of the command on the right. By default, the unnamed pipe cannot process multiple arguments. In Figure 5-17, the echo command on the right side of the unnamed pipe would produce the following:

filea

fileb

filec

The pipe passes this output to xargs, and xargs passes one whitespace-delimited argument to the touch command at a time as input.

Figure 5-17
xargs example

```
# echo file{a,b,c}
filea fileb filec
#
# ls -il file[a-c]
ls: cannot access file[a-c]: No such file or directory
#
# echo file{a,b,c} | xargs touch
#
# ls -l file[a-c]
-rw-r--r--. 1 root root 0 Mar 14 07:09 filea
-rw-r--r--. 1 root root 0 Mar 14 07:09 fileb
-rw-r--r--. 1 root root 0 Mar 14 07:09 filec
```

Figure 5-18
xargs and mv

```
# ls file*
filea  fileb  filec
#
# ls file* | xargs -I {} mv {} test.{}
# ls test.*
test.filea  test.fileb  test.filec
```

In Figure 5-18, we expand our usage of the xargs command. The -I option in the command is a string replacement option, and the curly braces are a placeholder for the standard input.

The output of the command **ls file*** will provide the whitespace-delimited arguments filea, fileb, and filec to xargs. The xargs command will place the current argument in the placeholder (**-I {}**). It will then execute the mv command to rename the current filename to test.<filename>. In our example, when xargs processes the argument filea, it will execute the command **mv filea test.filea**.

xargs is normally used with the find command. In the example shown in Figure 5-19, we use the xargs command to remove a list of commands.

In the example shown in Figure 5-20, we use the xargs command to print the command before it executes. You must confirm the command execution (**y**) or stop the command execution (**n** or CTRL-C).

EXAM TIP This tool is critical for Linux administrators; be prepared to demonstrate use of the find command.

Using locate

The locate command finds files by looking for the filename in a database. The database (by default, */var/lib/mlocate/mlocate.db*) is updated each day via the mlocate anacron job found in the directory */etc/cron.daily*. The output of the locate command is an absolute path to the file.

updatedb

The updatedb command may be used to update mlocate.db or create an independent database. The configuration file */etc/updatedb.conf* is used to configure the updatedb command.

Figure 5-19
xargs and find

```
# ls -il file[a-c]
1076996 -rw-r--r--. 1 root root 0 Mar 20 13:05 filea
1076997 -rw-r--r--. 1 root root 0 Mar 20 13:05 fileb
1076998 -rw-r--r--. 1 root root 0 Mar 20 13:05 filec
#
# find . -name "file[a-c]" | xargs rm
#
# ls -il file[a-c]
ls: cannot access file[a-c]: No such file or directory
```

Figure 5-20
find and xargs -p

```
# find . -name "file[a-c]" | xargs -p \rm
rm ./filea ./fileb ./filec ?...
```

Variable	Description
PRUNEFS	A space-delimited list of filesystem types (such as ext2 and ext3) that should be skipped when executing updatedb. Here's an example: PRUNEFS = "sysfs iso9660"
PRUNEPATHS	A space-delimited list of directories that should be skipped when executing updatedb. PRUNEPATHS = "/tmp /mnt"
PRUNENAMES	A space-delimited list of filenames that should be skipped when executing updatedb. PRUNENAMES = "/.bach .old"

Table 5-4 updatedb.conf

You may create locate databases using the command updatedb. You must have root privileges to execute this command. The command **updatedb -U /home/student1 -o /home/student1/mydatabase** will create a recursive file database starting from */home/student1*. To use the database, execute the command **locate -d /home/student1 /mydatabase <filename>**.

updatedb.conf

The file */etc/updated.conf* contains variables that determine how the updated command operates (see Table 5-4).

Using whereis

Before we talk about the whereis command, we need to discuss keywords. A keyword is a word that has a special significance to an operating system or application. For example, a command name would be an example of a keyword. The whereis command displays the location of the source code, binary files, and manual pages associated with a keyword.

The **-b** option returns the location of the binaries for the specified command. The **-m** option returns the location of man pages associated with a keyword. To see the location of the command's source code, use the **-s** option with the whereis command. If no option is used, all information is returned.

The keyword passwd is associated with the command /usr/bin/passwd and the file */etc/passwd*. Notice the results of the command **whereis passwd** in Figure 5-21.

```
# whereis passwd
passwd: /usr/bin/passwd /etc/passwd /usr/share/man/man1/passwd.1.gz /usr/share/man/man5/passwd.5.gz
#
# whereis -b passwd
passwd: /usr/bin/passwd /etc/passwd
#
# whereis -m passwd
passwd: /usr/share/man/man1/passwd.1.gz /usr/share/man/man5/passwd.5.gz
#
# whereis -s passwd
passwd:#
```

Figure 5-21 The whereis command

Understanding Commands and Precedence

Linux contains four types of commands:

- Alias
- Function
- Builtin
- External

Both aliases and functions are loaded into and executed from memory. Builtin and external commands are executed from a file.

Let's take a look at the different command types.

Alias

An alias is described as a command shortcut. Rather than typing the command **ls--color=auto** each time we want a color output, we can create an alias so each time we execute the command **ls** the command **ls -l --color=auto** is executed.

To create an alias, we will execute the command **alias <alias_name>='<command>'**. The command **alias ls='ls --color=auto'** creates an alias that produces a color output when we execute the **ls** command. To determine if the alias has been created, execute the command **alias** or **alias | grep <alias_name>**.

The alias **ls='ls color=auto'** is the default on most systems. Look at Figure 5-22 to see how the alias and unalias commands work.

It is important to remember that an alias is created in memory and only exists in the shell in which it is created. If we open a child shell, the alias we created in the parent will not be present. If we want an alias to be copied when we spawn a child shell, we must define the alias in the file *~/.bashrc*.

How do we force an alias to execute? We can explain this via the term *precedence*. Precedence determines the order in which specific command types are executed. Memory-based

Figure 5-22 alias

```
# alias | grep ls
alias l.='ls -d .* --color=auto'
alias ll='ls -l --color=auto'
alias ls='ls --color=auto'
#
# ls
anaconda-ks.cfg  Documents  initial-setup-ks.cfg  Pictures  Templates
Desktop          Downloads  Music                 Public    Videos
#
# unalias ls
#
# alias | grep ls
alias l.='ls -d .* --color=auto'
alias ll='ls -l --color=auto'
#
# ls
anaconda-ks.cfg  Documents  initial-setup-ks.cfg  Pictures  Templates
Desktop          Downloads  Music                 Public    Videos
#
```

commands (aliases and functions) have precedence over file-based commands (builtin and external commands). The precedence for Linux commands is as follows:

- Alias
- Function
- Builtin
- External

Based on the order of precedence, Linux will always look for an alias first.

Suppose we do not want an alias to execute. We can preceded the alias name with a backslash (\). The backslash tells the shell to ignore the alias and go to the next command in the order of precedence. Therefore, if we execute the command **\ls**, the alias will be ignored and in our case the external command will execute.

To remove an alias from memory, we would execute the command **unalias <alias_name>**. This would remove the alias from memory, but not from a configuration file. Supposed we had an alias defined in *~/.bashrc*. If we removed it from memory but did not remove it from *~/.bashrc*, and then opened a child shell, the alias would be loaded into memory. To completely remove an alias, execute the **unalias** command and, if the alias is also defined in *~/.bashrc*, remove it from *~/.bashrc*.

Function

A *function* is a list of commands performed as a group that can be called from other programs multiple times. Bash functions can pass and exit status code back to the calling program. In order to pass values back to the calling program, you must assign the value to a variable within the function.

To create a bash function on the command line, type the function name followed by opening and closing parentheses. Enclose the function commands between left and right curly braces and then complete the function by using the key sequence CTRL-D. This sequence will save the function to memory and exit the process creating the function. You can view this procedure in Figure 5-23.

A function only exists in the shell it is created in. Therefore, if you want a function to be persistent across child shells, make certain you define the function in *~/,bashrc*.

To view all functions loaded into memory, use the **typeset -f** or **declare -f** command. To remove a function from memory type the command **unset <function_name>**.

Builtin

Builtin commands are commands that are built in to the shell and execute as part of the shell process rather than spawning a child. To see a list of bash builtin commands, execute the command **compgen -b** or **enable**.

Figure 5-23 Creating a function

```
# pwd()
> {
> uname -r
> date +%m/%d%y
> }
#
```

```
[student1]$ echo $PATH
/usr/local/bin:/bin:/usr/bin:/usr/local/sbin:/usr/sbin:/home/student1/.local/bin:/home/student1/bin
```

Figure 5-24 PATH

In some cases, a keyword will represent multiple command types. For example, the keyword pwd is both a builtin and external command. In this situation, you would have to execute the command /usr/bin/pwd for the external command to execute or create an alias since aliases have precedence over builtin commands.

If an alias or function exists with the same name as the builtin, the command **builtin <builtin_command_name>** or **'<builtin_command_name>'** will force a builtin command to run. To receive help for builtin commands execute the command **help <builtin_command_name>**.

External

External commands are file-based commands. Once the shell has looked through the aliases, functions, and builtin commands, it will use the variable PATH to determine where to search for commands (Figure 5-24). The shell looks through each directory in the PATH variable in the order in which it has been presented until it finds the command.

Based on Figure 5-24, the first directory searched will be */usr/local/bin*, followed by */bin*, and so on.

Linux does not search the local directory for commands.

Hashed Commands

When you execute a command, the absolute path to the command is stored in a hash table. Before the shell looks for external commands, it will view the hash table to see if the command has executed before. The hash table contains the absolute path to commands and the number of times the commands have been executed (hits). The command hash, shown in Figure 5-25, will display those commands stored in the hash table.

The command **hash -r** will clear the hash table.

type

The type command evaluates a keyword and displays how the keyword will be interpreted as a command. The type command evaluates shell keywords, aliases, functions, builtins, and external commands. It displays command keywords in order of precedence.

The command **type <keyword>** will display the type of command that will execute when the keyword is entered on the command line. In Figure 5-26, using the type command with the keyword passwd executes the external command /usr/bin/passwd.

Type -a will display executable keywords in order of precedence. In Figure 5-27, line 1, we executed the command **type -a if**. From the output, we see that **if** is a shell keyword (builtin). Therefore, we know the command **help if** will tell us more about the keyword.

Figure 5-25 hash

```
# hash
hits    command
   7    /usr/bin/file
   1    /usr/bin/whereis
   2    /usr/bin/ls
   1    /usr/bin/su
   3    /usr/bin/clear
```

Figure 5-26
The type command

```
# type passwd
passwd is /usr/bin/passwd
```

Figure 5-27
Executing type -a

```
1 # type  -a if
  if is a shell keyword
  #
2 # type -a passwd
  passwd is /usr/bin/passwd
  passwd is /bin/passwd
  #
3 # type -a pwd
  pwd is a shell builtin
  pwd is /usr/bin/pwd
  pwd is /bin/pwd
```

On line 2, the command **type -a passwd** (line 2) shows there are two instances of the keyword passwd.

NOTE The directory */bin* is a symbolic link to the directory */usr/bin.*

On line 3 the command **type -a pwd** shows that the keyword pwd represents a shell builtin and an external command. Since a builtin command takes precedence over an external command, the builtin is listed first.

The type command can be used to determine what command is executing when you use a specific keyword, but it can also help keep you from creating an alias or function that will override a command. Before assigning a name to any of these constructs, execute the command type with the proposed name to make certain it is not a system keyword.

Using which

The **which -a <keyword>** command will list aliases and external commands associated with a keyword in order of precedence. The command **which <keyword>**, shown in Figure 5-28, will display (based on precedence) whether an alias or external command will be executed.

In Figure 5-29, we have created an alias and function for the keyword pwd. Notice the difference in the output between the **which -a pwd** and **type -a pwd** commands.

Figure 5-28
which

```
# which -a ls
alias ls='ls --color=auto'
        /usr/bin/ls
        /bin/ls
# type -a ls
ls is aliased to `ls --color=auto'
ls is /usr/bin/ls
ls is /bin/ls
```

Figure 5-29 Comparing which and type

```
1 # which -a pwd
  alias pwd='ls -ld /etc'
          /usr/bin/ls
          /bin/ls
  /usr/bin/pwd
  /bin/pwd
  #
2 # type -a pwd
  pwd is aliased to `ls -ld /etc'
  pwd is a function
  pwd ()
  {
      date
  }
  pwd is a shell builtin
  pwd is /usr/bin/pwd
  pwd is /bin/pwd
```

Exercise 5-3: Finding Files

In Exercise 5-3, you will practice using shell commands to navigate the Linux filesystem. For this exercise, you must be logged on to the virtual machine provided with the book as user student1 (password **student1**). Here are the steps to follow:

VIDEO Please watch the Exercise 5-3 video for a demonstration on how to perform this task.

1. Open a terminal session.
2. Verify you are in user student1's home directory (**pwd**).
3. Create the director *finddir* as a subdirectory of your home directory using the **mkdir finddir** command.
4. Use the command **ls -ld finddir** to verify the directory has been created.
5. Create the files *file1*, *file2*, and *file3* using one of the following methods:
   - Execute the **touch file{1,2,3}** command.
   - Execute the **touch file1 file2 file3** command.
6. Verify the files are created.
7. Execute the following commands:
   - **find -name file1**
   - **find -name file"[12]"**
   - **find -name "file*"**
   - **find -name "file[1-3]" ! -user student1**
8. Type the **locate file*** command. Remember, the locate database (mlocate.db) is only updated once per day.
9. Change your effective user ID to 0 by executing the command **su** and pressing ENTER. When asked for a password, enter the user root's password (**password**). Verify the change by executing the command **whoami** or **id**.

10. Create a locate database of user student1's home directory by executing the **updatedb -U ~student1 -o file.db** command. Verify the file exists by typing the **file ~student1/file.db** command.
11. Type **exit** to return to user student1.
12. Use the database created in user student1's home directory to locate file1 by executing the **locate -d ~student1/file.db file1** command.
13. Execute the following commands:
    - **find -name "file[1-3]" -exec ls -l {} \;**
    - **find -name "file[1-3]" -ok ls -l {} \;**
    - **find -name "file[1-3]" | xargs ls -l**
    - **find -name "file[1-3]" | xargs -p ls -l**
14. Determine what man pages exist for the keyword passwd by executing the command **whereis -m passwd**.
15. What binary files are associated with the keyword passwd (**whereis -b passwd**)?
16. Have the keyword pwd execute the date command by creating an alias (**alias pwd='date'**). Execute the following commands and notice and explain any differences in the outputs:
    - **which pwd**
    - **type pwd**
    - **which -a pwd**
    - **type -a pwd**
17. Execute the **unalias pwd** command.

Finding Content within Files

Earlier in this chapter, we discussed shell commands that can be used to search for files in the filesystem. Linux also provides three utilities to search for content within a file: grep, egrep, and fgrep.

grep

The grep utility may be used to search for specific content *within* a file. By default, grep will display the line on which the string is found.

The command **grep <option> <string>** may be used to search for a string in a file. For example, the command **grep student1 /etc/passwd**, shown in Figure 5-30, will search for the string "student1" in the file */etc/passwd*. If the string is found, by default, grep will print the line the string is on.

```
# grep student1 /etc/passwd
student1:x:1000:1000:Student1:/home/student1:/bin/bash
```

Figure 5-30 grep /etc/passwd

```
# grep student1 /etc/passwd /etc/shadow /etc/group
/etc/passwd:student1:x:1000:1001:Student1:/home/student1:/bin/bash
/etc/shadow:student1:$6$GSTfj2jt4vaqalWf$lZ0p.tGZIorNVjxHTSDl/GrIwA0odvAyZZt.mfE
CRtoonOm7VwWWtmkT2zZIDL/j0m6qa9FUtWp9BAPXyOvN6.:18039:0:99999:7:::
/etc/group:student1:x:1000:student1,student2,pradip,chin
/etc/group:vboxsf:x:982:student1
```

Figure 5-31 Grepping multiple files

The grep utility can also search for a text string across multiple files. The command **grep student1 /etc/passwd /etc/shadow /etc/group**, shown in Figure 5-31, will search for the string "student1" in */etc/passwd*, */etc/shadow*, and */etc/group*.

Adding the -n option to the command will display the number of the line on which the string was found.

When working with grep at the command line, you can use the following options:

- **-i** Ignores case when searching for the text
- **-l** Only displays the filename in which a string occurs when searching across multiple files for a string
- **-n** Displays matching line numbers
- **-r** Searches recursively through subdirectories of the path specified
- **-v** Displays all lines that *do not* contain the search string

The grep command uses basic regular expressions to extend its capabilities, as detailed in Table 5-5.

Metacharacter	Function	Example
*	The asterisk (*) will match the preceding character zero or more times.	**grep ro*** would find root, operator, usr.
\	Some basic regular expression metacharacters must be preceded by a backslash (\).	
?	The question mark (?) will match the preceding character zero or on time.	**grep ca?t** would find cat or ct.
^<string>	The string must be found at the beginning of a line.	**grep ^<root>** would find the string "root" at the beginning of a line.
$	The string must be found at the end of a line.	**grep bash$** would find the string "bash" at the end of a line.
.	Matches a single character	**grep r..t** will match any string that begins with an *r*, ends with a *t*, and has two characters in the middle (for example, **root r/ft**).

Table 5-5 grep Metacharacters

<table>
<tr><th>Metacharacter</th><th>Function</th><th>Example</th></tr>
<tr><td>+</td><td>Matches one or more occurrences of the character to the left.</td><td>**grep b+9** will match b9, b99, b999, bb9, and bbb9.</td></tr>
<tr><td>[abc]</td><td>Matches one character in the current location.</td><td>**grep student[123]** would match the strings student1, student2, and student3.</td></tr>
<tr><td>[^abc]</td><td>Matches one character in the current location, except the characters within the range.</td><td>**grep student[^123]** would match the strings studenta, student5, and studente.</td></tr>
<tr><td>[a-z]</td><td>Matches any single character in the range. Ranges can be [0-9], [a-z], or [A-Z].</td><td>**grep student[1-3]** would match the strings student1, student2, and student3.</td></tr>
<tr><td>\{n\}</td><td>Match *n* occurrences of the character to the left.</td><td>**grep student1\{2\}** matches student11.</td></tr>
<tr><td>\{n,m\}</td><td>Matches a minimum of *n* occurrences and maximum of *m* occurrences of the character to the left.</td><td>**grep student1\{2,3\}** matches student11 and student111.</td></tr>
<tr><td>\{n,\}</td><td>Matches *n* or more occurrences of the character to the left.</td><td>**grep student1\{2,\}** matches student11, student111, and student111.</td></tr>
<tr><td>'<stringa>\|<>stringb>'</td><td>OR. Matches the string on the left or string on the right. Multiple ORs (|) may be placed together.</td><td>**grep 'student1 \| student2'** would find the string student1 or student2.</td></tr>
</table>

Table 5-5 grep Metacharacters *(Continued)*

egrep

egrep extends the capabilities of the grep command. The egrep command has been deprecated but is still functional. The replacement command is **grep -E**.

Table 5-6 illustrates metacharacters used in extended regular expressions. Notice the absence of the \. This is because egrep is POSIX compatible and grep is not.

fgrep

The fgrep (Fixed Regular Expression Print) command interprets all characters based on their encoded value. Therefore, when fgrep sees the string r*, it sees the asterisk based on its encoded value rather than a metacharacter (no backslash necessary).

The fgrep command has been deprecated but is still functional. The replacement command is grep -F.

<table>
<tr><th>Metacharacter</th><th>Function</th><th>Example</th></tr>
<tr><td>\</td><td>The backslash is used to negate the special meaning of the character to the right.</td><td>**egrep 'r*t'** will search for the string r*t and not interpret the metacharacter *.</td></tr>
<tr><td></td><td>Some basic regular expression meta characters must be preceded by a backslash (\).</td><td>**grep a\{2,3\}**</td></tr>
<tr><td>*</td><td>The asterisk (*) will match the preceding character zero or more times.</td><td>**egrep ro*** would find root, operator, and usr.</td></tr>
<tr><td>?</td><td>The question mark (?) will match the preceding character zero or one time.</td><td>**egrep ca?t** would find cat or ct.</td></tr>
<tr><td>^<string></td><td>The string must be found at the beginning of a line.</td><td>**egrep ^<root>** would find the string root at the beginning of a line.</td></tr>
<tr><td><string>$</td><td>The string must be found at the end of a line.</td><td>**egrep bash$** would find the string bash at the end of a line.</td></tr>
<tr><td>.</td><td>Matches a single character.</td><td>**egrep r..t** will match any string that begins with an *r*, ends with a *t*, and has two characters in the middle (for example, **root r/ft**).</td></tr>
<tr><td>+</td><td>Matches one or more occurrences of the character to the left.</td><td>**egrep b9+** will match b9, b99, and b999.</td></tr>
<tr><td>[abc]</td><td>Matches one character in the current location.</td><td>**grep student[123]** would match the strings student1, student2, and student3.</td></tr>
<tr><td>[^abc]</td><td>Matches one character in the current location, except the characters within the range.</td><td>**egrep student[^123]** would match the strings studenta, student5, and studente.</td></tr>
<tr><td>[a-z]</td><td>Matches any single character in the range. Ranges can be [0-9], [a-z], or [A-Z].</td><td>**egrep student[1-3]** would match the strings student1, student2, and student3.</td></tr>
<tr><td>{n}</td><td>Matches *n* occurrences of the character to the left.</td><td>**egrep student1{2}** matches student11.</td></tr>
<tr><td>{n,m}</td><td>Matches a minimum of *n* occurrences and maximum of *m* occurrences of the character to the left.</td><td>**egrep student1{2,3}** matches student11 and student111.</td></tr>
<tr><td>{n, }</td><td>Matches *n* or more occurrences of the character to the left.</td><td>**egrep student1{2, }** matches student11, student111, and student111.</td></tr>
<tr><td>|</td><td>OR. Matches the string on the left or the string on the right. Multiple ORs (|) may be placed together.</td><td>**egrep 'student1 | student2'** would find the string student1 or student2.</td></tr>
</table>

Table 5-6 egrep Metacharacters

Exercise 5-4: Using grep

In Exercise 5-4, you will practice using Linux search tools. Log on as student1 (password student1) and then follow these steps:

1. We would like to view any entries that contain the string student1 in the files */etc/passwd*, */etc/shadow*, and */etc/group*. To do this, we would execute the command **grep student1 /etc/passwd /etc/shadow /etc/group**.
2. Add the -n option to the command in step 1. What did this add to the output?
3. What command would find the string root in the file */etc/passwd*? (**grep root /etc/passwd**)
4. The first field of a record in */etc/passwd* is the username. The command **grep ^root /etc/passwd** would display the user record for user root.
5. The last field for user accounts in the file */etc/passwd* contains the absolute path to their default shell. The command **grep bash$ /etc/passwd** would display all users whose default shell is bash.
6. Execute the commands **grep roo* /etc/passwd** and **grep ro\.** Explain the differences in the output.
7. Display any string that has two lowercase *o*'s together using the command **egrep o{2} /etc/passwd** or **grep -E o{2} /etc/passwd**.
8. Use the command **egrep 'root|Root'** to display the user record for user root or Root in */etc/passwd*.

VIDEO Please watch the Exercise 5-4 video for a demonstration on how to perform this task.

Chapter Review

In this chapter, we discussed the role of the Linux filesystem—to organize data such that it can be easily located and retrieved as well as reliably preserved—as well as the role of the various standard directories used in a typical Linux system, as specified in the Filesystem Hierarchy Standard (FHS). We also discussed various commands used to manage files. The role of the filesystem is to store and organize data such that it can be easily located and retrieved.

- The file command displays the type of content stored in a file.
- The type command identifies the type of command that will be executed based on precedence.
- Linux uses a hierarchical filesystem.

- The Linux filesystem hierarchy is based on the Filesystem Hierarchy Standard (FHS).
- The topmost directory is /.
- Other standard directories are created beneath / and serve functions defined in the FHS.
  - /bin
  - /boot
  - /dev
  - /etc
  - /home
  - /lib
  - /media
  - /mnt
  - /opt
  - /proc
  - /root
  - /sbin
  - /srv
  - /sys
  - /tmp
  - /usr
  - /var
- Linux file types are as follows:
  - Regular files
  - Symbolic and hard links
  - Named pipes
  - Character devices
  - Block devices
  - Sockets
- You can use the find utility to search for files or directories in the filesystem based on an expression.
- The find utility manually walks the filesystem hierarchy to search for files.
- You can use the locate utility to search for files or directories.
- The locate utility maintains a database of all files.

- When locate conducts a search, it searches the database instead of the filesystem.
- The which command will display aliases and external commands associated with a keyword.
- The whereis command displays the location of source files, external commands, and man pages associated with a keyword.
- The type <keyword> command displays the type of command that will be executed based on order of precedence.
- The type -a <keyword> command displays all file types associated with a keyword in order of precedence.
- The pwd command is used to display the current working directory.
- The cd command is used to change directories.
- The ls command is used to display directory contents.
- Using ls with the -l option displays the properties of files and directories.
- Using ls with the -R option displays directory contents recursively.
- The touch command is used to create new files or change the modification timestamp of an existing file.
- The mkdir command is used to create new directories.
- You can use cat to view a text file onscreen.
- You can also use less to view a text file onscreen.
- The less command pauses the display one line at a time.
- The head command can be used to display the first few lines of a text file.
- The tail command can be used to display the last few lines of a text file.
- The tail command used with the -f option can monitor a text file for changes.
- You can use rmdir to delete an empty directory.
- You can use rm -r to delete a populated directory.
- You can use rm to delete files.
- The cp command is used to copy files.
- The mv command is used to move files.
- The Linux filesystem allows you to create link files that point to other files or directories in the filesystem.
- Hard links point directly to the inode of another file.
- Symbolic links have their own inode.
- Links are created using the ln command.
- You can use grep to search for text within a file.

Questions

1. Which directory would contain boot configuration files?
   A. /bin
   B. /dev
   C. /etc
   D. /boot
2. What command would create a file that shares the same inode as filea?
   A. cat < filea > fileb
   B. ln -s filea fileb
   C. ln filea fileb
   D. ln -s fileb filea
3. What command will display how many files share the same inode as *filea*?
   A. cat < filea > fileb
   B. ln -l filea
   C. ls -l filea
   D. ln -sl filea
4. The inode number for *filea* is 1234. What command would display a list of files that share the same inode as *filea*?
   A. find / -name filea
   B. find / -name filea -a -inum 1234
   C. find / -inum 1234
   D. find / -name filea -o inum 1234
5. The command **find /etc useradd** will begin searching for the file *useradd* in which directory?
   A. /
   B. /etc
   C. /passwd
   D. /usr
6. A user would like to create a link between two files located in different filesystems. What command would they use?
   A. ln
   B. ln -s
   C. ls -l filea
   D. ln -sl filea

7. The command pwd is both a builtin and external command. Which command would display this information?
   A. type -a pwd
   B. which -a pwd
   C. type pwd
   D. which pwd
8. Which commands will display the location of the man pages for the keyword passwd. (Select two.)
   A. find / passwd
   B. locate passwd
   C. whereis -m passwd
   D. whereis passwd
9. Which commands will change your current working directory to your home directory? (Select two.)
   A. cd
   B. echo $HOME
   C. cd ~
   D. $HOME
10. A user has executed the command **mkdir -p cars/chevy/impala**. They immediately decide to remove the directories they just created. Which command would they use?
    A. rmdir cars
    B. rm -r cars
    C. rmdir etc
    D. rmdir usr
11. Which commands would display the first ten lines of the file */etc/passwd*? (Select two.)
    A. head +10 /etc/passwd
    B. head /etc/passwd
    C. head -10 /etc/passwd
    D. head 10 /etc/passwd
12. A user has created a symbolic link using the command **ln -s filea fileb**. Which command will display the permissions granted to a user accessing *fileb*?
    A. ls -l fileb
    B. ls -l filea
    C. ls -lL filea
    D. ls -lL fileb

13. Which of the following is *not* a valid Linux filename?
    A. Filea
    B. filea
    C. r*
    D. user one
14. What command would display the content type of a file?
    A. file
    B. ls -l
    C. cat <filename>
    D. less <filename>
15. What command other than alias may be used to determine if an alias is associated with a keyword?
    A. file <keyword>
    B. which -a <keyword>
    C. ls -l<keyword>
    D. type -a <keyword>
16. What commands would find files *filea*, *fileb*, and *filec* in student1's home directory and remove them, but require confirmation before removing them? (Select two.)
    A. find /student1 -name "file[a-c] -exec rm {} \;
    B. find /student1 -name "file[a-c] -ok rm {} \;
    C. find /student1 -name "file[a-c] | xargs rm
    D. find /student1 -name "file[a-c] | xargs -p rm
17. What command will create the directory tree *cars/chevy/vega*?
    A. mkdir cars/chevy/vega
    B. mkdir -p cars/chevy/vega
    C. mkdir /cars/chevy/vega
    D. mkdir cars;mkdir chevy;mkdir vega
18. You have just created the directory tree *fruit/apples/types* relative to the current working directory. What commands could you execute to delete the directory types? (Select two.)
    A. rmdir fruit
    B. cd fruit/apples and rmdir types
    C. rmdir fruit/apples/types
    D. rm -r fruit

19. You want to copy *file1* to an existing file, *file2*. You execute the command **cp file1 file2** and receive the message "cp: overwrite file2." What command or commands would you execute to troubleshoot the problem and prevent this message from occurring?

    A. **which -a** and then **\cp file1 file2**

    B. **which -a** and then **/cp file1 file2**

    C. **type -a cp** and then **cp file1 file2**

    D. **type -a cp** and then **\cp file1 file2**

20. Which commands will display all strings with two occurrences of a lowercase *o* (oo)? (Select three.)

    A. grep 'o{2}'

    B. grep 'o\{2\}'

    C. egrep o{2}

    D. grep -E 'o{2}'

21. Which commands will display the user record for student1 or root from the file */etc/passwd*? (Select three.)

    A. grep 'root \| student1' /etc/passwd

    B. grep -E '^student1|^root' /etc/passwd

    C. egrep '^student1|^root' /etc/passwd

    D. grep '^student1\|^root' /etc/passwd

22. Which expression will search for the string student1a through student9z?

    A. grep student[1a-9z]

    B. grep student[0-9][a-z]

    C. grep student[1-9][A-Z]

    D. grep student[1-9][a-z]

Answers

1. **D.** The */boot* directory contains boot configuration files.
2. **C.** The command **ln filea fileb** will create the file fileb, which would share the same inode as *filea*.
3. **C.** The command **ls -l filea** would display the number of files sharing the same inode.
4. **C.** The command **find / -inum 1234** would display a list of files with the same inode number. The command **find / -name filea -o -inum 1234** (answer D) would display all files with the inode number of 1234, but it would also display all files with the filename *filea*. It is possible to have multiple files named filea that would not have the inode number 1234, so this answer is incorrect.

5. **B.** The first argument of the find command specifies the start location of the search. If a start location is not specified, the search begins in the current working directory.
6. **B.** To link files in different filesystems, you must use a symbolic link; therefore, you would execute the command **ln -s**.
7. **A.** The command **type -a** will display builtins, external commands, aliases, and functions. The command **which -a** will only display external commands and aliases.
8. **C, D.** The **whereis -m passwd** command will only display the location of man pages associated with the keyword passwd. The command **whereis passwd** will display the location of the source code, binary, and man page files associated with the keyword passwd.
9. **A, C.** The commands **cd** and **cd ~** will change the current working directory to the user's home directory.
10. **B.** The command **rmdir** will only remove empty directories. Since the directory cars contains a subdirectory of chevy, the command would generate an error. Therefore, the command **rm -r cars** must be used.
11. **B, C.** The command **head <filename>** will display the first 10 lines of a file. The command **head -*n* <filename>** will display the first *n* lines of a file.
12. **D.** The **ls -l fileb** command will display the properties of *fileb*. The command **ls-lL fileb** will display the properties of the file it is linked to.
13. **D.** You may not use a null character, or whitespace characters in a filename. Although r* is a legal filename, it is not a good choice.
14. **A.** The file command uses the magic number to determine the type of content stored in the file. The **ls -l** command will display the code that represents the type of file (directory, ASCII, and so on).
15. **B.** The **which -a <keyword>** command will list aliases and external commands associated with a keyword in order of precedence.
16. **B, D.** Since the question states the command requires user confirmation prior to executing the command, we would need to use -ok with the find command and -p with the xargs command. Answers A and C would not require user intervention.
17. **B.** The command **mkdir -p** will create a directory tree. It is important to note that the directory tree must be created relative to the current working directory.
18. **B, C.** The rmdir command will only remove empty directories. Answer B will use cd to change directory to the parent of directory of types, and the rmdir command will remove the directory types. Answer C uses a relative path to remove the directory types. Answer D could work, but would strip too much, so it is not the best answer.

19. **D.** To troubleshoot the error, you must determine what command is executing by executing the command **which -a cp** or **type -a cp**. The output of these commands would tell you the **cp** command is aliased to **cp -i**, which is preventing the command from overwriting an existing file. To negate the alias, execute the command **\cp file1 file2**.
20. **B, C, D.** Remember that grep and egrep use two different regular expression engines, so the formatting of the expression is different, and grep requires a backslash before some of the expression metacharacters. It is also important to remember the command grep -E is the same as executing the command egrep.
21. **B, C, D.** The question asks for the commands that will display the records for the user root or student1. Since a user record in */etc/passwd* begins with the username, you are looking for the username string at the beginning of the line (^).
22. **D.** Each character position would require its own range specification. The question states that you need to look for student1a through 9z. The first character range position (after the *t*) would be [1-9] and the second character range position would be [a-z].

CHAPTER 6

Managing Ownership and Permissions

This chapter covers the following topics:

- Managing file ownership
- Mounting file and directory permissions
- File attributes and access control lists

There are two tasks to accomplish when managing user access to a Linux system:

- Control who can access the system.
- Define what users can do after they have logged in to the system.

Access control is implemented through defining users and groups, and authorizations are defined after end users log into the system. Let's begin by discussing file and directory ownership.

Managing File Ownership

To effectively control who can do what in the file system, System Administrators need to first consider who "owns" files and directories.

Any time a user creates a new file or directory, their user account is assigned as that file or directory's "owner." By default, the owner of a directory on a Linux system receives read, write, and execute permissions to the directory. In essence, they can do whatever they want with that directory. Likewise, the owner of a file on a Linux system receives read and write permissions to that file by default. For example, suppose the tcboony user logs into her Linux system and creates a file named *contacts.odt* using LibreOffice.org in her home directory. Because she created this file, tcboony is automatically assigned ownership of *contacts.odt*. Figure 6-1 shows the user and group settings of a file.

Notice in Figure 6-1 that there are two settings to discuss for *contacts.odt*. The first is the name of the user whom owns the file. In this case, it is tcboony. In addition, the

Figure 6-1 Viewing the owner and group of a file

```
[tcbonny@localhost ~]$ ls -l contacts.odt
-rw-r--r--. 1 tcboony staff 15 Aug 23 18:08 contacts.odt
              user    group
```

file belongs to the staff group. That's because staff is the primary group that tcboony belongs to.

Also view file ownership from the command line using the **ls -l** command. This has been done in tcboony's home directory in this example:

NOTE In this example, both instances of "l" are the lowercase letter L, not the number "one."

```
tcboony@openSUSE:~> ls -l
total 40
drwxr-xr-x 2 tcboony staff 4096 2011-03-10 16:43 bin
-rw-r--r-- 1 tcboony staff    0 2011-03-18 08:02 contacts.odt
drwxr-xr-x 2 tcboony staff 4096 2011-03-10 16:44 Desktop
drwxr-xr-x 2 tcboony staff 4096 2011-03-10 16:44 Documents
drwxr-xr-x 2 tcboony staff 4096 2011-03-10 16:44 Downloads
drwxr-xr-x 2 tcboony staff 4096 2011-03-10 16:44 Music
drwxr-xr-x 2 tcboony staff 4096 2011-03-10 16:44 Pictures
drwxr-xr-x 2 tcboony staff 4096 2011-03-10 16:44 Public
drwxr-xr-x 2 tcboony staff 4096 2011-03-10 16:43 public_html
drwxr-xr-x 2 tcboony staff 4096 2011-03-10 16:44 Templates
drwxr-xr-x 2 tcboony staff 4096 2011-03-10 16:44 Videos
```

Notice that the third column in the output displays the name of the file or directory's user (tcboony), while the fourth column displays the name of the group that owns it (staff). Even though file and directory ownership is automatically assigned at creation, it can be modified as explained in the following section.

Managing Ownership from the Command Line

File and directory ownership is not a fixed entity. Even though ownership is automatically assigned at creation, it can be modified. Users can specify a different user and/or group as the owner of a given file or directory. Only root can change the user who owns a file. To change the group that owns a file, become root or already belong to the group that the file is changing to.

This can be done with either graphical or command-line tools. Staying true to the form of the exam, the discussion focuses on two command-line utilities: chown and chgrp.

Using chown

The chown utility can be used to change the user or group that owns a file or directory. The syntax for using chown is **chown <user>:<group file or directory>**. For example, if there is a file named *myfile.txt* in */tmp* that is owned by root, to change the file's owner to the tcboony user, enter **chown tcboony /tmp/myfile.txt**, as shown here:

```
openSUSE:~ # ls -l /tmp/myfile.txt
-rw-r--r-- 1 root root 0 Mar 18 09:38 /tmp/myfile.txt
openSUSE:~ # chown tcboony /tmp/myfile.txt
openSUSE:~ # ls -l /tmp/myfile.txt
-rw-r--r-- 1 tcboony root 0 Mar 18 09:38 /tmp/myfile.txt
```

Also change both the user and the group all at once with a single chown command by entering **chown tcboony:staff /tmp/myfile.txt**, for example. This tells chown that the user to change ownership to is tcboony and the group to change ownership to is staff.

TIP Use the -R option with chown to change ownership on many files at once in the current directory and below. This is also known as changing ownership "recursively."

Using chgrp

In addition to chown, one can also use chgrp to change the group that owns a file or directory. Simply enter **chgrp <group file or directory>**. For example, to change the group ownership of the */tmp/myfile.txt* file discussed in the previous examples from root to staff, enter **chgrp staff /tmp/myfile.txt**.

Exercise 6-1: Managing Ownership

In this exercise, practice modifying file and directory ownership from the shell prompt of the Linux system. Perform this exercise using the virtual machine that comes with this book.

VIDEO Please watch the Exercise 6-1 video for a demonstration on how to perform this task.

Complete the following steps:

1. Log in to the system using login name student1 and password student1.
2. Open a terminal session by clicking Applications | Favorites | Terminal.
3. Switch to the root user account with the **su -** command using a password of password.

4. Verify the student1 user account is a member of the research group by doing the following:

NOTE The research group was configured in Exercise 4-2 of Chapter 4.

   a. At the shell prompt, enter **cat /etc/group**.
   b. Verify that the student1 user is a member of the research group.
   c. If the student1 user is not a member of the research group, add them using the groupmod command as follows:
      usermod -aG research student1

5. Change to the / directory by entering **cd /** at the shell prompt.
6. Create a new directory named *RandD* by entering **mkdir RandD** at the shell prompt.
7. At the shell prompt, enter **ls -l**. Notice that the root user account and the root group are the owners of the new directory.
8. Change ownership of the directory to the student1 user account and the research group by entering **chown student1:research RandD** at the shell prompt.
9. Enter **ls -l** again at the shell prompt. Verify that ownership of the *RandD* directory has changed to the student1 user account and the research group, as shown here:

```
[root@cent71-5t /# ls -l
total 104
drwxr-xr-x   2 student1 research  4096 Nov 25 17:34 RandD
```

Managing File and Directory Permissions

Managing ownership represents only a part of what needs to be done to control access to files and directories in the Linux file system. Ownership only specifies who *owns* what, not *what* one can or cannot do with files and directories. To do this, execute managing *permissions.*

How Permissions Work

Unlike ownership, permissions are used to specify exactly what an end user may do with files and directories in the file system. These permissions may allow an end user to view a file, but not modify it. They may allow an end user to open and modify a file. They may allow an end user to even run an executable file. Permissions can be configured to prevent an end user from even seeing a file within a directory.

Each file or directory in the Linux file system stores the specific permissions assigned to it. These permissions together constitute the *mode* of the file. Any file or directory can have the permissions shown in Table 6-1 in its mode.

Permission	Symbol	Effect on Files	Effect on Directories
Read	r	Allows a user to open and view a file. Does not allow a file to be modified or saved. Allows use of **less**, **more**, and **cat** commands.	Allows a user to list the contents of a directory (for example, executing the **ls** command).
Write	w	Allows a user to modify a file (for example, with the **vi**, **nano**, **gedit**, and **emacs** commands, and so on).	Allows a user to add or delete files from the directory. Good for commands such as **touch**, **rm**, **cp**, and so on.
Execute	x	Allows a user to run an executable file (for example, libreoffice is a program, so it can run as an executable).	Allows a user to enter a directory (for example, using the **cd** command).

Table 6-1 Linux Permissions

These permissions are assigned to each of three different entities for each file and directory in the file system:

- **User** This is the end user that has been assigned to be the file or directory's owner. Permissions assigned to the User apply only to that end user's account.
- **Group** This is the group that has been assigned to the file or directory. Permissions assigned to the Group apply to all accounts that are members of that group.
- **Other** This entity refers to all other users who have successfully authenticated to the system. Permissions assigned to this entity apply to these user accounts.

Linux first checks if the end user is the User; if so, they are assigned the User permission. If the end user is not the User, but belongs to the Group, they get the Group permission. Finally, if the end user is neither the user, nor a member of the group, they get the Other permission. For example, suppose the User permissions are read-only, and the Group and Other permissions are read/write; then the end user will have the weakest permissions of anyone since they are set to read-only.

Users run the ls -l command to view the permissions assigned to files or directories in the file system. Consider the example shown here:

```
tcboony@openSUSE:~> ls -l          # Remember, ls dash "el"
total 48
drwxr-xr-x 2 tcboony staff 4096 Nov 25 17:30 bin
drwxr-xr-x 2 tcboony staff 4096 Nov 25 18:33 Desktop
drwxr-xr-x 2 tcboony staff 4096 Nov 25 18:33 Documents
drwxr-xr-x 2 tcboony staff 4096 Nov 25 18:33 Downloads
drwxr-xr-x 2 tcboony staff 4096 Nov 25 18:33 Music
drwxr-xr-x 2 tcboony staff 4096 Nov 25 18:33 Pictures
-rw-r--r-- 1 tcboony staff  123 Nov 25 18:36 Project_design.odt
-rw-r--r-- 1 tcboony staff  104 Nov 25 18:36 Project_schedule.odt
drwxr-xr-x 2 tcboony staff 4096 Nov 25 18:33 Public
drwxr-xr-x 2 tcboony staff 4096 Nov 25 17:30 public_html
drwxr-xr-x 2 tcboony staff 4096 Nov 25 18:33 Templates
drwxr-xr-x 2 tcboony staff 4096 Nov 25 18:33 Videos
```

Table 6-2 Numeric Values Assigned to Permissions

Permission	Value
Read	4
Write	2
Execute	1

The first column displayed is the mode for each file and directory. The first character of the mode denotes the file type, which can be a regular file (-), a directory (d), a symbolic link (l), a block device (b), or character device (c). As can be seen, *Project_design.odt* and *Project_schedule.odt* are regular files, whereas *Desktop* is a directory.

A block device is a driver for some type of hardware, such as a hard disk drive, that transfers data in "blocks" from the hard disk to memory. A character device is a driver for hardware, such as a keyboard or a mouse, that transfers data one bit or byte at a time. A symbolic link is similar to a shortcut that gets redirected to the file it is "linked" to, as discussed in Chapter 5.

The next three characters are the permissions assigned to the entry's owner: the User. For example, *Project_schedule.odt* has rw- assigned to its User (tcboony). This means tcboony has read and write permissions to the file, but not execute. Because the file isn't a program or script, no executable permission needs to be set. If the file were a program or script and the execute permission were assigned, the permission would show as rwx. Because the User has read and write permissions, tcboony can open, edit, and save the file changes.

The next three characters are the permissions assigned to the Group. In this case, it is the staff Group. Any user on the system who is a member of the staff Group is granted r-- access to the *Project_schedule.odt* file. This means they have the read privilege, allowing them to open a file and view its contents, but they are not allowed to save any changes to the file.

Before we progress any further, permissions for each entity can also be represented numerically. This is done by assigning a value to each permission, as shown in Table 6-2.

Using these values, the permissions assigned to User, Group, or Other can be represented with a single digit. Simply add up the value of each permission. For example, suppose User is assigned read and write permissions to a file. To determine the numeric value of this assignment, simply add the values of read and write together (4 + 2 = 6). Often a file or directory's mode is represented by three numbers. Consider the example shown in Figure 6-2.

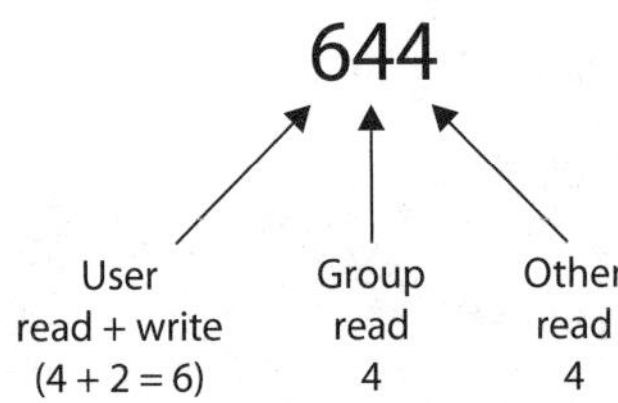

Figure 6-2 Representing permissions numerically

In this example, the associated file's User has read and write permissions (6), the Group has the read permission (4), and Other also has read permission (4). Using the **ls -l** command, this mode would be represented as **-rw-r- -r- -**.

So what if these permissions aren't correct? Use the **chmod** utility to modify them! Let's discuss how this is done next.

Managing Permissions from the Command Line

Although GUI is not covered on the exam, Linux administrators can modify permissions graphically. For example, using the file browser in the GNOME desktop environment, one can right-click any file or directory and then select Properties | Permissions to change the file permissions. The screen shown in Figure 6-3 is displayed.

However, for the Linux+ exam, the candidate must be able to accomplish the task with command-line tools using **chmod** to modify permissions. To use **chmod**, the end user must either own the file or be logged in as root.

Several different syntaxes can be used with **chmod**. The first is to enter **chmod <entity=permissions> <filename>** at the shell prompt. Substitute u for User, g for Group, and o for Other in the entity portion of the command. Also substitute r, w, and/or x for the permissions portion of the command. For example, to change the mode of *contacts.odt* to -rw-rw-r-- (giving User and Group read and write permissions while giving Other only read access), enter **chmod u=rw,g=rw,o=r contacts.odt** *or* **chmod ug=rw,o=r** at the shell prompt (assuming the file resides in the current directory). The permissions are adjusted as shown here:

```
openSUSE:/home/tcboony # chmod u=rw,g=rw,o=r contacts.odt
openSUSE:/home/tcboony # ls -l contacts.odt
-rw-rw-r-- 1 tcboony staff 0 Mar 18 08:02 contacts.odt
```

Figure 6-3 Setting permissions in file browser

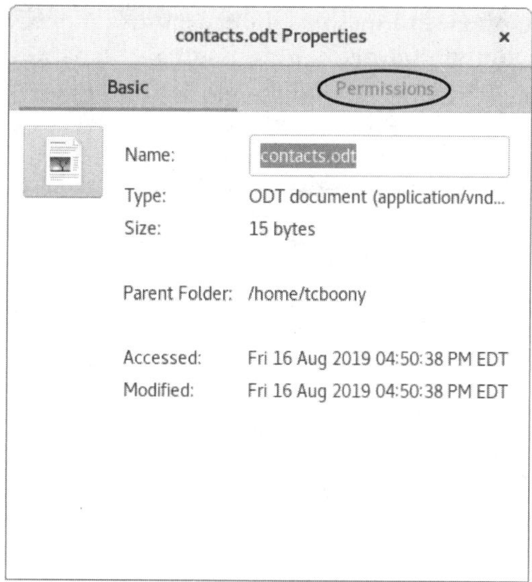

Also use chmod to toggle a particular permission on or off using the + or – sign. For example, to turn off the write permission just given to Group for the *contacts.odt* file, enter **chmod -gw contacts.odt** at the shell prompt. Once executed, the specified permission is turned off, as shown here:

```
openSUSE:/home/tcboony # chmod g-w contacts.odt
openSUSE:/home/tcboony # ls -l contacts.odt
-rw-r--r-- 1 tcboony staff 0 Mar 18 08:02 contacts.odt
```

To turn the permission back on, enter **chmod g+w contacts.odt**. Or, substitute u or o to modify the permission to the file or directory for User or Other, respectively.

There is a special setting for directories when working as a team on a project. When setting the special permission bit on the group user of the directory using **chmod g+s <directory>**, any files created in that directory thereafter will inherit the group ID of the directory instead of the primary group ID of the user who creates the file. See the example of a subdirectory called *temp* shown here:

```
openSUSE:/home/tcboony/temp # touch orange          # create the orange file
openSUSE:/home/tcboony/temp # chgrp wheel .         # change temp to wheel group
openSUSE:/home/tcboony/temp # chmod g+s .           # set special bit on temp dir
openSUSE:/home/tcboony/temp # touch apple           # create the apple file
openSUSE:/home/tcboony/temp # ls -l apple orange
-rw-r--r-- 1 tcboony wheel 0 Mar 18 08:02 apple     # apple inherits group of temp
-rw-r--r-- 1 tcboony staff 0 Mar 18 08:02 orange    # orange inherits group of user
```

Historically, the wheel group is a special group for system administrators. Members of this group are able to execute restricted commands within a standard user account, so be cautious adding files, directories, and commands to the wheel group. A better feature to provide administrative control is called **sudo** because it logs administrative activity. Further details are provided in Chapter 16.

Finally, one can also use numeric permissions with chmod, which Systems Administrator use most often. Just modify all three entities at once with only three characters. To do this, enter **chmod <numeric_permission> <filename>**.

Going back to the earlier example, suppose an end user wants to grant read and write permissions to User and Group, but remove all permissions from Other. That would mean User and Group's permissions would be represented numerically as 6. And, because Other gets no permissions, it would be represented by 0. Implement this by entering **chmod 660 contacts.odt** at the shell prompt. When done, the appropriate changes are made, as shown in the following example:

```
openSUSE:/home/tcboony # chmod 660 contacts.odt
openSUSE:/home/tcboony # ls -l contacts.odt
-rw-rw---- 1 tcboony staff 0 Mar 18 08:02 contacts.odt
```

TIP Use the -R option with chmod to change permissions on many files at once, recursively.

Let's practice managing permissions in the following exercise.

Exercise 6-2: Managing Permissions

In this exercise, you practice modifying permissions from the shell prompt of the Linux system. You also create a design document for a hypothetical Research and Design team and modify its permissions to control access. Perform this exercise using the virtual machine that comes with this book.

VIDEO Please watch the Exercise 6-2 video for a demonstration on how to perform this task.

Complete the following steps:

1. Log in to the system using login name student1 and enter the password. Start a terminal by clicking Applications | Terminal.
2. Switch to the root user account with the **su -** command, and enter the password.
3. Change to the */RandD* directory by entering **cd /RandD** at the shell prompt.
4. Create a design document for the team and restrict access to it by doing the following:
   a. Create a new file named *design_doc.odt* by entering **touch design_doc.odt** at the shell prompt.
   b. At the shell prompt, enter **ls -l**. Notice that the root user account and the root group are the owners of the new file.
   c. Change ownership of the file to the student1 user account and the research group using the chown command with the following command: **chown student1:research design_doc.odt**
   d. Enter **ls -l** again at the shell prompt. Verify that ownership of the file directory has changed to the student1 user account and the research group. Notice that User has rw- permissions to the file, but Group only has r-- permission.
   e. Grant Group rw- permissions by entering **chmod g+w design_doc.odt** at the shell prompt.
   f. Enter **ls -l** again at the shell prompt. Notice that User and Group now both have read/write access to the file.
   g. Notice that Other has read access to the file. To keep this document confidential, remove this access by entering **chmod 660 design_doc.odt** at the shell prompt.
   h. Enter **ls -l** again. Verify that Other has no permissions to this file.

5. Next, control access to the research directory itself using permissions. Do the following:
   a. Enter **ls -ld** at the shell prompt. Notice that User has full access to the *RandD* directory, but Group is missing the write permission to the directory. Also notice that Other can read the directory contents (r) and can enter the directory (x).
   b. Grant Group full access to the directory and remove Other access to the directory completely by entering **chmod 770 RandD** at the shell prompt.
   c. Enter **ls -ld** at the shell prompt. Verify that User and Group have full access and that Other has no access.

Working with Default Permissions

Whenever a new file or directory is created in the file system, a default set of permissions is automatically assigned.

By default, Linux assigns rw-rw-rw- (666) permissions to every file whenever it is created in the file system. It also assigns rwxrwxrwx (777) permissions to every directory created in the file system. However, these are not the permissions the files or directories actually end up with because of a security feature called umask. Let's take a look at an example.

Suppose tcboony was to create a new directory named revenue in her home directory and a file named *projections.odt* in the revenue directory. Based on what we just discussed, the revenue directory should have a mode of rwxrwxrwx and the *projections.odt* file should have a mode of rw-rw-rw-. However, this is not the case, as shown here:

```
tcboony@openSUSE:~> ls -ld revenue rev*/projectors.odt
drwxr-xr-x 2 tcboony staff 4096 2011-03-18 11:06 revenue-rw-r--r-- 1 tcboony
staff 0 2011-03-18 11:06 revenue/projections.odt
```

Notice that the *revenue* directory has a mode of drwxr-xr-x (755). This means the directory's User has read, write, and execute permissions to the directory. Group and Other have read and execute permissions to the directory. Likewise, notice that the *projections.odt* file has a mode of -rw-r--r-- (644). User has read and write permissions, whereas Group and Other have only the read permission.

These are not the default permissions Linux is supposed to assign! Why did this happen? It is because the default permissions are insecure. Think about it. The default directory mode would allow anyone on the system to enter any directory and delete any files they wanted to! Likewise, the default file mode would allow any user on the system to modify a file you created. What a nightmare!

To increase the overall security of the system, Linux uses a command called umask to automatically remove permissions from the default mode whenever a file or directory is created in the file system. The value of umask is a three- or four-digit number, as shown here:

```
openSUSE:~ # umask
0022
```

For most Linux distributions, the default value of umask is 0022 or 022. Each digit represents a permission value to be *removed.* The first digit (0) references—you guessed it—User. The middle digit (2) references Group, and the last digit (2) references Other. Because 0 (zero) is listed for User, no permissions are removed from the default mode for a file or directory user. However, because 2 is listed for Group and Other, *the write permission is removed from the default mode whenever a file or directory is created in the file system for Group and Other.* The function of umask is shown in Figure 6-4.

The default value of umask works for most Linux admins. However, there may be situations where you need to tighten or loosen the permissions assigned when a file or directory is created in the file system. To do this, change the value assigned to umask.

This can be done in two ways. First, to make a temporary change to umask, enter **umask <value>** at the shell prompt. For example, to remove the execute permission that is automatically assigned to Other whenever a new directory is created, enter **umask 023**. This would cause the write permission (2) to be removed from Group upon creation as well as write (2) and execute (1) from Other. This will effectively disallow anyone from entering the new directory except for the directory's User or members of Group. This is shown here:

```
openSUSE:~ # umask 023
openSUSE:~ # umask
0023
openSUSE:~ # mkdir /home/tcboony/temp
openSUSE:~ # ls -ld /home/tcboony/temp   # -d option will not descend a directory
...
drwxr-xr-x 2 tcboony staff  4096 Mar 18 11:06 revenue
drwxr-xr-- 2 root        4096 Mar 18 11:14 temp
```

Notice that, because the value of umask was changed, the execute permission (x) was removed from Other in the mode when the temp directory was created.

This method for modifying umask works great; however, it is not persistent. If the system restarted, the umask would revert to its original value. That is because the value of umask is automatically set each time the system boots using the umask parameter in */etc/profile*, */etc/bashrc*, */etc/login.defs*, or *~/.bashrc*, depending on the distribution (where "~" means the end-user's home directory).

To make the change to umask permanent, simply edit the appropriate configuration file in a text editor and set the value of umask to the desired value.

Next, let's look at special permissions.

Figure 6-4 How umask works

```
                          Files
         Default Mode : rw-rw-rw-
  Subtracted by umask : ----w--w-
                        ---------
              Result:   rw-r-r--

                    Directories
          Default Mode:  rwxrwxrwx
  Subtracted by umask:   ----w--w-
                         ---------
              Result:    rwxr-xr-x
```

Working with Special Permissions

Most of the tasks completed with permissions will be with the read, write, and execute permissions. However, there are several other special permissions to assign to files and directories in the file system. These are shown in Table 6-3.

These special permissions are referenced as an extra digit added to the *beginning* of the file or directory's mode. As with regular permissions, each of these special permissions has a numerical value assigned to it, as shown here:

- SUID: 4
- SGID: 2
- Sticky Bit: 1

Assign these special permissions to files or directories using **chmod**. Just add an extra number to the beginning of the mode that references the special permissions to associate with the file or directory.

For example, to apply the SUID and SGID permissions to a file named runme that should be readable and executable by User and Group, enter **chmod 6554 runme** at the shell prompt. This specifies that the file has SUID (4) and SGID (2) permissions assigned (for a total of 6 in the first digit). It also specifies that User and Group have read (4) and execute permissions (1) assigned (for a total of 5 in the second and third digits). It also specifies that Other be allowed to read (4) the file, but not be able to modify or run it (for a total of 4 in the last digit).

Permission	Description	Effect on Files	Effect on Directories
SUID	Set User ID. Can only be applied to binary executable files (not shell scripts).	When an executable file set with SUID is run, the end user temporarily runs the file at the User (owner) privilege of the file.	None.
SGID	Set Group ID. Can be applied to binary executable files (not shell scripts).	When an executable file with SGID set is run, the end user temporarily runs the file at the Group privilege of the file.	When the end user creates file in a directory that has SGID set, the group assigned to the new file is set to the group of the SGID-defined directory.
Sticky Bit		None.	When the Sticky Bit is set on a directory, users can only delete files within the directory for which they are the User (owner); otherwise, anyone can delete anyone's files.

Table 6-3 Special Permissions

Also set the special bits mnemonically. For example,

```
chmod ug=srx,o=r runme
```

is equivalent to **chmod 6554 runme**. To remove the sticky bit for the file user and file group, run

```
chmod u-s,g-s runme
```

Of course, **chmod ug-s runme** could have been executed.
For a directory, do one of the following:

chmod o+t dira
chmod ugo=rwx,o=trwx dira
chmod 1777 direca

Let's practice managing default and special permissions in the following exercise.

Exercise 6-3: Managing Default and Special Permissions

In this exercise, practice modifying default permissions with umask and start creating files. Also practice adding special permissions to directories. Perform this exercise using the virtual machine that comes with this book.

VIDEO Please watch the Exercise 6-3 video for a demonstration on how to perform this task.

Complete the following steps:

1. Verify that you are logged in to the system. Log in to the system using login name **student1** and password **student1**. Start a terminal by clicking Applications | Terminal.
2. If necessary, switch to the root user account with the **su -** command and a password of **password**.
3. Change to the /RandD directory by entering **cd /RandD** at the shell prompt.
4. Create several Research and Development documents in the RandD directory. However, make sure these documents are secure from prying eyes. Recall from the previous exercise that Other is automatically granted read access to files when created. You don't want this to happen. You need Other to have no access at all to any documents created. Do the following:
   a. Change the default permissions by entering **umask 027** at the shell prompt.
   b. Verify the value of umask by entering **umask** at the shell prompt. It should display 0027.
   c. Create a new file named *schedule.odt* by entering **touch schedule.odt** at the shell prompt.
   d. Enter **ls -l** at the shell prompt. Verify that User has rw-, Group has r--, and Other has --- permissions.

5. Having the write permission to a directory allows anyone in the research Group to delete any file in the directory. We want to configure the directory so that users in the research Group can only delete files they actually own. Do the following:
   a. At the shell prompt, enter **cd /**.
   b. At the shell prompt, add the Sticky Bit permission to the *RandD* directory by entering **chmod 1771 RandD**.
   c. At the shell prompt, enter **ls -l RandD** and notice that a "t" has been added to the last digit of the Other portion of the mode of the *RandD* directory. This indicates that the sticky bit has been set:

```
openSUSE:/ # ls -l
total 105
drwxrwx--t   2 tux  research  4096 Mar 18 11:25 RandD
...
```

File Attributes and Access Control Lists

File attributes allow an operator to provide additional capabilities to files on ext4 filesystems. For example, a file can be made to be append only or immutable. To change attributes, an administrator can use the chattr command, and to list attributes the administrator can use the lsattr command, as shown here:

```
openSUSE:/home/tcboony # chattr +i contacts.odt
openSUSE:/home/tcboony # lsattr contacts.odt
----i--------e- contacts.odt
openSUSE:/home/tcboony # chattr -i contacts.odt
openSUSE:/home/tcboony # lsattr contacts.odt
-------------e- contacts.odt
```

The preceding example shows the immutable bit being set using **chattr +i contacts.odt**, and then the immutable feature being removed with **chattr -i contacts.odt**. The "e" setting means extent format, which is always the case on ext4 filesystems.

Other modifiable file attributes include the following:

- **c** Compressed
- **j** Data journaling
- **S** Synchronous updates

Visit the chattr(1) and lsattr(1) man pages to learn about other modifiable attributes.

TIP File attributes are very lightly tested. Focus on understanding the command-line tools such as chattr and lsattr.

File Access Control Lists

Users can extend their file security settings by implementing a feature called access control lists, or ACLs. This feature allows users to define specific, more granular privileges to their files and directories. For example, user Nathan has read and write access to the files because he is a part of the group. However, since he is not a member of the project team, ACLs can reduce his privilege to read-only without changing the file's group membership.

To view the current ACL settings, use the getfacl command:

```
tcboony@openSUSE:~> getfacl contacts.odt
# file: contacts.odt
# owner: tcboony
# group: staff
user::rw-
group::rw-
other::r--
```

Since Nathan is a member of the group staff, he has read-write privileges. To give Nathan read-only privileges on the file, but still allow him read-write privileges on other files that belong to the staff group, set an ACL using setfacl.

In this example, we run setfacl with the -m option to modify the file's ACL value:

```
tcboony@openSUSE:~> setfacl -m u:nathand:r contacts.odt
tcboony@openSUSE:~> getfacl contacts.odt
# file: contacts.odt
# owner: tcboony
# group: staff
user::rw-
user:nathand:r--
group::rw-
mask::rw-
other::r--
```

User nathand now only has read access to the file *contacts.odt* even though he belongs to the group staff, which has a higher privilege of read-write. The mask value that appears is a security mechanism for automatically setting limiting privileges to a maximum value. For example, if the mask is set to r-- using the command **setfacl -m mask:r contacts.odt**, all users would only have read access even if their User or Group membership is higher.

Chapter Review

In this chapter, we discussed ownership and permissions. Users and groups only control who can access the system, but do not control what the user can do with files or directories in the file system. To do this, we need to implement ownership and permissions.

Whenever a user creates a file or directory, that user is automatically assigned to be its owner. In addition, the group the user belongs to becomes the file or directory's group owner. These defaults can be changed; however, only root can change a file or directory's owner. The owner can change its group.

To modify ownership, use the **chown** command. This command can change both the User and/or the Group that owns a file or directory. To only want to change the group, use the **chgrp** command. The permissions assigned to User, Group, and Other together constitute a file or directory's mode.

We then discussed the **chmod** tool, which is used to manage permissions from the shell prompt. The **chmod** utility can use any of the following syntaxes to assign permissions to User, Group, and/or Other:

- chmod u=rw,g=rw,o=r <file_or_directory>
- chmod ug=rw,o=r <file_or_directory>
- chmod 664 <file_or_directory>

By default, Linux automatically assigns new files with -rw-rw-rw- and new directories with drwxrwxrwx permissions upon creation. However, to increase security, the umask variable is used to automatically remove some privileges.

We also briefly discussed the special permissions one can assign. Assign these permissions numerically with chmod by adding an extra digit before the User digit in the command using the values just shown. For example, **chmod 6755 <command>** will set the SUID and SGID bit for the command. Now the program will run at the privilege of the User (owner), and Group permission of the command, not the end-user permissions.

Finally, additional file security settings can be created with ACLs and file attributes. Use the setfacl command to set granular permissions beyond chmod. The **chattr** command can be used to secure a file from accidental deletion from every user including root!

- Use the **ls -l** command to view ownership (note that this command uses a lowercase L, not a number one).
- Use the **chown** utility to configure user and group ownership of a file or directory.
- One must be logged in as root to change user ownership.
- One must be logged in as root or as the file/directory owner to change group ownership.
- Permissions are used to define what users may or may not do with files or directories in the file system.
- Linux uses the read, write, and execute permissions for files and directories.
- Linux permissions are assigned to User, Group, and Other.
- Permissions can be represented numerically: read=4, write=2, and execute=1.
- These permissions are too insecure for most situations, so the umask variable is used to subtract specific permissions from the defaults.
- The default value of umask is 022, which subtracts the write permission (2) from Group and Other.
- Modify the value of umask to change the default permissions assigned upon creation.
- Linux also includes three default special permissions: Sticky Bit, SUID, and SGID.
- Assign special permissions with chmod by adding an additional digit before the User digit in the command.

Questions

1. You need to change the owner of a file named /var/opt/runme from mireland, who is a member of the staff group, to dnelson, who is a member of the editors group. Assuming you want to change both user and group owners, which command will do this?

   A. chown mireland dnelson /var/opt/runme

   B. chown -u "dnelson" -g "editors" /var/opt/runme

   C. chown dnelson /var/opt/runme

   D. chown dnelson:editors /var/opt/runme

2. Which permission, when applied to a directory in the file system, will allow a user to enter the directory?

   A. Read

   B. Write

   C. Execute

   D. Access Control

3. A user needs to open a file, edit it, and then save the changes. What permissions does he need in order to do this? (Choose two.)

   A. Read

   B. Write

   C. Execute

   D. Modify

4. A file named *employees.odt* has a mode of -rw-r--r--. If mhuffman is not the file's owner but is a member of the group, what can he do with it?

   A. He can open the file and view its contents, but he can't save any changes.

   B. He can open the file, make changes, and save the file.

   C. He can change ownership of the file.

   D. He can run the file if it's an executable.

5. A file named *myapp* has a mode of 755. If dnelson does not own this file and is not a member of the group that owns the file, what can she do with it?

   A. She can change the group that owns the file.

   B. She can open the file, make changes, and save the file.

   C. She can change ownership of the file.

   D. She can run the file.

6. You need to change the permissions of a file named *schedule.odt* so that the file owner can edit the file, users who are members of the group that owns the file can edit it, and users who are not owners and don't belong to the owning group can view it but not modify it. Which command will do this?
   - **A.** chmod 664 schedule.odt
   - **B.** chmod 555 schedule.odt
   - **C.** chmod 777 schedule.odt
   - **D.** chmod 644 schedule.odt
7. The Linux system's umask variable is currently set to a value of 077. A user named jcarr (who is a member of the staff group) creates a file named *mythoughts.odt*. What can users who are members of the staff group do with this file?
   - **A.** They can view the file, but they can't modify or save it.
   - **B.** They can open, modify, and save the file.
   - **C.** They can open, modify, and save the file. They can also execute the file if it is an executable.
   - **D.** They have no access to the file at all.
8. An executable file has the SUID permission set and it is owned by root. If this file is run on the system by a guest user, which privilege will the program run at?
   - **A.** The user who created the file remains the owner.
   - **B.** The user who ran the file becomes the file's permanent owner.
   - **C.** The program will run at root privilege.
   - **D.** The root user becomes the file's owner.
9. Which command lists the file ACL?
   - **A.** setfacl --get
   - **B.** getfacl
   - **C.** getfacl --list
   - **D.** setfacl -g
10. Which of the following commands is used to make a file immutable?
    - **A.** chattr +i <filename>
    - **B.** chattr -i <filename>
    - **C.** chattr --immutable <filename>
    - **D.** chattr ++immutable <filename>

Answers

1. **D.** Entering **chown dnelson:editors /var/opt/runme** will change the user and group owners of the runme file to dnelson and editors.
2. **C.** The execute permission allows a user to enter a directory in the file system.

3. **A, B.** The user must have read and write permissions to open and modify a file.
4. **A.** In the mode shown, Group is given the read permission only. Because mhuffman is a member of the group, he can only open and view file contents. He can't modify and save the file.
5. **D.** Because dnelson isn't the owner and isn't a member of the owning group, she is granted the rights assigned to Other, which are read (4) and execute (1). This allows her to run the file.
6. **A.** Entering **chmod 664 schedule.odt** will grant User and Group read (4) and write (2) permissions. It will also grant Other read (4) permission.
7. **D.** Because umask is set to 077, all permissions (read=4, write=2, execute=1) are removed from Group and Other. Therefore, members of the owning group have no access to the file, so *mythoughts.odt*'s final permission will be 600.
8. **C.** The SUID permission causes the file's User (owner) to temporarily become the command's owner.
9. **B.** To list a file's ACL, use the getfacl command.
10. **A.** chattr +i <filename> will set the immutable bit on the file, making it unremovable, even by root. So if the program's user (owner) is root, the program runs as the root user.

CHAPTER 7

Managing Linux Filesystems

In this chapter, you will learn about

- An overview of partitions
- Creating partitions
- Managing filesystems
- Managing quotas

In this chapter, we will review the elements used to construct and manage a filesystem. We will also look into creating an encrypted filesystem and creating quotas for users and groups.

Partitions Overview

A new disk is a large storage space. Partitions are used to allocate the whole or portions of the drive into logical storage spaces (Figure 7-1).

The types of partitions available are dictated by the bootstrap method.

Master Boot Record

A Master Boot Record (MBR) is found on the first sector of a hard drive in systems that use Basic Input Output System (BIOS).

NOTE A sector is the smallest storage unit for a hard disk device. Traditionally this size was 512 bytes, but new hard drives using Advanced Format (AF) can increase the sector size to 4096 bytes. AF-capable hard drives can emulate a 512-byte sector.

The MBR was designed to fit in one 512-byte sector (see Figure 7-2) The first 446 bytes are allocated to boot code and error messages, the next 64 bytes contains the partition table, and the last 2 bytes store the disk signature. The disk signature points to the bootloader's root directory.

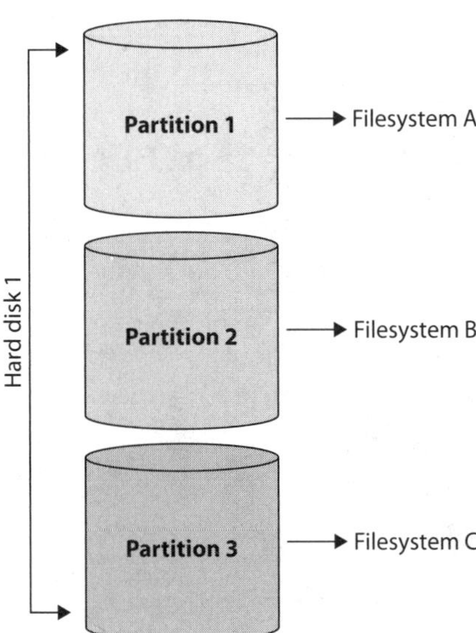

Figure 7-1 Disk divided into partitions

The MBR's partition table was designed to contain four 16-bit partition table entries. This limitation precluded BIOS-based systems from supporting more than four primary partitions.

The four-partition limitation was overcome by using an extended partition. An extended partition is a primary partition that may be divided into logical partitions. The extended partition tracks the logical partitions using an Extended Master Boot Record (EMBR). A logical partition is a partition that resides in an extended partition. Logical partition numbering starts at 5. A sample partitioning scheme is shown in Figure 7-3

NOTE BIOS supports 24-bit cylinder, head, sector (CHS) addressing and 32-bit logical block addressing (LBA). 32-bit addressing limits the maximum addressable disk size to 2.2TB.

GPT

GUID Partition Table (GPT), was designed to overcome some of BIOS's limitations and provide more security by adding redundancy.

The name GUID Partition Table refers to the assignment of a globally unique identifier to each partition. This concept is similar to the function of a universal unique

Figure 7-2 MBR

Master boot record		
Boot loader (bootstrap) 446 bytes	Partition table 64 bytes	Disk signature 2 bytes

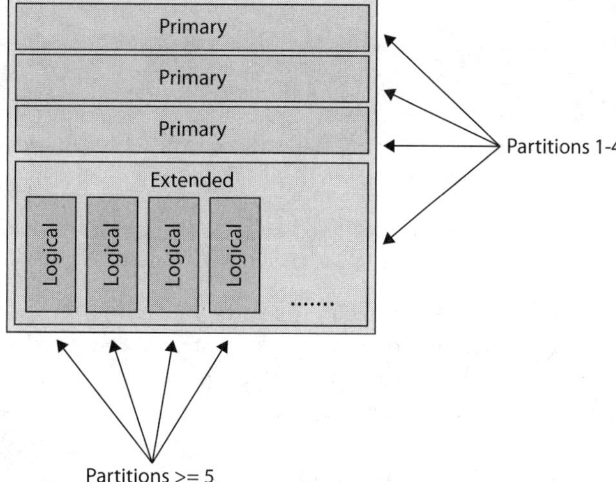

Figure 7-3 BIOS partitioning schema

identifier (UUID), which provides a unique identification number for filesystem and system devices.

GPT Partition Table Scheme

GPT is a single partition that extends across an entire disk device. Components of the partition are accessed via a logical block address. When viewing logical block numbers associated with the GPT partition scheme, you will see positive LBA numbers, which denote block locations offset from the beginning of the drive, and negative LBA numbers, which denote block locations offset from the end of the disk device (see Figure 7-4). The information stored in the positive number blocks are primary entries, and the information stored in negative number blocks are secondary (backup) entries.

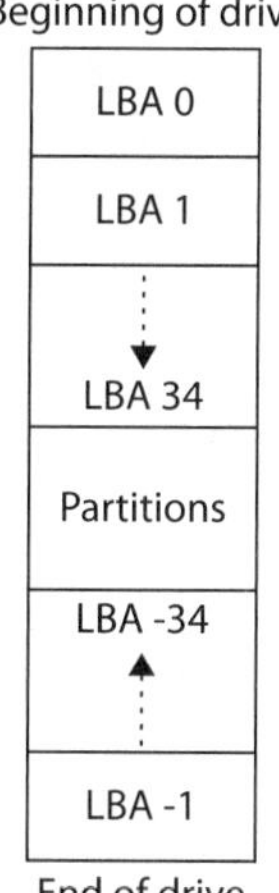

Figure 7-4 GPT LBA numbering

GPT Benefits

Let's examine some of the benefits of a GPT partition.

Sector Size GPT supports AF's 4KB sector.

Addressing GPT uses 64-bit LBA addressing, which increases disk size capabilities from 2.2 terabytes to approximately 8 zettabytes.

Redundancy Partition header and table information are stored at the beginning and end of the drive.

Advanced Device Names GPT supports human-readable partition names. These names are used by udev to create an entry in */dev/disk/by-partlabel.*

GPT assigns a GUID to each partition. This identifier can also be used to access the partition. This entry can be found in */dev/disk/by-partuuid.*

NOTE */dev/disk/by-partlabel* and */dev/disk/by-partuuid* are provided in addition to */dev/disk/by-id*, */dev/disk/by-uuid*, and */dev/disk/by-path* as methods of accessing a disk device.

Partition Table Components

Let's take a look at the various sections of a disk device using GPT partitioning (see Figure 7-5).

Protective MBR (LBA 0) The protective MBR is used to prevent MBR disk utilities from writing over the GPT partition. The MBR's bootloader is used so BIOS-based systems can benefit from GPT. GPT's MBR is modified to recognize GPT partitions.

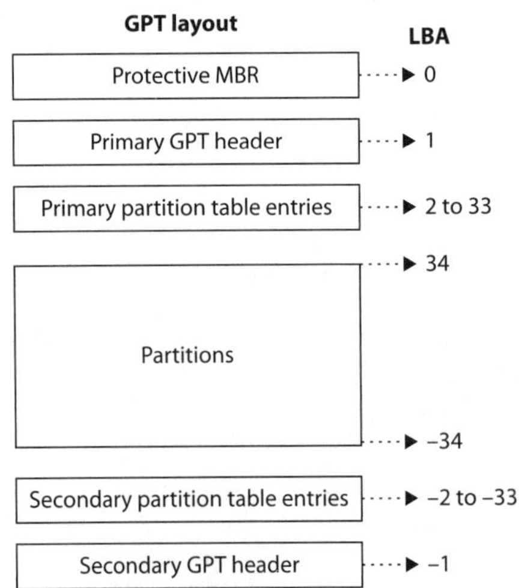

Figure 7-5 GUID Partition Table

GPT Header (LBA 1) The GPT header contains information regarding the structure of the partition table.

Partition Table Entries (LBA 2 to 33)

This section contains partition table entries for up to 128 logical partitions. Table 7-1 illustrates the information stored for each partition.

Partitions (LBA 34 to –34) This section defines user-defined partitions.

Secondary (Backup) Partition Table Entries (LBA –33 to –2)

This is a backup to the partition table entries found in LBA 2 to 33.

Secondary (Backup) GPT Header (LBA 1)

This is a backup to the header entry found in LBA 1.

Device Naming Conventions

A device name format is *xxyz,* where

- *xx* is the device type.
- *y* indicates the device's logical unit number.
- *z* indicates the partition number.

Device Type *xx*

Some examples of device types include sd (SCSI/SATA), hd (IDE), tty (text terminals), and pts (pseudo terminals).

Table Entry	Definition
Partition type (GUID)	The entry indicates the type of partition. This replaces the partition code in MBR. Here are some examples: Boot: 83BD6B9D-7F41-11DC-BE0B-001560B84F0F Home: 933AC7E1-2EB4-4F13-B844-0E14E2AEF915 Swap: 0657FD6D-A4AB-43C4-84E5-0933C84B4F4F LVM: E6D6D379-F507-44C2-A23C-238F2A3DF928 LUKS: CA7D7CCB-63ED-4C53-861C-1742536059CC
Unique GUID	Unique partition identifier (**ls -l /dev/disk/by-partuuid**).
Start LBA	Partition's starting block address.
End LBA	Partition's ending block.
Attributes	A 64-bit number used to define partition attributes.
Partition name	Human-readable partition name (**ls -l /dev/disk/by-partlabel**).

Table 7-1 Partition Table Entries

Logical Unit Number *y*

Next the device name will contain the device's logical unit number. A logical unit number is a unique identifier for a device within a group of devices.

For example, a system may have multiple SCSI devices (device type sd). To distinguish one SCSI device from another, each SCSI device will be assigned a unique identifier. Logical unit sda refers to the first (a=1) SCSI device. The second SCSI device would be sdb (b=2).

tty1 refers to the first text terminal.

pts/0 refers to the first slave pseudo terminal.

Partition Number

A block device may be split into numbered partitions. The device name for the first partition of the first SCSI device is sda1.

NOTE *sda1* is the name of the device. */dev/sda1* is the path to the device.

Integrated Drive Electronics (IDE)

An IDE interface does not contain devices controllers. The controller for an IDE drive is built into the disk device. The interface consists of a primary and a secondary channel (Table 7-2). Each channel supports two devices (master and slave). Within a specific channel, the master device controls communications on the channel.

The device hda is the name of the disk device attached to the IDE primary channel and is the master disk device on the channel.

Locating a Device

When the system boots, it classifies a device, provides it a device name, and stores the device specifications. Next the operating system must provide a means of accessing a device. Let's take a brief look at that process.

Major and Minor Numbers

On boot, the Linux kernel detects and initializes devices by scanning each system bus. When the kernel discovers a device, it determines the device class and assigns the device a major and a minor number. The device class is used to look up the driver associated with the device. The Linux Assigned Name and Number Authority (LANANA) maintains a list of device classes.

Table 7-2 IDE

	Master	Slave
Primary channel	hda	hdb
Secondary channel	hdc	hdd

Figure 7-6 Major and minor numbers

```
1 l# ls -l /dev/sd[ab]*
2
3 brw-rw----. 1 root disk 8,  0 Mar 31 09:19 /dev/sda
4
5 brw-rw----. 1 root disk 8, 16 Mar 31 09:19 /dev/sdb
6 brw-rw----. 1 root disk 8, 17 Mar 31 09:19 /dev/sdb1
7 brw-rw----. 1 root disk 8, 18 Mar 31 09:19 /dev/sdb2
8 brw-rw----. 1 root disk 8, 19 Mar 31 09:19 /dev/sdb3
9 brw-rw----. 1 root disk 8, 20 Mar 31 09:19 /dev/sdb4
10 brw-rw----. 1 root disk 8, 21 Mar 31 09:19 /dev/sdb5
11 brw-rw----. 1 root disk 8, 22 Mar 31 09:19 /dev/sdb6
12 brw-rw----. 1 root disk 8, 23 Mar 31 09:19 /dev/sdb7
13 brw-rw----. 1 root disk 8, 24 Mar 31 09:19 /dev/sdb8
```

Once the device class is determined, the kernel creates a device directory in */sys* and stores the properties of the device in that directory. After boot, the kernel continuously scans system buses for device additions, changes, or removals.

NOTE sys is the mount point for the sysfs pseudo-filesystem. sysfs provides device information to applications running in the system's user space.

Notice the output in Figure 7-6. Where the file size should be, you see two numbers (for example, 8, 0). The first number is the major number, and the second number is the minor number. Using this information, you can see when you access device sdb1 (Figure 7-6, line 6), you are using a Class 8 device driver to communicate with the first partition on the second SCSI disk device.

The device driver determines how the minor number is used. The minor number of a disk device informs the device driver which logical device to communicate with.

The total number of partitions on a disk device is dependent on the drive type. IDE devices may have up to 63 partitions; SCSI devices may have up to 15 partitions.

Notice sda (Figure 7-6, line 3) has no partitions, and the first minor number for sdb (Figure 7-6, line 5) is 16. Why is this? Let's learn why.

Minor numbers for a device class are sequential. The first minor number of a SCSI disk device represents the entire drive. We have learned that a SCSI drive may have up to 15 partitions. Therefore, 16 minor numbers are reserved for each SCSI drive. Minor numbers 0–15 are reserved for device sda, and the first minor number for device sdb is 16.

Table 7-3 shows an example of major and minor numbers for devices sda and sdb. sda's range of minor numbers is 0–15. The first minor number of the sequence, 0, is the logical unit number for the entire device (sda). The second minor number (1) is the logical unit number for the first partition of sda (sda1).

Table 7-3 Major Minor Numbers

Major Number	Minor Number	Device Name
8	0	sda
8	1	sda1
8	16	sdb
8	17	sdb1

sdb's range of minor numbers is 16–31. The first minor number of the sequence, 16, is the logical unit number for the entire device (sdb). The second minor number (17) is the logical unit number for the first partition of sdb (sdb1).

Device Tree

It is possible devices scanned during one boot process are not scanned in the same order in another boot process. Minor numbers influence the device name and are allocated sequentially, so this would cause a device's name to change. Although this does not affect the kernel's ability to access a device, an application trying to access a device by name would have a problem. This problem is solved by creating a path to a device in the systems device tree (*/dev*).

When the kernel discovers the addition, modification, or removal of a device on a system bus, it generates a uevent. The uevent informs udev of the addition, removal, or change. udev uses the class of the device, information stored in sys, and udev rules to create, remove, or modify the system device tree, /dev.

udev rules define how a specific device may be added or deleted and any actions that should occur before or after the device is added, modified, or removed. This makes device configuration persistent.

udev rules are found in */lib/udev/rules.d* or */etc/udev/rules.d*. The rules found in */lib/udev/rules.d* are system defaults, and those found in */etc/udev/rules.d* are custom rules. Rules in */etc/udev/rules.d* will override the rules in */lib/udev/rules.d*.

When enumerating a disk device, udev will create an entry in the following files:

- /dev/disk/by-path
- /dev/disk/by-id
- /dev/disk/by-uuid
- /dev/disk/by-partlabel (uefi)
- /dev/disk/by-partuuid (uefi)

/dev/disk/by-path The entries in /dev/disk/by-path, shown in Figure 7-7, provide a symbolic link between the physical path to the device and device name.

```
# ls -l /dev/disk/by-path | sort -k9 | grep sdb
lrwxrwxrwx. 1 root root 10 Apr  4 16:09 pci-0000:00:0d.0-ata-1.0-part1 -> ../../sdb1
lrwxrwxrwx. 1 root root 10 Apr  4 16:09 pci-0000:00:0d.0-ata-1.0-part2 -> ../../sdb2
lrwxrwxrwx. 1 root root 10 Apr  4 16:09 pci-0000:00:0d.0-ata-1.0-part3 -> ../../sdb3
lrwxrwxrwx. 1 root root 10 Apr  4 16:09 pci-0000:00:0d.0-ata-1.0-part4 -> ../../sdb4
lrwxrwxrwx. 1 root root 10 Apr  4 16:09 pci-0000:00:0d.0-ata-1.0-part5 -> ../../sdb5
lrwxrwxrwx. 1 root root 10 Apr  4 16:09 pci-0000:00:0d.0-ata-1.0-part6 -> ../../sdb6
lrwxrwxrwx. 1 root root 10 Apr  4 16:09 pci-0000:00:0d.0-ata-1.0-part7 -> ../../sdb7
lrwxrwxrwx. 1 root root 10 Apr  4 16:09 pci-0000:00:0d.0-ata-1.0-part8 -> ../../sdb8
lrwxrwxrwx. 1 root root  9 Apr  4 16:09 pci-0000:00:0d.0-ata-1.0 -> ../../sdb
```

Figure 7-7 /dev/disk/by-path

Table 7-4 Device path notation

Element	Definition
host	Adapter (SCSI controller)
bus	SCSI bus address
target	Storage device
lun	Logical unit number (partition)

The path to a device is notated as host:bus:target:lun and detailed in Table 7-4.

/dev/disk/by-id Each SCSI device is assigned a unique identifier called a World Wide Identifier (WWID) when the device is manufactured. The /dev/disk/by-id directory provides a symbolic link between the WWID of the device and the device name (see Figure 7-8). This allows applications to access a device even if the device path has changed.

The serial numbers in Figure 7-8 were created by VirtualBox.

/dev/disk/by-uuid A universally unique identifier (UUID) is a unique identification number applied to filesystem and system devices. A UUID number is assigned to each filesystem when it is created.

NOTE UUID numbers may also be applied to system devices such as network cards.

In Figure 7-9, you can see */dev/disk/by-uuid* contains symbolic links between a filesystem's UUID and the device name.

NOTE dm-0 and dm-1 in Figure 7-9 are LVM logical volumes. dm refers to device mapper.

```
# ls -l /dev/disk/by-id | sort -k9 | grep sdb*
lrwxrwxrwx. 1 root root  9 Apr  4 16:09 ata-VBOX_HARDDISK_VB4c12c352-8137b90e -> ../../sdc
lrwxrwxrwx. 1 root root 10 Apr  4 16:09 ata-VBOX_HARDDISK_VBeb78d713-ad74ebc8-part1 -> ../../sdb1
lrwxrwxrwx. 1 root root 10 Apr  4 16:09 ata-VBOX_HARDDISK_VBeb78d713-ad74ebc8-part2 -> ../../sdb2
lrwxrwxrwx. 1 root root 10 Apr  4 16:09 ata-VBOX_HARDDISK_VBeb78d713-ad74ebc8-part3 -> ../../sdb3
lrwxrwxrwx. 1 root root 10 Apr  4 16:09 ata-VBOX_HARDDISK_VBeb78d713-ad74ebc8-part4 -> ../../sdb4
lrwxrwxrwx. 1 root root 10 Apr  4 16:09 ata-VBOX_HARDDISK_VBeb78d713-ad74ebc8-part5 -> ../../sdb5
lrwxrwxrwx. 1 root root 10 Apr  4 16:09 ata-VBOX_HARDDISK_VBeb78d713-ad74ebc8-part6 -> ../../sdb6
lrwxrwxrwx. 1 root root 10 Apr  4 16:09 ata-VBOX_HARDDISK_VBeb78d713-ad74ebc8-part7 -> ../../sdb7
lrwxrwxrwx. 1 root root 10 Apr  4 16:09 ata-VBOX_HARDDISK_VBeb78d713-ad74ebc8-part8 -> ../../sdb8
lrwxrwxrwx. 1 root root  9 Apr  4 16:09 ata-VBOX_HARDDISK_VBeb78d713-ad74ebc8 -> ../../sdb
lrwxrwxrwx. 1 root root 10 Apr  4 16:09 lvm-pv-uuid-qokTSF-xqlc-tWTd-8eXW-r9LG-M9ey-VUZ4DM -> ../../sdb3
lrwxrwxrwx. 1 root root 10 Apr  4 16:09 lvm-pv-uuid-X61Dh2-CukT-trKd-dfHM-Ow4a-9dE3-cC2ggV -> ../../sdb2
```

Figure 7-8 /dev/disk/by-id

```
#ls -l /dev/disk/by-uuid | sort -k9n | grep sdb

lrwxrwxrwx. 1 root root 10 Apr  9 06:40 a05ba7d2-1136-42e7-ad26-95daf6087a18 -> ../../sdb1
lrwxrwxrwx. 1 root root 10 Apr  9 06:40 ce81200d-04a3-4a45-b6f4-9eebc8ab97dd -> ../../sdb7
lrwxrwxrwx. 1 root root 10 Apr  9 06:40 e7d2409a-29c1-4673-a365-54ada40980ac -> ../../sdb5
lrwxrwxrwx. 1 root root 10 Apr  9 06:40 3bfcbdf2-2708-4009-8d87-fb2bb7fbd76c -> ../../sdb6
lrwxrwxrwx. 1 root root 10 Apr  9 06:40 88e1fb57-b587-4137-a5e8-3ff64d5c3592 -> ../../sdb8

# ls -l /dev/disk/by-uuid | sort -k9n | grep dm
ls: cannot access ls: No such file or directory
lrwxrwxrwx. 1 root root 10 Apr  9 06:40 b1645c67-b27a-43ef-bbf1-ec415d92d10c -> ../../dm-0
lrwxrwxrwx. 1 root root 10 Apr  9 06:40 e593e336-16cd-403c-bbe1-b0a2b0312546 -> ../../dm-1
```

Figure 7-9 dev/disk/by/uuid

/dev/disk/by-partlabel This file is only found using GPT partitioning. This directory contains files that are a symbolic link between the device partition label and the device.

/dev/disk/by-partuuid This file is only found using GPT partitioning. Each partition is assigned a UUID. This directory contains files that are a symbolic link between the partition's UUID and the device.

Viewing Disk Partitions

There are times when you need to view how a disk device is partitioned. The commands **lsblk**, **fdisk -l**, and **parted -l** enable you to do that.

lsblk

The lsblk command, shown in Figure 7-10, displays a list of block devices and their partitions.

/dev/mapper /dev/mapper is a method of dividing a physical block device into virtual block devices.

The commands **ls -lha /dev/mapper** and **dmsetup ls** will display a list of logical volume devices.

Figure 7-10 lsblk

```
# lsblk
NAME         MAJ:MIN RM  SIZE RO TYPE MOUNTPOINT
sda            8:0    0    4G  0 disk
sdb            8:16   0   18G  0 disk
├─sdb1         8:17   0  500M  0 part /boot
├─sdb2         8:18   0  7.5G  0 part
│ └─USR-usr  253:0    0  7.5G  0 lvm  /usr
├─sdb3         8:19   0    3G  0 part
│ └─VAR-var  253:1    0    3G  0 lvm  /var
├─sdb4         8:20   0    1K  0 part
├─sdb5         8:21   0    1G  0 part /
├─sdb6         8:22   0    1G  0 part /home
├─sdb7         8:23   0    1G  0 part /tmp
└─sdb8         8:24   0    1G  0 part [SWAP]
sdc            8:32   0    4G  0 disk
sr0           11:0    1 1024M  0 rom
```

```
Disk /dev/sda: 4294 MB, 4294967296 bytes, 8388608 sectors
Units = sectors of 1 * 512 = 512 bytes
Sector size (logical/physical): 512 bytes / 512 bytes
I/O size (minimum/optimal): 512 bytes / 512 bytes
Disk label type: dos
Disk identifier: 0x102e2452

   Device Boot      Start         End      Blocks   Id  System

Disk /dev/sdb: 19.3 GB, 19327352832 bytes, 37748736 sectors
Units = sectors of 1 * 512 = 512 bytes
Sector size (logical/physical): 512 bytes / 512 bytes
I/O size (minimum/optimal): 512 bytes / 512 bytes
Disk label type: dos
Disk identifier: 0x000b5f25

   Device Boot      Start         End      Blocks   Id  System
/dev/sdb1   *        2048     1026047      512000   83  Linux
/dev/sdb2         1026048    16664575     7819264   8e  Linux LVM
/dev/sdb3        16664576    22964223     3149824   8e  Linux LVM
/dev/sdb4        22964224    37748735     7392256    5  Extended
/dev/sdb5        22966272    25063423     1048576   83  Linux
/dev/sdb6        25065472    27162623     1048576   83  Linux
/dev/sdb7        27164672    29261823     1048576   83  Linux
/dev/sdb8        29263872    31361023     1048576   82  Linux swap / Solaris


Disk /dev/mapper/USR-usr: 8002 MB, 8002732032 bytes, 15630336 sectors
Units = sectors of 1 * 512 = 512 bytes
Sector size (logical/physical): 512 bytes / 512 bytes
I/O size (minimum/optimal): 512 bytes / 512 bytes


Disk /dev/mapper/VAR-var: 3221 MB, 3221225472 bytes, 6291456 sectors
Units = sectors of 1 * 512 = 512 bytes
Sector size (logical/physical): 512 bytes / 512 bytes
I/O size (minimum/optimal): 512 bytes / 512 bytes
```

Figure 7-11 fdisk -l

fdisk -l

The command **fdisk -l**, shown in Figure 7-11, displays the partition table of all block devices.

The command **fdisk -l /dev/<device_name>**, shown in Figure 7-12, displays the partition information of the physical block device supplied in the argument **/dev/<device_name>**.

parted -l

The command **parted -l <device_name>**, shown in Figure 7-13, and the command **fdisk -l** will both display disk partition information. The parted command will print some detailed logical volume information.

To view an individual device using parted, execute the parted command (line 1 in Figure 7-14). Once you view the parted prompt (parted), use the select command (**select /dev/<device_name>**) to choose the device you want to review (line 7). Once you have selected the device, execute the command **print** (line 10) to print the device's partition table. Notice this method does not print /dev/mapper information.

```
# fdisk -l /dev/sdb

Disk /dev/sdb: 19.3 GB, 19327352832 bytes, 37748736 sectors
Units = sectors of 1 * 512 = 512 bytes
Sector size (logical/physical): 512 bytes / 512 bytes
I/O size (minimum/optimal): 512 bytes / 512 bytes
Disk label type: dos
Disk identifier: 0x000b5f25

   Device Boot      Start         End      Blocks   Id  System
/dev/sdb1   *        2048     1026047      512000   83  Linux
/dev/sdb2         1026048    16664575     7819264   8e  Linux LVM
/dev/sdb3        16664576    22964223     3149824   8e  Linux LVM
/dev/sdb4        22964224    37748735     7392256    5  Extended
/dev/sdb5        22966272    25063423     1048576   83  Linux
/dev/sdb6        25065472    27162623     1048576   83  Linux
/dev/sdb7        27164672    29261823     1048576   83  Linux
/dev/sdb8        29263872    31361023     1048576   82  Linux swap / Solaris
#
```

Figure 7-12 fdisk -l /dev/sdb

```
# parted -l
Model: VBOX HARDDISK (scsi)
Disk /dev/sda: 4295MB
Sector size (logical/physical): 512B/512B
Partition Table: msdos
Disk Flags:

Number  Start  End  Size  Type  File system  Flags


Model: ATA VBOX HARDDISK (scsi)
Disk /dev/sdb: 19.3GB
Sector size (logical/physical): 512B/512B
Partition Table: msdos
Disk Flags:

Number  Start   End     Size    Type      File system     Flags
 1      1049kB  525MB   524MB   primary   ext4            boot
 2      525MB   8532MB  8007MB  primary                   lvm
 3      8532MB  11.8GB  3225MB  primary                   lvm
 4      11.8GB  19.3GB  7570MB  extended
 5      11.8GB  12.8GB  1074MB  logical   xfs
 6      12.8GB  13.9GB  1074MB  logical   xfs
 7      13.9GB  15.0GB  1074MB  logical   xfs
 8      15.0GB  16.1GB  1074MB  logical   linux-swap(v1)


Model: Linux device-mapper (linear) (dm)
Disk /dev/mapper/VAR-var: 3221MB
Sector size (logical/physical): 512B/512B
Partition Table: loop
Disk Flags:

Number  Start  End     Size    File system  Flags
 1      0.00B  3221MB  3221MB  xfs


Model: Linux device-mapper (linear) (dm)
Disk /dev/mapper/USR-usr: 8003MB
Sector size (logical/physical): 512B/512B
Partition Table: loop
Disk Flags:

Number  Start  End     Size    File system  Flags
 1      0.00B  8003MB  8003MB  xfs
```

Figure 7-13 parted -l /dev/<device_name>

```
# parted

GNU Parted 3.1
Using /dev/sda
Welcome to GNU Parted! Type 'help' to view a list of commands.

(parted) select /dev/sdb
Using /dev/sdb

(parted) print
Model: ATA VBOX HARDDISK (scsi)
Disk /dev/sdb: 19.3GB
Sector size (logical/physical): 512B/512B
Partition Table: msdos
Disk Flags:

Number  Start   End     Size    Type      File system     Flags
 1      1049kB  525MB   524MB   primary   ext4            boot
 2      525MB   8532MB  8007MB  primary                   lvm
 3      8532MB  11.8GB  3225MB  primary                   lvm
 4      11.8GB  19.3GB  7570MB  extended
 5      11.8GB  12.8GB  1074MB  logical   xfs
 6      12.8GB  13.9GB  1074MB  logical   xfs
 7      13.9GB  15.0GB  1074MB  logical   xfs
 8      15.0GB  16.1GB  1074MB  logical   linux-swap(v1)
```

Figure 7-14 parted select

Creating Partitions

A partition is a section of a physical disk device treated as a logical block device. The commands fdisk, parted, and gdisk are applications used to create partitions on a disk device. gdisk is used specifically for devices with a GPT partition.

Partition Considerations

You must consider several questions when adding a partition.

Partition Availability

Can I add a partition?

A SCSI device can have up to 15 partitions, and an IDE device can have 63 partitions. As long as you do not exceed those limits, you are okay. In the example shown in Figure 7-15, we have used eight partitions on a SCSI device, so we can add another partition.

Disk Space

Do I have enough space?

You can determine if space is available to add additional partitions by determining the difference between the total number of sectors on the device (line 10 in Figure 7-15) and the ending sector of the last partition. Multiply that figure by the sector size (line 12 in Figure 7-15) to determine how much space is left on the drive.

Size

What size should the partition be?

```
# fdisk /dev/sdb
Welcome to fdisk (util-linux 2.23.2).
Changes will remain in memory only, until you decide to write them.
Be careful before using the write command.
Command (m for help): p
Disk /dev/sdb: 19.3 GB, 19327352832 bytes, 37748736 sectors
Units = sectors of 1 * 512 = 512 bytes
Sector size (logical/physical): 512 bytes / 512 bytes
I/O size (minimum/optimal): 512 bytes / 512 bytes
Disk label type: dos
Disk identifier: 0x000b5f25
   Device Boot      Start         End      Blocks   Id  System
/dev/sdb1   *        2048     1026047      512000   83  Linux
/dev/sdb2         1026048    16664575     7819264   8e  Linux LVM
/dev/sdb3        16664576    22964223     3149824   8e  Linux LVM
/dev/sdb4        22964224    37748735     7392256    5  Extended
/dev/sdb5        22966272    25063423     1048576   83  Linux
/dev/sdb6        25065472    27162623     1048576   83  Linux
/dev/sdb7        27164672    29261823     1048576   83  Linux
/dev/sdb8        29263872    31361023     1048576   82  Linux swap / Solaris
Command (m for help):
```

Figure 7-15 fdisk -l /dev/sdb

When considering the space required for a partition, you need to do research and some math. Most operating systems and applications have documentation, which suggests the amount of disk space required. Many third-party applications specify requirements based on the type of application, number of users accessing the application, and the projected amount of data. Once those figures are known, add in some extra space for growth

You might also want to consider using LVM (Logical Volume Manager), which enables you to dynamically increase the size of a partition and filesystem.

Swap Partition

Swap space is virtual memory space created on a swap filesystem. The swap filesystem may be created on a partition or in a file.

When active processes require more memory than is available; the operating system uses swap space by moving (swapping) inactive pages of memory to the block device.

When creating a swap partition, consider the following:

- The amount of physical memory
- The number of logical processors
- The current number of swap partitions
- Swap priorities

Each distribution may have its own swap space allocation suggestions. Table 7-5 is Red Hat's suggested swap space for systems that do not hibernate.

Table 7-5 Suggested Swap Space

RAM	Recommended Swap Size
< 2GB	Two times RAM
>2GB–8GB	Equal to RAM
>8GB–64GB	Minimum 4GB
>64B	Minimum 4GB

Based on the distribution's recommendations it may be more efficient to divide swap space across multiple drives and set swap priorities so swap partitions act as a raid stripe. Swap is discussed in depth later in this chapter

Partition Type

What type of partition should I use?

It is important to know what the partition will be used for and if there are any configuration factors to consider. Partition types are primary, extended, and logical. Some applications as well as certain directories (for example, /boot) must be placed on a primary partition.

Snapshots

Will I use snapshots?

If the filesystem you are placing on the partition supports snapshots and you are going to use them, you need to determine how much space you will need.

Block Size

What is the block size of the device?

To determine the block size of a device, execute the command **blockdev -getbsz <device>**.

fdisk

The fdisk utility is used to modify a partition table of a disk device. Any changes made while working within the application are stored in memory until the changes are written to the disk's partition table.

The command **fdisk <device_path>** is used to manage partitions for a specific device. The command **fdisk /dev/sda** allows us to modify the partition tables of */dev/sda*.

NOTE The following discussion focuses on a BIOS-based system.

Prior to making changes to a device, you need to know its current configuration. For our purposes, we will use the **fdisk -l /dev/sdb**. Refer back to Figure 7-12.

Table 7-6 provides a summary of the columns used to describe a partition.

Table 7-6 fdisk Partition Columns

Device	Device Path
Boot	An asterisk in this column indicates this partition is the boot partition.
Start	Partition's start sector.
End	Partition end sector.
Blocks	Number of blocks occupied by the partition.
Id	Also called a partition code.
System	Text description of the Id column.

Reviewing the information, we find that this disk device contains four primary partitions. One of the primary partitions is an extended partition that contains three logical partitions.

NOTE When partitioning a disk device, the extended partition should be the last primary partition and should take up the remaining available space on the drive.

With fdisk running, we now have a command prompt we can use to enter fdisk commands. Enter **m** to view a list of available commands, as shown next:

```
Command (m for help): m
Command action
  a   toggle a bootable flag
  b   edit bsd disklabel
  c   toggle the dos compatibility flag
  d   delete a partition
  g   create a new empty GPT partition table
  G   create an IRIX (SGI) partition table
  l   list known partition types
  m   print this menu
  n   add a new partition
  o   create a new empty DOS partition table
  p   print the partition table
  q   quit without saving changes
  s   create a new empty Sun disklabel
  t   change a partition's system id
  u   change display/entry units
  v   verify the partition table
  w   write table to disk and exit
  x   extra functionality (experts only)

Command (m for help):
```

Creating a Partition

To create a new partition, enter **n**. Then specify whether you want to create a primary (p), extended (e), or logical (l) partition.

NOTE Logical partitions may only be created in an extended partition. If an extended partition does not exist, you will not be offered the choice to create a logical partition.

To create a primary partition, enter **p** when prompted. To create an extended partition, enter **e**. You are then prompted to specify a partition number:

```
Command (m for help): n
Partition type:
  p   primary (0 primary, 0 extended, 4 free)
  e   extended
Select (default p): p
Partition number (1-4, default 1): 1
```

Pressing the ENTER key will apply the default partition number. The default partition number will be the next available partition. You can specify any number between 1 and 4. However, you cannot use a partition number that has been allocated.

The next entry is the starting sector. Accept the default. Although you can change the starting sector, you must be mindful of the following: If you choose a sector in an existing partition, you will receive a "value out of range" error. You can also choose a starting sector number greater than the default, but this wastes disk space. Many years ago, data was placed on the most efficient parts of the drive to improve efficiency and speed, thus causing a gap. This practice is no longer necessary.

You can specify the size of the partition by entering the last sector, the number of sectors, or the size in kilobytes, megabytes, or gigabytes. Specifying the last sector will start the partition at the end of the last sector +1 and end the partition on the sector specified by the last sector.

NOTE The use of start and stop cylinders has been deprecated.

After specifying the size, you should verify your new partition by entering **p**. This displays all partitions for the disk, as shown in the next example:

```
Command (m for help): p

Disk /dev/sdb: 1073 MB, 1073741824 bytes, 2097152 sectors
Units = sectors of 1 * 512 = 512 bytes
Sector size (logical/physical): 512 bytes / 512 bytes
I/O size (minimum/optimal): 512 bytes / 512 bytes
Disk label type: dos
Disk identifier: 0xd489eb71

  Device Boot       Start         End      Blocks   Id  System
/dev/sdb1            2048     2097151     1047552   83  Linux

Command (m for help):
```

You can verify the size by multiplying the number of blocks with the current block size or determine the number of sectors used and multiply by the sector size.

The ID column contains a filesystem code. By default, partitions are assigned a partition code of 83. If you are creating a partition that will contain a different filesystem type, you must change the filesystem code. This is done by entering **t** and then entering the number of the partition you want to change. fdisk will default to the last partition created. If you don't know the partition code, you can enter a lowercase **l** to list all valid partition codes (ID) and their descriptions.

For example, the partition code for a Linux swap partition is 82. To change the type of the partition, you could enter **t**, specify a partition number to change, and then type **82** for the partition code if you wanted to change the partition to a swap partition.

Deleting a Partition

You can also delete partitions using fdisk. To do this, enter **d** at the command prompt and then specify the partition number you want to delete. Any data that resides on the partition will be lost once you commit the change to disk.

You can also remove a partition that resides between two other partitions. To not waste the space, you can re-create the partition. fdisk has the intelligence to put in the appropriate start and stop sectors. In Figure 7-16, we removed the second partition, which occupied sectors 1026048 through 2050047. Notice what happened when we re-created the partition.

Writing Changes to the Partition Table

Once you have finished editing the partition table in memory, you must write the new partition table to disk using the write (w) command, like so:

```
Command (m for help): w

The partition table has been altered!
Calling ioctl() to re-read partition table.
Syncing disks.
```

Once the partition table is written, the write command will attempt to update the kernel with the new information, but if any of the disk partitions are mounted, the kernel update will fail ("ioctl device busy"). If the kernel is not aware of the new partition information, any attempt to place a filesystem on the partition will result in a "cannot stat" error.

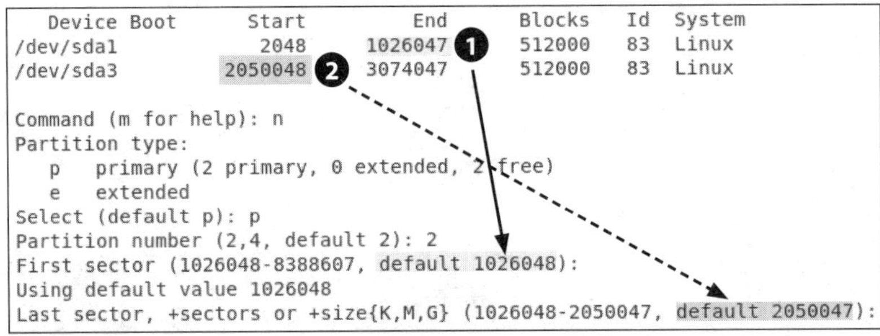

Figure 7-16 Deleting a partition

To force the kernel to read the new partition table into memory, execute the command **partprobe** or **partprobe <device_path>**.

parted

To use the parted command, enter **parted** at the shell prompt and then use the **select** command to specify which disk you want to manage. Be very careful, though, because if you don't manually specify a disk to manage, parted will automatically select the first hard disk for you—you know, the one with your system partitions and home partition on it? Accidentally deleting a partition on this disk could be bad! If you intend to work on a disk other than */dev/sda*, be sure you use the **select** command.

CAUTION The parted command writes partition changes immediately to the disk. Be absolutely certain of the changes you want to make before using parted!

After selecting the appropriate hard disk, you can create a new partition using the mkpart command at the parted prompt. You need to specify the following:

- **The type of partition to be created** For example, to create a standard Linux partition, you would specify a value of **linux**.
- **The starting point on the disk for the partition (in megabytes)** For example, to create a partition that starts at the 1GB point on the disk, you would specify a value of **1024**.
- **The ending point on the disk for the partition (in megabytes)** For example, to create a partition that ends at the 11GB point on the disk, you would specify a value of **11264**.

To view the partitions that have been created on the disk, you can use the print command at the parted prompt. In the following example, a 10GB partition is created on the second hard disk in the system (/dev/sdb):

```
# parted
GNU Parted 2.4
Using /dev/sda
Welcome to GNU Parted! Type 'help' to view a list of commands.
(parted) select /dev/sdb
Using /dev/sdb
(parted) mkpart linux 1024 11264
(parted) print
Model: VMware Virtual disk (scsi)
Disk /dev/sdb: 17.2GB
Sector size (logical/physical): 512B/512B
Partition Table: gpt

Number  Start   End     Size    File system  Name   Flags
1      1024MB  11.3GB  10.2GB               linux

(parted)
```

You can also use the following commands at the parted prompt to manage disk partitions:

- To rename a partition, enter **name <partition_name>**.
- To move a partition to a different location on the disk (which is a very handy thing to be able to do), enter **move <partition> <start_point> <end_point>**.
- To resize a partition on the disk (another very handy thing to be able to do), enter **resize <partition> <start_point> <end_point>**.
- To delete a partition from the disk, enter **rm <partition>**.

gdisk

To manage GPT partitions, use the gdisk utility. The utility can be used to perform the following tasks:

- Convert an MBR partition table to a GPT partition table.
- Verify a hard disk.
- Create and delete GPT partitions.
- Display information about a partition.
- Change the name and type of a partition.
- Back up and restore a disk's partition table.

For example, suppose you have added a second disk to your system and you want to create a GPT partition on it so you can use it to store information. To do this, you would first switch to the root user and then enter **gdisk /dev/sdb** at the shell prompt. gdisk uses many of the fdisk's commands. Enter **?** to view a list of gdisk commands, as shown here:

```
# gdisk /dev/sdb
GPT fdisk (gdisk) version 0.8.7

Partition table scan:
 MBR: not present
 BSD: not present
 APM: not present
 GPT: not present

Creating new GPT entries.

Command (? for help): ?
b       back up GPT data to a file
c       change a partition's name
d       delete a partition
i       show detailed information on a partition
l       list known partition types
n       add a new partition
o       create a new empty GUID partition table (GPT)
p       print the partition table
```

```
q       quit without saving changes
r       recovery and transformation options (experts only)
s       sort partitions
t       change a partition's type code
v       verify disk
w       write table to disk and exit
x       extra functionality (experts only)
?       print this menu

Command (? for help):
```

If you want to add a new partition to the disk, you would enter **n** at the gdisk prompt. When you do, you're prompted to specify the following:

- **The partition number** Partition numbers are sequential. EFI permits partition numbers from 1 to 128. You may supply a unique partition number or accept the suggested partition number.
- **The size of the partition** This can be done by specifying the beginning and ending sectors of the partition. You can also specify where on the disk you want the partition to start and end (such as at the 10GB and 20GB points on the disk).
- **The type of partition** The partition type numbers with gdisk are different from those used with MBR partitions. For example, to create a Linux partition, you use a partition type of **8300**. You can press an uppercase or lowercase **L** at the gdisk prompt to view a list of all possible partition types and their codes.

This process is shown in the following example:

```
Command (? for help): p
Disk /dev/sdb: 33554432 sectors, 16.0 GiB
Logical sector size: 512 bytes
Disk identifier (GUID): 1D3E9F48-D822-4DDF-AB94-C59B7A4E12C8
Partition table holds up to 128 entries
First usable sector is 34, last usable sector is 33554398
Partitions will be aligned on 2048-sector boundaries
Total free space is 12582845 sectors (6.0 GiB)

Number  Start (sector)    End (sector)  Size       Code  Name
   1            2048        20973567   10.0 GiB    8300  Linux filesystem

Command (? for help): w

Final checks complete. About to write GPT data. THIS WILL OVERWRITE EXISTING
PARTITIONS!!

Do you want to proceed? (Y/N): y
OK; writing new GUID partition table (GPT) to /dev/sdb.
The operation has completed successfully.
```

Once this is done, you can enter **p** at the gdisk prompt to view a list of the partitions on the disk. As with fdisk, the changes you make with gdisk are not actually committed to disk until you write them. If you like the changes you made to the disk partitioning, press **w** at the gdisk prompt. If you want to delete a partition, enter **d**. If you want to change a partition's type, enter **t** and then enter the partition type code you want to use. If you want to quit and start over without saving any changes, enter **q** instead.

Block Device Encryption

Block device encryption protects the data on the block device, even if the device is removed from the system, by encrypting data as it is written to the block device and decrypting data as it is read. To access the device, a passphrase must be entered during system startup to activate the decryption key. Each block device can have eight keys. The command **cryptsetup luksDump <device> | grep Slot** will display how many keys have been allocated. You may add or remove keys using variations of the cryptsetup command.

Creating an Encrypted Block Device

First, you need to create a block device. Linux Unified Key Setup (LUKS) supports physical volumes, logical volumes, RAID, and, of course, physical block devices.

Use the command **dd if=/dev/urandom of=<device_name>** to place random data on the block device. Placing random data on a drive makes it difficult for an attacker to distinguish between real and random data.

The command **crypsetup luksFormat <device>** (see Figure 7-17) formats the device as an encrypted device. Once the command has been entered, you will be asked to verify that you know all data will be destroyed. This requires a **YES** entry to go forward. After you enter the passphrase twice, the device will be formatted.

Each encrypted block device is assigned a UUID. We will use the UUID to give the encrypted device a device mapper name that's used to access the contents of the device.

The command **cryptsetup luksUUID /dev/<device_name>** (line 1 in Figure 7-18) illustrates how to obtain an encrypted block device's UUID. The command **crypsetup luksOpen <device> <device_name>** (line 4 in Figure 7-18) creates a device mapper name. Notice we have used **luks-<UUID>** as a device name. We are using the same UUID as the encrypted block device. This is certain to provide a unique device mapper name. The command **ls -l /dev/mapper** may be used to verify the device name has been created.

Figure 7-17 Encrypting a block device

```
[root@localhost ~]# cryptsetup luksFormat /dev/sda9

WARNING!
========
This will overwrite data on /dev/sda9 irrevocably.

Are you sure? (Type uppercase yes): YES
Enter passphrase for /dev/sda9:
Verify passphrase:
```

```
1 # cryptsetup luksUUID /dev/sda9
2 bfa7c906-b366-4232-9d11-d71f2d702d02
3
4 # cryptsetup luksOpen /dev/sda9 luks-bfa7c906-b366-4232-9d11-d71f2d702d02
5 Enter passphrase for /dev/sda9:
```

Figure 7-18 Naming the encrypted device

Managing Filesystems

A filesystem manages the storage and retrieval of data. Linux supports multiple filesystems via kernel modules and an abstraction layer called VFS (virtual filesystem).

Available Filesystems

To use a specific filesystem type, the appropriate kernel module must be available. To determine which filesystem modules are available, execute the command **ls -l /lib /modules/$(uname -r)/kernel/fs** (see Figure 7-19). Note that the output of Figure 7-19 has been edited.

To determine which kernel filesystem modules are currently loaded, execute the command **cat /proc/filesystems**. The term "nodev" (no device) in Figure 7-20 indicates the filesystem is not located on a block device but is loaded in memory. (The output of Figure 7-20 has been edited.)

The command **blkid**, shown in Figure 7-21, displays the UUID and filesystem type of a partition.

Figure 7-19 Displaying the available filesystems

```
# ls -l /lib/modules/$(uname -r)/kernel/fs

drwxr-xr-x. 2 root root   25 Jan 25 17:09 btrfs
drwxr-xr-x. 2 root root   24 Jan 25 17:09 ext4
drwxr-xr-x. 2 root root   60 Jan 25 17:09 fat
drwxr-xr-x. 2 root root   42 Jan 25 17:09 fuse
drwxr-xr-x. 2 root root   24 Jan 25 17:09 gfs2
drwxr-xr-x. 2 root root   25 Jan 25 17:09 isofs
drwxr-xr-x. 2 root root   24 Jan 25 17:09 jbd2
drwxr-xr-x. 2 root root   25 Jan 25 17:09 lockd
drwxr-xr-x. 6 root root  137 Jan 25 17:09 nfs
drwxr-xr-x. 2 root root   46 Jan 25 17:09 nfs_common
drwxr-xr-x. 2 root root   24 Jan 25 17:09 nfsd
drwxr-xr-x. 2 root root 4096 Jan 25 17:09 nls
drwxr-xr-x. 2 root root   23 Jan 25 17:09 udf
drwxr-xr-x. 2 root root   23 Jan 25 17:09 xfs
```

Figure 7-20 cat /proc/fs

```
# cat /proc/filesystems
nodev   sysfs
nodev   rootfs
nodev   proc
nodev   tmpfs
nodev   devtmpfs
nodev   debugfs
nodev   selinuxfs
        xfs
        ext3
        ext2
        ext4
```

```
# blkid /dev/sdb1
/dev/sdb1: UUID="a05ba7d2-1136-42e7-ad26-95daf6087a18" TYPE="ext4"
```

Figure 7-21 blkid

Building a Filesystem

Once you create a partition, you must prepare it for storing data. To do this, you create a filesystem on the partition. This is accomplished using one of several commands. In this part of the chapter, we look at mkfs, xfs, and mkswap.

Table 7-7 describes a few filesystem types.

Using mkfs

The mkfs utility is used to make an ext2, ext3, or ext4 filesystem on a partition. You specify which filesystem you want to use by entering the **-t** option and the type of filesystem. For example, if you want to create an ext4 filesystem on the first partition on the second hard disk drive in your system, you would enter **mkfs -t ext4 /dev/sdb1**. Here is an example:

```
# mkfs -t ext4 /dev/sdb1
mke2fs 1.42.8 (20-Jun-2013)
Filesystem label=
OS type: Linux
```

Filesystem Type	Description
ext3	Third extended filesystem. Successor to ext2, ext3 was a journaling filesystem. Journaling improved the reliability and recovery of the filesystem. ext3 has been deprecated.
ext4	Fourth extended filesystem. Successor to ext3 and supports larger volumes of up to 1 exbibyte (1.1 exabytes) and file sizes of up to 16 tebibytes (17.5 terabytes). ext4 also supports extents.
xfs	High-performance journaling filesystem that uses parallel I/O. It supports a maximum filesystem size of 500TB and a maximum file size of 16TB.
nfs	Network File System (NFS) is a filesystem protocol that allows a user to access files over a network
smb	Server Message Block (SMB) is used to provide shared access to files, printers, and serial ports.
cifs	A version of SMB.
ntfs	In the 1980s, Microsoft and IBM engaged in a joint project to develop OS/2 and the High Performance File System (HPFS). When the project broke up, Microsoft developed the New Technology File System (NTFS). New features include journaling, file compression, volume shadow copy, encryption, and quotas.

Table 7-7 Filesystem Types

```
Block size=4096 (log=2)
Fragment size=4096 (log=2)
Stride=0 blocks, Stripe width=0 blocks
524288 inodes, 2096474 blocks
104823 blocks (5.00%) reserved for the super user
First data block=0
Maximum filesystem blocks=2147483648
64 block groups
32768 blocks per group, 32768 fragments per group
8192 inodes per group
Superblock backups stored on blocks:
    32768, 98304, 163840, 229376, 294912, 819200, 884736, 1605632

Allocating group tables: done
Writing inode tables: done
Creating journal (32768 blocks): done
Writing superblocks and filesystem accounting information: done
```

NOTE The command **mkfs -t <fstype> /dev/mapper/<name>** will create a filesystem on encrypted block devices.

Here are some items to note in the preceding output:

- **Block size=4096** This specifies that the block size is 4KB. This value was determined to be optimal for the small 8GB partition that the filesystem was created on in this example. Smaller partitions will have small block sizes.
- **524288 inodes, 2096474 blocks** The filesystem has a maximum of 524,288 inodes and 2,096,474 blocks. This means it can hold a maximum of 524,288 files on the partition, even if the sum of their sizes is less than the total space available. If you multiply the total number of blocks (2,086,474) by the block size (4,096), you can calculate the total size of the partition (in this case, about 8GB).
- **Superblock backups stored on blocks: 32768, 98304, 163840, 229376, 294912, 819200, 884736, 1605632** A superblock lists filesystem metadata. If the superblock is damaged, the filesystem may be inaccessible. The superblock may be restored from copies found in each block group.

  Filesystems are divided into blocks groups (originally called cylinder groups). Block groups manage smaller sections of the filesystem. Each block group contains the following items:

  - Data blocks
  - A copy of the superblock
  - Block group meta data

  The metadata contains block and inode bitmaps as well as inode tables. Block and inode bitmaps track which data blocks or inodes are used. Inode tables contain inode information for files stored in the group.

tune2fs

tune2fs is used to adjust various filesystem parameters on ext2/3/4 filesystems. Here are some of the options you can use:

Option	Argument	Description
-L	<fs label>	Add or change the filesystem label. A label is a human-readable name for the filesystem.
-j		Add a journal to an ext2 filesystem
-c	*N*	Set the number of mounts (***n***) after which the filesystem will automatically be checked by fsck. This check is made at boot and by default is disabled.
-C	*N*	Set the current number of mounts.
-i		Set the fsck interval:
	d	Number in days.
	w	Number in weeks.
	m	Number in months.

The command **tune2fs -L** will place a label on the filesystem.

```
# tune2fs -L NewVol /dev/sdb1
tune2fs 1.42.8 (20-Jun-2013)
```

Creating an XFS Filesystem

The Extents File System (XFS) filesystem was created by Silicon Graphics (SGI) for its IRIX operating system. It's a very fast, flexible filesystem. It has been ported over to run on Linux as well, although in my opinion it doesn't function under Linux as well as it does under IRIX.

Creating an XFS filesystem is very easy. It is done in exactly the same manner as creating ext*x* filesystems using the mkfs command. First, create a standard Linux partition (type 83) using fdisk. Then, at the shell prompt, enter **mkfs -t xfs <device>**.

Swap

System memory may be physical RAM, random access memory, or virtual memory. Executing applications are stored in RAM. Swap space is virtual memory created on block devices.

When RAM becomes full, some memory must be released to make room to execute additional programs. To do this, memory management software will take pages of data stored in RAM that are not currently being used and swap them to virtual memory.

Creating a Swap Partition To create a swap partition you must first add a partition of type 82. Executing the **mkswap** command creates a swap area on a partition. The syntax for this command is **mkswap <device_path>** (for example, **mkswap /dev/sdb2**). You will see the output below.

```
# mkswap /dev/sdb2
Setting up swapspace version 1, size = 1959924 KiB
no label, UUID=1f51a8d7-ac55-4572-b68a-7a3f179aac61
```

Column	Definition
Total (memory)	Total installed memory
Total (swap)	Total amount of swap memory
Free (memory or swap)	Unused memory or allocated swap memory
Buffer	Used by kernel buffers
Cache	Memory used by page cache
Used (memory)	Used memory = Total – free – buffers – cache
Used (swap)	Swap memory being used
Available (memory)	How much memory is available for a process without swapping

Table 7-8 free Command Output

Even though you have created a swap partition, the swap space is not available to the operating system until you turn it on. Before you turn on the newly created swap space, execute the command **free**. The free command will display the total amount of memory and swap space available and used (see Table 7-8).

Next execute the command **swapon -s** to determine swap partitions currently in use. Execute the command **swapon </device_path>** to turn on the newly created swap space and then execute the **free** and **swapon -s** commands to verify the swap space is working.

The priority of a swap filesystem determines when it will be used. Higher-priority swap filesystems are used first. If the user does not specify a priority when creating the swap filesystem, the kernel will assign a negative priority number.

To set a priority for a swap space, add the option **-p <priority_number>**. For example, command **mkswap /dev/sdb2 -p 60** would assign a priority of 60 to the swap filesystem on /dev/sdb2.

Swap partitions with the same priority are accessed in a round-robin fashion. To increase the efficiency, consider creating multiple swap partitions with the same priority and use the highest priority number.

You can disable an existing swap partition by entering **swapoff <device>** at the shell prompt (for example, **swapoff /dev/sdb2**).

Creating a Swap File

A swap file may be used when you do not wish to create a new swap partition, but require additional swap space.

To create a swap file, use the dd, chmod, mkswap, and swapon commands. Use the dd command to create the file by copying input from the file */dev/zero* and writing it to another file.

CAUTION The keyword dd stands for disk destroyer. Be careful when using this command!

For our purposes we will use the dd options displayed in Table 7-9.

Table 7-9 dd Command Options

Option	Definition
if	Input file
of	Output file
bs	Block size
count	Number of blocks of block size bs to copy

The following command will create a 500MB file called swapfile in the directory */root*.

```
dd if=/dev/zero of=/root/swapfile bs=1024 count=500000
```

Next, change the permissions of the file to 600.

```
chmod 600 /root/swapfile
```

Place a swap filesystem on the file */root/swapfile* by executing this command:

```
mkswap /root/swapfile.
```

To make the new swap space available, execute the following command:

```
swapon /root/swapfile.
```

Mounting a Filesystem

A mount point is a logical connection between a directory and a filesystem. This allows you to access a filesystem on a storage device by changing directories.

Prior to mounting a partition, you must create a mount point (directory). For example, if you have created a partition to store public data, you might create the directory */public* and have that directory point to the partition.

The directories */mnt* and */media* serve as temporary mount points. */mnt* holds mount points for temporarily mounted filesystems, and */media* would be the mount point for temporarily mounted media (for example, CD-ROM or USB flash drive).

To use the mount command, you must have root access. The command syntax **mount -t <filesystem_type> <device> <mount_point>** creates a temporary mount point. If you don't know what type of filesystem is used by the partition, you can use the filesystem type auto (**mount -t auto**).

The following command would create a link from the directory */public* to the ext4 filesystem on the first partition on the second hard disk in your system:

```
# mount -t ext4 /dev/sdb1 /public
```

Now, whenever you execute the command **cd /public**, you will access the data stored on */dev/sdb1*.

mount Command Options

You can also use the -o option with the mount command to include a variety of mounting options with the command. For example, you could use **-o ro** to mount the partition as

Options	Definition
defaults	Implements the default options of rw, suid, dev, exec, auto, nouser, and async.
rw	Mounts a filesystem in read/write mode (default).
ro	Mounts a read-only filesystem
sync	Enables synchronous I/O. Changes are written immediately. Generally used for removable devices such as floppy disks.
async	Enables asynchronous I/O. Changes are cached and then written when the system isn't busy. Generally used for hard drives.
auto noauto	Indicates to automatically mount the filesystem at boot when the mountall command is executed Indicates to not the mount filesystem at boot.
atime noatime	atime updates the file access time the file's inode. Does not update the file's access time in the file's inode.
exec noexec	Allows executable binaries to execute. Does not allow executable binaries to execute.
suid nosuid	Allows suid. Ignores files' suid.
users nousers	Allows the device to be mounted by a regular user. (The device must be unmounted by that user or root.) The device may only be mounted and unmounted by root.
dev	Interprets a block device as a block and character device.

Table 7-10 Mount Options

read-only. See the man page for mount for a complete listing of all the available options. Table 7-10 describes the mount command options.

The mount command with no switches will display mounted filesystems. You can look through the output to verify that the device is mounted. The following line from the output of the mount command indicates that */dev/sdb1* is mounted on /public and uses the ext4 filesystem:

```
/dev/sdb1 on /public type ext4 (rw,relatime,data=ordered)
```

The command **cat /proc/mounts** will display a list of mounted filesystems. To view a specific mount point, execute the command **cat /proc/mounts | grep < mount_point>** or **mount | grep <mount_point>**.

The command **df -T** will display your partitions, filesystem type, where they're mounted, how much space has been used, and how much free space is still available.

To remount a filesystem with new options, execute the command **mount -o remount,<new_mount_options> <mount_point>**. The command **mount -o remount,ro /public** will remount the device associated with the /public mount point, read-only.

Mounting Removable Media

All Linux distributions support external storage devices. When a removable device is plugged in and enumerated (uevent), an entry is made into */var/log/messages*.

If a udev rule or automatic mount information is available for the device, the device name and filesystem mount point will be automatically applied. If the device needs to be enumerated, you can view device name details by executing the command **dmesg**. Rather than looking through the entire log, use the command **dmesg | tail -30** to view the last device enumerated. Other commands such as **lsblk** and **lsusb** may be helpful.

Once you have determined the device name, you may create a partition and mount the device.

Automatic Mounts

Devices can be automatically mounted by creating an entry in */etc/fstab* or creating a mount system unit.

/etc/fstab

The file */etc/fstab* contains the mount parameters for a device.

EXAM TIP Prior to making changes to */etc/fstab*, make a backup. Errors in */etc/fstab* can prevent your system from booting, but you can recover a backup version of */etc/fstab* by booting in rescue mode.

Here is an example:

```
# cat /etc/fstab
/dev/sda1      swap                    defaults                     0 0
/dev/sda2      /          ext4         defaults,acl,user_xattr      1 1
/dev/sda3      /home      ext4         defaults, acl,user_xattr     1 2
```

To specify a swap priority, add **pri=#** after specifying swap as the filesystem, as shown here:

```
/dev/sda1      swap       pri=60       defaults                     0 0
```

Table 7-11 describes the fields in */etc/fstab*. If you make changes to */etc/fstab*, you must execute the **systemctl daemon-reload** command.

Field	Function
1	Specifies the device and partition to be mounted (for example, */dev/sda3*).
2	The directory (mount point) where the partition is to be mounted.
3	The filesystem type of the partition.
4	Mount options.
5	Specifies whether the filesystem should be dumped: **0** means don't dump, whereas **1** means dump.
6	Specifies the order in which fsck should check the filesystem at reboot. The root partition should be set to a value of **1**. Other partitions should have a value of **2**.

Table 7-11 Fields in the /etc/fstab File

Figure 7-22
Mount by systemd unit

```
[Unit]
Description=Exercises mount

[Mount]
What=LabExercises
Where=/Exercises
Type=vboxsf
Options=defaults

[Install]
WantedBy=multi-user.target
```

If a device has either the auto or defaults option, this device will be mounted at boot or whenever the command **mount -a** is executed.

NOTE If the **mount -a** command is executed and the device is already mounted, the device will not be mounted again.

If a device record exists in */etc/fstab*, it may be mounted by executing the **mount <device> | <mount point>** command or unmounted by executing the **umount <device>** or **umount <mount_point>** commands.

Mount Unit

You may also automatically mount a device by creating a systemd mount unit (see Figure 7-22). User-defined units would be placed in */etc/systemd/system.*

The filename for the unit must be the same as the mount point. In the figure, the filename for the mount point LabExercises is *LabExercises.mount.*

Mounting an Encrypted Device

In order to automatically mount an encrypted device an entry must be made in the file */etc/crypttab*. If it does not exist, as user root, create the files with 744 permissions.

Each record (line) is divided into three space- or tab-delimited fields, as detailed in Table 7-12.

Once you have made an entry in */etc/crypttab*, create an entry in */etc/fstab* using the encrypted block device's device name.

Table 7-12
/etc/cryptab fields

Field	Description
1	Device name Example: **/dev/mapper/<name>**
2	Device Device path (/dev/sda4), UUID (**UUID=<uuid_number>**)
3	Absolute path to passphrase file (/etc/keyfile) (If a path is not present or is set to none, the user will enter a passphrase at boot.)

Unmounting a Partition

The umount command writes whatever device information is in memory to the device and then removes the mount point. You cannot unmount a filesystem if any user is accessing the filesystem.

The command **fuser -vm<mount_point>** will display users and processes accessing a filesystem. The command **fuser -vm /home** will display the user and process accessing the filesystem mounted on the directory /home.

To unmount a partition, simply enter **umount** followed by the device or the mount directory for the partition. To unmount /dev/sdb1 from the mount point /public, for example, enter **umount /dev/sdb1** or **umount /public**. Here is an example:

```
# umount /dev/sdb1
```

Maintaining Linux Filesystems

Just as with any other operating system, you need to monitor and maintain your Linux filesystems. In this part of the chapter, we cover the following topics:

- Checking partition and file usage
- Checking the filesystem integrity
- Checking for open files
- Identifying processes using files

df

In order to add files to a filesystem, you must have disk space and available inodes.

The df utility will display available space information for mounted filesystems, as shown here:

```
# df
Filesystem      1K-blocks    Used Available Use% Mounted on
/dev/sda2         6194480 4528228   1328540  78% /
devtmpfs           760928      32    760896   1% /dev
tmpfs              772004      96    771908   1% /dev/shm
tmpfs              772004    3832    768172   1% /run
tmpfs              772004       0    772004   0% /sys/fs/cgroup
tmpfs              772004    3832    768172   1% /var/lock
tmpfs              772004    3832    768172   1% /var/run
/dev/sda3         7985600   21380   7535524   1% /home
/dev/sdb1         5029504   10232   4740744   1% /mnt/extraspace
```

The command **df <filename>** displays information about the partition on which the specified file resides, as in this example:

```
# df /mnt/extraspace/myfile.txt
Filesystem      1K-blocks  Used Available Use% Mounted on
/dev/sdb1         5029504 10232   4740744   1% /mnt/extraspace
```

The default output displays size in blocks. The -h option displays space statistics in human-readable format:

```
# df -h
Filesystem       Size  Used Avail Use% Mounted on
/dev/sda2        6.0G  4.4G  1.3G  78% /
devtmpfs         744M   32K  744M   1% /dev
tmpfs            754M   96K  754M   1% /dev/shm
tmpfs            754M  3.8M  751M   1% /run
tmpfs            754M     0  754M   0% /sys/fs/cgroup
tmpfs            754M  3.8M  751M   1% /var/lock
tmpfs            754M  3.8M  751M   1% /var/run
/dev/sda3        7.7G   21M  7.2G   1% /home
/dev/sdb1        4.8G   10M  4.6G   1% /mnt/extraspace
```

Adding the -T option will display the filesystem type, as shown here:

```
# df -hT
Filesystem     Type      Size  Used Avail Use% Mounted on
/dev/sda2      ext4      6.0G  4.4G  1.3G  78% /
devtmpfs       devtmpfs  744M   32K  744M   1% /dev
tmpfs          tmpfs     754M   96K  754M   1% /dev/shm
tmpfs          tmpfs     754M  3.9M  751M   1% /run
tmpfs          tmpfs     754M     0  754M   0% /sys/fs/cgroup
tmpfs          tmpfs     754M  3.9M  751M   1% /var/lock
tmpfs          tmpfs     754M  3.9M  751M   1% /var/run
/dev/sda3      ext4      7.7G   43M  7.2G   1% /home
/dev/sdb1      ext4      4.8G   10M  4.6G   1% /mnt/extraspace
```

When a file is created, it is assigned an inode number. If a filesystem runs out of inodes, files can no longer be created, even if space exists. The **df -i** command lists inode usage of mounted filesystems:

```
# df -i
Filesystem     Inodes  IUsed  IFree IUse% Mounted on
/dev/sda2      402400 168063 234337   42% /
devtmpfs       190232    376 189856    1% /dev
tmpfs          193001      9 192992    1% /dev/shm
tmpfs          193001    503 192498    1% /run
tmpfs          193001     13 192988    1% /sys/fs/cgroup
tmpfs          193001    503 192498    1% /var/lock
tmpfs          193001    503 192498    1% /var/run
/dev/sda3      516096    516 515580    1% /home
/dev/sdb1      327680     12 327668    1% /mnt/extraspace
```

du

Another utility you can use to monitor disk space usage is the du utility. Its function is to provide you with a summary of disk space usage of each file, recursively, for a specified directory. The syntax is **du *directory***. Some useful options you can use with du include the following:

- **-c** Used to calculate a grand total
- **-h** Used to display output in human-readable format
- **--exclude *filename_or_pattern*** Used to exclude all files that match the specified filename or pattern

The -h option is the most useful one, in my experience. Here is an example of viewing the space used by files in the /tmp directory in human-readable format:

```
# du -h /tmp
4.0K	/tmp/.esd-485
4.0K	/tmp/.X11-unix
4.0K	/tmp/.XIM-unix
4.0K	/tmp/.Test-unix
4.0K	/tmp/.esd-1000
4.0K	/tmp/.font-unix
4.0K	/tmp/systemd-private-otNWQw/tmp
8.0K	/tmp/systemd-private-otNWQw
4.0K	/tmp/VMwareDnD
4.0K	/tmp/.ICE-unix
4.0K	/tmp/vmware-root
4.0K	/tmp/systemd-private-OSAy3Q/tmp
8.0K	/tmp/systemd-private-OSAy3Q
4.0K	/tmp/orbit-student
64K	/tmp
```

dumpe2fs

A filesystem uses a superblock and cylinder groups to manage the filesystem's metadata.

The output of the **dumpe2fs** command (**dumpe2fs <device>**) will show the statistics stored in both the superblock and block groups. The -h option, **dumpe2fs -h <device_path>**, limits the output to the information stored in the filesystem's superblock.

xfs tools

xfs has several administrative tools, including the df command. Let's examine some others.

xfs_admin xfs_admin uses xfs's debug utility, xfs_db, to modify various parameters (detailed in Table 7-13) of an unmounted xfs filesystem.

xfs_info xfs_info, shown in Figure 7-23, displays filesystem geometry.

xfs_metadump xfs_metadump is used to copy an xfs filesystem's metadata to a file using the command syntax **xfs_metadump <device_name> <output_filename>**.

Option	Argument	Description
-L	<label>	Assigns a label to the filesystem
-l		Prints the filesystem label
-U	<generate> <nil>	Generates a new UUID for the filesystem Sets a null UUID
-u		Displays the filesystems UUID

Table 7-13 Sample of xfs_admin Options

```
# xfs_info /dev/sdb5
meta-data=/dev/sdb5              isize=512    agcount=4, agsize=65536 blks
         =                       sectsz=512   attr=2, projid32bit=1
         =                       crc=1        finobt=0 spinodes=0
data     =                       bsize=4096   blocks=262144, imaxpct=25
         =                       sunit=0      swidth=0 blks
naming   =version 2              bsize=4096   ascii-ci=0 ftype=1
log      =internal               bsize=4096   blocks=2560, version=2
         =                       sectsz=512   sunit=0 blks, lazy-count=1
realtime =none                   extsz=4096   blocks=0, rtextents=0
```

Figure 7-23 xfs_info

Checking the Filesystem Integrity

The Filesystem Check utility (fsck) checks the integrity of a filesystem. To use this utility, you must first "umount" the filesystem you want to check. Then enter **fsck <device>** at the shell prompt. For example, if you want to check the filesystem on the first partition of the second hard drive in your system, you would enter **fsck /dev/sdb1**. The utility will then check the filesystem and display a report, as shown here:

```
# umount /dev/sdb1
# fsck /dev/sdb1fsck from util-linux 2.23.2
e2fsck 1.42.8(20-Jun-2013)/dev/sdb1:clean,12/402192 files,61153/1605632 blocks
```

Notice in this example that e2fsck was run. That's because fsck is a front end to several error checking utilities. fsck choses the correct utility based on the type of filesystem. If errors are encountered, a code will be displayed that represents the sum of the errors encountered:

- **0** No errors.
- **1** Filesystem errors corrected.
- **2** System should be rebooted.
- **4** Filesystem errors left uncorrected.
- **8** Operational error.
- **16** Usage or syntax error.
- **32** Fsck canceled by user request.
- **128** Shared library error.

After the check is complete, you can remount the partition using the mount command.

One very useful feature of e2fsck is its ability to restore a damaged superblock on *ext2/3/4* filesystems. Remember from earlier in this chapter that the superblock is the block at the beginning of the partition that contains information about the structure of the filesystem. Also, most Linux filesystems keep backup copies of the superblock at various locations in the partition. If the superblock gets corrupted, you can restore it using one of these backup copies. The syntax is **e2fsck -f -b *backup_superblock device***.

The -f option tells e2fsck to force a check, even if the filesystem seems to be clean. The -b option tells e2fsck which copy of the superblock it should use.

If you cannot remember the location of the backup superblocks, execute the command **mkfs -n <device>**.

Managing Quotas

Quotas are a method of limiting the number of files or the amount of disk space a user or group may use. Quotas are applied to filesystems. For our discussion we will create quotas on the /home filesystem

NOTE To install quotas, execute the command **yum -y install quota**.

Editing /etc/fstab

Remember to make a backup of the */etc/fstab* file prior to changing it.

You must enable quotas by filesystem. To do this, add the filesystem option usrquota to monitor user quotas and/or grpquota to manage group quotas. The entry will look like this:

```
defaults,usrquota,grpquota
```

Once you make the changes, you must remount the filesystem. You can do this by executing the command **mount -o remount <filesystem_name>** .

If the filesystem is busy you can use the command **mount -f -o remount < filesystem_name>**. In our example the command would be **mount -f -o remount | grep home**. Be aware you may be kicking someone out of a file.

Another method of working with a busy filesystem is executing the command **lsof | grep <filesystem_name>** to determine the process IDs and users who are using the filesystem. In our example the command would be **lsof | grep home**. At that point you can contact the users and ask them to close their files or use the kill command to kill the associated processes and then remount the filesystem.

The very last method of dealing with a busy file system would be using either the commands **fuser -k /<filesystem_name>** or **fuser -k -9 /<filesystem_name>**. Using our example the command would be **fuser -k /home**. Remember, this can be destructive. After running the command, remount the file system.

Creating database files

Once the filesystem is repaired, you must create the database files in the top directory of the file system.

For users we will use the quotacheck command to create the user database file *aquota .user* and/or the group database file, *aquota.group*. The quotacheck command uses these options:

Option	Description
-c	create
-u	user
-g	group

NOTE The quotacheck command may be used to rebuild existing tables, but should not be run on a filesystem that has quotas turned on. See the "Turning Quotas On and Off" section later in the chapter.

The command **quotacheck -cug /<filesystem_name>** will create the user and group database files in the top directory of a filesystem. To create the files in */home,* you would execute the command **quotacheck -cug /home**.

Once the files are created, you must create a database table in each file by executing the command **quotacheck -ug <filesystem_name>**. When you create the table it will contain the current filesystem usage statistics. To create the tables in */home*, execute the command **quotacheck -ug /home**.

Assigning a Quota

When assigning a quota you use three elements: hard limit, soft limit, and grace period. The number of files is specified in the number of inodes (an inode is created for each file), and the size is specified in blocks.

The hard limit specifies an exact limit. For our example we will assign a hard file limit of ten files and a hard limit size of 20MB.

The soft limit specifies a limit, which may be exceeded for the number of days specified by the grace period.

The grace period is the number of days after the soft limit is reached that the user or group has to go below the soft limit.

For our example user1 has a 10-file and 20MB hard limit, a five-file and 10MB soft limit, and a grace period of seven days of ten files. user1 has ten files on the file system and 4MB of disk space used on the filesystem. The soft limit is ten files, so the user may continue to create files until the grace period is met. During this period user1 can continue to add files or use additional disk space until either's hard limit is exceeded, but both must be less than the soft limit when the grace period expires.

Setting a Quota for a User or Group

The command **edquota -u <user_name>** is used to set a quota for a user, and the command **edquota -g <group_name>** is used to specify a quota for a group.

You can create a quota for a user using an existing user as a prototype. Assume you have created a quota for user1 and wish to create a quota for user2. To create the quota for use2, execute the command **edquota -p user1 user2**.

Use the command **edquoata -p <group_name> <group_name>** to create a group quota from an existing group. Once the quota is created, you use the commands **quota -u <username>** or **quota -g <group_name>** to view the quota settings.

To set the grace period, execute the command **edquota -t**. You can specify the time in days (5days or 5), hours (5hours), minutes (5minutes), or seconds (5seconds).

Turning Quotas On and Off

You can turn quotas on or off for all filesystems or a specific filesystem using the **quotaoff** command.

The command **quotaon -ap** will print the quota status for all filesystems.

One reason you may wish to turn off quotas on a filesystem is to repair a filesystem's quota tables. The quotacheck command requires quotas to be turned off to repair a quota table.

The command **quotaoff -u <filesystem_name>** (user), **quotaoff -g <filesystem_name>** (group), or **quotaoff -ug <filesystem_name>** (user and group) will turn off quota table modification for a specific filesystem. The command **quotaff -a** will turn off quotas for all filesystems. Verify the results by executing the command **quotacheck -ap**.

The command **quotaon** will turn quotas back on for all filesystems (-a), a specific filesystem, or a specific filesystem and table (**quotaon -u /home**).

Reporting on Quotas

There are two commands to gather quota reports:

- **repquota** Produces quota reports for a filesystem
- **repquota -a** Prints a quota report for all users and groups on all filesystems

Use the options **-u** (users) or **-g** (groups) to isolate the report to users or groups. The command **repquota -u <filesystem_name>** will report on all user quotas within a filesystem. The command **requota -g <filesystem_name>** will report on all group quotas within a filesystem. The command **repquota <filesystem_name>** will report on both user and group quotas for a filesystem.

The quota command displays quota information for a specific user or group. Users can only display their own quota information by executing the command **quota**. The user root, however, can display any user's quota information by executing the command **quota -u <user_name>** or quota information for any group by executing the command **quota -g <group_name>**.

Exercise 7-1: Managing Linux Partitions

In Exercise 7-1, you practice working with Linux partitions.

You can perform this exercise using the virtual machine that comes with this book. You must be logged on as user root (password **password**).

CAUTION Be sure to create a snapshot before proceeding.

1. View the partition table of /dev/sda using the **fdisk -l /dev/sda** command.
2. View the partition table of /dev/sda using parted:
   a. Execute the **parted** command.
   b. Type **select /dev/sda**.
   c. Type **print**.
   d. Type **quit** to exit parted.
3. Create a Linux swap partition on /dev/sda:
   a. Type **fdisk /dev/sda**.
   b. Enter **n** to create a new partition.
   c. Accept the default partition type.
   d. Accept the starting sector.
   e. Specify the size as 500MB.
   f. Use the **t** command to change the partition code:
      i. Enter the partition number to change.
      ii. Enter **82** for the partition code.
   g. Use the **p** command to verify the partition is created and has the correct partition code.
   h. Use the **w** command to write the changes to the partition table.
   i. Notice the kernel was not updated. DO NOT RUN partprobe.
4. Create a swap partition by executing the **mkswap <device_name>** command. The device name should be /dev/sda8.
   a. Notice the error message.
   b. Execute the **partprobe** command.
   c. Execute the **mkswap <device_name>** command.
5. Type the command **swapon -s** to determine existing swap spaces.
6. Type the command **free** to determine the total amount of swap space and how much swap space is free.
7. Execute the command **swapon /dev/sda8** and then use the **swapon -s** command to test that the swap space has been enabled.
8. Execute the command **free** to see the difference in swap space.
9. Disable /dev/sda8 swap space by executing the command **swapoff /dev/sda8** (verify the results of this command).

10. Using the steps in Question 3, create the following partitions (size 500MB) in the order specified:
    a. One Linux partition (partition code 83; device name should be /dev/sda9).
    b. Two LVM physical volumes (partition code 8e; device names should be /dev/sda10 and /dev/sda11).
    c. Two software RAID partitions (partition code fd; device names should be /dev/sda12 and /dev/sda13).
    d. Write the partition table.
11. Create an ext4 filesystem on /dev/sda9.
12. Use the command **dumpe2fs -h /dev/sda9** to display the filesystem superblock.
13. Create the directory /public.
14. Mount the filesystem on /dev/sda9 to the directory /public by executing the **mount -t ext4 /public** command.
15. Use the command **mount** or **mount | grep public** to ensure the filesystem is mounted.
16. Change directory to /public and execute the **touch file{1,2,3}** command.
17. Verify the files have been created by executing the **ls -l /public** command.
18. Make your current working directory /public.
19. Unmount the filesystem by typing the **umount /public** command.
20. Determine which user or process is accessing the filesystem attached to /public by executing the **fuser -vm /public** command.
21. Execute the **cd** command and verify with the **pwd** command you are no longer in /public.
22. Unmount /public and verify it is no longer mounted.
23. Execute the **fsck /dev/sda9** command.
24. Use the command **tune2fs -L public /dev/sda9** to add the label "public" to the filesystem on /dev/sda9.
25. Execute the **blkid /dev/sda9** command.
26. Execute the **findfs LABEL-public** command.
27. Mount the filesystem on /dev/sda9 by executing the **mount -L public /public** command.
28. Test that the filesystem has been mounted.
29. Unmount /dev/sda9.
30. Create a copy of /etc/fstab by executing the **cp /etc/fstab /etc/fstab.lab** command.

31. Execute the command **vi /etc/fstab** and go to the last line by using the key sequence ESC-GG.
    a. Enter several hash marks (####) and press RETURN. The hash marks are a visual reminder of where you have entered new configuration information. Enter the following line:
    /dev/sda9 /public defaults 0 0
    b. Save the file by using the ESC **: wq** sequence.
    c. Type the **mount -a** command.
    d. Test to see the filesystem in /dev/sda9 has been mounted.
32. Unmount /dev/sda9 and vi /etc/fstab:
    a. Place your cursor on the line configuring /dev/sda9.
    b. Use the key sequence ESC **i** to place vi in insert mode.
    c. Place a hash mark (#) at the beginning of the line so the line will be ignored.
    d. Use the key sequence ESC **o** to open a line below.
    e. Type **LABEL=public /public defaults 0 0.**
    f. Exit vi by executing the ESC **: wq** command.
    g. Use the **mount -a** command to remount /dev/sda9 using its label.

Chapter Review

In this chapter we discussed what a partition is and the difference between MBR and GPT partitioning. From there, we talked about the different partition types and how to manage partitions. Once the filesystem was created, you learned how to create a logical relationship between a directory and a filesystem placed on a partition (mount point) as well as manually and automatically mount filesystems.

- You must partition and format a disk before you can mount it in the Linux filesystem.
- The fdisk utility is used to create an MBR partition on hard disks.
- You have to set the partition type when partitioning disks.
- Partition changes are only saved in memory until you commit them to disk.
- Newer Linux distributions support GPT partitions, which are designed to address many of the shortcomings of the older MBR-type partitions.
- To manage GPT partitions, you use the gdisk utility or the parted utility.
- After partitioning a disk, you need to format it with mkfs.
- After formatting a disk, you can mount it using the mount command.

- You can also use /proc/mounts to view mounted filesystems.
- You can unmount a mounted filesystem using the umount command.
- All filesystems must be unmounted before Linux is shut down.
- Mounted filesystems won't be remounted on reboot unless they have an entry in the /etc/fstab file.
- The /etc/fstab file specifies mount points and other options for specific devices.
- You can monitor disk space and inode usage using the df and du utilities.
- The fsck utility is used to check and repair filesystems.
- The e2fsck utility can be used to restore a damaged superblock on ext2/3/4 filesystems.
- The tune2fs utility is used to adjust various filesystem parameters on ext2/3/4 filesystems.
- The dumpe2fs utility can display superblock and block group information for ext filesystems.
- The xfs_admin utility is the xfs equivalent of tune2fs.
- The xfs_info utility displays useful information about xfs filesystems.
- The xfs_metadump utility dumps xfs filesystem metadata (such as filenames and sizes) to a file.
- The fuser command displays the PIDs of processes using the specified files or filesystems.
- Removable devices must be mounted in the Linux filesystem before they can be accessed.
- /etc/fstab is used to automatically mount devices when the **mountall** or **mount -a** command is executed.
- If you don't know what type of filesystem is used, you can use **-t auto** to let mount try to determine the correct filesystem type.

Questions

1. You need to use fdisk to create an MBR partition for the fourth SATA hard drive in your system. Which is the correct command to do this?

   A. fdisk /dev/hdd

   B. fdisk /dev/sdd

   C. fdisk /dev/sda4

   D. fdisk /dev/sdb2

2. You've used fdisk to create a new MBR partition on the second hard drive in your Linux system. You want to use the partition as a second swap partition for your system. Which partition type do you need to change it to?
   A. 83
   B. 82
   C. 85
   D. 1
3. You need to format the first partition on the fourth SATA hard disk using the ext3 filesystem. Which is the correct command to do this?
   A. mkext3fs /dev/sdd1
   B. mkfs -t ext3 /dev/sdd1
   C. mkfs -t ext3 /dev/sda4
   D. mkreiserfs -t ext3 /dev/sdd1
4. On which block is the first redundant copy of a partition's superblock stored by default on an ext4 filesystem?
   A. 0
   B. 32768
   C. 98304
   D. 163840
5. You've created a new swap partition (/dev/sdb1) using the fdisk utility. You need to format and enable this partition. Which commands should you use to do this? (Choose two.)
   A. mkswap /dev/sdb1
   B. mkfs -t swap /dev/sdb1
   C. swapon /dev/sdb1
   D. swapon -a
   E. mkfs -t vfat /dev/sdb1
6. You created an ext4 filesystem on the first partition on the second SCSI hard disk in your system and now need to mount it in /mnt/extraspace in read-write mode. Which commands will do this? (Choose two.)
   A. mount -t ext4 /dev/sda1 /mnt/extraspace/
   B. mount -t ext4 /dev/sdb1 /mnt/extraspace/
   C. mount -a /dev/sdb1 /mnt/extraspace/
   D. mount -t ext /dev/sdb1 /mnt/extraspace/
   E. mount -t ext4 -o ro /dev/sdb1 /mnt/extraspace/

7. You have an ISO image file named discimage.iso in your home directory, and you want to mount it in the /mnt directory in your Linux filesystem so that you can extract several files from it. Which command will do this?
   A. mount ~/discimage.iso /mnt
   B. mount -a ~/discimage.iso /mnt
   C. mount -t iso9660 ~/discimage.iso /mnt
   D. mount -o loop ~/discimage.iso /mnt
8. You have mounted the /dev/sdb1 partition in the /mnt directory and now need to unmount it. Which commands will do this? (Choose two.)
   A. umount /mnt
   B. unmount /mnt
   C. umount /dev/sdb1
   D. mount --unmount /dev/sdb1
   E. unmount /dev/sdb1
9. Which file is used to automatically mount filesystems when the system initially boots?
   A. /etc/mtab
   B. /proc/mounts
   C. /etc/inittab
   D. /etc/fstab
10. Which fstab mount option causes pending disk writes to be committed immediately?
   A. async
   B. sync
   C. rw
   D. auto
11. Which command will provide you with a summary of inode consumption on your /dev/sda2 partition?
   A. df -i
   B. df -h
   C. df -hT
   D. du -inode
12. The /dev/sda1 partition on your Linux system currently has no volume label. Given that it is an ext4 partition, which command will set the label to "DATA"?
   A. dumpe2fs -L DATA /dev/sda1
   B. tune2fs -L DATA /dev/sda1

C. lsof /dev/sda1 --label "DATA"

D. mkfs -t ext4 -L "DATA" /dev/sda1

13. You are concerned about the condition of a hard drive containing a heavily used ext3 disk partition (/dev/sda2). To ensure data integrity, you want to increase the frequency of automatic fsck checks. Which utility should you use to configure this?

A. dumpe2fs

B. e2fsck

C. fsck

D. tune2fs

14. You need to mount an optical disc in /media/dvd. Which command will do this?

A. mount -t iso9660 /dev/cdrom /media/dvd

B. mount -t dvd /dev/cdrom /media/dvd

C. dvdmount -t iso9660 /dev/cdrom /media/dvd

D. mount -t iso9660 /dev/cdrom ~/dvd

15. You need to mount a USB flash drive on your Linux system. Given that your Linux system currently has one SATA hard drive (/dev/sda). What should be the flash drive's device name?

A. /dev/hdb

B. /dev/usb0

C. /dev/sdb

D. /dev/sda

Answers

1. **B.** The **fdisk /dev/sdd** command uses the correct syntax to create an MBR partition for the fourth SATA hard drive in your system.
2. **B.** Type 82 defines a Linux swap partition.
3. **B.** The **mkfs -t ext3 /dev/sdd1** command uses the correct syntax to format the first partition on the fourth SATA drive using the ext3 filesystem.
4. **B.** The first redundant copy of a partition's superblock is stored on block 32768 by default on an ext4 filesystem.
5. **A, C.** The **mkswap /dev/sdb1** command is used to create the swap filesystem, and the **swapon /dev/sdb1** command enables it as a swap partition.
6. **B, C.** Either the **mount -t ext4 /dev/sdb1 /mnt/extraspace/** command or the **mount -a /dev/sdb1 /mnt/extraspace/** command will mount the */dev/sdb1* partition in */mnt/extraspace/*.

7. **D.** The **mount -o loop ~/discimage.iso /mnt** command mounts the image file in the */mnt* directory.
8. **A, C.** Either the **umount /mnt** command or the **umount /dev/sdb1** command will unmount the partition from the filesystem.
9. **D.** The */etc/fstab* file is used to automatically mount filesystems at boot.
10. **B.** The sync option causes pending disk writes to be written immediately.
11. **A.** The **df -i** command displays a summary of inode consumption for all mounted filesystems.
12. **B.** The **tune2fs -L DATA /dev/sda1** command will set the volume label to **DATA**.
13. **D.** The **tune2fs** command with the **-c** option can be used to customize the frequency of automatic fsck checks.
14. **A.** The **mount -t iso9660 /dev/cdrom /media/dvd** command uses the correct syntax on most distributions, assuming a symbolic link named */dev/cdrom* has been created that points to */dev/sr0*.
15. **C.** The device will be referenced by */dev/sdb* because there is one other drive in the system.

CHAPTER 8

Configuring Volume Management

In this chapter, you will learn about

- Implementing logical volume management
- Creating archives and performing compression
- Enabling RAID with LVM

As filesystems grow and become larger, systems must be designed to make disk volumes manageable. Logical volumes allow administrators to create disk space without downtime, and RAID speeds data throughput and nullifies downtime by cutting the impact of disk failures. But it is still important to protect data by making duplicates called "backups."

Data compression improves data speeds through networks and reduces disk space use, thus cutting costs for organizations.

EXAM TIP Be prepared to be tested on this chapter in the Linux+ exam. About 4–6 percent of the exam questions come from this chapter.

Implementing Logical Volume Management

Logical volume management (LVM) is an option to use when partitioning Linux hard disk drives. It provides an alternative to the traditional process of creating disk partitions. Instead, volume groups are created from storage devices in the system. From the volume group, allocate space to specific logical volumes that are managed by the LVM. Instead of mounting partitions, administrators mount logical volumes at mount points in the filesystem. This provides administrators with a great deal of flexibility when allocating space on the system. For example, when a volume at */home* begins to run out of space, it is easy to reallocate space from a spare volume group and "grow" it onto */home*. That is very difficult to do with traditional disk partitions!

LVM allows adding space with no downtime. For example, to add capacity, simply install a new hard drive and then allocate its space to */home*. The size of the volume is increased on a live system without backing up and restoring data as would be done with traditional partitions.

In this part of this chapter, we're going to look at the following LVM topics:

- LVM components
- LVM configuration
- LVM snapshots
- LVM resizing
- LVM mirroring

LVM Components

LVM creates a virtual pool of memory space, called a *volume group*, from which *logical volumes* can be created. Linux uses logical volumes just like standard disk partitions created with fdisk. However, the way logical volumes are defined is quite a bit more complex. The basic structure of LVM consists of the following components:

- **Physical volumes** A physical volume can be either a partition or an entire hard disk.
- **Volume groups** A volume group consists of one or more physical volumes grouped together to form data pools. This means additional hard disks or partitions can be added to the volume group whenever more storage space is needed.
- **Logical volumes** These are defined from the volume group pool. Logical volumes can be formatted with a Linux filesystem and mounted just like physical partitions.

The way these components work together to provide storage for the Linux system is shown in Figure 8-1.

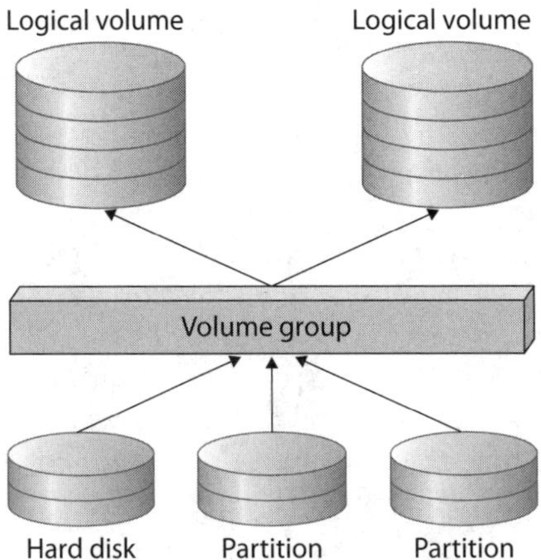

Figure 8-1 LVM components

LVM Configuration

To create and mount logical volumes, first create physical volumes, then volume groups, and finally logical volumes.

Creating LVM Physical Volumes

Disk partitions or even entire disks are physical LVM volumes. To use an existing partition, set the partition type to Linux LVM (8e) with fdisk, as shown here:

```
Command (m for help): t
Partition number (1,2, default 2): 1
Hex code (type L to list all codes): 8e
Changed type of partition 'Linux' to 'Linux LVM'
```

Once it has been determined which disks and partitions to use, run the pvcreate command at the shell prompt to define them as LVM physical volumes. The syntax is **pvcreate <device>**. In the following example, the first two partitions on */dev/sdb* are defined as physical volumes, as well as the entire */dev/sdc* hard disk:

```
openSUSE:~ # pvcreate /dev/sdb1
openSUSE:~ # pvcreate /dev/sdb2
openSUSE:~ # pvcreate /dev/sdc
```

Next, use the **pvscan -v** command to view all physical volumes on the system along with their size, as shown here:

```
openSUSE:~ # pvscan -v
   Volume Groups with the clustered attribute will be inaccessible.
   Wiping cache of LVM-capable devices
   Wiping internal VG cache
   Walking through all physical volumes
   PV /dev/sdc                          lvm2 [5.00 GiB]
   PV /dev/sdb1                         lvm2 [4.66 GiB]
   PV /dev/sdb2                         lvm2 [6.52 GiB]
   Total: 3 [16.18 GiB] / in use: 0 [0    ] / in no VG: 3 [16.18 GiB]
```

TIP If, at a later time, a hard disk drive fails, use the pvmove utility to move the data from the physical volume to be removed to another physical volume defined in the system.

Once the physical volumes are defined, volume groups can be created.

Creating LVM Volume Groups

The vgcreate utility is used to create volume groups on the system. The syntax is **vgcreate <volume_group_name> <physical_volume1> <physical_volume2> ....** In the following example, a volume group named DATA is created using the sdb1, sdb2, and sdc physical volumes:

```
openSUSE:~ # vgcreate DATA /dev/sdb1 /dev/sdb2 /dev/sdc
openSUSE:~ # pvscan -v
   Volume Groups with the clustered attribute will be inaccessible.
   Wiping cache of LVM-capable devices
   Wiping internal VG cache
   Walking through all physical volumes
   PV /dev/sdb1    VG DATA    lvm2 [4.65 GiB / 4.65 GiB free]
   PV /dev/sdb2    VG DATA    lvm2 [6.52 GiB / 6.52 GiB free]
   PV /dev/sdc     VG DATA    lvm2 [5.00 GiB / 5.00 GiB free]
   Total: 3 [16.16 GiB] / in use: 3 [16.16 GiB] / in no VG: 0 [0    ]
```

Notice in the output of the pvscan command that the three physical volumes are now members of the DATA volume group. After initially creating a volume group, use the following commands to manage it:

- vgexpand
- vgreduce
- vgremove

Once the volume group has been defined, logical volumes can be created.

NOTE Users can still use the ln command to hard link files across the volumes because a single filesystem is created with LVM. Use rm or the unlink commands to remove a hard link.

Creating LVM Logical Volumes

Use the lvcreate command to create logical volumes within a volume group. The syntax is **lvcreate -L <volume_size> -n <volume_name> <volume_group_name>**. In the following example, two 7GB volumes (named *research* and *development*, respectively) are defined from the DATA volume group:

```
openSUSE:~ # lvcreate -L 7G -n research DATA
openSUSE:~ # lvcreate -L 7G -n development DATA
openSUSE:~ # lvscan -v
   Volume Groups with the clustered attribute will be inaccessible.
   Finding all logical volumes
   ACTIVE            '/dev/DATA/research' [7.00 GiB] inherit
   ACTIVE            '/dev/DATA/development' [7.00 GiB] inherit
```

Use the lvscan command to view the logical volumes defined, as shown in the preceding example. Also notice that the two defined logical volumes are from the volume group, which itself is created by pooling together all the storage space from two disk partitions and one entire hard disk drive. Pretty cool!

To manage the logical volumes, use the following commands:

- **lvreduce** Used to reduce the size of a logical volume
- **lvremove** Used to remove a logical volume from the system

CAUTION Use extreme caution when working with lvreduce and lvremove! If the filesystem is larger than the size specified with lvreduce, there is a risk of chopping off chunks of data. The administrator should migrate any critical data to a different logical volume before using lvremove.

Once the logical volumes are complete, one can create filesystems on them and then mount them. Create a filesystem with mkfs, just as with traditional partitions, using the following syntax:

```
mkfs -t <filesystem> /dev/<volume_group>/<logical_volume>
```

Next, mount the logical volume using the mount command, just like mounting filesystems on traditional partitions. Use the following syntax:

```
mount -t <filesystem> /dev/<volume_group>/<logical_volume> /<mount_point>
```

LVM Snapshots

Linux systems run 24 hours a day, 7 days a week, making it hard to find a time in which to boot a system into single-user mode and get a clean backup. LVM snapshots allow administrators to create consistent backups on live systems, as well as allow systems to quickly revert to a clean state if corrupted after a snapshot is made.

A snapshot represents the state of a volume at the time the snapshot was taken, and it holds changes of the filesystem that occur over the life of the snapshot.

Making Snapshot Volumes

From the 2GB that are left from the DATA volume group, one can allocate snapshot space into a logical volume. Make sure to allow enough space to hold anticipated data changes; otherwise, if it gets full, the data will be lost. Use the -s flag with lvcreate to build the snapshot:

```
openSUSE:~ # lvcreate -L 1G -s -n snapshot DATA
lvcreate -- WARNING: the snapshot must be disabled if it gets full
lvcreate -- INFO: using default snapshot chunk size of 64 K for /dev/DATA
lvcreate -- doing automatic backup of "DATA"
lvcreate -- logical volume "/dev/DATA/snapshot" successfully created
```

To start using the snapshot, create a mount point to access the volume and then mount the device using the mount command:

```
openSUSE:~ # mkdir /mnt/snapshot
openSUSE:~ # mount /dev/DATA/snapshot /mnt/snapshot
mount: block device /dev/DATA/snapshot is write-protected, mounting read-only
```

To remove snapshots, use the umount and lvremove commands:

```
openSUSE:~ # umount /mnt/snapshot
openSUSE:~ # lvremove /dev/DATA/snapshot
lvremove -- do you really want to remove /dev/DATA/snapshot? [y/n]: y
lvremove -- doing automatic backup of volume group "DATA"
lvremove -- logical volume "/dev/DATA/snapshot" successfully removed
```

This will make the filesystem unavailable and remove any saved data in the snapshot.

Checking for Open Files

Although it is not necessary, some administrators feel more comfortable stopping certain jobs like databases or mail servers before engaging their snapshots. To observe which files are open for specific processes, use the **lsof** (list open files) command.

One useful option is -p. Follow this option with the process IDs monitored, and it will submit a listing of the files the process has open:

```
openSUSE:~ # lsof -p 5
COMMAND    PID USER   FD       TYPE DEVICE SIZE/OFF NODE NAME
kworker/0    5 root  cwd        DIR    8,5      260   64 /
kworker/0    5 root  rtd        DIR    8,5      260   64 /
kworker/0    5 root  txt    unknown                      /proc/5/exe
```

As disk space is utilized, there becomes less and less space for users to work. Increasing disk space in the past involved backing up the current drive, installing a larger drive, and then restoring the system—a risky process that could take an entire workday to accomplish, if nothing goes wrong.

Time and risk are reduced with logical volume management. Continuing with our current example, use lvextend to extend the current filesystem by 1GB and then use resize2fs to resize the filesystem to match, as shown here:

```
openSUSE:~ # lvextend -L +1G /dev/DATA/development
   Extending logical volume development to 8.0 GiB
   Logical volume development successfully resized
openSUSE:~ # resize2fs /dev/DATA/development
```

Creating Archives and Performing Compression

One of the key roles administrators must perform is data backups. When an organization puts thousands of hours of human effort into creating data, it is critical to secure that data. One of the best ways to do this is to copy the data to tape, disk, or cloud. This is called a "backup," and this redundant copy of data can be restored if a disaster occurs.

Hard drives have motors and other moving parts that slowly wear out over time. In fact, hard drives have a mean time between failure (MTBF) value assigned by the manufacturer. This value provides an estimate of how long a drive will last before it fails. Basically, it's not a matter of *if* a hard drive will fail; it's a matter of *when*.

There are several components to a backup plan. In this part of the chapter, we're going to discuss the following topics:

- Selecting a backup medium
- Selecting a backup strategy
- Linux backup and compression utilities

Let's begin by discussing how to select a backup medium.

Selecting a Backup Medium

Today, administrators use tape drives, hard drives, and the cloud to back up their data. Tape drives use magnetic tape to store data. They store a lot of data and are very reliable. However, they do wear out after years of use and are slower than backing up to disk.

Hard drives are cheap. An external 10TB hard drive costs less than US$300. Using external hard drives for backups has the advantage of being much faster than tape drives.

Of course, backing up to the cloud provides the benefits of high reliability and distance from the worksite. For example, if there were an earthquake at corporate headquarters, the data is protected because backups might be held continents away.

EXAM TIP The rsync utility provides a hot-backup solution over standard backups. The tool can be set up to synchronize locally or remotely at defined periods set up within cron (every hour, for example). If the main system goes down, simply switch over to the backup system.

Once the backup medium is selected, purchase the appropriate equipment and then connect and install it onto the system. Once everything is in place, define a backup strategy.

Selecting a Backup Strategy

When creating a backup plan, select a backup type and determine what to back up. First choose the backup type.

Selecting a Backup Type

Depending on the backup utility chosen, the Systems Administrator can implement at least three different types of backups:

- **Full** In a full backup, all specified files are backed up, regardless of whether or not they have been modified since the last backup. After being backed up, each file is flagged as having been backed up. This is generally the longest backup type.

- **Incremental** During an incremental backup, only the files that have been modified since the last backup (full or incremental) are backed up. After being backed up, each file is flagged as having been backed up. This is generally the fastest backup type.
- **Differential** During a differential backup, only the files that have been modified since the last full backup are backed up. Even though they have been backed up during a differential backup, the files involved are *not* flagged as having been backed up.

Running a full backup every time is thorough but exhaustive. However, it is the fastest to restore.

Many administrators mix full with incremental or differential backups to take advantage of the speed benefits. The restore order is important, so wise administrators label their backups with the date, order, and type of backup.

Finally, make sure to verify backups. Most backup utilities provide the option of checking backups after completion.

Determining What to Back Up

One option is to back up the entire system. This is safe but slow due to the sheer amount of data involved. Instead, prioritize backing up only critical data only, such as user data and configuration files. The theory behind this strategy is that in the event of a disaster, simply reinstall a new system and then restore the critical data. Consider backing up these important directories:

- /etc
- /home
- /root
- /var

Notice that this strategy doesn't back up Linux or its utilities. Instead, it only backs up configuration files, user data, log files, and Web/FTP files.

Linux Backup and Compression Utilities

When working with Linux, there are a host of different utilities for conducting backups. Many come with the operating system; others can be obtained from third parties. For the Linux+ exam, be familiar with the tools that are common to most distributions and run them from the shell prompt. The following topics are covered in this part of the chapter:

- Using gzip, bzip2, zip, and xz for compression
- Using tar and cpio for backups
- Using dd for disk cloning

Using gzip, bzip2, zip, and xz for Compression

Compression is used to help save space on hard drives and speed traffic through a network. In both cases, a minimized representation of the real data is saved or sent and then converted back to real data for processing.

```
openSUSE:~ # ls a.txt b.txt c.txt
a.txt        b.txt        c.txt
openSUSE:~ # gzip a.txt ; bzip2 b.txt ; xz c.txt
openSUSE:~ # ls a.txt.* b.txt.* c.txt.*
a.txt.gz     b.txt.bz2    c.txt.xz
```

The gzip, bzip2, zip, and xz utilities are installed by default on most Linux versions, with gzip being the most popular compression tool because it has been available the longest. The bzip2 tool provides even better compression than gzip, but requires more memory to perform the task. The xz program provides even better compression but is not as widely used.

Users can use the gunzip, bunzip, and unxz utilities to decompress their compressed files. The zip application provides the best support to compress and decompress to and from Microsoft Windows systems. Use the -r flag with zip and follow it with the name of the file to compress, as shown here to compress the *d.txt* file:

```
openSUSE:~ # zip -r d d.txt
openSUSE:~ # ls d.*
d.txt        d.zip
```

Use the unzip utility to decompress the zip file back to the normal state.

Using tar and cpio for Backup

The tar utility has been around for a very long time and is a commonly used backup tool. The acronym "tar" stands for tape archive. The tar utility takes a list of specified files and copies them into a single archive file (.tar). The .tar file can then be compressed with the gzip utility on the Linux system, resulting in a file with a .tar.gz or .tgz extension. This is called a *tarball.*

The tar utility can be used to send backup jobs to a variety of backup media, including tape drives and removable hard disk drives. The syntax for using tar to create backups is **tar -cvf <filename> <directory>**. The -c option tells tar to create a new archive. The -v option tells tar to work in verbose mode, displaying each file being backed up onscreen. The -f option specifies the name of the tar archive to be created.

For example, to create a backup of the */home* directory and name it backup.tar on an external USB hard drive mounted in */media/usb*, enter **tar -cvf /media/usb/backup.tar /home**, as shown in this example:

```
openSUSE:/ # tar -cvf /media/usb/backup.tar /home
tar: Removing leading '/' from member names
/home/
/home/tux/
/home/tux/.gftp/
```

```
/home/tux/.gftp/gftp.log
/home/tux/.gftp/bookmarks
/home/tux/.gftp/gftprc
/home/tux/.nautilus/
/home/tux/.local/
/home/tux/.local/share/
...
```

Notice in this example that the message `tar: Removing leading '/' from member names` is displayed. When a tar archive is created, absolute paths are converted to relative paths by default to simplify restores (for example, restoring to a different location). As a result, the leading / is removed.

NOTE The tar utility was created before subscripts became popular, so when making a tarfile, the user must add .tar in order for the file to be recognized as a tarfile.

Other tar options are shown in Table 8-1.

To back up to a tape drive, replace the <filename> parameter with the device name for the tape drive. On most distributions, the first SCSI or SATA tape drive in the system is referenced as */dev/st0* (that is, letter *s*, letter *t*, digit zero). Therefore, enter **tar -cvf /dev/st0 /home** to run the same backup as in the previous example, but send it to a tape drive instead.

To restore a tar archive, simply enter **tar -xvf <filename>**. For example, to extract the archive created, enter **tar -xvf /media/usb/backup.tar**. This will extract the archive into the current working directory.

The cpio utility can also be used to make archive files like tar.

Option	Function
-c --create	Create a new archive file.
-J --xz	Do one of two things. During archive creation, these options compress the new tar archive by running it through the xz utility. During extraction, they first decompress the tar archive using the xz utility.
-t --list	List the contents of an archive file.
-x --extract	Extract files from an archive.
-z --gzip --gunzip	Do one of two things. During archive creation, these options compress the new tar archive by running it through the gzip utility. During extraction, they first decompress the tar archive using the gunzip utility.
-j --bzip2 --bunzip	Do one of two things. During archive creation, these options compress the new tar archive by running it through the bzip2 utility. During extraction, they first decompresses the tar archive using the bunzip2 utility.

Table 8-1 The tar Command Options

For example, to back up multiple files in the current directory, use the -o option to write the data "out" to a file:

```
openSUSE:/ # ls z.txt y.txt x.txt | cpio -ov > /media/usb/backup.cpio
```

To restore files from a cpio archive, run **cpio** from the shell prompt using the -i option to read files "in." For example, to extract the archive just created, enter the following:

```
openSUSE:/tmp # cpio -iv < /media/usb/backup.cpio
x.txt
y.txt
z.txt
341 blocks
```

Like tar, cpio does not compress the archive by default. Use zip, gzip, bzip2, or xz to compress the archive after it has been created with cpio.

NOTE The previous examples were done on a USB drive, but high-security organizations discourage USB drives because it is easier for an insider threat to exfiltrate confidential data.

Using dd for Disk Cloning

The dd command is a great command for copying files, the master boot record (MBR), filesystems, and entire disk drives.

To copy a file with dd, use the syntax **dd if=<input_file> of=<output_file>**. Here's an example:

```
openSUSE:/ # dd if=./e.txt of=./e.bak
29+1 records in
29+1 records out
15112 bytes (15 kB) copied, 0.000263331 s, 57.4 MB/s
```

The dd command allows administrators to perform drive cloning.

To copy an entire partition or drive, enter **dd if=<device_file> of=<output_file>** at the shell prompt. The device file of the partition is used as the input file. All the contents of the partition are written to the output file specified. In the example that follows, the dd command is used to copy the entire hard drive, */dev/sda*, to an identical or larger hard drive:

```
openSUSE:/ # dd if=/dev/sda of=/dev/sdb bs=1024
dd: writing to '/dev/sdb':
7500249+0 records in
7500248+0 records out
3840126976 bytes (3.8 GB) copied, 108.441 s, 35.4 MB/s
```

The dd command can even create an image file of an entire hard disk. Again, the syntax is **dd if=<device_file> of=<output_file>**. The difference is that administrator simply specify the device file of the hard disk itself instead of a partition. In the next example, the entire */dev/sdb* hard drive is archived into the *drivebackup* file:

```
openSUSE:~ # dd if=/dev/sdc of=/mnt/bigdrive/drivebackup
16777216+0 records in
16777216+0 records out
8589934592 bytes (8.6 GB) copied, 157.931 s, 54.4 MB/s
```

Another useful feature of dd is that it can create a backup copy of the hard drive's MBR and partition table. The syntax is **dd if=<device_file> of=<output_file> bs=512 count=1**. This tells dd to grab just the first 512-byte block of the hard drive, which is where the MBR and partition table reside. This is shown in the following example:

```
openSUSE:/tmp # dd if=/dev/sda of=/root/mbrbackup bs=512 count=1
1+0 records in
1+0 records out
512 bytes (512 B) copied, 0.0123686 s, 41.4 kB/s
```

EXAM TIP The MBR is the first 512 bytes of the hard drive, which bootstraps the GRUB bootloader, which in turn bootstraps the kernel. The partition table, which defines the hard drive layout, is part of the MBR and starts at byte 440. To back up the MBR sans the partition table, run **dd if=/dev/sda of=/dev/sdb bs=440 count=1**.

Exercise 8-1: Backing Up Data

In Exercise 8-1, practice data backups. Perform this exercise using the virtual machine provided online.

VIDEO Please watch the Exercise 8-1 video for a demonstration on how to perform this task.

Complete the following steps:

1. With the system up and running, open a terminal session.
2. Change to the root user account by entering the **su -** command.
3. Enter **tar -cvf ./backup.tar /home** at the shell prompt.
4. Enter **ls** and then verify that the backup file exists.
5. Change to the */tmp* directory by entering **cd /tmp** at the shell prompt.
6. Enter **tar -xvf /root/backup.tar** to extract the tar file to the current directory.
7. Use the **ls** command to verify that the files from the tar archive were extracted to the current directory.
8. Enter **exit** to switch back to the standard user account.

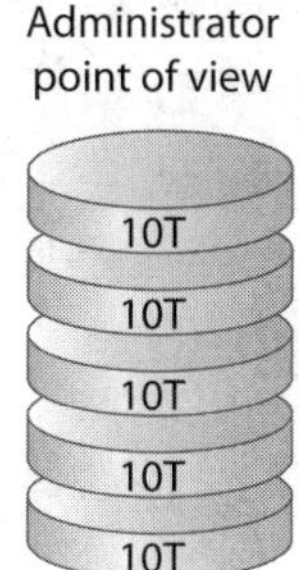

Figure 8-2
RAID 0 setup vs. user perspective

Enabling RAID with LVM

RAID stands for Redundant Array of Independent Disks and allows administrators to create filesystems over multiple hard drives. For example, an administrator can combine five 10TB hard drives and make them appear to users as a single 50TB hard drive. This is called RAID 0 (zero) or *striping*. RAID 0 provides superior data performance, as these drives can read and write striped data at the same time. The best applications include streaming media. The downside is that if a hard drive fails, the entire system fails and needs to be recovered from backup archives. See Figure 8-2 for the RAID 0 setup.

Other RAID concepts provide superior reliability. RAID 1 (one) offers the best in reliability because it clones or mirrors devices. On a hot-backup system, if a hard drive fails, it can be swapped with a good hard drive while the system is operating, thus allowing systems to run 24/7. The "insurance" is expensive because every hard drive requires a backup, so five 10TB hard drives will have a duplicate of five 10TB hard drives. See Figure 8-3 for the RAID 1 setup.

RAID 5 offers reliability at a much lower cost than RAID 1. Instead of duplicating all the hard drives, RAID 5 adds a single hard drive that calculates parity. When a drive dies on a hot-backup system, the administrator swaps it out with a good hard drive, and the system continues to operate. Unlike RAID 1, if two drives fail at the same time, the system fails and needs to be recovered with backups from tapes or the cloud. See Figure 8-4 for the RAID 5 setup.

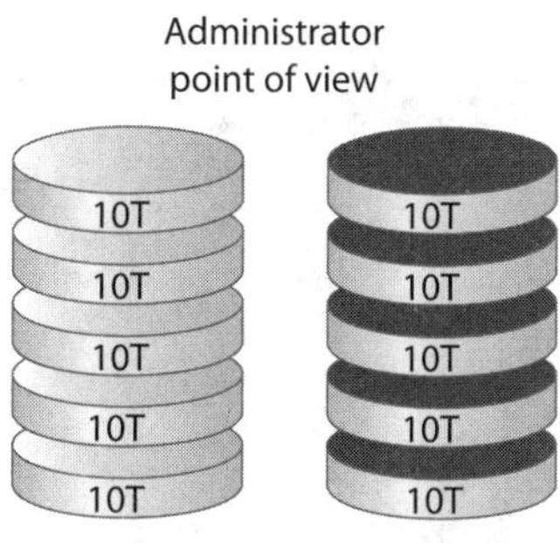

Figure 8-3
RAID 1 setup vs. user perspective

Figure 8-4 RAID 5 setup vs. user perspective

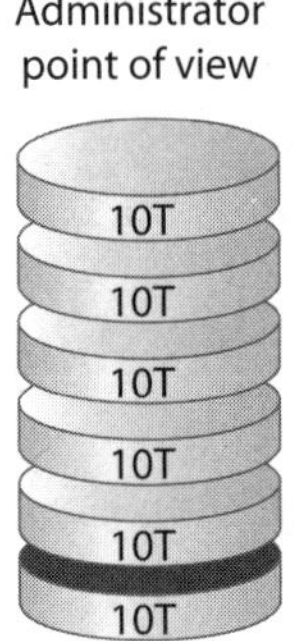

RAID 6 improves reliability over RAID 5 by providing an additional parity drive so that if two hard drives fail at the same time, the system can quickly recover by swapping in two good hard drives. The downside of RAID 5 and RAID 6 are performance. Performance is lost because the systems have to calculate parity. See Figure 8-5 for the RAID 6 setup.

RAID 1+0 (or RAID 10) provides administrators a balance between the reliability of RAID 1 and the performance of RAID 0. Figure 8-6 displays this setup, which combines the RAID 1 technique of mirroring each set of data with the RAID 0 technique of concatenating the data. RAID 10 requires much more hardware, but the uptime is tremendous.

Next, we look at the following RAID topics:

- Software RAID configuration
- Verifying RAID status

EXAM TIP Other RAID systems weigh differently on reliability and performance, such as RAID 3 and RAID 4, but knowledge of RAID 0, 1, 5, 6, and 10 are the only versions mentioned on the Linux+ exam.

Figure 8-5 RAID 6 setup vs. user perspective

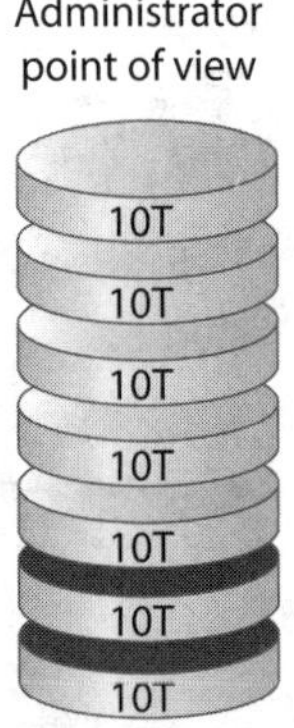

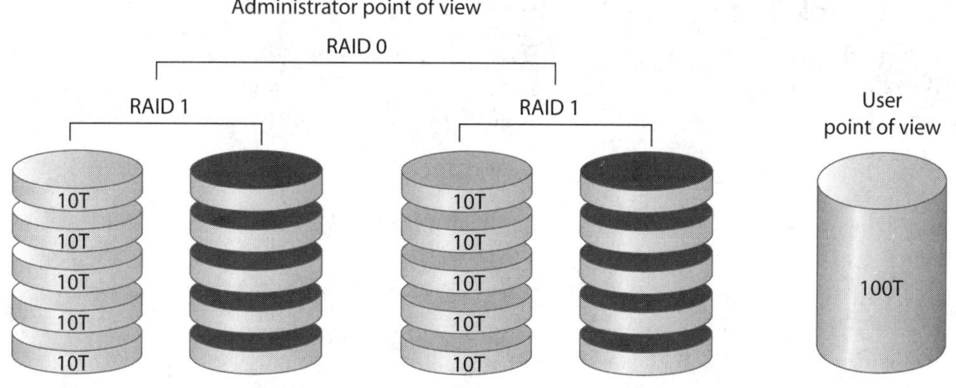

Figure 8-6 RAID 10 setup vs. user perspective

Software RAID Configuration

Of course, there are hardware RAID solutions, but to create any RAID system using Linux LVM starts with selecting the hard drives that will form the solution and then using the mdadm command to create the RAID device, as shown here:

```
openSUSE:~ # mdadm -C /dev/md0 --level=1 --raid-disks=2 /dev/sdb /dev/sdc
```

The preceding meta-device administration command uses -C to create a new meta-device called */dev/md0* at a RAID 1 level, which is disk mirroring. This system will use only two hard drives, */dev/sdb* and */dev/sdc*, as defined by --raid-disks.

Once the RAID 1 meta-device is created, treat it like any other filesystem. That is, create the filesystem and then mount it onto an empty directory. To make the filesystem permanent at boot time, update the */etc/fstab* file:

```
openSUSE:~ # mkfs.ext4 /dev/md0
mke2fs 1.42.9 (28-Dec-2013)
Filesystem label=
OS type: Linux
Block size=1024 (log=0)
Fragment size=1024 (log=0)
Stride=0 blocks, Stripe width=0 blocks
62744 inodes, 250880 blocks
12544 blocks (5.00%) reserved for the super user
First data block=1
Maximum filesystem blocks=33816576
31 block groups
8192 blocks per group, 8192 fragments per group
2024 inodes per group
...
openSUSE:~ # mkdir /raidone
openSUSE:~ # mount /dev/md0 /raidone
```

Verifying RAID Status

To verify the status of the running RAID system, again use the mdadm command. The mdmonitor service provides RAID monitoring and management. To get details of the current setup, including the devices and description of the array, use the --detail option with mdadm or view the */proc/mdstat* file:

```
openSUSE:~ # mdadm --detail /dev/md0
/dev/md0:
           Version : 1.2
     Creation Time : Wed Mar 27 10:48:01 2025
        Raid Level : raid1
        Array Size : 250880 (245.00 MiB 256.90 MB)
     Used Dev Size : 250880 (245.00 MiB 256.90 MB)
      Raid Devices : 2
     Total Devices : 2
       Persistence : Superblock is persistent
       Update Time : Wed Mar 27 10:48:04 2025
             State : clean
    Active Devices : 2
   Working Devices : 2
    Failed Devices : 0
     Spare Devices : 0
...
openSUSE:~ # less /proc/mdstat
Personalities : [raid1]
md0 : active raid1 sdc[1] sdb[0]
250880 blocks super 1.2 [2/2] [UU]
unused devices: <none>
openSUSE:~ # mdadm --detail /dev/md0 --scan » /etc/mdadm.conf
```

The */etc/mdadm.conf* configuration file created assembles RAID arrays properly after reboots and simplifies the description of the devices and arrays.

Use the mdadm command to manage hot spares; for example, **mdadm --fail** will mark the drive as faulty and prepare it for removal with the **mdadm --remove** command. After the hard drive has been physically removed and replaced, reenable it using **mdadm --add**. If the new device is part of the failed array, it will be used as part of RAID; otherwise, the drive will be seen as an available hot spare.

Exercise 8-2: RAID and Logical Volumes

In Exercise 8-2, practice using RAID and LVM. Perform this exercise using the virtual machine provided online.

To conduct this exercise, create four additional virtual hard drives within the hypervisor. To do this with VirtualBox, shut down the virtual Linux system, click Details in the upper right, and then click Storage (about halfway down in the Oracle VM VirtualBox Manager). See the following illustration.

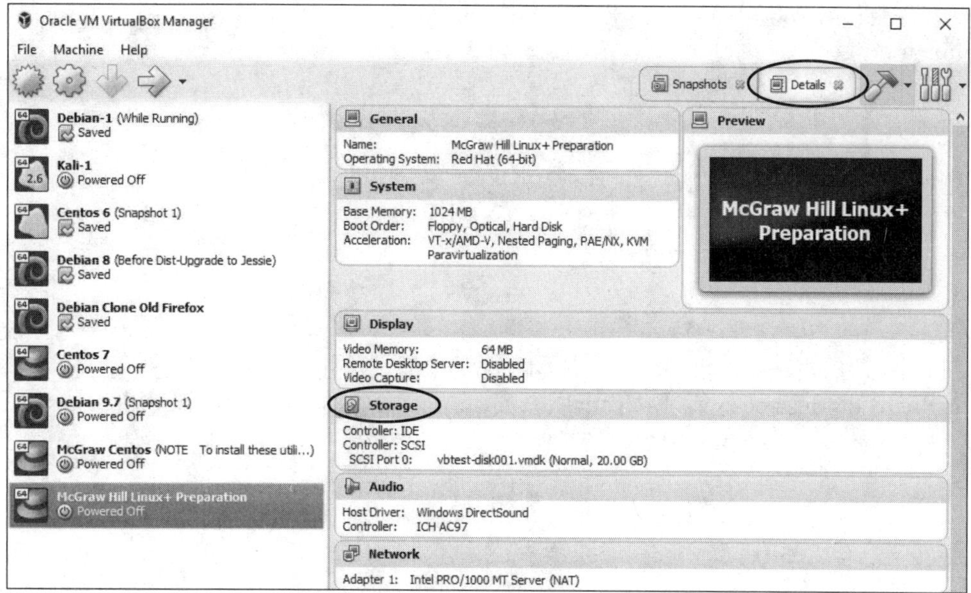

Click Controller: SCSI and then click the square icon just to the right with the green plus sign, as shown here.

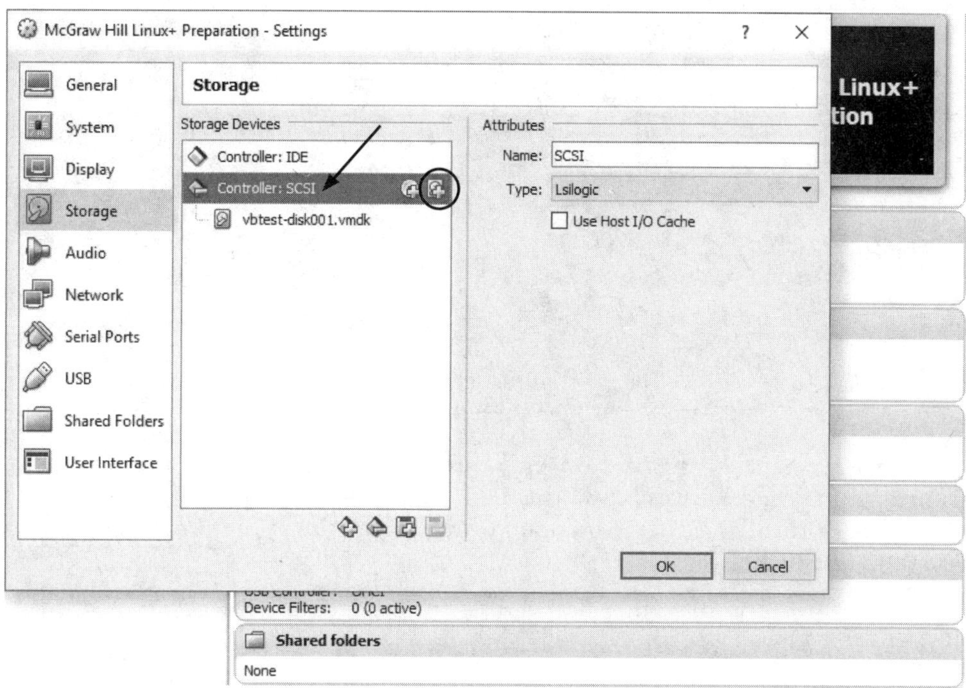

In the Virtualbox Question dialog box that appears, choose Create New Disk, as shown next.

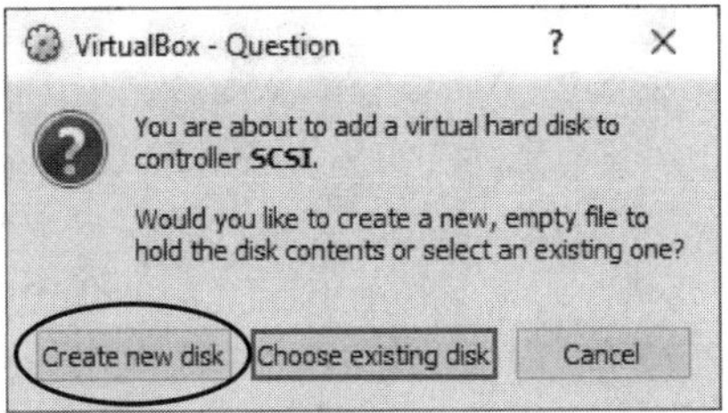

The next window will ask you which type of file you'd like to use for the new virtual hard disk. Choose VDI (VirtualBox Disk Image), as shown next, and then choose Dynamically Allocated in the next window.

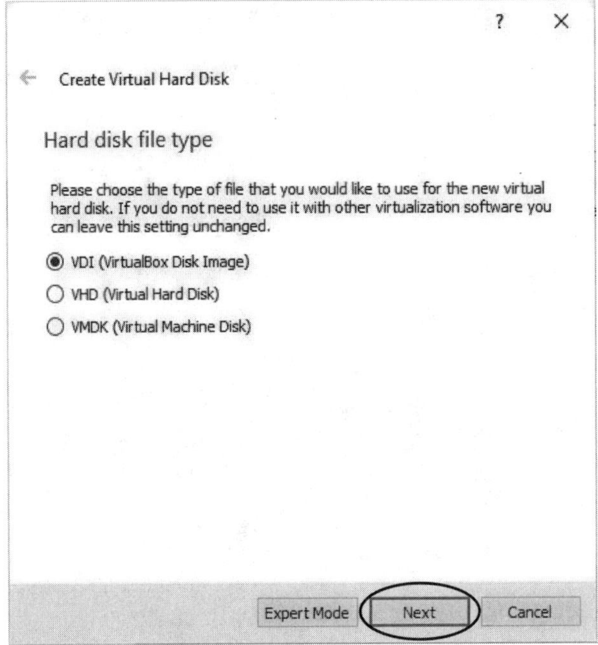

Change the name of the hard drive. For example, in the following illustration, we named our first hard drive as NewVirtualDisk10. The next hard drive we create will be named NewVirtualDisk11, and so on, up to 13. Set the size of the virtual hard disk to 256.0MB and click Create.

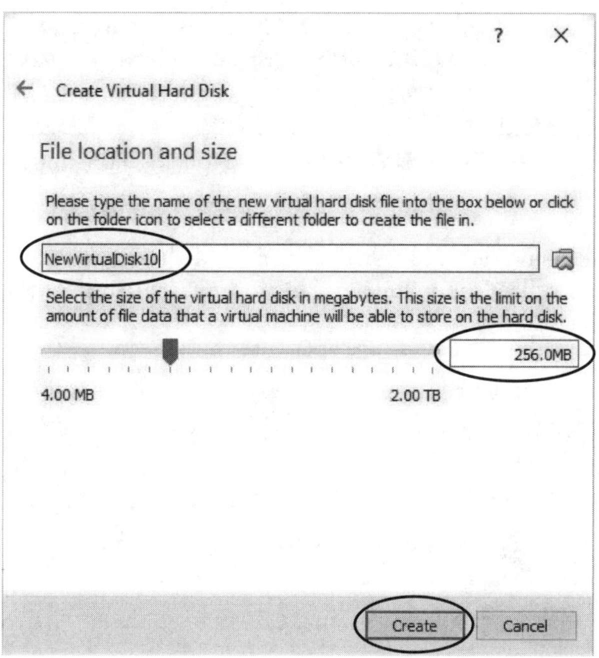

Repeat the steps to create a new disk until you have a total of *four additional 256MB virtual hard drives*. Click OK in the Storage Settings to finalize creation of the hard drive. The following illustration displays the final results; you should see your new hard drive added to the virtual machine. Power on the system to complete the next lab.

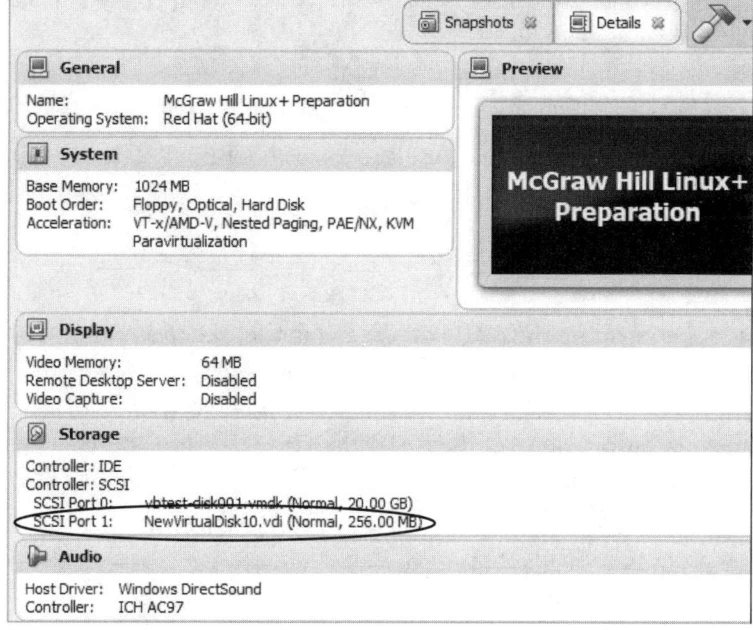

If you get an error during this process, it likely has to do with a naming conflict. Make sure the new hard drive name is different from earlier names. *Remember to take a snapshot of the virtual machine before starting the lab.*

VIDEO Please watch the Exercise 8-2 video for a demonstration on how to perform this task.

Once you have your four additional virtual hard drives using the virtual machine provided online, complete the following steps to practice using RAID and LVM:

1. With the system up and running, open a terminal session.
2. Change to the root user account by entering the **su -** command.
3. Convert two of the hard drives into physical volumes for LVM by running the following command:
   ```
   pvcreate /dev/sda10 ; pvcreate /dev/sda11 ; pvdisplay
   ```
4. Create the volume group called *labvg* using the default extent size:
   ```
   vgcreate labvg /dev/sda10 /dev/sda11 ; vgdisplay
   ```
5. Create a 200MB logical volume called *lablvm* from the new volume group:
   ```
   lvcreate -L 200M -n lablvm ; lvdisplay
   ```
6. Create the filesystem and mount it onto a new empty directory. Display the new logical volume settings using **lvdisplay**:
   ```
   mkfs.ext4 /dev/labvg/lablvm ; mkdir /lablvm
   mount /dev/labvg/lablvm /lablvm
   lvdisplay
   ```
7. Observe how much disk space is available using the **df -h** command. Resize the logical volume to 300MB:
   ```
   df -h
   lvresize -r -L 300M /dev/labvg/lablvm
   df -h
   ```
8. There is still not enough space. Add another 100MB:
   ```
   lvresize -r -L +100M /dev/labvg/lablvm
   df -h
   ```
9. Create a RAID 1 mirror using **mdadm**:
   ```
   mdadm -C /dev/md0 --level=1 --raid-disks=2 /dev/sda12 /dev/sda13
   ```
10. Create a filesystem on the RAID device and mount the filesystem:
    ```
    mkfs.ext4 /dev/md0 ; mkdir /labraid ; mount /dev/md0 /labraid
    ```
11. Save the meta-device settings into */etc/mdadm.conf* to be observed at boot time and then review the status of the RAID device:
    ```
    mdadm --detail --scan » /etc/mdadm.conf
    mdadm --detail
    cat /proc/mdstat
    ```

12. To mount the new LVM and RAID devices at boot time, add the entries to */etc/fstab*:

```
echo /dev/md0  /labraid ext4  defaults    0 0 » /etc/fstab
echo /dev/labvg/lablvm  /lablvm  ext4 defaults  0 0 » /etc/fstab
```

13. Enter **exit** to switch back to the standard user account.

Chapter Review

Logical volume management provides a solution to easily grow a filesystem while in use, and it eases archiving because of its snapshot capability. Physical volumes such as partitions are pooled together into volume groups. This data pool, or "volume group," can be divided into logical volumes. The logical volumes are formatted into filesystems. Instead of mounting partitions, logical volumes are mounted onto directories in the filesystem.

Administrators must conduct backups on a regular schedule: selecting a backup medium and backup strategy, and then implementing with backup and compression utilities.

Software RAID systems are a feature of logical volume management. RAID systems can be designed for performance (for example, RAID 0) or for data reliability (for example, RAID 1). To balance cost, reliability, and performance, RAID 5 and RAID 6 were implemented. For the best in reliability and performance, implement RAID 10.

Here are some key facts to remember about volume management:

- LVM enables administrators to dynamically add space to the system.
- To create LVM storage, use the following process:
  - Create physical volumes with the pvcreate command.
  - Create a volume group using the vgcreate command.
  - Create logical volumes using the lvcreate command.
- Use the lsof command at the shell prompt to display a list of open files.
- The -p option displays the PIDs of processes using specified files or filesystems.
- Backup medium choices include tape drives, removable hard drives, and/or the cloud.
- Administrators must select a backup strategy, such as full, incremental, or differential backups. Administrators combine them to design a backup strategy.
- Full backups back up everything and flag the files as having been backed up.
- Incremental backups back up everything that has been modified since the last full or incremental backup and flag the files as having been backed up.
- Differential backups back up everything that has been backed up since the last full backup. However, they don't flag the files as having been backed up.
- Rotate the backup media and verify the backup.

- Commonly backed-up filesystems include */etc*, */home*, */root*, and */var*.
- The tar and cpio utilities work with most backup media.
- The dd utility can copy an entire partition or even clone an entire hard drive.
- RAID 0, also known as striping, is designed for performance and not reliability.
- RAID 1 is known as mirroring and is designed for reliability.
- RAID 5 offers reliability by maintaining a single-parity drive.
- RAID 6 offers reliability by maintaining a dual-parity drive system.
- Use the mdadm command to configure, maintain, and monitor RAID.
  Use the --fail, --remove, and --add options to mark devices as faulty, removed, or added, respectively.

Questions

1. Which type of backup backs up all files modified since the last full backup and does not flag the files as having been backed up?
   A. Full
   B. Incremental
   C. Differential
   D. Partial
2. Create a backup of */etc* to a removable hard disk drive mounted at */mnt/USB*. Which tar command will do this?
   A. tar -cfv /mnt/USB/backup.tar /etc
   B. tar -xfv ~/backup.tar /etc
   C. tar -xzf /mnt/USB/backup.tar /etc
   D. tar -cfv /mnt/USB/backup.tar ~/etc
3. Which command will create a compressed cpio archive of all the files in the *Projects* directory within the user's home directory to */mnt/usbdrive/Projectsbackup.cpio.gz*?
   A. cpio -ov ~/Projects | gzip > /mnt/usbdrive/Projectsbackup.cpio.gz
   B. ls ~/Projects | cpio -ovz | > /mnt/usbdrive/Projectsbackup.cpio.gz
   C. ls ~/Projects | cpio -ov | gzip > /mnt/usbdrive/Projectsbackup.cpio.gz
   D. cpio -ovz ~/Projects > /mnt/usbdrive/Projectsbackup.cpio.gz
4. Which command can be used to create an image of the */dev/sda2* partition in the */mnt/usb/volback* file?
   A. dd if=/dev/sda2 of=/mnt/usb/volback
   B. cp /dev/sda2 /mnt/usb/volback
   C. dd if=/mnt/usb/volback of=/dev/sda2
   D. dd if=/dev/sda of=/mnt/usb/volback

5. Create a new GPT partition on the */dev/sdc* hard disk drive. After running **gdisk /dev/sdc** at the shell prompt, which command will create a new partition that is 100GB in size?

 A. n

 B. p

 C. new -size=100G

 D. t

6. After adding a third 1TB solid state drive (SSD) to a Linux server, it needs to be added as storage space to an LVM volume group named DATA on the system. Which command should be entered first to do this?

 A. vgexpand DATA /dev/sdc

 B. pvscan /dev/sdc DATA

 C. pvcreate /dev/sdc

 D. lvextend -L 1T -n DATA

7. Fill in the blank with the option to create a snapshot. (Choose two.)

 lvcreate -L 1G ____ -n snapshot DATA

 A. --clone

 B. -s

 C. --snapshot

 D. --snap

8. Which RAID system has two additional hard drives for parity?

 A. RAID 0

 B. RAID 1

 C. RAID 5

 D. RAID 6

9. Which commands will extend a logical volume filesystem from 500MB to 1000MB? (Choose two.)

 A. lvextend -L +500 /dev/lvm1

 B. lvextend -L +500M /dev/lvm1

 C. lvextend -L 1000 /dev/lvm1

 D. lvextend -L 1000M /dev/lvm1

10. Which command will compress files by default?

 A. tar

 B. cpio

 C. dd

 D. xz

Answers

1. **C.** A differential backup backs up all files modified since the last full backup and does not flag the files as having been backed up.
2. **A.** The **tar -cfv /mnt/USB/backup.tar /etc** command uses the correct syntax.
3. **C.** The **ls ~/Projects | cpio -ov | gzip > /mnt/usbdrive/Projectsbackup.cpio.gz** command will generate a listing of files in the *Projects* directory, send the list to the cpio command to create an archive, and send the archive to gzip for compression.
4. **A.** The **dd if=/dev/sda2 of=/mnt/usb/volback** command creates an image of the */dev/sda2* partition in the */mnt/usb/volback* file.
5. **A.** Within gdisk, type **n** to create a new partition. After doing so, the user is prompted to specify its size.
6. **C.** Before allocating space from a storage device to a volume group, first define it as an LVM physical volume. In this scenario, use the **pvcreate /dev/sdc** command.
7. **B, C.** The -s and --snapshot options create a snapshot with the lvcreate command.
8. **D.** RAID 6 has two additional hard drives for parity. (RAID 0 provides concatenation. RAID 1 provides mirroring. RAID 5 uses a single drive for parity.)
9. **B, D.** The lvextend command will extend a logical volume, and answers B and D show the correct syntax.
10. **D.** The xz command will compress files. The other options only archive data by default.

CHAPTER 9

Managing Linux Processes

In this chapter, you will learn about

- Understanding Linux processes
- Managing processes
- Scheduling processes

In this chapter, the candidate will learn how the Linux operating system handles executable programs and running scripts. Also, the reader will learn how to manage executables while they run on the system.

EXAM TIP For the Linux+ exam, become very familiar with how Linux handles running processes. Know how to use shell commands to view processes running on the system, and how to run processes in the foreground and background. Also, understand how to kill a process from the command line, and automate jobs using utilities "at" and "cron."

Understanding Linux Processes

The key to being able to effectively manage Linux processes is to first understand how processes function within the operating system. So, what exactly is a process? For our purposes, a *process* is a program that has been loaded from a long-term storage device, usually a hard disk drive, into system RAM and is currently being processed by the CPU on the motherboard.

Many different types of programs can be executed to create a process. On the Linux system, the types of programs listed in Table 9-1 can be loaded into RAM and executed by the CPU.

Remember that the Linux operating system can run many processes "concurrently" on a single CPU. Depending on how the Linux system is being used, it may have only a few processes or hundreds of processes running concurrently.

In the preceding paragraph, the term *concurrently* is in quotes because single-core CPUs cannot run multiple processes at the same time. Instead, Linux quickly switches between various processes running on the CPU, making it appear as if multiple processes run concurrently. However, the CPU actually only executes a single process at a time.

Type of Program	Description
Binary executables	These are programs that were originally created as a text file using a programming language such as C or C++. The text file was then run through a compiler, which converts the text language into machine language. This final binary file is processed by the CPU.
Internal shell commands	Some of the commands entered at the shell prompt are actual binary files in the filesystem that are loaded and run by the CPU. For example, entering **rm** at the shell prompt will load the rm binary into memory. Other commands, however, are not binary executables. Instead, they are rolled into a shell program itself, like the "bash" shell. For example, when entering **exit** at a shell prompt, it actually runs an internal shell command. There is no executable file in the filesystem named "exit."
Shell scripts	These are text files that are interpreted through the shell itself. They include commands to run binary executables within the text of any shell script. More details on shell scripts coming in Chapter 13.

Table 9-1 Linux Programs That Can Create Processes

All other processes currently "running" wait in the background for their turn. Linux maintains a schedule that determines when each process is allowed access to the CPU, called *multitasking*. Because the switching between processes happens so fast, it appears to the user that the CPU is executing multiple processes at the same time.

For true concurrency, consider either a multicore or hyperthreading CPU. Multicore CPUs can actually execute more than one process at a time because each core in the processor package is a separate CPU. Hyperthreading CPUs are designed such that a single processor can run more than one process at a time.

User Versus System Processes

The Linux operating system uses several types of processes. Some processes are created by the end user when they execute a command from the shell prompt or through the graphical interface. These processes are called *user processes*. User processes are usually associated with some kind of end-user program running on the system.

To view processes, the end user simply runs the ps (process status) command, as shown here:

```
cgreer@openSUSE:~> ps -a
 PID TTY          TIME CMD
28041 pts/0    00:00:00 ps
```

ps lists process IDs (PIDs), the terminal they are running within (TTY), how long the process has been running in CPU time (TIME), and the process command (CMD). In this example, we see one process: the ps user process.

The key point to remember about user processes is that they are called from within a shell and are associated with that shell session.

However, not all processes running on the system are user processes. In fact, most processes executing on a given Linux system will probably be of a different type, called *system processes* or *daemons*. Unlike a user process, a system process (usually) does not provide an application or an interface for an end user to use. Instead, it is used to provide a system service, such as a web server, an FTP server, a file service such as Samba, a print service such as CUPS, or a logging service. Such processes run in the background and usually don't provide any kind of user interface.

For example, consider the processes shown in Figure 9-1 when the end user executes the **ps -e** command. The figure is only showing a few lines of the output, but the -e option will display every process running on the system, not only the end-user processes.

NOTE Most system processes (but not all of them) are noted with a letter *d* at the end of the name, which stands for daemon. The system has many system processes running, and these are generally loaded after the kernel is booted; therefore, they are not associated with a shell. User processes are tied to the shell instance they were called from, but system processes are not.

By default, most Linux distributions boot with many daemons configured to automatically start at boot. Some of these daemons are critical to the overall function of the system; others are not.

```
rtracy@openSUSE:~
File  Edit  View  Search  Terminal  Help
27290 ?        00:00:00 evolution-sourc
27309 ?        00:00:00 evolution-alarm
27310 ?        00:00:05 tracker-store
27312 ?        00:00:00 deja-dup-monito
27331 ?        00:00:00 tracker-miner-f
27340 ?        00:00:00 evolution-calen
27347 ?        00:00:02 vmtoolsd
27373 ?        00:00:02 libsocialweb-co
27376 ?        00:00:00 obexd
27413 ?        00:00:00 gvfsd-burn
27437 ?        00:00:00 gvfsd-metadata
27501 ?        00:00:02 kworker/u4:2
27649 ?        00:00:00 kworker/1:0
27756 ?        00:00:02 gnome-terminal-
27766 ?        00:00:00 gnome-pty-helpe
27767 pts/0    00:00:00 bash
27913 pts/0    00:00:00 oosplash
27935 pts/0    00:00:05 soffice.bin
27995 ?        00:00:00 sshd
27998 ?        00:00:00 sshd
27999 pts/2    00:00:00 bash
28042 ?        00:00:00 kworker/1:1
28071 pts/0    00:00:00 ps
rtracy@openSUSE:~>
```

Figure 9-1 System processes

When implementing a new Linux system, whether as a server or as a workstation, it is wise to turn off all the daemons that are not needed. Running unnecessary daemons consumes system resources, such as memory and CPU time. More seriously, unnecessary daemons can also open up gaping security holes. Be aware of which system services are running. If the service is needed, keep it. If not, get rid of it!

How Linux Processes Are Loaded

All Linux process are loaded by one single process—either called the legacy "init" or the newer "systemd," depending on the distribution—that is started by the Linux kernel when the system boots. Understand that any process running on a Linux system can launch additional processes. The process that launched the new process is called the *parent process*. The new process itself is called the *child process*.

This parent/child relationship constitutes the *heredity* of Linux processes, as shown in Figure 9-2.

In Figure 9-2, the first parent process spawned three child processes. Each of these three child processes then spawned child processes of their own.

For any process on a Linux system, you need to be able to uniquely identify it as well as its heredity. Whenever a process is created on a Linux system, it is assigned two resources:

- **Process ID (PID) number** This is a number assigned to each process that uniquely identifies it on the system.
- **Parent Process ID (PPID) number** This is the PID of the process's parent process (that is, the process that spawned it).

By assigning these two numbers to each process, you can track the heredity of any process through the system. The Linux kernel uses the process table to keep track of the processes running on the system. The process table is maintained in memory by the operating system to facilitate switching between processes, scheduling processes, and

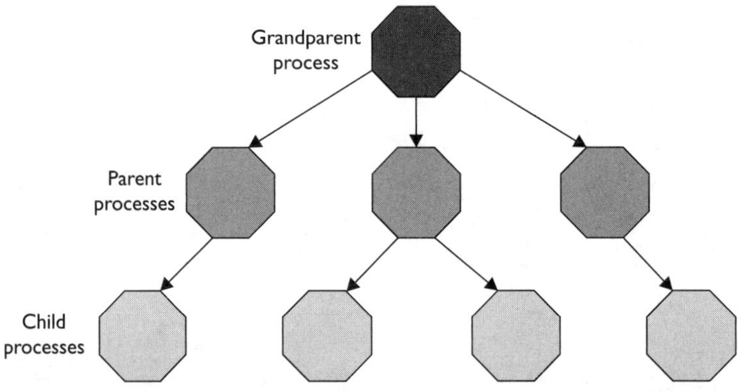

Figure 9-2 Generations of processes

prioritizing processes. Each entry in the table contains information about one specific running process, such as the process name, the state of the process, the priority of the process, and the memory addresses used by the process.

Notice in Figure 9-2 the "grandparent" process that spawned all the other processes. This figure is drawn conceptually to illustrate the nature of the parent/child relationships between processes. However, it also can be used to describe the hierarchy of generations in a Linux system. There really is a "grandparent" process that spawns all other processes. This is either the legacy init process or the modern systemd process (depending on the distribution).

NOTE Older distributions still use SysVinit or init. Modern Linux releases have migrated to systemd, which is the recommended choice today for security and performance. For the Linux+ exam, be familiar with both because in the real world, organizations use both.

The kernel loads the systemd or init process automatically during bootup. The systemd or init process then launches child processes, such as a login shell, that in turn launch other processes, such as that used by the vi utility, as shown in Figure 9-3.

Whereas other processes are assigned a PID randomly from the operating system's table of available PID numbers, the systemd or init process is always assigned a PID of 1. This brings up an interesting point. If the systemd or init process is the first process from which all other processes descend, what then is its PPID? Does it even have one? Actually, it does. Because the systemd or init process is launched directly by the Linux kernel (which always has a PID of 0), the PPID of the systemd process is always 0. This is shown in Figure 9-4.

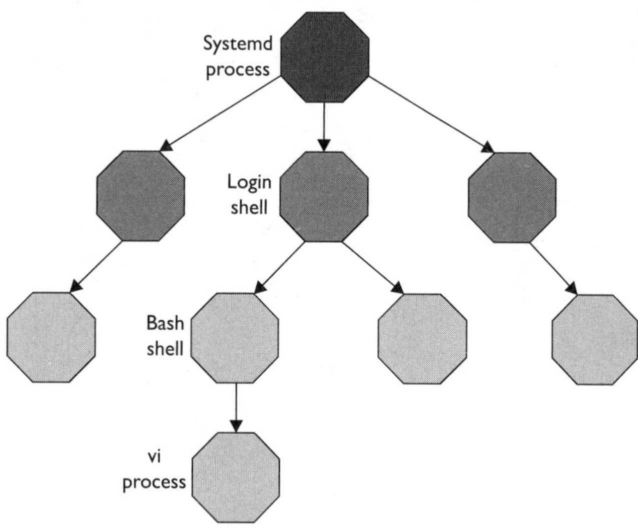

Figure 9-3 The systemd process as the grandparent of all other processes

Figure 9-4 The PPID of the systemd process

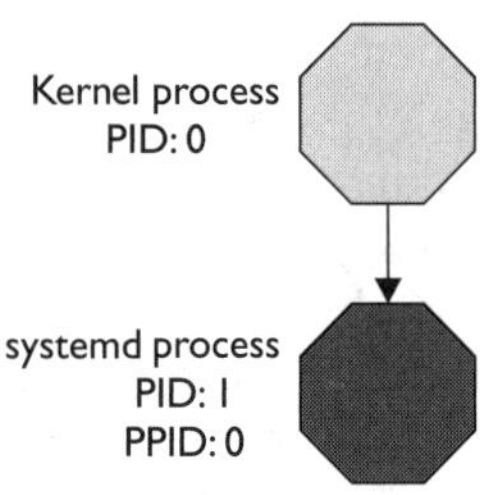

The systemd or init process is responsible for launching all system processes that are configured to automatically start on bootup. It also creates a login shell that is used for login.

This brings up an important point. Notice back in Figure 9-3 a second bash shell beneath the login shell. One might ask, "Couldn't I just run vi from within the login shell? Do I have to launch a second bash shell?"

Actually, in this figure, vi was, in fact, launched from the login shell. Why, then, does it show a second shell between the vi process and the login shell? Because any time a user runs a command from within any shell (whether it's a login shell or a standard shell session), a second shell session is created, called a *subshell*, and the process for the command entered is run within it. The subshell is a separate process in and of itself and has its own PID assigned. The PPID of the subshell is the PID of the shell where the command was entered.

The subshell process remains active for as long as the command is in use. The process for the command runs within the subshell and is assigned its own PID. The PPID of the command's process is, of course, the PID of the subshell it is running within. When the command process is complete and has exited, the subshell is terminated and control is returned back to the original shell session. This process of creating a new subshell and running the command process within it is called *forking*.

For example, in Figure 9-5, the user has issued the vi command at the shell prompt of a bash shell. A new subshell is created and the vi process is run within it. When the user exits vi, the subshell is destroyed and control is returned to the original shell instance.

Figure 9-5 Running a process from the shell prompt

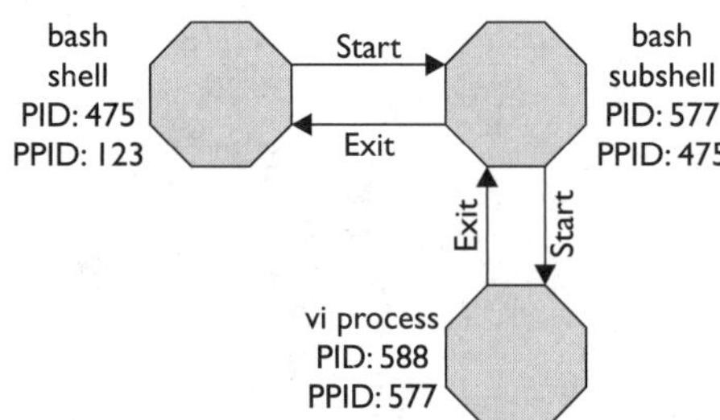

Managing Processes

Managing running processes is one of the key tasks performed on Linux systems. This section covers the following topics:

- Starting system processes
- Viewing running processes
- Prioritizing processes
- Managing foreground and background processes
- Ending a running process
- Keeping a process running after logout

Starting System Processes

There are two basic ways to start a process on a Linux system. For a user process, simply enter the command or script name at the shell prompt. For example, to run the vi program, simply enter vi at the shell prompt. When done, the vi process is created, as shown here:

```
cgreer@openSUSE:~> ps -a
 PID TTY          TIME CMD
3719 pts/1    00:00:00 vi
3729 pts/0    00:00:00 ps
```

For system processes, however, use either an init *script* or a service *file*, depending on whether the distribution uses init or systemd. If the distribution uses the init process, an init script is used by the init process to start processes on system boot. System services would manage processes that start the web server, File Transfer Protocol (FTP) server, Secure Shell (SSH) server, Domain Name Services, and so on.

These scripts are stored in a specific directory on the Linux system. Which directory they are stored in depends on the Linux distribution and the *runlevel* the system is starting at. For example, runlevel 0 is equivalent to halt, and runlevel 6 is a reboot. Most Linux distributions use one of two types of init scripts:

- **System V** Linux distributions that use System V init scripts store them in the */etc/rc.d* directory. Within */etc/rc.d* are a series of subdirectories named *rc0.d* through *rc6.d*. Each of these directories is associated with a particular runlevel. Within each of these subdirectories are symbolic links that point to the init scripts for the system daemons, which reside in */etc/rc.d/init.d*.
- **BSD** Other Linux distributions use BSD-style init scripts. These scripts reside in the */etc/init.d* directory. Within */etc/init.d* are a series of directories named *rc0.d* through *rc6.d*. As with System V init scripts, these directories are associated with specific runlevels. These directories contain links that point to the init scripts in */etc/init.d*.

In addition to using the init process to run these scripts, administrators can run these scripts from the command prompt. Simply enter **/etc/init.d/<script_name>** at the shell prompt (on a BSD-style system) or **/etc/rc.d/init.d/<script_name>** (on a System V–style system). If unsure of which script name to use, use the ls command to generate a listing of scripts in the script directory. This is shown in Figure 9-6.

The actual scripts in the *init* directory depend on which services are installed on the particular system. Whenever a service is installed on a system with a package manager like yum, rpm, and so on, a corresponding init script is automatically installed in the *init* script directory. Once there, an administrator can execute any script by simply running it from the command prompt. The syntax (on a BSD-style system) is as follows:

```
/etc/init.d/<script_name> start | stop | restart
```

For example, to enable file and print services with Microsoft Windows systems, start Samba by entering **/etc/init.d/smb start** at the shell prompt. To stop it, enter **/etc/init.d/smb stop**. To restart it, enter **/etc/init.d/smb restart**.

If the Linux distribution uses systemd instead of init, then the system services are managed using service files, which have a .service extension, or what Linux terms a "suffix."

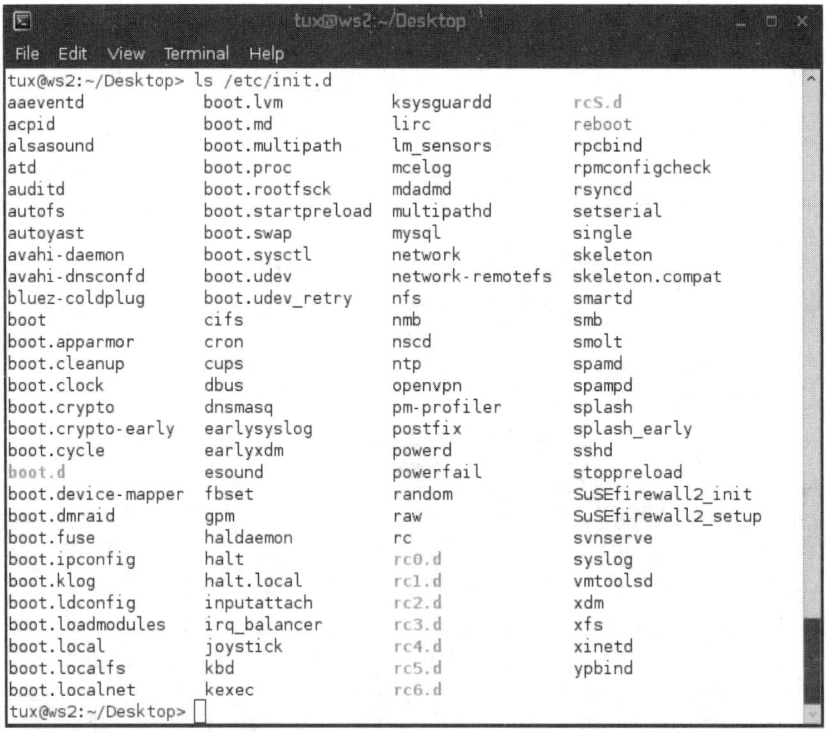

```
tux@ws2:~/Desktop
File  Edit  View  Terminal  Help
tux@ws2:~/Desktop> ls /etc/init.d
aaeventd            boot.lvm             ksysguardd         rcS.d
acpid               boot.md              lirc               reboot
alsasound           boot.multipath       lm_sensors         rpcbind
atd                 boot.proc            mcelog             rpmconfigcheck
auditd              boot.rootfsck        mdadmd             rsyncd
autofs              boot.startpreload    multipathd         setserial
autoyast            boot.swap            mysql              single
avahi-daemon        boot.sysctl          network            skeleton
avahi-dnsconfd      boot.udev            network-remotefs   skeleton.compat
bluez-coldplug      boot.udev_retry      nfs                smartd
boot                cifs                 nmb                smb
boot.apparmor       cron                 nscd               smolt
boot.cleanup        cups                 ntp                spamd
boot.clock          dbus                 openvpn            spampd
boot.crypto         dnsmasq              pm-profiler        splash
boot.crypto-early   earlysyslog          postfix            splash_early
boot.cycle          earlyxdm             powerd             sshd
boot.d              esound               powerfail          stoppreload
boot.device-mapper  fbset                random             SuSEfirewall2_init
boot.dmraid         gpm                  raw                SuSEfirewall2_setup
boot.fuse           haldaemon            rc                 svnserve
boot.ipconfig       halt                 rc0.d              syslog
boot.klog           halt.local           rc1.d              vmtoolsd
boot.ldconfig       inputattach          rc2.d              xdm
boot.loadmodules    irq_balancer         rc3.d              xfs
boot.local          joystick             rc4.d              xinetd
boot.localfs        kbd                  rc5.d              ypbind
boot.localnet       kexec                rc6.d
tux@ws2:~/Desktop>
```

Figure 9-6 init scripts in */etc/init.d*

Use the **systemctl** command at the shell prompt to start, stop, restart, or check the status of services on the system:

- To start a service, enter **systemctl start <service_name>**.
- To stop a service, enter **systemctl stop <service_name>**.
- To restart a service, enter **systemctl restart <service_name>**.
- To view the status of a service, enter **systemctl status <service_name>**.

For example, to enable the sshd daemon on a distribution that uses systemd, enter **systemctl start sshd** at the shell prompt.

Linux administrators must become more familiar with the init replacement, systemd, and the systemctl commands. The systemd utility is superior to SysVinit or init because it efficiently handles dependencies and performs parallel booting, thus getting systems up and running significantly faster.

EXAM TIP There were several candidates in line to replace SysVinit or init. These included systemd and a strong contender called Upstart. It is important to know a few systemd commands like systemctl and their options for the exam, but for Upstart, just know it was a candidate for SysVinit replacement.

Viewing Running Processes

This section covers how to view running processes on the system, and details the following tools:

- Using top
- Using ps
- Using pgrep

Using top

Linux provides a wide variety of tools to view running processes on the system. A popular utility is the "top" program because it lists processes and updates every three seconds, ranking by CPU utilization. Run top by simply entering **top** at the shell prompt. When done, the interface shown in Figure 9-7 is displayed.

In Figure 9-7, notice that top displays some of the running processes, one on each line. The following columns are used to display information about each process:

- **PID** The process ID of the process.
- **USER** The name of the user who owns the process.
- **PR** The priority assigned to the process. (We'll discuss process priorities later in this chapter.)
- **NI** This is the "nice" value of the process. (We'll talk about what this means later in this chapter.)

```
root@openSUSE:~
File  Edit  View  Search  Terminal  Help
top - 17:52:43 up 11 min,  3 users,  load average: 0.74, 0.72, 0.43
Tasks: 144 total,   2 running, 142 sleeping,   0 stopped,   0 zombie
%Cpu(s):  4.7 us,  1.7 sy,  0.0 ni, 93.7 id,  0.0 wa,  0.0 hi,  0.0 si,  0.0 st
KiB Mem:   1544012 total,   613836 used,   930176 free,    27880 buffers
KiB Swap:  2103292 total,        0 used,  2103292 free,   248316 cached

  PID USER      PR  NI    VIRT    RES    SHR S  %CPU  %MEM     TIME+ COMMAND
  634 root      20   0   68800  17724   7120 S 6.960 1.148   0:26.67 Xorg
 3476 rtracy    20   0  614076 147864  38720 S 4.308 9.577   0:28.47 gnome-she+
 3734 rtracy    20   0  246640  16812  12596 S 0.663 1.089   0:01.25 gnome-ter+
   31 root      20   0       0      0      0 S 0.331 0.000   0:03.49 kworker/1+
 3593 rtracy    20   0   34452  13248  11044 S 0.331 0.858   0:01.04 vmtoolsd
 3886 root      20   0    3636   1236    892 R 0.331 0.080   0:00.33 top
    1 root      20   0    5928   3236   2208 S 0.000 0.210   0:05.99 systemd
    2 root      20   0       0      0      0 S 0.000 0.000   0:00.01 kthreadd
    3 root      20   0       0      0      0 S 0.000 0.000   0:00.05 ksoftirqd+
    5 root       0 -20       0      0      0 S 0.000 0.000   0:00.00 kworker/0+
    6 root      20   0       0      0      0 S 0.000 0.000   0:00.85 kworker/u+
    7 root      rt   0       0      0      0 S 0.000 0.000   0:00.05 migration+
    8 root      -2   0       0      0      0 S 0.000 0.000   0:00.41 rcuc/0
    9 root      -2   0       0      0      0 S 0.000 0.000   0:00.00 rcub/0
   10 root      20   0       0      0      0 S 0.000 0.000   0:01.23 rcu_preem+
   11 root      20   0       0      0      0 S 0.000 0.000   0:00.00 rcu_bh
   12 root      20   0       0      0      0 S 0.000 0.000   0:00.00 rcu_sched
   13 root      rt   0       0      0      0 S 0.000 0.000   0:00.01 watchdog/0
   14 root      rt   0       0      0      0 S 0.000 0.000   0:00.02 watchdog/1
   15 root      -2   0       0      0      0 S 0.000 0.000   0:00.38 rcuc/1
```

Figure 9-7 Using top to view running processes

- **VIRT** The amount of virtual memory used by the process.
- **RES** The amount of physical RAM the process is using (its resident size) in kilobytes.
- **SHR** The amount of shared memory used by the process.
- **S** The status of the process. Possible values include the following:
  - **D** Uninterruptible sleep
  - **R** Running
  - **S** Sleeping
  - **T** Traced or stopped
  - **Z** Zombie

NOTE A zombie process has completed execution, but *after* its parent has died, thus being unable to cleanly exit. The zombie eventually clears up on its own, as init or systemd become the new parent. If that fails, attempt to kill the zombie or wait until the next scheduled reboot. The name sounds scary, but zombies are harmless to the system, only tying up a process slot.

- **%CPU** The percentage of CPU time used by the process.
- **%MEM** The percentage of available physical RAM used by the process.
- **TIME+** The total amount of CPU time the process has consumed since being started.
- **COMMAND** The name of the command that was entered to start the process.

One can sort top output not only by the default CPU utilization, but also by memory utilization (by pressing the M key), by PID (by pressing the N key), or back to %CPU (by pressing the P key).

Pressing H while top is running displays the help screen, which outputs the keystrokes required to sort by a particular category. This help screen is shown in Figure 9-8. To learn more about top, review the man page.

Using ps

The ps utility can be used to display running processes on the system. Unlike top, which displays processes dynamically, ps displays a *snapshot* of the current processes running.

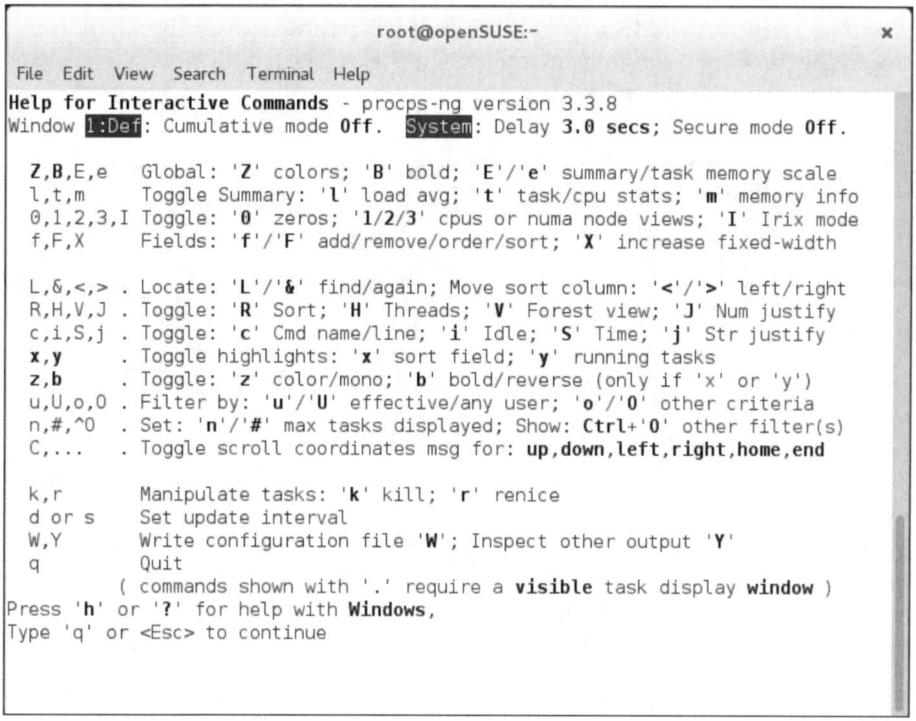

```
root@openSUSE:~
File  Edit  View  Search  Terminal  Help
Help for Interactive Commands - procps-ng version 3.3.8
Window 1:Def: Cumulative mode Off.  System: Delay 3.0 secs; Secure mode Off.

  Z,B,E,e    Global: 'Z' colors; 'B' bold; 'E'/'e' summary/task memory scale
  l,t,m      Toggle Summary: 'l' load avg; 't' task/cpu stats; 'm' memory info
  0,1,2,3,I  Toggle: '0' zeros; '1/2/3' cpus or numa node views; 'I' Irix mode
  f,F,X      Fields: 'f'/'F' add/remove/order/sort; 'X' increase fixed-width

  L,&,<,> .  Locate: 'L'/'&' find/again; Move sort column: '<'/'>' left/right
  R,H,V,J .  Toggle: 'R' Sort; 'H' Threads; 'V' Forest view; 'J' Num justify
  c,i,S,j .  Toggle: 'c' Cmd name/line; 'i' Idle; 'S' Time; 'j' Str justify
  x,y     .  Toggle highlights: 'x' sort field; 'y' running tasks
  z,b     .  Toggle: 'z' color/mono; 'b' bold/reverse (only if 'x' or 'y')
  u,U,o,O .  Filter by: 'u'/'U' effective/any user; 'o'/'O' other criteria
  n,#,^O  .  Set: 'n'/'#' max tasks displayed; Show: Ctrl+'O' other filter(s)
  C,...   .  Toggle scroll coordinates msg for: up,down,left,right,home,end

  k,r        Manipulate tasks: 'k' kill; 'r' renice
  d or s     Set update interval
  W,Y        Write configuration file 'W'; Inspect other output 'Y'
  q          Quit
          ( commands shown with '.' require a visible task display window )
Press 'h' or '?' for help with Windows,
Type 'q' or <Esc> to continue
```

Figure 9-8 Viewing the top help screen

Entering **ps** displays the processes associated with the *current* shell, as shown here:

```
openSUSE:~ $ ps
 PID TTY          TIME CMD
3947 pts/0    00:00:00 bash
3994 pts/0    00:00:00 ps
```

In this example, the following processes are displayed by ps:

- **bash** The current bash shell session.
- **ps** Because ps is in use to list current processes, its process is also listed.

Notice that the following information is displayed by default:

- **PID** The process ID of the process
- **TTY** The name of the terminal session (shell) that the process is running within
- **TIME** The amount of CPU time used by the process
- **CMD** The name of the command that was entered to create the process

Notice that only two processes were listed. By default, ps only shows processes associated with the current shell. Hence, only the shell and ps processes are displayed.

To see all processes running on the system, use the -e option with ps. Here is an example:

```
openSUSE:~ $ ps -e
 PID TTY          TIME CMD
   1 ?        00:00:06 systemd
   2 ?        00:00:00 kthreadd
   3 ?        00:00:00 ksoftirqd/0
   5 ?        00:00:00 kworker/0:0H
   7 ?        00:00:00 migration/0
   8 ?        00:00:00 rcuc/0
   9 ?        00:00:00 rcub/0
  10 ?        00:00:01 rcu_preempt
  11 ?        00:00:00 rcu_bh
  12 ?        00:00:00 rcu_sched
  13 ?        00:00:00 watchdog/0
  14 ?        00:00:00 watchdog/1...
```

As can be seen in this example, the -e option results in many more processes being displayed by the ps command. Also notice that most of the processes shown have a question mark (?) in the TTY column. This indicates the process is a system process. Remember that system processes (daemons) are loaded by the init or systemd process at startup and are therefore not associated with any shell. Because of this, a ? is displayed in the TTY column in the output of ps.

The ps command has other options displayed within the ps(1) man page. For example, the -f option will provide "full" detail. Combined with -e, as shown here, it will result in a "full" listing of every process running on the system:

```
openSUSE:~ $ ps -ef
UID         PID  PPID  C STIME TTY          TIME CMD
root          1     0  0 17:41 ?        00:00:06 /sbin/init showopts
root          2     0  0 17:41 ?        00:00:00 [kthreadd]
root          3     2  0 17:41 ?        00:00:00 [ksoftirqd/0]
root          5     2  0 17:41 ?        00:00:00 [kworker/0:0H]
root          7     2  0 17:41 ?        00:00:00 [migration/0]
root          8     2  0 17:41 ?        00:00:00 [rcuc/0]
root          9     2  0 17:41 ?        00:00:00 [rcub/0]
root         10     2  0 17:41 ?        00:00:01 [rcu_preempt]
root         11     2  0 17:41 ?        00:00:00 [rcu_bh]
root         12     2  0 17:41 ?        00:00:00 [rcu_sched]
root         13     2  0 17:41 ?        00:00:00 [watchdog/0]
root         14     2  0 17:41 ?        00:00:00 [watchdog/1]...
```

The -f option displays additional information, including the following:

- **UID** The user ID of the process's owner
- **PPID** The PID of the process's parent process
- **C** The amount of processor time utilized by the process
- **STIME** The time that the process started

For further detail, use the -l (lowercase L) option with the ps command. The -l option displays the long format of the ps output. Here is an example combined with -e and -f:

```
openSUSE:~ $ ps -efl
F S UID        PID  PPID  C PRI  NI ADDR SZ WCHAN  STIME TTY          TIME CMD
1 S root         2     0  0  80   0 -     0 kthrea 11:09 ?        00:00:00 [kth]
1 S root         3     2  0 -40   - -     0 migrat 11:09 ?        00:00:00 [mig]
1 S root         4     2  0  80   0 -     0 run_ks 11:09 ?        00:00:00 [kso]
5 S root         5     2  0 -40   - -     0 watchd 11:09 ?        00:00:00 [wat]
1 S root         6     2  0 -40   - -     0 migrat 11:09 ?        00:00:00 [mig]
1 S root         7     2  0  80   0 -     0 run_ks 11:09 ?        00:00:00 [kso]
5 S root         8     2  0 -40   - -     0 watchd 11:09 ?        00:00:00 [wat]
1 S root         9     2  0  80   0 -     0 worker 11:09 ?        00:00:00 [eve]
1 S root        10     2  0  80   0 -     0 worker 11:09 ?        00:00:00 [eve]
1 S root        11     2  0  80   0 -     0 worker 11:09 ?        00:00:00 [net]
...
```

With the -l option, the user can view the following information about processes running on the system:

- **F** The flags associated with the process. This column uses the following codes:
  - **1** Forked, but didn't execute
  - **4** Used root privileges
- **S** The state of the process. This column uses the following codes:
  - **D** Uninterruptible sleep
  - **R** Running
  - **S** Interruptible sleep
  - **T** Stopped or traced
  - **Z** Zombie

- **PRI** The priority of the process.
- **NI** The nice value of the process.
- **ADDR** The memory address of the process.
- **SZ** The size of the process.
- **WCHAN** The name of the kernel function in which the process is sleeping. A dash (–) in this column means the process is currently running.

EXAM TIP Knowledge of various column outputs for ps is not critical for the exam. For example, no need to know that -l will list process states and -f will not. Just know that ps lists PIDs and process names, and -e will list every process.

The ps command has two flavors: System V and BSD. We have demonstrated System V examples. BSD examples do not use a leading dash (-). For example, to list all processes in BSD style, use the command ps aux instead of ps -elf. Learn more from the ps(1) man page.

Using pgrep

The ps command is very useful for viewing process information. However, sometimes the output of ps can be overwhelming, especially when just looking for a specific process. For example, to view just the "bash" processes running, run the following:

```
openSUSE:~ $ ps -e | grep bash
3947 pts/0    00:00:00 bash
3998 pts/1    00:00:00 bash
```

Another option for doing the same thing is to use the pgrep command. As its name implies, pgrep combines the functionality of ps and grep into a single utility. When running pgrep, the end user specifies certain selection criteria to view. Then the command searches through all the currently running processes and outputs a list of processes that match the criteria specified, as shown here:

```
openSUSE:~ $ pgrep bash
3947
3998
```

Use the following options with pgrep to create the selection criteria:

- **-l** Lists the process name and process ID
- **-u <user_name>** Matches on the specified process owner

The pgrep command lists only the PID of the matching processes by default. To view the name of the process as well as its PID, use the -l option with the pgrep command. For example, to view a list of all processes owned by the cgreer user, use the following command:

```
openSUSE:~ $ pgrep -l -u cgreer
3947 bash
3998 bash
```

Prioritizing Processes

Recall from the first part of this chapter that Linux is a multitasking operating system. It rotates CPU time between each of the processes running on the system, creating the illusion that all of the processes are running concurrently.

Because Linux is a multitasking operating system, one can specify a priority level for each process. Doing so determines how much CPU time a given process gets in relation to other processes on the system.

By default, Linux tries to equalize the amount of CPU time given to all processes on the system. However, there may be times to adjust the priority assigned to a process. Depending on how the system is deployed, a particular process may be set to have a higher priority than other processes. This can be done using several Linux utilities. In this section, we review the following topics:

- Setting priorities with nice
- Changing priorities with renice

Setting Priorities with nice

The nice utility can be used on Linux to launch a program with a different priority level. Recall from our previous discussion of top and ps that each process running on the system has a PR and NI value associated with it, as shown in Figure 9-9.

```
root@openSUSE:~
File  Edit  View  Search  Terminal  Help
top - 19:45:24 up  2:03,  4 users,  load average: 0.12, 0.04, 0.05
Tasks: 149 total,   2 running, 147 sleeping,   0 stopped,   0 zombie
%Cpu(s):  3.5 us,  1.3 sy,  0.0 ni, 95.2 id,  0.0 wa,  0.0 hi,  0.0 si,  0.0 st
KiB Mem:   1544012 total,   788312 used,   755700 free,    37736 buffers
KiB Swap:  2103292 total,        0 used,  2103292 free,   387936 cached

  PID USER      PR  NI    VIRT    RES    SHR S  %CPU  %MEM     TIME+ COMMAND
  634 root      20   0   68800  17724   7120 S 4.631 1.148   0:49.28 Xorg
 3476 rtracy    20   0  620012 154720  38864 S 3.639 10.02   1:32.26 gnome-she+
 3593 rtracy    20   0   34452  13248  11044 S 0.662 0.858   0:16.79 vmtoolsd
 4341 root      20   0    3636   1244    892 R 0.662 0.081   0:00.12 top
 3734 rtracy    20   0  246824  17044  12620 S 0.331 1.104   0:02.06 gnome-ter+
    1 root      20   0    5928   3236   2208 S 0.000 0.210   0:06.18 systemd
    2 root      20   0       0      0      0 S 0.000 0.000   0:00.01 kthreadd
    3 root      20   0       0      0      0 S 0.000 0.000   0:00.06 ksoftirqd+
    5 root       0 -20       0      0      0 S 0.000 0.000   0:00.00 kworker/0+
    7 root      rt   0       0      0      0 S 0.000 0.000   0:00.06 migration+
    8 root      -2   0       0      0      0 S 0.000 0.000   0:00.48 rcuc/0
    9 root      -2   0       0      0      0 S 0.000 0.000   0:00.00 rcub/0
   10 root      20   0       0      0      0 R 0.000 0.000   0:01.42 rcu_preem+
   11 root      20   0       0      0      0 S 0.000 0.000   0:00.00 rcu_bh
   12 root      20   0       0      0      0 S 0.000 0.000   0:00.00 rcu_sched
   13 root      rt   0       0      0      0 S 0.000 0.000   0:00.07 watchdog/0
   14 root      rt   0       0      0      0 S 0.000 0.000   0:00.09 watchdog/1
   15 root      -2   0       0      0      0 S 0.000 0.000   0:00.43 rcuc/1
   16 root      rt   0       0      0      0 S 0.000 0.000   0:00.09 migration+
   17 root      20   0       0      0      0 S 0.000 0.000   0:00.04 ksoftirqd+
```

Figure 9-9 Viewing PR and NI values

The PR value is the process's kernel priority. The *higher* the number, the *lower* the priority of the process. The lower the number, the higher the priority of the process. The NI value is the **nice** value of the process, from the adage "nice guys finish last." The nice value is factored into the kernel calculations that determine the priority of the process. The nice value for any Linux process ranges between –20 and +19. The *lower* the nice value, the *higher* the priority of the process.

An administrator cannot directly manipulate the priority of a process, but can manipulate the process's nice value. The easiest way to do this is to set the nice value when starting the command using the nice command. Any time a program starts, the default "niceness" is 0 (zero). But, the default for starting a program *with* nice is 10. To set higher priorities (that is, negative niceness), one must be the administrative user or root. The syntax is **nice -n <nice_level> <command>**.

The following shows launching various subshells with different priorities using nice:

```
openSUSE:~ $ nice bash
openSUSE:~ $ nice -n 19 bash
openSUSE:~ $ ps -o pid,pri,ni,cmd
 PID PRI   NI CMD
8279  19    0 bash
8389   9   10 bash
8470   0   19 bash
8511   0   19 ps -o pid,pri,ni,cmd
```

The ps -o option allows us to list the columns to view from ps. Notice that PID 8389 runs at the default nice value of 10, and PID 8470 runs at 19.

The nice command works great for modifying the nice value when running a command to start a process. But to change the nice value of a running command, the user must use the renice command.

Changing Priorities with renice

Instead of having to kill a process and restart it with nice to set its nice value, use the renice command to adjust the nice value of a process that is currently running on the system. The syntax for using this command is **renice <nice_value> <PID>**.

For example, in the last example, the PID of the vi process is 8488. To adjust the priority of the vi process to a lower level without unloading the program, enter **renice 4 8488** at the shell prompt, as shown in this example:

```
openSUSE:~ $ renice 15 8389
8389: old priority 10, new priority 15
openSUSE:~ $ ps -o pid,pri,ni,cmd
 PID PRI   NI CMD
8279  19    0 bash
8389   4   15 bash
8470   0   19 bash
8511   0   19 ps -o pid,pri,ni,cmd
```

As this example shows, the nice value of the PID 8389 process was increased from 10 to 15. This caused the overall priority of the process to go from 9 to 4, thus decreasing the process's overall priority level.

Only root can *decrease* nice values (that is, *raise* priority) with renice. For example, if an end user attempts to return the niceness of PID 8470 back to 10, they will not be allowed, as shown here:

```
openSUSE:~ $ renice 10 8389
renice: failed to set priority for 8389 (process ID): Permission denied
```

Let's now shift gears and talk about foreground and background processes.

EXAM TIP Make sure to understand nice and renice basics, such as how to use them, their defaults, and minimum and maximum settings.

Managing Foreground and Background Processes

In this part of the chapter, we need to discuss running processes in the foreground and background. We'll address the following topics:

- Running processes in the background
- Switching processes between background and foreground

Running Processes in the Background

Recall from our earlier discussion of processes that when entering any command at the shell prompt, a subshell is created and the process runs within it. As soon as the process exits, the subshell is destroyed. While the process is running, the "$" shell prompt is unavailable, so the user is unable to run another command until the current process completes. For example, the sleep command simply "sleeps" in the foreground for a number of seconds (doing nothing) and then prompts the user for the next command. Here's an example:

```
openSUSE:~ $ sleep 20     # waits 20 seconds before returning prompt
                         < waits for 20 seconds >
openSUSE:~ $
```

Programs by default run in the foreground, whether they are a text-based shell programs or graphical programs. However, it is possible to run a program in the *background*. These programs launch normally, but control is immediately returned to the shell. Then you can use the shell to launch other programs or perform other shell tasks.

To run a program in the background, simply append an ampersand (**&**) character to the command. This tells the shell to run the program in the background. So, let's use sleep again, but for a much longer period this time. The following command will still run, but the end user is allowed to continue working:

```
openSUSE:~ $ sleep 216000 &                 # sleep for 60 hours
[1]  9148
         < prompt returns immediately >
openSUSE:~ $
```

Notice that two values are displayed on the screen after the process was run in the background. The first value, [1], is the job ID assigned to the background job, and the second value is the PID of the process. View all background jobs running on the system by entering **jobs** at the shell prompt:

```
cgreer@openSUSE:~> jobs
[1]+  Running                                    sleep 216000 &
```

In this example, the output of the jobs command displays the status of the job as well as the name of the command that was run to create the background job. To see the process ID, use the ps command.

Switching Processes Between Background and Foreground

Just because a process was started in the background or the foreground does not mean it has to stay there. Switch a process between foreground and background while it is running by using the following commands:

- **fg** This command will move a background process to the foreground.
- **bg** This command will move a foreground process to the background.

To use the bg utility, first put the foreground job to sleep by pressing CTRL-Z (that is, press the left CTRL key and the Z key at the same time). This will cause the process to pause and then a job ID is assigned to the process. Next, enter **bg** to move the process to the background, where it will continue from where it left off.

In the next example, the sleep program is loaded into the foreground and then put to sleep using CTRL-Z, where it is assigned a job ID of 1. It is then sent to the background using the bg command. Finally, the job is returned to the foreground with fg.

```
cgreer@openSUSE:~> sleep 10000
CTRL-Z
[1]+  Stopped                  sleep 10000
cgreer@openSUSE:~> bg
[1]+ sleep 10000 &
cgreer@openSUSE:~> fg
sleep 10000
```

The bg and fg commands are shell commands; to learn more about these, read the bash(1) man page.

NOTE CTRL-Z is often shown as ^Z. Control characters are *not* case sensitive, unlike most every other commands in Linux. There are other control characters; for example, ^C will "cancel" a job, causing it to stop and quit, and ^D means "done" or "end of input," to notify Linux that there is no further input.

Ending a Running Process

Up to now we have run, viewed, prioritized, and moved processes from background to foreground. The final topic we need to cover is how to end a process that is running on the system.

Normally, enter CTRL-C (^C) to end a running process. But if the job is running in the background, ^C will not work. Also, processes sometimes hang and become difficult to close properly. In this section, we discuss how to kill such processes:

- Using kill and killall
- Using pkill

Using kill and killall

The kill command is used to terminate a process using the process ID. The syntax for using kill is **kill -<signal> <PID>**. The PID parameter is the process ID of the process to kill. The command kill is a misnomer because end users can also pause and resume jobs using kill by sending a specific kill signal to the process. There are 64 kill signals an end user can send to a process, but the exam focuses only on the following ones:

- **SIGHUP** This is kill signal 1. This signal restarts the process. After a restart, the process will have exactly the same PID that it had before. This is a very useful option for restarting a service, such as a website, for which an end user made changes to a configuration file.
- **SIGINT** This is kill signal 2. This signal sends a CTRL-C key sequence to the process.
- **SIGKILL** This is kill signal 9. This is a brute-force kill and should only be used as a last resort. If the process is hung badly, this option will force it to stop, but the child processes orphan and later convert to zombies. If these are not removed, the users can wait until the next scheduled reboot. Avoid using SIGKILL on databases, mail servers, and print servers because their data could become corrupted.
- **SIGTERM** This is kill signal 15, and the default. This signal tells the process to terminate gracefully, gently killing the child processes, and then the parent.

When using kill, you can use the signal name, such as SIGTERM, or the signal value, such as 15. End users use ps to first identify the PID of the process before using kill to stop it. Here, the sleep process is running with a PID of 8312:

```
openSUSE:~ # ps
 PID TTY          TIME CMD
8278 pts/0    00:00:00 su
8279 pts/0    00:00:00 bash
8312 pts/0    00:00:00 sleep
8313 pts/0    00:00:00 ps
openSUSE:~ # kill -SIGTERM 8312
openSUSE:~ #
```

Also, any of the following could be used to kill, or specifically *terminate*, our sleep process:

- kill 8312
- kill -15 8312
- kill -TERM 8312
- kill -s TERM 8312
- kill -s 15 8312
- kill -s SIGTERM 8312

The exam may show any of these forms, so they are listed here for the candidate's preparation. Again, using SIGKILL will work, but it is best to try gentler signals first. Only if these signals fail should one use the harsher SIGKILL signal. When experiencing a hung process that needs to be killed, use the following sequence:

1. Send a SIGTERM. Usually, this will fix the problem and allow the process to exit cleanly. If it doesn't, then go on to step 2.
2. Send a SIGKILL.

In addition to kill, one can also use killall to kill processes by name, which is more convenient than running ps or pgrep to determine the PID first and then running the kill command.

The killall command syntax is similar to the kill command. For example, to kill the sleep process in the preceding example with killall instead of kill, one would run **killall -15 sleep**. This command sends the SIGTERM signal to the process named vi. Again, -15 is the default kill signal for killall, so **killall sleep** would also work.

NOTE If the end user is running multiple sleep processes, the killall command will terminate all of them.

To learn more about kill(1) and killall(1), review their man pages. These tools are very useful, such as using the -u option with killall to end processes owned by a specific user.

EXAM TIP For users of the dd command, sending signal SIGUSR1 reports the **dd** I/O status. Simply run killall -10 dd while dd is running in the background and the user will be informed of dd's data transfer progress.

Using pkill

Like killall, the pkill command can also stop a running process by name. The pkill command is a cousin of the pgrep command reviewed earlier. In fact, they use exactly the same options and even share the same man page!

Again like killall, pkill will kill all processes that match the argument name. For example, to kill all running processes named "sleep" with the SIGTERM signal, execute **pkill -SIGTERM sleep** at the shell prompt. Again, since SIGTERM is the default, **pkill sleep** terminates the process in the same manner.

EXAM TIP For the Linux+ exam, make sure to know that the top utility may be used to kill processes as well using the K key!

Keeping a Process Running After Logout

The last topic to address in this objective is how to keep a process running after logging out from the system. As discussed, signals are sent to running processes to indicate that a system event has occurred and that the process needs to respond.

A commonly used signal is the hang-up signal (SIGHUP). When a user logs out of a terminal session, Linux sends a SIGHUP signal to all the programs associated with that terminal.

However, a process can also be told to ignore SIGHUP signals, which allows it to remain running even after the end user logs out! This is done by using the nohup utility to run the program. This causes the process created by the command to ignore all SIGHUP signals.

For example, suppose a shell script called updatemydb, which automatically updates a database, runs nightly for six hours. For security reasons, the end user does not want to stay logged in to the system while updatemydb runs.

To allow the script to run, and have the security of logging out, the end user can start the script with the nohup command. They just enter **nohup updatemydb &** at the shell prompt and then log out. If the command generates output that is usually sent to the stdout, nohup will redirect the output to the *~/nohup.out* file.

It is important to note that a command run under nohup is only immune to SIGHUP signals. All other kill signals still work. For example, terminating the program using the SIGTERM signal using the kill command will be successful.

Let's practice working with Linux processes in Exercise 9-1.

Exercise 9-1: Working with Linux Processes

In this exercise, practice using shell commands to manage processes running on the system. Perform this exercise using the virtual machine provided online.

VIDEO Please watch the Exercise 9-1 video for a demonstration on how to perform this task.

Complete the following steps:

1. Boot the Linux system and log in as a standard user.
2. Open a terminal session.

3. Switch to the root user account by entering **su -** and provide the password.
4. Practice starting system processes by doing the following:
   a. At the shell prompt, enter the **systemctl status at** command.
   What's the status of the at daemon? (For most distributions, the atd daemon is not configured to run by default.)
   b. Start the atd daemon by entering **systemctl start atd** at the shell prompt.
   c. Enter **systemctl status atd** again at the shell prompt. The atd service should now be shown as running.
5. Practice using the top utility by following these steps:
   a. Enter **top** at the shell prompt.
   b. View the running processes.
   c. Press H to access the top help screen. Which keystroke will sort the display by CPU stats?
   d. Press T to sort the display by CPU stats. Which processes are using the most CPU time on the system?
   e. Press M to sort the display by memory usage. Which processes are using the most memory?
   f. Add columns by pressing F.
   g. Add the PPID column to the display by pressing B and then SPACEBAR. Note that the PPID of each process is added to the display.
   h. Exit top by pressing q.
6. Practice using the ps utility to view processes by doing the following procedure:
   a. Enter **ps** at the shell prompt. What processes are associated with the current shell session?
   b. View all running processes on the system by entering **ps -ef | more** at the shell prompt.
   c. Press SPACEBAR until the atd service comes into view. What username does atd run under? (On most distributions, it should run under the at user.)
   d. Enter **ps -el | less** at the shell prompt.
   e. Locate the Status (S) column.
   f. Press SPACEBAR and look for the atd service. What is the status of the service? (Because it isn't being used at the moment, it's probably sleeping.)
7. Practice managing process priorities by completing the following steps:
   a. Enter **top** at the shell prompt.
   b. What are the priority (PR) and nice (NI) values associated with the top process? (For most distributions, these values should be 16 and 0, respectively.)

c. Press Q to stop the top process.

d. Enter **nice -n -20 top** at the shell prompt.
Now what are the PR and NI values for the top process?

e. Note the PID for the top process.

f. Open a new terminal window and use su to switch to the root user.

g. Adjust the nice value of the top process while it's running by entering **renice 1 <top_PID>** at the shell prompt.

h. Switch back to the first terminal session where top is running. What are its PR and NI values now?

i. Press Q to exit top.

8. Practice switching processes between the foreground and the background by performing the following procedure:

   a. Load top again by entering **top** at the shell prompt.

   b. In the terminal where top is running, press CTRL-Z.

   c. Note the background job ID number assigned to the process.

   d. Enter **bg <background_job_ID>** at the shell prompt.
   The output from top disappears while the process runs in the background.

   e. Press CTRL-C.

   f. Enter **fg <background_job_ID>** at the shell prompt.
   The output from top reappears as the process now runs in the foreground.

9. Practice killing processes by completing the following steps:

   a. Ensure that top is still running.

   b. Switch to the other terminal session where logged in as root.

   c. Enter **ps -e | grep top** at the shell prompt.

   d. Note the PID of the top process.

   e. Enter **kill -SIGTERM <top_PID>** at the shell prompt.

   f. Switch back to the terminal session where top was running. Verify that top has exited.

   g. Load top again at the shell prompt.

   h. Switch back to the other terminal session where logged in as root.

   i. Kill the top process by entering the **killall -15 top** command.

   j. Switch back to the first terminal window and verify that top has exited.

10. Exit out of top by pressing ESC and then exit out of the screen by entering **exit**.

Scheduling Processes

There are many occasions when a process needs to run automatically without any end-user intervention. Backups are a good example. One key problem with backups is that system administrators forget to do them! One of the worst things one can do in the backup strategy is to rely on a human being to remember to run them.

Instead, configure the Linux system to run programs automatically. This removes the human element from the equation and ensures that the specified programs execute regularly and on time. Three key utilities are used to schedule processes to run in the future. We'll discuss the following topics in this part of the chapter:

- Using the **at** daemon
- Using the **cron** daemon
- Using the **anacron** service

Using the at Daemon

Using the "at" utility is a great way to schedule a process. The at service is a system daemon (called atd) that runs in the background on the system. Most Linux distributions install this service during the basic installation of the system. If not, it may need to be installed manually with a package manager like rpm, dpkg, yum, apt-get, and so on.

If the distribution uses init, then the startup script used to start the atd daemon is located in the init script directory, which should be either */etc/init.d* or */etc/rc.d/init.d*, depending on the distribution. To check the status of at, run the following command:

```
YouTV:~ # systemctl status atd.service
```

To start that atd daemon, run the following as root:

```
YouTV:~ # systemctl start atd.service
```

To ensure that atd starts at boot time, run the following as root:

```
YouTV:~ # systemctl enable atd.service
```

Next, the administrator needs to specify which end users can and cannot create at jobs. This can be done by editing the following files:

- */etc/at.allow* Users listed in this file are allowed to create `at` jobs.
- */etc/at.deny* Users listed in this file are not allowed to create `at` jobs.

NOTE Because the atd service checks the */etc/at.allow* file first, if an end user is listed in both */etc/at.allow* and */etc/at.deny*, they will be allowed to use at!

To use at to schedule jobs, complete the following steps:

1. At the shell prompt enter the following:

   ```
   openSUSE:~ # at time
   ```

Type of Reference	Syntax	Description
Fixed	HH:MM	Specifies the exact hour and minute when the commands should run. The at daemon assumes that the hour/minute specified is today unless that time has already passed; then it assumes tomorrow. Add **am** or **pm** to the value to specify morning or afternoon, respectively.
	noon	Specifies that a command run at 12:00 P.M.
	midnight	Specifies that a command run at 12:00 A.M.
	teatime	Specifies that a command run at 4:00 P.M.
	MMDDYY or MM/DD/YY or MM.DD.YY	Specifies the exact month, date, and year when a command is to run.
	HH:MM MMDDYY	Specifies the exact month, date, year, and time when a command is to run.
Relative	now	Specifies that the command run immediately.
	now + value	Specifies that the command run at a certain time in the future. For example: **now +5 minutes** **now +3 days**
	today	Specifies that the command run today. For example: **2 pm today**
	tomorrow	Specifies that the command be run tomorrow. For example: **2 pm tomorrow**

Table 9-2 The at Command Time Syntax Options

The at daemon is very flexible as to how to specify the *time* value for the command. Observe the syntax shown in Table 9-2.

After running the at command, the at> prompt is displayed, as shown here:

```
openSUSE:~ # at now +10 minutes
warning: commands will be executed using /bin/sh
at>
```

2. At the at> prompt, enter command(s) to run at the scheduled time. If the commands normally display output on the screen, an e-mail of the output is sent to the end user's account.

   Alternatively, one can also redirect output to a file using > or >>. Here's an example:

```
openSUSE:~ # at now +10 minutes
warning: commands will be executed using /bin/sh
at> updatedb_script > $HOME/outfile
```

3. Press ENTER to add additional commands. To run multiple commands within the same job, each command should be on its own line.
4. When done entering commands, press CTRL-D to see <EOT>, and the at> prompt will disappear, the job will be scheduled, and a job number will be assigned, as shown here:

```
openSUSE:~ # at now +10 minutes
warning: commands will be executed using /bin/sh
at> updatedb_script > $HOME/outfile
at> <EOT>
job 3 at 2021-04-02 08:57
openSUSE:~ #
```

Once this is configured, use the atq command to view a list of pending at jobs. Output similar the following is shown:

```
openSUSE:~ # atq
3       2021-04-02 08:57 a root
```

As a regular user, the atq command will display only the jobs associated with the current user account. As root, atq displays all pending jobs for all users. To remove a pending job from the list, use the **atrm <job_number>** command.

In addition to the at daemon, use the cron daemon to schedule *repeatable* jobs (such as nightly backups or database updates), as discussed below.

NOTE Another utility related to at(1) is batch(1). The batch command is *not* tested on the Linux+ exam but is a nice way to schedule a job. Instead of scheduling a specific time, the batch utility waits for *low* system load, and then starts the job.

Using the cron Daemon

The at daemon is great, but can only schedule a job to run once in the future. Jobs often require running on a regular schedule. For example, backups may need to run daily or weekly, and Linux provides a tool for this.

The cron daemon, crond, can handle repetitious schedules. Unlike at, cron runs commands on a schedule specified by an end user. For example, many organizations setup cron jobs to run their nightly or weekly backups. That way, backups occur automatically on a regular schedule.

The discussion continues with these following topics:

- How cron works
- Using cron to manage scheduled system jobs
- Using cron to manage scheduled user jobs

How cron Works

The crond daemon is a service that runs continuously in the background and checks a special file called *crontab* once every minute to see if there is a scheduled job it should run. If the distribution uses init, then the cron daemon is managed using the cron init script in the *init* directory. If the distribution uses systemd, use the systemctl command to manage the crond daemon.

By default, crond is configured to run automatically every time the system boots on most Linux distributions. If not, to start it manually, do the following as root:

```
YouTV:~ # systemctl start crond.service
```

To check the crond daemon status, run the following:

```
YouTV:~ # systemctl status crond.service
```

To ensure that crond starts at boot time, run the following as root:

```
YouTV:~ # systemctl enable crond.service
```

One can configure cron to run system jobs or user-specific jobs, which is covered next.

NOTE Extensions, or what Linux calls *suffixes* (such as .service, .c, .doc, and .txt), are ignored by Linux, but are important to applications such as systemctl, gcc, LibreOffice, gedit, and so on. Read more at the suffixes(7) man page.

Using cron to Manage Scheduled System Jobs

Using cron to schedule system jobs is extremely useful for a Linux system administrator. Administrators can configure systems to perform a wide variety of tasks on a regular schedule automatically; for example, system backups or rotating and compressing log files.

To schedule system jobs, use crond and the */etc/crontab* file to configure which jobs to run and when:

```
openSUSE:/etc # head -5 /etc/crontab
SHELL=/bin/sh
PATH=/usr/bin:/usr/sbin:/sbin:/bin:/usr/lib/news/bin
MAILTO=root
#
# check scripts in cron.hourly, cron.daily, cron.weekly, and cron.monthly
#
```

In this example, the */etc/crontab* file contains commands that are used to run scripts found in four different directories:

- */etc/cron.hourly* Contains cron scripts that are run every hour
- */etc/cron.daily* Contains cron scripts that are run every day

- */etc/cron.weekly* Contains cron scripts that are run weekly
- */etc/cron.monthly* Contains cron scripts that are run once a month

All scripts found in any of these directories are automatically run by cron according to the specified schedule. For example, the */etc/cron.daily* directory contains a variety of scripts that are used to clean up the system and rotate the logs once each day. These scripts are shown here:

```
openSUSE:/etc/cron.daily # ls
logrotate                    suse-clean_catman           suse.de-backup-rpmdb
mdadm                        suse-do_mandb               suse.de-check-battery
packagekit-background.cron  suse.de-backup-rc.config  suse.de-cron-local
```

If an end user has a system task that needs to be run on one of these four schedules, they can simply create a script file and copy it into the appropriate *cron* directory in */etc*.

NOTE System cron jobs run as the root user!

Using cron to Manage Scheduled User Jobs

End users can create their own scheduled jobs using a *crontab* file associated with their user account. Their *crontab* file is saved in either */var/spool/cron/crontabs/<username>*, */var/spool/cron/tabs/<username>*, or */var/spool/cron/<username>*, depending on the Linux version.

A *crontab* file is simply a text file that uses one line per job. Each line has six fields, separated by tabs, as detailed in Table 9-3. The *crontab* file also accepts characters such as the asterisk (*), comma (,) , and hyphen (-) to fine-tune the schedule for various domains and ranges. Also, the forward slash (/) can be used for "skips." For example, ***/2** in the hour field means every 2 hours, instead of showing **0,2,4,6,8,10,12,14,16,18,20,22**.

Table 9-3 The crontab File Fields

Field	Description
1	Minutes. This field specifies the minutes past the hour that the command should be run.
2	Hour. This field specifies the hour of the day when the command should be run. The cron daemon prefers military time, so use a value of 0 to 23 in this field.
3	Day. This field specifies the day of the month that the command should be run.
4	Month. This field specifies the month of the year when the command should be run.
5	Day of the week. Sunday is 0, Saturday is 6, and 1-5 means Monday through Friday.
6	The name of the command or script, using the full path, to be run.

An end user creates and edits their *crontab* file by running the following from the command prompt:

```
actionshots:~ # crontab -e
```

After this command has been entered, the default editor is opened to create or modify the *crontab* file.

NOTE To change the default editor to gedit, for example, enter the following: **actionshots:~ #EDITOR=/usr/bin/gedit ; export EDITOR**

To schedule a backup job that runs at 5:10 P.M. every day, after running **crontab -e**, enter the following:

```
# min   hr     dom     mon     dow      command
10      17      *       *       *      /bin/tar -cvf ~/homebak.tar ~
```

After editing the file, save and quit. A new or modified *crontab* file is completed in */var/spool/cron*. In addition, the cron service is reloaded so the new configuration can be applied.

To display the *crontab* file updates, run the following:

```
actionshots:~ # crontab -l
```

Finally, **crontab -r** removes the *crontab* file.

End users who incorrectly configure cron jobs can cause system failure; therefore, many system administrators restrict end users from using cron. This is done by utilizing the */etc/cron.allow* and */etc/cron.deny* files.

By default, only the */etc/cron.deny* file is created automatically, and it contains only one restriction by default for the guest user account. All other users are allowed to create *crontab* files to schedule jobs. If the administrator creates the */etc/cron.allow* file, then *only* the users in that file will be allowed to create *crontab* files; all others will be denied.

NOTE Because the crond service checks the */etc/cron.allow* file first, if an end user is listed in both */etc/cron.allow* and */etc/cron.deny*, they will be allowed to use cron!

Let's practice working with Linux processes in Exercise 9-2.

Exercise 9-2: Scheduling Linux Processes

In this exercise, practice using the cron and at commands to schedule processes to run in the future on the system. Perform this exercise using the virtual machine provided online.

VIDEO Please watch the Exercise 9-2 video for a demonstration on how to perform this task.

Complete the following steps:

1. Boot the Linux system and log in as a standard user.
2. Open a terminal session.
3. Switch to the root user account by entering **su -** followed by the root password.
4. Practice using the at daemon by doing the following:
   a. At the shell prompt, enter the **systemctl status atd** command.
   b. Verify that the at daemon is running. If it isn't, enter **systemctl start atd** at the shell prompt.
   c. Enter **at now +5 minutes** at the shell prompt.
   d. Enter **ps -ef > ~/psoutput.txt** at the at> prompt.
   e. Press CTRL-D.
   f. Generate a listing of pending at jobs by entering the **atq** command. The job just created will be displayed.
   g. Wait for the pending at job to complete.
   h. Use the cat command to check the *~/psoutput.txt* file and verify that the output from the ps command was generated correctly.
   i. Enter **at 2 pm tomorrow** at the shell prompt.
   j. Enter **ps -ef > ~/psoutput.txt** at the at> prompt.
   k. Press ENTER.
   l. Press CTRL-D.
   m. Generate a listing of pending at jobs by entering **atq** and notice the job just created. Note its job number.
   n. Remove the pending job by entering the **atrm <job_number>** command.
   o. Enter **atq** again. The pending job should be gone.
5. Practice using cron by completing the following steps:
   a. Log out of the root user account by entering **exit**.
   b. Enter **crontab -e** at the shell prompt.
   c. Press INSERT.
   d. Configure the system to create a backup of the user's home directory every day at 5:05 P.M. by entering the following:

      ```
      05    17    *    *    *    /bin/tar -cvf ~/mybackup.tar ~/
      ```

      If waiting until 5:05 P.M is inconvenient, specify a time value that is only two or three minutes in the future.
   e. Press ESC.

f. Enter **:x** and notice the message on the screen indicating that a new crontab has been installed.

g. Enter **crontab -l** and verify that the job was created correctly.

h. Wait until the time specified in the *crontab* file and then check the user's home directory and verify that the *mybackup.tar* file was created.

i. Remove the user's *crontab* file by entering **crontab -r** at the shell prompt.

Using the anacron Service

Some distributions use anacron along with cron to automate the running of tasks. The two services are similar, except that cron assumes the computer system will remain up and running 24 hours a day, 7 days a week. That is fine for servers and desktops, but not for laptops or desktops that are likely to be off or asleep during certain periods of the day. If the system is not on, cron will not run.

The anacron service works around this issue. If a job is scheduled in anacron, but the system is off, then the missed job will automatically run when the system comes back up.

Just as cron uses the */etc/crontab* file, anacron uses the */etc/anacrontab* file. This file uses the following fields:

```
period   delay   job-identifier   command
```

The first field specifies the recurrence period (in days). For example, use any one of the following values in this field:

- **1** The task recurs daily.
- **7** The task recurs weekly.
- **30** The task recurs monthly.

The second field specifies the delay (in minutes) anacron should wait before executing a skipped job after the system starts up.

The third field contains the job identifier. This is the name that will be used for the job's timestamp file and must be unique for each anacron job. This file is created in the */var/spool/anacron* directory and contains a single line with a timestamp that indicates the last time the particular job was run. The fourth field specifies the command or script that should be run.

Consider the following example in which anacron is configured to run the /usr/bin/updatedb.sh script once a day. If the system is down when the anacron job is supposed to run, the script will execute 30 minutes after the system boots up.

```
openSUSE:/ # cat /etc/anacrontab
1       30      updatedbtime.log      /usr/bin/updatedb.sh
```

Notice that this file does not specify the exact time when the job will run. This is configured by the START_HOURS_RANGE variable in the */etc/anacrontab* file. In the following example, the start range is set to 3–22, which specifies a time range from 3 A.M. to 10 P.M.

```
openSUSE# cat /etc/anacrontab
...
START_HOURS_RANGE=3-22
```

It's important to note that anacron also adds a random number of minutes to whatever value specified in the second field of the *anacrontab* file. The number of minutes that can be added is constrained by the RANDOM_DELAY variable within the */etc/anacrontab* file. By default, this variable is set to a value of 45, which causes anacron to add a random number of minutes between 0 and 45 to the delay time in the anacrontab file. This is shown here:

```
openSUSE# cat /etc/anacrontab
...
RANDOM_DELAY=45
```

EXAM TIP Focus on studying cron and at, more than anacron.

Chapter Review

In this chapter, the reader learned that Linux is a multitasking operating system.

When a daemon is loaded, a system process is created. When an end user enters a command at the shell prompt, a user process is created. User processes are associated with a shell session; system processes are not. Managing running processes is one of the key tasks performed on Linux systems. Configuring the Linux system to run specified programs automatically ensures that the programs execute regularly and on time.

Here are some key facts to remember about Linux processes:

- When the init process or the systemd process loads a daemon, a system process is created.
- A process that spawns another process is called the *parent.*
- The new process that was created by the parent is called the *child.*
- All Linux processes can trace their heredity back to the init or systemd process (depending on the distribution), which is the first process loaded by the kernel on system boot.
- For distributions that use systemd, use the systemctl command to start and stop system services.
- Use the top utility to view system processes.

- By default, the ps command only displays running processes in the current shell.
- nice values range from –20 to +19
- The lower the nice value, the higher the priority of the process.
- The syntax for using renice is **renice <nice_value> <PID>**.
- Only root can assign a nice value less than 0 and use renice to set a lower nice value than the current one.
- By default, processes launched from the shell prompt run in the foreground, and the shell prompt is locked until the process is complete.
- To run a process in the background append an & character to the end of the command.
- When executed, the background process is assigned a job ID number.
- To move a process running in the background to the foreground, enter **fg <job_ID>** at the shell prompt.
- To move a foreground process into the background, press CTRL-Z to stop the process and then enter **bg <job_ID>** to move the process to the background.
- Use the kill, pkill, top, or killall command to terminate a job.
- Common kill signals used with kill or killall include
  - SIGHUP (1)
  - SIGINT (2)
  - SIGKILL (9)
  - SIGTERM (15), the default
- To kill a process with kill, enter **kill -<signal> <PID>** at the shell prompt.
- To kill a process with killall, enter **killall -<signal> <process_name>**.
- One can load a program using the nohup command to allow the process to continue running after logging out.
- To schedule a process to run once in the future, use the at command.
- The at time value can be a fixed time, such as the following:
  - HH:MM
  - noon
  - midnight
  - teatime
- Use the atq command to view a list of pending at jobs.
- Use the atrm command to remove a pending at job.

- A *crontab* file contains one line for each command to run; each line contains six fields:
  - **1** Minutes
  - **2** Hour
  - **3** Day
  - **4** Month
  - **5** Day of the week
  - **6** Command to execute
- A user can create a *crontab* file by entering **crontab -e** at the shell prompt.

Questions

1. After entering **vi** at the shell prompt, what type of process was created on the Linux system?

   A. User

   B. System

   C. Daemon

   D. System V

2. Which process could be the grandparent of all processes running on a Linux system? (Choose two.)

   A. bash

   B. init

   C. sh

   D. ps

   E. systemd

3. When running a Fedora Linux system that uses SysVinit scripts, where are these scripts stored in the filesystem?

   A. /etc/init.d

   B. /etc/rc.d/init.d

   C. /etc/sysv/init.d

   D. /etc/init.d/rc.d

4. Use ps to display extended information about only the processes associated with the current terminal session. Which command will do this?

   A. ps

   B. ps -e

C. ps -f

D. ps -ef

5. What is a zombie process?

   A. A process that has finished executing but whose parent process has not released the child process's PID

   B. A process that has stopped executing while waiting for user input

   C. A process that is being traced by another process

   D. A process that has gone to sleep and cannot be interrupted

6. Which ps option can be used to display all currently running processes?

   A. -c

   B. -e

   C. -f

   D. -l

7. The myapp process has a nice value of 1. Which of the following nice values would increase the priority of the myapp process? (Choose two.)

   A. –15

   B. 5

   C. 19

   D. 0

   E. 2

8. Which of the following shell commands will load the myapp program with a nice value of –5? (Choose two.)

   A. myapp -n -5

   B. nice -5 myapp

   C. renice -5 myapp

   D. nice -n -5 myapp

   E. nice --5 myapp

9. The myapp process (PID 2345) is currently running on the system. Which of the following commands will reset its nice value to –5 without unloading the process? (Choose two.)

   A. myapp -n -5 -p 2345

   B. renice -n -5 2345

   C. renice -5 2345

   D. nice -n -5 2345

10. Load the myapp program from the shell prompt and run it in the background. Which command will do this?

A. myapp -b

B. myapp &

C. myapp --bg

D. myapp

11. Which kill signal sends a CTRL-C key sequence to a running process?

A. SIGHUP

B. SIGINT

C. SIGKILL

D. SIGTERM

12. A user needs to kill a hung process by its process' name, not its PID. Which utilities could best be used? (Choose two.)

A. killall

B. kill

C. hangup

D. SIGKILL

E. pkill

13. You want to run the rsync command to synchronize the home directory with another server on the network, but you know this command will take several hours to complete and you don't want to leave the system logged in during this time. Which commands will leave rsync running after logout?

A. SIGHUP

B. nohup

C. stayalive

D. kill -NOHUP

14. It's currently 1:00 in the afternoon. To schedule the myapp program to run automatically tomorrow at noon (12:00). Which of the following at commands is best to use? (Choose two.)

A. at 12 pm tomorrow

B. at tomorrow -1 hour

C. at now +1 day

D. at today +23 hours

E. at now +23 hours

15. Which of the following crontab lines will cause the /usr/bin/myappcleanup process to run at 4:15 A.M. on the first of every month?

A. `15 4 1 * * /usr/bin/myappcleanup`

B. `15 4 * 1 * /usr/bin/myappcleanup`

C. `1 4 15 * * /usr/bin/myappcleanup`

D. `4 1 * * 15 /usr/bin/myappcleanup`

Answers

1. A. Because the command was entered from the shell prompt, a user process was created.

2. B, E. On some distributions, the init process is the grandparent of all other Linux processes on the system. Other distributions use the systemd process instead. All other processes can trace their heredity to init or systemd, depending on the distribution.

3. B. The init scripts for distributions that use SysVinit scripts are stored in */etc/rc.d/init.d.*

4. C. The ps -f command will display extended information about processes associated with the current shell session.

5. A. A zombie process is one where the process has finished executing, but the parent process wasn't notified and, therefore, hasn't released the child process's PID.

6. B. The ps -e command can be used to display a list of all running processes on the system.

7. A, D. The lower the nice value, the higher the priority of the process. Therefore, nice values of 0 and –15 will increase the priority of the myapp process.

8. D, E. The **nice -n -5 myapp** and **nice --5 myapp** commands will load myapp with a nice value of –5.

9. B, C. The **renice -5 2345** and **renice -n -5 2345** commands will reset the nice value of the myapp process while it's running.

10. B. The **myapp &** command will cause myapp to run in the background.

11. B. The SIGINT kill signal sends a CTRL-C key sequence to the specified process.

12. A, E. The killall utility uses the process name in the command line and can be used to kill the process in this scenario. Also use the pkill command to search for and kill a hung process by its name.

13. **B.** The nohup command can be used to load a program so that it will ignore the SIGHUP signal that is sent when the user logs out, thus allowing the process to remain running.
14. **A, E.** Enter **at 12 pm tomorrow** or **at now +23 hours** to cause the atd daemon to run the specified command at 12:00 on the following day.
15. **A.** The **15 4 1 * * /usr/bin/myappcleanup** crontab line will cause the myappcleanup process to be run at 4:15 A.M. on the first day of every month no matter what day of the week it is.

CHAPTER 10

Managing Linux Software

In this chapter, you will learn about

- Defining package managers
- Red Hat Package Manager (RPM)
- yum
- dnf
- zypper
- Debian package management
- Installing packages from a source
- Managing shared libraries

As a Linux system administrator, you need to know how to install and manage software on a Linux system. The exam includes questions testing your knowledge of the RPM, yum, dnf, and zypper package management tools.

What Is a Package Manager?

Regardless of which package manager your distribution uses, it will perform tasks similar to all package managers, including the following:

- Installing software
- Updating software that has already been installed
- Uninstalling software
- Querying installed software
- Verifying the integrity of installed software

Table 10-1 defines some of the terms associated with package management (the terms are ordered by the syntax of a package, discussed later).

Term	Definition
Package	A package is a group of files (for example, documentation, library files, or scripts) used by a package manager to install an application or applications.
Package group	A group of individual packages that have a similar purpose. The Gnome Desktop package group contains all packages or groups of packages required.
Version number	A version number defines the edition of a package. A version number format is Edition.Major Change.Minor Change. (Minor change may be a feature addition or bug fix.)
Release number	Identifies a version released to the public.
Architecture	Architecture refers to the processor (for example, x86_64) the package will be able to run on. Some packages will run on multiple architectures, and others are not architecture dependent.
Source code	Source code consists of a text file or files made up of instructions written in a programming language (for example, C, C++, Visual Basic), which are later translated into object code by a compiler. Having source code to an application enables a programmer to modify the application to their specific needs.
Repository	A software repository is a location used by package managers to retrieve stored packages.

Table 10-1 Package Management Terms

Red Hat Package Manager (RPM)

The Red Hat Package Manager, RPM, was originally developed in 1997 to install and upgrade software packages in Red Hat Linux distributions. RPM also contains facilities to query the package database and verify the integrity of installed packages.

RPM packages are used on Red Hat Enterprise, CentOS, and Fedora-based systems. The command **rpm --help** will display RPM help information.

Package Names

The syntax of an RPM package name is as follows:

<package name>-<version_number>-<release_number>.<architecture>.rpm
<package name>-<version_number>-<release_number>.<distributor_designator>.rpm

The following list explains these elements, using an example of a package named bash-3.2-32.el5:

- **Package name** This part of the filename simply identifies the name of the package. In this example, the name of the package is bash.
- **Version number** This part of the filename specifies the version of the software in the package. In our example, the version number 3.2 indicates we are looking at the third edition of the software, which has had two major changes since the third edition was released.

- **Release number** This part of the filename indicates the current release of the software version. In our example, the software release is 32.
- **Distribution designator** The distribution designator indicates that the package has been compiled for a specific Linux distribution. In our example, the distribution designator is el5 (Red Hat Enterprise 5).
- **Architecture type** This part of the filename specifies the CPU architecture that the software inside the package will run on. In our example, the architecture is specified as x86_64, which means the software will run on 64-bit x86 CPUs. You may also see the following architectures specified in a package's filename:
  - **i386** Specifies that the software will run on an Intel 80386 or later CPU
  - **i586** Specifies that the software will run on an Intel Pentium or later CPU
  - **i686** Specifies that the software will run on Intel Pentium 4 or later CPUs
  - **x86_64** Specifies that the software will run on 64-bit x86 CPUs
  - **athlon** Specifies that the software is intended to run on an AMD Athlon CPU
  - **ppc** Specifies that the software is intended to run on the PowerPC CPU
  - **noarch** Specifies that the package is not architecture dependent

RPM modes

The command syntax for managing rpm packages is as follows:

```
rpm <mode> <mode_options> <package_name(s) | <package_filename>
```

The rpm command may require either the package name or package filename as an argument. The package name is used when referencing the databases in */var/lib/rpm*. The package filename is the path to the storage location of the package.

RPM uses multiple modes to manage packages, as detailed in Table 10-2.

Mode	Option	Description
install	-i --install	Installs a package file.
upgrade	-U --upgrade	Upgrades the operating system. This option will upgrade current packages and install new operating system packages as necessary. The freshen option will only update installed packages.
erase	-e --erase	Removes a package.
query	-q --query	The query option retrieves package information from the RPM database.
verify	-V --verify	The verify option compares information from the package database with installed files.

Table 10-2 RPM Modes

Installing an RPM Package

To install, erase, update, or freshen a package, you must have root privileges. The command **rpm -i <package_name>** will install a package on your system.

You use the command **rpm -i ftp://<ftp_address> <package_name>** to install a package from an ftp server. An example would be **rpm -i ftp://ftp.download.com/publi/rpms/package**. If the site requires a password, you may execute the command **rpm -i <user_name>:<password>@ftp://ftp.download.com/publi/rpms/package**.

Table 10-3 contains a partial list of RPM installation options.

Upgrading an RPM Package

The RPM upgrade option will upgrade current packages and install new operating system packages as necessary. When using the -U option, RPM considers the checksum information of the original file, the current file installed, and the new file to be installed.

The command **rpm -q --changelog <package_name>** will display package file changes. If the checksum of all three files are the same, the new file will be installed. Even though the files are the same, the new version may have an ownership or permission change.

If the checksums of the original and current files are the same but the new file is different, an upgrade will be performed. This time RPM assumes a change in the package file's content.

If the checksums of the original and new files are the same but the current file is different, RPM does not make any changes. It assumes the current file is valid.

If the checksums of the current file and the file to be installed are the same but are different from the original file, RPM will install the new file. The assumption is that some permission or ownership has changed.

If the checksums of all three files are different, RPM installs the new file but saves a modified copy of the original file (current file) to *<filename>.rpmsave*. The reason behind

Option	Description
--test	Checks for possible installation issues (for example, dependency) without installing the package.
--force	Forces the installation of a package, even if the package is installed on the system. Forces the installation of an older package over a newer package.
--nodeps	Indicates to not check package dependencies.
-K --checksig	Verifies the package is not corrupted by checking the MD5 checksum. You may check the signature of an existing package by executing the command **rpm -K -nosignature <package_name>**.
--prefix <path>	Installs the package in the directory specified by the argument <path>.
-v	Verbose. Prints progress information.
-vv	Prints debugging information.

Table 10-3 RPM Installation Options

this is that RPM cannot look at the contents of the package's files. It assumes the new file is valid but saves the current file since it still has viable information.

When RPM upgrades a package, it retains the configuration files. Some upgrade options are displayed in Table 10-4.

EXAM TIP A key exam concept is to understand that the -i option installs a package, the -F option only updates existing packages, and the -U option is used to upgrade existing packages and will install additional packages if necessary.

Removing (Erasing) an RPM Package

The erase option removes a package. It is best to use the -vv (verbose debug) option when executing the following command:

The command **rpm -e <package_name>** removes a package. During the package removal, **rpm -e**

- Checks to make certain no other package depends on the package to be erased.
- Determines whether any of the package config files have been modified and saves a copy of any modified files.
- Determines if a file that's part of the package is required by another package. If it's not, the file is erased.
- Removes all traces of the package and associated files from the RPM database.

Finally, note that a package may contain a pre-uninstall and post-uninstall scripts. These scripts would be executed as part of the erase process. The erase command will not erase a package if there are dependencies, unless the --nodeps option is specified. Also, consider using the --test option prior to actually erasing a package.

Verify Mode

RPM tracks changes to packages and files. The verify option compares files and packages installed on the system and compares them with the RPM database, and also verifies package dependencies are met. The output of the verify option is a series of codes that may be used to determine if the system configuration has changed or the RPM database is corrupt.

The verify option is also capable of executing a package-specific verification script if one was provided by the publisher.

Option	Description
--oldpackage	Permits a newer version package to be upgraded with an older version package.
--force	The --force option has the same effect as --oldpackage.
-F	The -F (freshen) option will only upgrade installed packages.

Table 10-4 RPM Upgrade Options

Verify compares the following install information with the RPM database:

- File ownership
- File group ownership
- File permissions
- File checksum
- File size
- Validity of symbolic links
- File major and minor numbers (used only for block and character device files)
- File modification time

To verify a package, execute the command **rpm -V <package_name>** or **rpm --verify <package_name>**. Adding an additional **v** will display files associated with the package, even if there are no errors.

To verify all packages, execute the command **rpm -Va**.

Additional verify options allow you to verify packages that contain a certain file or are in a package group. You may also use verify options to exclude size, modification, and other checks.

The output of the command is a series of columns:

SM5DLUGT <attribute marker>

If the code designator appears in the column, then the condition exists. For example, if the letter 5 appears in column 3, then the current checksum differs from the original checksum, which means the file has been modified. In most cases this may not be an issue, but it could be a sign that an attacker has altered files on your Linux system.

Table 10-5 defines the different verify codes.

Table 10-6 defines the RPM verify attribute codes. Attribute codes appear only if the attribute is applied to the file.

Table 10-5 RPM Verify Codes

Column	Code	Definition
1	S	Indicates a size difference
2	M	Indicates a mode (permissions) difference
3	5	Indicates a signature difference
4	D	Indicates a difference in major and minor numbers
5	L	Indicates a difference in symbolic links
6	U	Indicates a difference in file ownership
7	G	Indicates a difference in file group ownership
8	T	Indicates a difference in modification time

Table 10-6 RPM Verify Attribute Codes

Attribute Code	Definition
c	Configuration file
d	Documentation file
g	Ghost file (that is, a file not included in the package)
l	License file
r	Readme file
P	Capability (that is, packages that require this package)

Figure 10-1 contains the edited output of the **rpm -Va** command:

- Line 2 indicates the configuration file */var/lib/unbound/root.key* has a different size, file signature, and modification time.
- Line 3 states that the file */var/run/pulse* is missing.
- Line 4 shows us that the ghost file */var/lib/setroubleshoot/email_alert_recipients* permissions have changed.
- Line 5 indicates the owner and group owner of the ghost file */var/run/avahi-daemon* have changed.

Querying the RPM Database

The query mode allows a user to search for package data in the RPM database. Several query options are shown in Table 10-7.

Note that you can combine options and queries. For example, if you are having difficulty with a command or want to know additional information about a command, you could combine options.

The command **rpm -qcf /usr/bin/passwd** will display the configuration files for the passwd command. Consider using the command **rpm -qif /usr/bin/passwd** to find out package information for the package that contains the passwd command.

rpm2cpio

The command rpm2cpio produces a cpio archive from an RPM package. The syntax is as follows:

rpm2cpio <package_name> | cpio <cpio_options>

Table 10-8 lists some cpio options.

```
1 [root@localhost ~]# rpm -Va
2 S.5....T.  c /var/lib/unbound/root.key
3 missing     /var/run/pulse
4 .M.......  g /var/lib/setroubleshoot/email_alert_recipients
5 ....L....  c /etc/pam.d/fingerprint-auth
6 .....UG..  g /var/run/avahi-daemon
```

Figure 10-1 Error codes for rpm -Va

Option	Definition
-q <package_name> --query	Display the package name and version if the package is installed.
-qa	Display all packages installed on the system. You can combine this with grep to find specific packages (for example, **rpm -qa | grep kernel**).
-qf <absolute_path_filename> rpm -q --whatprovides <filename>	Determine which package a file came from. The file cannot be a symbolic link.
-qi <package_name>	Display package information. This information includes version, vendor, architecture, installation date, and other package information.
-ql <package_name>	List files in a package.
-qR -q --requires	List package dependencies.
-q --whatrequires "<package_name>"	List packages dependent on this package.
-qd <package_name>	List package documentation.
-qp <package_name>	Query the uninstalled package.

Table 10-7 RPM Query Options

Table 10-8 cpio Options

Option	Definition
-t	List contents
-i	Extract
-d	Create subdirectories
-v	Verbose output

To list the contents of a package, execute the command **rpm2cpio <package_filename> | cpio -t**. To extract an entire package, execute the command **rpm2cpio <package_filename> | cpio -idv**. You may extract a file from an RPM package using the command **rpm2cpio <package_filename> | cpio -idv <filename>**.

NOTE The extraction will occur in the current working directory. It is advisable that you use an empty directory.

Exercise 10-1: RPM

In Exercise 10-1, you practice using some of the RPM commands you have just learned. Be sure to use the CentOS image we have provided you and log in as user **root** with a password of **password**. Follow these steps:

VIDEO Please watch the Exercise 10-1 video for a demonstration on how to perform this task.

1. Create a snapshot.
2. Determine the installation date of the bash package by executing the **rpm -qi bash** or **rpm -qif /bin/bash** command.
3. Look at the package that installed the command /bin/bash by executing the command **rpm -qf /bin/bash** and then review the output of the command in step 2. Where do you see the package information?
4. What other packages are required (package dependencies) by the bash package? Execute the **rpm -qR bash** or **rpm -q --requires bash** command.
5. Determine what packages are required by the lsscsi package and then try to remove the lsscsi package by executing the command **rpm -e --test lsscsi** (this will simulate removing the package). Compare the output of the **rpm -q --whatrequires "lsscsi"** command with the output of the **rpm -e --test lsscsi** command.
6. Use the **rpm -qc bash** command to determine which configuration files are provided with the bash package,
7. Determine what configuration files are affecting a command. Use the command **rpm -qcf /usr/bin/passwd** to determine the configuration files used by the passwd command.
8. Verify the package that provides the command lsscsi by executing the following commands:
   rpm -V lsscsi; sleep 5; rpm -qvf /usr/bin/lsscsi; sleep 5; rpm -Vv lsscsi.
9. View the output of the **rpm -qVf /etc/at.deny** command. According to the output, what has changed since the file was installed?
10. View the list of files in the bash package. Execute the command **cd /run/media/root/"CentOS 7 x85_64"/Packages**; next, execute the **rpm2cpio $(rpm -qf /bin .bash).rpm | cpio -t** command.

    The rpm2cpio command requires a package filename. The command **rpm -qf** will provide a package name but not a package filename. **$(rpm -qf /bin/bash)** will output the package name, and **.rpm** adds the suffix .rpm to the end of the package name.

yum

Yum, or Yellow Dog Updater Modified, is a package manager that is a command-line front end to RPM. Yum allows users with root privileges to add, remove, and search for available packages. Yum also allows the user to use history to roll back or redo previous yum transactions.

Yum's main configuration file is */etc/yum.conf*, which we discuss next.

```
[main]
cachedir=/var/cache/yum/$basearch/$releasever
keepcache=0
debuglevel=2
logfile=/var/log/yum.log
exactarch=1
obsoletes=1
gpgcheck=1
plugins=1
installonly_limit=5
bugtracker_url=http://bugs.centos.org/set_project.php?project_id=23&ref=\
http://bugs.centos.org/bug_report_page.php?category=yum

distroverpkg=centos-release


#  This is the default, if you make this bigger yum won't see if the metadata
# is newer on the remote and so you'll "gain" the bandwidth of not having to
# download the new metadata and "pay" for it by yum not having correct
# information.
#  It is esp. important, to have correct metadata, for distributions like
# Fedora which don't keep old packages around. If you don't like this checking
# interupting your command line usage, it's much better to have something
# manually check the metadata once an hour (yum-updatesd will do this).
# metadata_expire=90m

# PUT YOUR REPOS HERE OR IN separate files named file.repo
# in /etc/yum.repos.d
```

Figure 10-2 A sample *etc/yum.conf* file

/etc/yum.conf

The file */etc/yum.conf* is a global yum configuration file that contains a list of directives assigned a value (see Figure 10-2). If the directive's value is 0, the directive is not asserted; if the directive value is 1, the directive is asserted.

Directives configured in */etc/yum.repos.d* take precedence over directives configured in */etc/yum.conf*. Table 10-9 reviews some directives found in */etc/yum.conf*.

Directive	Definition
[main]	The main configuration section of */etc/yum.conf*.
[repository]	Repository configurations. Repository configurations may also be found in */etc/yum.repos.d*.
$releaseserver	The release version of the operating system. This value is determined from the variable distroverpkg in */etc/yum.conf*.
$arch	Specifies the CPU: I686 (i386) or x86_64 (64 bit).
$basesearch	Base architecture of the system. i386 is a 32-bit system and x86_64 is a 64-bit system.
distroverpkg=	Used by yum to determine the distribution version. If the line distroverpkg is not available, the value is obtained from the file */etc/redhat-release*.
cachedir	Specifies the location where downloads are saved.
debuglevel	Specifies the amount of detail displayed in debug output. The value range is 0–10. The higher the value, the more debug information is displayed. The default debug level is 2. If the debug level is 0, debug output is disabled.

Table 10-9 yum.conf Directives

Directive	Definition
keepcache=0|1	Yum, by default, stores package files in the directive specified by cachedir. The keepcache directive determines if the packages are retained after install. A value of 1 retains the package information so it may be used when a network connection is not available.
logfile	Location of the yum logfile.
discoverpkg=0|1	Location of the current kernel version (*/etc/redhat-release*).
exactarch=0|1	A value of 0 disregards the system architecture. A value of 1 limits package downloads to those matching the system architecture.
obsoletes=0|1	A value of 1 checks to see if a package obsoletes another package. If so, the obsolete package is replaced. A value of 0 disables obsolete package checking.
gpgcheck=0|1	This value may be set in */etc/yum.conf* or in individual repository files. If set in */etc/yum.conf*, it sets the value for all repositories. (The repo file takes precedence over the value in */etc/yum.conf*.) A value of 1 enables GNU Privacy Guard (GPG), checking for all packages in all repositories. A value of 0 disables GPG checking.
plugins=0|1	A value of 1 include plug-ins defined in */etc/yum/pluginconf.d* and */usr/lib/yum-plugins* as part of yum's configuration. A value of 0 disables plug-ins. Individual plug-ins may be enabled or disabled by editing the enabled directive in the plug-in configuration. To enable a plug-in, the enable directive would be equal to 1.
installonly_limit=	Maximum number of versions of any single package that may be installed. The default value is 3 but should not be less than 2.
retries=	This directive determines the number of times yum will try to retrieve a file before returning an error code. A value of 0 will set a continuous retry. The default value is 10.
reposdir=	The absolute path to the directory where a specific repository is located. Can be used to point to private repositories.
assumeyes=	Determines the answer to yum prompts. A value of 1 will answer yes to all system prompts.

Table 10-9 yum.conf Directives *(Continued)*

/etc/yum/repos.d

As stated earlier, packages are stored in repositories. For yum to install a package, it must know how to locate the repositories. The location of repositories is defined in the repository section, [repository], of *yum.conf* or repository files in */etc/yum/repos.d*. The directive in */etc/yum.repos.d* (**include /etc/yum.repos.d**) in */etc/yum.conf* tells yum to include the repository definition files in */etc/yum.repos.d*. The directive reposdir= points to a specific repository directive.

Repository Definition Files

Repository definition files contain information on how to access a specific repository. Figure 10-3 shows edited output of the file *CentOS-Base.repo*. We examine some of the directives in this section.

```
[base]
name=CentOS-$releasever - Base
mirrorlist=http://mirrorlist.centos.org/?release=$releasever&arch=$basearch&repo=os&infra=$infra
#baseurl=http://mirror.centos.org/centos/$releasever/os/$basearch/
gpgcheck=1
gpgkey=file:///etc/pki/rpm-gpg/RPM-GPG-KEY-CentOS-7

#released updates
[updates]
name=CentOS-$releasever - Updates
mirrorlist=http://mirrorlist.centos.org/?release=$releasever&arch=$basearch&repo=updates&infra=$infra
#baseurl=http://mirror.centos.org/centos/$releasever/updates/$basearch/
gpgcheck=1
gpgkey=file:///etc/pki/rpm-gpg/RPM-GPG-KEY-CentOS-7
```

Figure 10-3 A sample repos configuration file

Section Name Each repository definition starts with a repository name enclosed in left and right brackets. In Figure 10-3, we find two repositories: base and updates.

name= The name directive is a description of the repository definition file.

mirrorlist= The mirrorlist directive defines a location that contains a list of base URLs.

baseurl= This directive is a URL to the directory where repository data is located. The directive has several formats:

- If the repository is located on the local machine, you use file:///<path_to_repository>.
- If the repository is on an FTP server or is sent over HTTP, you use ftp|http://<path_to_repository>.
- To add a username or password, you use ftp|http://<username>:<password>@<path_to_repository>.

gpg There are two directives associated with gpg:

- The directive gpgcheck= takes a value of 0 and 1. A value of 1 tells yum to check GPG signatures.
- gpgkey defines the location yum will use to import the GPG key.

enable The enable directive also takes a value of 0 or 1. If the value is 0, yum will not use the repository defined in the section as a data source.

Plug-Ins

Plug-ins are used to enhance the capabilities of yum. For example, the plug-in refresh-package automatically refreshes the package kit metadata each time yum is executed. Package kit is a graphics application used to install, uninstall, and update packages via yum.

Yum plug-ins have configuration files (*<plugin_name>.conf*) located in the directory */etc/yum/pluginconf.d*.

Plug-ins may be enabled or disabled by the directive plug-ins in */etc/yum.conf* or the enabled directive in the plug-in configuration file. The enable directive in the plug-in configuration file takes precedence.

A plug-in may be also be disabled on the command line when executing a yum command by adding the option **--disableplugin=<plugin_name>**. The command **yum update --disableplugin=downloadonly** disables the downloadonly plug-in while executing the **yum update** command.

Whenever you execute a yum command, enabled plug-ins are displayed.

Yum Commands

Yum commands permit the use of glob expressions, which are strings that contain metacharacters such as * and ?. The expressions must be escaped (surrounded by \ \) or quoted (using ' ').

Table 10-10 introduces some basic yum commands.

Command	Description
yum list available	This command displays a list of all available packages in enabled repositories. This command may be used with the grep command (for example, **yum list available | grep kernel**).
yum list installed	This command lists all packages installed on your system.
yum list all	Displays a list of installed packages and packages available on enabled repositories.
yum list installed <package_name>	Lists installed packages with a specific package name (for example, **yum list installed kernel**).
yum list <package_name>	Lists installed and available packages with a specific package name (for example, **yum list kernel**.
yum list update <package_name>	This command checks for updates for the specified package.
yum info <package_name>	This command displays information about the specified package, including its version and dependencies.
yum deplist <package_name>	Displays a list of package dependencies.
yum provides <file_name> yum whatprovides <file_name>	This command identifies the RPM package that provides the specified filename. You must use the absolute path to the file.
yum search <search_string>	Searches the package names and descriptions of packages on enabled repositories.
yum grouplist	Displays a list of installed and available package groups.
yum groupinfo <group_name>	Displays the description and contents of a package group (for example, **yum groupinfo "Gnome Desktop"**).
yum repolist	Displays a list of enabled repositories.
yum clean packages	Removes cached package data.
yum clean all	Removes cached packages and metadata.

Table 10-10 Basic yum Commands

Command	Description
yum install <package_name>	This command installs the specified package.
yum groupinstall <package group>	Installs a package group.
yum install <filename>	Installs the package associated with a file.
enablerepo=<repo_name> \install <package_name>	Installs a package from a specific repository.
yum check-update	Searches enabled repositories for package updates.
yum list updates	This command generates a list of updates for all installed packages.
yum update	Updates packages to the current version.
yum update <package_name>	Updates a package to the current version.
yum upgrade	Updates packages to the current version and deletes obsolete packages.
yum remove <package_name> yum erase <package_name>	This command uninstalls the specified package.
yum clean packages	Removes cached package data.
yum clean all	Removes cached packages and metadata.

Table 10-11 yum Install, Erase, and Update Commands

Installing Packages

In this section, we review commands and options used to install packages using the yum package manager. Table 10-11 reviews the commands used to install, update, and remove applications.

EXAM TIP Note that some packages for Linux have different names than expected, such as the httpd package for apache2, or the bind package for the DNS nameserver. For example:

```
sysA# yum install bind
```

Table 10-12 lists the yum command options.

Option	Description
--noplugin --disableplugin=<plugin>	Disable plugins when executing this command. Disable a specific plugin.
--enableplugin=<plugin>	Enable a plug-in (for this command) that may have been disabled using the directive **enable=0**.
download --downloaddir	These options save a package to a directory rather than installing the package. Here is the command syntax: **yum install <package_name> --downloadonly \ --downladdir=<directory_name** This plug-in requires installation using the command: **yum install yum-plugin-downloadonly**

Table 10-12 yum Command Options

Exercise 10-2: Yum

In Exercise 10-2, you practice using some of the yum commands you have just learned. Be sure to use the CentOS image we have provided you and log in as user **root** with a password of **root**. Follow these steps:

VIDEO Please watch the Exercise 10-2 video for a demonstration on how to perform this task.

1. Create a snapshot.
2. Look at the package that installed the command /bin/bash by executing the **yum provides /bin/bash** command.
3. What other packages are required (package dependencies) by the bash package? Execute the **yum deplist bash** command.
4. Execute the command **yum repolist** to display a list of enabled repositories.
5. Use the command **yum list installed** to list the packages installed on your system.
6. Execute the command **yum list kernel** to list installed kernel packages.
7. Execute the command **yum list available kernel*** to list available kernel packages.
8. Use the command **yum check-update** to check the enabled repositories for available package updates.
9. Select one of the packages on the list and execute the **yum update <package_name>** command.
10. Execute the command **yum update** to update all the packages on your system.

dnf

dnf, or dandified yum, is a package manager that has replaced yum in Fedora and will replace yum in Red Hat Enterprise 8. One of the most major improvements is dependency resolution. Table 10-13 contains a list of DNF configuration files.

Most of the yum commands may be executed in dnf by changing yum to dnf. Refer to the preceding section on yum, as we will not duplicate the commands here. Also, note that the command deplist has been removed.

Table 10-13 dnf Configuration Files

File	Description
/etc/dnf	Contains dnf configuration files and directories
/etc/dnf/dnf.conf	Global configuration file
/var/lcache/dnf	Contains DNF cache files
/etc/yum.repos.d	Contains repository configuration files

zypper

zypper is the SUSE command-line package manager that's a front end to the RPM package manager.

NOTE SUSE also offers a GUI-based, all-purpose systems administration tool called YaST that manages packages, users, security, networking, and so on.

Installing, Updating, and Removing Packages

The command **zypper in <package_name>** is used to install a package. You may also use the install command to replace one package with another using the syntax **zypper in <new_package> <old_package>**. To replace vi with nano, execute the command **zypper in nano -vi**.

Updating Packages

Zypper is capable of patching existing packages and updating the system.

The command **zypper list-patches** will display a list of required patches. The command **zypper patch** will install existing patches.

System-wide package updates may be applied using the command **zypper update**. To apply updates to a specific package, execute the command **zypper update <package_name>**.

Removing Packages

To remove a package, execute the command **zypper remove <package_name>** or **zypper rm <package_name>**.

Package Info

The zypper if (info) command may be used to obtain package information. The syntax is **zypper if <option> <package_name>**.

Table 10-14 lists some package info options.

Table 10-14 Package Info Options

Option	Description
--provides	Displays packages that provide a file
--requires	Displays a list of package dependencies
-t	Displays the type of package: **package** RPM package **patch** Released patch **product** Group of packages used to install an application **pattern** Group of packages used to provide a function

```
#  | Alias                     | Name                            | Enabled | GPG Check | Refresh | Type
---+---------------------------+---------------------------------+---------+-----------+---------+-----
1  | repo-debug                | Debug Repository                | No      | ----      | ----    | NONE
2  | repo-debug-non-oss        | Debug Repository (Non-OSS)      | No      | ----      | ----    | NONE
3  | repo-debug-update         | Update Repository (Debug)       | No      | ----      | ----    | NONE
4  | repo-debug-update-non-oss | Update Repository (Debug, Non-OSS) | No   | ----      | ----    | NONE
5  | repo-non-oss              | Non-OSS Repository              | Yes     | ( p) Yes  | No      | NONE
6  | repo-oss                  | Main Repository                 | Yes     | ( p) Yes  | No      | NONE
7  | repo-source               | Source Repository               | No      | ----      | ----    | NONE
8  | repo-source-non-oss       | Source Repository (Non-OSS)     | No      | ----      | ----    | NONE
9  | repo-update               | Main Update Repository          | Yes     | ( p) Yes  | No      | NONE
10 | repo-update-non-oss       | Update Repository (Non-Oss)     | Yes     | ( p) Yes  | No      | NONE
```

Figure 10-4 Using zypper -lr to list repository information

Working with Repositories

Every zypper repository has a unique identification number (see Figure 10-4), alias name, and repository name and priority. The command **zypper repos** or **zypper lr** will display a list of repositories and their alias names. The output also indicates if the repository is enable and has been refreshed.

Table 10-15 displays commands used to refresh repository information.

Repository configuration information may be found by executing the command **zypper repos -d**.

Adding a Repository

The command **zypper ar <url>** or **zypper addrepo <url>** will add a repository. Once the repository is added, you can add an alias name. First, use **zypper -lr** to find the new repository's ID number. Then use the command **zypper nr <id_number> <repo_name>** or **zypper namerepo <id_number> <repo_name>**.

Removing a Repository

The command **zypper rr <repo_name>** or **zypper removerepo <repo_name>** will remove a repository.

Enabling and Disabling Repositories

A repository may be modified by using the commands **zypper mr** or **zypper modifyrepo**.

If you look at Figure 10-4, you will see the repository ID 7, rep-oss, is enabled. To disable the repository, issue the command **zypper mr -d** 7 or **zypper modifyrepo -d** 7. To enable a repository, change the -d to -e.

Table 10-15 zypper Refresh Repository Commands

Command	Description
zypper ref zypper refresh	Download package metadata.
zypper ref -f	Force download of metadata even if the metadata has not expired.

Debian Package Management

Distributions based on the Debian distribution use the Debian Package Manager (dpkg) instead. In this part of the chapter, we discuss how to manage Debian software packages. The following topics are addressed:

- Debian package naming
- Installing packages with dpkg
- Viewing package information with apt-cache
- Installing packages with apt-get
- Using aptitude

Debian Package Naming

Debian packages use a naming convention similar to that used by RPM packages. The syntax is **<package_name>_<version>_<architecture>.deb** (for example, 3dchess_0.8.1-16_i386.deb):

- **packagename** Like with RPM, this is simply the name of the package. In the example here, the name of the application in the package is **3dchess**.
- **version** Specifies the version number of the package. In this example, it is **0.8.1-16**.
- **architecture** Specifies the hardware architecture the package will run on. In the example here, **i386** indicates the package will run on Intel 80386 or later CPUs.

Installing Packages with dpkg

The key command-line utility used to manage Debian packages is **dpkg**. The syntax for using dpkg is

dpkg <options> <action> <package_name> or <package_filename>

You can use the actions and options listed in Tables 10-16 and 10-17 with the dpkg command.

Some options are associated with other options. Table 10-17 illustrates the associations.

Viewing Package Information with apt-cache

In addition to dpkg, you can also use several apt (Advanced Package Tool) tools to manage packages on a Debian-based system. The apt-cache command is used to query package information from the Debian package database. Common apt-cache commands are shown in Table 10-18.

Option	Description
-i	Installs the specified package.
-r	Uninstalls the specified package but does not delete its configuration files.
-P	Uninstalls the specified package and deletes all its configuration files.
--configure	Reconfigures the specified package (can also be done with dpkg-reconfigure).
-p	Displays information about the specified package. The package must already be installed.
-I	Displays information about a package that isn't currently installed on the system.
-l	Lists all installed packages on the system.
-L	Lists all files that were installed by the specified package on the system.
-S <filename>	Identifies the package that installed the specified file.

Table 10-16 dpkg Command Actions

Option	Associated Options	Description
-B	-r	When you're uninstalling a package that other packages are dependent on, this option disables those packages.
-G	-i	This option tells dpkg to not install the specified package if a newer version of the same package is already installed.
-E	-i	This option tells dpkg to not install the specified package if the same version of that package is already installed.
--ignore	-i or -r	This option causes dpkg to ignore dependency information when installing or removing a package.
--no-act	-i or -r	This option tells dpkg to check for problems (such as unresolved dependencies) when installing or removing a package.
--recursive	-i	This option allows you to install multiple packages at once using * in the package filename part of the command. All matching packages in the current directory as well as subdirectories will be installed.

Table 10-17 dpkg Command Options

Common apt-cache Command	Description
apt-cache showpkg <package_name> or apt-cache show <package_name>	Displays information about the package.
apt-cache stats	Displays the number of packages installed, dependency information, and other package cache statistics.
apt-cache unmet	Reports any missing dependencies in the package cache.
apt-cache depends <package_name>	Displays all of the package's dependencies.
apt-cache pkgnames <package_name>	Checks to see whether or not a package is installed on the system. Leaving out the package name displays a list of all the packages installed on the system.
apt-cache search <keyword>	Searches package descriptions for the specified keyword.

Table 10-18 Common apt-cache Commands

Installing Packages with apt-get

In addition to apt-cache, the apt suite of tools also includes the apt-get utility, which is the equivalent of the yum utility on an RPM system.

The */etc/apt/sources.list* file defines the repositories from which apt-get can install packages. As with yum, these repositories can reside on a local optical disc (such as your installation disc), a local hard drive, or a server on the Internet (via the HTTP or FTP protocol). A sample *sources.list* file is shown here:

```
root@Ubuntu-Desktop:/etc/apt# cat sources.list
#deb cdrom:[Ubuntu 9.10 _Karmic Koala_ - Release i386 (20091028.5)]/
karmic main restricted
deb http://us.archive.ubuntu.com/ubuntu/ karmic main restricted
deb-src http://us.archive.ubuntu.com/ubuntu/ karmic main restricted
```

Package repositories are identified in this file with the prefix deb, whereas source file repositories are identified with deb-src. After the prefix, the URL to the repository is specified.

The syntax for using apt-get is pretty straightforward:

apt-get options command package_name

Commonly used apt-get commands and options are listed in Tables 10-19 and 10-20, respectively.

Using aptitude

All the apt tools we have looked at thus far in this chapter have been command-line utilities. However, this tool suite also provides a text-based, menu-driven package management utility that is really handy, called aptitude. Aptitude must be installed. You run

apt-get Command	Description
Install	Installs the latest version of a specified package
Remove	Removes the specified package
Update	Displays updated information about all packages available in your configured package repositories
Upgrade	Upgrades all installed packages to the newest version
dist-upgrade	Upgrades all installed packages to the newest version, but avoids upgrading packages if the upgrade would break a dependency
Check	Verifies the integrity of installed packages as well as the package database
Clean	Removes outdated information from the package database

Table 10-19 Common apt-get Commands

apt-get Option	Associated Command	Description
-d	upgrade install	Downloads the specified package but doesn't install it
-s	All commands	Simulates the actions associated with the specified command but doesn't actually perform them
-f	install remove	Checks for unmet dependencies and fixes them, if possible
-q	All commands	Suppresses progress information
-y	All commands	Sends a default "yes" answer to any prompts displayed in the action
--no-upgrade		Tells apt-get not to upgrade a package if an older version of the package has already been installed

Table 10-20 Common apt-get Options

aptitude by simply entering **aptitude** at the shell prompt. When you do, the interface shown in Figure 10-5 is displayed.

You can use aptitude to do just about anything you can do with dpkg or apt-get. You can install packages, uninstall packages, and update packages. For example, to install

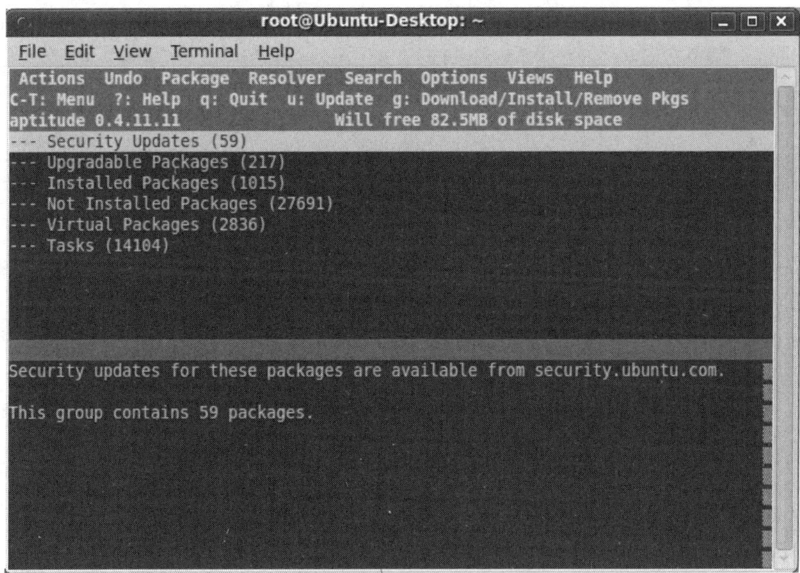

Figure 10-5 Using aptitude to manage packages

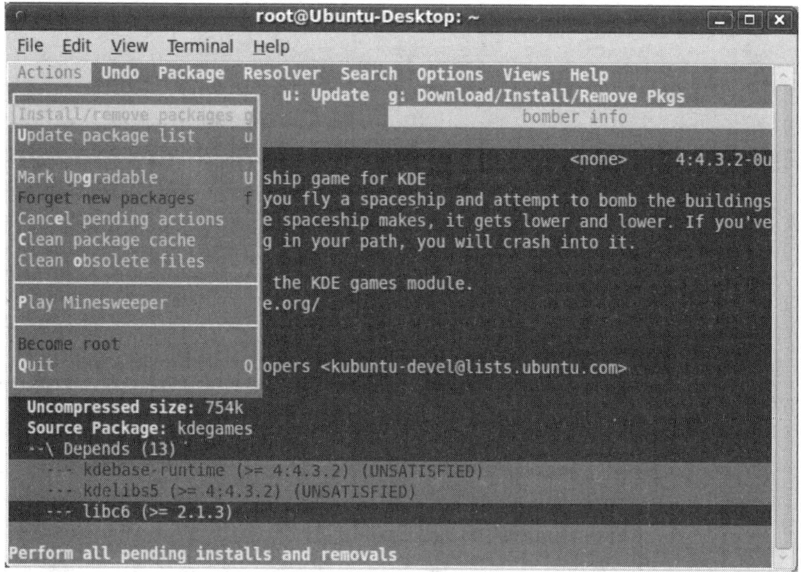

Figure 10-6 Accessing aptitude menus

a new package, you would arrow down to and select Not Installed Packages; then you would browse to the package you want to install and press G. You can also press CTRL-T to access the aptitude menus, as shown in Figure 10-6. The aptitude utility can also be used in command-line mode using the syntax shown in Table 10-21.

aptitude Command	Description
aptitude install <package_name>	Downloads and installs the specified package
aptitude remove <package_name>	Uninstalls the specified package
aptitude purge <package_name>	Uninstalls the specified package and also deletes its associated configuration files and data files
aptitude update	Updates the list of available packages
aptitude full-upgrade	Upgrades all the installed packages on your system to the latest version
aptitude search <search_term>	Searches for patterns that contain the specified search term

Table 10-21 Command-Line aptitude Commands

EXAM TIP The **wget** and **curl** commands are utilities available to download software and source code when a web browser such as Firefox cannot be used; for example, from the comand-line interface. Running **wget http://downloads.metasploit.com/data/releases/framework-latest.tar.bz2** will download the metasploit source code. Running **curl -o ftpd.tgz https://security.appspot.com/downloads/vsftpd-3.0.3.tar.gz** will download the FTP server source code.

Installing Packages from a Source

In addition to installing software using a package manager, you can also install software on Linux from source code. In fact, many of the applications and services you will install on a Linux system will be delivered as source code, not as a binary executable. When you install the software on your local system, you actually compile the source code from the installation files into a binary executable that can be run.

Distributing software in this manner has many advantages. Key among these is the fact that you don't have to create a separate executable and installation package for each delivery architecture and platform. You can have the installation process detect the type of system the software is being installed on and compile the software appropriately. The key disadvantage to this approach is the fact that it makes the installation process much more complex. Users must have a compiler installed on their system; otherwise, they won't be able to compile the source code into a binary executable. In addition, the user must know the proper procedure for compiling the source code and installing the resulting executable.

Fortunately, a standard process for completing this task has been adopted by most developers. This process is composed of preparing the installation files, compiling the executable, installing the executable, and uninstalling software compiled from source code.

Preparing the Installation Files

The first step in installing an application from source code is to download the appropriate installation files from the Internet. For example, if you wanted to install the pure-ftpd service, you would navigate to the website https://www.pureftpd.org/project/pure-ftpd/ and download the installation files.

One thing you'll notice about installation files used to install from source code is that they are usually distributed as a tarball file. Tarball files usually have a .tar.gz extension. Because these applications are distributed as tarballs, you must first use the command gunzip to decompress the archive and the tar command to extract the archive.

You must execute the command **tar -xvf <tar_filename>** to untar them after downloading them from the Internet before you can do anything else. This is done using the tar command. The tar command is used to create archive files. It can also be used to extract files from archives such as tarballs.

Once you have downloaded the tarball, create a directory to extract the file to and then copy the file to that directory. Execute the cd command to change directory where you copied the tarball. Enter **tar -zxvf <filename>** to decompress and extract the archive to the current directory. For example, suppose you downloaded the pure-ftpd-1.0.29.tar.gz file.

To extract this file, you would enter **tar -zxvf pure-ftpd-1.0.29.tar.gz** at the shell prompt. The files are extracted to the current directory. This directory contains the source code files that will be used to create the executable program. It also contains a variety of utilities needed to help create the executable. Here is a sample list of files:

```
openSUSE:/root/work# ls
AUTHORS                          README.Donations       depcomp
CONTACT                          README.LDAP            gui
COPYING                          README.MacOS-X         install-sh
ChangeLog                        README.MySQL           m4
FAQ                              README.PGSQL           man
HISTORY                          README.TLS             missing
INSTALL                          README.Virtual-Users   pam
Makefile.am                      README.Windows         pure-ftpd.png
Makefile.gui                     THANKS                 pure-ftpd.spec
Makefile.in                      aclocal.m4             pure-ftpd.spec.in
NEWS                             compile                puredb
README                           config.h.in            pureftpd-ldap.conf
README.Authentication-Modules    configuration-file     pureftpd-mysql.conf
README.Configuration-File        configure              pureftpd-pgsql.conf
README.Contrib                   configure.ac           pureftpd.schema
README.Debian                    contrib                src
```

With the files extracted, you next need to prepare the installation files to be compiled. This is done using the configure command shown in the preceding example. To run this command, first verify that you're in the directory created when the tarball was extracted; then enter **./configure** at the shell prompt, as shown here:

```
openSUSE:/root/work # ./configure
checking for a BSD-compatible install... /usr/bin/install -c
checking whether build environment is sane... yes
checking for a thread-safe mkdir -p... /bin/mkdir -p
checking for gawk... gawk
checking whether make sets $(MAKE)... yes
checking for ranlib... ranlib
checking for gcc... gcc
checking whether the C compiler works... yes
checking for C compiler default output file name... a.out
...
```

The configure file is a script that does two things when it is run. First, it checks your system to make sure all the necessary components required to compile the program are available. One of the most important things it checks for is the existence of a compiler compatible with the C programming language. If you don't have a C compiler, such as the GNU C Compiler (gcc) or the GNU C++ Compiler (gcc-c++), the configure command will display an error on the screen instructing you to install a compiler and then run configure again. It also verifies that your overall system environment is compatible with the program you're going to install.

Second, it also creates a very important file called Makefile. Because most source code applications are designed to be deployed on a variety of distributions and architectures, the installation program needs to know how to customize the source code files such that the resulting executable will run on your particular system. One of the last things the configure script does is create a series of Makefile files. The Makefile file contains specific instructions for how the executable should be compiled to run on your platform.

Although not required, it's usually a good idea to check the Makefile file after running configure to verify that the program is going to be installed in the manner you want.

If you see something you want to change, you can use a text editor to make the appropriate changes and save the file.

Once configure has been run and the Makefile file is ready, the next step in the process is to actually compile the executable. Let's discuss how this is done next.

Compiling the Executable

At this point in the process, the program you want to install still exists only as source code. Before you can run it, you must convert the text-based source code into a binary executable file. This is done using the make command. The make command calls your system's C compiler (such as gcc) and directs it to read the source code files, using the specifications and options listed in the Makefile file, and then generates a compiled executable file. This is done by entering **make** at the shell prompt without any options while you are still in the directory created when you untarred the tarball file. Here is an example:

```
openSUSE:/root/work # make
make  all-recursive
make[1]: Entering directory '/home/tux/Downloads/pure-ftpd-1.0.29'
Making all in puredb
make[2]: Entering directory '/home/tux/Downloads/pure-ftpd-1.0.29/puredb'
Making all in src
make[3]: Entering directory '/home/tux/Downloads/pure-ftpd-1.0.29/puredb/src'
gcc -DHAVE_CONFIG_H -I. -I../..    -I/usr/local/include -DCONFDIR=\"/etc\" -
DSTATEDIR=\"/var\"   -g -O2 -MT puredb_read.o -MD -MP -MF .deps/puredb_read.Tpo -c
-o puredb_read.o puredb_read.c
mv -f .deps/puredb_read.Tpo .deps/puredb_read.Po
rm -f libpuredb_read.a
ar cru libpuredb_read.a puredb_read.o
...
```

Be aware, however, that make only creates the executable. Before you can use it, it needs to be actually installed on the system; doing this will copy the executable, startup scripts, and documentation files to the appropriate directories in your filesystem. Let's discuss how this is done next.

Installing the Executable

To actually install the program on your system, you use the make command a second time. However, this time you specify a target with **make install**. This tells make to install the program using the information specified in the INSTALL portion of the Makefile file.

To do this, make sure you're still in the directory created when you untarred the tarball file. Then enter **make install** at the shell prompt. The make utility will then follow the instructions in the Makefile file to install the application, as shown here:

```
openSUSE:/home/rtracy/Downloads/pure-ftpd-1.0.29 # make install
Making install in puredb
make[1]: Entering directory '/home/tux/Downloads/pure-ftpd-1.0.29/puredb'
Making install in src
make[2]: Entering directory '/home/tux/Downloads/pure-ftpd-1.0.29/puredb/src'
make[3]: Entering directory '/home/tux/Downloads/pure-ftpd-1.0.29/puredb/src'
make[3]: Nothing to be done for 'install-exec-am'.
make[3]: Nothing to be done for 'install-data-am'.
...
```

At this point, the application or service is ready to run. Simply enter the appropriate commands at the shell prompt.

Exercise 10-3: Building Software from Source Code

In this exercise, you practice installing the Pure-FTPd software from a tarball.

You can perform this exercise using the virtual machine that comes with this book. Make certain you are logged in as user **root** with a password of **root**. Follow these steps:

VIDEO Please watch the Exercise 10-3 video for a demonstration on how to perform this task.

1. Use the **cd /LABS/Chapter_10/work** command. Use the **ls** command to verify the file *pure-ftpd-1.0.29.tar.gz* exists in the directory.

NOTE There are two copies of the compressed file. One is in */LABS/Chapter_10/work* and the other in */LABS/Chapter_10/source*. Make certain you use the file in */LABS/Chapter_10/work*. The file in */LABS/Chapter_10/source* is a backup copy.

2. Enter **tar -zxvf ./ pure-ftpd-1.0.29.tar.gz** at the shell prompt.
3. Use the **cd** command to change to the directory created by tar. This should be *pure-ftpd-1.0.29*.
4. Enter **ls** to view the files extracted from the tarball.
5. Enter **./configure** at the shell prompt. The configure script will check your system and verify that the software can be installed. You must have a C compiler installed on your system. If configure reports that you're missing a compiler, use the **yum -y install gcc** command.
6. When the configure script is done, compile the executable by entering **make** at the shell prompt.
7. When the compilation is complete, install the executable by entering **make install** at the shell prompt.
8. Start the service by entering **/usr/local/sbin/pure-ftpd &** at the shell prompt.
9. Test the system by entering **ftp localhost** at the shell prompt.
10. When prompted, enter **anonymous** for a username. You should be logged in to the FTP server at this point.
11. Enter **quit** to close the connection.

    At this point, you have a functioning FTP server running on your Linux system!

Uninstalling Software Compiled from Source Code

Uninstalling software of this variety is very similar to the installation process.

For most applications or services that are installed using the standard build process we discussed earlier, you must (in most cases) have access to your installation files to uninstall the associated software. The issue here is that many Linux administrators delete the installation source files once the installation process is complete to save disk space. If you do this, you've just deleted the files you'll need if you ever decide to uninstall the software. We recommend that you create a protected directory in your filesystem somewhere that only root can access and keep your source installation files in it. Yes, it does take up a little bit of disk space, but you'll have the files you need if uninstalling ever becomes necessary.

The uninstall process can vary slightly from product to product. Some applications or services may include an uninstall script in the files you extract from the tarball. If this is the case, you can execute this script to uninstall the application from your system.

Other products may include an UNINSTALL target in their Makefile file. If this is the case, you must first run configure from the directory created when you originally extracted the downloaded tarball file, just as you did when you first installed the software. Then, instead of running **make install**, you run **make uninstall**. This will cause the make utility to follow the instructions in the uninstall portion of the Makefile file to remove the software from your system. For example, you can use the make uninstall command to remove the Pure-FTPd service from the system.

How do you know what method to use? The tarball you downloaded should include a README file of some sort that documents both the install and uninstall processes for the particular software you are working with. Check this file first. If the information isn't available, then check the FAQ or knowledge base on the website of the organization that produced the software. One of these resources should provide you with the steps you need to follow to uninstall the software.

Managing Shared Libraries

In addition to checking for software package dependencies, you may also need to verify that your system is configured properly to access the libraries an application needs to run. In this part of the chapter, you will learn how to do this. The following topics are addressed:

- How shared libraries work
- Managing shared library dependencies

Let's begin by discussing how shared libraries work.

How Shared Libraries Work

On Linux, applications running on the system can share code elements called *shared libraries*. This is very useful. Shared libraries make it such that software developers don't have to reinvent the wheel each time they write a new program.

If you think about it, many functions are commonly used across many programs. For example, the process for opening a file, saving a file, and closing an open file are the same no matter what application is being used. Without shared libraries, programmers would have to include the code for completing these basic tasks in each application they write. What a waste of time and resources!

Instead, with shared libraries, software developers can focus on the code elements that are unique to the individual application. For common elements that are shared across applications, they can simply link to the prewritten code in a shared library and not worry about rewriting the code. Using shared libraries speeds up development time.

There are two types of shared libraries on Linux:

- **Dynamic** Dynamic shared libraries exist as files in the Linux filesystem. Programmers simply insert links to the functions in these shared libraries in their program code. The functions are called from the dynamic shared libraries when the program is run, not integrated into the program itself. A configuration file on the system contains a list of installed dynamic shared libraries and where they are located in the filesystem. Using dynamic shared libraries decreases the overall size of the executable after it's compiled. However, they do create a dependency issue. If the program calls a function from a dynamic shared library that isn't installed on the system (or has become unavailable for some reason), the application will malfunction.
- **Static** Static libraries are associated with a specific program and version of a program. They have the suffix .a. They are no longer used.

Shared library files use a special naming format to help you identify the type of shared library it is. This syntax is as follows:

libname.type.version

Most shared library files use the prefix "lib" followed by the name of the shared library. The *type* part of the filename identifies the type of shared library. The string "so" indicates the file is a dynamic shared library, whereas an "a" indicates the file is a static library. The *version* part of the filename specifies the version number of the library. For example, libfreetype.so.6.4.0 is a dynamic shared library.

ldconfig

Paths to library files are contained in the following:

- /lib
- /etc/ld.so.conf
- /etc/ld.so.conf.d
- LD_LIBRARY_PATH

The file */etc/ld.so.conf* may contain absolute paths to library configuration files and an include statement. The include statement points to files inside the */etc/ld.so.conf.d* directory. Each file in this directory contains a path to library files for specific applications.

Searching through each of these sources would take time. The **ldconfig** command creates the binary file */etc/ld.so.cache*, which is used is used when a command tries to load library files.

Each module can provide a service (symbol) to other modules or require a symbol from another module. The command **depmod -a** reads a list of modules in */lib/modules<kernel version>* and creates a list of dependencies in the file */lib/modules<kernel version>/modules.dep*. **depmod -a** is executed as part of the boot process. A user may also execute the command **depmod -A** to update modules.dep if something has changed.

When an application is executed, it is the responsibility of the command **ld.so** to make certain the necessary library files are loaded when a command executes. The command **ldd <absolute_path_to_command>** will display the libraries required by the command.

lib/modules

The directory lib modules contains kernel modules. The modules for the current kernel would be found in */lib/modules/`uname -r`*.

lsmod

The **lsmod** command is used to view modules currently loaded. The same information may be obtained by looking at the file */proc/modules*.

modinfo

The command **modinfo** displays information concerning a specific module. The syntax for the command is **modinfo <option> <module_name>**.

/etc/modprobe.d

This directory contains files for specific applications. Each file contains directives used to load and unload a module.

modprobe

modprobe is a front end to the commands insmod (insert module) and rmmod (remove module). modprobe is aware of dependencies and is intelligent enough to load a module dependency priory to loading a module. It also may use the configuration file */etc/modprobe.conf* or files in */etc/modprobe.d*.

NOTE The file */etc/modprobe.conf* may not exist. It has been deprecated.

The modprobe command uses the following options and arguments.

Options and Arguments	Description
<module_name>	Loads the module specified by the argument <module_name> and its dependencies.
-r <module_name>	Unloads (removes) the module specified by the argument <module_name>
-L	Lists available modules
-c	Lists module dependencies

Two other commands we must discuss are insmod and rmmod. The command **insmod <module_name>** will load a module without loading its dependencies. The command **rmmod <module_name>** will remove a module.

Chapter Review

The chapter began with a definition of terms used in package management. Our goal was to review multiple methods of installing packages.

We first reviewed Red Hat Package Manager and went over rpm commands to add, erase, and upgrade packages. You also learned to query the RPM database to retrieve package information. Next, we reviewed the capabilities of the yum package manager. Yum is also able to add, remove, and upgrade packages as well as search for and report package information. You learned that yum is being deprecated and is being replaced by dnf. You saw that dnf uses different configuration files than RPM, with the exception of */etc/yum.repos.d*. You also learned that many of the commands in yum are duplicated in the dnf package. You then learned that zypper is SUSE's package manager and investigated some of its command syntax.

To this point, all the package managers we investigated were front ends to RPM. We then reviewed the Debian Package Manager (dpkg).

Tar files provide a method of installing and uninstalling files. We reviewed how to create tar files, extract source code and applications from tar files, and install a package from a tar file.

Finally, you learned about shared libraries and modules.

Here are some key facts to remember about managing Linux software:

- RPM packages are installed using the Red Hat Package Manager.
- RPM packages are compiled for a specific architecture and sometimes a specific Linux distribution.
- You can tell what architecture a package file is intended for by looking at the filename, which contains the following information:
  - Package name
  - Version number
  - Release number
  - Architecture type
- You can enter **rpm --checksig** to verify the digital signature of an RPM package before you install it.
- You can enter **rpm -i** to install a package file on your system.
- To uninstall an RPM package, you use the **rpm -e** command.
- You can update an existing package to a newer version using the **rpm -U** command.
- To query a package, you use the -q option with rpm.

- To verify a package, you use the -V option with rpm.
- The yum utility allows you to download and then install a package and all its dependencies.
- The yum **install <packagename>** command installs a package.
- The yum **remove <packagename>** command uninstalls a package.
- The *yum.conf* file is the global configuration file for yum.
- Repository information can be stored in the repository section of yum.conf or in a file in the */etc/yum.repos.d* directory.
- To install from source code, you first download and extract a tarball file.
- In the installation directory, you run configure, make, and make install.
- The configure command checks your system to verify compatibility and creates the Makefile file.
- The make command compiles a binary executable from the source code text using the specifications in the Makefile file.
- The **make install** command installs the compiled executable.
- The **make uninstall** command is typically used to uninstall an executable installed from source.
- Distributions based on the Debian distribution use the Debian Package Manager (dpkg).
- Debian packages include dependency information.
- You use the dpkg command to install, uninstall, query, and verify Debian packages.
- The **apt-cache** command is used to query package information from the Debian package database (called the package cache).
- The **apt-get** command automatically downloads and installs packages (along with all dependent packages) for you.
- The aptitude utility uses a text-based, menu-driven interface to manage Debian packages.
- Applications running on a Linux system can share code elements called *shared libraries.*
- Linux applications can use either dynamic or static shared libraries.
- The dynamic shared library configuration file is */etc/ld.so.conf.*
- The */etc/ld.so.conf* file contains a list of paths in the filesystem where shared library files are stored.
- To view a list of all the shared libraries available on your Linux system, enter **ldconfig -p** at the shell prompt.

- You can view libraries required by a specific application by entering **ldd -v <command>**.
- The library cache is */etc/ld.so.cache*.
- The *ld.so.cache* file contains a list of all the system libraries and is refreshed when the system is initially booted.
- If you add library files to a directory not listed in the *ld.so.conf* file, you must use the ldconfig command to rebuild the library cache manually.
- The command **depmod -A** will rebuild library dependencies.
- You can also add a new library file path to the LD_LIBRARY_PATH environment variable.

Questions

1. You've just downloaded a file named *FC-6-i386-DVD.iso* to the */home/tux* directory on your Linux system. What command would you use to generate a checksum value?
   A. checksum /home/tux/FC-6-i386-DVD.iso
   B. sum /home/tux/FC-6-i386-DVD.iso
   C. verify /home/tux/FC-6-i386-DVD.iso
   D. rpm -V /home/tux/FC-6-i386-DVD.iso
2. You've just downloaded a file named *FC-6-i386-DVD.iso* and have generated a checksum value. The value generated is slightly different from that shown on the download website. What does this imply?
   A. The downloaded copy is different from the original, but the download is still usable as long as the differences are minor.
   B. The version number is incremented by 1 when the file was downloaded.
   C. The downloaded copy is different from the original copy and shouldn't be used.
   D. The downloaded copy is exactly the same as the original copy.
3. You've just downloaded a file named *BitTorrent-5.0.1.tar.gz* to your home directory. Assuming the current directory is ~, what command would you enter at the shell prompt to extract all the files from this archive?
   A. gzip -d ./BitTorrent-5.0.1.tar.gz
   B. tar -axvf ./BitTorrent-5.0.1.tar.gz
   C. tar -xvf ./BitTorrent-5.0.1.tar.gz
   D. tar -zxvf ./BitTorrent-5.0.1.tar.gz

4. Where does RPM store its database of installed packages?
   A. /var/lib/rpm
   B. /etc/rpm
   C. /var/rpmdb
   D. /tmp/rpm
5. You've just downloaded an RPM package file named *evolution-2.6.0-41.i586.rpm* to your home directory. Assuming the current directory is ~, what command could you use to check the digital signature of the downloaded file to verify that it hasn't been tampered with?
   A. rpm --checksig evolution-2.6.0-41.i586.rpm
   B. rpm --verify evolution-2.6.0-41.i586.rpm
   C. rpm -tamperproof evolution-2.6.0-41.i586.rpm
   D. rpm --signature evolution-2.6.0-41.i586.rpm
6. You've just downloaded an RPM package file named *evolution-2.6.0-41.i586.rpm* to your home directory. Assuming the current directory is ~, what commands could you use to install the package on your system, displaying a progress indicator as the installation is completed? (Choose two.)
   A. rpm -i evolution-2.6.0-41.i586.rpm
   B. rpm -ihv evolution-2.6.0-41.i586.rpm
   C. rpm -U evolution-2.6.0-41.i586.rpm
   D. rpm -install --progress evolution-2.6.0-41.i586.rpm
   E. rpm --Uhv evolution-2.6.0-41.i586.rpm
7. You need to uninstall the Pure-FTPd service from your Linux system. You've switched to the directory where the original installation files are located. What's the first command you need to enter to uninstall this package?
   A. ./configure
   B. make
   C. make remove
   D. make uninstall
8. You've installed an RPM package file named *evolution-2.6.0-41.i586.rpm* on your Linux system. What command would you use to uninstall this package?
   A. rpm -U evolution
   B. rpm -U --remove evolution
   C. rpm -i --remove evolution
   D. rpm -e evolution

9. You currently have an RPM package file named *evolution-2.2.0-2.i586.rpm* installed on your Linux system. You've recently downloaded the *evolution-2.6.0-41.i586.rpm* package from www.sourceforge.net. What command would you use to install the newer version of this package?

 A. rpm -U evolution-2.6.0-41.i586.rpm

 B. rpm -i evolution-2.6.0-41.i586.rpm

 C. rpm -i --upgrade evolution-2.6.0-41.i586.rpm

 D. rpm -e evolution-2.2.0-2.i586.rpm

10. You currently have an RPM package file named *evolution-2.6.0-41.i586.rpm* installed on your Linux system. What command would you enter to display summary information about the package?

 A. rpm -s evolution

 B. rpm -qs evolution

 C. rpm -qi evolution

 D. rpm -V --summary evolution

11. You've used the rpm command with the **-q --requires** option to determine the components required by the RPM package. One of the required components is /usr/bin/perl. What command would you enter to find out which RPM package provides this component?

 A. rpm -q --whatprovides /usr/bin/perl

 B. rpm -qs --requires /usr/bin/perl

 C. rpm -qi --requires /usr/bin/perl

 D. rpm -q --provides perl

12. You've used the rpm command with the -V option to verify an RPM package installed on your system. The output from the command listed the following error code:

```
S.5....T     c     /opt/kde3/share/config/kdm/kdmrc
```

 What does this error code indicate? (Choose three.)

 A. There's a problem with the size of the file.

 B. There's a problem with the mode of the file.

 C. There's a problem with the timestamp of the file.

 D. There's a problem with the checksum.

 E. There's a problem with a file's ownership.

13. You need to extract a single file out of an RPM package. Which utility can be used to do this?

 A. tar

 B. rpm

C. dpkg

D. rpm2cpio

14. You need to install the GNU C Compiler (gcc) package on your system. Which yum command will do this?

A. yum gcc

B. yum install gcc

C. yum update gcc

D. yum installpkg gcc

15. Which yum command generates a list of available updates for all installed packages on a Linux system?

A. yum list updates

B. yum info

C. yum list available

D. yum list all

16. What does the configure script do in an application's installation directory? (Choose two.)

A. It compiles the source code into a binary executable.

B. It checks the local system to verify that the necessary components are available.

C. It copies the binary executable and other files, such as documentation, to the appropriate directories in the filesystem.

D. It creates the Makefile file.

E. It verifies that the installation files haven't been corrupted or tampered with.

17. What does the **make** command do when installing an application from source code?

A. It compiles the source code into a binary executable.

B. It checks the local system to verify that the necessary components are available.

C. It copies the binary executable and other files, such as documentation, to the appropriate directories in the filesystem.

D. It creates the Makefile file.

18. What does the **make install** command do when installing an application from source code?

A. It compiles the source code into a binary executable.

B. It checks the local system to verify that the necessary components are available.

C. It copies the binary executable and other files, such as documentation, to the appropriate directories in the filesystem.

D. It creates the Makefile file.

19. Which action, when used with the dpkg command, uninstalls a specified package and deletes all its configuration files?
    A. -r
    B. -p
    C. -P
    D. -U
20. You want to use apt-get to download and install the 3dchess package on your Linux system. Which command can you use to do this?
    A. apt-get install 3dchess
    B. apt-get -d install 3dchess
    C. apt-get upgrade 3dchess
    D. apt-get -s install 3dchess
21. Which type of shared library is integrated directly into an executable file when it is initially compiled?
    A. Dynamic
    B. Shared
    C. Static
    D. Linked
22. Which file is checked by applications on startup for the location of shared libraries on the Linux system?
    A. /etc/ld.so.conf
    B. /etc/ld.so.cache
    C. /lib/ld.so
    D. /usr/lib/ld.so

Answers

1. **B.** The sum /home/tux/ FC-6-i386-DVD.iso command will generate a checksum value for the file specified.
2. **C.** A variance in the checksum values indicates the two copies of the file are different in some way. You shouldn't use the file in this situation because it probably is corrupt or has been tampered with.
3. **D.** To extract the file, you would enter **tar -zxvf ./BitTorrent-5.0.1.tar.gz**.
4. **A.** The RPM database is stored in /var/lib/rpm.
5. **A.** The **rpm --checksig evolution-2.6.0-41.i586.rpm** command would be used to check the file's digital signature.

6. **B, E.** Either the **rpm -ihv evolution-2.6.0-41.i586.rpm** command or the **rpm -Uhv evolution-2.6.0-41.i586.rpm** command will install the file and display a progress indicator composed of hash marks on the screen as the installation progresses.
7. **A.** The **./configure** command would be used first to generate the Makefile file. This file contains the UNINSTALL target that can then be used with the make utility to uninstall the software.
8. **D.** To erase rpm from the system, you would enter **rpm -e evolution**.
9. **A.** The **rpm -U evolution-2.6.0-41.i586.rpm** command will upgrade the existing RPM to the newer version.
10. **C.** The **rpm -qi evolution-2.6.0-41.i586.rpm** command will query the package and display summary information on the screen.
11. **A.** The **rpm -q --whatprovides /usr/bin/perl** command displays the name of the package that provides this component.
12. **A, C, D.** The S, 5, and T in the error code indicate that there is a problem with the file's size, MD5 checksum, and timestamp. The c indicates that the file is a configuration file, so these errors may or may not be significant.
13. **D.** The rpm2cpio utility can be used to create a cpio archive file from the RPM package. You can then extract individual files from the archive using the cpio utility.
14. **B.** The **yum install gcc** command can be used to download and install the gcc package on your Linux system, including all packages it is dependent on.
15. **A.** The **yum list updates** command can be used to generate a list of available updates for all installed packages on a Linux system.
16. **B, D.** The configure script is used to check the local system to make sure it has the components required to install and run the software. It also creates the Makefile file.
17. **A.** The **make** command compiles the text-based source code into a binary executable that can be run on the system.
18. **C.** The **make install** command actually installs the program and its associated support files (such as documentation and configuration files) into the appropriate directories in the filesystem.
19. **C.** The -P option, when used with the dpkg command, uninstalls a specified package and deletes all its configuration files.
20. **A.** The **apt-get install 3dchess** command can be used to download and install the 3dchess package on your Linux system, along with all other packages it is dependent on.
21. **C.** Static shared libraries are integrated directly into an executable file when it is initially compiled.
22. **B.** The */etc/ld.so.cache* file is checked by applications on startup for the location of shared libraries on the Linux system.

CHAPTER 11

Managing the Linux Boot Process

In this chapter, you will learn about:

- The bootstrap phase
- The bootloader phase
- The kernel phase
- System V
- systemd

To make the Linux boot process more easily digestible, we're going to break it down into the following phases:

- The bootstrap phase
- The bootloader phase
- The kernel phase
- System initialization

Figure 11-1 illustrates the BIOS boot process. Boot-specific messages are written to */var/log/boot.log*. The systemd command **journalctl -b** will display boot messages from your last boot, but may also be configured to store boot logs from previous boots.

The Bootstrap Phase

Bootstrapping is the startup process responsible for initializing system hardware and finding the location of instructions responsible for loading the operating system (bootloader).

You should be familiar with the following bootstrap methods:

- BIOS
- EFI/UEFI
- PXE

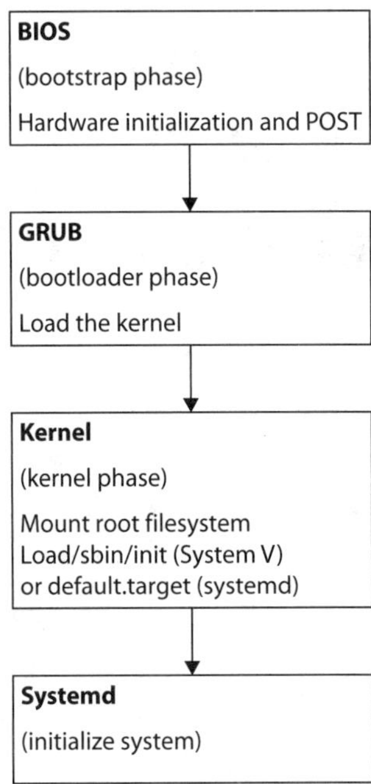

Figure 11-1 System boot process

BIOS

BIOS, or Basic Input/Output System, is the traditional bootstrap program stored on a flash memory chip on the system motherboard. Once power has been applied, BIOS initializes the motherboard POST (power-on self-test). If POST encounters any problems, it will either display an error message onscreen or play a series of beeps. The website bioscentral.com has a listing for most motherboard POST error codes.

Once POST is complete, BIOS will look through the list of devices for bootloader code. The order in which this list is searched can be manipulated by entering BIOS. Figure 11-2 shows that our system will search for removable devices and then a list of hard drives. Figure 11-3 shows it will search the network for a bootable image and then look at local removable drives, followed by local hard drives.

When searching these devices, BIOS looks in the first sector of a disk device (boot sector) searching for a master boot record (MBR), illustrated in Figure 11-4.

The master boot record is divided into three sections. The first 446 bytes of the MBR contain the first stage of the master boot code. The master boot code contains error messages (such as "missing operating system") and the code required for loading the second stage of the bootloader. The next 64 bytes contain the drive's partition table, and the last 2 bytes contain a disk signature. The disk signature identifies the device that contains the /boot directory, which contains files required by the boot process.

Once BIOS has begun loading the bootloader, control of the boot process is turned over to the bootloader.

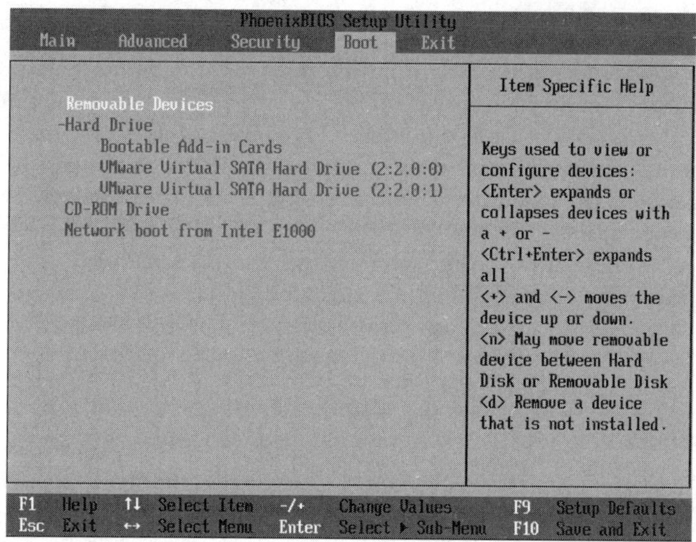

Figure 11-2 Selecting a boot device

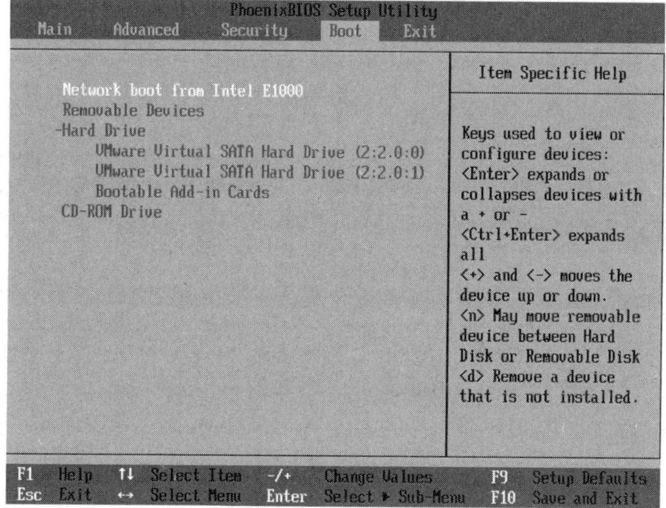

Figure 11-3 Selecting a removeable or network boot device

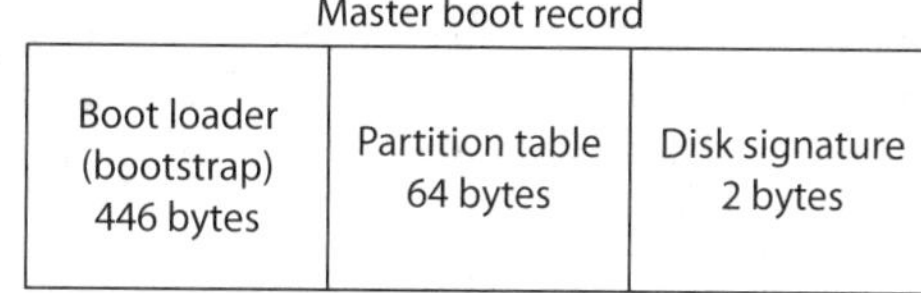

Figure 11-4 The master boot record (MBR) details

UEFI ESP

BIOS did not keep pace with advancements in technology. It was limited to 16-bit addressing, could only access 1MB of memory, could not boot from drives larger than 2.1TB, and could manage only a limited number of devices.

Unified Extensible Firmware Interface (UEFI) is an OS-neutral, architecture-independent software interface between firmware and the operating system designed to overcome the limitations of BIOS. One of UEFI's most important features is its ability to execute applications prior to the operating system loading.

Some features of UEFI include the following:

- It provides a user interface prior to the operating system being available.
- It operates in 32- or 64-bit mode.
- It has access to all system memory and devices.
- It can mount partitions and read some filesystems (FAT12, FAT16, FAT32, and VFAT).
- It has network capabilities without the OS being loaded.
- It can boot drives larger than 2.1TB.
- You can add applications that can be executed as part of the boot process or from UEFI's command shell.
- It supports remote diagnostics and storage backup.
- It can be configured via the OS using the command efibootmgr.

TIP If UEFI is implemented, the directory /sys/firmware/efi will exist and the command efibootmgr should be available.

UEFI controls the boot process using UEFI boot services. While the operating system is running, UEFI provides a connection between the OS and firmware.

After hardware initialization, UEFI looks for a storage device with an EFI system partition (ESP). This partition is a FAT32 partition that contains the bootloader code, applications, and device drivers. Applications contained in ESP can be part of the boot process or utilities that can be chosen by the user at boot time.

The partition is normally mounted on /boot/efi. Vendor-specific applications or EFI utilities will be stored in the /boot/efi directory. For example, Red Hat EFI files are stored in /boot/efi/EFI/redhat, and CentOS stores its bootloader information in /boot/efi/EFI/centos. If multiple operating systems are available, each has its own directory in /boot/efi.

Depending on the contents of the ESP, several things could happen. You could be prompted to execute a UEFI application or load a specific operating system, or UEFI could automatically load another bootloader, such as GRUB.

PXE

PXE (pronounced *pixie*), or Preboot Execution Environment, is an OS-neutral client/server facility that can be used to remotely boot operating systems or provision computer systems from a network server. PXE requires the client system have a network card that supports PXE and has PXE enabled as a boot device in flash memory.

When power is applied to a PXE client, the enabled NIC card "looks" for a DHCP server by broadcasting a series of DHCP discover packets, which are requests from the client to obtain an IP address from a DHCP server. The Dynamic Host Configuration Protocol (DHCP) server is used to automatically assign an IP address to the client and provide the client with the location of one or more TFTP servers. A Trivial File Transfer Protocol (TFTP) server uses the User Datagram Protocol (UDP) to transfer files from a host to a client.

The DHCP server will also provide the location of the TFTP configuration files on the server. Once the client system knows the location of the TFTP server, it downloads and executes the appropriate boot image from the *pxelinux.cfg* directory.

ISO

An ISO image is a file that contains the contents of an entire CD or DVD. We can use an ISO to distribute a large program such as an operating system or we can access the ISO remotely to install an operating system on a client. Access to the ISO can be made via FTP, HTTP, or NFS servers. Note that the connection ports mentioned below are default service ports.

FTP is more efficient in transferring larger files. FTP can transfer data in binary mode (bit by bit) or ASCII, and it uses port 20 for a data connection and port 21 for control information. SFTP, or Secure FTP, connects using SSH on port 22. FTP connections can require a password.

Hypertext Transfer Protocol (HTTP) connections are single-direction connections via port 80. Examples of HTTP servers are Apache and Nginx.

An ISO boot may also be achieved by using a custom GRUB2. The custom GRUB entry would specify the path to the ISO file (mounted as a loopback device) and, if necessary, a path to the vmlinux or vmlinuz (kernel) and initrd or intitramfs files.

The Bootloader Phase

Once the bootstrap phase has completed, the bootloader is used to load the Linux kernel. Although multiple bootloaders are available, we will confine our discussion to GRUB, or Grand Unified Bootloader, and GRUB2.

GRUB (Legacy)

The GRUB Legacy bootloader is divided into separate chunks called *stages*. These stages include the following:

- **Stage 1** This stage of GRUB is usually stored in the MBR. Its only real job is to point to the location of Stage 1.5 or Stage 2.

- **Stage 1.5** This stage of GRUB is located in the first 30KB of the hard drive immediately after the MBR, but before the first partition. Stage 1.5 contains filesystem drivers. These filesystem drivers may be found in /boot/grub.
- **Stage 2** This stage of GRUB is stored in a disk partition. Stage 2 presents a text menu on the screen that allows the user to select the kernel image that should be loaded. You can configure GRUB with a default image and a timeout value. If the user doesn't select an option within the timeout period, the system will automatically boot the default kernel image. A typical GRUB menu is shown in Figure 11-5.

grub.conf

The GRUB menu is configured from the default GRUB configuration file */boot/grub/menu.lst*. Some distributions use */boot/grub/grub.conf* as the configuration file. The file */boot/grub/grub.conf* is linked to */boot/grub/menu.lst*. The grub.conf file is divided into two sections: global and title (see Figure 11-6).

Device Names GRUB accesses devices via the BIOS. Integers distinguish drives and partitions based on the order that GRUB discovers them on the bus. In GRUB Legacy, device and partition numbering begins at 0.

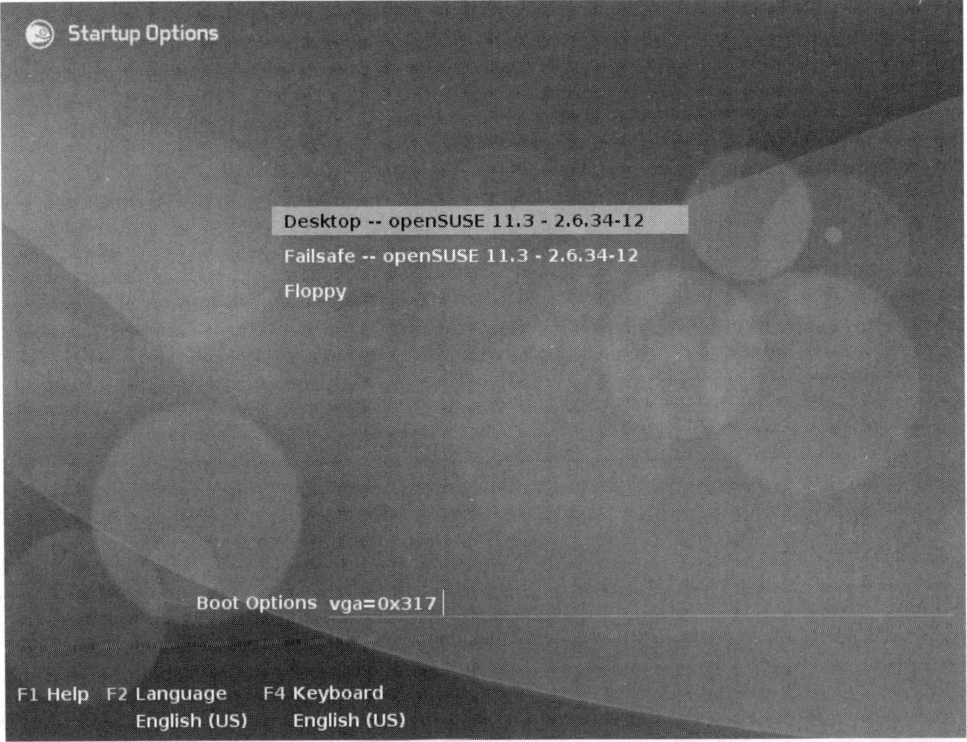

Figure 11-5 GRUB boot menu

```
# grub.conf generated by anaconda
#
# Note that you do not have to rerun grub after making changes to this file
# NOTICE:  You have a /boot partition.  This means that
#          all kernel and initrd paths are relative to /boot/, eg.
#          root (hd0,0)
#          kernel /vmlinuz-version ro root=/dev/sda3
#          initrd /initrd-version.img
#boot=/dev/sda
default=0
timeout=5
splashimage=(hd0,0)/grub/splash.xpm.gz
hiddenmenu
title CentOS (2.6.9-42.0.8.EL)
        root (hd0,0)
        kernel /vmlinuz-2.6.9-42.0.8.EL ro root=LABEL=/ rhgb quiet
        initrd /initrd-2.6.9-42.0.8.EL.img
title CentOS-4 i386 (2.6.9-42.EL)
        root (hd0,0)
        kernel /vmlinuz-2.6.9-42.EL ro root=LABEL=/ rhgb quiet
        initrd /initrd-2.6.9-42.EL.img
```


Figure 11-6 Contents of the *grub.conf* file

GRUB cannot distinguish the difference between hard disk types, such as SCSI and IDE. Therefore, GRUB uses the device type **hd** for hard disks. The syntax for naming a device is **<device_type><drive_number>,<partition_number>**. Therefore, hd0,0 represents the first partition on the first hard disk, */dev/sda1*.

Global Settings The global settings, detailed in Table 11-1, define some of the operating parameters.

Section	Description
default	The default setting determines the default operating system to load. Available operating systems are defined in a line beginning with the word "title." The directive **default=0** specifies the default operating system stanza to boot from. The stanzas begin with the word Title and are numbered from 0.
timeout	The timeout setting sets the time in seconds GRUB will wait for operator intervention before it will proceed to the title section referred to in the default setting.
splashimage	splashimage defines the image used when the GRUB menu is displayed. in In Figure 11-6, notice that the path to the file begins with (hd0,0). This translates to */dev/sda1*, which is mounted to */boot*. Therefore, the path to the image file is */boot/grub/splash.xpm.gz*. No operating system is loaded, so we cannot use */boot/grub/splash.xpm.gz* in the GRUB configuration file.
password	This global setting (not included in Figure 11-6) could contain a plaintext or encrypted password that would be required before editing any GRUB settings or executing any GRUB commands during the boot process. To place a plaintext password, edit the file with an editor and add the global setting **password <space> <grub_password>**. To create an encrypted password, open another terminal and execute the command **grub-md5-crypt** and then enter the password you want to use. (The password will not be printed on the screen.) You will then be asked to verify the password. The encrypted results can then be cut and pasted into the *grub.conf* file.

Table 11-1 The grub.conf Global Settings

Section	Description
title	The title line contains a description of the OS to be booted.
root	This setting specifies the location of GRUB's root directory (/boot) for the operating system being loaded. hd0,0 specifies the device /dev/sda1.
kernel	Specifies the kernel (vmlinuz or vmlinux) to load and how to mount the operating system's kernel. Additional kernel parameters may be added to this line. In the example shown in Figure 11-6, the operating system kernel will be mounted read-only. Note that rhgb indicates a Red Hat graphical boot and displays boot information; quiet indicates that most boot messages will be hidden.
initrd	initrd contains a filesystem that has the executables and drivers required to boot the kernel. This section specifies the initrd file to use.

Table 11-2 Legacy Grub stanza

Title The title section, detailed in Table 11-2, defines the files and parameters used to load an operating system.

GRUB Interactive Boot

GRUB's interactive mode allows a user to change the boot process or issue GRUB commands. To enter interactive mode, press ESC once GRUB's splash image appears. If the hiddenmenu directive is part of global settings, you will not see the splash image, so you must press ESC before the number of seconds specified by the directive timeout has passed.

Using the keys found in Table 11-3, you can temporarily edit boot parameters, such as the boot device, kernel parameters, and runlevel.

Key	Description
ESC	Returns to previous menu level.
Up or down arrow	Moves between lines.
ENTER	Selects the current line.
E	Edits the current line.
A	Appends text to the current line. (The cursor moves to the end of the line.) Pressing A from the main GRUB menu will place the cursor at the end of the kernel (vmlinuz) line.
D	Deletes the current line.
C	Executes a GRUB shell command.
B	Boots the system.
P	Enters the GRUB password. If you have added a password to the GRUB configuration file, you must enter the password to edit the boot process.

Table 11-3 GRUB Interactive Keys

The end of the kernel line contains boot options. If you are trying to boot your system and SELinux is freezing, adding selinux=0 to the end of the kernel line (vmlinuz) would turn off SELinux. To do this, you would press ESC when the splash image appears to stop the boot process. Use the up or down arrow to place the cursor on the operating system you want to change and press A to append **selinux=0** to the end of the kernel line. You could also specify a different runlevel by placing a runlevel number at the end of the kernel line.

If your system is not booting, you can stop the boot process and load a specific program. To do this, enter **init=<program_name>** as a boot option. For example, to skip loading the init process and load the bash shell instead, you would enter **init=/bin/bash**. When you boot the system, the bash shell is loaded and you have full root-level access to the system, allowing you to diagnose and repair whatever is keeping the system from booting normally.

Be aware that the root (/) filesystem will be mounted in read-only mode on some distributions. If this is the case, you will need to remount it in read-write mode before you can make changes to a configuration file by entering **mount -o remount,rw,sync -t <filesystem> <device_name> <mount_point>** at the shell prompt. After making the necessary changes, you can tell the kernel to resume the normal boot process via init by entering **exec /sbin/init** at the shell prompt.

TIP You won't be prompted to provide your root password. Because of this, you can use this technique to rescue a system if you've forgotten its root user's password.

The grub command key (C) opens a GRUB shell that allows you to execute GRUB shell commands. Pressing TAB will display a list of available commands, and the command **help <grub_command>** will display help text.

GRUB Password Protection

Although the ability to customize GRUB and its menu items can be very useful, it also can be a bit of a security risk. As noted, it can potentially provide anyone who has the know-how root-level access to your system without providing a password.

To increase the security of the GRUB menu, you can add a GRUB password. Once the menu is configured this way, you can only modify your GRUB boot options after the correct password has been supplied. The simplest way to do this is to edit your GRUB configuration file and enter the following:

```
password <password>
```

Here's an example:

```
password natasha01
```

To make the configuration more secure, you can encrypt the GRUB password in the configuration file. This way, even if a user gets access to the GRUB configuration file, they won't be able to read the password you specify. To encrypt the password, do the following:

1. Open a terminal session and switch to root.
2. At the shell prompt, enter **grub-md5-crypt**.
3. When prompted, enter the password you want to assign to the GRUB menu.

   When this is complete, the hashed form of the password is displayed on the screen. An example follows:

   ```
   fs2:~ # grub-md5-crypt
   Password:
   Retype password:
   $1$WLZwz/$DP3wgbtInP1KJOL.Wg3t00
   ```

4. Open the GRUB configuration file in a text editor.

TIP It's easier to copy and paste using gedit or vi.

5. In the GRUB configuration file, enter **password --md5 <hashed_password>**. Here is an example:

   ```
   password --md5 $1$WLZwz/$DP3wgbtInP1KJOL.Wg3t00
   ```

6. Save your changes to the file and reboot the system.

Reinstalling GRUB

If you want to reinstall the GRUB bootloader, you may do so, as root, using the command **grub-install** or using a few grub shell commands.

The command **grub-install <device>** may be used to place a bootloader on a drive.

NOTE BIOS must be aware of the drive.

To install a bootloader via the GRUB shell, do the following:

```
#grub
>root (hd0,0)      #This sets GRUB's root (/boot) directory.
>setup (hd0)       #Installs the bootloader on device /dev/sda
>quit
```

GRUB2

GRUB2 is a newer version of the original GRUB bootloader. GRUB2 works in a completely different manner than the original GRUB Legacy bootloader. Be aware that GRUB version 1.98 or later is actually considered "GRUB2." Any version of GRUB earlier than 1.98 is considered "GRUB Legacy." You can run one of two commands at the shell prompt (as root) to see which version of GRUB your particular Linux system is using:

- grub-install -v
- grub2-install -v

An example is shown here:

```
# grub2-install -v
grub2-install (GRUB2) 2.00
```

One important difference between Legacy GRUB and GRUB2 is device names. Whereas Legacy GRUB started device numbering at 0, GRUB2 starts numbering at 1.

Table 11-4 lists the configuration files and directory used by Grub2.

File	Description
grub.cfg	This file replaces */boot/grub/menu.lst* as GRUB's main configuration file. This file is created using the grub2-mkconfig command and may not be edited
/etc/default/grub	This file contains default variables used when configuring grub2
/etc/grub.d	Contains GRUB scripts.

Table 11-4 GRUB2 Configuration Files

/etc/default/grub

The file */etc/default/grub* contains GRUB configuration variables, as detailed in Table 11-5.

/etc/grub.d

The directory */etc/grub.d* contains scripts used to build GRUB's menu (see Figure 11-7). Scripts are processed in order of their script number. Table 11-6 describes some of those scripts.

Figure 11-7 Files found in /etc/grub.d

```
[root@localhost grub.d]# ls -l
total 72
-rwxr-xr-x. 1 root root  8702 Jan 30 08:58 00_header
-rwxr-xr-x. 1 root root  1043 Jul  4  2018 00_tuned
-rwxr-xr-x. 1 root root   232 Jan 30 08:58 01_users
-rwxr-xr-x. 1 root root 10781 Jan 30 08:58 10_linux
-rwxr-xr-x. 1 root root 10275 Jan 30 08:58 20_linux_xen
-rwxr-xr-x. 1 root root  2559 Jan 30 08:58 20_ppc_terminfo
-rwxr-xr-x. 1 root root 11169 Jan 30 08:58 30_os-prober
-rwxr-xr-x. 1 root root   214 Jan 30 08:58 40_custom
-rwxr-xr-x. 1 root root   216 Jan 30 08:58 41_custom
-rw-r--r--. 1 root root   483 Jan 30 08:58 README
```

Variable	Description
GRUB_TIMEOUT	Boots the default entry in *n* number of seconds if no user action takes place.
GRUB_HIDDEN_TIMEOUT	Displays a blank screen (or a splash image if you configure it to do so) for a specified number of seconds. After the end of the timeout period, the system will boot. While the screen is blank, the user can press SHIFT to display the menu.
GRUB_DEFAULT	Indicates the default operating system to boot after the number of seconds in GRUB_TIMEOUT is reached. This entry may be a number or a menu entry title.
GRUB_SAVED_DEFAULT	If this parameter is set to true, GRUB will automatically select the last selected operating system from the menu as the default operating system to be used on the next boot. As you can see, this parameter could potentially conflict with the GRUB_DEFAULT parameter. Therefore, you can use either one, but not both.
GRUB_DISTRIBUTOR	Used when creating menu titles. Sets the operating system's name.
GRUB_CMDLINE_LINUX	Linux kernel parameters.

Table 11-5 GRUB2 /etc/default/grub Variables

Interactive Boot

You can press ESC to interrupt the boot process. The keys detailed in Table 11-7 may be used.

Changing GRUB2

To make changes to GRUB's configuration, you can edit the file */etc/default/grub* or the scripts in */etc/grub.d*. You can even create a custom script. Once a user makes changes to this directory, they must execute the command **grub2-mkconfig -o <config_filename>**.

TIP Make certain you have a backup of the current *grub.cfg* file and copy the output of the grub2_mkconfig command to *grub.cfg*.

grub.d Script Files	Description
00_header	This file replaces */boot/grub/menu.lst* as GRUB's main configuration file. This file may not be edited. Configuration changes to GRUB 2 are made in */etc/default/grub*.
10_linux	Identifies Linux kernels and places them in the menu.
30_os_prober	Searches for non-Linux operating systems and puts the results in memory.
40_custom	Template for adding custom menu entries.

Table 11-6 Grub Script Files in/etc/grub.d

Key	Description
E	Edit the current menu entry.
CTRL-X	Boot the system. You must be editing a menu entry to use this key sequence.
TAB	List available GRUB commands. The command **help <grub_command>** will display help documentation. You must be editing a menu entry to use this key sequence.
CTRL-C	Enter a GRUB shell. When finished executing GRUB shell commands, you can exit the shell using the command **normal_exit**. You must be editing a menu entry to use this key sequence.
ESC	Discard edits and return to the previous screen.

Table 11-7 Interactive Boot Control Keys

Exercise 11-1: Working with GRUB2

In Exercise 11-1, you practice customizing your GRUB2 menu. You can perform this exercise using the virtual machine. (Be sure to log in as user root using the password root.)

VIDEO Please watch the Exercise 11-1 video for a demonstration on how to perform this task.

Complete the following steps:

1. Boot your Linux system and log in as user root using the password root.
2. Create a snapshot.
3. Enter **vi /etc/default/grub** at the shell prompt.
4. Change the GRUB_TIMEOUT value to 15 seconds.
5. Change the GRUB_DEFAULT parameter to automatically load the first menu entry if the user makes no selection within the timeout period.
6. Save your changes and exit the vi editor.
7. Make a copy of */boot/grub2/grub.cfg* using the following command:
```
cp  boot/grub2/grub.cfg  /boot/grub2/grub.cfg.$(date +%m%d).old
```
8. Execute the following command to create a new configuration file:
```
grub2-mkconfig -o /boot/grub2/grub.cfg.$(date +%m%d).new
```
9. Copy the new file to */boot/grub.cfg* using the following command:
```
cp  /boot/grub2/grub.cfg.$(date +%m%d).new  /boot/grub2.cfg
```
10. Reboot your system and verify the changes have been applied to the bootloader.

The Kernel Phase

The purpose of the bootloader is to load the system kernel. The GRUB bootloader will load a kernel named either vmlinuz or vmlinux. The difference between the two is that vmlinuz is a compressed file (gzip) whereas vmlinux is not a compressed file.

NOTE Most distributions use vmlinuz.

These kernel images are located in /boot.

The kernel decompresses and mounts the initial RAM disk (initrd) specified by the bootloader. This RAM disk is a temporary filesystem that contains kernel modules and applications necessary to access the devices and filesystems required to boot the operating system.

NOTE initrd is a fixed-size block device with a filesystem. initramfs is a cpio archive that is not limited in size. See Chapter 8 for more about cpio.

The kernel will first initialize memory and then configure the attached hardware by using drivers found in initrd. initrd also includes the nash shell and linuxrc. The nash (not a shell) shell is a subset of the bash shell containing the commands necessary to execute linuxrc. linuxrc is responsible for mounting the "real" root filesystem and begins initializing the operating system. When all device drivers are loaded, the kernel mounts the root filesystem in read-write mode and begins operating system initialization. We will discuss both System V and systemd initialization.

System V Initialization

Once the kernel is running, the init process that begins initrd is unmounted and the system scheduler is started (process 0).

The init process is the last step of the boot process. The init process executes the command /sbin/init, which reads a file called */etc/inittab*. This is a configuration file that brings the operating system to a predefined runlevel.

Runlevel

A runlevel defines what services and resources are available. Table 11-8 describes the seven runlevels.

Runlevel	Mode	Description
0	Halt	Halts the system.
1	Single User	Single user only. Also known as maintenance mode. (Text mode.)
2	Local Multiuser	Multiuser access. Networking is available but network filesystems are not. (Text mode.)
3	Full Multiuser	Multiuser access. Both networking and network filesystems are available. (Text mode.)
4	Not Used	
5	Graphics Mode	Full multiuser mode (Graphics mode.)
6	Reboot	Brings the system to runlevel 0 and then back to the default runlevel.

Table 11-8 System V Runlevels

/etc/inittab

The command /sbin/init uses the configuration file */etc/inittab* to initialize the system. Configuration lines in */etc/inittab* have the following format.

<line_id> :<applicable_run_level> :<action>: <command>

On line 21 in Figure 11-8, you can see the line ID is si. Since no runlevel numbers are assigned, this line will be executed for all runlevels. The action is sysinit, and the command will execute the script */etc/rc.d/rc.sysinit.*

Line 18 of Figure 11-8 specifies the default runlevel. In our example, the operating system will boot to runlevel 5. To change the default runlevel, change the number in this line with an editor.

The next seven lines define what will be executed to boot to a specific runlevel. Look at line 28 in Figure 11-9. Notice the applicable runlevel is our default runlevel (runlevel 5).

If you look at the command executed for runlevel 5, you will see it is a path to the directory */etc/rc.d/rc5.d*. This directory contains numbered filenames prefixed by the

Figure 11-8 An excerpt from /etc/inittab showing the default runlevel

```
18 id:5:initdefault:
19
20 # System initialization.
21 si::sysinit:/etc/rc.d/rc.sysinit
```

Figure 11-9 The etc inittab runlevel definition lines

```
l0:0:wait:/etc/rc.d/rc 0
l1:1:wait:/etc/rc.d/rc 1
l2:2:wait:/etc/rc.d/rc 2
l3:3:wait:/etc/rc.d/rc 3
l4:4:wait:/etc/rc.d/rc 4
l5:5:wait:/etc/rc.d/rc 5
l6:6:wait:/etc/rc.d/rc 6
```

letter *S* (start) or *K* (kill); see Figure 11-10. The start scripts are using when starting the runlevel, and the kill scripts are used when stopping the runlevel. These files are symbolic links to scripts in the directory */etc/init.d*, which contains scripts used to manage system daemons.

NOTE A daemon is a background application waiting for an event or time to run.

The files preceded with a letter *S* are services that must to be started for the runlevel and will pass the argument **start** to the scripts they are linked to. The filenames preceded with a letter *K* are services that must be stopped for the runlevel and will pass the argument **stop** to the scripts they are linked to.

The number that follows the *S* or *K* in the filename determines the sequence in which the scripts are run. This ensures that services that other services are dependent on are started first. For example, a script assigned the number 01 will be run before a script assigned the number 02. This means a file in rc5.d named S02network is run after S01dbus but before S03syslog.

The action **wait** will not allow the init process to go any further until each script has completed successfully.

A daemon may have a start script in a runlevel and not have a corresponding kill script. For example, the CUPS service has start script S56cups in runlevels 2, 3 and 5, but the kill script K10cups is in runlevel 1.

/etc/rc.local

The script file */etc/rc.d/rc.local* is a symbolic link of */etc/rc.d/rc3.d/S099*. This file is executed at boot time or when changing runlevels. It can contain local commands that you want to run as part of the boot process. It is advisable to run these commands in the background so the boot process does not hang if an error occurs.

```
K01dnsmasq           K73ipmi       S08mcstrans      S26hidd
K02avahi-dnsconfd    K73ypbind     S10network       S26lvm2-monitor
K02NetworkManager    K74nscd       S11auditd        S28autofs
K02oddjobd           K74ntpd       S12restorecond   S50hplip
```

Figure 11-10 Start and kill scripts (/etc/rc.d/rc5.d)

Changing Runlevels

The **init <runlevel>** command is used to change runlevels. The init command calls the script */etc/rc.d/rc*. This runs all the kill scripts and then runs all the start scripts in the target runlevel's directory (for example, */etc/rc.d/rc5.d*). The **runlevel** command, shown here, will display the previous runlevel (3) and current runlevel (5).

```
[root@localhost ~]# runlevel
3 5
```

Managing Daemons

System daemons may be started by initialization scripts found in */etc/init.d*, by the server daemon xinetd (the Extended Internet Service daemon), or on the command line. It is also possible to add or remove a daemon from a runlevel.

/etc/init.d

You can manage daemon scripts in */etc/init.d* from the command prompt by executing the command **/etc/init.d/<script_name> <argument>**.

Most scripts support the following arguments:

- **start** Use this parameter to start the associated service.
- **stop** Use this parameter to stop the associated service.
- **status** Use this parameter to view the status of the service, such as whether it is currently running.
- **restart** Use this parameter to stop and then start the associated service. This is a very useful option if you've made extensive configuration changes to the service and it needs to be restarted to apply the changes.
- **condrestart** Restarts the service if it is currently running.
- **reload** Use this parameter to reread the service's configuration file without restarting the service itself. Not all daemons support this option.

For example, to stop the CUPS service enter the command **/etc/init.d/cups stop**, as shown next.

```
[root@localhost ~]# /etc/init.d/cups stop
Stopping cups:                                          [  OK  ]
```

You may also use the service command to manage a daemon. Here, we start the cups daemon by executing the command **service cups start**.

```
[root@localhost rc5.d]# service cups start
Starting cups:                                          [  OK  ]
```

Many daemons place a file in */var/lock/susbsys* when they start and remove the entry when they end. The conditional restart case statement (**condrestart;;**) in the daemon scripts checks to see if the file exists before proceeding with a conditional restart.

chkconfig

The chkconfig command may be used to display or change the runlevel at which a daemon starts and stops. In the following example, we use the command **chkconfig --list cups** to view the runlevels at which CUPS is turned on and off.

```
[root@localhost rc5.d]# chkconfig --list cups
cups            0:off    1:off    2:on     3:on     4:on     5:on     6:off
```

You may also discover at what run levels a specific daemon is turned on by looking for the chkconfig statement in the daemon's script in */etc/init.d*. Next, we use the command **chkconfig --level 23 cups off** to turn the CUPS service off in runlevels 2 and 3.

```
[root@localhost rc5.d]# chkconfig --level 23 cups off
[root@localhost rc5.d]# chkconfig --list cups
cups            0:off    1:off    2:off    3:off    4:on     5:on     6:off
```

Shutting Down the System

As with any other operating system, you need to shut down a Linux system properly. This ensures any pending disk write operations are actually committed to disk before the system is powered off.

You can use several commands to properly shut down a Linux system, including the following:

- **init 0** Switches the system to runlevel 0, which halts the system
- **init 6** Switches the system to runlevel 6, which reboots the system
- **halt** Shuts down the system
- **reboot** Reboots the system

In addition to these commands, you can also use the shutdown command to either shut down or reboot the system. It has several key advantages over the preceding commands:

- You can specify that the system go down after a specified period of time. This gives your users time to save their work and log out before the system goes down. It also allows you to shut down the system at a specified time even if you're not there to do it.
- It allows you to send a message to all logged-in users warning them that a shutdown is pending.
- It does not allow other users to log in before the pending shutdown.

The syntax for using shutdown is **shutdown +*m* -h|-r <message>**. The ***+m*** option specifies the amount of time (in minutes) before shutting down the system. You can also use the **now** option instead of ***+m*** to specify that the system go down immediately. If you need the system to go down at a specific time, you can replace ***+m*** with the time (entered as ***hh:mm***) when the shutdown should occur. The -h option specifies that the system be halted, whereas the -r option specifies that the system be rebooted. Some examples of using shutdown are shown here:

```
shutdown +10 -h Please save your work and log out.
```

When you enter this command, all other logged-in users see the following message:

```
tux@ws1:~/Desktop>
Broadcast message from root@ws1 (pts/3) (Thu Feb 17 10:29:59 2011):

Please save your work and log out.
The system is going DOWN for system halt in 10 minutes!
```

If you've scheduled a shutdown using the shutdown command and later need to cancel that shutdown, enter **shutdown -c** at the shell prompt.

You can also use the wall command to send messages to users to inform them of system events, such as a system reboot or a runlevel change. To use wall, you must send the message to the stdin of the wall command. An example is shown here:

```
# echo "The system is going down for a reboot." | wall

Broadcast Message from rtracy
        (/dev/pts/1) at 16:26 ...

The system is going down for a reboot.
```

Working with systemd

The traditional init process starts services one at a time in sequential fashion. systemd is a system and service manager created by Red Hat developers Lennart Poettering and Kay Sievers.

Units

The main configuration file for services is called a unit. Default units are found in */usr/lib/systemd/system*. Modified and custom units are contained in */etc/systemd/system*. Unit files in */etc/systemd/system* override the entries in */usr/lib/systemd/system*.

The command **systemctl -t help**, shown here, will display a list of available units.

```
[root@localhost boot]# systemctl -t help
Available unit types:
service
socket
busname
target
snapshot
device
mount
automount
swap
timer
path
slice
scope
```

The command **systemctl list-units -type=<unit_type>** will display all active units of a specific type. The edited output in the following illustration shows the results of the command **systemctl list-units -type=mount**, which displays all active units of type mount. Adding the -all option, **systemctl list-units -type=mount -all,** will display both active and available units of type mount.

```
[root@localhost boot]# systemctl list-units --type=mount
UNIT                              LOAD   ACTIVE SUB     DESCRIPTION
-.mount                           loaded active mounted /
boot.mount                        loaded active mounted /boot
```

A unit file consists of sections that contain configuration directives. The contents of the vsftpd.service unit file are shown here.

```
[Unit]
Description=Vsftpd ftp daemon
After=network.target

[Service]
Type=forking
ExecStart=/usr/sbin/vsftpd /etc/vsftpd/vsftpd.conf

[Install]
WantedBy=multi-user.target
```

NOTE Daemon names end in the letter *d*. The unit type for daemons is service.

The unit section will be found in all unit configuration files. It contains a description of the unit and generic unit options. Some unit options are explained in Table 11-9.

The service section is configuration information only found in units of type service. Other unit types may have different sections. For example, a mount unit contains a mount section. Table 11-10 contains a few service directives.

Operating parameters for a specific unit may be viewed by executing the command **systemctl show <unit_name>**.

Option	Description
Description	Describes the service.
Documentation	Location of documentation for this unit.
After	Defines the service that must be started before this service.
Before	Defines services that must be started after this service.
Requires	Units that this unit requires to operate. If any required units do not start, the unit is not activated.
Wants	Units that if not started will not prevent the unit from starting.
Conflicts	Units that conflict with this unit.

Table 11-9 Unit Section Directives

Option	Description
Type	systemd contains multiple unit categories called types. systemd types are target, service, device, mount, slice, timer, socket, and scope.
ExecStart	Contains the absolute path and arguments for the command used to start the service.
ExecStartPre	Commands to be executed before ExecStart.
ExecStartPost	Commands to be executed after ExecStart.
ExecStop	Commands required to stop the service. If this directive does not exist, the process will be killed when the service is stopped.
ExecStopPost	Commands executed after ExecStop.

Table 11-10 Service Section Directives

Option	Description
Alias	Space-delimited list of additional names for this unit. Alias names may be used for most systemctl commands, except for **systemctl enable**.
RequiredBy	List of units that require this unit.
WantedBy	List of units that depend on but do not require this unit.
Also	This contains a list of units that will be installed when the unit is started and uninstalled when the unit is removed.

Table 11-11 Unit Install Directives

The install section, detailed in Table 11-11, contains directives associated with the activation of the unit.

Dependencies

To display a list of units that a unit is dependent on, execute the command **systemctl list-dependencies <unit_name>**. To display a list of units that are dependent on a unit, execute the command **systemctl list-dependencies --reverse <unit_name>**.

The output of this command will be a tree-like structure that lists the units that apply. The left margin will contain a green dot if the unit is active and a red dot if inactive.

Status

The command **systemctl status <unit_name>** will display the operational status of a unit. In Figure 11-11, we see the output of the command **systemctl status cups.service**.

```
● cups.service - CUPS Printing Service
   Loaded: loaded (/usr/lib/systemd/system/cups.service; enabled; vendor preset: enabled)
   Active: active (running) since Mon 2019-05-06 11:28:31 EDT; 11h ago
 Main PID: 7510 (cupsd)
    Tasks: 1
   CGroup: /system.slice/cups.service
           └─7510 /usr/sbin/cupsd -f

May 06 11:28:31 localhost.localdomain systemd[1]: Started CUPS Printing Service.
```

Figure 11-11 The results of the systemctl status cups command

Option	Description
Loaded	Loaded into memory
Inactive (dead)	Unit not running
Active Running	Running with one or more active processes
Active Excited	Completed configuration
Active Waiting	Running and listening for a request
Enabled	Will start when system boots
Disabled	Will not start when system boots
Static	Must be started by another service (cannot be enabled)

Table 11-12 Unit Status Definitions

Table 11-12 defines the terms provided in the output.

Failed Units

To list all failed units, execute the command **systemctl -failed**. To list all failed units of a specific type, execute the command **systemctl -failed -type=<unit_type>**.

Controlling Services

You may control services as in System V using the syntax **systemctl <command> <unit>**. Table 11-13 provides a list of control commands.

Targets

A unit defines a specific service. A target is a grouping of units and or other targets to provide a specific function. A target name is suffixed by .target. The command **systemctl --type=target** will list all active targets. The command **systemctl -type=target -all** will list all available targets.

The first target for systemd is default.target. The file */etc/systemd/system/default.target* is linked to the default runlevel target file. You may also execute the command **systemctl get-default** to display the default runlevel. Table 11-14 displays the systemd runlevels and their System V equivalents.

Command	Description
systemctl enable	Turn service on at boot.
systemctl disable	Do not turn service on at boot.
systemctl start	Start service.
systemctl stop	Stop service.
systemctl mask	Make a unit unavailable by creating a symbolic link to */dev/null*.
systemctl unmask	Remove mask.

Table 11-13 Controlling Services

Runlevel (System V)	Target (systemd)	Description
0	runlevel0.target poweroff.target	Shut down and power off.
1	runlevel1.target rescue.target	Rescue mode.
2	runlevel2.target multi-user.target	Text-based multiuser mode.
3	runlevel3.target multi-user.target	Text-based multiuser mode.
4	runlevel4.target multi-user.target	Text-based multiuser mode. Runlevel 4 is not used in Linux systems using System V initialization.
5	runlevel5.target graphical.target	Graphics multiuser mode.
6	runlevel6.target reboot.target	System reboot.

Table 11-14 The systemd Runlevels

To view the current runlevel, execute the command **systemctl get-default**. To change the default runlevel, type the command **systemctl set-default <runlevel_target>**. To change the current runlevel, type the command **systemctl isolate <runlevel_target>**. Note that isolate is used when switching runlevels to stop anything that is not part of the new runlevel.

Kernel Panic

A kernel panic (also called a kernel oops) is a protective measure generated by the kernel to prevent the risk of data loss or corruption when the kernel detects an unrecoverable error. Panics occur due to configuration or software problems; missing, misconfigured, or failed hardware or hardware drivers; or system resource problems. System utilities kexec, kdump, and crash are used to store and troubleshoot a kernel panic. These tools may be installed during system installation or at a later time.

When a kernel panic occurs, the kdump utility, by default, saves the crash dump to memory. kdump may store the dump data on a remote machine.

kdump requires system memory reserved specifically for storing kernel crash information. The memory is reserved during the boot process via the crashkernel directive on the GRUB command line. The amount of memory reserved is dependent on the type of hardware and the total amount of system memory. You may also set this setting to allocate the correct amount of memory automatically.

The kexec utility boots the kernel from another kernel but does not use BIOS. This preserves the current system state so you may analyze the crash dump data using the crash command.

Chapter Review

In this chapter, you learned about the boot process. The bootstrap phase is used to initialize system hardware, and we explored the difference between the BIOS, UEFI, and PXE bootstraps. We then explored the configuration the GRUB Legacy and GRUB2 bootloaders. You learned how to configure the bootloaders and use them in interactive mode. We continued the boot process by discussing how the kernel and root filesystem are loaded. Finally, we reviewed both the System V and systemd initialization processes as well as how to control services.

- In the bootstrap phase, the computer's BIOS chip has control of the system.
- The BIOS tests the system hardware using the power-on self-test (POST) routine and then locates a storage device with boot files on it.
- BIOS turns control of the system over to a bootloader.
- The bootloader points to and loads a temporary kernel.
- The first stage of a BIOS bootloader resides in the master boot record (MBR) of the boot device or in the boot partition on the drive.
- The Linux kernel is located in */boot* and is named *vmlinuz-version.gz* or *vmlinux.*
- The GRUB Legacy bootloader was widely used by many Linux distributions.
- GRUB Legacy is divided into three stages: Stage 1, Stage 1.5, and Stage 2.
- Some distributions use */boot/grub/grub.conf*; others use */boot/grub/menu.lst* to configure GRUB Legacy.
- GRUB Legacy refers to hard disks in the system as hd*x,* where *x* is the number of the drive in the system.
- Partitions on the drive are referred to as hd*x,y,* where *y* is the number of the partition on the drive.
- /boot is the root directory for GRUB.
- GRUB Legacy allows you to modify its configuration file directly so you may add directives or new menu entries.
- GRUB Legacy allows you to create new boot menu items interactively by accessing the grub> prompt.
- You can replace the init process with a different program (such as the bash shell) from the GRUB menu to troubleshoot a system that won't boot.
- You can add an encrypted password to your GRUB menu to restrict access.
- Version 1.98 or later of GRUB is considered "GRUB2."

The configuration files used by GRUB2 are as follows:

- The */boot/grub/grub.cfg* file
- The files within the */etc/grub.d* directory
- The */etc/default/grub* file

- With GRUB2, the menu.lst file has been replaced by the */boot/grub2/grub.cfg* file.
- The GRUB2 configuration is stored in several script files within the */etc/grub.d* directory.
- After making a change to the GRUB2 configuration, you must run the **grub2-mkconfig -o <output_file>** command.
- Linux defines seven runlevels (0–6):
    - **0** Halts the system.
    - **1** Runs Linux in single-user mode.
    - **2** Runs Linux in multiuser mode with networking disabled.
    - **3** Runs Linux in multiuser mode with networking enabled.
    - **4** Unused.
    - **5** Runs Linux in multiuser mode with networking enabled. The graphical user interface is used.
    - **6** Reboots the system.
- The */etc/inittab* file is used to configure what happens in each runlevel.
- */etc/inittab* also defines the default runlevel that your system will boot into.
- System services are started and stopped using an init script.
- The syntax for running init scripts is **/etc/init.d/<script_name> start | stop | restart**.
- Your system's init directory contains a series of subdirectories named rc.0 to rc.6, each of which contains symbolic links to init scripts that should be run for the respective runlevel.
- You can change runlevels on the fly using the init command by entering **init <runlevel>** from the shell prompt.
- When you change runlevels, the init process runs the rc script, which shuts down services associated with the current runlevel and starts scripts associated with the runlevel you're switching to.
- You can configure services to run a specific runlevel using the chkconfig command.
- Entering **chkconfig --list** will list each service and the runlevels at which they are configured to run.
- To configure a service to start at a particular runlevel, enter **chkconfig -level <run_levels> <service_name> on| off**.

- Most Linux distributions today have migrated away from init to systemd.
- The systemd daemon uses the concept of *targets*, which function in a way similar to runlevels.
- The traditional init runlevels are shown here with their equivalent systemd boot target files:
  - runlevel 3 = multi-user.target or runlevel3.target
  - runlevel 5 = graphical.target or runlevel5.target
- On a system that uses systemd, you use the **systemctl** command to manage services and boot targets.

Questions

1. What is the role of the BIOS during system boot? (Choose two.)
   A. It tests system hardware.
   B. It creates an initrd image in a RAM disk.
   C. It locates a bootable storage device.
   D. It provides a menu that lets you choose which operating system to boot.
   E. It points to your operating system kernel.
2. Where can your Linux bootloader reside? (Choose two.)
   A. In the BIOS
   B. In an initrd image
   C. In the MBR of a storage device
   D. In the bootable partition
   E. In the system chipset
3. Where does the Linux kernel reside?
   A. In /boot
   B. In the MBR
   C. In /proc
   D. In /kernel
4. You want to install GRUB into the first partition on the first SATA hard disk drive of your system. Which shell command will do this?
   A. grub /dev/sda1
   B. grub-install /dev/sda1
   C. grub-install /dev/sda
   D. grub /dev/hda1

5. Which file is used to configure the legacy GRUB bootloader? (Choose two.)
   - A. /etc/menu.lst
   - B. /etc/grub.conf
   - C. /boot/grub/grub.conf
   - D. /boot/grub/menu.lst
6. Which of the following GRUB configuration file directives points to the partition on the hard drive where /boot resides?
   - A. root
   - B. boot
   - C. kernel
   - D. partition
7. When you're configuring your GRUB configuration file, which of the following points to /dev/sda2 on a SATA hard drive?
   - A. hd1,2
   - B. hd0,2
   - C. sd0,2
   - D. hd0,1
8. Which of the following configuration files is *not* used by the GRUB2 bootloader?
   - A. /boot/grub/grub.cfg
   - B. /etc/grub.d
   - C. /etc/default/grub
   - D. /boot/grub/menu.lst
9. Which GRUB2 configuration script file can detect a Windows installation on the same hard disk as Linux?
   - A. 00_header
   - B. 10_linux
   - C. 30_os-prober
   - D. 40_custom
10. Which configuration parameter in */etc/default/grub* specifies how long the user has to make a menu selection from the GRUB menu before the default operating system is booted?
    - A. GRUB_TIMEOUT
    - B. GRUB_DEFAULT
    - C. GRUB_SAVED DEFAULT
    - D. GRUB_HIDDEN_TIMEOUT

11. Which runlevel uses a graphical user interface by default?

A. 2

B. 3

C. 4

D. 5

12. Which runlevels use a command-line user interface by default? (Choose two.)

A. 0

B. 2

C. 3

D. 5

E. 4

13. To which file can you add commands that you want executed each time the system boots?

A. rc

B. /boot/local

C. rc.local

D. rc.systinit

14. Where are the init scripts stored on an older Fedora Linux system?

A. /etc/rc.d/init.d

B. /etc/init.d

C. /etc/init

D. /etc/rc.d/init.d/rc*x*.d

15. Which commands can be used on an older openSUSE Linux system to start the Secure Shell server (sshd) daemon? (Choose two.)

A. /etc/rc.d/init.d/sshd start

B. /etc/init.d/sshd restart

C. /etc/rc.d/init.d/sshd reload

D. /etc/init.d/sshd start

E. /etc/init.d/sshd reload

F. /etc/rc.d/init.d/sshd restart

16. Which file is used to set the default runlevel of a Linux system that uses the init daemon?

A. /etc/inittab

B. /etc/runlevel.conf

C. /etc/init.conf

D. /etc/sysconfig/init

17. Which command can be used to switch runlevels while the system is running?

A. runlevel

B. chrun

C. mode

D. init

18. The following link files are located in the */etc/init.d/rc3.d* directory. If the system is configured to boot into runlevel 3 by default, which file is run by init before any of the others?

A. S09cups

B. S05cifs

C. S06kbd

D. S10cron

19. Your older openSUSE Linux system is currently in runlevel 5. You enter the **init 3** command at the shell prompt as root to switch to runlevel 3. There is a kill script for the CUPS service in the */etc/init.d/rc3.d* directory and a start script for the same service in the *rc5.d* directory. What happens to the CUPS service as the runlevel is changed?

A. The rc script leaves the service running because it is configured to run in both runlevels.

B. The rc script runs the kill script to stop the service but does not run the start script to run it.

C. The rc script runs the start script to start the service but does not run the kill script to stop it.

D. The rc script runs the kill script to stop the service and then runs the start script to restart the service.

20. Your Linux system uses systemd instead of init. You need to switch the system into runlevel 3. Which command should you use?

A. systemctl isolate graphical.target

B. systemctl isolate multi-user.target

C. systemctl isolate runlevel5.target

D. systemctl isolate nongraphical.target

Answers

1. **A, C.** The BIOS tests your system hardware during the POST routine and then locates a bootable storage device.
2. **C, D.** The Linux bootloader can be stored in the MBR of the storage device and in the bootable partition on the disk.
3. **A.** The Linux kernel resides in /boot in the filesystem.
4. **B.** The **grub-install /dev/sda1** command will install GRUB into the first partition on the first hard disk drive.
5. **C, D.** The */boot/grub/menu.lst* file is used to configure GRUB. The file */boot/grub/grub.conf* is a symbolic link to */boot/grub/menu.lst*.
6. **A.** The root directive in the GRUB configuration file specifies the partition on the hard drive where /boot resides.
7. **D.** The term **hd0,1** in a GRUB configuration file points to the second partition on the first hard drive in the system.
8. **D.** The */boot/grub/menu.lst* is used by GRUB Legacy. It's not used by GRUB2.
9. **C.** The 30_os-prober GRUB2 script can detect other operating systems, such as Windows, installed on the same system as Linux. It can use the information it finds to add menu items to the GRUB menu that will launch those operating systems.
10. **A.** The GRUB_TIMEOUT parameter is used by GRUB2 to specify how long the user has to make a menu selection from the GRUB menu before the default operating system is booted.
11. **D.** Runlevel 5 uses a graphical user interface by default.
12. **B, C.** Runlevels 2 and 3 use a command-line interface by default.
13. **C.** You can enter commands in *rc.local* on System V–type systems to have them automatically run each time the system boots.
14. **A.** The init scripts on a Fedora system are stored in */etc/rc.d/init.d*.
15. **B, D.** Either the **/etc/init.d/sshd restart** or the **/etc/init.d/sshd start** command can be used on an openSUSE Linux system to start the Secure Shell server (sshd) daemon.
16. **A.** The */etc/inittab* file is used to set the default runlevel of a Linux system.
17. **D.** The init command can be used to switch runlevels while the system is running.
18. **B.** The S05cifs link file (which starts the cifs daemon) is run before any of the other files due to the number assigned to the file.
19. **A.** Because CUPS is configured to run in both runlevels (and is therefore assumed to be running currently), the rc script does nothing. It just leaves the daemon running.
20. **B.** The **systemctl isolate multi-user.target** command will switch the system into the systemd equivalent of init runlevel 3.

CHAPTER 12

Managing Hardware Under Linux

In this chapter, you will learn about

- Discovering devices
- Configuring hardware devices
- Configuring Bluetooth
- Configuring Wi-Fi
- Configuring Storage devices
- Understanding Printing
- Using facility priority with dmesg
- Using the abrt Command

In this chapter we are going to review how system devices are discovered and made available to system applications as well as some of the commands you may use to obtain information concerning system hardware.

NOTE All of the figures and examples in this chapter were created using the same virtual machine image you have access to. Remember that even though we are using the same image device, when you execute the commands in this chapter, the information may not be the same. You will learn why in this chapter.

Discovering Devices

Part of the system boot process is discovering hardware devices. The discovery process starts with searching through system buses for devices. When a device is found, its properties are discovered and then named (enumerated) so applications may access the device.

Table 12-1 contains a list of device terms we will use in our discussion.

Kernel and User Space

To protect kernel information from users, system memory is divided into kernel space and user space. The kernel memory is only accessible to the kernel, and the user memory is accessible to users and applications.

Table 12-1 Device Terms

Term	Definition
Bus	A system device used to transfer data between devices
Port	A physical connection to a bus
Device	A system component capable of receiving or providing data
Driver	A file or group of files used to control a hardware device

Some kernel data is made available to users via directories such as */proc* and */sys*.

/sys and sysfs

The sysfs filesystem is a memory-based filesystem mounted on the directory */sys*. sysfs provides user space with the properties and dynamic operational statistics of system hardware and filesystems.

NOTE Do not confuse */sys* with */proc/sys*. */proc/sys* contains kernel operating parameters, which may be manipulated by changing entries in the */proc/sys* directory (temporary changes) or */etc/sysctl.conf* file (permanent changes).

On boot, the Linux kernel modules detect and initialize devices by scanning each system bus. Device manufacturers assign each device with a vendor and device ID. The Linux kernel assigns the device a major and minor number based on the vendor and device ID.

Next, the kernel creates a directory in */sys*. Each directory contains subdirectories (Table 12-2) that contain device attributes. Table 12-3 lists some device attribute directories.

Table 12-2 */sys* (sysfs) Directories

Directory	Purpose
block	Contains block device (disk and partition) information
bus	A system device used to connect components. A data bus transfers information. An address bus contains the memory location where data should be read from or written. A control bus carries device control information between the CPU and system devices.
device	Hierarchical presentation of devices
firmware	System firmware
fs	Mounted filesystems and devices using the filesystem type
kernel	Kernel status
modules	Loaded modules
power	Information about power management

Directory	Device Attributes
dev	Major and minor number (used to create entry in */dev*)
device	Operation statistics
driver	Symbolic link to device driver (*/sys/bus<bus_type>/drivers/<device>*)

Table 12-3 sys Device Attribute Directories

block

The block directory contains an entry for each system block device. This information is used by the lsblk command (see Figure 12-1).

The entries in the directory are symbolic links to directors in */sys/devices* (lines 1–9 in Figure 12-2). The block device directory contains operational information for the devices (lines 11–15 in Figure 12-2).

NOTE For a closer view of Figure 12-2 and other selected images from this chapter, download the full-resolution images from the online content for this book.

We can also use the systool command to examine system buses. The systool command is part of the sysfsutil package, which is not installed by default. Executing the

```
# lsblk
NAME          MAJ:MIN RM  SIZE RO TYPE MOUNTPOINT
sda             8:0    0    4G  0 disk
sdb             8:16   0   18G  0 disk
├─sdb1          8:17   0  500M  0 part /boot
├─sdb2          8:18   0  7.5G  0 part
│ └─USR-usr   253:0    0  7.5G  0 lvm  /usr
├─sdb3          8:19   0    3G  0 part
│ └─VAR-var   253:1    0    3G  0 lvm  /var
├─sdb4          8:20   0    1K  0 part
├─sdb5          8:21   0    1G  0 part /
├─sdb6          8:22   0    1G  0 part /home
├─sdb7          8:23   0    1G  0 part /tmp
└─sdb8          8:24   0    1G  0 part [SWAP]
sdc             8:32   0    4G  0 disk
sr0            11:0    1 1024M  0 rom
```

Figure 12-1 Output of the lsblk command

```
 1 # cd /sys/block
 2 #
 3 # ls -l
 4 total 0
 5 lrwxrwxrwx. 1 root root 0 May 27 09:30 dm-0 -> ../devices/virtual/block/dm-0
 6 lrwxrwxrwx. 1 root root 0 May 27 09:30 dm-1 -> ../devices/virtual/block/dm-1
 7 lrwxrwxrwx. 1 root root 0 May 27 09:30 sda -> ../devices/pci0000:00/0000:00:10.0/host2/target2:0:0/2:0:0:0/block/sda
 8 lrwxrwxrwx. 1 root root 0 May 27 09:26 sdb -> ../devices/pci0000:00/0000:00:11.0/0000:02:03.0/usb1/1-1/1-1:1.0/host3/target3:0:0/
   3:0:0:0/block/sdb
 9 lrwxrwxrwx. 1 root root 0 May 27 09:30 sr0 -> ../devices/pci0000:00/0000:00:07.1/ata2/host1/target1:0:0/1:0:0:0/block/sr0
10 #
11 # cd /sys/block/sda
12 # ls
13 alignment_offset  dev                events            ext_range  power  removable  sda2  sda5  sda8  slaves     trace
14 bdi               device             events_async      holders    queue  ro         sda3  sda6  sda9  stat       uevent
15 capability        discard_alignment  events_poll_msecs inflight   range  sda1       sda4  sda7  size  subsystem
```

Figure 12-2 View of */sys/block*

```
#systool -pc block
Class = "block"

  Class Device = "dm-0"
  Class Device path = "/sys/devices/virtual/block/dm-0"

  Class Device = "dm-1"
  Class Device path = "/sys/devices/virtual/block/dm-1"

  Class Device = "sda"
  Class Device path = "/sys/devices/pci0000:00/0000:00:10.0/host2/target2:0:0/2:0:0:0/block/sda"
    Device = "2:0:0:0"
    Device path = "/sys/devices/pci0000:00/0000:00:10.0/host2/target2:0:0/2:0:0:0"


  Class Device = "sr0"
  Class Device path = "/sys/devices/pci0000:00/0000:00:07.1/ata2/host1/target1:0:0/1:0:0:0/block/sr0"
    Device = "1:0:0:0"
    Device path = "/sys/devices/pci0000:00/0000:00:07.1/ata2/host1/target1:0:0/1:0:0:0"
```

Figure 12-3 systool -c block

command systool will display a list of supported buses, classes, devices, and modules. This package is installed on your system. Figure 12-3 illustrates the use of the command **systool -c block** to display block devices. The -p option displays the path to the block devices.

NOTE Figure 12-3 has been edited for brevity.

bus

A bus is a system device used to transfer data between devices. The */sys/bus* directory contains operational statistics for all system buses. Lines 1–6 in Figure 12-4 display different bus types. On lines 12–14 in Figure 12-4, you can see the files found in the */sys//bus/usb* directory.

Each directory in */sys/bus* contains devices and drivers directories. The device directory (lines 21–25 in Figure 12-4) contains entries for devices discovered on the bus. Most of these files are symbolic links to the directory */sys/devices*. The drivers directory (lines 30–36 in Figure 12-4) contains device driver information for all discovered devices on the bus.

You can also use the command **systool -pb scsi** to display SCSI bus information. Figure 12-5 displays the instances of a SCSI bus (-b scsi) and paths (-p).

class

A device class contains devices that perform similar operations, such as block (block device). Figure 12-6 illustrates listings found in */sys/class*.

PCI

Peripheral Component Interconnect (PCI) is a system specification that defines the implementation of the PCI bus. The bus supports 32- or 64-bit addressing and ultra DMA burst mode, and it can auto-detect PCI peripheral boards. Multiple PCI buses may be joined using a bridge.

```
# cd /sys/bus
#
# ls
ac97          clocksource  edac          i2c    machinecheck  mipi-dsi  nvmem        platform  serio    thunderbolt  workqueue
acpi          container    event_source  iio    mdio_bus      nd        pci          pnp       snd_seq  usb          xen
clockevents   cpu          hid           ishtp  memory        node      pci_express  scsi      spi      usb-serial
#
# cd /sys/bus/usb
#
# ls -l
total 0
drwxr-xr-x. 2 root root    0 May 27 09:21 devices
drwxr-xr-x. 9 root root    0 May 27 09:26 drivers
-rw-r--r--. 1 root root 4096 May 28 08:23 drivers_autoprobe
--w-------. 1 root root 4096 May 28 08:23 drivers_probe
--w-------. 1 root root 4096 May 28 08:23 uevent
#
# cd devices
# ls -l
total 0
lrwxrwxrwx. 1 root root 0 May 27 09:22 1-0:1.0 -> ../../../devices/pci0000:00/0000:00:11.0/0000:02:03.0/usb1/1-0:1.0
lrwxrwxrwx. 1 root root 0 May 27 09:26 1-1 -> ../../../devices/pci0000:00/0000:00:11.0/0000:02:03.0/usb1/1-1
lrwxrwxrwx. 1 root root 0 May 27 09:26 1-1:1.0 -> ../../../devices/pci0000:00/0000:00:11.0/0000:02:03.0/usb1/1-1/1-1:1.0
lrwxrwxrwx. 1 root root 0 May 27 09:22 usb1 -> ../../../devices/pci0000:00/0000:00:11.0/0000:02:03.0/usb1
lrwxrwxrwx. 1 root root 0 May 27 09:22 usb2 -> ../../../devices/pci0000:00/0000:00:11.0/0000:02:00.0/usb2

# cd /sys/bus/usb/drivers
[root@localhost drivers]# ls -l
total 0
drwxr-xr-x. 2 root root 0 May 28 08:25 hub
drwxr-xr-x. 2 root root 0 May 27 09:26 uas
drwxr-xr-x. 2 root root 0 May 28 08:24 usb
drwxr-xr-x. 2 root root 0 May 28 13:57 usbfs
drwxr-xr-x. 2 root root 0 May 28 13:57 usbhid
drwxr-xr-x. 2 root root 0 May 28 13:57 usbserial_generic
drwxr-xr-x. 2 root root 0 May 27 09:26 usb-storage
```

Figure 12-4 View of */sys/bus*

```
 #systool -pb scsi
Bus = "scsi"

  Device = "1:0:0:0"
  Device path = "/sys/devices/pci0000:00/0000:00:07.1/ata2/host1/target1:0:0/1:0:0:0"

  Device = "2:0:0:0"
  Device path = "/sys/devices/pci0000:00/0000:00:10.0/host2/target2:0:0/2:0:0:0"

  Device = "host0"
  Device path = "/sys/devices/pci0000:00/0000:00:07.1/ata1/host0"

  Device = "host1"
  Device path = "/sys/devices/pci0000:00/0000:00:07.1/ata2/host1"

  Device = "host2"
  Device path = "/sys/devices/pci0000:00/0000:00:10.0/host2"

  Device = "target1:0:0"
  Device path = "/sys/devices/pci0000:00/0000:00:07.1/ata2/host1/target1:0:0"

  Device = "target2:0:0"
  Device path = "/sys/devices/pci0000:00/0000:00:10.0/host2/target2:0:0"
```

Figure 12-5 Using systool to display bus devices

```
# ls /sys/class

ata_device  bsg          drm_dp_aux_dev  i2c-adapter  misc            powercap      scsi_device   spi_master     typec
ata_link    cpuid        gpio            input        msr             power_supply  scsi_disk     spi_transport  usbmon
ata_port    devcoredump  graphics        iommu        nd              ppdev         scsi_generic  thermal        vc
backlight   dma          hidraw          leds         net             pwm           scsi_host     tpm            vtconsole
bdi         dmi          hmm_device      mdio_bus     pci_bus         raw           sound         tpmrm          watchdog
block       drm          hwmon           mem          pcmcia_socket   rtc           spi_host      tty
```

Figure 12-6 View of */sys/class*

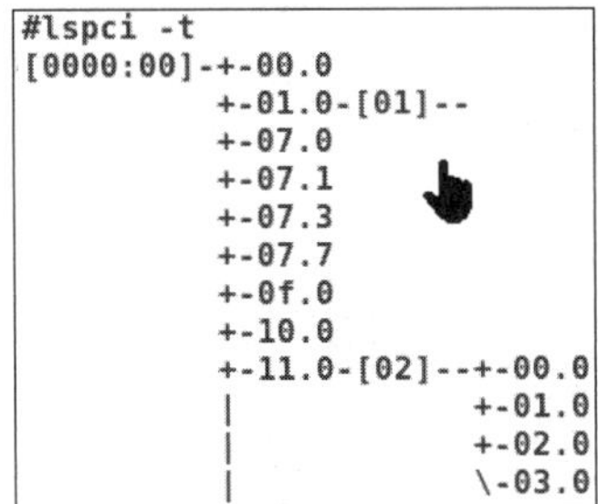

```
#lspci -t
[0000:00]-+-00.0
          +-01.0-[01]--
          +-07.0
          +-07.1
          +-07.3
          +-07.7
          +-0f.0
          +-10.0
          +-11.0-[02]--+-00.0
          |            +-01.0
          |            +-02.0
          |            \-03.0
```

Figure 12-7 PCI hierarchical structure

PCI limits the number of buses to 256 per system. Each bus can host up to 32 devices. Larger systems may require additional PCI buses. This is accomplished by using domains.

The PCI bus is a hierarchical structure (shown in Figure 12-7) that starts at the top bus (0).

The format of the lspci command's output is Bus:Device:Function Class Vendor Name.

NOTE The -D option will display the domain number (Domain:Bus:Device:Function) when executing the lspci command. If the -D option is not used, the domain is assumed to be 0000.

Figure 12-8 shows an edited output of the lspci command. Line 1 shows the first device (00) located on bus 02. The device is a USB controller manufactured by VMware and its name is USB1.1 UHCI Controller. Lines 2–4 show us three other devices located on bus 02.

The class of device, manufacturer, and device name are stored as a numeric value. This information may be found in */usr/share/hwdata/pci.ids*. (Device classes are stored at the end of the file.)

Notice the class ID for the USB controller (shown in line 3 of Figure 12-9) is 0c03, and the vendor information for the device <vendor:device> is 15ad (VMware): 0770 (USB2 EHCI Controller).

```
1 02:00.0 USB controller: VMware USB1.1 UHCI Controller
2 02:01.0 Ethernet controller: Intel Corporation 82545EM Gigabit Ethernet Controller (Copper) (rev 01)
3 02:02.0 Multimedia audio controller: Ensoniq ES1371/ES1373 / Creative Labs CT2518 (rev 02)
4 02:03.0 USB controller: VMware USB2 EHCI Controller
```

Figure 12-8 Output of the lspci command

```
1 02:01.0 Ethernet controller [0200]: Intel Corporation 82545EM Gigabit Ethernet Controller (Copper) [8086:100f] (rev 01)
2 02:02.0 Multimedia audio controller [0401]: Ensoniq ES1371/ES1373 / Creative Labs CT2518 [1274:1371] (rev 02)
3 02:03.0 USB controller [0c03]: VMware USB2 EHCI Controller [15ad:0770]
```

Figure 12-9 Using lspci to view vendor and class ID

```
#lspci -v | grep -A8  USB2
02:03.0 USB controller: VMware USB2 EHCI Controller (prog-if 20 [EHCI])
        Subsystem: VMware USB2 EHCI Controller
        Physical Slot: 35
        Flags: bus master, fast devsel, latency 64, IRQ 17
        Memory at fd5ef000 (32-bit, non-prefetchable) [size=4K]
        Capabilities: [40] PCI Advanced Features
        Kernel driver in use: ehci-pci

#lspci -vv | grep -A8  USB2
02:03.0 USB controller: VMware USB2 EHCI Controller (prog-if 20 [EHCI])
        Subsystem: VMware USB2 EHCI Controller
        Physical Slot: 35
        Control: I/O- Mem+ BusMaster+ SpecCycle- MemWINV- VGASnoop- ParErr- Stepping- SERR- FastB2B- DisINTx-
        Status: Cap+ 66MHz- UDF- FastB2B- ParErr- DEVSEL=fast >TAbort- <TAbort- <MAbort- >SERR- <PERR- INTx-
        Latency: 64 (1500ns min, 63750ns max)
        Interrupt: pin A routed to IRQ 17
        Region 0: Memory at fd5ef000 (32-bit, non-prefetchable) [size=4K]
        Capabilities: [40] PCI Advanced Features
                AFCap: TP+ FLR+
```

Figure 12-10 The -v and -vv options of lspci

The -v and -vv options display additional bus information, as shown in Figure 12-10.

In Figure 12-11, we combine the -t and -v options. The -t option displays a tree structure and the -v option prints more detailed information.

Host Bus Adapter (HBA)

A host bus adapter, also called a host adapter or host controller, is an expansion card used to connect multiple devices, using a single controller, with a computer system. Here are some examples of host adapters:

- IDE, SCSI, and SATA controllers
- ISCSI and Fiber Channel controllers
- Network controllers

To view HBA adapters, you may execute the command **lspci -nn | grep -i hba** or **systool -c <adapter_class>**.

You could also look for information in */sys/class*.

```
#lspci -t
          +-11.0-[02]--+-00.0
          |            +-01.0
          |            +-02.0
          |            \-03.0


#lspci -tv
          +-11.0-[02]--+-00.0  VMware USB1.1 UHCI Controller
          |            +-01.0  Intel Corporation 82545EM Gigabit Ethernet Controller (Copper)
          |            +-02.0  Ensoniq ES1371/ES1373 / Creative Labs CT2518
          |            \-03.0  VMware USB2 EHCI Controller
```

Figure 12-11 The -t and -v options of lspci

Figure 12-12 */lib/udev/rules.d* directory (edited for brevity)

```
1 #pwd
2 /lib/udev/rules.d
3  #ls --format=single-column
4 01-md-raid-creating.rules
5 10-dm.rules
6 11-dm-lvm.rules
7 11-dm-mpath.rules
8 13-dm-disk.rules
9 60-cdrom_id.rules
10 60-keyboard.rules
11 60-net.rules
12 60-persistent-storage.rules
13 99-vmware-scsi-udev.rules
```

udev

udev stands for *userspace /dev*. The */dev* directory provides access to system devices. After the kernel module detects a device and has made the appropriate entries in */sys*, it generates a uevent. The udev service, systemd-udevd.service, responds to the uevent and matches the attributes of the device specified in */sys* to a udev configuration rule, which ensures a device's configuration is persistent across system reboots.

NOTE Many of the device discovery commands in this udev section receive a more detailed explanation later in this chapter.

Location of udev Rules

udev rules are located in */lib/udev/rules.d* (system default rules) and */etc/udev/rules.d* (custom rules). In Figure 12-12, you see each rule begins with a number and then a short name. The udev daemon searches for rules in dictionary order (numbers first, then short name). Later rules (higher number) can override earlier rules.

Figure 12-13 displays a section of the rule 60-persistent-storage.rules, which creates the entries by-label, by-uuid, by-id, by-partlabel, and by-partuuid in */dev* for a disk device.

Notice the entry 99-vmware-scsi-udev.rules in both */lib/udev/rules.d* (line 13 in Figure 12-12) and */etc/udev/rules.d* (line 5 in Figure 12-14). This tells us that the default rule in */lib/udev/rules.d* has been customized and udev will use the rule */etc/udev/rules.d* rather than the rule in */lib/udev/rules.d*.

```
# by-label/by-uuid links (filesystem metadata)
ENV{ID_FS_USAGE}=="filesystem|other|crypto", ENV{ID_FS_UUID_ENC}=="?*", SYMLINK+="disk/by-uuid/$env{ID_FS_UUID_ENC}"
ENV{ID_FS_USAGE}=="filesystem|other", ENV{ID_FS_LABEL_ENC}=="?*", SYMLINK+="disk/by-label/$env{ID_FS_LABEL_ENC}"

# by-id (World Wide Name)
ENV{DEVTYPE}=="disk", ENV{ID_WWN_WITH_EXTENSION}=="?*", SYMLINK+="disk/by-id/wwn-$env{ID_WWN_WITH_EXTENSION}"
ENV{DEVTYPE}=="partition", ENV{ID_WWN_WITH_EXTENSION}=="?*", SYMLINK+="disk/by-id/wwn-$env{ID_WWN_WITH_EXTENSION}-part%n"

# by-partlabel/by-partuuid links (partition metadata)
ENV{ID_PART_ENTRY_SCHEME}=="gpt", ENV{ID_PART_ENTRY_UUID}=="?*", SYMLINK+="disk/by-partuuid/$env{ID_PART_ENTRY_UUID}"
ENV{ID_PART_ENTRY_SCHEME}=="gpt", ENV{ID_PART_ENTRY_NAME}=="?*", SYMLINK+="disk/by-partlabel/$env{ID_PART_ENTRY_NAME}"
```

Figure 12-13 Persistent storage rules example

Figure 12-14 */etc/udev/rules.d*

```
1  #pwd
2 /etc/udev/rules.d
3  #ls --format=single-column
4 70-persistent-ipoib.rules
5 99-vmware-scsi-udev.rules
```

```
#udevadm info -q property -n /dev/sdb
DEVLINKS=/dev/disk/by-id/usb-Kingston_DataTraveler_2.0_C860008862E4ED606A1C00A0-0:0 /dev/disk/by-path/pci-0000:02:03.0-usb-0:1:1.0
-scsi-0:0:0:0
DEVNAME=/dev/sdb
DEVPATH=/devices/pci0000:00/0000:00:11.0/0000:02:03.0/usb1/1-1/1-1:1.0/host6/target6:0:0/6:0:0:0/block/sdb
DEVTYPE=disk
ID_BUS=usb
ID_DRIVE_THUMB=1
ID_INSTANCE=0:0
ID_MODEL=DataTraveler_2.0
ID_MODEL_ENC=DataTraveler\x202.0
ID_MODEL_ID=6545
ID_PART_TABLE_TYPE=dos
ID_PATH=pci-0000:02:03.0-usb-0:1:1.0-scsi-0:0:0:0
ID_PATH_TAG=pci-0000_02_03_0-usb-0_1_1_0-scsi-0_0_0_0
ID_REVISION=PMAP
ID_SERIAL=Kingston_DataTraveler_2.0_C860008862E4ED606A1C00A0-0:0
ID_SERIAL_SHORT=C860008862E4ED606A1C00A0
ID_TYPE=disk
ID_USB_DRIVER=usb-storage
ID_USB_INTERFACES=:080650:
ID_USB_INTERFACE_NUM=00
ID_VENDOR=Kingston
ID_VENDOR_ENC=Kingston
ID_VENDOR_ID=0930
MAJOR=8
MINOR=16
MPATH_SBIN_PATH=/sbin
SUBSYSTEM=block
TAGS=:systemd:
USEC_INITIALIZED=80555195
```

Figure 12-15 Sample udevadm info command

udevadm

udevadm is a utility that can manage and obtain information about a system device.

udevadm info The command **udevadm info** (Figure 12-15) searches the udev database for device information. The format of the command is as follows:

udevadm info --query=<query_type> | -q <type> --path=<device_path> |-p <device_path

or

udevadm info --query=<query_type> | -q <type> --name=<device_name> | -n <device_name>

Table 12-4 lists the query types for udevadm info.

The attribute walk option (-a) of **udevadm info** may assist you in troubleshooting. Its output will display a device and its attributes as well as the attributes of all its parent devices. An example of the command is **udevadm -a --name=/dev/sda**.

Table 12-4 udevadm Info Query Types

Query Type	Definition
Name	Displays the device name
symlink	Displays the symbolic link attached to a device
Path	The physical path to the device
property	Displays the device properties
All	Displays the properties of parent devices

udevadm monitor The command **udevadm monitor** listens for uevents and displays them on the console. By default, **udevadm monitor** will display the kernel uevent and the udev process.

You can restrict the output to kernel uevents (-k or --kernel) or udev events (-u or --udev). In addition, the option -p will display the properties of devices associated with the event.

udevadm control The command **udevadm control** is used to control the systemd-udevd.

Creating udev Rules

A udev rule is used to match a uevent with some action. The rules are created by using a comma-delimited set of key/value entries. These keys can be either match keys or assign keys.

It is important to remember that udev rules are read in order of priority (lower number to higher number). When you're initially creating rules, use the command line. Once a rule has been completed, test the rule before adding it to */etc/udev/rules.d*.

udev rules support the following characters:

*
?
[ ]

udev supports substitutions, such as $(pwd), and also maintains a built-in list of substitution strings (Table 12-5).

String	Definition
$$	$
%%	%
%r or $root	*/dev*
%p or $devpath	Value of DEVPATH
%k or $kernel	Kernel device name (for example, */dev/sdb*)
%n or $number	Device number
%M or $major	Device's major number
%m or $minor	Device's minor number
%E{variable} $attr{variable}	Value of an environmental variable
%s $attr{attribute}	Value of a sysfs attribute
%c or $result	Output of an executed PROGRAM

Table 12-5 udev Built-in Substitutions

```
#systool -pb scsi
Bus = "scsi"

  Device = "1:0:0:0"
  Device path = "/sys/devices/pci0000:00/0000:00:07.1/ata2/host1/target1:0:0/1:0:0:0"

  Device = "2:0:0:0"
  Device path = "/sys/devices/pci0000:00/0000:00:10.0/host2/target2:0:0/2:0:0:0"

  Device = "host0"
  Device path = "/sys/devices/pci0000:00/0000:00:07.1/ata1/host0"

  Device = "host1"
  Device path = "/sys/devices/pci0000:00/0000:00:07.1/ata2/host1"

  Device = "host2"
  Device path = "/sys/devices/pci0000:00/0000:00:10.0/host2"

  Device = "target1:0:0"
  Device path = "/sys/devices/pci0000:00/0000:00:07.1/ata2/host1/target1:0:0"

  Device = "target2:0:0"
  Device path = "/sys/devices/pci0000:00/0000:00:10.0/host2/target2:0:0"
```

Figure 12-16 Properties of */dev/sdb*

Prior to creating rules for a device, you must know its properties. Executing the **udevadm info** command will enable you to display device properties. In Figure 12-16, we executed the command **udevadm info -q property -n /dev/sdb** to view the properties of the drive.

NOTE For the examples in this chapter, we will be using a DataTraveler flash drive enumerated as */dev/sdb*.

Match Keys Match keys are used to match conditions that must exist for the rule to apply. Table 12-6 reviews some of the match keys.

Table 12-6 udev Rule Match Keys

Key	Definition
ACTION	The name of the event (that is, add or remove)
add	Adds a rule
remove	Removes a rule
DEVPATH	The device path
KERNEL	Kernel name for the device
BUS	Bus type (for example, scsi or usb)
SUBSYSTEM	Subsystem of the device (for example, usb)
ATTR{filename}	Matches a device attribute
DRIVER	Matches a device driver name
ENV{key}	Matches an environmental variable

Table 12-7 udev Match Operators

Match Operator	Definition
==	Double equal sign search to find a match between the match key and value.
!=	Not equal to. The key and value are not a match.

When matching a key with a value, you use one of the operators in Table 12-7. The value must be enclosed in double quotes (" ").

The following key/value pairs would match our device:

NOTE udev requires one rule per line. If a rule will exceed a single line, use a \ to join multiple lines.

```
SUBSYSTEM=="block", ENV{ID_SERIAL_SHORT}==\
"C860008862E4ED606A1C00A0-0:0"
```

This could also have been written as follows:

```
SUBSYSTEM=="block",  %E{ID_SERIAL_SHORT}=="C860008862E4ED606A1C00A0-0:0"
```

Or it may have been written like this:

```
SUBSYSTEM=="block", $attr{ID_SERIAL_SHORT}==\
"C860008862E4ED606A1C00A0-0:0"
```

Assign Keys Once you have matched the device, you can assign values using the assign operators in Table 12-8 and the assign keys in Table 12-9.

Assignment keys are used to add an action or value to a device.

Once you have completed your rule, you need to test it. The command **udevadm test --action <udev_rule>** will test the rule without implementing it. If no error messages are displayed, the rule has no functional errors.

udev automatically detects changes to rules files when a rule is added or changed. Therefore, most changes will take place immediately. Existing devices may require the command **udevadm control --reload** for rule changes to be applied.

Table 12-8 udev Assignment Operators

Assign Operator	Definition
=	Assigns a value to a key. If the key had any values assigned to it, they all will be replaced by this assignment.
+=	Adds a value to an existing key.

Assign Key	Definition
ACTION==	The name of the event (add or remove).
add	Adds a device.
remove	Removes a device.
NAME	Assigns a name to the device node. This will overwrite the existing name. Any rules assigned to the previous name will be ignored. The following rule will assign the node name MYUSB to our flash drive: **SUBSYSTEM=="block", ENV{ID_SERIAL_SHORT}==\ "C860008862E4ED606A1C00A0-0:0", NAME="MYUSB"**
SYMLINK	A symlink is established when the device is first enumerated; therefore, you can add a symlink to a device. This is especially useful if you have two devices of the same type because you can assign them different symlinks. The + before the = indicates to add a symlink to existing symlinks: **SYMLINK+="8GUSB"**
OWNER, GROUP, MODE	Assigns a device owner, group owner, and permissions: **OWNER="<user_name>"** **GROUP="<group_name>"** **MODE="0655"**
ATTR{key}	Assigns an attribute to a device. If double equal signs (==) are used, this key is used to match rather than to assign: **ATTR{<attribute_name>}=="<value>"**
ENV{key}	Creates an environmental variable. If double equal signs (==) are used, this key is used to match rather than to assign.
RUN	Executes a program. The following line will execute the script found in test.sh: **RUN+="test.sh"**
GOTO <label>	Skips rules until after the LABEL.
LABEL	Creates a label (see GOTO).
IMPORT{type}	Loads variables into the environment.
program	Executes a program and imports the output.
file	Imports a text file.
OPTIONS	
last_rule	Ignores any additional rules set for the defined device. Here's an example: **KERNEL="/dev/sda",OPTIONS="last-rule"**
ignore_device	Ignores a device. The following rule effectively disables USB devices: **BUS=="usb", KERNEL="sd*", SUBSYSTEM="block"\ OPTIONS+="ignore-device**
ignore_remove	Adds a udev rule for all partitions found on the device
all_partitions	

Table 12-9 udev Assignment Keys

Configuring Hardware Devices

In this section, you will learn general elements and commands that are used to configure hardware devices.

lsdev

The lsdev command displays information about installed hardware.

NOTE The command /usr/bin/lsdev is no longer available in RHEL 7. The command is available in Fedora (29) and SUSE as part of the procinfo package. To install the package in Fedora, execute the command **dnf install procinfo**. To install the package in a SUSE distribution, execute the command **zypper in procinfo**. Fedora and SUSE OVA images are available for download with this book.

lsdev retrieves information from */proc/interrupts*, */proc/ioports*, and */proc/dma* and displays the following columns:

- Device Name
- DMA
- IRQ
- I/O Ports

Figure 12-17 shows output of the lsdev command.

DMA

Direct Memory Access (DMA) enables devices to transfer data directly without the need of the CPU controlling the transfer.

DMA is implemented on the motherboard using the DMA controller chip (DCC). The DCC has four leads that connect it to the memory controller chip (MCC). Each of these leads is referred to as a *DMA channel.* Two DCC chips may be connected together

```
Device              DMA   IRQ  I/O Ports
ACPI                           1000-1003 1004-1005 1008-100b 100c-100f 1010-1015
ata_piix                14 15  0170-0177 01f0-01f7 0376-0376 03f6-03f6 1060-106f
cascade               4
dma                            0080-008f
dma1                           0000-001f
dma2                           00c0-00df
e1000                          2000-203f
ehci_hcd:usb2              17
keyboard                       0060-0060 0064-0064
uhci_hcd:usb1              18
```

Figure 12-17 lsdev (output edited for brevity)

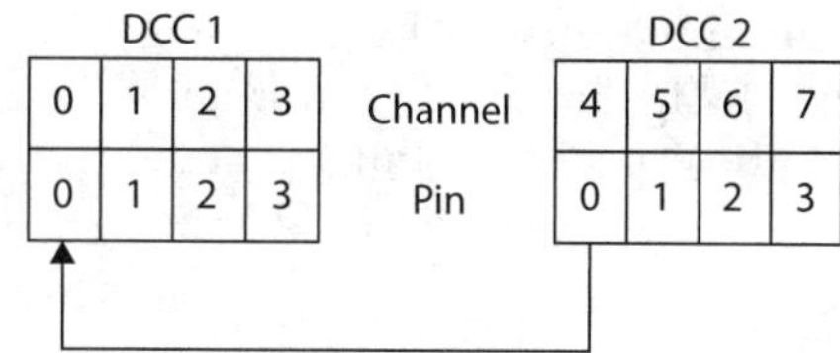

Figure 12-18
DMA controller

via channel 0 on the first chip and channel 4 on the second chip (cascade), as shown in Figure 12-18. Only one device may be assigned per channel. By default, channels 1 and 2 are reserved.

Ultra DMA is a method that allows devices to bypass the DMA controller and transmit data in bursts of either 33 or 66 Mbps. (Normal DMA transfer speeds are approximately 7.2 Mbps).

The file */proc/dma* (shown in Figure 12-19) will display active DMA channels.

IRQ

Every device is assigned an interrupt. Each interrupt is assigned a priority (interrupt request level) based on the importance of the device it is associated with.

Programmable Interrupt Controller

A programmable interrupt controller (PIC) can manage eight interrupts per controller. The interrupt request line of a device is electrically attached to an interrupt line on the PIC.

Systems using PIC chips have one PIC chip (master) managing interrupts 0–7 and a second PIC chip (slave) managing interrupts 8–15.

Devices configured to use interrupt 2 use interrupt 9. Interrupt 9 is used for peripherals or the SCSI host adapter. Interrupt 2 is used by the slave PIC to signal the master PIC. The master PIC is connected to the CPU.

Advanced Programmable Interrupt Controller (APIC)

The Advanced Programmable Interrupt Controller (APIC) has eight additional interrupts to manage PCI interrupts and can support 255 physical interrupt request lines. This system consists of a Local APIC (LAPIC) and an I/O APIC

NOTE It is easy to confuse APIC (Advanced Programmable Interrupt Controller) with ACPI, which stands for Advanced Configuration and Power Interface.

Figure 12-19
/proc/dma

```
[root@localhost ~]# cat /proc/dma
 2: floppy
 4: cascade
```

The LAPIC is built in to the CPU and is used to accept and generate interrupts. The I/O APIC contains a table that directs interrupt requests to one or more LAPICs.

If a system has APIC capabilities, but grub.conf contains the entry noapic, the system will use PIC.

/proc/interrupts

Figure 12-20 displays an edited output of the file */proc/interrupts*, which contains the following information:

- The interrupt number.
- Number of times the interrupt has been requested (per CPU). If the system contains multiple CPUs, there would be a column for each CPU.
- Type of interrupt.
- Interrupt name.

Interrupt Request Channels

The first system resource you need to be familiar with is the interrupt request channel. Interrupt request channels are also referred to as *IRQs* or just *interrupts.*

When a device is installed in a PC system, it needs some means of letting the CPU know when it needs attention. Many devices in your PC need lots of CPU time; other devices need the CPU only on occasion. We need a way to make sure the busy devices get the attention they need without wasting time on devices that don't need as much. This is done through interrupts.

The CPU in your system has one wire on it called the interrupt (INT) wire. If current is applied to this wire, the CPU will stop what it is doing and service the device that placed current on the wire. If no current is present on the wire, the CPU will continue working on whatever processing task has been assigned to it.

```
# cat /proc/interrupts
          CPU0
  0:       131    XT-PIC-XT        timer
  1:       754    XT-PIC-XT        i8042
  2:         0    XT-PIC-XT        cascade
  5:     22126    XT-PIC-XT        ahci, Intel 82801AA-ICH
  8:         0    XT-PIC-XT        rtc0
  9:         0    XT-PIC-XT        acpi
 10:     13953    XT-PIC-XT        eth0
 11:         0    XT-PIC-XT        ohci_hcd:usb1
 12:     12240    XT-PIC-XT        i8042
 14:         0    XT-PIC-XT        ata_piix
 15:         0    XT-PIC-XT        ata_piix
```

Figure 12-20 */proc/interrupts* (edited for brevity)

The interrupt system in a PC is very similar to a typical classroom. In a classroom setting, the instructor usually presents the material she has prepared to the students. If a student has a question, he can raise his hand and interrupt the instructor's presentation. After the question is answered, the instructor resumes the presentation.

PC interrupts work in much the same manner. Like the instructor, the CPU goes about its business until it is interrupted. Once interrupted, the CPU diverts its attention to the device that raised the interrupt. Once the device's request has been satisfied, the CPU goes back to what it was doing before.

The advantage to using interrupts is that the CPU services system devices only when they need it. It doesn't waste processing time on devices that are idle.

The PIC chip is connected to the INT wire on the CPU as well as the interrupt wires in your motherboard's expansion bus. When a device needs attention, it applies current to its interrupt wire. The PIC is alerted by this event and applies current to the CPU's INT wire. The CPU acknowledges the interrupt, and the PIC then tells the CPU which interrupt number was activated. The CPU can then service the device.

Early PCs had only eight interrupts and a single PIC, as just related. However, a modern PC has many more interrupts. Newer systems use an Advanced Programmable Interrupt Controller (APIC) chip that supports up to 255 IRQ lines.

When working with interrupts, you should keep in mind the following important facts:

- Every device in the PC must be assigned an interrupt.
- Two PCI devices can share interrupts.
- Some system devices have interrupts assigned to them by default. Some of these can be changed or disabled, but many cannot:
    - IRQ 0: System timer
    - IRQ 1: Keyboard
    - IRQ 3: COM 2
    - IRQ 4: COM 1
    - IRQ 5: LPT 2
    - IRQ 6: Floppy drive
    - IRQ 7: LPT 1
    - IRQ 8: Real-time clock
- Interrupts 0, 1, and 8 are hardwired. Under no circumstances can you use these interrupts for any other device in the system.
- If a device with a default interrupt assignment isn't installed in the system or is disabled, you can use its interrupt for another device.

In addition to interrupts, devices also require an I/O address to function in a PC system. Let's talk about I/O addresses next.

Figure 12-21 */proc/ioports* (edited for brevity)

```
# cat /proc/ioports
0000-001f : dma1
0020-0021 : pic1
0040-0043 : timer0
0050-0053 : timer1
0060-0060 : keyboard
0064-0064 : keyboard
0070-0071 : rtc_cmos
  0070-0071 : rtc0
0080-008f : dma page reg
00a0-00a1 : pic2
00c0-00df : dma2
00f0-00ff : fpu
0170-0177 : 0000:00:01.1
  0170-0177 : ata_piix
01f0-01f7 : 0000:00:01.1
  01f0-01f7 : ata_piix
0376-0376 : 0000:00:01.1
  0376-0376 : ata_piix
03c0-03df : vga+
```

I/O port

An I/O port is a memory address used to communicate with a hardware device. The file */proc/ioports* will contain a list of I/O ports being used (Figure 12-21).

Input/Output Addresses

Input/output (I/O) addresses go by a variety of names in a PC system. You may hear them referred to as *I/O ports, port addresses,* or simply as *ports.*

I/O addresses allow communications between the devices in the PC and the operating system. I/O addresses are very similar to mailboxes. To send a letter to someone, you must know their mailing address. You write their address on the letter, and the mail carrier delivers it to the box with that address. Likewise, the person you wrote to can respond to your letter and leave it in their mailbox for the mail carrier to pick up.

I/O addresses work in much the same manner. They serve as mailboxes for the devices installed in the system. Data can be left for a device in its I/O address. Data from the device can be left in the I/O address for the operating system to pick up.

On a personal computer, there are 65,535 port addresses for devices to use.

NOTE I/O addresses are written using hexadecimal notation. The decimal numbering system that we use in our everyday work is a base-10 numbering system. When we count, we start at 0 and proceed to 9, and then we start over again at 10. Alternatively, hexadecimal is a base-16 numbering system. Like decimal numbering, hexadecimal starts at 0 and proceeds to 9. However, instead of starting over, hexadecimal continues on with six additional numbers represented by the letters A through F. Therefore, if you were to count in hex, you would say: 0, 1, 2, 3, 4, 5, 6, 7, 8, 9, A, B, C, D, E, F. Because hex and decimal numbers can sometimes be easily mistaken with each other, we usually put an *h* either before or after any hex number.

When working with I/O addresses, you should keep the following important facts in mind:

- All devices must have an I/O address assigned.
- Most devices will use a range of I/O addresses.
- Devices must use unique I/O ports.
- Default I/O port assignments include the following:
  - 0000h: DMA controller
  - 0020h: PIC 1
  - 0030h: PIC 2
  - 0040h: System timer
  - 0060h: Keyboard
  - 0070h: CMOS clock
  - 00C0h: DMA controller
  - 00F0h: Math co-processor
  - 0170h: Secondary IDE hard disk controller
  - 01F0h: Primary IDE hard disk controller
  - 0200h: Joystick
  - 0278h: LPT2
  - 02E8h: COM4
  - 02F8h: COM2
  - 0378h: LPT1
  - 03E8h: COM3
  - 03F0h: Floppy disk drive controller
  - 03F8h: COM1

lshw

The lshw (list hardware) command may be used to display detailed hardware configuration information. lshw is a replacement for the deprecated hwinfo command and should be executed by a user with root privileges.

The syntax for lshw is **lshw -<format> <options>**.

The output of the command lshw is a detailed description of system hardware, starting at the top of the device tree.

In Figure 12-22, we have used the short format option (**lshw -short**). This option displays the hardware path (bus address), device name, class of device, and storage path.

```
#lshw -short
H/W path                  Device      Class        Description
/0/100/10                 scsi0       storage      53c1030 PCI-X Fusion-MPT Dual Ultra320 SCSI
/0/100/10/0.0.0           /dev/sda    disk         21GB VMware Virtual S
/0/100/10/0.0.0/1         /dev/sda1   volume       500MiB EXT4 volume
/0/100/10/0.0.0/2         /dev/sda2   volume       8196MiB Linux LVM Physical Volume partition
/0/100/10/0.0.0/3         /dev/sda3   volume       3076MiB Linux LVM Physical Volume partition
/0/100/10/0.0.0/4         /dev/sda4   volume       8707MiB Extended partition
/0/100/10/0.0.0/4/5                   volume       1GiB Linux filesystem partition
/0/100/10/0.0.0/4/6       /dev/sda6   volume       500MiB EXT4 volume
/0/100/10/0.0.0/4/7       /dev/sda7   volume       500MiB EXT4 volume
/0/100/10/0.0.0/4/8       /dev/sda8   volume       1GiB Linux swap volume
/0/100/10/0.0.0/4/9       /dev/sda9   volume       500MiB Linux filesystem partition
/0/100/11                             bridge       PCI bridge
/0/100/11/0                           bus          USB1.1 UHCI Controller
/0/100/11/0/1             usb2        bus          UHCI Host Controller
/0/100/11/0/1/1                       input        VMware Virtual USB Mouse
/0/100/11/0/1/2                       bus          VMware Virtual USB Hub
/0/100/11/1               ens33       network      82545EM Gigabit Ethernet Controller (Copper)
/0/100/11/2                           multimedia   ES1371/ES1373 / Creative Labs CT2518
/0/100/11/3                           bus          USB2 EHCI Controller
/0/100/11/3/1             usb1        bus          EHCI Host Controller
```

Figure 12-22 Command lshw using -short output format (edited for brevity)

NOTE The command lshw requires the format option -businfo to display the bus address.

Additional format options are -html and -xml. When these format options are used, the output must be redirected to a file.

We can focus our output on a specific class or multiple classes of devices by adding the option **-class <class_name>**. Here are the available classes:

address	generic	printer
bridge	input	processor
bus	memory	storage
communication	multimedia	system
disk	network	tape
display	power	volume

The command **lshw -short -class storage -class disk -class volume** (shown in Figure 12-23) displays hardware information on devices of class storage, disk, and volume.

The command **lshw -html -short -class volume > lshw_html_out** will produce a file in HTML format. In Figure 12-24, we have used Firefox to display the output.

NOTE The command dmidecode is used to display information from the DMI (Desktop Management Interface) table. This table contains system hardware and software information. Although this command is not part of the exam, you will find it an excellent way for gathering system information.

```
 #lshw -short -class storage
H/W path               Device      Class          Description
==========================================================
/0/100/7.1             scsi2       storage        82371AB/EB/MB PIIX4 IDE
/0/100/10              scsi0       storage        53c1030 PCI-X Fusion-MPT Dual Ultra320 SCSI
 #

 #lshw -short -class disk
H/W path               Device      Class          Description
==========================================================
/0/100/7.1/0.0.0       /dev/cdrom  disk           VMware IDE CDR10
/0/100/7.1/0.0.0/0     /dev/cdrom  disk
/0/100/10/0.0.0        /dev/sda    disk           21GB VMware Virtual S
 #


 #lshw -short -class volume
H/W path               Device      Class          Description
==========================================================
/0/100/7.1/0.0.0/2                 volume         15EiB Windows FAT volume
/0/100/10/0.0.0/1      /dev/sda1   volume         500MiB EXT4 volume
/0/100/10/0.0.0/2      /dev/sda2   volume         8196MiB Linux LVM Physical Volume partition
/0/100/10/0.0.0/3      /dev/sda3   volume         3076MiB Linux LVM Physical Volume partition
/0/100/10/0.0.0/4      /dev/sda4   volume         8707MiB Extended partition
/0/100/10/0.0.0/4/5                volume         1GiB Linux filesystem partition
/0/100/10/0.0.0/4/6    /dev/sda6   volume         500MiB EXT4 volume
/0/100/10/0.0.0/4/7    /dev/sda7   volume         500MiB EXT4 volume
/0/100/10/0.0.0/4/8    /dev/sda8   volume         1GiB Linux swap volume
/0/100/10/0.0.0/4/9    /dev/sda9   volume         500MiB Linux filesystem partition
```

Figure 12-23 lshw -short -class storage -class disk -class volume

```
/root/lshw_html_out
file:///root/lshw_html_out

H/W path               Device      Class          Description
==========================================================
/0/100/7.1/0.0.0/2                 volume         15EiB Windows FAT volume
/0/100/10/0.0.0/1      /dev/sda1   volume         500MiB EXT4 volume
/0/100/10/0.0.0/2      /dev/sda2   volume         8196MiB Linux LVM Physical Volume partition
/0/100/10/0.0.0/3      /dev/sda3   volume         3076MiB Linux LVM Physical Volume partition
/0/100/10/0.0.0/4      /dev/sda4   volume         8707MiB Extended partition
/0/100/10/0.0.0/4/5                volume         1GiB Linux filesystem partition
/0/100/10/0.0.0/4/6    /dev/sda6   volume         500MiB EXT4 volume
/0/100/10/0.0.0/4/7    /dev/sda7   volume         500MiB EXT4 volume
/0/100/10/0.0.0/4/8    /dev/sda8   volume         1GiB Linux swap volume
/0/100/10/0.0.0/4/9    /dev/sda9   volume         500MiB Linux filesystem partition
```

Figure 12-24 lshw formatted as html output

Exercise 12-1: Discovering Devices

This exercise reviews some of the tools you have learned to view block devices.

VIDEO Please watch the Exercise 12-1 video for a demonstration on how to perform this task.

1. View the block devices on your system by executing the **lsblk** command.
2. Now view the block device entries in */sys* by executing the **ls -l /sys/block** command.
3. You can also view system block device using the **systool -c block** command.
4. You know that a bus is a device. View SCSI bus devices by executing the **ls /sys/bus/scsi/devices** or **systool -b scsi** command.

5. The command **lspci -t | more** will display the PCI bus hierarchy. Adding the -v option (**lspci -tv | more**) will add information about devices.
6. Prior to creating a udev rule, you'll want to view the properties of the device. To display the properties of the device */dev/sda*, you could execute this command: **udevadm info -q property -n /dev/sda**
7. Display active DMA channels by executing the **cat /proc/dma** command.
8. To see interrupt request statistics, view the file */proc/interrupts*.
9. The command **/proc/ioports** will display the memory address ranges used to communicate with hardware devices.
10. The lshw command will list hardware devices. To display types of storage devices execute the **lshw -class storage** command.
11. The lsblk command will display block storage devices by devices and partitions. The command **lshw -class volume** will display more detailed partition information.

Configuring Bluetooth

Bluetooth is a device interconnect designed to replace RS232 with wireless communication operating between 2.4 GHz and 2.485 GHz.

A Bluetooth master (transmitter) can connect up to seven devices (receivers) via a piconet. Piconets may also be called personal area networks (PANs). Although the technology is not currently refined, multiple piconets may be connected. Multiple networked piconets are called a scatternet.

Classes

Bluetooth classes determine the transmission range of the Bluetooth device. Table 12-10 details the Bluetooth classes and their transmission ranges.

Bluetooth Commands

Bluetooth commands are provided by the bluez package. The package must be installed (**yum -y install bluez**) and the service must be started (**systemctl start bluetooth**). To see if Bluetooth is active, execute the command **systemctl status bluetooth**.

Table 12-10 Bluetooth Class Transmission Ranges

Class	Maximum Distance
1	300 feet
2	30 feet
3	3 feet
4	1.5 feet
5	500 feet

Argument	Description
Controller Arguments	
agent on	Turns on Bluetooth support. If the controller is a USB adapter, it will remain on as long as it is plugged in.
discoverable on	Makes the controller visible to other Bluetooth devices.
discoverable off	Hides the controller from other Bluetooth devices
pairable on	Makes the controller ready for pairing
Device Arguments	
info <device_MAC_address>	Display device information
connect <device_MAC_address>	Makes the device ready for pairing
pair <device_MAC_address>	Pairs the device with the controller

Table 12-11 bluetoothctl options

The command **bluetoothctl list** displays a list of available Bluetooth controllers. The command **bluetoothctl show** displays a list of controllers and their status.

The command **bluetoothctl scan on** will display a list of available controllers that have not been paired.

To configure a Bluetooth device, you need to know the device's MAC address. The command **hcitool scan** will provide a controller's MAC address and name.

Once you know the controller's address, execute the command **bluetoothctl select <controller_MAC_address>**. This will apply any bluetoothctl commands issued in the next three minutes to that controller.

Some additional bluetoothctl options may be found in Table 12-11. Notice that some commands are applicable to the controller whereas others are applicable to the device. All arguments that end in <device_MAC_address> are associated with a device.

Configuring Wi-Fi

Wi-Fi is a generic name for a wireless technology that uses radio waves to access a network via wireless access points. You can determine if a Wi-Fi network device is installed by using the tools discussed next.

Scanning for Network Devices

The following commands may be used to scan for network interfaces:

- ip link show
- ifconfig -a
- ncmli connection show
- ncmli device status
- netstat -i

Table 12-12 Network Interface Names

Interface Name	Description
lo	Loopback
eth or ens	Ethernet interface
wlan	Wireless network interface. Most wireless interface names begin with the letter w.

Table 12-12 contains a partial list of interface names.

Configuring a Wi-Fi Network

Next we will explore configuring a Wi-Fi connection using the command iwconfig.

EXAM TIP Although the iwconfig command is on the exam, you should know it has been deprecated and replaced by the iw command.

We have installed the software package wireless-tools (which contains the commands iwconfig, iwlist, and iwspy) on your system. This is how we did it.

1. Installed the repo file for the EPEL repository (**yum -y install epel-release**).
2. Installed wireless-tools (**yum -y wireless-tools**).

Be sure you understand the following Wi-Fi terms:

- **Frequency** A frequency is the pipe that carries a signal. Most Wi-Fi adapters will provide a frequency of 2.4Ghz, or both 2.4 and 5Ghz frequencies. The frequencies may be modulated using direct sequence spread (DSS) or orthogonal frequency division (OFDM). Frequencies may be divided into channels.
- **Channel** A channel is like a pipe set inside a frequency as a path for data. Each channel has an upper and lower frequency and is separated from other channels by 5MHz. Overlapping channels share bandwidth. If you look at Channel 1 on 2.4Ghz, you'll notice it has a lower frequency of 2401MHz and an upper frequency of 2423MHz (20MHz bandwidth). Channel 2 has a lower frequency of 2406MHz and an upper frequency of 2428.
- **ESSID** Extended Service Set Identification (ESSID) is the identifier (name) used by a wireless device to connect to a router or access point.
- **Router** A router is a device that routes data between two or more networks.
- **Access point** An access point is a device that connects wireless devices to a network. Most access points have routers built in.

iwconfig

The iwconfig command is used to setup a wireless interface. Executed without any options or arguments, **iwconfig** will list all available wireless interfaces. To view the status of a specific interface, execute the command **iwconfig <interface_name>**.

Most wireless interfaces begin with the letter *w*, for example, wlan0. To view the status of interface wlan0, execute the command **iwconfig wlan0**.

You may need to know what access points can be seen by a wireless interface. The command **iwlist <interface_name> scan** will search for available access points.

The command **iwconfig <interface_name> essid <essid_name>** will connect you to a wireless access point. Assuming an essid name of network_one, the following command will connect wlan0 to network_one: **iwconfig wlan0 essid network_one**.

You can use a specific channel by adding the channel option: **iwconfig wlan0 channel 11**.

Once the changes are made, execute the command **iwconfig wlan0 commit**. This will ensure all changes are applied to the interface.

Configuring Storage Devices

In this section, we introduce the various types of storage devices and commands associated with them.

IDE

Integrated Drive Electronics (IDE) refers to a technology in which the disk controller is integrated into the drive. The controller on one drive can control two devices (master and slave). IDE I/O cards or motherboards that support IDE contain two IDE channels (primary and secondary).

A single motherboard can support four devices:

- Primary master
- Primary slave
- Secondary master
- Secondary Slave

If a system contains multiple IDE drives, the primary master drive is the default boot drive. Newer versions of IDE drives (ATA-4 forward) support Ultra DMA. ATA-6, which is also called Parallel ATA (PATA), can reach data transfer speeds of 133 Mbps.

SCSI

Small Computer System Interface (SCSI) is a parallel interface used to connect peripheral devices. SCSI devices are connected in a chain through an internal ribbon or external cable. It is important that the last SCSI device has a terminator installed.

Table 12-13 SCSI Device Types

Device	Description
Narrow SCSI	Supports eight devices (0–7) Data transfer: 8 bits Speed: 10 MBps
Wide SCSI	Supports 16 devices (0–15) Data transfer: 16 bits Speed: 20 MBps
Ultra SCSI	Data transfer: 8 bits Speed: 20 MBps
Ultra2 SCSI	Data transfer: 16 bits Speed: 40 MBps
Wide Ultra2SCSI	Data transfer: 16 bits Speed: 80 MBps
Ultra3 SCSI	Data transfer: 16 bits Speed: 160 MBps

SCSI devices are defined by the number of bits they transfer at a time and speed per second. Some SCSI device types are listed in Table 12-13.

SCSI Device ID and Priorities

Each SCSI device is assigned an ID. The device ID may be set using a thumb wheel, jumper, or firmware. The device ID determines the priority of the device. Here are some points to keep in mind:

- The host bus adapter (HBA) is always assigned the highest priority (7).
- Narrow SCSI device priority order is 7, 6, 5, 4, 3, 2, 1, 0.
- Wide SCSI device priority order is 7, 6, 5, 4, 3, 2, 1, 0, 15, 14, 13, 12, 11, 10, 9, 8.

SATA

A Serial AT Attachment (SATA) drive communicates bit by bit (serial communications) to a dedicated hard disk channel via a high-speed serial cable.

The cable contains seven pins (two data pair and three ground wires). One pair of wires is used to receive data, and the other pair is used to transmit acknowledgements. This wiring scheme is much simpler than the 40-pin or 80-pin ribbon connector required by IDE and removes many of the electrical limitations imposed by the IDE cable.

SATA data transfer rates range from 150 MBps to 600 MBps.

eSATA

An eSATA port is used to connect external SATA devices to a system. Power for the device is supplied by an external power supply.

eSATAp

An eSATAp (powered eSATA) port is capable of supplying power to the external SATA device. An eSATAp port can also support USB.

Optical Drives

Optical drives have the ability to store large amounts of data. Data is written on a photoconductive surface using a high-intensity laser. Data is represented by pits and lands. Pits represent a binary 0, and lands represent a binary 1. A lower intensity laser is used to read the data. There are three major types of optical media:

- CD
- DVD
- Blue-ray

Solid State Drives

Solid state drives (SSDs) use flash memory circuitry to store data. Information stored in flash memory is retained when system power is removed. Data is stored as if the device was an actual hard drive (cylinder/head/sector, or CHS). In most cases, SSD drives use the same interface as SATA, but they can implement other interfaces.

Since data is accessed electronically rather than mechanically, SSD data is accessed faster than on a traditional hard drive. However, an SSD's performance may degrade over time.

USB

USB is a high-speed Plug and Play interface that allows multiple devices to connect via a single bus. A USB bus can support 127 devices in a star topology. The speed of the bus is limited to the speed of the slowest device on the bus. Standard bus speeds are as follows:

- USB 1.0: 12 Mbps
- USB 2.0: 480 Mbps
- USB 3.0: 800 Mbps

NOTE USB 3.0 is capable of 800 Mbps, but multiple USB devices may be connected to the USB interface via a USB hub, which could slow down the connection.

Make sure you are familiar with the following terms for our discussion of USB devices:

- **USB** Refers to a bus type used for data transfer
- **Port** A physical connection to a bus
- **Thumb drive** Refers to the physical size of a drive
- **Flash drive** A storage device that contains a USB interface and flash memory

USB devices may draw power from the USB connection or require an external power supply.

NOTE For the following examples, we have attached a Kingston 4G DataTraveler flash drive to a virtual machine.

Connecting a USB Device

When a flash drive is connected, the kernel creates a uevent, udev configures the device, and dbus informs user applications the device is available. We can view some of this activity using the dmesg command.

dmesg dmesg is a command used to read and control the kernel ring buffer. The ring buffer is a cyclical storage space of specific size used to contain kernel log messages. Once a ring buffer's space has been used, data will be overwritten (starting from the beginning of the buffer). In many cases, log information found in the ring buffer will be handled by the syslog facility kernel.

Figure 12-25 illustrates kernel log entries during the discovery process of the USB flash drive.

The dmesg command displays the contents of the ring buffer. The ring buffer contains kernel messages. Table 12-14 displays two dmesg command options.

Line 1 of Figure 12-26 illustrates how you may search for specific objects by adding the grep command (**dmesg | grep usb**).

```
[  315.048403] usb 1-1: new high-speed USB device number 2 using ehci-pci
[  315.283444] usb 1-1: New USB device found, idVendor=0930, idProduct=6545
[  315.283451] usb 1-1: New USB device strings: Mfr=1, Product=2, SerialNumber=3
[  315.283479] usb 1-1: Product: DataTraveler 2.0
[  315.283484] usb 1-1: Manufacturer: Kingston
[  315.283489] usb 1-1: SerialNumber: C860008862E4ED606A1C00A0
[  315.473822] usb-storage 1-1:1.0: USB Mass Storage device detected
[  315.476678] scsi host3: usb-storage 1-1:1.0
[  315.476751] usbcore: registered new interface driver usb-storage
[  315.479338] usbcore: registered new interface driver uas
[  316.564135] scsi 3:0:0:0: Direct-Access     Kingston DataTraveler 2.0 PMAP PQ: 0 ANSI: 4
[  316.565705] sd 3:0:0:0: Attached scsi generic sg2 type 0
[  317.997706] sd 3:0:0:0: [sdb] 15240576 512-byte logical blocks: (7.80 GB/7.26 GiB)
```

Figure 12-25 dmesg Kernel Events

Table 12-14 Options Used with the dmesg Command

Option	Description
-L	Add color to the output
-T	Display timestamp

```
[ 5790.274589] usb 1-1: Manufacturer: Kingston
[ 5790.274591] usb 1-1: SerialNumber: C860008862E4ED606A1C00A0
[ 5790.442630] usb-storage 1-1:1.0: USB Mass Storage device detected
[ 5790.458073] scsi host3: usb-storage 1-1:1.0
[ 5790.458407] usbcore: registered new interface driver usb-storage
[ 5790.461915] usbcore: registered new interface driver uas
```

Figure 12-26 Using dmesg to look for USB events

lsusb -t

The command lsusb -t produces a hierarchical view of USB hubs and devices attached to the hubs. Lines 1 and 5 of Figure 12-27 display the USB hub, driver, and transfer speed. 12M indicates 12 megabits per second (USB 1.0) and 480 indicates 480 megabits per second (USB 2.0). Lines 3, 4, and 6 shows the devices that are attached.

lsusb

Figure 12-28 displays a list of USB devices. Looking at line 3, you can see information concerning the flash storage device. Notice this device is connected to Bus 001. Device 002 indicates this is the second device on the bus.

Root Hub Line 4 in Figure 12-28 refers to the first device as a root hub. The root hub is responsible for communicating with devices attached to hub ports and the hub controller. The hub controller performs the following tasks:

- It monitors devices being placed on or removed from the hub.
- It manages power for devices on the host's ports.
- It manages communications on the controller's bus.

```
1 # lsusb -t
2 /:  Bus 02.Port 1: Dev 1, Class=root_hub, Driver=uhci_hcd/2p, 12M
3     |__ Port 1: Dev 2, If 0, Class=Human Interface Device, Driver=usbhid, 12M
4     |__ Port 2: Dev 3, If 0, Class=Hub, Driver=hub/7p, 12M
5 /:  Bus 01.Port 1: Dev 1, Class=root_hub, Driver=ehci-pci/6p, 480M
6     |__ Port 1: Dev 2, If 0, Class=Mass Storage, Driver=usb-storage, 480M
```

Figure 12-27 Displaying a USB device tree

```
1 #lsusb
2
3 Bus 001 Device 002: ID 0930:6545 Toshiba Corp. Kingston DataTraveler 102/2.0 / HEMA Flash Drive 2 GB / PNY Attache 4GB Stick
4 Bus 001 Device 001: ID 1d6b:0002 Linux Foundation 2.0 root hub
5 Bus 002 Device 003: ID 0e0f:0002 VMware, Inc. Virtual USB Hub
6 Bus 002 Device 002: ID 0e0f:0003 VMware, Inc. Virtual Mouse
7 Bus 002 Device 001: ID 1d6b:0001 Linux Foundation 1.1 root hub
```

Figure 12-28 List of USB devices

Figure 12-29 Sample of USB device IDs

```
092f  Northern Embedded Science/CAVNEX
        0004  JTAG-4
        0005  JTAG-5
0930  Toshiba Corp.
        653c  Kingston DataTraveler 2.0 Stick (512M)
        653d  Kingston DataTraveler 2.0 Stick (1GB)
        653e  Flash Memory
        6540  TransMemory Flash Memory
        6544  TransMemory-Mini / Kingston DataTraveler 2.0 Stick
        6545  Kingston DataTraveler 102/2.0 / HEMA Flash Drive 2 GB / PNY Attache 4GB Stick
```

The ID numbers in the lsusb output are contained in two fields: **<manufacturer>:<device_id>**. If you look at the table found at www.linux-usb.org/usb-ids (shown in Figure 12-29), you will see 930 is the manufacturer ID for Toshiba and the device ID 6545 is a Kingston DataTraveler flash drive.

You can find out additional information by executing the command **lsusb -D /dev/bus/usb/<bus_number><device_number>**. The output of the command **lsusb -D /dev/bus/usb/001/002** displays additional information concerning the flash drive (see Figure 12-30).

sginfo

sginfo is a deprecated utility package used to query SCSI and IDE drive parameters. This command is not installed by default. Executing the command **yum -y install sg3_utils** will install a set of generic utilities used to query disk parameters. Table 12-15 shows options for the sginfo command.

```
#lsusb -D /dev/bus/usb/001/002
Device: ID 0930:6545 Toshiba Corp. Kingston DataTraveler 102/2.0 / HEMA Flash Drive 2 GB / PNY Attache 4GB Stick
Device Descriptor:
  bLength                18
  bDescriptorType         1
  bcdUSB               2.00
  bDeviceClass            0 (Defined at Interface level)
  bDeviceSubClass         0
  bDeviceProtocol         0
  bMaxPacketSize0        64
  idVendor           0x0930 Toshiba Corp.
  idProduct          0x6545 Kingston DataTraveler 102/2.0 / HEMA Flash Drive 2 GB / PNY Attache 4GB Stick
  bcdDevice            1.00
  iManufacturer           1 Kingston
  iProduct                2 DataTraveler 2.0
  iSerial                 3 C860008862E4ED606A1C00A0
```

Figure 12-30 lsusb -D (edited for brevity)

Table 12-15 sginfo Options

Option	Description
-i <device>	Display device information
-d <device>	Display defect list

Table 12-16
hdparm Options

Option	Description
-v <device>	Disk Settings
-I <device>	Detailed Disk Statistics

hdparm

hdparm is another utility used to query hard disk statistics and can change drive operating parameters. Use extreme caution when changing drive parameters. Table 12-16 shows options for the hdparm command.

lsscsi

The lsscsi command is used to get SCSI device and host information. To install the utility, execute the command **yum -y install lsscsi**. The lsscsi command will display a list of SCSI devices and hosts (as shown in Figure 12-31). The output on the left indicates scsi [host: channel: target_number and lun]. Here's a breakdown of the output:

- The host number indicates the number assigned to the adapter card.
- The channel indicates the bus number.
- The target number is the device number.
- The LUN is the logical unit number.

In larger systems, there may be an additional number at the beginning: [domain:host: channel: target_number and lun]

Table 12-17 shows options for the lsscsi command.

Figure 12-31
lsscsi

```
# lsscsi
[1:0:0:0]    cd/dvd  NECVMWar VMware IDE CDR10 1.00  /dev/sr0
[2:0:0:0]    disk    VMware,  VMware Virtual S 1.0   /dev/sda
```

Table 12-17
lsscsi Command Options

Option	Description
<no option>	List SCSI devices
-H --hosts	List SCSI host adapters
-l --long	List SCSI device information
-d	Display major and minor numbers

Understanding Printing

We created file-based printers to demonstrate the commands in this section. To do this, we removed the comment symbol (#) before the directive FileDevice in the file */etc/cups/cup-files.conf* and changed the value to Yes (that is, FileDevice Yes).

To specify a printer device name, use the syntax **file:///dev/tty[2-5]**. A printer named tty2printer has been configured as a raw printer on */dev/tty2* (file:///dev/tty2).

To view printer output on these terminals from the GUI environment, use the key sequence CTRL-ALT-F[2-4] (F2 would be function key 2). To move between the text terminals, use the key sequence ALT-F[2-5]. To return to the GUI, use the key sequence ALT-F1.

The Common UNIX Printing System provides tools that manage printing. The directory that contains CUPS configuration files is */etc/cups*.

The CUPS daemon executes in the background, waiting for print requests. The CUPS daemon may be configured in the file */etc/cups/cupsd.conf*.

Adding Printers

Printers may be added via the command line, GUI, or web access.

lpadmin

The lpadmin command is used to add and configure printers and printer classes. Printer configuration information is stored in */etc/printers.conf*. Printer class information is stored in */etc/cups/classes.conf*.

A printer class is a group of printers associated with a single print queue. As print jobs are submitted to the queue, they are sent to the next available printer on the queue.

Prior to creating a printer, we will execute **lpinfo -v** (shown in Figure 12-32) to determine available devices.

We also want to use the **lpinfo -m** command to determine what drivers are available. The command **lpinfo -m | grep -i Epson** will list all the driver files. Find the appropriate model and write down the PPD filename.

Table 12-18 displays some lpadmin options.

NOTE We have not created tty3printer on your image. You will do this as part of the printer lab (step 14).

Figure 12-32
lpinfo -v

```
#lpinfo -v
network ipp
network ipps
network http
network https
network socket
network lpd
serial serial:/dev/ttyS0?baud=115200
network beh
direct parallel:/dev/lp0
network smb
```

<table>
<tr><th>Option</th><th>Definition</th></tr>
<tr><td>-E</td><td>Enables (starts) a printer and allows the print queue to accept print jobs.</td></tr>
<tr><td>-p</td><td>Printer name used when adding a printer or changing printer attributes.</td></tr>
<tr><td>-v</td><td>Device name (local).</td></tr>
<tr><td>-s</td><td>Server name.</td></tr>
<tr><td>-m</td><td>Printer driver.</td></tr>
<tr><td>-d</td><td>Make the printer the default printer.</td></tr>
<tr><td>-c <class_name></td><td>Add a printer to a class. If the class does not exist, create it.</td></tr>
<tr><td>-r <class_name></td><td>Remove a printer from a class.</td></tr>
<tr><td>-x <class|printer_name></td><td>Remove a printer or class.</td></tr>
<tr><td>-u allow:<user></td><td>Comma-delimited list of users allowed to use the printer.
@<group_name> specifies a group.</td></tr>
<tr><td>-u deny:<user></td><td>Comma-delimited list of users not allowed to use the printer.
@<group_name> specifies a group.</td></tr>
</table>

Table 12-18 lpadmin Options

The command **lpadmin -p tty3printer -v file:///dev/tty3 -m raw** creates printer tty3printer on */dev/tty3* using raw printing. Raw printing bypasses a printer driver and sends characters directly to the printer. The command **lpstat -p tty3printer** (line 2 in Figure 12-33) shows the printer is disabled. We need to start the printer and allow the printer's print queue to accept print jobs by issuing the command **lpadmin -p tty3printer -E**. Viewing Figure 12-33, notice the printer is enabled (line 8). You could execute the command **lpadmin -p tty3printer -v file:///dev/tty3 -m raw -E** to create and enable the printer. The command **lpadmin -d** sets the default system printer.

A printer class groups two or more printers. Instead of printing to a specific printer, you may print to the printer class. If one printer in the class is busy, the print job will be serviced by another printer in the class. The command **lpadmin -p tty3printer -c testclass** will add printer tty3printer to the printer class testclass. If the class does not exist, it will be created.

```
1 #lpstat -p tty3printer
2 printer tty3printer disabled since Tue 04 Jun 2019 10:45:12 AM EDT -
3         reason unknown
4
5  #lpadmin -p tty3printer -E
6
7  #lpstat -p tty3printer
8 printer tty3printer is idle.  enabled since Tue 04 Jun 2019 11:03:29 AM EDT
```

Figure 12-33 Determining the status of tty3printer

Figure 12-34 Using lpstat -c to view printer classes

```
1  #lpstat -c
2 members of class testclass:
3         tty3printer
4
5  #lpstat -c testclass
6 members of class testclass:
7         tty3printer
8
9  #lpadmin -p tty2printer -c testclass
10
11  #lpadmin -p tty2printer -c testclass2
12  #
13  #lpstat -c
14 members of class testclass:
15         tty3printer
16         tty2printer
17 members of class testclass2:
18         tty2printer
```

NOTE You cannot assign a printer as a default printer or assign a printer to a class until it has been created.

To remove a printer from a class, use the command **lpadmin -p <printer_name> -r <class_name>**. If you are removing the last printer in the class, the class will be deleted.

The command **lpstat -c** will display a list of all printer classes and printers that are members of that class (see line 1 of Figure 12-34). To view members of a specific printer class, use the command **lpstat -c <printer_class>** (see line 5). On lines 9 and 11, we added tty2printer to the classes testclass and testclass2.

To remove a printer from a class, execute the command **lpadmin -p <printer_name> -r <printer_class_name>**.

Web Interface

You can administer a printer via a web browser. Open a browser and enter **localhost:631** (see Figure 12-35). This is the port for the CUPS web interface. From this interface, you can manage all printer functions.

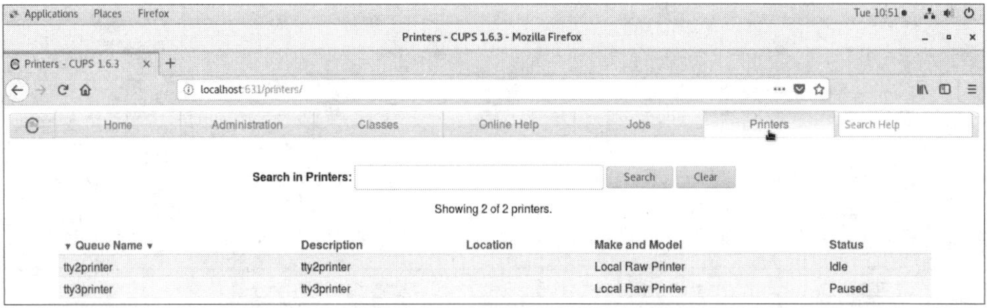

Figure 12-35 The CUPS web interface

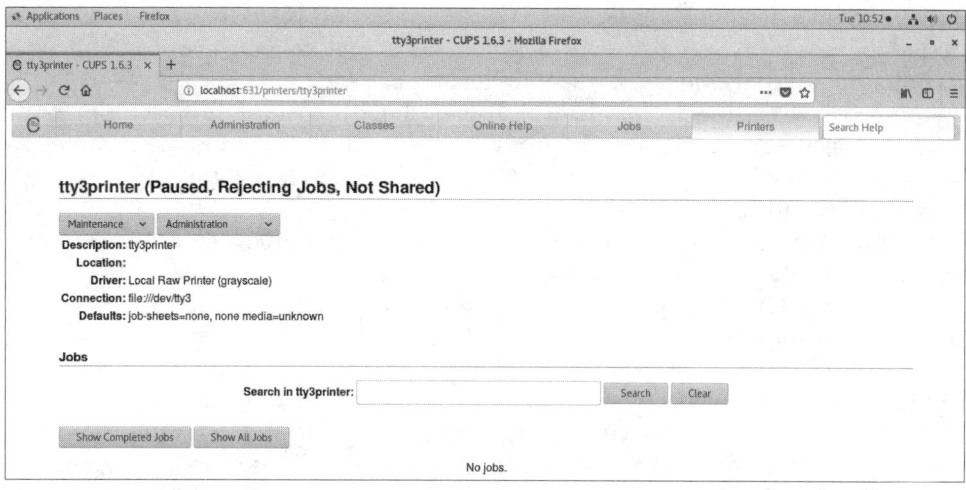

Figure 12-36 Web interface for managing a printer

Selecting the Printers tab will display the available printers. Selecting a printer opens a management window for that printer (see Figure 12-36).

Printing to a Printer

The commands lpr, lpd, and lp may be used to print to a printer. If no printer is specified, the default printer will be used. To determine the default printer, execute the command **lpstat -d**.

The command **lp -d tty2printer /etc/hosts** will print the file */etc/hosts* to tty2printer.

When the job is submitted, a job ID will be displayed. The job ID consists of <printer_queue name>-<job_id> (see Figure 12-37).

To print to a printer class, use the command **lp -d <printer_class_name> <filename>**.

Managing Printers and Print Queues

A printer queue is created each time a printer or printer class is added. The queue name is the same as the printer or printer class added.

accept, reject, cupsenable, cupsdisable

A print queue can accept print jobs or reject print jobs. When it's accepting print jobs, print requests may be entered into the queue and passed to the printer. When it's rejecting print jobs, a submitted print job receives an error message. A reason for rejecting print jobs may be a broken printer.

Figure 12-37 Output of the print job

```
#lp -d tty2printer /etc/hosts
request id is tty2printer-5 (1 file(s))
```

To reject jobs for a print queue, execute the command **reject <queue_name>**. To accept jobs for a print queue, execute the command **accept <queue_name>**. Once a job has been spooled to the queue, it is sent to the printer.

A printer is either enabled or disabled. If the printer is enabled, it is accepting print jobs from the print queue. A disabled printer is not accepting jobs from the print queue. In this case, print jobs are stored in the queue until the printer is enabled or the print jobs are moved to another queue.

To disable a printer, execute the command **cupsdisable <printer_name>**. To enable a printer, execute the command **cupsenable <printer_name>**.

The command **lpstat -p <printer_name>** will print the printer status. The command **lpq -P <queue_name >** will print the status of a print queue. The status will include any print jobs held in the queue. The command **lpstat -o** will display all print jobs, and the command **lpstat -o <queue_name>** will display print jobs for a specific queue.

The following conditions were applied prior to executing the commands shown in Figure 12-38. The commands **cupsdisable tty2printer** and **cupsdisable tty3printer** were executed to disable printers tty2printer and tty3printer, and the commands **lp -d tty2printer /etc/hosts** and **lp -d tty3printer /etc/hosts** was executed.

The **lpstat -o** command on line 1 of Figure 12-38 will display all print jobs in all queues. You can look at jobs on specific queues by executing the command **lpstat -o <queue_name>** (lines 5–9). The lpq command (**lpq -P <queue_name**>) on lines 11 and 16 displays the status and jobs queued for the respective queue names.

Cancelling Print Jobs

The cancel command is used to cancel print jobs. The command **cancel <job_id>** (Figure 12-39, line 5) will cancel a specific print job.

The command **cancel <queue_name>** (line 10) will cancel all jobs in the queue. The command **cancel -a** will remove all jobs from all queues.

```
1  #lpstat -o
2 tty3printer-6           root              1024   Tue 04 Jun 2019 12:37:42 PM EDT
3 tty2printer-7           root              1024   Tue 04 Jun 2019 12:54:01 PM EDT
4
5  #lpstat -o tty3printer
6 tty3printer-6           root              1024   Tue 04 Jun 2019 12:37:42 PM EDT
7
8  #lpstat -o tty2printer
9 tty2printer-7           root              1024   Tue 04 Jun 2019 12:54:01 PM EDT
10
11  #lpq -P tty2printer
12 tty2printer is not ready
13 Rank    Owner   Job     File(s)                        Total Size
14 1st     root    7       hosts                          1024 bytes
15
16  #lpq -P tty3printer
17 tty3printer is not ready
18 Rank    Owner   Job     File(s)                        Total Size
19 1st     root    6       hosts                          1024 bytes
```

Figure 12-38 Using lpstat and lpq to view print queues

```
 #lpstat -o
tty3printer-6           root            1024    Tue 04 Jun 2019 12:37:42 PM EDT
tty3printer-7           root            1024    Tue 04 Jun 2019 12:54:01 PM EDT

 #cancel 7

 #lpstat -o
tty3printer-6           root            1024    Tue 04 Jun 2019 12:37:42 PM EDT

 #cancel tty3printer

_#lpstat -o
```

Figure 12-39 Cancelling print jobs

lpmove

The lpmove command moves print jobs from one queue to another. In line 2 of Figure 12-40, you can see job 6 is in the print queue tty3printer. The command **lpmove <job_id> <printer_queue>** will move a print job from one queue to another.

The output of the lpstat command on lines 8 and 9 indicates both print jobs are in tty2printer's queue. The command **lpmove <old_print_queue> <new_print_queue>** will move all jobs from the old print queue to another. Executing the command **lpmove tty2printer tty3printer** will move all the print jobs in tty2printer to tty3printer (lines 13–15).

Removing a Printer or Printer Class

Prior to removing a printer, you need to disable the printer using the command **cupsdisable <printer_name>**. Then stop the queue from accepting any additional print jobs by executing the command **reject <queue_name>**. Next, use the cancel or lpmove command to remove all jobs from the current queue. Verify there are no jobs left in the queue (**lpstat -o <queue_name**. Delete the printer or class by executing the command **lpadmin -x <printer_name>|<class_name>**.

```
1   #lpstat -o
2  tty3printer-6           root            1024    Tue 04 Jun 2019 12:37:42 PM EDT
3  tty2printer-7           root            1024    Tue 04 Jun 2019 12:54:01 PM EDT
4
5   #lpmove 6 tty2printer
6
7   #lpstat -o
8  tty2printer-6           root            1024    Tue 04 Jun 2019 12:37:42 PM EDT
9  tty2printer-7           root            1024    Tue 04 Jun 2019 12:54:01 PM EDT
10
11  #lpmove tty2printer  tty3printer
12
13  #lpstat -o
14 tty3printer-6           root            1024    Tue 04 Jun 2019 12:37:42 PM EDT
15 tty3printer-7           root            1024    Tue 04 Jun 2019 12:54:01 PM EDT
```

Figure 12-40 Moving printer jobs

Exercise 12-2: Printing

For Exercise 12-2, you need to be user root (password root). Remove all printer classes and all printers except tty2printer.2print by following these steps:

VIDEO Please watch the Exercise 12-2 video for a demonstration on how to perform this task.

1. Determine what printers and print classes are currently on your system by executing the **lpstat -p** command. You should have the printer tty2printer.
2. Determine if there are any print jobs in the print queues by executing the command **lpstat -o** or **lpstat <queue_name>**.
3. Create the class labclass and add tty2printer to the class labclass by executing the **lpadmin -p tty2printer -c labclass** command.
4. Verify your command by executing the command **lpstat -c -p tty2printer**.
5. Create a raw printer (tty3printer) using device */dev/tty3*. The printer should be a member of the printer class labclass and be the default printer: **lpadmin -E -p tty3printer -v file:///dev/tty3 -m raw && lpadmin -p tty3printer -c labclass\ && lpadmin -d tty3printer**
6. Verify the printer was created correctly using the **lpstat -p**, **lpstat -c**, and **lpstat -d** commands.
7. Disable printers tty2printer and tty3printer using the **cupsdisable <printer_name>** command. Test your results using the **lpstat -p <printer_name>** command.
8. Be sure to do this lab question as written. Print the files */etc/hosts* and */etc/shells* to both printers tty2printer and tty3printer. You may use the commands **lp -d tty2printer /etc/hosts ; lp -d tty2printer /etc/shells** and **lp -d tty3printer /etc/hosts/; lp -d tty3printer etc/shells.**
9. Verify the jobs are in the queues using the **lpstat -o** command.
10. Print (lp) the file */etc/passwd* to the (-d) labclass queue and verify the job has been printed (lpstat -o).
11. Prevent queues tty2printer and tty3printer from accepting print jobs by executing the **reject tty2printer** and **reject tty3printer** commands. Verify the results by executing the **lpstat -p tty2printer** and **lpstat -ptty3printer** commands.
12. Print the file */etc/group* to printer tty2printer and class labclass. What happened? Why?
13. Move all the print jobs in class labclass and tty3printer to tty2printer. Remember that tty2printer's queue is not accepting jobs, so you must fix that first. Once you are finished, check all the print queues:
    a. Execute **accept tty2printer** so the queue will start accepting jobs and verify the queue is accepting jobs.
    b. Execute **lpmove labclass tty2printer** and **lpmove tty3printer tty2printer**.
    c. Check the results with the **lpstat -o <queue_name>** command.

14. Remove tty3printer from class labclass by executing the **lpadmin -p tty3printer -r labclass** command. Verify this by executing the **lpstat -c ttyprinter3** command.
15. Remove the printer tty3printer and class labclass:
    a. First, execute the **lpstat -a -c** command.
    b. Next, execute the **lpadmin -x tty3printer**; **lpadmin -x labclass** command.
    c. Verify by executing the **lpstat -a -c** command.

Using Facility Priority with dmesg

The dmesg command is used to display kernel ring buffer information. You may also search the dmesg ring buffer using syslog facility and priority names (see Table 12-19).

NOTE dmesg uses the term "level" to describe a syslog priority.

The command **dmesg -T -f kern -l notice | grep sdb** (shown in Figure 12-41) will display all messages in the ring buffer that have a kernel message (-f or --facility) of level notice (-l or --level) and contain the string sdb. The -T option will display the message timestamp.

Table 12-19 Syslog Facilities and Priorities

Syslog Facility	Syslog Priority
kern	Emerg
user	Alert
mail	Crit
daemon	Err
auth	Warn
syslog	Notice
lpr	Info
news	Debug

```
#dmesg -T -f kern -l notice | grep sdb
[Tue Jun  4 11:44:02 2019] sd 3:0:0:0: [sdb] 15240576 512-byte logical blocks: (7.80 GB/7.26 GiB)
[Tue Jun  4 11:44:02 2019] sd 3:0:0:0: [sdb] Write Protect is off
[Tue Jun  4 11:44:02 2019] sd 3:0:0:0: [sdb] Attached SCSI removable disk
```

Figure 12-41 Adding a timestamp to dmesg output

Using the abrt Command

abrt, the Automatic Bug Reporting Tool, is a utility that collects information concerning application and kernel crashes and stores the information in the base directory */var/spool/abrt*. The directory contains the following items:

- The absolute path to the executable.
- The rpm packages associated with the error.
- The number of times the problem has occurred (count).
- The timestamp of the error.
- The daemon notifies the program abrt-applet, which informs the user a bug report has been generated.
- The steps taken leading up to the error (backtrace).
- List of libraries loaded.
- */var/log/messages* entries associated with the error.

If the user is in a GUI environment, an icon will appear, as shown in Figure 12-42.

Selecting the icon will open the application gnome-abrt (see Figure 12-43). Selecting an entry on the left with a single left-click will display a general description of the error. Double-clicking the error will generate a report.

If you are using a text environment, you will see a message beginning with "abrt":

```
ABRT has detected 1 problem(s) For more info run:\
abrt-cli list --since 02054477227
```

To view the information associated with the notification, type **abrt-cli list**. This output will display the following information:

- The error ID
- The time at which the error occurred
- The command executed
- The associated rpm packages
- The user ID of the user executing the command
- The directory that contains the error information
- Where the error was reported

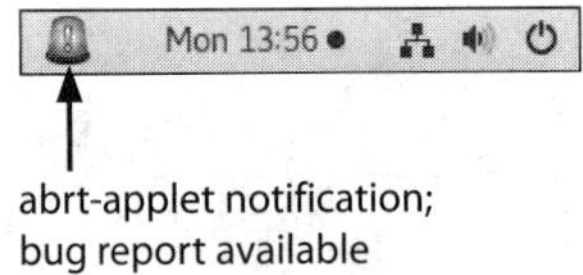

Figure 12-42 abrt Notification

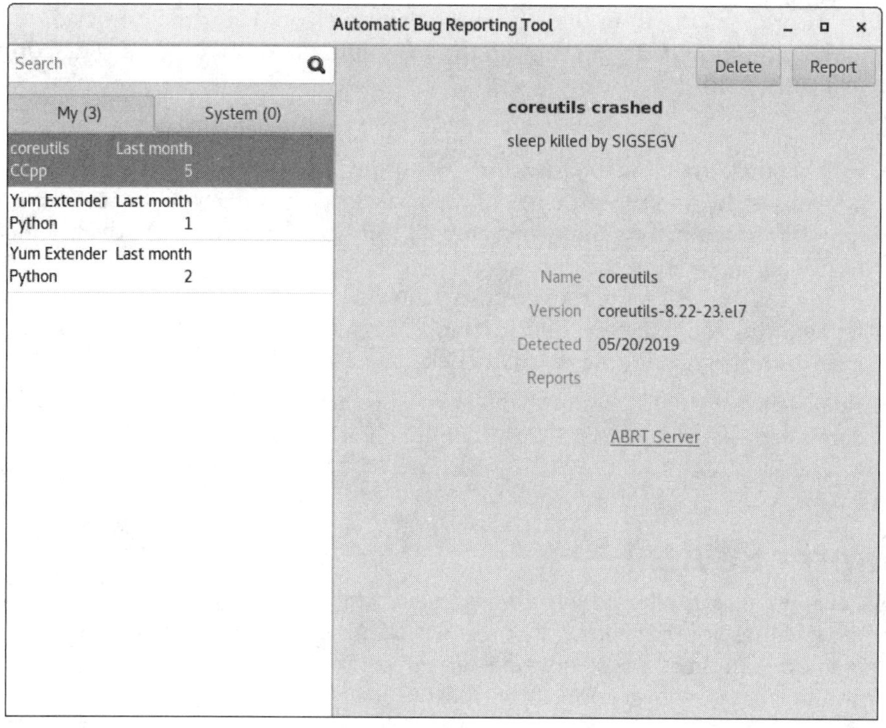

Figure 12-43 Generating an abrt report via the GUI

A more detailed output that contains the environment in which the command was executed and the steps taken to execute the command may be obtained by executing the command **abrt-cli info <directory of spool file>**.

To remove an entry from the list, execute the command **abrt-cli remove <directory of spool file>**. This will also remove the directory.

Exercise 12-3: abrt

This exercise will have you create a system fault and then view the fault using abrt.

VIDEO Please watch the Exercise 12-3 video for a demonstration on how to perform this task.

1. Create a background job that will run the sleep command for 100 seconds (**sleep 100 &**) and note the process ID number (second number). If you forget the process ID, you can execute the **jobs -l** command.
2. This step will force a segmentation fault that will be handled by abrtd. A segmentation fault is created when an application tries to access restricted memory. Execute the **kill -11 abrt-cli<pid_from_step_2>** command.

3. If you are working from the GUI, note the fault icon. Click the icon to display abrt fault notices. Click an entry in the left column to display a general description of a fault.
4. At the command line, execute the **abrt-cli list** to display faults command.
5. Execute the **abrt-cli info <directory_of_spool_file>** command. Each message contains an id, and the last entry of the message is the directory that contains the fault information. The command **abrt-cli info -d <directory>** will display the information stored in the directory.

   You can cut and paste the directory name into the abrt-cli info command by highlighting the directory, right-clicking, and selecting Copy. Place the cursor next to the space after the -d, right-click, and select Paste.
6. Remove the entry by executing the **abrt-cli remove <directory_of_spool_file>** command. Verify by executing the command **abrt-cli list**.

Chapter Review

In this chapter, you discovered how to search for, add, modify, or remove hardware. You began by learning how the kernel discovers devices and writes configuration and statistical data to */sys*. You then learned how the */dev* directory is built so users can access devices. During this process, you developed the skills to search for hardware information using the lsdev, lspci, lshw, systool, and udev commands.

You continued your discovery by learning about Bluetooth, Wi-Fi, and a variety of storage devices. You finished the chapter by learning how to add, modify, and delete printers and printer classes as well as how to use information from abrt to help troubleshoot your system. Here are some key points from this chapter:

- A device is a system component capable of receiving or providing data.
- A bus is a system device used to transfer data between devices.
- A port is a physical connection to a bus.
- A driver is a file or group of files used to control a hardware device.
- Kernel space is memory accessible to the kernel.
- User space is memory accessible to users and user applications.
- Kernel information is made available to users via */proc* and */sys*.
- The sysfs filesystem is a memory-based filesystem mounted on the directory */sys*. sysfs provides user space with the properties and dynamic operational statistics of system hardware and filesystems.
- Major numbers designate a device class.

- lsblk will print a list of block devices.
- systool -c block will display a list of block devices.
- systool -pb <bus> will display bus information, including the path to the bus.
- A device class contains devices that perform similar operations.
- Peripheral Component Interconnect (PCI) is a system specification that defines the implementation of the PCI bus.
- PCI bus is a hierarchical structure.
- The output of the lspci command is Domain:Bus:Device:Function Class Vendor Name.
- A host bus adapter is an expansion card used to connect multiple devices using a single controller to a computer system.
- **lspci -nn | grep -i hba** or **systool -c <adapter_class>** will display host adapters.
- udev, or userpsace /dev, is used to build */dev* from information found in */sys*.
- udev rules are located in */lib/udev/rules.d* (system default rules) and */etc/udev/rules.d* (custom rules).
- udev rules ensure a device's configuration is persistent across system reboots.
- The udev daemon searches for rules in dictionary order (numbers first) then short name.
- udevadm is a utility that controls the operation of udev and can manage and obtain information about system devices.
- udevadm info searches the udev database for device information.
- udevadm monitor listens for uevents and displays them on the console.
- udevadm control is used to control the systemd-udevd.
- The lsdev command displays information about installed hardware
- lsdev retrieves information from */proc/interrupts*, */proc/ioports*, and */proc/dma*.
- Direct Memory Access (DMA) enables devices to transfer data directly without the need of the CPU controlling the transfer.
- Ultra DMA is a method that allows devices to bypass the DMA controller and transmit data in bursts of either 33 or 66MBps.
- The file */proc/dma* displays active DMA channels.
- Every device is assigned an interrupt (IRQ).
- Interrupts are assigned a priority (interrupt request level) based on the importance of the device they are associated with.
- Two types of interrupt controllers are PIC and APIC.
- */proc/interrupts* displays active interrupts.
- I/O port is a memory address used to communicate with a hardware device.

- */proc/ioports* will contain a list of I/O ports being used.
- The lshw (list hardware) command may be used to display detailed hardware configuration information.
- lshw replaces hwinfo.
- lshw has multiple output formats: short, businfo xml, and html.
- Bluetooth is a device interconnect designed to replace RS232 with wireless communication.
- A Bluetooth master (transmitter) can connect up to seven devices (receivers) via a piconet.
- Multiple networked piconets are called a scatternet.
- The command hcitool is used to configure Bluetooth connections.
- The command hciconfig is used to configure and view the properties of a Bluetooth device.
- Integrated Drive Electronics (IDE) refers to a technology in which the disk controller is integrated into the drive.
- Small Computer System Interface (SCSI) is a parallel interface used to connect peripheral devices.
- Each SCSI device is assigned an ID.
- The SCSI device ID determines the priority of the device.
- A Serial AT Attachment (SATA) drive communicates bit by bit (serial communications) to a dedicated hard disk channel via a high-speed serial cable.
- An eSATA port is used to connect external SATA devices to a system. Power for the device is supplied by an external power supply.
- An eSATAp (powered eSATA) port is capable of supplying power to the external SATA device. An eSATAp port can also support USB.
- Solid state drives (SSDs) use flash memory circuitry to store data.
- Information stored in flash memory is retained when system power is removed.
- SSDs store data as if the device was an actual hard drive (cylinder/head/sector, or CHS).
- In most cases, SSDs use the same interface as SATA, but can implement other interfaces.
- USB is a high-speed Plug and Play interface that allows multiple devices to connect via a single bus.
- A USB bus can support 127 devices in a star topology.
- The speed of the bus is limited to the speed of the slowest device on the bus.
- dmesg is a command used to read and control the kernel ring buffer.

- The ring buffer is a cyclical storage space of a specific size used to contain kernel log messages.
- lsusb displays a list of USB devices.
- The root hub is responsible for communicating with devices attached to hub ports and the hub controller.
- The Common UNIX Printing System includes tools that manage printing.
- CUPS configuration files are located in */etc/cups*.
- The lpadmin command is used to add and configure printers and printer classes.
- A printer class is a group of printers associated with a single print queue.
- Printer class information is stored in */etc/cups/classes.conf*.
- lpinfo -v determines the available devices.
- lpinfo -m lists printer drivers (*/usr/share/cups/model*).
- lpstat is used determine the status of printers, classes, and queues.
- The CUPS web interface is port 631 (localhost:631).
- Print queues accept and reject print jobs (via accept or reject).
- Printers are enabled or disabled (via cupsenable or cupsdisable).
- cancel is used to cancel print jobs.
- lpmove moves print jobs between queues.
- abrt, the Automatic Bug Reporting Tool, is a utility that collects information concerning application and kernel crashes.
- abrt stores the information in the base directory */var/spool/abrt*.

Questions

1. Which directory contains device operational and statistical information discovered during the boot process?
   A. /dev
   B. /proc/sys
   C. /sys
   D. /devices
2. What is a bus? (Choose two.)
   A. A system device
   B. A system port
   C. A system driver
   D. Used to transfer data between devices

3. When are major and minor numbers discovered?
   A. During the device discovery process
   B. When creating an entry in /dev
   C. When a device is accessed
   D. When a device is created
4. Which of the following commands will display block devices? (Select all that apply.)
   A. lsblk
   B. systool -c block
   C. lshw -short -class volume
   D. ls -l /sys/block
5. Which of the following commands would display uevents? (Choose two.)
   A. udevadm info
   B. udevadm monitor
   C. dmesg
   D. grep ueven /varlog/messages
6. What will the command **dmesg -f kern -l notice | grep sdb** do?
   A. Display all uevents associated with /dev/sdb.
   B. Display kernel messages containing the string sdb generated by facility kernel and priority notice.
   C. Display all kernel events associated with /dev/sdb.
   D. Display all kernel messages.
7. udevadm control:
   A. Is used to modify systemd-udevd operating parameters
   B. Controls how the kernel discovers devices
   C. Has been deprecated
   D. Used to control device discovery
8. Select all udev match operators. (Choose two.)
   A. =
   B. ==
   C. +=
   D. !=
9. Before writing a udev rule for a device, what command would you execute?
   A. lsblk
   B. systools

C. udevadm info

D. udevadm reload

10. What command would you run after you have created a udev rule and before you place it in */etc/udev/rules.d*?

A. udevadm monitor

B. udevadm test

C. udevadm trigger

D. udevadm reload

11. You have made changes to an existing udev rule. What command must you run?

A. udevadm monitor

B. udevadm test

C. udevadm trigger

D. udevadm reload

12. Which file contains a list of active direct memory access channels?

A. /proc/interrupts

B. /etc/dma

C. /proc/dma

D. /proc/memory

13. What format option must be used when executing the lshw command to display the bus path information? (Choose two.)

A. xml

B. html

C. businfo

D. short

14. A Bluetooth device can support which of the following network types? (Choose three.)

A. Piconet

B. Scatternet

C. Personal area network (PAN)

D. Wide area network (WAN)

15. To display a hierarchical view of USB devices, you would execute which command?

A. lsusb

B. lsusb -t

C. lsusb -D

D. usbdev -t

16. The configuration file for the CUPS daemon is:
   A. /etc/cups/cups.conf
   B. /etc/cups/cupsd.conf
   C. /etc/cups/classes.conf
   D. /etc/cupsd.conf
17. Prior to configuring a printer, it might be wise to execute which of the following commands? (Choose two.)
   A. lpadmin --test
   B. lpinfo -v
   C. lpinfo -m
   D. lpinof -t
18. To manage CUPS using the browser interface, you would open your browser and enter:
   A. :631
   B. 631
   C. localhost:631
   D. localhost:cups
19. Which command will display whether a specific printer is enabled or disabled?
   A. lpstat -p <printer_name>
   B. lpstat -o <printer_name>
   C. lpstat -c <printer_name>
   D. lpstat -d <printer_name
20. PrinterA has gone bad and you want to move all its print jobs to PrinterB. Using the letters, place the commands in the proper order.
   A. lpmove PrinterA PrinterB
   B. reject Printera
   C. cupsdisable Printera
   D. lpstat -o PrinterB

Answers

1. **C.** During the boot process, kernel modules discover device information and populate */sys*. Operational statistics are also stored in */sys*.
2. **A, D.** A bus is a system device used to transfer data between devices.
3. **A.** The major and minor numbers are discovered during the kernel device discovery process. The major number is associated with the device class. The minor number is used by the device driver.

4. **A, B, C, D.** Each of these choices will display a listing of block devices.
5. **B, C.** The command **udevadmin monitor** can display both kernel and udev events associated with hardware discovery. The dmesg command may be used to display kernel events.
6. **B.** You can use the facility (-f) priority (-l) filters found in syslog to filter the dmesg output. This question is asking to display the facility kernel and priority notice.
7. **A. udevadm control** is used to modify systemd-udevd operating parameters.
8. **B, D.** == and != are udev match operators. = and += are assignment operators.
9. **C. udevadm info** would provide you all the device attributes that can be used to write udev rules.
10. **B.** The **udevadm test** command allows you test a udev rule for errors.
11. **D. udevadm reload** will reload the rules so new or changed rules will be available.
12. **C.** The file */proc/dma* contains a list of active direct memory access channels.
13. **C, D.** The command lshw by itself requires the businfo format option to display bus path information. The short option includes the display of the bus path.
14. **A, B, C.** Bluetooth consists of a network of a master and receivers. This network is called a piconet. Multiple piconets may be joined together (scatternet). Piconets may also be called personal area networks (PANs). A Bluetooth device would not be appropriate for a wide area network (WAN).
15. **B.** The command **lsusb -t** produces a hierarchical view of USB hubs and devices attached to the hubs. **lsusb** will list USB devices, **lsusb -D** will display detailed information about a USB device, and **usbdev -t** is not a valid command.
16. **B.** */etc/cups/cupsd.conf* is the configuration file for the CUPS daemon.
17. **B, C. lpinfo -v** will display devices available to attach printers. **lpinfo -m** will display available drivers.
18. **C.** Port 631 is use to access the CUPS web tool. Entering **localhost:631** will start the CUPS web configuration tool.
19. **A. lpsat -p <printer_name>** will display whether a printer is enabled or disabled. **lpstat -o** will display jobs in the printer queue. **lpstat -c <printer_name>** will display the printer classes the printer belongs to. **lpstat -d <printer_name>** is not a working command.
20. **C, B, A, D.** First disable the printer. This will prevent the print queue from sending any other print jobs. Then prevent the print queue from accepting any more jobs. Once this is done, move the print jobs to another queue and then view the queue to make certain the jobs have moved.

CHAPTER 13

Writing Shell Scripts

In this chapter, you will learn about

- Understanding shell script components
- Using control operators
- Processing text streams

This chapter covers how to create and control basic shell scripts on a Linux system. Shell scripts are text files that contain a variety of commands that can be used to automate tasks and process information.

NOTE Most of the scripts found in this chapter can be found on the image provided with the book in the directory */Labs/Chapter_13*.

Understanding Shell Script Components

A script is a series of commands that are interpreted and executed by a shell.

Shebang (#!)

The first line of a script, also called the shebang line, contains the absolute path to the command-line interpreter used when executing the script. For example, line 1 in Figure 13-1 indicates we will use the Bash shell for our script.

The command **chsh -l** or **cat /etc/shells** displays a list of available command-line interpreters.

Comments (#)

Comments are designed to explain purpose. Once you have specified the shell interpreter, you'll want to create a comment that details the purpose of the script.

Figure 13-1 Shebang

```
1 #!/bin/bash
2
3 #This is a sample script
4 #which will display Hello World
5
6 echo "Hello World"      #The echo command will display Hello World
```

Use comments liberally (Figure 13-2). They are great reminders when you or another user has to troubleshoot or add to a script several weeks later. For example, when you edit a script, you should consider creating a comment that contains the date of and reason for the edit. All comments begin with the # symbol, which tells the interpreter to ignore all text to the right of the symbol to the end of the line.

Executing a Script

It is not necessary to have execute permissions on a script, but you must have read permissions.

The command **source <script_name>** or **bash <script_name>** will execute a script as long as you have read permissions to the file. The command **bash -x <script_name>** is used to debug a script.

If your script is executable, you must supply the absolute path to the script if the directory in which the script is located is not contained in the variable **PATH** (**echo $PATH**).

You can use the command **chmod u+x <filename>** to provide the owner of the file with execute permissions.

Variables

Variables store data. We will consider three variable types:

- **string** A string variable contains alphanumeric characters.
- **integer** An integer variable contains numbers that will be used in a mathematical expression.
- **constant** A constant (read-only) variable may not be changed or removed (that is, unset).

A variable's type determines how the variable will be used. The variable type string contains alphanumeric characters and may not be used in mathematical expressions.

```
#!/bin/bash

# Declaring functions

timestamp()                                 #create function to display current date and time
{                                           #start function commands
echo "Current time $(date +%m/%d/%y" "%R)"  #display mm/dd/yyyy HH:MM
sleep 2                                     #idle for 2 seconds
clear                                       #clear scren
}

#Start of script

clear                                       #clear screen
timestamp                                   #call timestamp function

echo -n "Enter your first name: "; read     #input stored to read variable REPLY
echo -n "Enter your last  name: "; read lname   #input stored to variable lname


echo -e  " \v Full Name: $REPLY $lname \v\v"   #Vertical line feed and print value of variables REPLY and lname

timestamp                                   #call timestamp function
```

Figure 13-2 Comments

The variable type integer contains only numbers. If a string is supplied as a value for an integer type variable, the value of the variable becomes 0. The last variable type is a constant. Constants are variables that may be neither changed nor deleted.

The Bash interpreter does not assign a variable type when one is created. Bash considers a variable a string if its content contains an alphanumeric value. If the variable contains numbers, Bash will allow the variable to be used in arithmetic expressions.

The declare command enables you to assign a variable type to a variable. For example, the command **declare flower=rose** creates a local string variable named flower and assigns it a value of rose. To view the properties of a variable execute the command **declare -p <variable_name>**.

You can use the command **echo $flower** to display the content of a variable. The **declare -p** command is more efficient because it will display any attributes assigned to the variable as well as the content.

To create a variable of type integer, execute the command **declare -i <variable_name>=<value>**.

Let's look at the difference between declaring a variable type and not declaring a variable type. In Figure 13-3 lines 1 and 5, we have assigned numerical values of 100 and 110, respectively, to the variable sum. On line 9, we assign the variable sum a value of Fred.

In line 1 in Figure 13-4, we use the declare command to set the variable sum to type integer. On line 4 we change the value of the variable to 110. On line 7 we change the value of the variable to Fred. Since the variable sum is assigned an integer type and we changed the value to a string, the value of the variable is changed to 0.

Reading User Input

There are times when you need to prompt a user for a response and use the response in a script. The read command reads user input and assigns the value of the input to a variable specified by the argument in the read statement. If no variable name is supplied, the default variable REPLY is used.

In Figure 13-5, lines 1–7 contain the script read_script, and lines 10–12 show the script executing.

Figure 13-3
Bash sum

```
1 # sum=100
2 # echo $sum
3 100
4 #
5 # sum=110
6 # echo $sum
7 110
8 #
9 # sum=Fred
10 # echo $sum
11 Fred
```

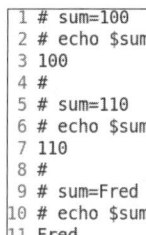

Figure 13-4
Assigning a variable type

```
1 # declare -i sum=100
2 # declare -p sum
3 declare -i sum="100"
4 # declare sum=110
5 # declare -p sum
6 declare -i sum="110"
7 # declare sum=Fred
8 # declare -p sum
9 declare -i sum="0"
```

```
1 #!/bin/bash
2
3
4 echo -n "Enter your first name: "; read         #input stored to read variable REPLY
5 echo -n "Enter your last  name: "; read lname   #input stored to variable lname
6
7 echo "$REPLY $lname"
8
9 # bash read_statement
10 Enter your first name: George
11 Enter your last  name: Washington
12 George Washington
```

Figure 13-5 Using the read command

Line 4 of the script requests user input, but does not specify a variable; therefore, the user's first name will be stored to the variable REPLY. Line 5 assigns the user's input to the variable lname.

You can use the **-t** option to limit the time a user has time to respond. The command **echo -n "Enter your name: " ; read -t 5** allows the user five seconds. The script will terminate after five seconds.

Positional Parameters

A command-line, system-generated tabular output or a system flat-line database may have up to nine arguments, positions, or fields, all of which can be identified numerically based on their position (see Figure 13-6).

In Figure 13-7 you can see fred is in position 1, george is in position two, and Andrew is in position 3. The $ followed by the position of the argument, column, or field points to the value of the argument. For Figure 13-7, the command **echo $2** would display george.

Let's modify the read script by using positional parameters. Notice in Figure 13-8 the script uses the echo command to display the first and second arguments of the command line (see script output line 7 in Figure 13-8).

Additional command-line and command information may be found by using parameter codes detailed in Table 13-1. Remember the $ character is a metacharacter that may be interpreted as "the value of."

	argument1	**argument2**	**argument3**
Position	1	2	3
	column1	**column2**	**column3**

Figure 13-6 Positional parameters

	fred	**george**	**andrew**
Position	1	2	3

Figure 13-7 Arguments in positions

```
#!/bin/bash

echo "$1 $2"   #Display the arguments entered in position 1 and position 2


# bash positional_parameters George Washington
George Washington
```

Figure 13-8 Positional parameters in a script

Table 13-1 Additional Parameter Shortcuts

Parameter	Description
$0	Name of command or script
$#	Number of command-line arguments
$*	List of command-line arguments
$$	Current process's PID
$!	PID of the last background job
$?	Command exit status code

Functions

A function is a named section of a program that contains a series of commands designed to perform a specific task. Rather than writing the same code over and over, you can create a function and then have the script call (execute) the function.

A function is defined as follows:

```
function_name()
     {
          <command>
          <command>
     }
```

Figure 13-9 displays the script function_script. Lines 5–10 in Figure 13-9 define the function timestamp, which is called on lines 15 and 23.

```
1 #!/bin/bash
2
3 # Declaring functions
4
5 timestamp()                                #create function to display current date and time
6 {                                          #start function commands
7 echo "Current time $(date +%m/%d/%y" "%R)"     #display mm/dd/yyyy HH:MM
8 sleep 2                                    #idle for 2 seconds
9 clear                                      #clear scren
10 }
11
12 #Start of script
13
14 clear                                     #clear screen
15 timestamp                                 #call timestamp function
16
17 echo -n "Enter your first name: "; read    #input stored to read variable REPLY
18 echo -n "Enter your last  name: "; read lname  #input stored to variable lname
19
20
21 echo -e  " \v Full Name: $REPLY $lname \v\v"   #Vertical line feed and print value of variables REPLY and lname
22
23 timestamp                                 #call timestamp function
```

Figure 13-9 Example of a function in a script

Command Substitution

Command substitution is a way of embedding a command into an output. There are two methods of embedding a command: **`<command>`** and **$(<command>)**. The ` (backtick) is found on most keyboards in the top-left corner under the ~ (tilde).

An example of command substitution may be found on line 7 of Figure 13-9. This command could have been written **echo "Current time: `date +%m/%d/%y" "%R`"**.

Using Control Operators

Control operators change the flow of a command. In scripting, control operators are used to form test conditions in an expression.

Expressions

An expression uses operators to evaluate a condition and determine if the condition is true (exit status code 0) or false (exit status code 1).

String Operators

String operators are used by expressions to test strings (see Table 13-2). The comparison is based on ASCII alphabetical order.

Relationship Operators

Relationship operators are traditionally used for integers. Table 13-3 displays some relationship operators.

Arithmetic Operators

With an arithmetic expression, you use one of the arithmetic operators shown in Table 13-4.

Boolean Operators

Boolean operators are used to join multiple expressions. In line 7 of Figure 13-10, we use the operator -a (AND Boolean) to specify two conditions that must be true to make the expression true. Some of the Boolean operators are displayed in Table 13-5.

String Operator	Description
=	Are both strings equal?
>	Is the string on the left greater than the string on the right? [$a \> $b]
<	Is the string on the left less than the string on the right? [$a \< $b]

Table 13-2 String Operators

Table 13-3 Relationship Operators

Relationship Operator	Description
-eq	Equal to [$a -eq $b]
-ne	Not equal to [$a -ne $b]
-ge	Greater than or equal to [$a -ge $b]
lt	Less than [$a -lt $b]
le	Less than or equal to [$a -le $b]
<=	Less than or equal to ((“$a” <= “$b”))
>	Greater than ((“$a” > “$b”))
>=	Greater than or equal to ((“$a” >= “$b”))

Table 13-4 Arithmetic Operators

Arithmetic Operator	Description
+	Add a+b
-	Subtract a b
*	Multiply a*b
/	Divide a/b

```
#!/bin/bash

#Start of Script

if [ $EUID -ge 1000 ]; then                    #Test to see if the users effective user id is greater than or equal to 1000
  echo "Regular User"                           #Display Regular Users
   elif [ $EUID -gt 99 -a $EUID -lt 1000 ]      # If EUID was not 1000 but is greater than 99 and less than 1000
    echo "System Account"                       #Display System Account
   else                                         #If none of the conditions are true
    echo "System Admin Account"                 #Display System Admin Account
fi                                              # End of if statement
```

Figure 13-10 Using Boolean Operators

Table 13-5 Boolean Operators

Boolean Operators	Description
-a	Boolean AND Both expressions must be true
-o	Boolean OR Either expression must be true
!	Boolean NOT Invert expression

File Test Operators

File test operators (Table 13-6) are used to test the properties of files. Permission and ownership tests are based on the user executing the script.

File Test Operator	Description
-a or -e	Does the file exist? [-a /root/George]
-s	Is the file size greater than 0? [-s /etc/bashrc]
-f	Is the file a text file? [-f /etc/bashrc]
-d	Is the file a directory? [-d /etc]
-b	Is the file a block device? [-b /dev/sda]
-c	Is the file a character device? [-c /dev/tty1]
-p	Is the file a named pipe? [-p /run/dmeventd-client]
-L or -h	Is the file a symbolic link?
-r	Does the file have read permissions for the user executing the test?
-w	Does the file have write permissions for the user executing the test?
-x	Does the file have execute permissions for the user executing the test?
-u	Does the file have suid applied?
-g	Does the file have sgid applied?
-k	Does the file have sticky bit applied?
-O <username>	Is the file owned by the user specified by the argument <username>?
-G <group_name>	Is the file owned by the user specified by the argument <group_name>?

Table 13-6 File Test Operators

```
#!/bin/bash


#Script start

echo -e  "\v\vTesting -f /root/.bashrc \v"
if [ -f /root/.bashrc ]; then                          #Test to see if the file /root/.bashrc is a text file
 echo -e "true \v"
  else
    echo -e "not true \v"
fi

echo -e  "\v\vTesting -u /usr/bin/passwd \v"
if [ -u /usr/bin/passwd ]; then                        #Test to see if the file /usr/bin/passwd has suid applied
 echo -e "true \v"
  else
    echo -e "not true \v"
fi

echo -e  "\v\vTesting -d /etc \v"                      #Test to see if /etc is a directory
if [ -d /etc ]; then
 echo -e "true \v"
  else
    echo -e "not true \v"
fi

echo -e  "\v\vTesting -b /dev/sda \v"
if [ -b /dev/sda ]; then                               #Test to see if /dev/sda is a block device.
 echo -e "true \v"
  else
    echo -e "not true \v"
fi
```

Figure 13-11 File test operator script

Figure 13-11 illustrates the script file_test_operator_script, which contains an example of the file test expressions.

Control Structure

Control structures are used to determine the flow of a script.

test

The test command is a shell builtin that allows you to evaluate conditions using the syntax **test <expression>**. Executing the command **test $EUID -eq 0;echo $?** on the command line would indicate if your effective user ID is 0. This expression could also be written as **[$EUID -eq 0];echo $?**.

NOTE When using the left and right brackets, remember to include a space after the left bracket and before the right bracket.

The test command may also be applied in scripts The script test_script, shown in Figure 13-12, displays an example of the test command.

```
#!/bin/bash

#start script

if test "$UID --eq 0"
  then
  echo "UID equals 0"
fi
```

Figure 13-12 A test command script

```
#!/bin/bash


#Declare Variables

passwd_file=/etc/passwd                              #set the value of the variable passwd_file

clear                                                #clear the screen
read -p "Enter a username:" username                 #Ask the user to enter a username and place it in the variable username
grep ^$username $passwd_file > /dev/null             #Search /etc/passwd for the content of the variable username at the beginning of the line
status=$?                                            #Set the value of the variable status equal to the exit status of the previous command

if [ $status -eq 0 ]; then                           #Determine if the exit status of the previous command  is 0
  echo "User $username found in $passwd_file"        #Display user found
   else                                              #Execute the command below if the exit status code was > 0
    echo "User $username is not found in $passwd_file"  #Display user not found
fi                                                   #End if statement
```

Figure 13-13 Sample if then test script 1

if then else

The if statement expands the use of the test command by allowing us to direct the flow of the script based on the exit status of the test statement. If the test condition evaluates to true (exit status 0), the command or commands directly under the test statement are executed. If the test condition evaluates to false (exit status 1), one of two flow control elements may be used. The else statement indicates the commands to be executed if the original test condition is true. The elif statement opens another test condition. All if statements end in fi.

Figure 13-13, which shows if_then_script_1, and Figure 13-14, which shows multi-user_script, illustrate examples using if, else, and elif.

NOTE For a closer view of Figure 13-13 and other selected images from this chapter, download the full-resolution images from the online content for this book.

case

Using case is a more efficient way of making choices. It uses the first argument or expression of the command line to determine what it will do.

A case statement is broken into stanzas, which have the following structure:

```
case <$<variable> in
<string>)
   <command>
    <command>
;;
<string>)
   <command>
    <command>
;;
esac
```

```
#!/bin/bash

#Start of Script

if [ $EUID -ge 1000 ]; then                   #Test to see if the users effective user id is greater than or equal to 1000
  echo "Regular User"                         #Display Regular Users
   elif [ $EUID -gt 99 -a $EUID -lt 1000 ]    # If EUID was not 1000 but is greater than 99 and less than 1000
    echo "System Account"                     #Display System Account
   else                                       #If none of the conditions are true
    echo "System Admin Account"               #Display System Admin Account
fi                                            # End of if statement
```

Figure 13-14 if then else

```
1 #!/bin/bash
2
3 case $1 in                    #use the first argument of the command line as the string to match
4
5   start)                      #if the string is start execute this stanza
6    echo start
7   ;;                          #end of stanza
8
9   stop)                       #if the string is stop execute this stanza
10   echo stop
11  ;;                          #end of stanza
12
13  *)                          #if user has entered a string which does not match any of the strings in the case statement
14   echo "incorrect entry"
15  ;;
16
17 esac                         #end of case statement
```

Figure 13-15 Sample case statement

The case statement examines the input argument against the string that begins a stanza. If the string matches, that stanza is executed. Notice that the very last stanza in Figure 13-15 (script case_script, line 13) begins with *). This entry is used to handle any user entry that does not match any of the strings in the case statement. Figure 13-16 shows the results of using a case statement.

Using Looping Structures

The if/then/else and case structures are called *branching structures*. Depending on how a condition evaluates, the script branches in one direction or another. You can also use *looping* control structures within a shell script. Looping structures come in three varieties: while loop, until loop, and for loop.

While Loop

A while loop executes over and over until a specified condition is no longer true. The structure of a while loop is as follows:

```
while condition
do
     script commands
done
```

A while loop will keep processing over and over and over until the condition evaluates to false. Figure 13-17 shows while_loop_script and illustrates the use of a while loop.

Figure 13-16 Case script output

```
[root@localhost book]# bash case_script start
start

[root@localhost book]# bash case_script stop
stop

[root@localhost book]# bash case_script fred
incorrect entry
```

```
#!/bin/bash

#Declare variables

declare -i x=0

#Start Script

while [ $x -lt 10 ]                         #While the value of the variable x is less than 10
  do                                        #Execute the commands between do and done for each iteration
    x=$x+1                                  #Increment the value of x by 1
    echo "the variable x is less then 10"   #Display
  done                                      # End of commands for this iteration
```

Figure 13-17 While loop

Until Loop

In addition to a while loop, you can also use an until loop in your script. It works in the opposite manner. An until loop runs over and over as long as the condition is false. As soon as the condition is true, it stops. The structure for an until loop is as follows:

```
until condition
do
     script commands
done
```

For Loop

You can also use a for loop, which operates in a different manner than until and while loops. The until and while loops keep looping indefinitely until the specified condition is met. A for loop, on the other hand, loops a specific number of times.

It is very common to use the seq command within a for loop to create the sequence of numbers to determine how many times it will loop. There are three options for creating a number sequence with seq:

- If you specify a single value, the sequence starts at 1, increments by one, and ends at the specified value.
- If you specify two values, the sequence starts at the first value, increments by one, and ends at the second value.
- If you specify three values, the sequence starts at the first value, increments by the second value, and ends at the third value.

An example of a for loop script using seq can be seen in Figure 13-18 (for_loop_seq script).

```
#!/bin/bash


#Start Script

for x in `seq 0 1 10`                      #Start sequence at 0 increment by 1 end at 10
 do
 echo "The current number is $x"
 done
```

Figure 13-18 For loop script using seq

```
#!/bin/bash

#Start Script

for i in {0..10..1}                    #Replaces seq  start at 0 end at 10 increment by 1
  do
   echo "The current number is $i"
  done
```

Figure 13-19 for loop using { } for sequence

You may also see scripts that use a different sequence notation. For example, **{0..10..1}** is the same as **seq 0 1 10**. Figure 13-19 (for_loop_new_sequence script) illustrates the use of **{0..10..1}**.

Exercise 13-1: Creating a Basic Shell Script

For Exercise 13-1, use the image provided with the book. Log on as user root using the password root. We have supplied the scripts used in this chapter in the directory */LABS/Chapter_13/source* and duplicated the scripts in */LABS/Chapter_13/work*.

Follow these steps:

VIDEO Please watch the Exercise 13-1 video for a demonstration on how to perform this task.

1. We suggest you review these scripts as well as edit or create your own. Use the scripts in the lab directory and keep them in the book directory to recover anything you might mess up.
2. When you create a script, consider your objectives and how you will test the script to make certain it meets its objectives.
3. Draw the script out first before you start typing. Your diagram should show the flow of the script. You can write your script from the diagram.
4. Test commands on the command line before you place them in the script.
5. Write snippets. Create small units of code and apply them to the scripts. You will find you are always going to reuse code. Many of the scripts in this chapter were created from snippets. This saves a great deal of time.
6. When you test your commands, snippets and script make certain you are testing based on the objectives you outlined before you started writing the script.

Enjoy!

Processing Text Streams

When you're processing text streams within a script or piping output at the shell prompt, you might need to filter the output of one command so that only certain portions of the text stream are actually passed along to the stdin of the next command. You can use a variety of tools to do this. In this part of the chapter, we'll look at using the following commands:

- tr
- cut
- expand and unexpand
- fmt
- join and paste
- nl
- od
- pr
- sed
- awk
- sort
- split
- head
- tail
- uniq
- wc

Let's begin by looking at the tr command.

tr

The tr (translate) command is used to change or translate characters. The tr command accepts input from a command via an unnamed pipe, like so:

<command> |tr <option> <character_set_old> <character_set_new>

Figure 13-20 shows how you can translate lowercase letters to uppercase letters.

Figure 13-21 illustrates how to use the tr command to translate the letter *r* to 1, *o* to 2, and *t* to 3.

```
[root@localhost ~]# grep root /etc/passwd | tr [a-z] [A-Z]
ROOT:X:0:0:ROOT:/ROOT:/BIN/BASH
OPERATOR:X:11:0:OPERATOR:/ROOT:/SBIN/NOLOGIN
```

Figure 13-20 Using tr to translate lowercase to uppercase

```
# grep root /etc/passwd | tr rot 123
1223:x:0:0:1223:/1223:/bin/bash
2pe1a321:x:11:0:2pe1a321:/1223:/sbin/n2l2gin
```

Figure 13-21 Using tr to translate letters to numbers

Figure 13-22
tr squeeze

```
[root@localhost ~]# who

root      :0           2019-05-16 13:48 (:0)
root      pts/0        2019-05-16 13:48 (:0)

[root@localhost ~]# who | tr -s "  " " "

root :0 2019-05-16 13:48 (:0)
root pts/0 2019-05-16 13:48 (:0)
```

The tr command can use the -s (squeeze) option to replace multiple occurrences. In Figure 13-22, we use the squeeze option to remove multiple spaces between fields so there is only one space between fields. The command **who | tr -s " " " "** replaces two contiguous spaces with one.

cut

The cut command is used to print columns or fields that you specify from a file to the standard output. Table 13-7 shows options that can be used with cut.

Option	Description
-b	Extracts specific bytes from a file. By default, the character count starts at the beginning of a line. Here are some examples: **cut -b 1,3,5** will cut the first, third, and fifth bytes. **cut -b -3** will cut from the first to third byte. **cut -b 3-** will cut from the third byte to the end of the line. **cut -b 1-3** will cut the first three bytes.
-c	Extracts a character from a given position. Tabs are considered characters. Here are some examples: **cut -c 1,3,5** will cut the first, third, and fifth characters. **cut -c -3** will cut from the first to third character. **cut -c 3-** will cut from the third character to the end of the line. **cut -c 1-3,7,8** will cut the first three characters.
-d	Specifies the delimiter used by cut. If a space is used as a delimiter, use " ".
-f	Extracts fields. Here's an example: **cut -d : -f 1 /etc/passwd** extracts the first field of the file */etc/passwd*.

Table 13-7 cut Options

Figure 13-23 Using the cut command to extract fields

```
[root@localhost ~]# who

root     :0           2019-05-16 13:48 (:0)
root     pts/0        2019-05-16 13:48 (:0)

[root@localhost ~]# who | tr -s "   " " " |cut -d " " -f1,3
root 2019-05-16
root 2019-05-16
```

In Figure 13-23, we execute the who command and then use the **tr -s** command to remove multiple contiguous spaces so there is only one space between the fields. The cut command, using a space as a delimiter, extracts the real username (field one) and time (field 3).

expand and unexpand

The expand command converts tabs to spaces. The default number of spaces is eight, but you can specify the number of spaces using the **-t <number_of_spaces>** options.

The command syntax is **expand -t <number> <filename>**.

Line 3 in Figure 13-24 displays the content of the file *expandtest*. In order to see the tabs, we must use the command **cat -vte** (line 6). Notice that the output on line 8 displays the location of tabs (^I).

On line 10, we execute the command expand to replace the tabs with spaces (8) and redirect the results to the file *expandresult*. Looking at the content of the file *expandresult* (line 14), you can see all the tabs have been removed and replaced with spaces.

The unexpand command converts spaces to tabs. By default, eight contiguous spaces are converted into tabs. However, you can use the **-t** option to specify a different number of spaces.

unexpand will only convert leading spaces at the beginning of each line. To force it to convert all spaces of the correct number to tabs, you must include the **-a** option with the unexpand command.

In Figure 13-25, the file *expandresult* (line 2) consists of spaces. We then execute the command **unexpand -a expandresult > unexpandresult** to convert the spaces to tabs (line 4). You can see on line 7 that the spaces have been converted into tabs (^I).

Figure 13-24 Using the expand command

```
1 [root@localhost share]# cat expandtest
2
3 this    is      a       tab
4
5
6 [root@localhost share]# cat -vte expandtest
7
8 this^Iis^Ia ^Itab$
9
10 [root@localhost share]# expand expandtest > expandresult
11
12
13 [root@localhost share]# cat -vte expandresult
14 this    is      a       tab$
```

Figure 13-25 Using the unexpand command

```
[root@localhost share]# cat -vte expandresult
this    is      a       tab$

[root@localhost share]# unexpand -a expandresult > unexpandresult

[root@localhost share]# cat -vte unexpandresult
this^Iis^Ia^Itab$
```

fmt

You can use the fmt command to reformat a text file and send the results to the standard output device. It is commonly used to change the wrapping of long lines within the file to a more manageable width. The syntax for using fmt is **fmt <option> <filename>**.

For example, you could use the **-w** option with the fmt command to narrow the text of a file to 80 columns by entering **fmt -w 80 <filename>**. An example is shown in Figure 13-26.

join and paste

The join command prints a line from each of two specified input files that have identical join fields. The first field is the default join field, delimited by whitespace. You can specify a different join field using the **-j <field>** option.

For example, suppose you have two files. The first file (named *firstnames*) contains the following content:

```
1 Mike
2 Jenny
3 Joe
```

The second file (named *lastnames*) contains the following content:

```
1 Johnson
2 Doe
3 Jones
```

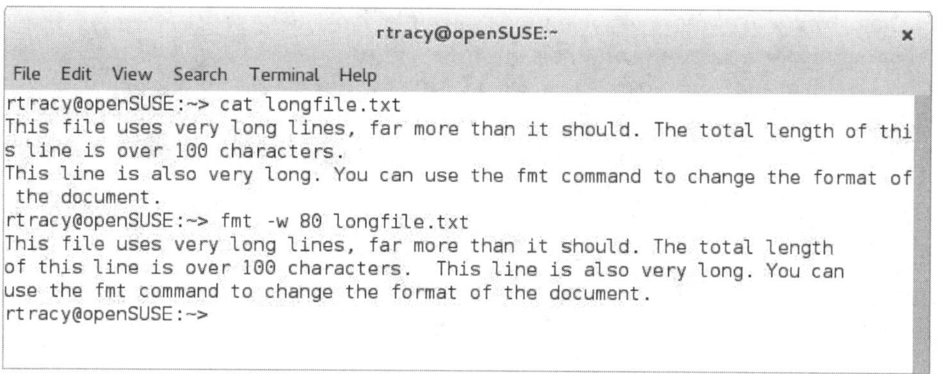

Figure 13-26 Using fmt to change the number of columns in a text file

You can use the join command to join the corresponding lines from each file by entering **join -j 1 firstnames lastnames**. This is shown here:

```
# join -j 1 firstnames lastnames
1 Mike Johnson
2 Jenny Doe
3 Joe Jones
```

The paste command works in much the same manner as the join command. It pastes together corresponding lines from one or more files into columns. By default, the tab character is used to separate columns. You can use the **-d<n>** option to specify a different delimiter character. You can also use the **-s** option to put the contents of each file into a single line.

For example, you could use the paste command to join the corresponding lines from the *firstnames* and *lastnames* files by entering **paste firstnames lastnames**. An example is shown here:

```
# paste firstnames lastnames
1 Mike    1 Johnson
2 Jenny   2 Doe
3 Joe     3 Jones
```

Next, let's look at the nl command.

nl

The common usage for nl is line numbering. This can be accomplished by executing the command **nl <filename>**.

When creating a text document, you can break the document up into three sections (header, body, and footer) and assign independent numbering schemes to each section. By default, nl only numbers the body section.

Table 13-8 shows the command-line option and the text file designator for a document marked up for nl. Figure 13-27 illustrates an example of dividing a document into sections with nl designators.

The numbering schemes for each section are applied in the command line using the designator and one or more of the options shown in Table 13-9.

The syntax for a section would be **<-h|-b|-f> <a|t|n>**.

The command **nl -h a -b n -f t -v 20 -i2 nltest** will start the numbering of the file *nltest* at 20 (**-v 20**) and increment the numbers by two (**-i 2**). All lines in the header section will be numbered (**-h a**), none of the lines in the body section will be numbered

Table 13-8 nl Section Designators

Section	Option	Designator
Header	-h	\:\:\:
Body	-b	\:\:
Footer	-f	\:

Figure 13-27 Document formatted with nl designators

```
\:\:\:

This is the header section
To define line numbering for this section use the -h option

Line A

Line B
Line C


\:\:

This is the body  section
To define line numbering for this section use the -b option

Line A

Line B
Line C

\:

This is the footnote section
To define line numbering for this section use the -f option

Line A

Line B
Line C
```

Option	Description
a	Number all lines. By default, nl will not number empty lines. (Applied to section.)
n	Do not number lines. (Applied to section.)
t	Do not number empty lines. (Applied to section.)
-n	Format line numbers using one of the following format codes: **ln** Left justified with no leading zeros (for example, **nl -nln <filename>**) **rn** Right justified with no leading zeros (for example, **nl -nrn <filename>**) **rz** Right justified with leading zeros (for example, **nl -nrz <filename>**) (Applied to document.)
-s	Change the separator between the number and the line. By default, a tab is used. **nl -s -** uses the - character as a separator. **nl -s " - "** surrounds the - character with spaces.
-v #	Starting line number. Changes the starting line number of the document.
-i #	Increment line count by *n*. **nl -i2** will increment line numbers by 2.

Table 13-9 nl Numbering Options

Figure 13-28 Numbering a document by section

```
[root@localhost book]# nl -h a  -b n -f t -v 20 -i 2 nltest

    20
    22  This is the header section
    24  To define line numbering for this section use the -h option
    26
    28  Line A
    30
    32  Line B
    34  Line C
    36
    38


       This is the body  section
       To define line numbering for this section use the -b option

       Line A

       Line B
       Line C



    40  This is the footnote section
    42  To define line numbering for this section use the -f option

    44  Line A

    46  Line B
    48  Line C
```

(**-b n**), and the footer will not number empty lines (**-f t**). Figure 13-28 displays the output of the command.

od

The od command converts the contents of a binary file into hex, octal, or decimal notation to the standard output device. The command is used to locate changes or unwanted characters in a file.

NOTE The file *helloworld.odt* can be found on your image in */LABS/Chapter_13/source.*

The syntax for using od is **od <options> <filename>**. Here are some of the more commonly used options:

- **-b** Octal dump
- **-d** Decimal dump
- **-x** Hex dump
- **-c** Character dump

pr

The pr command is used to format text files for printing. It formats the file with pagination, headers, and columns. The header contains the date and time, filename, and page number. You can use the following options with pr:

- **-d** Double-space the output.
- **-l <page_length>** Set the page length to the specified number of lines. The default is 66.
- **-o <margin>** Offset each line with the specified number of spaces. The default margin is 0.

Next, we need to look at sed and awk.

sed

sed is a data stream editor that reads one line of a file at a time into a buffer (pattern space) and makes a single change to a line at a time. sed does not change the content of the edited file. To save changes, you must redirect the output to a file.

The syntax of a sed command is **sed <options> <address> <expression>**. Some sed options are listed in Table 13-10.

The command **sed '=' /etc/passwd** will print the file */etc/passwd* (see Figure 13-29). Each line will be preceded by a line number.

The command **sed 1,3p /etc/passwd** should print the range of lines (address) from line 1 through line 3 of the file */etc/passwd*. When viewing the output in Figure 13-30, it looks as if the whole file has been printed. However, what we are viewing is the pattern buffer.

Option	Description
-e	Expression. This option is used when placing more than one expression in a sed command.
-n	Do not print the pattern space.
-f <instruction_file>	Obtain sed filtering instructions from a file.
c	Append text.
d	Delete text.
i	Insert a line.
a	Append a line.
r <filename>	Read in a file.
s	Substitute one string pattern for another.

Table 13-10 sed Command Options

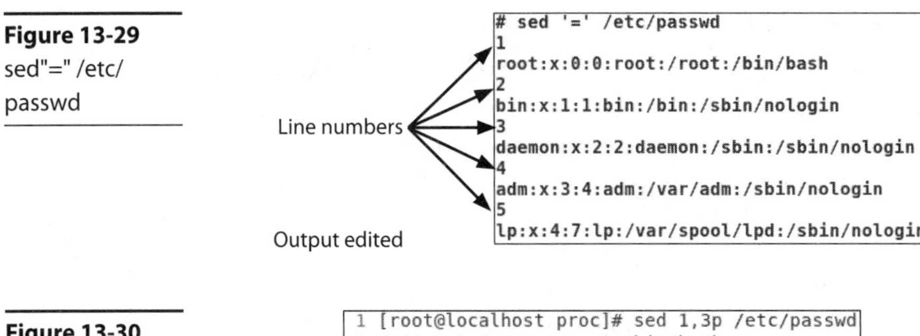

Figure 13-29 sed"=" /etc/passwd

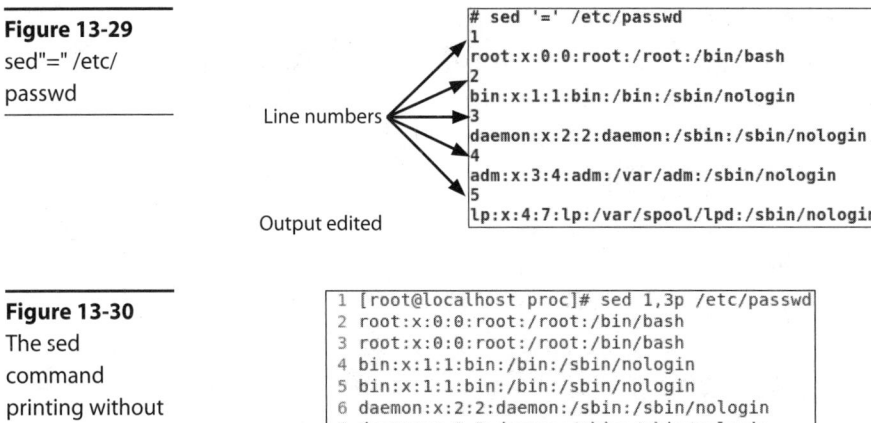

```
[root@localhost proc]# sed 1,3p /etc/passwd
root:x:0:0:root:/root:/bin/bash
root:x:0:0:root:/root:/bin/bash
bin:x:1:1:bin:/bin:/sbin/nologin
bin:x:1:1:bin:/bin:/sbin/nologin
daemon:x:2:2:daemon:/sbin:/sbin/nologin
daemon:x:2:2:daemon:/sbin:/sbin/nologin
adm:x:3:4:adm:/var/adm:/sbin/nologin
lp:x:4:7:lp:/var/spool/lpd:/sbin/nologin
sync:x:5:0:sync:/sbin:/bin/sync
```

Figure 13-30 The sed command printing without suppressing pattern space

To prevent printing the pattern space, you must use the **-n** option (see Figure 13-31).

You can print a number of lines from a starting address. The command **sed -n 3, +3p /etc/passwd** will begin printing from the third line of */etc/passwd* and print the next three lines (see Figure 13-32).

sed will only make one edit per line (see Figure 13-33) The command **sed -n 's/root/fred/p /etc/passwd** will search each line for the first instance of the string root and change the string to fred.

```
[root@localhost proc]# sed -n 1,3p /etc/passwd
root:x:0:0:root:/root:/bin/bash
bin:x:1:1:bin:/bin:/sbin/nologin
daemon:x:2:2:daemon:/sbin:/sbin/nologin

[root@localhost proc]#
```

Figure 13-31 The sed command suppressing the pattern space

```
# cat -n /etc/passwd | sed -n 3,+3p
     3  daemon:x:2:2:daemon:/sbin:/sbin/nologin
     4  adm:x:3:4:adm:/var/adm:/sbin/nologin
     5  lp:x:4:7:lp:/var/spool/lpd:/sbin/nologin
     6  sync:x:5:0:sync:/sbin:/bin/sync
```

Figure 13-32 The sed command printing three consecutive lines

```
# sed -n 's/root/fred/p' /etc/passwd
fred:x:0:0:root:/root:/bin/bash
operator:x:11:0:operator:/fred:/sbin/nologin
```

Figure 13-33 Using sed to search and replace a single instance of a string per line

```
# sed -n 's/root/fred/gp' /etc/passwd
fred:x:0:0:fred:/fred:/bin/bash
operator:x:11:0:operator:/fred:/sbin/nologin
```

Figure 13-34 Using sed to search and replace multiple instances of a string per line

```
# sed -n 's/^root/fred/p' /etc/passwd
fred:x:0:0:root:/root:/bin/bash
```

Figure 13-35 Using sed with regular expressions

In order to make multiple edits on a single line, add the **g** option to the end of the sed expression (**sed -n 's/root/fred/gp' /etc/passwd**). You can view the output in Figure 13-34.

You can use regular expressions as part of your search expression. The command **sed -n 's/^root/fred/p' /etc/passwd** will search for the string root at the beginning of the line in /etc/passwd and change it to fred (see Figure 13-35).

We will use the file *sedawk* for the next few examples. Figure 13-36 displays the contents of sedawk.

The command **cat sedawk | sed '/Jane/s/14/16'** will search each line of the file *sedawk* for the string Jane. When it finds a line with the string Jane, it will search for the string 14 and replace it with the string 16 (see Figure 13-37).

Figure 13-36 sedawk file

```
Jane    F    14    Algebra    90
George  M    13    French     88
Angela  F    14    Algebra    78
Jane    F    14    French     75
Bruce   M    15    Algebra    62
Bruce   M    15    French     89
George  M    13    Algebra    55
Angela  F    14    French     92
```

Figure 13-37 Using sed to search for a string in a line

```
# cat sedawk | sed /Jane/s/14/16/
Jane    F    16    Algebra 90
George  M    13    French  88
Angela  F    14    Algebra 78
Jane    F    16    French  75
Bruce   M    15    Algebra 62
Bruce   M    15    French  89
George  M    13    Algebra 55
Angela  F    14    French  92
```

Figure 13-38 Using sed to search a range of lines

```
# cat sedawk | sed 3,5s/Algebra/German/
Jane     F        14       Algebra 90
George   M        13       French  88
Angela   F        14       German  78
Jane     F        14       French  75
Bruce    M        15       German  62
Bruce    M        15       French  89
George   M        13       Algebra 55
Angela   F        14       French  92
```

Figure 13-39 Using sed to make multiple edits

```
# sed -ne 's/Jane/Margaret/p' -e 's/Bruce/Bill/p' sedawk
Margaret        F       14      Algebra 90
Margaret        F       14      French  75
Bill    M       15      Algebra 62
Bill    M       15      French  89
```

The command **cat sedawk | sed 3,5s/Algebra/German** will search lines 3–5 (address) for the string Algebra and replace it with the string German (see Figure 13-38).

We can define multiple expressions. The command **sed -ne 's/Jane/Margaret/p' -e 's/Bruce/Bill/p ' sedawk** will search the file *sedawk* and replace the name Jane with Margaret and the name Bruce with Bill (see Figure 13-39).

To append a line, use the **a** option. The command **sed '3 a \This is an append test\'** (shown in Figure 13-40) will add the text "This is an append test" after line 3.

To insert a line, use the **i** option. The command **sed '3 i \This is an insert test\'** (shown in Figure 13-41) will insert the text "This is an insert test" before line 3.

Figure 13-40 Using sed to append a line

```
# sed '3 i \This is an insert test' sedawk
Jane     F        14       Algebra 90
George   M        13       French  88
This is an insert test
Angela   F        14       Algebra 78
Jane     F        14       French  75
Bruce    M        15       Algebra 62
Bruce    M        15       French  89
George   M        13       Algebra 55
Angela   F        14       French  92
```

Figure 13-41 Using sed to insert a line

```
# sed '3 a \This is an append test' sedawk
Jane     F        14       Algebra 90
George   M        13       French  88
Angela   F        14       Algebra 78
This is an append test
Jane     F        14       French  75
Bruce    M        15       Algebra 62
Bruce    M        15       French  89
George   M        13       Algebra 55
Angela   F        14       French  92
```

```
# cat sedawk | sed 3,5d
Jane    F       14      Algebra 90
George  M       13      French  88
Bruce   M       15      French  89
George  M       13      Algebra 55
Angela  F       14      French  92
```

Figure 13-42 Using sed to delete a range of lines

To delete a line, use the **d** option. The command **cat sedawk | sed 3,5d** (shown in Figure 13-42) will delete lines 3–5 of the file *sedawk*. Remember, sed will not change the file but instead displays the changes that would occur. To save the change, redirect the output to a file.

awk

awk is an application used to process text files. The GNU implementation of awk is gawk. Either command, gawk or awk, may be executed. awk processes a single line at a time. It treats each line as a record that is divided into fields. Fields are separated by a delimiter. The default delimiter is a space or tab.

Table 13-11 lists some awk options.

awk also has a set of a built-in variables. A partial list of these variables is shown in Table 13-12.

awk uses the same escape sequences to do character insertions as the echo command. Some of these are listed in Table 13-13.

Option	Description
-f <instruction_file>	Obtain awk filtering instructions from the file specified by the argument <instruction_file>.
-F <delimiter>	Use the character(s) specified by the argument <delimiter> as the field delimiter.

Table 13-11 awk Options

Table 13-12 awk Variables

Variable	Description
FILENAME	Filename of current input file
NF	Number of fields in a record
NR	Number of current record
FS	Current delimiter (input field separator)

Character	Description
\f	Insert form feed (advance to next page).
\n	Insert new line character (line feed and return cursor to the beginning of the line).
\r	Return cursor to the beginning of the line.
\t	Insert tab.

Table 13-13 Character Insertion Codes

Filtering Command Output

The next several commands use awk (gawk) to filter the output of a command.

Most commands use a whitespace character to separate the columns of output. Each column (field) is assigned a position number from 1 to 9. We will use the position number to reference a specific output field.

In the following example, the output of the **ls -l** command is filtered by awk to display the first field of the output (permissions) and the ninth field of the output (filename).

```
# ls -l | gawk '{ print $1,$9 }'
total
-rw------- anaconda-ks.cfg
drwxr-xr-x Desktop
-rw-r--r-- install.log
-rw-r--r-- install.log.syslog
-rw-r--r-- sedawk
```

To make the output more readable, let's add spaces between the fields by adding several spaces surrounded by double quotes.

```
# ls -l | gawk '{ print $1 "      " $9 }'
total
-rw-------      anaconda-ks.cfg
drwxr-xr-x      Desktop
-rw-r--r--      install.log
-rw-r--r--      install.log.syslog
-rw-r--r--      sedawk
```

In the following illustration, we replace the spaces with a tab.

```
# ls -l | gawk '{ print "The file "$9" has the permissions " $1 }'
The file  has the permissions total
The file anaconda-ks.cfg has the permissions -rw-------
The file Desktop has the permissions drwxr-xr-x
The file install.log has the permissions -rw-r--r--
The file install.log.syslog has the permissions -rw-r--r--
The file sedawk has the permissions -rw-r--r--
```

Finally, we add descriptive text for clarity.

```
# ls -l | gawk '{ print $1,"\t" $9 }'
total
-rw-------       anaconda-ks.cfg
drwxr-xr-x       Desktop
-rw-r--r--       install.log
-rw-r--r--       install.log.syslog
-rw-r--r--       sedawk
```

Filtering the Content of a File

In the following example, we extract information from the file */etc/passwd* and create formatted output. Notice the **-F** option is used to specify the colon (:) character as a delimiter.

```
#  gawk -F: '{ print "The user "$1 " has a userid of " $3"." }' /etc/passwd
The user root has a userid of 0.
The user bin has a userid of 1.
The user daemon has a userid of 2.
The user adm has a userid of 3.
The user lp has a userid of 4.
The user sync has a userid of 5.
The user shutdown has a userid of 6.
The user halt has a userid of 7.
```

The remainder of the examples use the file *sedawk* (shown next) as a data source.

```
Jane    F    14    Algebra    90
George  M    13    French     88
Angela  F    14    Algebra    78
Jane    F    14    French     75
Bruce   M    15    Algebra    62
Bruce   M    15    French     89
George  M    13    Algebra    55
Angela  F    14    French     92
```

NOTE The *sedawk* file is available in the directory */LABS/Chapter_13/source.*

In the following example, we are filtering for all female students (**$2 =="F"**) who have grades greater than 80 ($5 > 80).

```
# cat sedawk | awk '$2 == "F" && $5 > 80 { print $1 " is passing." }'
Jane is passing.
Angela is passing.
```

In the next example, we are filtering for all students whose name begins with an A or B.

```
# cat sedawk | awk '/^[AB]/ { print $0 }'
Angela  F       14      Algebra 78
Bruce   M       15      Algebra 62
Bruce   M       15      French  89
Angela  F       14      French  92
```

Using a Script File

You can create awk script files and apply them to data. Figure 13-43 is a script file called *sedawkscript.*

Figure 13-43 The file *sedawkscript*

```
BEGIN{
        total_grade_n=0
        print " "
}
        {
        total_grade_n=total_grade_n + $5
        print "In " $4 " "$1 " received " $5
        }

END{
        print " "
        print " "
        print NR " grades were reported."
        print "The average grade is " total_grade_n/NR "."
}
```

Figure 13-44 Using sedawkscript

```
# cat sedawk | sort -k4,4 -k5,5nr | awk -f sedawkscript
Jane has achieved a grade of 90 in Algebra.
Angela has achieved a grade of 78 in Algebra.
Bruce has achieved a grade of 62 in Algebra.
George has achieved a grade of 55 in Algebra.
Angela has achieved a grade of 92 in French.
Bruce has achieved a grade of 89 in French.
George has achieved a grade of 88 in French.
Jane has achieved a grade of 75 in French.
The total number of grades reported equals 8
The average grade equals 78.625
```

NOTE The file *sedawkscript* is available in the directory */LABS/Chapter_13/source.*

The script file is divided into three sections. Each section is enclosed within curly braces (that is, { }). The BEGIN section is used to declare variables. The next section is a set of commands to process, and the END section is used to create a report.

The command **cat sedawk | sort -k4,4 -k5,5nr | awk -f sedawkscript** (see Figure 13-44) will sort the file *sedawk* by class and grade and then filter the result through the awk script (sedawkscript). The report will produce the list of student grades, total number of grades reported, and the average grade.

sort

The sort command is used to sort a field or fields in output. Fields are sorted in the order they are presented on the command line. Table 13-14 describes some of the sort command's options.

The command **ls -l | sort -k 5,5n -k 9,9** (see Figure 13-45) will sort the output of the **ls -l** command on the file's size and then the file's name.

Option	Description
-t <delimiter>	Delimiter.
-n	Numeric sort.
-r	Reverse sort order.
-k	Specifies the field to sort on. Here are some examples: **-k1** or **-k1,1** Sorts on Field 1. **-k 1.3,1.5** Sorts on the third through fifth character in Field 1.

Table 13-14 The sort Command Options

Figure 13-45 Using ls with sort

```
# ls -l | sort -k5,5n -k9,9
total 92
-rw-r--r-- 1 root root   176 Aug  5 16:31 sedawk
-rw-r--r-- 1 root root   236 Aug  5 16:31 sedawkscript
-rw------- 1 root root  1773 Jul 29 18:48 anaconda-ks.cfg
drwxr-xr-x 2 root root  4096 Jul 29 19:17 Desktop
drwxr-xr-x 4 root root  4096 Aug  6 02:08 labs
-rw-r--r-- 1 root root  5894 Jul 29 18:48 install.log.syslog
-rw-r--r-- 1 root root 33583 Jul 29 18:48 install.log
```

Option	Description
-l #	Defines the number of lines allowed per file. The default is 1000 lines.
-b #	Defines the size of each file in bytes.

Table 13-15 The split Command Options

split

The split command will split a large file into smaller pieces. Options used with the split command are explained in Table 13-15. The syntax for the split command is as follows:

split <-l | -b> <input_filename> <output_prefix>

The standard naming convention for the files created by split are *x*aa, *x*ab, *x*ac, and so on. The output prefix would replace the **x** with the argument specified in **<;output_prefix>;**. For example, if the output prefix argument is set to **sp**, the output files would be named *spaa*, *spab*, *spac*, and so on.

head

The command **head <filename>** will print the first 10 lines of a file. The command **head -<n> <filename>** will display the first *n* lines of a file.

tail

The command **tail<filename>** will print the last 10 lines of a file. The command **tail -<n> <filename>** will display the last *n* lines of a file.

uniq

The uniq command reports or omits repeated lines. The syntax is **uniq <options> <input> <output>**. You can use the following options with the uniq command:

- **-d** Only print duplicate lines.
- **-u** Only print unique lines.

For example, suppose our *lastnames* file contained duplicate entries:

```
1 Johnson
1 Johnson
2 Doe
3 Jones
```

You could use the **uniq lastnames** command to remove the duplicate lines. This is shown in the following example:

```
# uniq lastnames
1 Johnson
2 Doe
3 Jones
```

Be aware that the uniq command only works if the duplicate lines are adjacent to each other. If the text stream you need to work with contains duplicate lines that are not adjacent, you can use the sort command to first make them adjacent and then pipe the output to the standard input of uniq.

Finally, let's look at the wc command.

wc

The wc command prints the number of newlines, words, and bytes in a file. The syntax is **wc <options> <filename>**. You can use the following options with the wc command:

- **-c** Print the byte counts.
- **-m** Print the character counts.
- **-l** Print the newline counts.
- **-L** Print the length of the longest line.
- **-w** Print the word counts.

For example, to print all counts and totals for the *firstnames* file, you would use the **wc firstnames** command, as shown in this example:

```
# wc firstnames
 3 6 21 firstnames
```

Let's practice processing text streams in Exercise 13-2.

Exercise 13-2: Processing Text Streams

For this exercise, use the image supplied with the book. Log on as user root using the password root.

Here are the steps to follow:

VIDEO Please watch the Exercise 13-2 video for a demonstration on how to perform this task.

1. Use the command **cd /LABS/Chapter_13/work** to change to the directory that contains the scripts. Directory **/LABS/Chapter_13** also contains a source directory. Those are originals you can copy to the work directory in case of an oops.
2. To display only the file owner, group owner, file size, and filename, use the following command:
   ls -l | cut -d " " -f3,4,5,9
3. Sort the output by file owner and file size:
   ls -l | cut -d " " -f3,4,5,9 | sort -k3 -k9n
4. Save the output of the command in step 3 to *labfile* by executing this command:
   ls -l | cut -d " " -f3,4,5,9 | sort -k3 -k9n >labfile

5. To change the owner name of each file to fred, use the following command:
   sed -n's/root/fred/p' labfile
6. Print the first line of the file *labfile* to determine its structure:
   head -1 labfile
7. Use awk to print "The file <filename> is owned by <owner>" using this command:
   awk '{print "The file " $4 " is owned by " $1}' labfile

Chapter Review

In this chapter, you learned how to create basic shell scripts on a Linux system. You also learned how to use control structures (if and case) to control the flow of a script and how to use loops (while, until, and for) to repeat a series of commands for a specific period.

You also learned how to manipulate text using commands like tr, cut, sed, and awk. Shell scripts are text files that contain a variety of commands that can be used to automate tasks and process information. Here are some key takeaways from this chapter:

- Bash shell scripts should begin with **#!/bin/bash** to specify that the Bash shell should be used to run the script.
- You should include a comment at the beginning of each script that describes what it does.
- You can run shell scripts by using **/bin/bash <script_filename>** or by adding the execute permission to the script file.
- You can read user input in a script using **read <variable_name>** in a script.
- To make your scripts more powerful, you can add branching structures to them.
- Control structures allow you to configure your scripts so that they branch or loop according to conditions you supply.
- To make a script that branches in two directions, you can use an if/then/else structure.
- If the condition you specify in the structure is true, one set of commands (under then) is executed.
- If the condition is false, the commands under the else portion of the structure are executed.
- You can use the test command in an if/then/else structure to test a condition.
- If you want more than two branches in your script, you can use the case structure.
- With a case structure, you can evaluate multiple conditions and execute a series of commands that are executed according to which condition is true.
- You can also use looping control structures within a shell script.
- Looping structures come in three varieties: the while loop, the until loop, and the for loop.

- A while loop executes over and over until a specified condition is no longer true.
- You can also use an until loop in your script.
- An until loop runs over and over as long as the condition is false. As soon as the condition is true, it stops.
- To loop a specific number of times, you can use a for loop.
- It is very common to use the seq command within a for loop to create the sequence of numbers to determine how many times it will loop.
- There are three options for creating a number sequence with seq:
  - If you specify a single value, the sequence starts at 1, increments by one, and ends at the specified value.
  - If you specify two values, the sequence starts at the first value, increments by one, and ends at the second value.
  - If you specify three values, the sequence starts at the first value, increments by the second value, and ends at the third value.
- You can process text streams to manipulate and modify text within a script or within a pipe.
- You can use the following utilities to process a text stream:
  - cut
  - expand
  - unexpand
  - fmt
  - join
  - paste
  - nl
  - od
  - pr
  - sed
  - awk
  - sort
  - split
  - tr
  - uniq
  - wc
- Command substitution allows you to run a command and have its output pasted back on the command line as an argument for another command.

Questions

1. Which of the following elements must be included at the beginning of every shell script?
   - A. #Comment
   - B. #!/bin/bash
   - C. exit 0
   - D. #begin script
2. You've created a shell script named myscript in your home directory. How can you execute it? (Choose two.)
   - A. Enter **/bin/bash ~/myscript** at the shell prompt.
   - B. Enter **myscript** at the shell prompt.
   - C. Select Computer | Run in the graphical desktop; then enter **~/myscript** and select **Run**.
   - D. Enter **run ~/myscript** at the shell prompt.
   - E. Enter **chmod u+x ~/myscript**; then enter **~/myscript** at the shell prompt.
3. Which command will create a new variable named TOTAL and set its type to be "integer"?
   - A. variable -i TOTAL
   - B. declare -i TOTAL
   - C. declare TOTAL -t integer
   - D. TOTAL=integer
4. You need to display the text "Hello world" on the screen from within a shell script. Which command will do this?
   - A. echo "Hello world"
   - B. read Hello world
   - C. writeln "Hello world"
   - D. print "Hello world"
5. From within a shell script, you need to prompt users to enter their phone number. You need to assign the value they enter into a variable named PHONE. Which command will do this?
   - A. read "What is your phone number?" $PHONE
   - B. read $PHONE
   - C. read PHONE
   - D. ? "What is your phone number?" PHONE

6. Which command can be used from within an if/then/else structure to evaluate whether or not a specified condition is true?
   A. eval
   B. ==
   C. test
   D. <>
7. Which command will evaluate to true within an if/then/else structure in a shell script if the variable num1 is less than the variable num2?
   A. eval num1 < num2
   B. test num1 < num2
   C. test num1 -lt num2
   D. test "num1" != "num2"
8. In a shell script, you need to prompt the user to select from one of seven different options presented with the echo command. Which control structure would best evaluate the user's input and run the appropriate set of commands?
   A. A while loop
   B. A for loop
   C. An until loop
   D. if/then/else
   E. case
9. Which control structure will keep processing over and over until a specified condition evaluates to false?
   A. A while loop
   B. A for loop
   C. An until loop
   D. if/then/else
   E. case
10. Which control structures are considered to be branching structures? (Choose two.)
    A. A while loop
    B. A for loop
    C. An until loop
    D. if/then/else
    E. case

11. Which control structure will keep processing over and over as long as the specified condition evaluates to false?
    - **A.** A while loop
    - **B.** A for loop
    - **C.** An until loop
    - **D.** if/then/else
    - **E.** case
12. Which control structure will process a specified number of times?
    - **A.** A while loop
    - **B.** A for loop
    - **C.** An until loop
    - **D.** if/then/else
    - **E.** case
13. Consider the following use of the seq command: **seq 3 9**. What sequence of numbers will this command generate?
    - **A.** 3, 4, 5, 6, 7, 8, 9
    - **B.** 3, 6, 9
    - **C.** 1, 4, 7, 10, 13, 16, 19, 22, 25
    - **D.** 9, 18, 27
14. Which command can be used to print columns or fields that you specify from a file to the standard output using the tab character as a delimiter?
    - **A.** cut
    - **B.** pr
    - **C.** fmt
    - **D.** sort
15. Which command can be used to process a text stream and remove all instances of the tab character and replace them with eight spaces?
    - **A.** cut
    - **B.** replace -t 8
    - **C.** expand
    - **D.** unexpand

16. Which command can process a file or text stream and add a number to the beginning of each new line?
    A. join
    B. paste
    C. fmt
    D. nl
17. The first column of the file *logfile.txt* contains last names. Which commands will sort the file by last names? (Choose two.)
    A. sort < logfile.txt
    B. sort logfile.txt
    C. sort < logfile.txt -o "screen"
    D. sort < logfile.txt > screen
    E. sort -n logfile.txt
    F. cat /var/log/messages | awk 'syslog {print 6,7,8}'
18. You need to search for and replace the word "June" with the word "July" in a file named *proj_sched.txt* in your home directory and send the output to a new file named *new_proj_sched.txt*. Which command will do this?
    A. cat ~/proj_sched.txt | sed s/June/July/
    B. cat ~/proj_sched.txt | awk s/June/July/
    C. cat ~/proj_sched.txt | awk s/June/July/ 1> new_proj_sched.txt
    D. cat ~/proj_sched.txt | sed s/June/July/ 1> new_proj_sched.txt

Answers

1. **B.** The **#!/bin/bash** element must be included at the beginning of every Bash shell script.
2. **A, E.** You can enter **/bin/bash ~/myscript** or **chmod u+x ~/myscript** to make the script execute.
3. **B.** The **declare -i TOTAL** command will create the TOTAL variable and type it as integer.
4. **A.** The **echo "Hello world"** command will display the text "Hello world" on the screen from within a shell script.
5. **C.** The **read PHONE** command in a shell script will assign the value entered by the user into a variable named $PHONE.
6. **C.** The **test** command can be used from within an if/then/else structure to evaluate whether or not a specified condition is true.

7. **C.** The **test num1 -lt num2** command will evaluate to true within an if/then/else structure if the variable num1 is less than the variable num2.
8. **E.** The case structure is the best option presented to evaluate the user's choice of multiple selections and run the appropriate set of commands as a result.
9. **A.** A while loop will keep processing over and over until the specified condition evaluates to false.
10. **D, E.** The if/then/else and case structures are considered to be branching structures because they branch the script in one of several directions based on how a specified condition evaluates.
11. **C.** The until loop control structure will keep processing over and over as long as the specified condition evaluates to false.
12. **B.** The for loop control structure will process a specified number of times.
13. **A.** The **seq 3 9** command will generate the following sequence of numbers: 3, 4, 5, 6, 7, 8, 9. The first number specifies the starting number, and the second number specifies the ending number in the sequence. Because an increment is not specified, the sequence increments by one.
14. **A.** The **cut** command can be used to print columns or fields that you specify from a file to the standard output using the tab character as a delimiter.
15. **C.** The **expand** command can be used to process a text stream and remove all instances of the tab character and replace them with eight spaces.
16. **D.** The **nl** command can be used to process a file or text stream and add a number to the beginning of each new line.
17. **A, B.** The **sort < logfile.txt** command and the **sort logfile.txt** command will both send the contents of the *logfile.txt* file to the sort command to sort its lines alphabetically and display them on the screen.
18. **D.** The **cat ~/proj_sched.txt | sed s/June/July/ 1> new_proj_sched.txt** command will search the *proj_sched.txt* file for the word "June" and replace all instances with the word "July." The output from sed will be written to a file named *new_proj_sched.txt*.

CHAPTER 14

Managing Linux Network Settings

In this chapter, you will learn about

- Understanding IP networks
- Configuring network addressing parameters
- Troubleshooting network problems
- Understanding network-based filesystems

Up to this point in the book, we have focused on configuring and using Linux as a stand-alone computer system. However, Linux can also be configured to function in a networked environment. Unlike many operating systems, Linux was designed from the ground up with networking in mind.

One of Linux's greatest features is that most any distribution can be configured to fill a wide variety of roles on the network—all for little or no cost. For example, one can configure a Linux system as any of the following:

- A networked workstation
- A secure shell (SSH), file and print server
- A database server
- A Dynamic Host Configuration Protocol (DHCP) server
- A Domain Name System (DNS) name server
- A web and network time protocol (NTP) server
- An e-mail and virtual private networking (VPN) server
- A load balancing, clustering, or containers server
- A domain controller, logging, monitoring, and authentication server
- A Lightweight Directory Access Protocol (LDAP) directory server
- A gateway router and proxy server
- A packet-filtering, stateful, or application-level firewall
- A certificate authority (CA) server

With most other operating systems, one has to pay lots of money to get these additional functionalities. In this chapter, we focus on enabling basic networking on your Linux system as well as how to set up a variety of Linux services.

EXAM TIP As a candidate, you should be very comfortable with Linux networking basics before taking your Linux+ exam. The exam assumes you have a solid understanding of the Internet Protocol (IP). Be sure to understand how IP addressing works with both IPv4 and IPv6. You should be able to look at an IP address and identify it as Class A, B, or C. Also be certain to know what the DNS server and default gateway router addresses are used for when configuring network settings on a Linux system.

Knowledge of the ifconfig and ip commands to manage the network interfaces installed in your system is important, as is knowledge of how to use commands such as dig, ping, netstat, and traceroute to verify your network configuration.

Understanding IP Networks

For the Linux+ exam, you need be proficient with the IP protocol (both versions 4 and 6) and know how to configure the protocol such that a system can participate on the network. A brief review of IP addressing and protocols follow:

- What is a protocol?
- How IPv4 addresses work
- How IPv4 subnet masks work
- Specifying the DNS server and default gateway router addresses
- Using IPv6

What Is a Protocol?

So what exactly is a protocol? Strictly speaking, a *protocol* is a set of rules, and, in the context of networking, a protocol is the set of rules that govern communication between two systems. A good analogy for a protocol is a human language. Before two people can communicate, they must speak the same language; otherwise, no information can be transferred between them.

For the Linux+ exam, you need to be familiar with the IP protocol, which is the networking protocol used on the Internet. IP works in conjunction with other protocols, such as the Transmission Control Protocol (TCP), the User Datagram Protocol (UDP), and the Internet Control Message Protocol (ICMP), to be discussed shortly.

NOTE The two versions of the IP protocol are called IPv4 and IPv6. We are going to discuss IPv4 first in this chapter and later explore IPv6.

To understand the TCP/IP protocol, you need to understand the OSI Reference Model. The OSI Reference Model was designed by delegates from major computer and telecom companies back in 1983. The goal was to design a network communications model that was modular so that products from different vendors could interoperate. Prior to this, networking solutions tended to be proprietary, forcing implementers to purchase all of their components from the same vendor. By defining the OSI Reference Model, the industry created a standard that allows administrators to pick and choose components from a variety of vendors.

The OSI Reference Model divides the communication process between two hosts into seven layers, as shown in Figure 14-1.

These layers break down the overall communication process into specific tasks. Information flows down through the layers on the sending system and then is transmitted on the network medium. The information then flows up the layers on the receiving side.

The OSI Reference Model layers are defined as follows:

- **Layer 1: Physical** Defines electrical formats between hosts. Devices include cables and hubs.
- **Layer 2: Data Link** Defines rules to access the Physical layer. Information received is organized into *datagrams*. Devices include switches and bridges.
- **Layer 3: Network** Enables the routing of the data to outside networks. Both IP and ICMP operate at this layer. Devices include routers and stateless firewalls.
- **Layer 4: Transport** Ensures *packet* integrity and reliability. TCP and UDP operate at this layer. Devices include packet filter firewalls.
- **Layer 5: Session** Responsible for maintaining connections between network hosts called *sessions*. Devices include stateful firewalls.

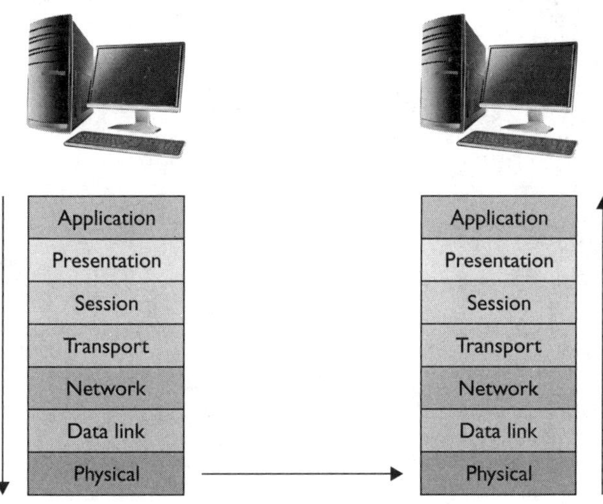

Figure 14-1 The OSI Reference Model

- **Layer 6: Presentation** Responsible for ensuring that data is formatted and presented correctly. Most compression and encryption occur here.
- **Layer 7: Application** Where "apps" or applications such as FTP, SMTP, SSH, and Telnet operate. Devices include Application layer firewalls.

The Internet Protocol itself is used only to make sure each packet arrives at the destination system and to reassemble and resequence it when it arrives at the destination system. This is shown in Figure 14-2.

TCP is one of the two original components of the IP protocol suite and provides a guaranteed connection, whereas UDP is considered *connectionless* because verification of packets reaching their final destination is not done.

Using TCP is like using signature confirmation with a shipping company. When one sends a package, the shipper requires the receiver to sign for the package, allowing the sender to verify that the package was received correctly.

TCP is used by applications that require a high degree of data integrity, including web servers, e-mail servers, FTP servers, and so on. With UDP, packets are sent unacknowledged. It assumes that error checking and correction are either not necessary or will be performed by the application, thus avoiding the processing overhead of TCP.

UDP is similar to sending a postcard through the mail. Essentially, the sender assumes that the mail carrier is reasonably reliable and that the data on the postcard is not important enough to require the receiver to sign for it. Some applications that make use of UDP include the following:

- Streaming audio and video
- VoIP

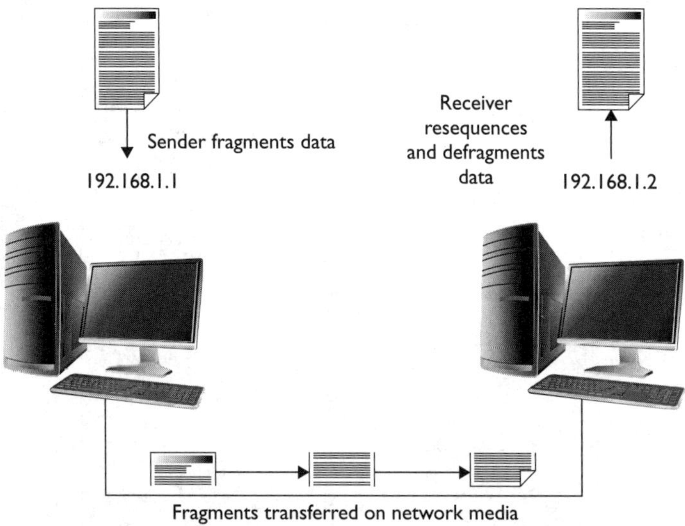

Figure 14-2 Transferring data with the IP protocol

ICMP is another core protocol in the Internet Protocol suite. It differs in purpose from TCP and UDP, which are transport protocols. The primary role of ICMP is to test and verify network communications between hosts. Commands that use the ICMP protocol are ping and traceroute.

For example, to test network connectivity, the ping utility will send ICMP Echo Request packets to a remote host. If the host receives them, it will respond to the sender, which verifies a successful connection. The traceroute utility is used to trace the router used by a packet from source to destination.

For the Linux+ exam, you are required to understand the concept of IP ports, provided at the Transport layer. Ports allow a single host with a single IP address to provide multiple network services. Each service uses the same IP address but operates using a different port number.

For example, assume a network server with an IP address of 192.168.1.1. This system could be configured as both a web server and an FTP server, running at the same time. Each service will listen for requests. The web server listens on port 80, and the FTP server listens on ports 20 and 21. Therefore, requests sent to port 80 are handled by the web service, and data sent to ports 20 and 21 is handled by the FTP daemon.

NOTE The FTP service is somewhat unique in that it uses two ports. One is for the control connection (port 21) and the other (port 20) is for transferring data.

Port numbers can range from 0 to 65536. The way these ports are used is regulated by the Internet Corporation for Assigned Names and Numbers (ICANN). IP ports are lumped into three different categories:

- **Well-known ports** Reserved for specific services, well-known ports are those numbered from 0 to 1023. Here are some examples:
  - Ports 20 and 21: FTP
  - Port 22: Secure Shell (SSH, SCP, SFTP, STelnet)
  - Port 23: Telnet
  - Port 25: SMTP
  - Port 53: DNS
  - Port 80: HTTP
  - Port 110: POP3
  - Port 123: NTP (time synchronization)
  - Ports 137, 138, and 139: NetBIOS
  - Port 143: IMAP
  - Port 389: LDAP
  - Port 443: HTTPS
  - Port 514: Syslog remote logging

- **Registered ports** ICANN has reserved ports 1024 through 49151 for special implementations that organizations can apply for.
- **Dynamic ports** Dynamic ports are also called *private ports.* Ports 49152 through 65535 are designated as dynamic ports. They are available for use by any network service. They are frequently used by network services that need to establish a temporary connection.

How IPv4 Addresses Work

Every host on an IP-based network must have a unique IP address. An IP address is a Network layer (3) address that is logically assigned to a network host. Because the IP address is a logical address, it is not permanent.

The IP address is different from the MAC address. The MAC address is a Data Link layer (2) hardware address that is burned into a ROM chip on every network board sold in the world. The MAC address is hard-coded and cannot be changed; theoretically, every MAC address in the world is unique.

NOTE The Address Resolution Protocol (ARP) is used to map IP addresses to MAC addresses. ARP makes local area networks (LANs) faster. To view the current ARP table on your Linux system, simply run arp -a.

An IP address consists of four numbers, separated by periods. In decimal notation, each *octet* must be between 0 and 255. Here are some examples of valid IP addresses:

- 12.34.181.78
- 192.168.1.1
- 246.270.3.8

NOTE IPv4 addresses are sometimes called "dotted quad" addresses. Each number in the address is actually an eight-bit binary number called an *octet.* Because each octet is a binary number, it can be represented as 0's and 1's. For example, the address 192.168.1.1 can be represented in binary form as follows: 11000000.10101000.00000001.00000001

The fastest way to convert from decimal to binary, and vice versa, for the exam is to understand the decimal value of each binary field, as shown in Table 14-1. Note thc only values that become part of the conversion to decimal are those with a 1. Once all the

Field Value	*128*	*64*	*32*	*16*	*8*	*4*	*2*	*1*	**Total**
Binary	1	0	1	0	1	0	1	1	**10101011**
Decimal	128	0	32	0	8	0	2	1	**179**

Table 14-1 Binary-to-Decimal Conversion Calculator

decimal values are determined, take the sum for the final conversion result. For example, use the table to determine the value of each bit in the binary number 10101011.

Therefore, 10101011 = 128 + 0 + 32 + 0 + 8 + 0 + 2 + 1 = 179.

EXAM TIP In the real world, there are subnet calculators to perform these conversions, but you are not allowed to bring a calculator into the exam room.

Some IP addresses are reserved and cannot be assigned to a host. For example, the last octet in a host IP address cannot be the *lowest* subnet value, or 0. This is reserved for the address of the network segment itself that the host resides on. For example, the default network address for the host assigned an IP address of 192.168.1.1 is 192.168.1.0.

In addition, the last octet of an IP address assigned to a host cannot be the *highest* subnet value, or 255. This is reserved for sending a broadcast to all hosts on the segment. In the preceding example, the default broadcast address for a host with an IP address of 192.168.1.1 would be 192.168.1.255.

Every host on an IP-based network must have a *unique* IP address assigned to it. If the host resides on a public network, such as the Internet, it must use a *globally* unique IP address obtained from the IANA. Once an IP address is assigned, no one else in the world can use it on a public network.

This introduces an important problem with IP version 4. The 32-bit addressing standard allows for a maximum of 4,294,967,296 unique addresses. This seemed like a lot of addresses when IPv4 was originally defined. However, today the number of addresses is depleted.

One method to mitigate the shortage of IPv4 addresses is to utilize network address translation (NAT). A NAT router can present a single registered IP address to a *public* network and hide thousands of *private* IP addresses on the network behind it. This is shown in Figure 14-3.

Within each class of IP address are blocks of addresses called *private* or *reserved* IP addresses. These addresses can be used by anyone who wants to use them. This allows administrators to use private addresses on your local network and still be able to connect to public networks, such as the Internet. All traffic from the private network appears to be originating from the registered IP address configured on the public side of the NAT router.

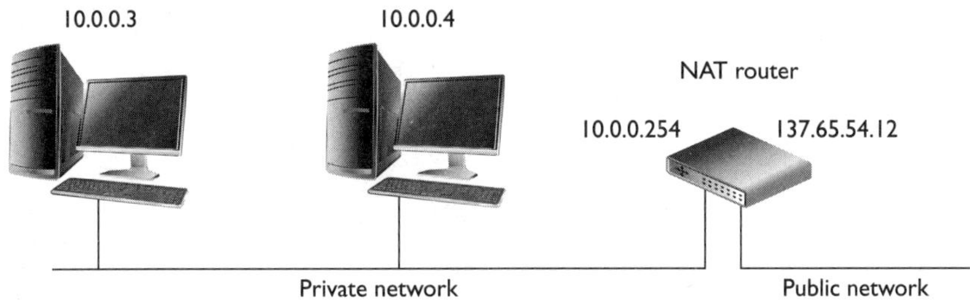

Figure 14-3 Using a NAT router to separate public and private networks

Here are the private IP address ranges:

- 10.0.0.0–10.255.255.255 (Class A)
- 172.16.0.0–172.31.255.255 (Class B)
- 192.168.0.0–192.168.255.255 (Class C)

These are nonroutable addresses, meaning that if you try to use them on a public network, such as the Internet, routers will not forward data to or from them. This allows anyone in the world to use these private IP address ranges without worrying about conflicts.

How IPv4 Subnet Masks Work

When configuring a system with an IP address, you must also assign a *subnet mask*. This parameter defines the network a system belongs to. The IP address is divided into two parts:

- Network address
- Node or host address

Part of an IPv4 address is used to identify the network the host resides on. The rest identifies a specific host (node) on the network. The key point to remember is that every system on the same network segment must have exactly the same numbers in the network portion of the address. However, they each must have a unique node portion. This is shown in Figure 14-4.

How much of the address is used for the network and how much is used for the node is defined by the subnet mask. Default subnet masks are divided into three classes, as defined next, in decimal and binary forms:

	Decimal Notation	Binary Notation
Class A Mask:	255.0.0.0	11111111.00000000.00000000.00000000
Class B Mask:	255.255.0.0	11111111.11111111.00000000.00000000
Class C Mask:	255.255.255.0	11111111.11111111.11111111.00000000

Subnet mask octets with 1's identify the network portion of the IP address, and the 0's define the host portion. For example, an IP address of 192.168.1.1 with a mask of 255.255.255.0 specifies a subnet where the first three octets of the address are the network and the last octet is the node. This is shown in Figure 14-5.

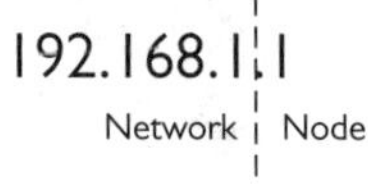

Figure 14-4 Network vs. node in an IP address

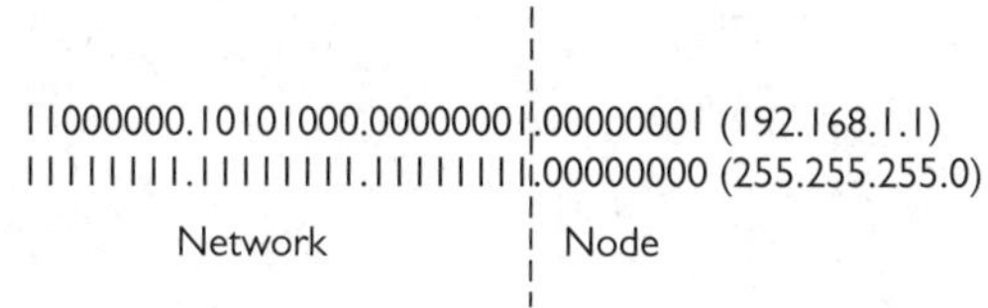

Figure 14-5 Using the subnet mask to define the network and node portions of an IP address

IP addresses are divided into five different classes, with their own default subnet masks. You only need to be concerned with the first three address classes:

- **Class A** The decimal value of the *first octet must be between 1 and 126*. In a Class A address, the first octet is the network address and the last three octets are the node. Class A allows only 126 total possible networks, but offers 16.7 million possible node addresses.
- **Class B** The decimal value of *the first octet must be between 128 and 191*. In a Class B address, the first two octets are the network and the last two octets are the node address. Using Class B addressing allows 16,384 possible networks with 65,534 possible nodes each.
- **Class C** The decimal value of *the first octet must be between 192 and 223*. In a Class C address, the first three octets are the network address, while the last octet is the node address. A huge number of Class C networks are available at 2,097,152. However, only 254 hosts can exist on any given Class C network.

EXAM TIP To calculate the number of hosts per network, count the number of 0's, or *Z*, in the subnet. For example, there are eight 0's in a Class C network. The number of hosts per network, or *N*, is defined as follows:

$N = 2^Z-2$

or

$254 = 2^8 - 2 = 256 - 1$ (the network address) – 1 (the broadcast address)

Subnet masks are often noted using a type of shorthand called *CIDR notation.* This is done by adding a slash (/) and the number of 1's used in the mask after the IP address (for example, 192.168.1.1/24). The /24 parameter indicates 24 bits are used for the subnet mask, which in longhand is 192.168.1.1/11111111.11111111.1111111.00000000, or in decimal is 192.168.1.1/255.255.255.0.

Default subnet masks are not required; for instance, you could define a mask of 255.255.255.0 for a Class A address or anything in between. For example, a subnet mask of 11111111.11111111.11111100.00000000, or a CIDR of 22, or 255.255.252.0 in decimal, is allowed. This results in $N = 2^{10} - 2$, or 1,022 hosts per network. Network administrators perform this type of subnetting because debugging a 1,000-host network is much easier than troubleshooting a network of 16 million hosts.

Network ID	Available Addresses	Broadcast Address
10.0.0.0	10.0.0.1–10.0.3.254	10.0.3.255
10.0.4.0	10.0.4.1–10.0.7.254	10.0.7.255
10.0.8.0	10.0.8.1–10.0.11.254	10.0.11.255
10.0.12.0	10.0.12.1–10.0.15.254	10.0.15.255

Table 14-2 Creating Subnets with a 10-bit Subnet Mask

In this case, for a 10.0.0.0 network, the first subnet would range from

```
00001010.00000000.00000000.00000000 - 00001010.00000000.00000011.11111111
```

or in decimal from 10.0.0.0, the network ID through 10.0.3.255, the broadcast address. Addresses from 10.0.0.1 through 10.0.3.254 are host addresses for the first subnet.

The next subnet would range from

```
00001010.00000000.00000100.00000000 - 00001010.00000000.00000111.11111111
```

or in decimal from 10.0.4.0 (the network ID) through 10.0.7.255 (the broadcast address). Addresses from 10.0.4.1 through 10.0.7.254 are host addresses for the second subnet.

The network administrator would continue assigning host addresses until they run out of systems, or usable IP addresses. In the real world, subnetting calculators exist to complete this process. Two additional examples are shown in Table 14-2 for a subnet of 10.0.0.0/22.

An important point to remember is that in order for two hosts on the same network segment to communicate, they need to have *exactly* the same network address, which means they must have *exactly* the same subnet mask. For example, suppose you have three systems, as shown in Figure 14-6.

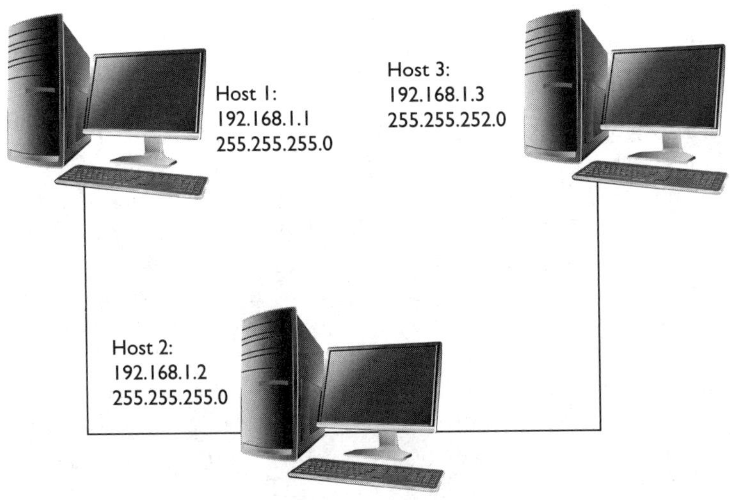

Figure 14-6 Hosts with wrong subnet masks

Host 1 and Host 2 both have the exact same network address and subnet mask, and therefore can communicate on the IP network segment. However, Host 3 uses a subnet mask of 255.255.252.0 instead of 255.255.255.0. Therefore, Host 3 has a different network address than Host 1 and Host 2 and will not be able to communicate with them without the use of a network router.

Configuring Network Addressing Parameters

To install an Ethernet network interface in your system, you need to complete the following tasks:

- Assigning NIC nomenclature
- Configuring IPv4 parameters
- Configuring routing parameters
- Configuring name resolver settings
- Configuring IPv6

Assigning NIC Nomenclature

Linux's systemd uses *predictable network interface names*. One key benefit is that specific aliases can be permanently assigned to specific network interfaces. For example, an onboard network adapter is assigned the index number provided by the BIOS to construct the alias. A commonly assigned alias created using this parameter is eno1, where

- en is the Ethernet interface.
- o1 is the onboard device index number (in this case, device number 1).

At this point, the network interface is loaded and active.

Configuring IPv4 Parameters

Network interfaces can be configured using a non-changing static IP address, or dynamic IP address. Table 14-3 highlights the advantages and disadvantages of each method.

Option	Description	Advantages	Disadvantages
Static address assignment.	Configure a network host with a non-changing IP address.	Great for servers in the network.	The host consumes the address regardless of whether the system is on or off.
Dynamic address assignment.	Linux contacts a DHCP server and assigns an available IP address for a specified *lease* time.	The system engages and gets an IP address. Once it's powered off, the address can be reassigned to others.	You must have a DHCP server installed and configured before you can use this option.

Table 14-3 IP Address Assignment Options

```
root@openSUSE:/
File  Edit  View  Search  Terminal  Help
openSUSE:/ # ifconfig
ens32     Link encap:Ethernet  HWaddr 00:0C:29:B0:9F:B5
          inet addr:10.0.0.83  Bcast:10.0.0.255  Mask:255.255.255.0
          inet6 addr: fe80::20c:29ff:feb0:9fb5/64 Scope:Link
          UP BROADCAST RUNNING MULTICAST  MTU:1500  Metric:1
          RX packets:92 errors:0 dropped:0 overruns:0 frame:0
          TX packets:71 errors:0 dropped:0 overruns:0 carrier:0
          collisions:0 txqueuelen:1000
          RX bytes:13685 (13.3 Kb)  TX bytes:12624 (12.3 Kb)

lo        Link encap:Local Loopback
          inet addr:127.0.0.1  Mask:255.0.0.0
          inet6 addr: ::1/128 Scope:Host
          UP LOOPBACK RUNNING  MTU:65536  Metric:1
          RX packets:8 errors:0 dropped:0 overruns:0 frame:0
          TX packets:8 errors:0 dropped:0 overruns:0 carrier:0
          collisions:0 txqueuelen:0
          RX bytes:544 (544.0 b)  TX bytes:544 (544.0 b)
```

Figure 14-7 Using ifconfig to view network interface information

To statically assign IP address parameters to a Linux system, use the ifconfig command or the newer ip command. Running ifconfig without any options displays the current status of all network interfaces in the system, as shown in Figure 14-7. The iwconfig command performs similarly to ifconfig, but works with wireless networks.

EXAM TIP ifconfig lists multiple interfaces, not just one. The extra interface labeled "lo" is the *loopback* interface and is usually assigned a special IP address of 127.0.0.1. This is a virtual interface, not an actual hardware interface. It is used for network testing, internal communications, diagnostics, and so on.

Notice in Figure 14-7 that two network interfaces are displayed: ens32 and lo. The ens32 interface is the Ethernet network interface installed in the system. The lo interface is the local loopback virtual network interface. This interface is required for many Linux services to run properly.

Another utility you can use to manage IP addressing on a Linux system is the newer ip command. Practice using this command because it may supersede ifconfig, route, and others because it can also manage IPv6. This command is also available on Windows, Chrome, and Macintosh computers. To view the current configuration, enter **ip addr show** at the shell prompt, as shown here:

```
[root@localhost ~]# ip addr show
1: lo: <LOOPBACK,UP,LOWER_UP> mtu 65536 qdisc noqueue state UNKNOWN
   link/loopback 00:00:00:00:00:00 brd 00:00:00:00:00:00
   inet 127.0.0.1/8 brd 127.255.255.255 scope host lo
      valid_lft forever preferred_lft forever
   inet6 ::1/128 scope host
      valid_lft forever preferred_lft forever
```

```
2: ens32: <BROADCAST,MULTICAST,UP,LOWER_UP> mtu 1500 qdisc pfifo_fast
state UP qlen 1000
   link/ether 00:0c:29:b0:9f:b5 brd ff:ff:ff:ff:ff:ff
   inet 10.0.0.83/24 brd 10.0.0.255 scope global ens32
      valid_lft forever preferred_lft forever
   inet6 fe80::20c:29ff:feb0:9fb5/64 scope link
      valid_lft forever preferred_lft forever
```

EXAM TIP The **ethtool** command allows administrators to list and alter the hardware settings of the network card.

Some of the more important parameters include those shown in Table 14-4.

To use the ip command to configure IP addressing parameters, enter **ip addr add <ip_address> dev <interface>** at the shell prompt. For example, to set the IP address assigned to the ens32 network interface to 10.0.0.84, enter the following:

[root@localhost ~]# **ip addr add 10.0.0.84 dev ens32**

NOTE The actual ip commands allow shortening the options, so
ip address add 10.0.0.84 dev ens32
and even
ip a a 10.0.0.84 dev ens32
are possible ways to run the command and get the same results.

To remove an IP address from an interface, just enter **ip addr del <ip_address> dev <interface>** at the shell prompt.

The ip command can also disable and enable a network interface. To disable an interface, enter **ip link set <interface> down** at the shell prompt. To bring a disabled interface back online, enter **ip link set <interface> up** at the shell prompt. Also, **systemctl** can restart the network interface. To do this, simply enter **systemctl restart network** on a Red Hat strain system, or **systemctl restart networking** on a Debian strain system.

This IP address assignment is not persistent. It will be lost on reboot. To make it persistent, configure the file */etc/sysconfig/network-scripts/ifcfg-ens32* on this CentOS system. Sample parameters for this interface are shown here:

```
[root@localhost ~]# cat /etc/sysconfig/network-scripts/ifcfg-ens32
BOOTPROTO='dhcp'
NAME='ens32'
NETMASK=''
NETWORK=''
```

ip addr Parameter	Description
link	The MAC address of the network board
inet	The IPv4 address/mask assigned to the interface
inet6	The IPv6 address/mask assigned to the interface
brd	The broadcast address of the network segment

Table 14-4 ip addr show Output

Option	Description	Other Possible Values
BOOTPROTO="static"	This option specifies that the interface use a static IP address assignment.	Set to dhcp to dynamically assign an address.
IPADDR="192.168.1.81"	Assigns an IP address of 192.168.1.10 to the interface with a subnet mask of 255.255.255.0.	
NETMASK="255.255.255.0"	Assigns the NETMASK to CIDR /24.	
BROADCAST="192.168.1.255"	Specifies the broadcast address.	

Table 14-5 Configuring Persistent Parameters for a Network Interface

Some other options available in this configuration file are listed in Table 14-5.

The lines for IPADDR, NETMASK, NETWORK, and BROADCAST are not required if BOOTPROTO is set to "dhcp."

If the system DHCP leases are too short from the DHCP server, at the DHCP server, modify the */etc/dhcpd.conf* file. Modify the max-lease-time variable to obtain longer lease times.

EXAM TIP The */etc/hostname* file configures the Linux system's hostname and can be made persistent by using the hostnamectl command. Here's an example:
[root@localhost ~]# **hostnamectl set-hostname server-one**

The final network utility is the NetworkManager daemon, which has two interface utilities: nmtui and nmcli. The **nmtui** command provides a curses-based text-user interface with NetworkManager, as shown in Figure 14-8. The nmcli command is used to create, display, edit, delete, activate, and deactivate network connections with a command-line interface. What's great about both of these tools is that *they will update the network related configuration files automatically!* To view the existing network connections, simply enter nmcli con or just **nmcli**, as shown here:

```
[root@localhost ~]# nmcli
ens32: connected to Wired connection 1
     "Intel 82540EM Gigabit Ethernet Controller (PRO/1000 MT Desktop Adapter)"
     ethernet (e1000), 08:00:27:6B:12:8C, hw, mtu 1500
     ip4 default
     inet4 10.0.2.15/24
     route4 169.254.0.0/16
     inet6 fe80::a00:27ff:fe6b:128c/64

lo: unmanaged
     loopback (unknown), 00:00:00:00:00:00, sw, mtu 65536

DNS configuration:
     servers: 10.153.10.100 10.153.10.103
     interface: ens32
```

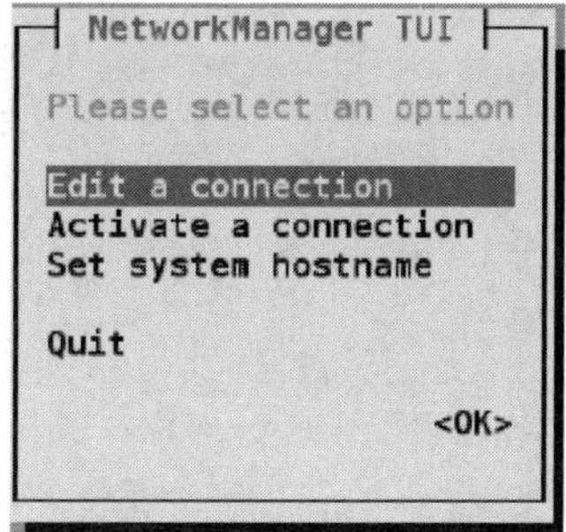

Figure 14-8 nmtui main screen

To determine the IP address of the ens32 connection, use the show option to nmcli:

```
[root@localhost ~]# nmcli con show ens32 | grep IP4.ADDRESS
IP4.ADDRESS[1]:                10.0.2.15/24
```

To add an IP address alias on the ens32 connection, use the modify option to nmcli and then activate the connection with the up option:

```
[root@localhost ~]# nmcli con modify ens32 +ipv4.addresses 10.0.2.14/24
[root@localhost ~]# nmcli con up ens32
Connection successfully activated
```

Again, use modify to remove the alias:

```
[root@localhost ~]# nmcli con modify ens32 -ipv4.addresses 10.0.2.14/24
[root@localhost ~]# nmcli con up ens32
Connection successfully activated
```

If the BOOTPROTO option is defined as DHCP, and the DHCP server happens to be down when a request for an IP address is made, it is not necessary to reboot. Simply run dhclient at the shell prompt after the DHCP server is available. To acquire an address for a specific interface enter **dhclient <interface>**. For example, **dhclient ens32** specifies that the interface get its IP address from the DHCP server. This is shown in Figure 14-9.

```
root@openSUSE:/
File  Edit  View  Search  Terminal  Help
openSUSE:/ # dhclient ens32 -v
Internet Systems Consortium DHCP Client 4.2.5-P1
Copyright 2004-2013 Internet Systems Consortium.
All rights reserved.
For info, please visit https://www.isc.org/software/dhcp/

Listening on LPF/ens32/00:0c:29:b0:9f:b5
Sending on   LPF/ens32/00:0c:29:b0:9f:b5
Sending on   Socket/fallback
DHCPDISCOVER on ens32 to 255.255.255.255 port 67 interval 3
DHCPOFFER from 10.0.0.1
DHCPREQUEST on ens32 to 255.255.255.255 port 67
DHCPACK from 10.0.0.1
bound to 10.0.0.83 -- renewal in 41783 seconds.
```

Figure 14-9 Using dhclient to obtain an IP address lease

Exercise 14-1: Working with Network Interfaces

In Exercise 14-1, you practice using the ifconfig command to manage your network interface. You can perform this exercise using the CentOS virtual machine that comes with this book.

VIDEO Please watch the Exercise 14-1 video for a demonstration on how to perform this task.

Complete the following:

1. Boot your Linux system and log in as your student1 user.
2. Open a terminal session.
3. Switch to your root user account by entering **su -** followed by the password.
4. At the shell prompt, enter **ip addr show**. Record the following information about your Ethernet interface:
    - MAC address
    - IP address
    - Broadcast address
    - Subnet mask
5. At the shell prompt, use the cd command to change to the */etc/sysconfig/network-scripts* directory.
6. Use the ls command to identify the configuration file for your network board.
7. Use the cat command to view the contents of the configuration file for your Ethernet network interface board.
8. Bring your interface down by entering ip link set **<interface_name>** down at the shell prompt.
9. Bring your interface back up by entering ip link set **<interface_name>** up at the shell prompt.
10. Change the IP address assigned to your Ethernet network interface to 192.168.1.100 by entering ip addr add 192.168.1.100 dev **<interface_name>** at the shell prompt.
11. Enter **ip addr show** again and verify that the change was applied.
12. Use the **ip addr show** command again to change your IP configuration parameters back to their original values.
13. If you have a DHCP server on your network segment, modify your network interface configuration to use DHCP and then dynamically assign an IP address to your Ethernet board by entering **dhclient <interface_name>** at the shell prompt.

Configuring Routing Parameters

Within the IP protocol, routers do just what their name implies: they route data across multiple networks to deliver information to a destination. Routers operate at the Network layer and are used to connect various networks together.

Routers are usually implemented in conjunction with a gateway and need to be defined when setting a static network. The router hardware itself may be as simple as a computer system with two NICs installed, or it may be a specialized hardware appliance dedicated to routing.

Routers determine the best way to get data to the right destination by maintaining a routing table of available routes. Routers use an algorithm that evaluates distance, congestion, and network status to determine the best route to the destination. Even if not configured as a router, every Linux system maintains a routing table in RAM to determine where to send data on a network.

To configure the default router address on a Red Hat class system, update the */etc/sysconfig/network-scripts/ifcfg-<interface>* file with the GATEWAY parameter, as shown here:

```
[root@localhost ~]# tail -7 /etc/sysconfig/network-scripts/ifcfg-ens32
DEVICE=ens32
BOOTPROTO=static
ONBOOT=yes
IPADDR=192.168.1.81
NETMASK=255.255.255.0
BROADCAST=192.168.1.255
GATEWAY=192.168.1.1
```

To configure the default router address on a Debian class system, update the */etc/default/interfaces* file and add a line for the gateway, as shown here:

```
[root@localhost ~]# tail -7 /etc/network/interfaces
auto ens32
iface ens32 inet static
       address 192.168.1.81
       netmask 255.255.255.0
       broadcast 192.168.1.255
       ## default gateway for ens32
       gateway 192.168.1.1
```

NOTE Use IP addresses, not hostnames, in this file. If the DNS server were to go down or become unreachable, routing would be disabled.

After adding the gateway settings, simply restart the network, as shown here:

```
[root@localhost ~]# systemctl restart network
```

For the CompTIA Linux+ exam, you need be familiar with how to manage routes with the route command at the shell prompt. Use the route command to display or modify the routing table on the Linux host. If you enter route without options, it simply displays the current routing table, as shown in this example:

```
[root@localhost ~]# route
Kernel IP routing table
Destination     Gateway         Genmask         Flags Metric Ref    Use Iface
default         10.0.0.1        0.0.0.0         UG    0      0        0 ens32
10.0.0.0        *               255.255.255.0   U     0      0        0 ens32
loopback        *               255.0.0.0       U     0      0        0 lo
```

Note that the default gateway is 10.0.0.1 because it is listed under the Gateway setting, and the "G" is shown under Flags (the "U" means that the connection is "up").

You can add routes to the host's routing table by entering **route add -net <network_address> netmask <netmask> gw <router_address>**. For example, suppose you need to add a route to the 192.168.2.0/24 network through the router with an IP address of 10.0.0.254. In this case, you would enter the following:

```
[root@localhost ~]# route add -net 192.168.2.0/24 gw 10.0.0.254
```

To remove existing routes, use **route del -net <network_address> netmask <netmask> gw <router_address>**. Here's an example:

```
[root@localhost ~]# route del -net 192.168.2.0/24 gw 10.0.0.254
```

Finally, to set the default route, enter **route add default gw <router_address>** at the shell prompt. For example, if you want to add 10.0.0.254 as your default gateway router, enter this:

```
[root@localhost ~]# route add default gw 10.0.0.254
```

NOTE Changes made with the route or ip route command are not persistent and are lost on reboot.

The ip command can also be used to manage routing. For example, to view the routing table, enter **ip route show** or simply **ip route** at the shell prompt, as shown here:

```
[root@localhost ~]# ip route
default via 10.0.0.1 dev ens32
10.0.0.0/24 dev ens32  proto kernel  scope link  src 10.0.0.83
127.0.0.0/8 dev lo  scope link
```

To add a static route to the routing table, enter **ip route add <network/prefix> via <router_ip_address> dev <interface>** at the shell prompt. The following example shows adding route 10.0.0.254 to the 192.168.5.0/24 network:

```
[root@localhost ~]# ip route add 192.168.5.0/24 via 10.0.0.254 dev ens32
[root@localhost ~]# ip route show
default via 10.0.0.1 dev ens32
10.0.0.0/24 dev ens32  proto kernel  scope link  src 10.0.0.83
127.0.0.0/8 dev lo  scope link
192.168.5.0/24 via 10.0.0.254 dev ens32
```

To remove a route from the routing table, enter **ip route del <network/prefix>** at the shell prompt. For example, to remove the 192.168.5.0/24 route, enter the following:

```
[root@localhost ~]# ip route del 192.168.5.0/24
```

Configuring Name Resolver Settings

When one opens a browser window and enters http://www.google.com in the URL field, the browser, IP stack, and operating system have no clue where to go to get the requested information. To make this work, the local system needs to first resolve the domain name into an IP address.

In the old days, basic hostname-to-IP-address resolution was performed by the */etc/hosts* file, which contains IP-address-to-hostname mappings.

NOTE The */etc/hosts* file still exists on Linux systems. In fact, it is the first name resolver used by default. Only if a record for the requested domain name does not exist in the *hosts* file will the operating system then try to resolve the hostname using DNS. Because of this, it is important to manage the *hosts* file very carefully. Many network hacks exploit this function of the operating system. A malicious website or malware may try to rewrite the */etc/hosts* file with name mappings that point to fake websites on the Internet that look like popular auction or banking sites but instead are elaborate pharming websites designed to steal the user's personal information.

The *hosts* file contains one line per host record. The syntax is

```
<IP_address>  <host_name>  <alias>
```

For example, consider the following *hosts* file entry:

```
192.168.1.1      mylinux.mydom.com      mylinux
```

This record resolves either the fully qualified DNS name of mylinux.mydom.com or the alias (CNAME) of mylinux to an IP address of 192.168.1.1. Usually this file only contains the IP address and hostname of the local system, but other entries may be added as well.

Using the *hosts* file to resolve hostnames works just fine; however, it really isn't feasible as the sole means of name resolution. The file would have to be huge in order to resolve all the domain names used by hosts on the Internet. In addition, one would have to manually add, remove, and modify hostname mappings in the file whenever a domain name changed on the Internet. What a nightmare!

A better option is to submit the domain name to a DNS server. When a DNS server receives a name resolution request, it matches the domain name submitted with an

IP address and returns it to the requesting system. The system can then contact the specified host using its IP address. Here's how it works:

1. The system needing to resolve a hostname sends a request to the DNS server it has been configured to use on IP port 53. If the DNS server is authoritative for the zone where the requested hostname resides, it responds with the appropriate IP address. If not, the process continues on to step 2.

NOTE A DNS server is considered to be authoritative if it has a record for the domain name being requested in its database of name mappings.

2. The DNS server sends a request to a root-level DNS server. There are 13 root-level DNS servers on the Internet. Every DNS server is automatically configured with the IP addresses of these servers. These root-level DNS servers are configured with records that resolve to authoritative DNS servers for each top-level domain (.com, .gov, .edu, .au, .de, .uk, .ca, and so on).
3. The DNS server responds to the client system with the IP address mapped to the hostname, and the respective system is contacted using this IP address.

NOTE Once this process happens for a particular name mapping, most DNS servers will cache the mapping for a period of time. That way, if a resolution request for the same hostname is received again, they can respond directly to the client without going through this whole process again.

Therefore, to make this system work, the administrator must provide the system with the IP address of the DNS server to use. This is configured in the */etc/resolv.conf* file. This file defines the search prefix and the name servers to use. Here is some sample content from a CentOS system's *resolv.conf* file:

```
search mydom.com
nameserver 8.8.8.8
nameserver 8.8.4.4
nameserver 192.168.2.1
```

As can be seen in this example, the file contains two types of entries:

- **search** Specifies the domain name that should be used to fill out incomplete hostnames. For example, if it's trying to resolve a hostname of WS1, the name will be automatically converted to the fully qualified domain name of WS1.mydom.com. The syntax is **search <domain>**.
- **nameserver** Specifies the IP address of the DNS server to use for name resolution. You can configure up to three DNS servers. If the first server fails or is otherwise unreachable, the next DNS server is used. The syntax is **nameserver <DNS_server_IP_address>**.

Use the */etc/nsswitch.conf* (name service switch) file to define the order in which services will be used for name resolution. Here are two lines of the file you need to be concerned with:

```
hosts:          files dns
networks:       files dns
```

These two entries specify that the */etc/hosts* file (files) is consulted first for name resolution. If there is no applicable entry, the query is then sent to the DNS server (dns) specified in the */etc/resolv.conf* file. To search "dns" first and then "files," change the order within */etc/nsswitch.conf*, as shown here:

```
hosts:          dns files
networks:       dns files
```

TIP Use the dnsdomainname command to show the system's DNS domain name.

Configuring IPv6

As mentioned earlier, the world's supply of registered IP addresses is exhausted. To address this issue, most organizations reduce the number of registered IP addresses that they need by implementing a NAT router. However, using a NAT router is a short-term solution. To fully address this issue, a new version of the IP protocol was released that handles the number of IP addresses the modern computing world needs.

To accomplish this, IP version 6 (IPv6) is rolling out around the world. IPv6 is expected to completely replace IPv4 over the next decade. Instead of 32 bits, IPv6 defines 128-bit IP addresses, which allows for 340,282,366,920,938,463,463,374,607,431,768, 211,456 total unique IP addresses. (Hopefully, this will be enough!)

IPv6 addresses are composed of eight four-character hexadecimal numbers (called *quartets*), separated by colons instead of periods. Each quartet is represented as a hexadecimal number between 0 and FFFF. For example, a valid IPv6 address is 128 bits and appears like 35BC:FA77:4898:DAFC:200C:FBBC:A007:8973.

For an IPv6 address of 1:2:3:a:b:c:d:e, assume each quartet is led by zeros, so this address is the same as 0001:0002:0003:000a:000b:000c:000d:000e.

EXAM TIP Because IPv6 addresses are so long, they will frequently be abbreviated. If the address contains a long string of multiple zeros, omit them by specifying ::. If 0000 occurs more than once in an address, the abbreviation can only be used once. For example, the IPv6 address 2001:0000:3a4c:1115:0000:0000:1a2f:1a2b can be shown as either 2001::3a4c:1115:0000:0000:1a2f:1a2b or 2001:0000:3a4c:1115::1a2f:1a2b.

There are actually several configuration options when it comes to IPv6 addressing. The first is to use static assignment. As with IPv4, static IPv6 address assignments require you to manually assign the entire 128-bit IPv6 address and prefix to the host.

This can be done from the shell prompt using a command-line utility such as ifconfig or ip. Alternatively, you can manually enter the address and prefix in the appropriate interface configuration file in */etc/sysconfig/network* or use nmcli.

The final IPv6 address configuration option is to use DHCP. As with IPv4, IPv6 address assignments can be made automatically using an updated version of DHCP called DHCPv6.

Troubleshooting Network Problems

Getting the network interface installed is only half the battle. To enable communications, you need to use a variety of testing and monitoring tools to make sure the network itself is working properly. You need to understand the following topics to pass the Linux+ exam:

- Using a standardized troubleshooting model
- Using ping
- Using netstat
- Using traceroute
- Using nc
- Using name resolution tools

NOTE If necessary, install these utilities by running the following on CentOS strain systems as root:
yum install nfs-utils nmap-ncat samba-client iproute

Using a Standardized Troubleshooting Model

Being a good troubleshooter is a key part of being an effective Linux system administrator. Some new administrators seem to have an intrinsic sense to troubleshoot problems; others turn five-minute solutions into five-hour puzzles. The reason for this is that troubleshooting is part art form, part science. Just as it is difficult for some to learn to draw, sculpt, or paint, it is also difficult for some to learn to troubleshoot.

There are three keys to troubleshooting effectively:

- Using a solid troubleshooting procedure
- Obtaining a working knowledge of troubleshooting tools
- Gaining a lot of experience troubleshooting problems

The last point is beyond the scope of this book. The only way to gain troubleshooting experience is to spend a couple years in the field. However, we can work with the first two points. In the last part of this chapter, we will focus specifically on troubleshooting network issues. However, the procedure we discuss here can be broadly applied to any system problem.

Many new system administrators make a key mistake when they troubleshoot system or network problems. Instead of using a methodical troubleshooting approach, they start trying to implement fixes before they really know what the problem is. The administrator tries one fix after another, hoping that one of them will repair the problem.

Even though troubleshooting models are not *covered on the Linux+ exam*, here is a suggested troubleshooting model as a starting point for a new systems administrator:

- **Step 1: Gather information**. This is a critical step. Determine exactly what has happened. What are the symptoms and error messages? How extensive is the problem?
- **Step 2: Identify what has changed**. In this step, identify what has changed in the system. Has new software or hardware been installed? Did a user change something?
- **Step 3: Create a hypothesis**. Develop several hypotheses that could explain the problem. Check FAQs and knowledgebases available on the Internet. Consult with peers to validate your hypotheses. Narrow the results down to one or two likely causes.
- **Step 4: Determine the appropriate fix**. Use peers, FAQs, and experience to identify the steps needed to fix the problem. Identify side effects of implementing the fix and account for them. Often, the fix may have side effects that are worse than the original problem.
- **Step 5: Implement the fix**. Note that in this troubleshooting model, much research is done before implementing a fix! This increases the likelihood of success. After implementing the fix, be sure to verify that the fix actually repaired the problem.
- **Step 6: Ensure user satisfaction**. Educate users as to how to keep the problem from reoccurring. Communicate with the users' supervisors and ensure they know that the problem has been fixed.
- **Step 7: Document the solution**. Finally, document the solution. If it occurs again a year later, the team can quickly identify the problem and know how to fix it.

Using this methodology, you can learn to be a very effective troubleshooter, gaining hands-on experience in the real world.

In addition to using a troubleshooting methodology, you also need to know how to use a variety of network troubleshooting tools for your Linux+ exam.

Using ping

The ping utility is one of the handiest tools in the networking virtual toolbox. The ping command is used to test connectivity between hosts on the network. Ping works by sending an ICMP echo request packet from the source system to the destination. The destination system then responds with an ICMP echo response packet. This process is shown in Figure 14-10.

If the ICMP echo response packet is received by the sending system, you know three things:

- Your network interface is working correctly.
- The destination system is up and working correctly.
- The network hardware between your system and the destination system is working correctly.

CAUTION Be warned that many host-based firewalls used by many operating systems are configured by default to not respond to ICMP echo request packets. This is done to prevent a variety of denial of service (DoS) attacks that utilize a flood of ping requests. This configuration can give the false impression that the destination system is down.

The basic syntax for using ping is **ping <destination_IP_address>**. This causes ICMP echo request packets to be sent to the specified host. For example, enter **ping 192.168.2.1** to test a host with this address. This is shown in Figure 14-11.

Notice in Figure 14-11 that the results of each ping sent are shown on a single line. Each line displays the size of the echo response packet (64 bytes), where it came from (192.168.2.1), its time-to-live value (63), and the round-trip time (4.25 ms to 1.01 ms).

NOTE The time-to-live (TTL) value specifies the number of routers the packet is allowed to cross before being thrown away.

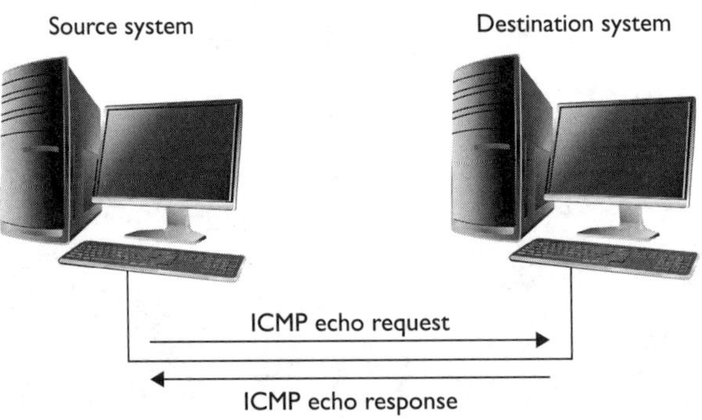

Figure 14-10 Using ping

```
root@openSUSE:/
File  Edit  View  Search  Terminal  Help
openSUSE:/ # ping 192.168.2.1
PING 192.168.2.1 (192.168.2.1) 56(84) bytes of data.
64 bytes from 192.168.2.1: icmp_seq=1 ttl=63 time=4.25 ms
64 bytes from 192.168.2.1: icmp_seq=2 ttl=63 time=2.52 ms
64 bytes from 192.168.2.1: icmp_seq=3 ttl=63 time=1.01 ms
64 bytes from 192.168.2.1: icmp_seq=4 ttl=63 time=1.07 ms
64 bytes from 192.168.2.1: icmp_seq=5 ttl=63 time=1.09 ms
```

Figure 14-11 Pinging a host by IP address

By default, the ping utility will continue sending ping requests to the specified host until CTRL-C is pressed to stop it. Use the -c option with the ping command to specify a number of times to ping. For example, enter **ping -c 10 192.168.2.1** to ping 10 times and then exit.

Pinging by hostname is shown in Figure 14-12.

Pinging with a hostname can be a valuable troubleshooting tool because it signals if there is a problem with the DNS server. For example, pinging by IP address works but pinging by hostname does not.

Using netstat

The netstat utility is another powerful tool in the virtual toolbox. This utility can do the following:

- List network connections
- Display the routing table
- Display information about the network interface

The syntax for using netstat is to enter netstat <option> at the shell prompt. Use the options listed in Table 14-6.

EXAM TIP The "show sockets" (ss) command is the replacement command for netstat, but with more functionality to better examine network status. Try running the command **ss -neopa** and observe the status from all sockets.

```
root@openSUSE:/
File  Edit  View  Search  Terminal  Help
openSUSE:/ # ping www.google.com
PING www.google.com (74.125.239.144) 56(84) bytes of data.
64 bytes from nuq05s02-in-f16.1e100.net (74.125.239.144): icmp_seq=1 ttl=54 time=30.7 ms
64 bytes from nuq05s02-in-f16.1e100.net (74.125.239.144): icmp_seq=2 ttl=54 time=31.2 ms
64 bytes from nuq05s02-in-f16.1e100.net (74.125.239.144): icmp_seq=3 ttl=54 time=30.9 ms
64 bytes from nuq05s02-in-f16.1e100.net (74.125.239.144): icmp_seq=4 ttl=54 time=31.5 ms
64 bytes from nuq05s02-in-f16.1e100.net (74.125.239.144): icmp_seq=5 ttl=54 time=29.5 ms
```

Figure 14-12 Pinging by hostname

Table 14-6 netstat Options

netstat Option	Description
-a	Lists all listening and non-listening sockets
-i	Displays statistics for your network interfaces
-r	Displays your routing table

Using traceroute

When information is sent to an IP host that does not reside on your local network segment, the packets will be sent to the default gateway router. This router will then use a variety of routing protocols to figure out how to get the packets to the destination. In the process, the packets are transferred from router to router to router to get them there, as shown in Figure 14-13.

This is the advantage of an IP-based network. A network administrator can connect multiple networks together using routers and transfer data between them. The routing protocols used by routers dynamically determine the best route for packets to take based on system load. The route taken can change as network conditions change.

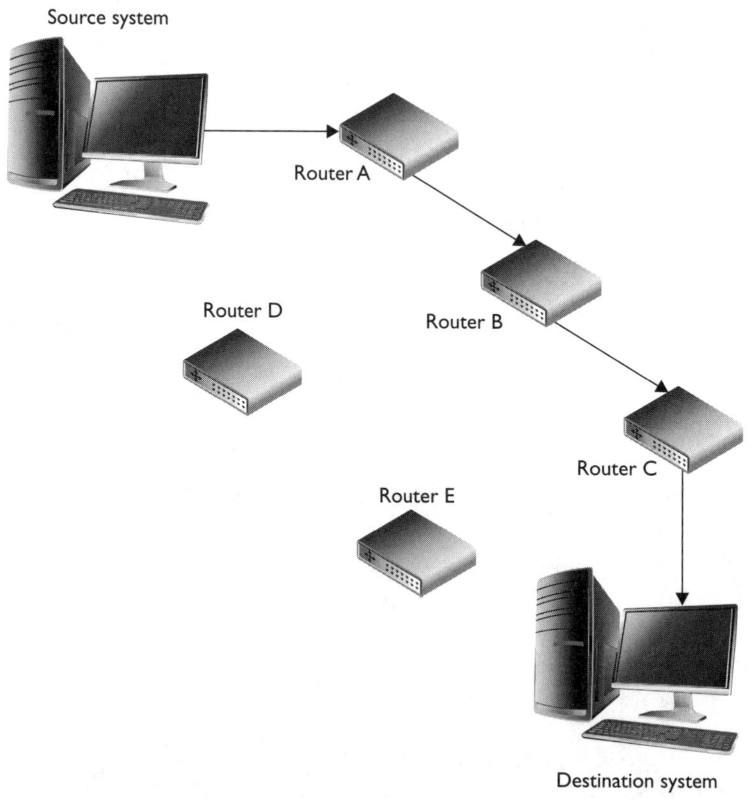

Figure 14-13 Routing in an IP network

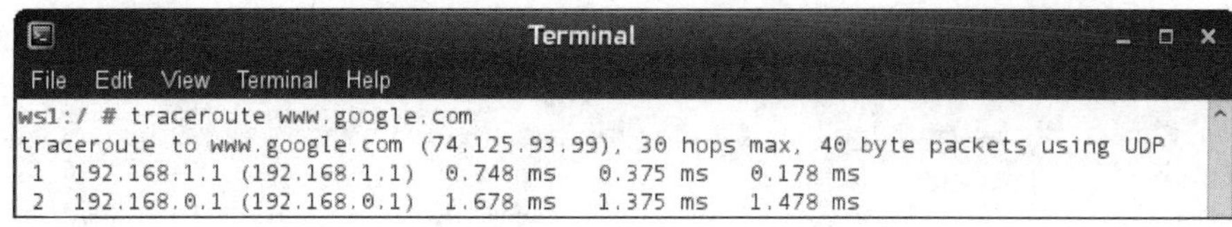

Figure 14-14 Using traceroute

The traceroute utility is used to trace the route a packet traverses through these routers to arrive at its destination. It does this using the same ICMP echo request and ICMP echo response packets used by the ping utility, but it manipulates the TTL parameter of those packets. As a result, an ICMP echo response packet is sent back to the source system from each router the packets cross as they work their way through the network to the destination host, providing a list that shows the route between the source and destination systems.

This utility can be a very useful in troubleshooting communication problems between networks, because it can track down which router is not working correctly. The syntax for using this utility is **traceroute <destination_hostname_or_IP_address>**. The traceroute command creates one line for each router the packets cross as they make their way to the destination. This is shown in Figure 14-14.

As you can see in Figure 14-14, the IP address of the router is displayed along with round-trip time statistics.

The "my traceroute" (**mtr**) command is a network diagnostics tool that combines the functionality of traceroute and ping. To see mtr www.yahoo.com results, see Figure 14-15. The output displays the quality of the connections.

My traceroute

Hostname: www.yahoo.com 1.00 Pause Restart About Quit

Hostname	Loss	Snt	Last	Avg	Best	Worst	StDev
10.0.2.2	0.0%	80	5	1	0	5	0.84
RAC2V1S	1.2%	80	128	50	3	317	74.69
142.254.155.165	0.0%	80	358	62	8	358	78.94
ae63.brfdwifb02h.midwest.rr.com	0.0%	80	331	106	19	917	132.78
be42.gnfdwibb01r.midwest.rr.com	0.0%	80	258	81	13	845	125.56
bu-ether16.chcgildt87w-bcr00.tbone.rr.com	0.0%	80	185	71	15	772	109.61
66.109.5.225	0.0%	80	112	72	14	699	106.61
UNKNOWN-216-115-102-X.yahoo.com	0.0%	80	43	73	13	625	103.62
ae-0.pat2.bfy.yahoo.com	0.0%	80	65	86	27	554	94.03
UNKNOWN-216-115-101-X.yahoo.com	0.0%	80	74	95	38	611	103.03
et-19-1-0.msr2.bf1.yahoo.com	0.0%	80	54	96	39	534	90.32
et-19-0-0.clr2-a-gdc.bf1.yahoo.com	0.0%	80	83	96	39	467	83.36
eth-18-3.bas2-1-flk.bf1.yahoo.com	0.0%	80	162	90	38	505	86.85
media-router-fp1.prod1.media.vip.bf1.yahoo.com	0.0%	79	89	93	39	464	87.15

Figure 14-15 Output of the mtr command

Using nc

The netcat, or nc, command is a very useful tool for testing network communications between hosts. It goes one step beyond the ping command and actually establishes a connection between two network hosts. One way to use this command is to open a listening socket on one host and then connect to that socket from another host. In the following example, the listening socket is enabled using the "dash el" option using port 2388:

```
[root@10.0.0.83 ~]# nc -l 2388
```

With a listening socket established on the server, the client can connect to it using the nc command again, this time entering the IP address of the server and the listening port:

```
[root@fs5 ~]# nc 10.0.0.83 2388
```

Once the connection is established, any text typed at the prompt of the client system will appear on the netcat server, as shown here:

```
[root@fs5 ~]# nc 10.0.0.83 2388
This is a test.
[root@10.0.0.83 ~]# nc -l 2388
This is a test.
```

EXAM TIP Make sure the appropriate ports in the firewalls are open on both systems; otherwise, the test will fail!

Using Name Resolution Tools

Using DNS for name resolution works great—until it doesn't work! Fortunately, there are several tools available to troubleshoot name resolution on a network:

- dig
- host
- nslookup

NOTE To install these utilities, run the following on CentOS strain systems as root: # yum install bind-utils

dig

The Domain Information Groper, or dig, utility performs DNS lookups on the network and displays detailed information about the hostname being resolved from the DNS server, as configured in the */etc/resolv.conf* file. The syntax is **dig <hostname>**, as shown in Figure 14-16.

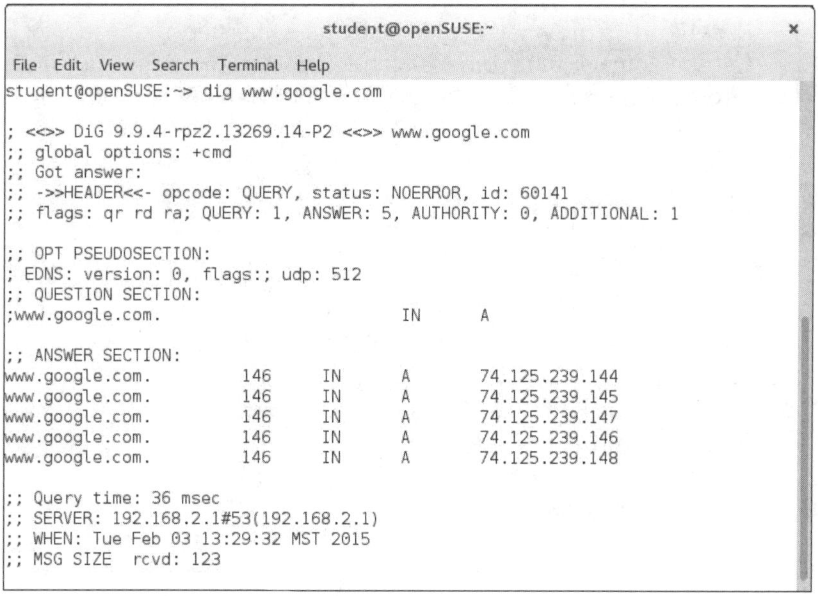

```
student@openSUSE:~
File  Edit  View  Search  Terminal  Help
student@openSUSE:~> dig www.google.com

; <<>> DiG 9.9.4-rpz2.13269.14-P2 <<>> www.google.com
;; global options: +cmd
;; Got answer:
;; ->>HEADER<<- opcode: QUERY, status: NOERROR, id: 60141
;; flags: qr rd ra; QUERY: 1, ANSWER: 5, AUTHORITY: 0, ADDITIONAL: 1

;; OPT PSEUDOSECTION:
; EDNS: version: 0, flags:; udp: 512
;; QUESTION SECTION:
;www.google.com.                IN      A

;; ANSWER SECTION:
www.google.com.         146     IN      A       74.125.239.144
www.google.com.         146     IN      A       74.125.239.145
www.google.com.         146     IN      A       74.125.239.147
www.google.com.         146     IN      A       74.125.239.146
www.google.com.         146     IN      A       74.125.239.148

;; Query time: 36 msec
;; SERVER: 192.168.2.1#53(192.168.2.1)
;; WHEN: Tue Feb 03 13:29:32 MST 2015
;; MSG SIZE  rcvd: 123
```

Figure 14-16 Using dig to resolve a hostname

The output from dig is considerably more extensive than that displayed by other DNS troubleshooting tools such as nslookup and host in that it displays more than just the IP address of the host. It also lists the authoritative name server for the host and zone.

host

The host command resolves hostnames. Whereas the dig command provides extensive name resolution information, host provides simple, quick information. The syntax is similar to that of dig. Enter host <hostname> at the shell prompt. An example of using host is shown here:

```
[root@localhost ~]# host www.google.com
www.google.com has address 74.125.239.49
www.google.com has address 74.125.239.48
www.google.com has address 74.125.239.50
www.google.com has address 74.125.239.52
www.google.com has address 74.125.239.51
www.google.com has IPv6 address 2607:f8b0:4005:800::1011
```

nslookup

In addition to host and dig, **nslookup** can test name resolution, as shown here:

```
[root@localhost ~]# nslookup www.google.com
Server:          192.168.1.1
Address:         192.168.1.1#53

Non-authoritative answer:
Name:    www.google.com
Address:  172.217.8.196
```

EXAM TIP Use the whois command to get ownership information of a website domain, if the owner has not blocked it. The command **whois <domain_name>** will list their name, phone number, and address.

Exercise 14-2: Working with Network Commands

In Exercise 14-2, you will practice using network commands to manage and troubleshoot your network interface. This exercise assumes that you have a connection to the Internet. You can perform this exercise using the CentOS virtual machine that comes with this book.

VIDEO Please watch the Exercise 14-2 video for a demonstration on how to perform this task.

Complete the following steps:

1. Boot your Linux system and log in as your student1 user.
2. Open a terminal session.
3. Switch to your root user account by entering **su -** followed by the password.
4. Test connectivity by entering **ping www.google.com** at the shell prompt. Your system should resolve the hostname into an IP address and send ICMP echo request packets to it. (If your system isn't connected to the Internet, this step won't work.)

NOTE If you are unable to ping the remote website, verify that an IP address has been assigned using the ifconfig command. If an address has not been assigned, enter systemctl restart network to reload the network configuration.

5. Display summary information about your network interface by entering **netstat -s | more** at the shell prompt. Review the information displayed.
6. Trace the route to www.google.com by entering **traceroute www.google.com** at the shell prompt. Note the various routers crossed as your packets traverse the Internet to www.google.com.
7. Generate extended name resolution about www.google.com by entering **dig www.google.com** at the shell prompt.

Understanding Network-based Filesystems

There are two network-based filesystems you need to be familiar with for the Linux+ exam:

- Network File System (NFS)
- Samba

NFS allows users to mount network filesystems on vendor-neutral networks. Samba allows Linux systems to mount network filesystems on Windows-based networks. You should understand the basics of accessing these filesystems.

Network File System (NFS)

Most networks allow sharing of filesystems over NFS. In order for NFS to function properly, all systems need to run NFS. For Windows systems, this means installing PC-NFS. NFS Manager is built into macOS.

Once the NFS servers are properly set up, their "shares" are accessible to NFS clients. To view the possible shares, run the showmount command:

```
[root@localhost ~]# showmount -e system5
Export list for system5:
/music
/sales
/users
```

To access a shared NFS directory, use the mount command and the name of the NFS server (system5), as shown:

```
[root@localhost ~]# mkdir /mnt/sys5
[root@localhost ~]# mount -t nfs system5:/sales /mnt/sys5
```

There may be situations where an administrator attempts to mount a network filesystem, but the remote system is down. NFS has a feature called *automounting* to alleviate this issue, which will automatically mount the remote filesystem once it becomes available.

Samba

For organizations that heavily rely on Windows systems, instead of installing PC-NFS on several Windows computers, they could take advantage of the SMB protocol available on Windows networks. Once the Samba server is set up, the shared filesystems are viewable using the smbclient command:

```
[root@localhost ~]# smbclient -L win2 -U jim_angel

Server=[WIN2] User=[JIM_ANGEL] Workgroup=[WORKGROUP] Domain=[]

       Sharename       Type      Comment
       ---------       ----      -------
       ADMIN$          Disk      Remote Admin
       public          Disk      Public

       Music           Disk      Default share
       HPblack         Printer   HPblack
```

To access shared filesystem from Windows, use the mount command preceded by two forward slashes. This signifies that the mount is using SMB. An example follows from a system called win2:

```
[root@localhost ~]# mkdir /mnt/win2
[root@localhost ~]# mount //win2/Music /mnt/win2
```

NOTE Both NFS and Samba allow for shared directories to be available at boot time. Just add the shares to the */etc/fstab* file.

Chapter Review

In this chapter, you learned how to set up networking on a Linux system. You will most likely work with Ethernet network boards and the IP protocol in most modern organizations.

The Internet Protocol (IP) works in conjunction with the Transmission Control Protocol (TCP) or the User Datagram Protocol (UDP) to fragment, transmit, defragment, and resequence network data to enable communications between hosts. We also looked at the Internet Control Message Protocol (ICMP), which is another core protocol in the IP protocol suite. The primary role of ICMP is to test and verify network communications between hosts.

Each host on the network must have a correctly configured, unique IP address assigned to it, and the correct subnet mask assigned. The subnet mask defines how much of a given host's IP address is the network address. When viewed in binary form, any bit in the subnet mask that has a 1 in it represents a network address, and any bit with a 0 in it represents the host address. IP addresses are categorized into the following classes:

- **Class A** 255.0.0.0 = 11111111.00000000.00000000.00000000 binary
- **Class B** 255.255.0.0 = 11111111.11111111.00000000.00000000 binary
- **Class C** 255.255.255.0 = 11111111.11111111.11111111.00000000 binary

Hosts on the same network segment must have the same network address for them to communicate. Therefore, the same subnet mask must be assigned to each host.

To resolve domain names into IP addresses, the Linux system must also be configured with the IP address of the organization's DNS server. In addition, the system must be configured with the address of the default gateway to communicate with hosts on other network segments.

We also reviewed public and private IP addressing. Public networks are allowed on the Internet. Private networks are only allowed in local area networks (LANs). NAT routers hide a private network behind one or more public interfaces. IPv6 addresses are composed of eight four-character hexadecimal numbers, separated by colons instead of periods.

To assign the DNS server address or the default gateway address, edit the */etc/resolv.conf* configuration file. To bring a network interface down, enter **ifdown** at the shell prompt. To bring it up, enter **ifup**. To use a DHCP server to dynamically assign IP address information to a Linux host, enter **dhclient <interface>** at the shell prompt.

This chapter discussed several command-line utilities one can use to test and monitor the network, such as ping, traceroute, and mtr.

The **nc** command establishes a connection between two hosts. First open a listening socket on one host and then connect to that socket from another host.

Tools available for name resolution include dig, host, and nslookup. The **whois** command details the owner, phone number, and address of the domain owner.

Finally, the exam covers two utilities that allow remote mounts of filesystems. NFS is best for vendor-neutral environments, whereas Samba allows sharing from Windows systems.

Be sure you understand these key points about managing network settings:

- A protocol is a common networking language that must be configured for network hosts to communicate.
- The Internet Protocol (IP) works in conjunction with TCP or UDP to fragment, transmit, defragment, and resequence network data.
- The Internet Control Message Protocol (ICMP) is used to test and verify network communications between hosts with traceroute and ping.
- Ports allow a single host with a single IP address to provide multiple network services.
- Each host on an IPv4 network must have a unique IP address assigned as well as the correct subnet mask.
- The subnet mask defines how much of a given host's IP address is the network address and how much is the IP address.
- Hosts on the same network segment must have the same subnet mask and must be assigned to each host.
- A network host must be configured with the IP address of a DNS server to resolve domain names into IP addresses.
- A network host must be configured with the IP address of the segment's default gateway router for it to communicate with hosts on other network segments.
- IPv6 addresses are composed of eight four-character hexadecimal numbers, separated by colons instead of periods.
- Within each class of IP address are blocks of addresses called private or reserved IP addresses:
  - 10.0.0.0–10.255.255.255 (Class A)
  - 172.16.0.0–172.31.255.255 (Class B)
  - 192.168.0.0–192.168.255.255 (Class C)
- A NAT router hides a private network behind one or more public interfaces.
- You can enter **ifconfig** or **ip addr show** at the shell prompt to view the details of your installed network interfaces.
- To assign an IP address to a network interface, use **ifconfig** or **ip addr add** at the shell prompt.
- To make IP address assignments persistent, enter them in the appropriate file under the */etc/* directory.
- Use the **ip** command to manage network interfaces.

- Enter the organization's DNS server address in the */etc/resolv.conf* file.
- To dynamically assign an IP address to a Linux host, enter **dhclient <interface>** at the shell prompt.
- Use ping to test connectivity between systems. The syntax is **ping <destination_host>**.
- Use the **netstat** command to view a variety of network interface information using the -a, -i, and -r options.
- Use the traceroute utility to trace the route your packets follow to reach a remote system. The syntax is **traceroute <destination_host>**.
- The **mtr** command combines both ping and traceroute by displaying routes and how long it takes to reach them.
- Use the **route**, **ip route**, or **netstat -r** command to view your system's routing table.
- To test TCP or UDP communications, use the **nc** command.
- Use the **route** or **ip route** command to add or remove routes from the route table.
- Use the dig, host, and nslookup commands to test DNS name resolution.
- The whois command provides domain ownership and IP address information.

Questions

1. Which of the following statements are true of the MAC address? (Choose two.)

A. It's hard-coded in the network board.

B. It's logically assigned by the operating system.

C. A MAC address is globally unique.

D. The network administrator can configure its value.

E. It is used by the DNS server to resolve domain names.

2. Which transport protocol is used by network applications that need very low latency and can tolerate a certain degree of unreliability?

A. User Datagram Protocol

B. Transmission Control Protocol

C. Internet Protocol

D. Internet Control Message Protocol

3. Which layer of the OSI model enables the routing of data?

A. Data Link

B. Network

C. Transport

D. Session

E. Application

4. You've just set up an e-mail server on your Linux system and enabled the SMTP and POP3 daemons to allow users to send and receive mail. Which ports must be opened in your system's host firewall to allow this? (Choose two.)
   - **A.** 20
   - **B.** 21
   - **C.** 25
   - **D.** 110
   - **E.** 119
   - **F.** 80
5. Which of the following are valid IP addresses that can be assigned to a network host? (Choose two.)
   - **A.** 192.168.254.1
   - **B.** 11.0.0.0
   - **C.** 257.0.0.1
   - **D.** 192.345.2.1
   - **E.** 10.200.0.200
6. Your network interface has been assigned an IP address of 10.0.0.1. What is this binary equivalent of this decimal address?
   - **A.** 10001010.00000000.00000000.00000001
   - **B.** 00001010.00000001.00000001.00000001
   - **C.** 10100000.00000000.00000000.00000001
   - **D.** 00001010.00000000.00000000.00000001
7. You need to use ifconfig to assign an IP address of 176.23.0.12 and a subnet mask of 255.255.0.0 to your eth0 interface. Which of the following commands will do this?
   - **A.** ifconfig eth0 176.23.0.12 netmask 255.255.0.0
   - **B.** ifconfig 176.23.0.12 netmask 255.255.0.0
   - **C.** ifconfig eth0 176.23.0.12 mask 255.255.0.0
   - **D.** ifconfig dev=eth0 ipaddr=176.23.0.12 subnetmask=255.255.0.0
8. You've opened your */etc/sysconfig/network/resolv.conf* file in the vi editor. You want to specify a DNS server address of 10.200.200.1. Which of the following directives would you enter in this file to do this?
   - **A.** host 10.200.200.1
   - **B.** resolver 10.200.200.1
   - **C.** dnsserver 10.200.200.1
   - **D.** nameserver 10.200.200.1

9. You want to use your organization's DHCP server to dynamically assign an IP address to your ens1 network interface. Which of the following commands would you enter at the shell prompt to do this?
   A. dhcp ens1
   B. dhclient ens1
   C. get address dynamic ens1
   D. ip address=dhcp dev= ens1
10. You need to verify that a remote host with a hostname of fs1.mycorp.com is up and running. Which of the following commands would you enter at the shell prompt to do this?
   A. finger fs1.mycorp.com
   B. ping fs1.mycorp.com
   C. netstat -s fs1.mycorp.com
   D. verify fs1.mycorp.com

Answers

1. **A, C.** MAC addresses are hard-coded into the firmware of every Ethernet network board. Theoretically, no two network boards in the world should have the same MAC address. However, a few types of network boards actually do allow you to manually configure the MAC address.
2. **A.** The User Datagram Protocol is an unacknowledged, connectionless protocol that sends packets without requesting a confirmation of receipt. This makes it ideal for network applications that need very low latency but can tolerate a certain degree of unreliability, such as streaming video.
3. **B.** The Network layer of the OSI model enables the routing of data between networks. In an IP network, this functionality is provided by the Internet Protocol (IP itself).
4. **C, D.** The SMTP daemon uses port 25 by default, whereas the POP3 daemon uses port 110 by default.
5. **A, E.** 192.168.254.1 and 10.200.0.200 are both valid IP addresses that can be assigned to network hosts.
6. **D.** The binary equivalent of the first octet (10) is 00001010. The binary equivalent of the second and third octets (0) is 00000000 each. The binary equivalent of the fourth octet (1) is 00000001.
7. **A.** The **ifconfig eth0 176.23.0.12 netmask 255.255.0.0** command will assign the IP address and subnet mask to the eth0 interface.

8. **D.** The **nameserver 10.200.200.1** directive specifies a DNS server with an IP address of 10.200.200.1.
9. **B.** The **dhclient ens1** command will configure the ens1 interface with IP address information from a DHCP server.
10. **B.** The **ping fs1.mycorp.com** command is the best to use to test the network.

CHAPTER 15

Understanding Network Security

In this chapter, you will learn about

- Understanding how encryption works
- Implementing secured tunnel networks
- Configuring high-availability networking
- Understanding single sign-on
- Defending against network attacks
- Encrypting files with GPG

Hackers have figured out that a minimal amount of information can yield huge profits, and they will stop at nothing to get it. As a result, ethical hackers have to be obsessive about information security.

Network security is focused on protecting valuable electronic information of organizations and users. Therefore, the demand for IT professionals who know how to secure networks and computers is at an all-time high. Linux system administrators need to be very aware of the security issues affecting networks. In this chapter, we will cover how to use encryption to increase the security of Linux networks.

TIP Information security is a huge topic that cannot adequately be addressed in this book. I highly recommend that you enhance your knowledge by getting the Security+ certification from CompTIA, or the CISSP certification from (ISC)². The IT world has become the modern equivalent of the Wild West from American history. Linux+ certified engineers must know how to thoroughly protect data from malicious users!

Understanding How Encryption Works

Harken back to elementary school days when you may have passed notes to friends. To keep those notes secret, you may have used a code such as this:

```
Key:                  ZABCDEFGHIJKLMNOPQRSTUVWXY
Plain Text:           ABCDEFGHIJKLMNOPQRSTUVWXYZ
```

NOTE This symmetric encryption technique is called a *letter shift*.

For example, the plain text "JAKE LIKES PAM" would encrypt to the cipher "IZJD KHJFR OZL."

This basic concept of using keys to scramble and descramble messages can be used to encode network communications as well. In today's security-conscious world, the need to encrypt the contents of network communications is critical, as hackers listen to traffic for passwords, social security numbers, national insurance numbers, personal account numbers, and so on. Using network monitoring tools such as Wireshark, or the Linux command-line tools **tcpdump** and **tshark**, makes it relatively easy for hackers to sniff out network transmissions and read them.

To protect this information, network communications must be encrypted. Unlike simple codes used in the fourth grade, network cryptography today uses much more sophisticated encoding mechanisms. There are three general approaches:

- Symmetric encryption
- Asymmetric encryption
- Integrity checking via hashing

Symmetric Encryption

The fourth-grade encryption system just mentioned is an example of symmetric encryption, which uses a single private key. The key used to encrypt a message is the same key used to decrypt the message. This means the sender and the receiver must both have the exact same key, as shown in Figure 15-1. Symmetric algorithms include Blowfish, 3DES, and AES.

NOTE Symmetric encryption is sometimes called *secret key encryption*. Because of the high risk of the secret key being stolen, another encryption mechanism is commonly used today, called *asymmetric encryption*.

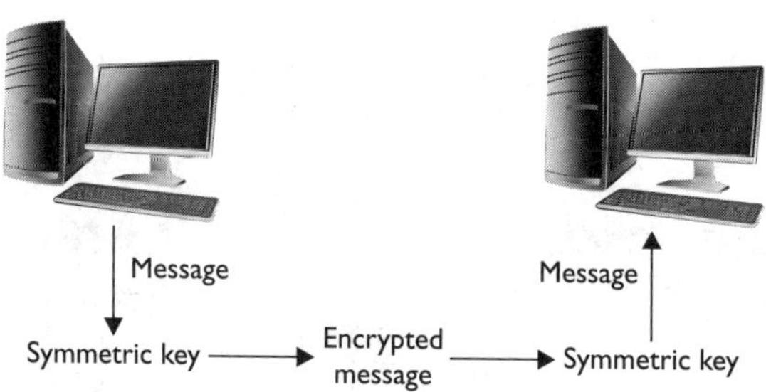

Figure 15-1 Symmetric encryption

Asymmetric Encryption

Unlike symmetric encryption, asymmetric encryption uses two keys instead of one: a public key known by everyone, and a private key only known by the owner. Data encrypted with the public key is decrypted with the private key. Data signed with the private key is verified with the public key. Examples of asymmetric encryption include RSA, DSA, and Diffie-Hellman.

NOTE Digital signatures are not GIF or JPEG images of a written signature. They are codes that only each owner has. Because the data comes with the individual code (that is, the sender's private key), you can verify that the message came from that individual using the sender's public key.

Because of its high difficulty to break, public key cryptography is a widely used method for encrypting data. Online shopping only exists because of asymmetric encryption, keeping secret the customer's address, phone, and credit card number.

To verify that an online store is legitimate, a *certificate authority (CA)* is used, such as VeriSign, Entrust, or DigiCert. The CA assures customers that they are shopping at tmall.com, for example, and not a spoof site like fake-tmall.com, by providing the store with a signed certificate that only they own. The fake site appears to be tmall.com but is programmed to steal customer credit cards. This asymmetric process is called Public Key Infrastructure, or PKI.

Administrators can mint their own certificates and use them to encrypt both network transmissions and files in the filesystem. These are called *self-signed* certificates.

Integrity Checking via Hashing

When downloading software, pictures, or music, how does the user know that the file has not been accidentally altered or intentionally modified? To validate that the file has not been altered, the user can use a technique called one-way encryption, or *hashing*. For example, when visiting OpenSUSE to download the operating system, you will also see a list of hash values, as shown here:

```
Filename: openSUSE-Leap-15.0-DVD-x86_64.iso
Path: /distribution/leap/15.0/iso/openSUSE-Leap-15.0-DVD-x86_64.iso
Size: 3.6G (3917479936 bytes)
Last modified: Wed, 16 May 2018 17:47:07 GMT (Unix time: 1526492827)
SHA-256 Hash: c477428c7830ca76762d2f78603e13067c33952b936ff100189523e1fabe5a77
SHA-1 Hash: 64b710bdb8e49d79146cd0d26bb8a7fc28568aa0
MD5 Hash: 5d4d4c83e678b6715652a9cf5ff3c8a3
BitTorrent Information Hash: 21b15d6ff16b245d2f48c5265a7a5463b2d9373b
```

NOTE You can reach OpenSUSE's link of mirror download sites by visiting https://opensuse.org. From there, click the link that states "Get the most complete Linux distribution" or "latest regular-release version" and then select "Pick Mirror."

In this case, three hash values are listed: SHA-256, SHA-1, and MD5.

File integrity checking is completed by ensuring the downloaded file hash matches the vendor's published hash value. There are several hashing tools, but the two most popular are MD5 and SHA. There are multiple versions of SHA, with SHA-256 being one of the best because it is less likely for two different files to calculate the same result, which is called a *collision*.

Hashes are like serial numbers for files. A specific file should only give one result. So the MD5 hash for OpenSUSE v15.0 is 5d4d4c83e678b6715652a9cf5ff3c8a3. If an administrator decides to download OpenSUSE v15.0 from a mirror, they have to ask themselves, is this a mirror we can trust? The administrator can verify the file by checking the hash with the **md5sum** command. This outputs a message digest, like so:

```
theogj@ws1:~> md5sum openSUSE-Leap-15.0-DVD-x86_64.iso
5d4d4c83e678b6715652a9cf5ff3c8a3
```

In this case, since the hash value matches the hash value on the OpenSUSE website, the administrator knows they have a clean download. If the value returned were any value other than 5d4d4c83e678b6715652a9cf5ff3c8a3, then something is wrong with the downloaded file. In most cases, the user downloaded only a portion of the file and has to attempt the download again. In rare cases, a mismatch could signal the file has been altered with malware. A hash mismatch would look something like this:

```
ariaecj@ws1:~> md5sum openSUSE-Leap-15.0-DVD-x86_64.iso
7qwm66m390s9fkwilcm0909wwickj28d
```

The OpenSUSE website also lists SHA-1 and SHA-256 hash values. These can be verified using the **sha1sum** and **sha256sum** commands, respectively. Sometimes vendors will list the highest quality hashing value to date, SHA-512. In this case, use the sha512sum command to verify file integrity.

Implementing Secured Tunnel Networks

In the early days of UNIX/Linux, network connection tools between systems included telnet, rlogin, and rsh. Users would use rcp or FTP to copy files between systems. However, because of hackers, these utilities must never be used over public networks because they lack encryption.

These days, you can use the SSH package to accomplish these same tasks securely *with* encryption. In this section, the following topics are addressed:

- How SSH works
- Configuring SSH
- Logging in to SSH without a password
- Virtual Private Networks

How SSH Works

SSH provides the functionality of telnet, rlogin, rsh, rcp, and FTP, but with encryption. To do this, SSH provides the following encryption-enabled components:

- sshd This is the ssh daemon that runs on the server.
- ssh The ssh client used to connect to the SSH server from a remote system.
- scp This utility securely copies files between systems.
- sftp This utility securely copies files between systems, acting like FTP.
- slogin Like SSH, this utility is used to access the shell prompt remotely.
- ssh-keygen Used to create users' public/private keys. Can also create self-signed certificates.

To establish a secure connection, SSH uses both asymmetric and symmetric encryption. First, the SSH client creates a connection with the system, where the SSH server is running on IP port 22. The SSH server then sends its public keys to the SSH client. The SSH server stores its keys in the following files:

- **Private key** */etc/ssh/ssh_host_key*
- **Public key** */etc/ssh/ssh_host_key.pub*

The client system receives the public key from the SSH server and checks to see if it already has a copy of that key. The SSH client stores keys from remote systems in the following files:

- */etc/ssh/ssh_known_hosts*
- *~/.ssh/known_hosts*

By default, if the client does not have the server's public key in either of these files, it will ask the user to add it. Having done this, the client now trusts the server system and generates the symmetric key. It then uses the server's public key to encrypt the new secret key and sends it to the server. The server decrypts the symmetric key using its private key, and now both systems have the same secret key and can use faster symmetric encryption during the duration of the SSH session. The user is presented with a login prompt and can now authenticate securely because everything she types is sent in encrypted format.

After this secure channel has been negotiated and the user has been authenticated through the SSH server, data can be securely transferred between both systems.

EXAM TIP By default, SSH is set up to use privileged port 22. This is defined in the */etc/services* file. Hackers also know the default port is 22. Often, network administrators will use a port that is not 22 to make it harder for hackers to invade the network.

Option	Description
AllowUsers	Restricts logins to the SSH server to only the users listed. Specify a list of users separated by spaces.
DenyUsers	Prevents users listed from logging in through the SSH server. Specify a list of users separated by spaces.
PermitRootLogin	Specifies whether root can authenticate through the SSH server. Set the value to "no" to disallow users from logging in as root.

Table 15-1 Options in the *sshd_config* File

Configuring SSH

To use SSH, install the openssh package. This package includes both the sshd daemon and the ssh client. (SSH is usually installed by default on most Linux distributions.)

The process of configuring SSH involves configuring both the SSH server and the SSH client. You configure the sshd server using the */etc/ssh/sshd_config* file. The ssh client, on the other hand, is configured using the */etc/ssh/ssh_config* file or the *~/.ssh/config* file.

Let's look at configuring the SSH server (sshd) first. There are many directives within the */etc/ssh/sshd_config* file. The good news is that after you install the openssh package, the default parameters work very well in most circumstances. After making changes to this file, restart sshd as root by using **systemctl restart sshd**. Some of the more useful parameters in this file include those shown in Table 15-1.

EXAM TIP Set **PermitRootLogin** to **no** to disallow logging in as root.

The SSH client on a Linux system is configured using the */etc/ssh/ssh_config* file. The */etc/ssh/ssh_config* file is used to specify default parameters for all users running SSH on the system. A user can override these defaults using the *~/.ssh/config* file in their home directory. The precedence for configuring SSH client settings is as follows:

1. Any command-line options included with the ssh command at the shell prompt.
2. Settings in the *~/.ssh/config* file.
3. Settings in the */etc/ssh/ssh_config* file.

As with the sshd daemon, the default parameters used in the *ssh_config* file usually work without a lot of customization. Some of the more common parameters used to customize the SSH client are listed in Table 15-2.

Option	Description
Port	Specifies the port number to connect to on the SSH server system to initiate an SSH request
User	Specifies the user to log in to the SSH server as

Table 15-2 Options in the *ssh_config* File

Firewall Configuration: Allowed Services
Start-Up
Interfaces
Allowed Services
Masquerading
Broadcast
IPsec Support
Logging Level
Allowed Services for Selected Zone
External Zone
Service to Allow
DHCP Client
Add
Allowed Service
SSH
Remove

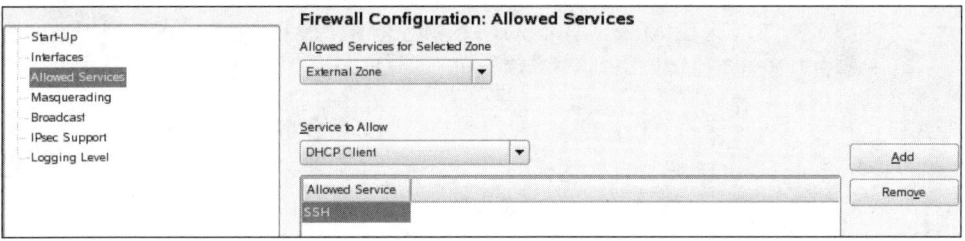

Figure 15-2 Configuring the firewall to allow SSH traffic

EXAM TIP Before connecting to an SSH server, make sure port 22 is open on the host-based and network-based firewalls.

Figure 15-2 shows the YaST Firewall module on a SUSE Linux Enterprise Server, configured to allow SSH traffic.

After configuring the firewall, you can log in to the remote Linux system by entering

```
openSUSE:~ # ssh -l <user_name> <ip_address>
```

TIP Don't forget the -l parameter for logon name; otherwise, the SSH client will attempt to authenticate the user as $USER to the remote system. If the credentials are the same on both the client and server systems, authentication will be successful. But if they are not, authentication will be unsuccessful.

For example, to connect to a remote Linux system with a hostname of fedora (which has an IP address of 10.0.0.85) as the user "student" using the SSH client on a local computer system, enter **ssh -l student fedora** at the shell prompt, as shown in Figure 15-3.

Notice in Figure 15-3 that the user is prompted to accept the public key from the fedora host because this was the first connection to this SSH server. Once done, the user is authenticated to the remote system as the student user (notice the change in the shell prompt). Now the user has access to the fedora server and works as if they are sitting right at the console of fedora. To close the connection, just enter **exit** at the shell prompt.

```
rtracy@openSUSE:~> ssh -l student fedora
The authenticity of host 'fedora (10.0.0.85)' can't be established.
RSA key fingerprint is 03:8f:61:c0:ba:3f:fc:00:3b:f1:03:1e:5f:f5:18:42.
Are you sure you want to continue connecting (yes/no)? yes
Warning: Permanently added 'fedora,10.0.0.85' (RSA) to the list of known hosts.
student@fedora's password:
Last login: Fri Jan 23 20:11:46 2015
[student@fedora ~]$ █
```

Figure 15-3 Connecting remotely via SSH

TIP To use SSH from Windows workstations, download PuTTY from the Internet and use it to connect to an SSH server.

Exercise 15-1: Working with SSH

In Exercise 15-1, you set up an SSH server on a Linux system and then connect to it using an SSH client from another Linux system.

Set up at least two Linux systems for this and the remaining exercises in this chapter. Either use two live Linux systems, two Linux virtual machines, or a mixture of both.

VIDEO Watch the Exercise 15-1 video for a demonstration on how to perform this task.

Complete the following steps:

1. Configure the SSH server system by doing the following:
   a. Boot the Linux system that you want to function as an SSH server and log in as a standard user (for example, student1).
   b. Open a terminal session.
   c. Switch to your root user account by entering **su -** followed by your root user's password.
   d. At the shell prompt, use the package management utility of your choice to ensure the openssh package has been installed.
   e. At the shell prompt, enter **vi /etc/ssh/sshd_config**.
   f. Locate the PermitRootLogin setting. If it has been commented out, remove the # character from the beginning of the line.
   g. Press INS; then set PermitRootLogin to a value of **no**.
   h. Press ESC; then enter **:x** to save your changes and exit the editor.
   i. At the shell prompt, enter **service sshd restart** to restart the SSH service and apply the change.
   j. If necessary, open port 22 in the host firewall of the system where the SSH server is running. The steps for doing this will depend on your particular distribution.
2. Create an SSH connection from a client system by doing the following:
   a. Start your second system, which will function as an SSH client, and log in as a standard user.
   b. Open a terminal session.

c. Open an SSH session with the first Linux system by entering **ssh -l <user_name> <IP_address_of_SSH_server>** at the shell prompt. For example, to connect to a system with an IP address of 192.168.1.125 as the student1 user on that system, enter **ssh -l student1 192.168.1.125** at the shell prompt.

d. If prompted, enter **yes** to accept the public key from the SSH server.

e. Enter the password for the user you specified on the SSH server system.

f. Enter **exit** at the shell prompt to log off from the remote system.

3. Practice working with SSH utilities from your client system by doing the following:

a. Run the ifconfig command on the remote system using SSH by entering **ssh -l <user_name> <IP_address_of_SSH_server> /sbin/ifconfig** at the shell prompt.

b. Enter the password of the remote user when prompted. You should see the networking configuration assigned to the various interfaces on the remote system. Notice that the connection automatically closed once the command finished running.

c. Copy a file using a secure SSH connection by doing the following:

i. Create a new file in your user's home directory by entering **echo "This is my new file." > ~/mytestfile.txt** at the shell prompt.

ii. Copy this new file to the home directory for your remote user account on your SSH server system by entering **scp ~/mytestfile.txt <user_name>@<IP_address_of_SSH_server>:** at the shell prompt.

iii. Enter the remote user's password when prompted. You should see that the file was copied.

iv. Use the **ssh** command to establish an SSH connection again with your SSH server system using the same username you entered previously to copy the file.

v. Verify that the file exists in the remote user's home directory.

vi. Enter **exit** to close the connection.

d. Use the sftp command to copy the *mytestfile.txt* file down from the SSH server system to the local */tmp* directory by doing the following:

i. At the shell prompt of your workstation system, enter **sftp <user_name>@<IP_address_of_SSH_server>**.

ii. Enter the remote user's password when prompted.

iii. At the sftp> prompt, enter **get mytestfile.txt /tmp/**.

iv. At the sftp> prompt, enter **exit**.

v. At the shell prompt, enter **ls /tmp**. You should see the *mytestfile.txt* file that was copied down from the SSH server system.

Now that you know how to use the SSH server and SSH client, you're ready to advance your knowledge by learning how to tunnel unencrypted traffic through an SSH connection.

Logging In to SSH Without a Password

Administrators can also configure the SSH server to allow authentication without a password. For example, the systems administrator Eric is setting up the system for encrypted remote backups using scp and wants to run these weekly. He decides running backups as a cron job is the best way to do this, but realizes that this will not work because scp always asks for a password. So, now he must inform the server that a *trusted* client needs access, so no longer ask for a password from this user at this client.

For this to work, the public key of the user on the client system must be stored at the server. The file on the server is called *~/.ssh/authorized_keys*. To do this, Eric needs to securely copy the public key from the client system to the server system and add it to *~/.ssh/authorized_keys*. (The private key, of course, remains on the client system.) Now Eric can use scp and SSH to log in to the server without a password; this is also known as *public key authentication*.

To configure public key authentication, first create the public/private key pair on the client system. This can be done using the **ssh-keygen** command by following these steps:

1. At the shell prompt of the client system, enter **ssh-keygen -t rsa** or **ssh-keygen -t dsa**, depending on which encryption method your SSH server supports. To be safe, simply use both commands to make two key pairs—one for RSA encryption and the other for DSA encryption.
2. When prompted for the file in which the *private* key will be saved, press enter to use the default filename of *~/.ssh/id_rsa* or *~/.ssh/id_dsa*. The associated public key will be saved as *~/.ssh/id_rsa.pub* or *~/.ssh/id_dsa.pub*, respectively.
3. When prompted, enter a passphrase for the key. Assigning a passphrase to the key renders the key useless if someone does not know it.

At this point, the key pair is created. An example of creating an RSA key pair is shown here:

```
ejeff@ws1:~> ssh-keygen -t rsa
Generating public/private rsa key pair.
Enter file in which to save the key (/home/ejeff/.ssh/id_rsa):
Enter passphrase (empty for no passphrase):
Enter same passphrase again:
Your identification has been saved in /home/ejeff/.ssh/id_rsa.
Your public key has been saved in /home/ejeff/.ssh/id_rsa.pub.
The key fingerprint is:
ba:14:48:14:de:fd:42:40:f2:4b:c8:8b:03:a4:6d:fc ejeff@ws1
The key's randomart image is:
+--[ RSA 2048]----+
| .  +oo          |
|oo + = o         |
|o + = + o        |
| o + + o .       |
|  o E o S .      |
|   .   o .       |
|      o          |
|     . .         |
|      .          |
+-----------------+
ejeff@ws1:~>
```

Next, copy the public key just created to the SSH server. An easy (and secure) way to do this is to use the scp command. The syntax is

```
scp ~/.ssh/<key_name>.pub <user_name>@<address_of_SSH_server>:<filename>
```

In the example shown here, the RSA public key for the local ejeff user on WS1 is copied to the home directory of the ejeff user on WS3 and saved in a file named *keyfile*:

```
ejeff@ws1:~> scp ~/.ssh/id_rsa.pub ws3:keyfile
Password:
id_rsa.pub                                   100%  392     0.4KB/s   00:00
ejeff@ws1:~>
```

At this point, the contents of the key file just copied need to be appended to the end of the *~/.ssh/authorized_keys* file in the home directory of the user connecting to the SSH server. An easy way to do this is to connect to the SSH server system using a standard SSH session and then use the cat command to append the contents of the key file to the end of the *~/.ssh/authorized_keys* file. Here's an example:

```
ejeff@ws1:~> ssh -l ejeff ws3
Password:
Last login: Thu Jun  2 15:05:34 2022 from 192.168.1.84
ejeff@WS3:~> mkdir ~/.ssh
ejeff@WS3:~> cat keyfile » ~/.ssh/authorized_keys
ejeff@WS3:~>
```

Now test the configuration to see if public key authentication works by establishing a new SSH session with the server. In this case, Eric will be prompted for the key file's passphrase instead of a username and password. Once the passphrase is entered, Eric will be authenticated to the SSH server. Notice in the next example that no password was requested to establish the SSH session:

```
ejeff@ws1:~> ssh -l ejeff ws3
Last login: Thu Jun  2 16:13:39 2022 from 192.168.1.84
ejeff@WS3:~>
```

The final step is to use the ssh-agent command to eliminate the need to enter the passphrase every time an SSH connection is established, as detailed next. The ssh-agent command caches the keys once added to the agent with ssh-add.

1. At the shell prompt of the client system, enter **ssh-agent bash**.
2. At the shell prompt, enter **ssh-add ~/.ssh/id_rsa** or **ssh-add ~/.ssh/id_dsa**, depending on which key file created.
3. When prompted, enter the key file's passphrase. You will be prompted that the identity has been added. An example follows:

```
ejeff@ws1:~> ssh-agent bash
ejeff@ws1:~> ssh-add ~/.ssh/id_rsa
Enter passphrase for /home/ejeff/.ssh/id_rsa:
Identity added: /home/ejeff/.ssh/id_rsa (/home/ejeff/.ssh/id_rsa)
ejeff@ws1:~>
```

Once this is done, the ssh-agent process stores the passphrase in memory and listens for SSH requests. It then automatically provides the key passphrase when requested.

Exercise 15-2: Configuring Public Key Authentication

In Exercise 15-2, you generate an RSA key pair on the client system and copy the public key to the SSH server to enable public key authentication.

You'll need at least two Linux systems for this exercise. Use either two live Linux systems, two Linux virtual machines, or a mixture of both.

VIDEO Watch the Exercise 15-2 video for a demonstration on how to perform this task.

Complete the following steps:

1. Generate an RSA key pair on your client system by doing the following:
   a. Log in to your client system as a standard user.
   b. Open a terminal session.
   c. Enter **ssh-keygen -t rsa** at the shell prompt.
   d. When prompted for the file in which the private key will be saved, press ENTER to use the default filename of *~/.ssh/id_rsa*.
   e. When prompted, enter a passphrase for the key.
2. Configure the server system to use public key authentication by doing the following:
   a. Copy the public key you just created to your SSH server system by entering the following:
   scp ~/.ssh/id_rsa.pub <user_name>@<address_of_SSH_server>:mykeyfile
   b. Enter the remote user's password when prompted.
   c. Establish an SSH session with the remote system as the user you intend to authenticate as using public key authentication. Use the following command:
   ssh -l <user_name> <address_of_SSH_server>
   d. Enter the remote user's password when prompted.
   e. At the shell prompt of the remote system, check to see if the *.ssh* hidden directory already exists by entering **ls -la** at the shell prompt. If the *.ssh* directory doesn't exist, create it using the **mkdir ~/.ssh** command. Otherwise, go on to the next step.
   f. Enter **cat mykeyfile » ~/.ssh/authorized_keys** at the shell prompt of the remote system.
   g. Enter **exit** at the shell prompt to close the SSH session.

3. Test the new configuration by doing the following:
   a. Enter **ssh -l <user_name> <address_of_SSH_server>** at the shell prompt of your client system.
   b. When prompted, enter the passphrase you assigned to your RSA private key. At this point, you should be automatically authenticated to the SSH server.
   c. Close the session by entering **exit** the shell prompt.
4. Configure ssh-agent to remember your private key passphrase by doing the following:
   a. Enter **ssh-agent bash** at the shell prompt of your client system.
   b. At the shell prompt, enter **ssh-add ~/.ssh/id_rsa**.
   c. When prompted, enter the key file's passphrase. When you do, you should be prompted that the identity has been added.
   d. Enter **ssh -l <user_name> <address_of_SSH_server>** at the shell prompt of your client system. You should be automatically authenticated to the SSH server without being prompted for the private key passphrase.

Automatically Updating *authorized_keys*

The manual method to update *~/.ssh/authorized_keys* can be automated with **ssh-copy-id** if you already know the username and password of the remote system. Here's an example:

```
ejeff@ws1:~> ssh-copy-id ejeff@ws3
ejeff@ws3's password:
Number of key(s) added: 1
ejeff@ws1:~>
```

The ssh-copy-id command will automatically update the *authorized_keys* file on the SSH server.

Virtual Private Networks

A virtual private network (VPN) allows users to connect to remote servers over untrusted networks but make it appear they are part of the internal network. To ensure the confidentiality of the network, encryption and tunneling protocols are used to create this private network. This security is provided through IPSec. To reduce traffic congestion without sacrificing security, DTLS (Datagram Transport Layer Security) is implemented.

VPNs are used by employees wanting to work from home and connect to the corporate office, for example. Figure 15-4 shows an example of a home office connecting to the corporate network via VPN.

VPN connections can be made either in transport mode or tunnel mode. Tunnel mode encrypts the headers and the message. Use tunnel mode when data is transported over public networks. Transport mode is used over trusted networks (for example, moving data from office to office). Transport mode only encrypts the message, not the headers.

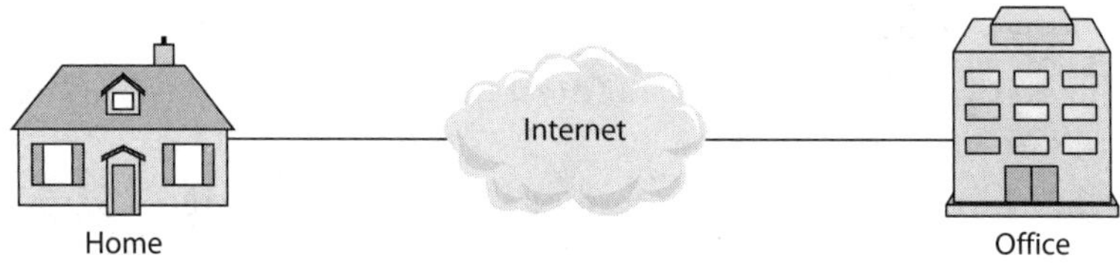

Figure 15-4 VPN connection from a home office to corporate headquarters

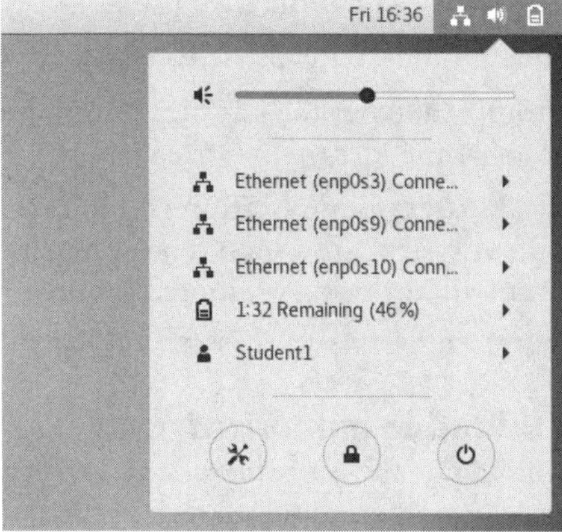

Figure 15-5 Step 1 of creating a VPN connection

To set up the VPN client from Linux, click in the upper-right corner of the screen on the network icon, as shown in Figure 15-5.

Next, click "Wired Settings" (see Figure 15-6). Then click the + sign to the right of VPN to initiate the VPN connection, as shown in Figure 15-7.

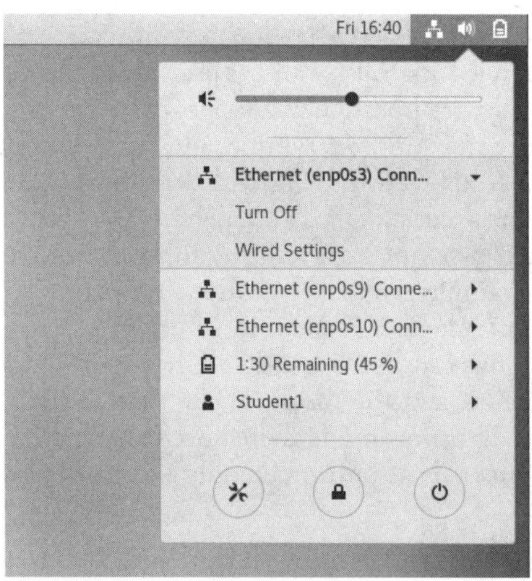

Figure 15-6 Step 2 of creating a VPN connection

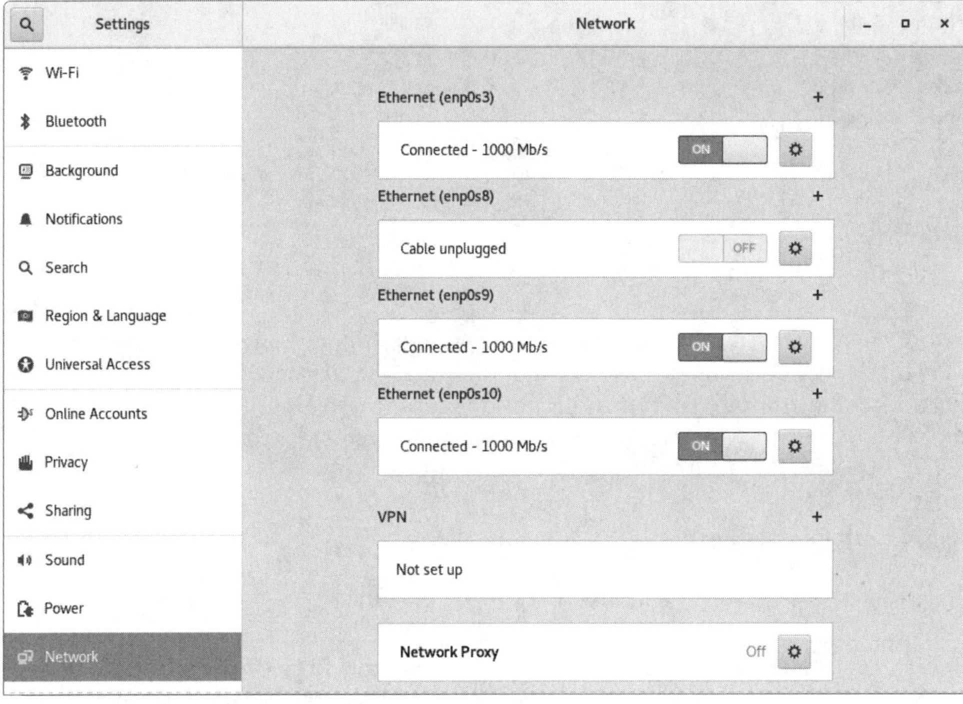

Figure 15-7 Step 3 of creating a VPN connection

After obtaining the credentials, save them to a file and import them into the VPN client for an easy connection to the VPN server.

NOTE A common command-line VPN client used on Linux systems is OpenVPN.

There are several implementations of VPNs. One type is using SSH, and another is the SSL VPN, which use TLS as the encryption protocol. Some administrators find these easier to set up over IPSec-based VPNs because they can be deployed over a web browser.

EXAM TIP If the VPN settings are all correct, and the system will not connect, make sure the proper ports are opened on the firewalls.

Configuring High-Availability Networking

The consequence of not being able to access data is destruction. That is, if data is not available, it is as if it has been destroyed, so availability is an important component of security. Network availability can be enhanced by converting the local network adapter

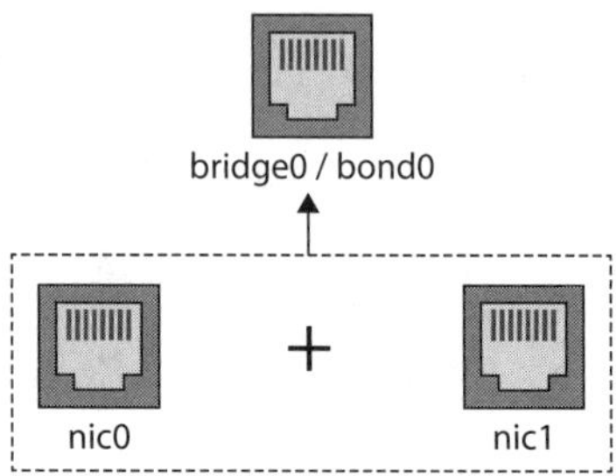

Figure 15-8 Setup for network bridging and bonding

into a concept called *network bridging* or *bonding.* Bridging dual-homes two or more networks together for fault tolerance. Bonding dual-homes network segments to boost network throughput. Dual-homed networking is shown in Figure 15-8.

At this point, we will cover the two major types of redundant networks:

- Network bridge control
- Network bonding

For the Linux+ exam, you need to understand only the basics of bridging and bonding.

NOTE Overlay networks allow administrators to give multiple IP addresses to a local network card. Fox example, running the following makes a single network card act like three network cards:
[root@cent71-5t dkosuth]# ifconfig eth0 inet 192.168.2.2
[root@cent71-5t dkosuth]# ifconfig eth0:0 inet 192.168.2.3
[root@cent71-5t dkosuth]# ifconfig eth0:1 inet 192.168.2.4

Network Bridge Control

You set up bridging with the **brctl** command. Here is an example using the addbr function to create the bridge and addif to add interfaces to the bridge:

```
[root@cent71-5t dkosuth]# brctl addbr trilby
[root@cent71-5t dkosuth]# brctl addif trilby enp0s9 enp0s10
[root@cent71-5t dkosuth]# brctl show
bridge name bridge id         STP enabled interfaces
trilby      8000.0800271eb6e8 no          enp0s10
                                          enp0s9
```

Spanning Tree Protocol (STP) is not enabled by default, but when it is enabled, it provides methods to seek the shortest path between two Ethernets and prevents network loops when multiple bridges are on the network. To enable STP, run the following:

```
[root@cent71-5t dkosuth]# brctl stp trilby on
[root@cent71-5t dkosuth]# brctl show
bridge name bridge id         STP enabled interfaces
trilby      8000.0800271eb6e8 yes         enp0s10
                                          enp0s9
```

Network Bonding

Network bonding aggregates multiple network interface cards into a single bond interface that provides redundancy, increased throughput, and high availability. To construct the bond on CentOS, you must define the bond script file at */etc/sysconfig/network-scripts/ifcfg-bond0*:

```
[root@cent71-5t bertollini]# cat /etc/sysconfig/network-scripts/ifcfg-bond0
DEVICE=bond0
NAME=bond0
TYPE=Bond
BONDING_MASTER=yes
IPADDR=10.1.1.150
PREFIX=24
ONBOOT=yes
BOOTPROTO=none
BONDING_OPTS="mode=1 miimon=100"
```

The BONDING_OPTS setting describes the bonding mode, as listed in Table 15-3. The miimon parameter is the link check interval in milliseconds.

Next, modify the network interface configuration files and add the bond definitions. Here is an example for interface enp0s9:

```
[root@cent71-5t bertollini]# cat /etc/sysconfig/network-scripts/ifcfg-enp0s9
TYPE=Ethernet
BOOTPROTO=none
DEVICE=enp0s9
ONBOOT=yes
HWADDR="08:a2:37:69:60:09"
MASTER=bond0
SLAVE=yes
```

The administrator would make similar settings for the other network interfaces that are part of the bond and then restart the network by running **systemctl restart network.service**.

Understanding Single Sign-On

Single sign-on (SSO) is an identity management feature that allows one login and password to every system on the network. So, no matter if an engineer is working in the Austin, Texas, office or the Mumbai, Maharashtra, office, they can use the same login and password to access their data.

Policy	Mode	Description
Round-robin	0	Packets sent in order across all NICs (the default policy).
Active-passive	1	One NIC sleeps and activates if another fails.
Aggregation	4	NICs act as one, which results in higher throughput.
Load balancing	5	Traffic equally balanced over all NICs.

Table 15-3 Network Bonding Policies

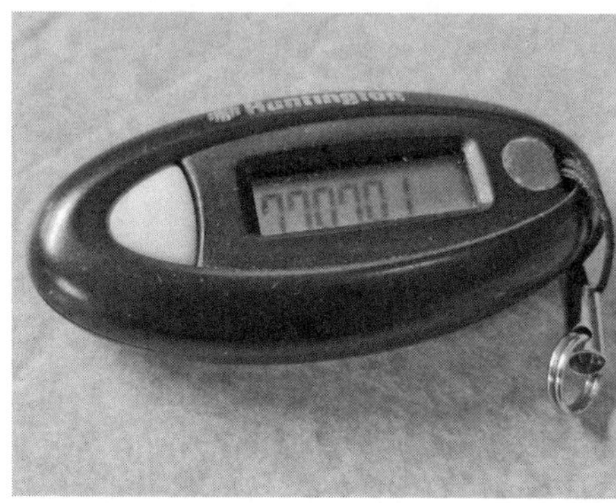

Figure 15-9 One-time password (OTP) hardware token

SSO systems have several features, including one-time passwords (OTPs). These systems provide the user a software token (e.g., FreeOTP) or a hardware token, as shown in Figure 15-9, that produces a random value every 30 seconds. When the user logs on to the system, to further authenticate themselves they must provide the updated random value. This provides an additional layer of security. If a hacker obtains the user's password but cannot guess the random value, they will still be locked out.

Several utilities provide SSO services, including the following:

- RADIUS
- LDAP
- Kerberos
- TACACS+

For the Linux+ exam, you simply need to understand the basics of each single sign-on service.

EXAM TIP Every user must have a unique user ID that is not shared with anyone else. Shared accounts make it difficult to determine who caused a negative occurrence.

RADIUS

Remote Authentication Dial-In User Service (RADIUS) is an authentication protocol that allows local and remote users to connect via modems. Users log in and get authenticated by the RADIUS server. After the user is authenticated, they are granted an IP address and access to the network. Since RADIUS is an open standard, it is vendor neutral.

RADIUS uses ports 1812 and 1813. Figure 15-10 diagrams how users remotely access the RADIUS client to log on to the network.

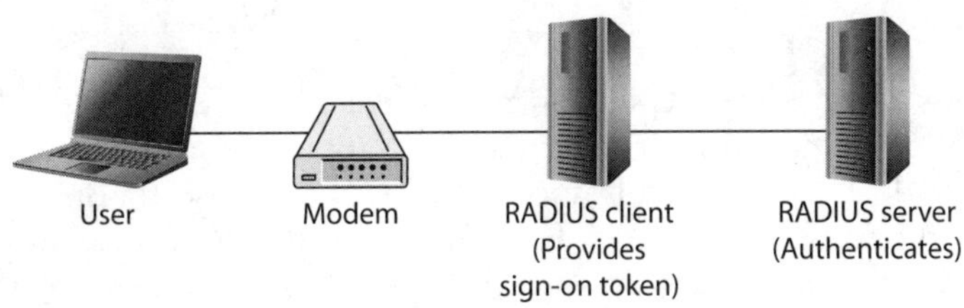

Figure 15-10 RADIUS client and server setup

LDAP

Lightweight Directory Access Protocol (LDAP) is an open source Active Directory service. LDAP is vendor neutral, so it can operate well in Linux, Windows, and Mac environments. The directory service follows the X.500 standard, which defines usernames, passwords, computers, networks, wireless devices, printers, and more.

LDAP v3 provides the most security, implementing TLS. LDAP uses ports 389, or port 636 if combined with SSL.

Kerberos

Kerberos is the name of the three-headed dog that guards Hades according to Greek mythology. The Kerberos utility for systems administrators guards the network by providing strong authentication to protect the corporate network.

Kerberos is the preferred system over public networks because users can access services such as e-mail and SSH *without* transmitting their password across the network. This way, hackers cannot even read the hashed version of the user's password. Kerberos uses a system called "tickets" to allow users access to services.

Kerberos tickets work similarly to tickets used to see a movie. For example, when you go to the movie complex, they may be showing 20 different titles. Let's say you want to see *Candace, Eric, Albert, and Edward: The Movie* at 2 P.M. You can only use the ticket for that movie at that time. When the movie ends, the ticket expires.

In a similar way, a user gets a ticket from Kerberos to access e-mail that starts now and expires in 60 minutes. Because encrypted tickets get passed instead of passwords, it makes it extremely difficult for a hacker to discover the credentials. Once the ticket expires, a new encrypted key with a new expiration can be requested.

Make sure the clocks match between the client and the server. If they are more than five minutes apart, Kerberos will fail. Kerberos will also fail if firewall port 88 is closed.

To initiate a Kerberos session, run **kinit <username>@<hostname>.com** and enter the user's password. To view the addresses associated with the current Kerberos tickets, run **klist -a**. To get details on current tickets, such as length, expiration times, renewal times, and so on, run **klist -v**.

TACACS+

Terminal Access Controller Access Control System Plus, or TACACS+ (pronounced "tack-us-plus"), combines authentication, authorization, and accounting. TACACS+ is also more secure that other protocols, such as RADIUS, because not only is the password encrypted, but the entire transaction is encrypted. Also, TACACS+ can place authentication, authorization, and accounting on three different servers, unlike RADIUS, which combines authentication and authorization. TACACS+ is not compatible with its predecessor, TACACS.

TACACS+ uses TCP port 49 to operate. Because it uses TCP instead of UDP as RADIUS does, the connections are much more reliable. TACACS+ was originally designed for Cisco networks, but other vendors now support TACACS+.

Defending Against Network Attacks

It would be nice if we lived in a world where we could connect networks together and be able to trust others to respect our systems. Unfortunately, such a world doesn't exist. If our Linux systems are connected to a network, we need to be concerned about network attacks. If our network is connected to a public network, such as the Internet, we need to be extremely concerned about network attacks.

As with most of the topics discussed in this book, network security is a huge topic that can fill many volumes. Therefore, we will discuss basic steps administrators can take to defend against network attacks. We will cover several important areas of the Linux+ exam, including the following:

- Mitigating network vulnerabilities
- Implementing a firewall with firewalld
- Implementing a firewall with iptables

Let's begin by discussing some steps to take to mitigate network vulnerabilities.

Mitigating Network Vulnerabilities

The good news is that there are some simple steps systems administrators can take to mitigate the threat to Linux systems from network attacks. These include the following:

- Disabling unused services
- Installing security updates

Let's first discuss staying abreast of current network threats.

Disabling Unused Services

One of the simplest steps administrators can take to mitigate threats from a network attack is to disable unused network services. Depending on the Linux distribution, there are probably a number of services running that do not need to operate. To view a list of installed services and whether or not they are running, enter **systemctl list-unit-files** at the shell prompt. This command will list each service and its status, as shown here:

```
[root@cent71-5t gwenj]# systemctl list-unit-files
UNIT FILE                                          STATE
exercises.mount                                    enabled
lcfileshare.mount                                  enabled
tmp.mount                                          disabled
brandbot.path                                      disabled
```

In addition to systemctl, you can also use the **nmap** command to view open IP ports on the Linux system. Again, each port that is open on the Linux system represents a potential vulnerability. Some open ports are necessary; others are not.

NOTE The nmap package is usually not installed by default.

The syntax for using nmap is **nmap -sT <host_IP_address>** for a TCP port scan and **nmap -sU <host_IP_address>** for a UDP port scan. In Figure 15-11, the nmap utility is used to scan for open TCP ports.

Figure 15-11 shows a number of services running on the host that was scanned. Use this output to determine what should be left running on the system. To disable a service, use **systemctl disable <service_name>** to ensure it will not start after reboot. Run **systemctl stop <service_name>** to disable the running service.

```
root@openSUSE:~
File Edit View Search Terminal Help
openSUSE:~ # nmap -sT 10.0.0.3

Starting Nmap 6.40 ( http://nmap.org ) at 2015-01-20 19:33 MST
Nmap scan report for 10.0.0.3
Host is up (0.0011s latency).
Not shown: 982 filtered ports
PORT      STATE  SERVICE
22/tcp    open   ssh
80/tcp    open   http
113/tcp   closed ident
139/tcp   open   netbios-ssn
389/tcp   open   ldap
427/tcp   open   svrloc
443/tcp   open   https
445/tcp   closed microsoft-ds
524/tcp   open   ncp
631/tcp   open   ipp
636/tcp   open   ldapssl
5801/tcp  open   vnc-http-1
5901/tcp  open   vnc-1
5989/tcp  open   wbem-https
6901/tcp  open   jetstream
8008/tcp  open   http
8009/tcp  open   ajp13
```

Figure 15-11 Using nmap to scan for open ports

EXAM TIP The legacy tool to manage services was called chkconfig. To check the status of all daemons, run **chkconfig -l**. To disable the service, run **chkconfig <service_name> off**.

The netstat utility also lists open ports. An example of using netstat with the -l option to view a list of listening sockets on a Linux host is shown in Figure 15-12.

Similar to netstat, using the -i option with lsof will also list network services and their ports, as shown here:

```
[root@cent71-5t gwenj]# lsof -i
COMMAND     PID   USER    FD   TYPE DEVICE SIZE/OFF NODE NAME
systemd       1   root   45u  IPv4  25466      0t0  TCP *:sunrpc (LISTEN)
systemd       1   root   46u  IPv4  25467      0t0  UDP *:sunrpc
systemd       1   root   47u  IPv6  25468      0t0  TCP *:sunrpc (LISTEN)
systemd       1   root   48u  IPv6  25469      0t0  UDP *:sunrpc
avahi-dae 3214  avahi   12u  IPv4  24455      0t0  UDP *:mdns
avahi-dae 3214  avahi   13u  IPv4  24456      0t0  UDP *:53940
rpcbind   3218    rpc    4u  IPv4  25466      0t0  TCP *:sunrpc (LISTEN)
rpcbind   3218    rpc    5u  IPv4  25467      0t0  UDP *:sunrpc
rpcbind   3218    rpc    6u  IPv6  25468      0t0  TCP *:sunrpc (LISTEN)
rpcbind   3218    rpc    7u  IPv6  25469      0t0  UDP *:sunrpc
rpcbind   3218    rpc   10u  IPv4  24207      0t0  UDP *:844
rpcbind   3218    rpc   11u  IPv6  24210      0t0  UDP *:844
```

```
root@openSUSE:~
File  Edit  View  Search  Terminal  Help
openSUSE:~ # netstat -l
Active Internet connections (only servers)
Proto Recv-Q Send-Q Local Address           Foreign Address         State
tcp        0      0 *:59082                 *:*                     LISTEN
tcp        0      0 *:ssh                   *:*                     LISTEN
tcp        0      0 localhost:ipp           *:*                     LISTEN
tcp        0      0 localhost:smtp          *:*                     LISTEN
tcp        0      0 *:mysql                 *:*                     LISTEN
tcp        0      0 *:ssh                   *:*                     LISTEN
tcp        0      0 localhost:ipp           *:*                     LISTEN
tcp        0      0 *:44472                 *:*                     LISTEN
tcp        0      0 localhost:smtp          *:*                     LISTEN
udp        0      0 *:43439                 *:*
udp        0      0 *:35268                 *:*
udp        0      0 *:ipp                   *:*
udp        0      0 10.0.0.83:ntp           *:*
udp        0      0 localhost:ntp           *:*
udp        0      0 *:ntp                   *:*
udp        0      0 *:mdns                  *:*
udp        0      0 *:10123                 *:*
udp        0      0 *:dhcpv6-client         *:*
udp        0      0 *:59465                 *:*
udp        0      0 fe80::20c:29ff:feb0:ntp *:*
udp        0      0 localhost:ntp           *:*
```

Figure 15-12 Using netstat to view a list of listening sockets

Installing Security Updates

One of the most important steps administrators can take to defend against network attacks is to regularly install operating system updates. A simple fact of life that we have to deal with in the IT world is that software isn't written perfectly. Most programs and services have some defects. Even the Linux kernel has defects that can represent serious security risks.

As software is released and used, these defects are discovered by system administrators, users, and hackers. As they are discovered, updates are written and released to fix the defects. Most distributions can be configured to automatically check and install updates. The tool used to update the system will vary depending on which Linux distribution you are using.

Implementing a Firewall with firewalld

Today, most organizations connect their corporate networks to the Internet. Doing so enhances communications and provides access to a wealth of information. Unfortunately, it also exposes their network to a serious security threat. If users can reach the Internet, an uninvited person from the Internet can also reach into their network. To keep this from happening, the organization needs to implement a firewall.

The two types are network-based firewalls and host-based firewalls. A *host-based firewall* controls traffic in and out of a single computer system, whereas a *network-based firewall* is used to control traffic in and out of an entire network.

In this part of the chapter, you spend some time learning how to use Linux in both capacities. We'll discuss the following topics:

- How firewalls work
- Implementing a packet-filtering firewall

How Firewalls Work

So what exactly is a firewall? A *firewall* acts like a gatekeeper between networks. Its job is to monitor the traffic that flows between the networks, both inbound and outbound. The firewall is configured with rules that define the type of traffic allowed. Any traffic that violates the rules is denied, as shown in Figure 15-13.

Firewalls can be implemented in a variety of ways. One of the most common types is a *packet-filtering firewall,* where all traffic moving between the private and public networks must go through the firewall. As it does, the firewall captures all incoming and outgoing packets and compares them against the access control list (ACL) configured by the network administrator.

The firewall ACL filters traffic based on the origin address, destination address, origin and destination ports, protocol used, or type of packet. If a packet abides by the rules, it is forwarded on to the next network. If it does not, it is logged and dropped, as shown in Figure 15-14.

Packet-filtering firewalls are considered *stateless* firewalls, which means they do not look at the state of the connection. *Stateful* firewalls maintain the state of the connection and

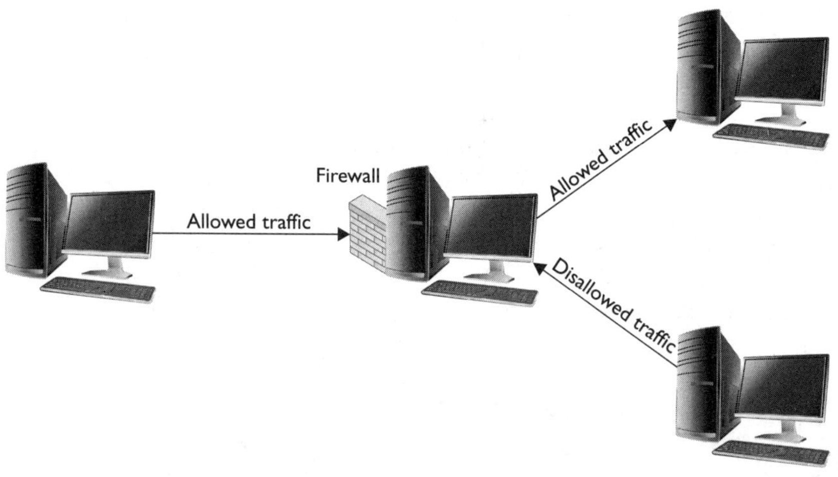

Figure 15-13 How a firewall works

are commonly used today. For example, if traffic is normally blocked from the Country of Belchre, traffic initiating from the Country of Belchre will be rejected.

But if a trusted user within the LAN requests a connection with the Country of Belchre, they will be allowed, and traffic related to this connection will be allowed because it was initiated by an internal, trusted user. This takes a huge part of the workload off the network administrator. They no longer have to respond to hundreds of requests to adjust the ACL for users who justifiably need to reach normally banned websites.

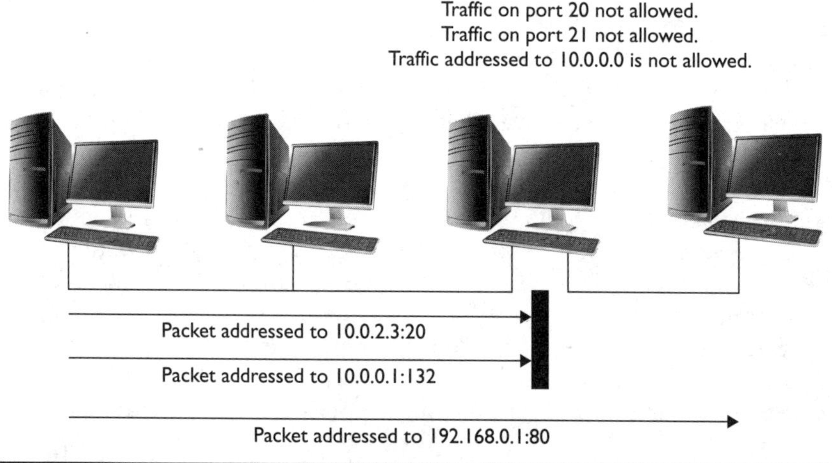

Figure 15-14 Using a packet-filtering firewall

But this also introduces *phishing* e-mails. If a hacker can trick a trusted user into clicking a link that forwards to a banned website in the Country of Belchre that the hacker controls, the hacker now has breached the firewall and now can attack the victims.

NOTE There are also kernel-proxy, web-application, application-level gateways, circuit-level next-generation firewalls, and so on. These operate higher up the OSI Model and are beyond the scope of the Linux+ exam.

Implementing a Packet-Filtering Firewall

A Linux system can be configured to function as many network devices, such as router or firewalls. Currently, there are many firewall appliances on the market based on Linux. For our purposes, we will focus on creating a basic packet-filtering firewall using firewalld and the legacy tool iptables.

The first step in setting up a packet-filtering firewall on a Linux system is to design the implementation. Answer the following questions when designing in the firewall:

- Will the firewall deny all incoming traffic except for specific allowed traffic?
- Will all outgoing traffic be blocked except for specific types or destinations?
- What ports must be opened on the firewall to allow traffic through from the outside? For example, is there a publicly accessible website behind the firewall? If so, then ports 80 and 443 must be opened.

Next, configure the firewall using the firewalld service. The firewalld service offers zone-based firewalling, making it easier to create common setups. The firewalld service supports IPv4 and IPv6 and is part of systemd. Also, permanent and temporary or runtime configurations are available.

To enable the firewalld service, use systemctl, as shown here:

```
[root@cent71-5t kimberli]# systemctl enable firewalld
[root@cent71-5t kimberli]# systemctl start firewalld
[root@cent71-5t kimberli]# systemctl status firewalld
firewalld.service - firewalld - dynamic firewall daemon
  Loaded: loaded (/usr/.../firewalld.service; enabled; vendor preset: enabled)
  Active: active (running) since Thu 2022-04-04 00:09:58 EDT; 1 day 22h ago
    Docs: man:firewalld(1)
Main PID: 3334 (firewalld)
   Tasks: 2
  CGroup: /system.slice/firewalld.service
          └─3334 /usr/bin/python -Es /usr/sbin/firewalld --nofork --nopid

Apr 04 00:09:56 cent71-5t systemd[1]: Starting firewalld - dynamic firewall...
Apr 04 00:09:58 cent71-5t systemd[1]: Started firewalld - dynamic firewall ...
Hint: Some lines were ellipsized, use -l to show in full.
[root@cent71-5t kimberli]#
```

If there are multiple network interfaces, IP forwarding needs to be enabled, as shown next:

```
[root@cent71-5t kellij]# echo 1 > /proc/sys/net/ipv4/ip_forward
[root@cent71-5t kellij]# echo 1 > /proc/sys/net/ipv6/ip_forward
```

NOTE For IPv6 forwarding, set */proc/sys/net/ipv6/conf/all/forwarding* to 1. This will enable forwarding for all network interfaces enabled on the system.

The firewalld feature has several predefined zones of trust to manage IP packets. Table 15-4 lists some of the common zones available with firewalld.

Use the firewall-cmd tool to display available zones and to switch to a different default. For example, here's how to change from the home zone to internal zone:

```
[root@cent71-5t jake]# firewall-cmd --get-default-zone
home
[root@cent71-5t jake]# firewall-cmd --set-default-zone=internal
success
[root@cent71-5t jake]# firewall-cmd --get-default-zone
internal
[root@cent71-5t jake]#
```

To list all the configured services and interfaces allowed through the zone, run the **firewall-cmd --list-all** option, as shown here:

```
[root@cent71-5t edwina]# firewall-cmd --list-all
internal (active)
 target: default
 icmp-block-inversion: no
 interfaces: enp0s3
```

Zone	Outgoing Connections	Incoming Connections
work	Allowed	SSH, IPP, and DHCPv6 client allowed
home	Allowed	SSH, IPP, multicast DNS, DHCPv6 client, and Samba client allowed
internal	Allowed	SSH, IPP, multicast DNS, DHCPv6 client, and Samba client allowed
external	Allowed and masqueraded to IP address of outgoing network interface	SSH allowed
dmz	Allowed	SSH allowed
public	Allowed	SSH and DHCPv6 client allowed
trusted	Allowed	Allowed
drop	Allowed	Dropped
block	Allowed	Rejected with icmp-host-prohibited message

Table 15-4 The firewalld Zones

```
sources:
services: ssh mdns samba-client dhcpv6-client
ports:
protocols:
masquerade: no
forward-ports:
source-ports:
icmp-blocks:
rich rules:
```

After the system is rebooted, the firewall settings return to their default values. To add a service and make the runtime values permanent, use the **--permanent** flag:

```
[root@cent71-5t camilla]# firewall-cmd --permanent --add-service=telnet
success
[root@cent71-5t camilla]# firewall-cmd --reload
```

The **--reload** option makes it so that the change occurs immediately; otherwise, the change does not take effect until reboot.

NOTE The --reload operation only loads the known existing service, so if the administrator did *not* use --permanent, as shown previously, the telnet service would not be enabled. For example, telnet is not enabled after --reload:
[root@cent71-5t matia]# firewall-cmd --add-service=http --zone=home
[root@cent71-5t matia]# firewall-cmd --reload
**[root@cent71-5t matia]# firewall-cmd --list-services --zone=home ssh **
mdns samba-client dhcpv6-client

Exercise 15-3: Implementing Network Security Measures with firewalld

In Exercise 15-3, you practice using firewalld settings by adding web services to the public zone. You can perform this exercise using the virtual machine that comes with this book. Complete the following steps:

VIDEO Please watch the Exercise 15-3 video for a demonstration on how to perform this task.

1. Boot your Linux system and log in as the root user. Install firewalld if necessary.
2. Set the firewall to use the home zone as follows:
   ```
   firewall-cmd --set-default-zone=home
   ```
3. Add web services and secure web services to the public zone:
   ```
   firewall-cmd --zone=home --add-service=http
   firewall-cmd --zone=home --add-service=https
   ```
4. Prove that you were successful in adding these services:
   ```
   firewall-cmd --list-services --zone=home
   ```
5. Learn more about firewalld by running **firewall-cmd --help**.

Implementing a Firewall with iptables

The firewalld service is actually the front end to iptables, but firewalld can maintain existing connections even after a change in settings. Most Linux distributions include iptables, but if not it can be downloaded from www.netfilter.org or from the vendor's repositories. The Linux kernel itself completes the packet-filtering tasks using netfilter.

The netfilter infrastructure uses the concept of "tables and chains" to create firewall rules. A *chain* is simply a rule that is implemented to determine what the firewall will do with an incoming packet. The netfilter infrastructure uses the *filter table* to create packet-filtering rules. Within the filter table are three default chains:

- **FORWARD** The FORWARD chain contains rules for packets being transferred between networks through the Linux system.
- **INPUT** The INPUT chain contains rules for packets that are being sent to the local Linux system.
- **OUTPUT** The OUTPUT chain contains rules for packets that are being sent from the local Linux system.

Each chain in the filter table has four policies:

- ACCEPT
- DROP
- QUEUE
- REJECT

To create a chain of multiple rules, each rule in a chain is assigned a number. The first rule you add is assigned the number 1. The iptables utility can add rules, delete rules, insert rules, and append rules. The syntax for using iptables is **iptables -t <table> <command> <chain> <options>**. Use the following commands with iptables:

- **-L** Lists all rules in the chain
- **-N** Creates a new chain

You can work with either the default chains listed previously or create your own chain. You create your own chain by entering **iptables -N <chain_name>**. You can add rules to a chain by simply using the -A option. You can also use one of the other options listed here:

- **-I** Inserts a rule into the chain
- **-R** Replaces a rule in the chain
- **-D** Deletes a rule from the chain
- **-F** Deletes all the rules from the chain (called *flushing*)
- **-P** Sets the default policy for the chain

EXAM TIP The candidate should be comfortable with the iptables options listed in Table 15-5.

You can also use the following options with iptables:

- **-p** Specifies the protocol to be checked by the rule. You can specify all, tcp, udp, or icmp.
- **-s <ip_address/mask>** Specifies the source address to be checked. If you want to check all IP addresses, use 0/0.
- **-d <ip_address/mask>** Specifies the destination address to be checked. If you want to check all IP addresses, use 0/0.
- **-j <target>** Specifies what to do if the packet matches the rule. You can specify the ACCEPT, REJECT, DROP, or LOG action.
- **-i <interface>** Specifies the interface where a packet is received. This only applies to INPUT and FORWARD chains.
- **-o <interface>** Specifies the interface where a packet is to be sent. This applies only to OUTPUT and FORWARD chains.

NOTE The options presented here represent only a sampling of what can be done with iptables. To see all the options available, see the iptables man page.

The best way to learn how to use iptables is to look at some examples. Table 15-5 has some sample iptables commands to start with.

You can use iptables to create a sophisticated array of rules that control how data flows through the firewall. Most administrators use the -P option with iptables to set up the firewall's default filtering rules. Once the default is in place, use iptables to configure exceptions to the default behavior needed by the particular network.

iptables Command	Function
iptables -L	Lists existing rules
iptables -D FORWARD 1	Deletes the first rule in the FORWARD chain
iptables -t filter -F	Deletes all rules from the filter table
iptables -P INPUT DROP	Sets a default policy for the INPUT chain that drops all incoming packets
iptables -P FORWARD DROP	Configures your FORWARD chain to drop all packets
iptables -A INPUT -s 0/0 -p icmp -j DROP	Configures the firewall to disregard all incoming ping packets addressed to the local Linux system
iptables -A INPUT -i eth0 -s 192.168.2.0/24 -j DROP	Configures the firewall to accept all incoming packets on eth0 coming from the 192.168.2.0 network

Table 15-5 Some iptables Commands

Remember that any rules created with iptables are not persistent. If you reboot the system, they will be lost by default. To save the rules, use the **iptables-save** command to write firewall tables out to a file. Then use the **iptables-restore** command to restore the tables from the file created.

Exercise 15-4: Implementing Network Security Measures with iptables

In Exercise 15-4, you practice scanning for open IP ports and implementing a simple host-based firewall. Perform this exercise using the virtual machine that comes with this book.

VIDEO Please watch the Exercise 15-4 video for a demonstration on how to perform this task.

1. Boot your Linux system and log in as your student1 user.
2. Open a terminal session and switch to your root user account by entering **su -** followed by the password **student1**.
3. Scan your system for open ports by completing the following steps:
   a. At the shell prompt, enter **nmap -sT <your_IP_address>**. What TCP/IP ports are in use on your system?
   b. At the shell prompt, enter **nmap -sU <your_IP_address>**. What UDP/IP ports are in use on your system?
4. Configure a simple firewall with iptables by doing the following:
   a. From a remote system, ping your Linux system and verify that it responds.
   b. Open a terminal session.
   c. At the shell prompt, **su -** to root.
5. Configure the kernel to use the iptables filter by entering **modprobe iptable_filter** at the shell prompt.
6. List the current rules for the filter table by entering **iptables -t filter -L** at the shell prompt.
7. At the shell prompt, enter **iptables -t filter -A INPUT -s 0/0 -p icmp -j DROP**. This command creates a rule that will drop all incoming packets using the ICMP protocol from any source destined for the local system.
8. View your new rule by entering **iptables -t filter -L** at the shell prompt. You should see the following rule added to your INPUT chain:
   ```
   DROP       icmp --  anywhere             anywhere
   ```
9. Using your remote system, ping your Linux system's IP address. The packets should be dropped, as shown in this sample output:
   ```
   Pinging 192.168.1.10 with 32 bytes of data:
   Request timed out.
   Request timed out.
   ```

Configuring a Firewall with UFW

The uncomplicated firewall (UFW) makes firewall configuration simple. After installing UFW, start with a simple set of rules:

```
[root@cent71-5t camilla]# ufw default allow outgoing
[root@cent71-5t camilla]# ufw default deny incoming
[root@cent71-5t camilla]# ufw allow ssh
[root@cent71-5t camilla]# ufw allow 80/tcp
```

This example blocks all incoming traffic except for SSH and HTTP. The **ufw status** command will show all the rules that are enabled as well as whether UFW is active or inactive. Default firewall policies can be defined within the file */etc/default/ufw*, such as whether or not to enable IPV6 and whether to drop or reject packets.

To override the default UFW rules, create *before.rules* and *after.rules* files within the */etc/ufw* directory. Before rules run before the user settings when UFW runs, such as adding ping or loopback features. After rules run after the administrator's command-line rules.

NOTE For IPv6 settings, there are also *before6.rules* and *after6.rules* files within */etc/ufw*.

Dynamic Firewall Rulesets

Because hackers never rest, searching globally for weak spots 24 hours a day, seven days a week, automating intrusion detection is a necessity, and that is what *dynamic firewall rulesets* provide.

Imagine setting up an SSH server for remote staff to access. Once hackers become aware of this service, they will start their attack using brute-force login attempts. A utility such as DenyHosts automatically monitors these attempts and blocks further attempts from attacking IP addresses by automatically updating iptables and a file called */etc/hosts.deny*. As the name implies, */etc/hosts.deny* lists IP addresses that are disallowed access to the network and is a feature of TCP Wrappers.

NOTE TCP Wrappers also include a file of allowed hosts called */etc/hosts.allow*. This allow file is usually empty, with all access controls listed in */etc/hosts.deny*. The following example denies FTP except from the funutation domain, and the last line denies all other TCP Wrappers services:
ALL EXCEPT vsftpd : .funutation.com
ALL : ALL

Similarly, Fail2Ban monitors more than just SSH, parsing log files such as */var/log/auth.log*, */var/log/vsftpd.log*, and */var/log/apache2/access.log* to monitor attacks to SSH, FTP, Web Services, and so on. Fail2Ban looks for numerous bad login attempts and other network security threats to lock out abusers, updating iptables and */etc/hosts.deny*. As threats begin to dissipate, addresses can be "unbanned," realizing that most threats are coming from spoofed IP addresses. The system comes with configurations that also include qmail, Postfix, and Courier Mail Server.

The final dynamic firewall tool discussed is called "IP set," which can dynamically update iptables and firewalld against attacks from IP addresses and ports. The primary command used to implement IP sets is ipset. The ipset command is used to create rules that expire, enhance iptables, monitor and stop brute-force attempts, detect and block port scans, and forward hostile packets to honeypots.

Encrypting Files with GPG

Just as you can encrypt network transmissions between Linux systems using SSH, you can also use encryption to protect files in the Linux file system. There are a wide variety of tools to do this. Some are open source; others are proprietary. A great utility for encrypting files is the open source GNU Privacy Guard (GPG) utility. We'll discuss the following topics in this section:

- How GPG works
- Using GPG to encrypt files

Let's begin by discussing how GPG works.

NOTE Knowledge of GPG is *not* part of the requirements on the Linux+ exam. This section was added for your information.

How GPG Works

GNU Privacy Guard (GPG) is an open source implementation of the OpenPGP standard (RFC 4880). It allows users to encrypt and digitally sign data and communications. For example, users can encrypt files and digitally sign e-mail messages.

GPG provides a cryptographic engine that can be used directly from the shell prompt using the gpg command-line utility. It can also be called from within shell scripts or other programs running on the system. For example, GPG is integrated into several Linux e-mail clients such as Evolution and KMail as well as instant messaging applications such as Psi.

GPG supports many encryption algorithms, including AES, 3DES, Blowfish, MD5, SHA, and RSA.

NOTE The *gpg.conf* file is also located in the *~/.gnupg* directory. You can use this file to customize the way GPG works on your system.

Using GPG to Encrypt Files

To encrypt a file using GPG, follow these steps:

1. Use GPG to generate your keys. To do this, enter **gpg --gen-key** at the shell prompt. An example is shown here:

```
cgreer@openSUSE:~> gpg --gen-key
gpg (GnuPG) 2.0.22; Copyright (C) 2013 Free Software Foundation, Inc.
This is free software: you are free to change and redistribute it.
There is NO WARRANTY, to the extent permitted by law.

Please select what kind of key you want:
   (1) RSA and RSA (default)
   (2) DSA and Elgamal
   (3) DSA (sign only)
   (4) RSA (sign only)
Your selection?
```

2. Select the type of key you want to create. Usually you will use the default option (1), which uses RSA and RSA. You are prompted to specify the size of the key, as shown here:

```
RSA keys may be between 1024 and 4096 bits long.
What keysize do you want? (2048)
```

3. Specify the size of key you want to create. Using the default size of 2048 bits is usually sufficient. You are prompted to configure the key lifetime, as shown here:

```
Please specify how long the key should be valid.
         0 = key does not expire
      <n>  = key expires in n days
      <n>w = key expires in n weeks
      <n>m = key expires in n months
      <n>y = key expires in n years
Key is valid for? (0)
```

4. Specify when the key will expire. As shown in step 3, you can specify that the key expire in a certain number of days, weeks, months, or years.
5. Construct your user ID for the key. The first parameter you need to specify is your real name. The name you specify is very important because it will be used later during the encryption process. In the next example, I entered **cgreer** for the real name:

```
GnuPG needs to construct a user ID to identify your key.
Real name: cgreer
```

6. When prompted, enter your e-mail address.
7. When prompted, enter a comment of your choosing. You are prompted to confirm the user ID you have created for the key. An example is shown here:

```
You selected this USER-ID:
   "cgreer <cgreer@openSUSE>"

Change (N)ame, (C)omment, (E)mail or (O)kay/(Q)uit?
```

8. If the information is correct, enter **O** to confirm the ID. You are prompted to enter a passphrase for the key.

9. Enter a unique passphrase for the key. After doing so, you are prompted to perform various actions on the system while the key is generated. An example is shown here:

```
We need to generate a lot of random bytes. It is a good idea to perform
some other action (type on the keyboard, move the mouse, utilize the
disks) during the prime generation; this gives the random number
generator a better chance to gain enough entropy.
+++.++++++++++.++++++++++.++++++++++.++++++++++..+++++.++++++++++>++++++++++
..................................>+++++...........................<+++++.
................................>+++++...........<+++++.......+++++
```

10. Move your mouse and type on the keyboard. GPG uses these actions to generate random numbers to make the key. If you are not doing enough, you'll be prompted to increase activity to generate enough entropy to create the key. An example is shown here:

```
Not enough random bytes available.  Please do some other work to give
the OS a chance to collect more entropy! (Need 137 more bytes)
```

At this point, the key pair has been generated! The key files are stored in the *~/.gnupg* directory in the user's home directory. The following files are created in this directory:

- *secring.gpg* This file is the GPG secret keyring.
- *pubring.gpg* This file is the GPG public keyring.
- *trustdb.gpg* This file is the GPG trust database.

To create a backup of your GPG key pair, enter **gpg --export-secret-keys -armor <key_owner_email_address> > <filename>.asc** at the shell prompt. This is shown in the following example:

```
gpg --export-secret-keys --armor cgreer@openSUSE > cgreer-privatekey.asc
cgreer@openSUSE:~> ls
addnum          firstnames      mytestfile.txt      cgreer-privatekey.asc
```

For security, do not leave this file on your hard disk. Instead, copy it to a USB flash drive and lock it away. This will allow you to restore the private key should the original get corrupted.

Now use the key pair to encrypt files and messages. For example, to encrypt a file in the Linux file system, do the following:

1. At the shell prompt, enter **gpg -e -r <key_user_name> <filename>**. As shown here, I encrypted *mytestfile.txt*. The -e option tells GPG to encrypt the file. Remember that I specified a key username of cgreer when I created the key user ID, so that's what I enter here.

```
cgreer@openSUSE:~> gpg -e -r cgreer mytestfile.txt
```

2. Use the ls command to view the new encrypted file GPG created. The original file is left intact. The new file will have the same filename as the original file with a *.gpg* extension added. In the example here, the name of the new file is *mytestfile.txt.gpg*.

Once the file has been encrypted, it can then be decrypted using the gpg command. The syntax is **gpg --output <output_filename> --decrypt <encrypted_filename>**. For example, to decrypt the *mytestfile.txt.gpg* file created earlier, enter **gpg --output mytestfile.txt.decrypted --decrypt mytestfile.txt.gpg**. This is shown in the following example:

```
cgreer@openSUSE:~> gpg --output mytestfile.txt.decrypted --decrypt   \
mytestfile.txt.gpg

You need a passphrase to unlock the secret key for
user: "cgreer (<cgreer@openSUSE>"
2048-bit RSA key, ID FB8BF16C, created 2023-01-24 (main key ID 9DF54AB2)

gpg: encrypted with 2048-bit RSA key, ID FB8BF16C, created 2023-01-24
     "cgreer (<cgreer@openSUSE>"
cgreer@openSUSE:~> cat mytestfile.txt.decrypted
This is a text file that I wrote.
cgreer@openSUSE:~>
```

At this point, you are able to encrypt and decrypt files on your local system. But what do you do if you need to exchange encrypted files with someone else and you want both of you to be able to decrypt them? To do this, you must exchange and install GPG public keys on your systems.

To do this, copy your public keys to a public key server on the Internet. This is done by entering **gpg --keyserver hkp://subkeys.pgp.net --send-key <key_ID>** at the shell prompt. Notice that this command requires you to know the ID number associated with your GPG public key. This number is actually displayed when you initially create the GPG key pair; you can generate it again from the command line by entering **gpg --fingerprint <key_owner_email>**, as shown here:

```
cgreer@openSUSE:~> gpg --fingerprint cgreer@openSUSE > key_ID.txt
cgreer@openSUSE:~> cat key_ID.txt
pub   2048R/9DF54AB2 2023-01-24
     Key fingerprint = AF46 4AB3 1397 B88E BC6A  FBDA 465F 82C4 9DF5 4AB2
uid                  cgreer       <cgreer@openSUSE>
sub   2048R/FB8BF16C 2023-01-24
```

In this example, the output was saved from the command to a file named key_ID.txt to keep it handy, but this is optional. The ID number of the key is contained in the first line of output from the command. The number needed appears in bold in this example.

Once you have the ID number, you can then copy your GPG public key to a public key server on the Internet. Using the preceding information for my system, enter **gpg --keyserver hkp://subkeys.pgp.net --send-key 9DF54AB2** at the command prompt.

This option works great if you want to be able to exchange keys with a large number of other users. However, if you are only concerned about doing this with a limited number of people, just directly exchange keys between systems.

To do this, users can export public keys and send them to each other. To do this, enter **gpg --export --armor <key_owner_email> > <public_key_filename>** at the shell prompt. For example, to export the public key to the file named *gpg.pub* created earlier, enter the following:

```
cgreer@openSUSE:~> gpg --export cgreer@openSUSE > gpg.pub
```

Each user can then copy their key file to the other users. For example, to send a key to the charly user account on another Linux host named fedora, enter the following:

```
cgreer@openSUSE:~> scp gpg.pub charly@fedora:
```

Once this is done, each user can import the other users' public keys into their GPG keyring using the **gpg --import <public_key_filename>** command. For example, use scp to copy the public key file from the openSUSE system to the fedora system, and then used gpg to import the public key:

```
[charly@fedora ~]$ gpg --import gpg.pub
gpg: key 9DF54AB2: public key "cgreer <cgreer@openSUSE>" imported
gpg: Total number processed: 1
gpg:               imported: 1  (RSA: 1)
[charly@fedora ~]
```

Remember, each user needs to repeat this process. Then they can use each other's GPG keys to encrypt and decrypt files. You can view the keys in your GPG keyring using the **gpg --list-keys** command, as shown in the following example:

```
[charly@fedora ~]$ gpg --list-keys
/home/charly/.gnupg/pubring.gpg
--------------------------------
pub   2048R/9DF54AB2 2023-01-24
uid                  cgreer <cgreer@openSUSE>
sub   2048R/FB8BF16C 2023-01-24
[charly@fedora ~]$
```

In this example, you can see that the public key created earlier on openSUSE is now imported into the charly user's GPG keyring on fedora. The keyring file itself is located in the *~/.gnupg/* directory within my home directory and is named *pubring.gpg*.

Before we end this chapter, we need to discuss the topic of *key revocation.* From time to time, you may need to revoke a key, which withdraws it from public use. This should be done if the key becomes compromised, gets lost, or if you forget the passphrase associated with the key.

To revoke a key, you create a *key revocation certificate*. As a best practice, you should create a key revocation certificate immediately after initially creating your key pair. This is done in case something gets corrupted and the revocation certificate can't be created should it be required for some reason later on. Creating the key revocation certificate doesn't actually revoke the key pair; only when you issue the key revocation certificate does the key get revoked. Therefore, the key revocation certificate is a placeholder just in case it's needed later.

To create (not issue) the key revocation certificate, enter **gpg --output revoke.asc --gen-revoke <key_ID>** at the shell prompt. Remember, use the --fingerprint option with the gpg command to view the key ID number. In the example that follows, a key revocation certificate is created for the GPG key pair generated for the charly user on the fedora system:

```
[charly@fedora ~]$ gpg --fingerprint charly@fedora
pub   2048R/899AB9E6 2023-01-24
      Key fingerprint = A469 942C F5C9 555A B4A4  F975 1B3A CB26 899A B9E6
uid                  charly <charly@fedora>
```

```
sub   2048R/A86F1A4B 2023-01-24
[charly@fedora ~]$ gpg --output revoke.asc --gen-revoke 899AB9E6
sec  2048R/899AB9E6 2023-01-24 charly <charly@fedora>
Create a revocation certificate for this key? (y/N) y
Please select the reason for the revocation:
 0 = No reason specified
 1 = Key has been compromised
 2 = Key is superseded
 3 = Key is no longer used
 Q = Cancel
(Probably you want to select 1 here)
Your decision? 1
Enter an optional description; end it with an empty line:
> This key has been compromised
>
Reason for revocation: Key has been compromised
This key has been compromised
Is this okay? (y/N) y
You need a passphrase to unlock the secret key for
user: "charly <charly@fedora>"
2048-bit RSA key, ID 899AB9E6, created 2023-01-24
ASCII armored output forced.
Revocation certificate created.
Please move it to a medium which you can hide away; if Mallory gets
access to this certificate he can use it to make your key unusable.
It is smart to print this certificate and store it away, just in case
your media become unreadable.  But have some caution:  The print system of
your machine might store the data and make it available to others!
```

Avoid keeping the key revocation certificate on your system's hard disk. Instead, copy it to the same flash drive as your key pair backup and lock it away! If someone were to get ahold of this file, they could revoke the certificate without the administrator's knowledge or consent.

NOTE Again, knowledge of GPG is *not* part of the requirements on the Linux+ exam. This section was added for your edification.

So what should you do if the certificate actually does get compromised and you end up needing to revoke it? Import the revocation certificate in the same manner we discussed for standard certificates. Enter **gpg --import <revocation_certificate_filename>** at the shell prompt:

```
[charly@fedora ~]$ gpg --import revoke.asc
gpg: key 899AB9E6: "charly <charly@fedora>" revocation certificate imported
gpg: Total number processed: 1
gpg:    new key revocations: 1
gpg: 3 marginal(s) needed, 1 complete(s) needed, PGP trust model
gpg: depth: 0  valid:   1  signed:   0  trust: 0-, 0q, 0n, 0m, 0f, 1u
```

Once this is done, verify that the key was revoked by entering **gpg --list-keys <key_ID>** at the shell prompt. If you used the manual method discussed earlier in this chapter to distribute the public key, you must import the key revocation certificate on any other systems where your public key was imported.

If you are using a public key server on the Internet to distribute your keys to other users, you would need to issue the key revocation certificate there as well. Enter **gpg --keyserver <public_key_server_URL> --send <key_ID>** at the shell prompt. This lets everyone who is using your public key know that the key has been compromised and should no longer be used.

Exercise 15-5: Using GPG to Encrypt Files

In Exercise 15-5, you use GPG to encrypt a file and send it to a second Linux system. Then export the public key, copy it to the second Linux system, and decrypt the file that was sent.

NOTE You'll need at least two Linux systems for this exercise. Use two live Linux systems, two Linux virtual machines, or a mixture of both.

Complete the following steps:

1. Generate your GPG key pair by following these steps:
    a. Boot your first Linux system and log in as a standard user.
    b. Open a terminal session.
    c. Enter **gpg --gen-key** at the shell prompt.
    d. When prompted to select the type of key you want to create, press ENTER to use the default option (1), which uses RSA and RSA.
    e. When prompted to specify the size of the key, press ENTER to use the default size of 2048 bits.
    f. When prompted to specify when the key will expire, press ENTER to select the default option (0), which specifies that the key never expires.
    g. Enter **y** when prompted to confirm this selection.

NOTE We're doing this for demonstration purposes. In the real world, you should configure your keys to expire after a certain length of time. That way, if your key ever gets compromised, it will become invalid after a period of time.

    h. Construct the user ID for the key by first specifying a username that is at least five characters long. Write down the username you entered because you will need it later.
    i. When prompted, enter your e-mail address. Write down the e-mail address you entered because you will need it later.
    j. When prompted, enter your full name as a comment.
    k. When prompted to confirm the user ID you created for the key, enter **O** (the letter, not a zero) to confirm it.

  l. When prompted to enter a passphrase for the key, enter a unique passphrase.
  m. When prompted, move the mouse, type characters on your keyboard, or open and close your optical disc drive door. After you have done this, your key pair is generated!
2. Encrypt a file with GPG by doing the following:
  a. At the shell prompt, enter **gpg -e -r <key_user_name> mytestfile.txt**. Replace **<key_user_name>** with the real name you entered when creating your key. You created the *mytestfile.txt* file in Exercise 15-1. If you don't have this file, create a new one with this name.
  b. At the shell prompt, use the ls command to verify that the *mytestfile.txt.gpg* file was created.
3. Decrypt the file you just created by doing the following:
  a. Enter **gpg --output mytestfile.txt.decrypted --decrypt mytestfile.txt.gpg** at the shell prompt to decrypt the file.
  b. Use the cat command to display the contents of the *mytestfile.txt.decrypted* file and verify that it matches the content of the original file.
4. Send the encrypted file to a different system and decrypt it there by doing the following:
  a. Boot your second Linux system and log in as a standard user.
  b. Use the ping command to verify that it can communicate over the network with the first Linux system, where you create the GPG key pair.
  c. Switch back to your first Linux system.
  d. From the shell prompt of your first Linux system, export your key by entering the following:

```
gpg --export --armor <key_owner_email> > gpg.pub
```

  e. Use the scp command to copy the *gpg.pub* and *mytestfile.txt.gpg* files from your first Linux system to your second Linux system.
  f. Switch over to your second Linux system.
  g. Verify that the *gpg.pub* file was copied to your user's home directory.
  h. Import the public key from your first Linux system into the GPG keyring by entering **gpg --import ~/gpg.pub** at the shell prompt.
  i. Verify that the public key was imported by entering **gpg --list-keys** at the shell prompt.
  j. Decrypt the encrypted file you copied over from the first Linux system by entering **gpg --output mytestfile.txt.decrypted --symmetric mytestfile.txt.gpg** at the shell prompt.
  k. When prompted, enter the passphrase you assigned to the GPG key when you created it on the first system.
  l. Use the cat command to display the contents of the *mytestfile.txt.decrypted* file and verify that it matches the content of the original file on the first Linux system.

5. Perform maintenance tasks on your GPG key pair by doing the following:
   a. Create a backup of your GPG key pair by entering **gpg --export-secret-keys --armor <key_owner_email_address> > gpgkey.asc** at the shell prompt.
   b. Create a key revocation certificate by entering **gpg --output revoke.asc --gen-revoke <key_ID>** at the shell prompt. Remember, you can use the --fingerprint option with the gpg command to view the key ID number.

VIDEO Please watch the Exercise 15-5 video for a demonstration on how to perform this task.

Chapter Review

This chapter covered how to use encryption to secure data on a Linux system and network security systems. We first looked at encrypting network communications with SSH, high-available networks with bonding, and then reviewed defending networking attacks using firewalld and iptables.

Be familiar with the following key facts about network security:

- With symmetric encryption, the key used to encrypt a message is the same key used to decrypt the message. The sender and the receiver must both have the exact same key.
- Symmetric encryption processes much faster than asymmetric encryption.
- One of the difficulties associated with symmetric encryption is how to securely distribute the key to all the parties that need to communicate with each other.
- Asymmetric encryption uses two keys instead of one: the public key and the private key.
- Data that has been encoded with the public key can be decoded only with its private key. Data that has been signed with the private key can be verified only with its public key.
- A certificate authority (CA) is responsible for issuing and managing encryption keys.
- The private key is given only to the key owner.
- The public key can be made available to anyone who needs it.
- The primary role of the CA is to verify that parties involved in an encrypted exchange are who they say they are.
- Administrators can mint their own certificates, called self-assigned certificates.
- Hashing is used for file integrity checking. Hash values are unique to every file. When this fails, it is called a collision.
- Popular hash algorithms include MD5 and SHA.

- SSH uses private/public key encryption along with secret key encryption:
  - The SSH client first creates a connection with the system where the SSH server is running on IP port 22.
  - To use the SSH client on your local computer, connect to the sshd daemon on the remote Linux system by entering **ssh -l <user_name> <ip_address>** at the shell prompt.
- VPNs use IPSec in tunnel mode for providing encryption and authentication.
- Tunnel mode is best over untrusted networks, such as from home to office.
- VPNs in transport mode use IPSec to encrypt packets and are a good solution over trusted networks.
- High-availability networks are implemented within Linux by way of bridging or bonding technologies.
- Network bridging provides fault tolerance.
- Network bonding boosts network throughput.
- Use the **brctl** command to set up a network bridge.
- Network bonding requires updating network scripts and enabling the bonding policy.
- Bonding options include active-passive, aggregation, and load balancing.
- Single sign-on (SSO) allows users the convenience of using one username and password for all their data from most anywhere.
- Popular SSO services include RADIUS with dial-up modem access, LDAP for vendor-neutral environments, Kerberos, which hides passwords by using tickets that expire, and TACACS+ for high availability and reliability.
- Linux systems can be configured as firewalls using firewalld, iptables, netfilter, or UFW.
- The **nmap**, **netstat**, and **lsof -i** utilities are used to examine vulnerable open IP ports.
- To enable IP forwarding, run **echo 1 > /proc/sys/net/ipv4/ip_forward**
- The firewalld feature offers nine default zones, including work, home, internal, external, dmz, and public.
- Run **firewall-cmd --get-default-zone** to view the current zone setting.
- Run **firewall-cmd --permanent** to make runtime values permanent after reboot.
- The **ufw** command simplifies building firewalls. Default firewall policies are listed in the */etc/default/ufw* file. Inside the */etc/ufw* directory, create *before.rules* and *after.rules* to enhance the firewall.
- Dynamic firewall ruleset providers include DenyHosts, which updates */etc/hosts.deny*, Fail2Ban, which updates iptables, and IP set, which updates firewalld. These utilities create firewall rules when they sense attacks to SSHD, FTPD, HTTPD, and other services.

Questions

1. Which of the following statements are true of symmetric encryption? (Choose two.)
   A. It uses a private/public key pair.
   B. Both the sender and the recipient must have a copy of the same key.
   C. RSA is a form of symmetric encryption.
   D. Blowfish is a form of symmetric encryption.
2. Which tools can scan for open network ports? (Choose two.)
   A. tcpwatch
   B. lsof
   C. nmap
   D. wireshark
   E. webgoat
3. Which host key files store the private keys used by the SSH version 2 server? (Choose two.)
   A. /etc/ssh/ssh_host_key
   B. /etc/ssh/ssh_host_key.pub
   C. /etc/ssh/ssh_known_hosts
   D. /etc/ssh/ssh_host_rsa_key
   E. /etc/ssh/ssh_host_dsa_key
4. Which parameter in the */etc/ssh/sshd_config* file specifies which version of SSH the sshd daemon should use?
   A. HostKey
   B. Protocol
   C. SSHVersion
   D. ListenAddress
5. Which parameter in the */etc/ssh/sshd_config* file configures the SSH server to disable root logins?
   A. RootAccess
   B. AllowRootLogin
   C. PermitRootLogin
   D. DenyRootLogin
6. Which option to iptables will list the current firewall rules?
   A. iptables -N
   B. iptables -L

C. iptables -I

D. iptables -R

7. Which of the following shell commands will load the SSH client and connect as the sseymour user to an SSH server with an IP address of 10.0.0.254?

A. sshd -l sseymour 10.0.0.254

B. ssh -u sseymour 10.0.0.254

C. ssh -l sseymour 10.0.0.254

D. sshd -u sseymour 10.0.0.254

8. Which of the following are hashing algorithms? (Select two.)

A. RSA

B. DSA

C. MD5

D. SHA

9. You've just created a DSA private/public key pair for use with SSH public key authentication. What is the name of the public key file?

A. ~/.ssh/id_rsa

B. ~/.ssh/id_dsa

C. ~/.ssh/id_rsa.pub

D. ~/.ssh/id_dsa.pub

10. You've copied your RSA public key to the home directory of a user on an SSH server. Which file do you need to add the public key to in order to enable public key authentication?

A. ~/.ssh/authorized_keys

B. /etc/ssh/authorized_keys

C. ~/.ssh/id_rsa

D. ~/ssh_host_key.pub

Answers

1. **B, D.** With symmetric encryption, both the sender and the recipient must have a copy of the same key. Blowfish is a form of symmetric encryption.
2. **B, C.** Use **nmap** and **lsof -i** to view open network ports on a system.
3. **D, E.** The private keys used by the SSH version 2 server are stored in */etc/ssh/ssh_host_rsa_key* and */etc/ssh/ssh_host_dsa_key*. The private keys for SSH version 1 are stored in */etc/ssh/ssh_host_key*.
4. **B.** The Protocol parameter in the */etc/ssh/sshd_config* file specifies which version of SSH the sshd daemon should use.

5. **C.** The **PermitRootLogin** parameter is set to no to disallow logging in as root.
6. **B.** Use **iptables -L** to list the current firewall ruleset with iptables.
7. **C.** The **ssh -l sseymour 10.0.0.254** command will load the SSH client and connect as the sseymour user to an SSH server with an IP address of 10.0.0.254.
8. **C, D.** The integrity checking algorithms include SHA and MD5. RSA and DSA are asymmetric encryption algorithms.
9. **D.** The *~/.ssh/id_dsa.pub* file is the DSA public key that can be used for SSH public key authentication.
10. **A.** You need to add the public key to the *~/.ssh/authorized_keys* file in the home directory of the user you want to authenticate as using public key authentication.

CHAPTER 16

Securing Linux

In this chapter, you will learn about

- Securing the system
- Controlling user access
- Managing system logs
- Enhancing group and file security

In today's world, security is a key issue in every organization. A Linux systems administrator needs to be aware of the security threats affecting the architecture. This chapter covers how to can increase the security of the Linux system.

EXAM TIP Computer system security is an ever-evolving topic. The security issues of last year teach those to prepare for the security incidents of tomorrow. This is reflected in your Linux+ exam. Do not be overly concerned with specific security threats. Instead, focus on commands, key security principles, and practices.

Securing the System

One of the most important and most frequently overlooked aspects of Linux security is securing the system itself. Topics addressed here include:

- Securing the physical environment
- Securing access to the operating system

Securing the Physical Environment

Convenience or security? That is the question. Many firms desire easy access to their computer systems. Organizations must balance security with convenience. If data on the system is mission critical or contains sensitive information, it should be less convenient to access, thus keeping it more secure.

Consider the following cases when determining physical access to Linux systems:

- A rogue supplier steals the hard drive from a server containing clients' tax identification numbers.
- A rogue employee steals week-old backup tapes from the shelf located outside the secure server room. The data contains customer logins and password hints.
- A passerby steals a pancake-style server from an unlocked closet, gleaning private health records of patients.

As a Linux administrator, one of the most important steps you can take is to limit who can access data-processing systems. Servers need the highest degree of physical security and should be locked in a server room. Access to the server room should be strictly controlled.

NOTE Biometric systems offer multifactor authentication. These scan retinas, match fingerprints, or observe voice patterns to control access to data.

In addition to controlling access to the office, you can further protect your organization's workstations and servers by securing access to the operating system.

Securing Access to the Operating System

After physically securing access to computer systems, the next line of defense is the access controls built into the Linux operating system itself. Of course, Linux provides user accounts and passwords to control who can do what with the system. This is an excellent feature, allowing users to protect their data no matter their level of responsibility or the criticality of the data. After the end users' work is complete, teach them to log out or lock their screen (as shown in Figure 16-1) as a good security practice to protect their data.

CAUTION You should never leave a server logged in. If you do, at least use a screensaver that requires a password to resume operations. Otherwise, best security practice is that if the user is not using the server console, they should log out.

To allow users to log out and leave without killing an important process, use the nohup command to initially load the command. Any process loaded by nohup will ignore any hang-up signals it receives, such as those sent when logging out. The syntax for using nohup is **nohup <command> &**. For example, in Figure 16-2, the **find -name named &** command has been loaded using nohup, allowing the find command to continue to run even if the shell were logged out.

Finally, administrators need to also protect servers from data loss. Private corporate strategies could reach competitors, harming the organization's image. One method to

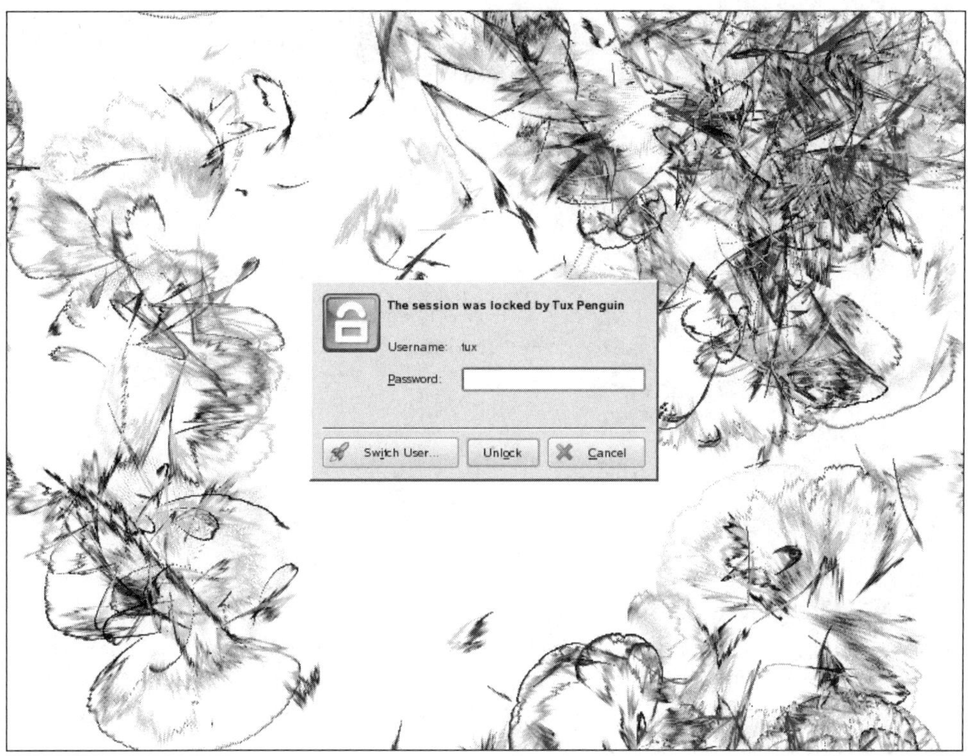

Figure 16-1 Locking the desktop

protect data leaks is to *disable USB ports*. In Linux you can do this by removing the USB module after Linux installation and every kernel update:

```
root# rm /lib/modules/$(uname -r)/kernel/drivers/usb/storage/usb-storage.ko.xz
```

Successful security practices boil down to end-user training. Social engineering attacks mitigate technical controls put in place by the system administrator to secure the network. If end users do not cooperate, corporate policies such as acceptable use policies and computer usage policies must be enforced.

```
root@openSUSE:~
File  Edit  View  Search  Terminal  Help
openSUSE:~ # nohup find / -name named &
[1] 2658
nohup: ignoring input and appending output to 'nohup.out'
```

Figure 16-2 Using nohup

Controlling User Access

A key aspect of both Linux workstation and Linux server security is to implement and use user access controls to constrain what users can do with the system. Earlier in this book, we discussed how to create and manage users, groups, and permissions to do this. However, you can take additional measures to increase the security of your systems. In this section, we review the following:

- To root or not to root?
- Implementing a strong password policy
- Locking accounts after failed authentications
- Configuring user limits
- Disabling user login
- Security audit using find

Let's begin by discussing the proper care and feeding of the root user account.

To Root or Not to Root?

As discussed earlier in this book, every Linux system, whether a workstation or a server, includes a default administrator account named root. This account has full access to every aspect of the system. As such, it should be used with great care. As a Linux+ candidate, you need understand the following:

- Proper use of the root user account
- Using su
- Using sudo

Proper Use of the Root User Account

A key mistake made by new Linux users is excessive use of the root account. There's a time and a place when the root user account should be used; however, most of the work on a Linux system should be done as a non-root user. The rule of thumb is this: only use root when absolutely necessary. If a task can be completed as a non-root user, then use a non-root user account.

Why is the proper use of the root user account of concern? Imagine the havoc an intruder could wreak if they were to happen upon an unattended system logged in as root! All of the data on the system could be accessed and copied. Major configuration changes could be made to the daemons running on the system. Heaven only knows what kind of malware could be installed.

The point is, a system logged in as root represents a serious security risk. Everyone, including the system administrator, should have a standard user account that they always use to access the system. If the system administrator requires root privilege, they should temporarily use the privilege and then return back to normal privilege. Linux provides two ways to do this that are important for the Linux+ exam: su and sudo.

Using su

The su command stands for "substitute user." This command allows one to change to a different user account at the shell prompt. The syntax is **su <options> <user_account>**. If no user account is specified in the command, su assumes switching to the root user account. Here are some of the more useful options you can use with su:

- **-** Loads the target user's profile. For example, when you use the **su -** command to switch to the root user account, this also loads root's environment variables.
- **-c <command>** Temporarily switches to the target user account, runs the specified command, and returns to the original account.
- **-m** Switches to the target user account but preserves the existing profile.

Everyone with the root password can use su to switch to the root user, but providing all users root privileges is a very poor security practice. Also, becoming root with su will not log the activities of the user. Sometimes users need root access temporarily to add a printer or a new network device. There must be a way to do this without having to locate the system administrator, and that method is with sudo.

Using sudo

Suppose there is a power user on a Linux system. This user might be a programmer, a project manager, or a database administrator. A user in this category may frequently need to run some root-level commands. To allow them to run a limited number of root-level commands, and to log their administrator activity, you can teach them to use sudo.

The **sudo** command allows a given user to run a command as a different user account. As with su, it could be any user account on the system; however, it is most frequently used to run commands as root. The sudo command uses the */etc/sudoers* file to determine what user is authorized to run which commands. This file uses the following aliases to define who can do what:

- **User_Alias** Specifies the user accounts allowed to run commands
- **Cmnd_Alias** Specifies the commands users can run
- **Host_Alias** Specifies the hosts users can run commands on
- **Runas_Alias** Specifies the usernames commands can be run as

To edit the */etc/sudoers* file, run either **sudo -e /etc/sudoers**, **sudoedit /etc/sudoers**, or simply the **visudo** command as the root user. The */etc/sudoers* file is loaded in using the default editor, which is usually vi but may be modified using the EDITOR, VISUAL, or SUDO_EDITOR environment variable. Your changes are written to */etc/sudoers.tmp* until committed. This is shown in Figure 16-3.

NOTE To modify the default editor for programs like sudoedit, place the following line into the user's *~/.bashrc* file:
EDITOR=/usr/bin/nano; export EDITOR
This example implements nano to now be the default editor.

```
root@openSUSE:~
File  Edit  View  Search  Terminal  Help
## sudoers file.
##
## This file MUST be edited with the 'visudo' command as root.
## Failure to use 'visudo' may result in syntax or file permission errors
## that prevent sudo from running.
##
## See the sudoers man page for the details on how to write a sudoers file.
##


##
## Host alias specification
##
## Groups of machines. These may include host names (optionally with wildcards),
## IP addresses, network numbers or netgroups.
# Host_Alias    WEBSERVERS = www1, www2, www3

##
## User alias specification
##
## Groups of users.  These may consist of user names, uids, Unix groups,
## or netgroups.
# User_Alias    ADMINS = millert, dowdy, mikef

"/etc/sudoers.tmp" 81L, 3009C                              1,1           Top
```

Figure 16-3 Editing /etc/sudoers with visudo

The */etc/sudoers* file is configured by default such that users must supply their password when using sudo, instead of the root password like with su. This sudo feature makes the system more secure because the root password is shared with fewer users.

To configure the */etc/sudoers* configuration file, modify User_Alias to define an alias containing the user accounts (separated by commas) allowed to run commands as root. The syntax is

```
User_Alias <alias> = <user1>, <user2>, <user3>, ...
```

For example, to create an alias named PWRUSRS that contains the cheryl, theo, and aria user accounts, you would enter the following in the */etc/sudoers* file:

```
User_Alias PWRUSRS = cheryl, theo, aria
```

NOTE All alias names within */etc/sudoers* must start with a capital letter!

Next use Cmnd_Alias to define the commands, using the full path, that you want the defined users to run. Separate multiple commands with commas; for example, if the users are programmers who need to be able to kill processes, define an alias named KILLPROCS that contains the kill command, as shown here:

```
Cmnd_Alias KILLPROCS = /bin/kill, /usr/bin/killall
```

Then use Host_Alias to specify which systems the users can run the commands on. For example, to allow them to run commands on a system named openSUSE, use the following:

```
Host_Alias MYHSTS = openSUSE
```

Finally, to glue the aliases together to define exactly what will happen, the syntax is this:

```
User_Alias Host_Alias = (user) Cmnd_Alias
```

For example, to allow the specified users to run the specified commands on the specified hosts as root, enter the following:

```
PWRUSRS     MYHSTS = (root) KILLPROCS
```

Now that the updates to */etc/sudoers* is complete, exit visudo by pressing ESC and then enter **:wq** (this assumes that EDITOR is defined as */usr/bin/vi*). The visudo utility will verify the syntax and, if everything is correct, will exit. At this point, the end users defined within */etc/sudoers* can execute commands as the root user by entering **sudo <command>** at the shell prompt. For example, the cheryl user could kill a process named vmware-toolbox (owned by root) by entering **sudo killall vmware-toolbox** at the shell prompt. After the cheryl user supplies her password, *not* the root password, and the process is killed.

In addition to managing the root user account properly, administrators also should implement a strong password policy.

Implementing a Strong Password Policy

Another serious security weakness to organizations is the use of weak passwords. A weak password is one that can be easily guessed or cracked. Here are some examples:

- A last name
- A mother's maiden name
- A birthday
- Any word that can be found in the dictionary
- Using "password" as the password
- Blank passwords

These types of passwords are used because they are easy to remember. Unfortunately, they are also easy to crack. Administrators need to train their users to use strong passwords, such as passphrases. A strong password uses the following:

- Twelve or more characters (the longer the better!)

- A combination of numbers, special characters, and letters
- Upper- and lowercase letters
- Words not found in the dictionary

For example, a password such as M3n0v31273!! is a relatively strong password because it meets the criteria, but it is hard to remember. A passphrase such as "To &3 or NOT to &3" is strong and easier to remember. The Linux password management utilities are configured by default to check user passwords to ensure they meet the criteria for strong passwords. For example, if you try to use a weak password with the passwd command, you are prompted to use a stronger one, as shown here:

```
[root@localhost ~]# passwd theo
New Password:BAD PASSWORD: it is WAY too short
BAD PASSWORD: is too simple
Retype new password:
```

In addition to using strong passwords, administrators should also configure user accounts such that passwords expire after a certain period of time. This is called *password aging.* Why age passwords? The longer a user has the same password, the more likely it is to be compromised. Forcing users to periodically change passwords keeps intruders guessing. The length of time allowed for a given password varies from organization to organization. More security-minded organizations mandate password ages of 27–30 days. Less paranoid organizations use aging of 90 or more days.

Administrators can configure aging for passwords using the **chage** command. The syntax for using chage is **chage <option> <user>**. The following options are available with chage:

- **-m <*days*>** Specifies the minimum number of days between password changes
- **-M <*days*>** Specifies the maximum number of days between password changes
- **-W <*days*>** Specifies the number of warning days before a password change is required

For example, in Figure 16-4, the chage command has been used to specify a minimum password age of five days, a maximum password age of 90 days, and seven warning days for the ksanders user.

In addition, Linux systems should *not* be configured to store passwords within the */etc/passwd* file. Many processes running in a Linux system need access to */etc/passwd*

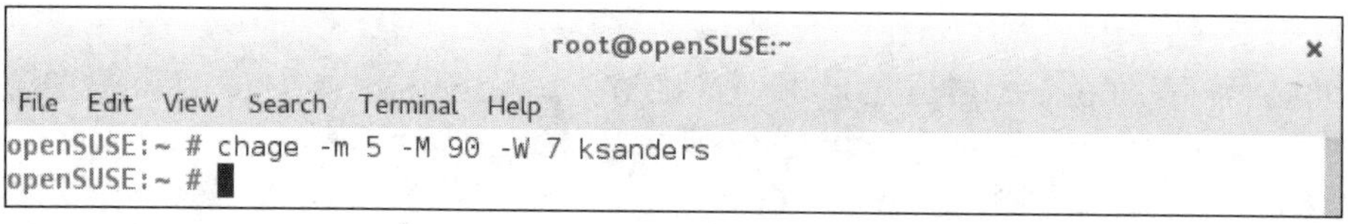

```
root@openSUSE:~
File Edit View Search Terminal Help
openSUSE:~ # chage -m 5 -M 90 -W 7 ksanders
openSUSE:~ #
```

Figure 16-4 Using chage to set password aging

to complete various tasks, so storing passwords in */etc/passwd* exposes them to a serious security hole. Administrators who find systems with password hashes located in */etc/passwd* can use the pwconv command to easily move user password hashes from */etc/passwd* and into */etc/shadow*.

EXAM TIP For even greater security, administrators may set boot passwords on the system BIOS, UEFI, or even within GRUB.

Password Security Threats

Administrators must train their users to use common sense when working with passwords. A recent issue at a middle school shows how important it is to protect passwords. The attendance secretary kept her password on a sticky note. A student noticed this and logged in. The student then used the school's attendance-tracking software to send out automated prank phone calls to all the parents. Complex computer security systems cannot stop this type of attack.

Social Engineering Threats

Administrators should also train users on how to deal with social engineering attempts. This is actually one of the most effective tools in the intruder's toolbox. Social engineering exploits human weaknesses instead of technical weaknesses in the system. Here's how a typical social engineering exploit works.

The intruder calls an employee of an organization posing as another employee. The intruder tells the employee that he is "Fred" from Sales and is on the road at a client site. He needs to get a very important file from the server and cannot remember his password. He then asks the employee if he can use their password "just this once" to get the files he needs.

Most employees want to be team players and help out in an emergency. They are all too willing to hand out their password, granting the intruder easy access to the system.

Finally, administrators need to mitigate the flood of *phishing e-mails* plaguing organizations. Phishing e-mails appear to come from a legitimate organization, such as a bank, a friend, or an e-commerce website. They convince the user to click a link that takes them to a malicious website where they are tricked into revealing their password.

Train users to *hover* their mouse over a link (*without* clicking it) to see where the link actually leads. If the link is not pointing to the organization's URL, there's a pretty good chance the message is an exploit.

The best way to combat social engineering is end-user training. Enforce policies of not writing down passwords and not clicking on e-mail links, as well as shredding sensitive data and forwarding any calls asking for passwords to the security office.

In addition to configuring password aging, you can also increase the security of your Linux systems by limiting logins and resources. Let's review how this is done next.

EXAM TIP Password security threat practices comprise a very important topic, but are not an area of focus for the Linux+ exam. Be sure you study the basics of the pwconv command as well as the columns and permissions of the */etc/passwd* and */etc/shadow* files for better exam results.

Locking Accounts After Failed Authentications

Administrators can secure user account access using Pluggable Authentication Modules (PAM). PAM controls authentication of users for applications such as login, ssh, su, and others. For example, use PAM to require specific password lengths and characters or to disallow users from logging in from specific terminals.

Linux locates the PAM configuration files in the */etc/pam.d* directory. Configuration files for services such as login, ssh, and others are located here. Partial contents of the */etc/pam.d/sshd* appear as follows:

```
...
auth required pam_nologin.so
auth sufficient pam_ldap.so
account sufficient pam_ldap.so
password required pam_ldap.so
password required pam_limits.so
session required pam_selinux.so
session include password-auth
...
```

The first column represents authentication tasks, grouped by account, authentication, password, and session:

- **account** Provides account verification services (for example, has the password expired? Is the user allowed access to a specific service?).
- **auth** Used to authenticate the user, request a password, and set up credentials.
- **password** Requests the user enters a replacement password when updating the password.
- **session** Manages what happens during setup or cleanup of a service (for example, mounting the home directory or setting resource limits).

The second column represents the control keyword to manage the success or failure processing:

- **required** If required fails, the entire operation fails *after* running through all the other modules.
- **requisite** Operation fails immediately if requisite fails.
- **sufficient** If successful, this is enough to satisfy the requirements of the service.
- **optional** Will cause an operation to fail if it is the only module in the stack for that facility.

The third column displays the module that gets invoked, which can take additional options and arguments. For example, pam_ldap.so provides authentication, authorization, and password changing to LDAP servers. The pam_nologin.so module prevents non-admin users from logging in to a system if the */etc/nologin* file exists. The default security context is set with the pam_selinux.so module.

Using pam_tally2 to Manage Failed Authentications

To deny access after three failed login attempts, add the following two lines to */etc/pam.d/sshd*:

```
auth required pam_tally2.so deny=3 onerr=fail
account required pam_tally2.so
```

The pam_tally2.so module is the login counter. The argument **deny=3** sets the login counter for failed attempts, and **onerr=fail** will lock the account after three failures in this case.

To view the tally of failed logins, the root user can run the **/sbin/pam_tally2** command, as shown here:

```
[root@localhost ~]# pam_tally2
Login        Failures    Latest failure           From
hollis       3           06/15/2024 12:12:13      localhost
```

After the security issue has been investigated, the root user can reset the account to allow logins, as follows:

```
[root@localhost ~]# pam_tally2 -u hollis -r
Login        Failures    Latest failure           From
hollis       3           06/15/2024 12:12:13      localhost
[root@localhost ~]# pam_tally2 -u hollis -r
Login        Failures    Latest failure           From
hollis       0
```

Using faillock to Manage Failed Authentications

The other utility used to view failed login attempts is faillock. The following will display failed login attempts using faillock for user hollis:

```
[root@localhost ~]# faillock --user hollis
hollis:
When                   Type        Source              Valid
2023-10-12 06:15:03    TTY         pts/0               V
```

To reset the failed-login counter for the user, run the following:

```
[root@localhost ~]# faillock --user hollis --reset
```

Authentication utilities such as ssh and login need to use the pam_faillock.so module to implement the faillock capabilities.

Configuring User Limits

Limit settings allow for a better-tuned Linux system. For example, administrators can limit how many times users may log in, how much CPU time can be consumed, how much memory can be used on a Linux system, and more. There are two ways administrators can restrict access to resources:

- Using ulimit
- Using pam_limits

Using ulimit to Restrict Access to Resources

Administrators use the ulimit command to configure limits on system resources. However, limits configured with ulimit are applied only to programs launched from the shell prompt. The syntax for using ulimit is ulimit **<options> <limit>**. You can use the following options with ulimit:

- **-c** Sets a limit on the maximum size of core files in blocks. If this option is set to a value of 0, core umps for the user are disabled.
- **-f** Sets a limit on the maximum size (in blocks) of files created by the shell.
- **-n** Sets a limit on the maximum number of open file descriptors.
- **-t** Sets a limit on the maximum amount of CPU time (in seconds) a process may use.
- **-u** Sets a limit on the maximum number of processes available to a single user.

Use the -a option with ulimit to view the current value for all resource limits. This is shown in Figure 16-5.

Finally, use **ulimit** to set resource limits. For example, to set a limit of 250 processes per user, enter **ulimit -u 250** at the shell prompt. The user could then own no more than 250 concurrent shell processes.

Using pam_limits to Restrict Access to Resources

Administrators can also limit user access to Linux system resources using a PAM module called pam_limits, which is configured using the */etc/security/limits.conf* file. This file contains resource limits defined using the following syntax:

```
<domain>      <type>      <item>      <value>
```

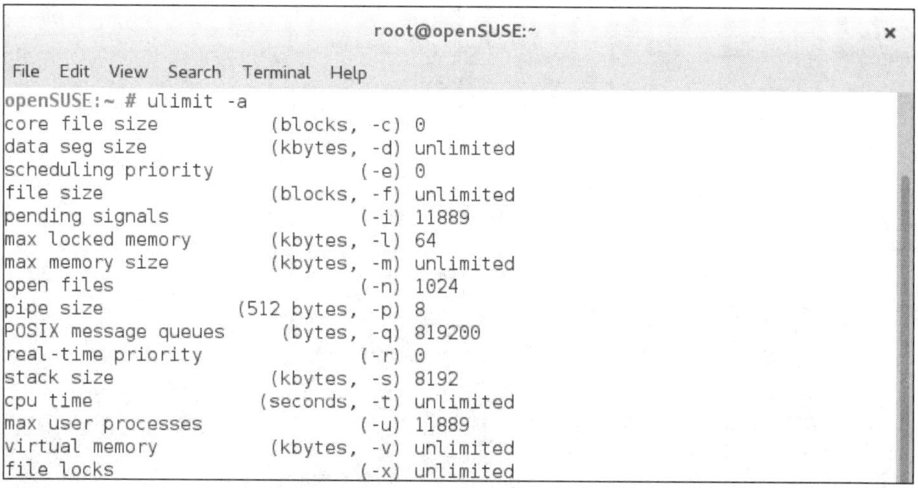

```
root@openSUSE:~
File  Edit  View  Search  Terminal  Help
openSUSE:~ # ulimit -a
core file size          (blocks, -c) 0
data seg size           (kbytes, -d) unlimited
scheduling priority             (-e) 0
file size               (blocks, -f) unlimited
pending signals                 (-i) 11889
max locked memory       (kbytes, -l) 64
max memory size         (kbytes, -m) unlimited
open files                      (-n) 1024
pipe size            (512 bytes, -p) 8
POSIX message queues     (bytes, -q) 819200
real-time priority              (-r) 0
stack size              (kbytes, -s) 8192
cpu time               (seconds, -t) unlimited
max user processes              (-u) 11889
virtual memory          (kbytes, -v) unlimited
file locks                      (-x) unlimited
```

Figure 16-5 Viewing current resource limits with ulimit

Resource	Description
core	Restricts the size of core files (in KB)
fsize	Restricts the size of files created by the user (in KB)
nofile	Restricts the number of data files a user may have open concurrently
cpu	Restricts the CPU time of a single process (in minutes)
nproc	Restricts the number of concurrent processes a user may run
maxlogins	Sets the maximum number of simultaneous logins for a user
priority	Sets the priority to run user processes with
nice	Sets the maximum nice priority a user is allowed to raise a process to

Table 16-1 Configuring Resource Limits

This syntax is described here:

- **<domain>** Describes the entity to which the limit applies. You can use one of the following values:
  - **<user>** Identifies a specific Linux user
  - **@<group_name>** Identifies a specific Linux group
  - * Specifies all users
- **<type>** Defines a hard or soft limit. A hard limit cannot be exceeded, whereas a soft limit can be temporarily exceeded.
- **<item>** Specifies the resource being limited via values shown in Table 16-1.
- **<value>** Specifies a value for the limit.

For example, to configure the aria user with a soft CPU limit of 15 minutes, modify the */etc/security/limits.conf* file in a text editor and enter the following:

```
aria      soft      cpu      15
```

This limit is useful for users running CPU-intensive programs that are hogging cycles away from other users.

Likewise, limit the cheryl user to a maximum of two concurrent logins by entering the following in the */etc/security/limits.conf* file:

```
cheryl      hard      maxlogins      2
```

This would prevent any further logins to the system after two initial logins were successful for the cheryl user.

Disabling User Login

From time to time, it may be important to disable all logins to your Linux system (for example, if an administrator prefers a clean, total system data backup). To do this, all current users must log out. The **w** command lists all currently logged-in users and shows what they are doing. For example, in Figure 16-6, two users are currently logged in: ksanders and rtracy.

```
root@openSUSE:~
File Edit View Search Terminal Help
openSUSE:~ # w
 19:05:56 up 29 min,  4 users,  load average: 0.51, 0.28, 0.26
USER     TTY      FROM             LOGIN@   IDLE   JCPU   PCPU WHAT
rtracy   :0       console          18:43   ?xdm?   2:57   0.31s /usr/lib/gdm/gd
rtracy   console  :0               18:43   29:13   0.00s  0.31s /usr/lib/gdm/gd
rtracy   pts/0    :0               18:43    4.00s  0.78s  1.70s /usr/lib/gnome-
ksanders pts/1    10.0.0.60        19:05   27.00s  0.17s  0.17s -bash
```

Figure 16-6 Generating a list of logged-in users

After the administrator has politely asked the users to log off, they can brute-force log out a user, and reasonably protect their jobs, using the **pkill -KILL -u <username>** command. For example, in Figure 16-7, the pkill command is used to log off the ksanders user.

Now, to disable all future logins, create a file in */etc* named *nologin*. As long as this file exists, no one but root is allowed to log in. In addition, any text you enter in the */etc/nologin* file will be displayed if a user attempts to log in. In the example shown in Figure 16-8, the text "The system is currently unavailable for login" is entered in the */etc/nologin* file. Thus, when a user tries to log in, this is the error message displayed.

NOTE Administrators can enable a script to notify users of scheduled shutdowns. Within the script use the printf command to send the message, for example:
printf "System Going down for service at 5PM Today"

```
root@openSUSE:~
File Edit View Search Terminal Help
openSUSE:~ # w
 19:05:56 up 29 min,  4 users,  load average: 0.51, 0.28, 0.26
USER     TTY      FROM             LOGIN@   IDLE   JCPU   PCPU WHAT
rtracy   :0       console          18:43   ?xdm?   2:57   0.31s /usr/lib/gdm/gd
rtracy   console  :0               18:43   29:13   0.00s  0.31s /usr/lib/gdm/gd
rtracy   pts/0    :0               18:43    4.00s  0.78s  1.70s /usr/lib/gnome-
ksanders pts/1    10.0.0.60        19:05   27.00s  0.17s  0.17s -bash
openSUSE:~ # pkill -KILL -u ksanders
openSUSE:~ # w
 19:10:10 up 33 min,  3 users,  load average: 0.13, 0.17, 0.21
USER     TTY      FROM             LOGIN@   IDLE   JCPU   PCPU WHAT
rtracy   :0       console          18:43   ?xdm?   3:21   0.31s /usr/lib/gdm/gd
rtracy   console  :0               18:43   33:27   0.00s  0.31s /usr/lib/gdm/gd
rtracy   pts/0    :0               18:43    2.00s  0.79s  2.16s /usr/lib/gnome-
```

Figure 16-7 Forcing a user to log off

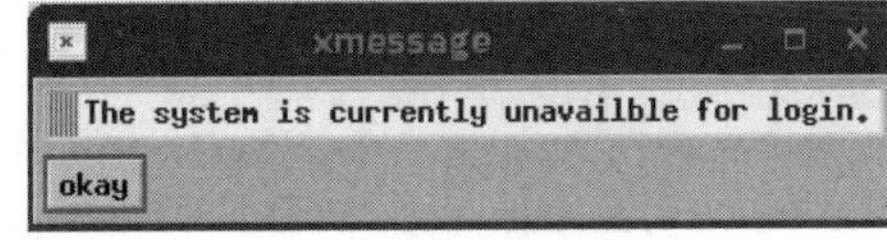

Figure 16-8 "Login denied" message from */etc/nologin*

This behavior is actually configured in the */etc/pam.d/login* file, shown here:

```
[root@localhost ~]# cat /etc/pam.d/login
#%PAM-1.0
auth     requisite       pam_nologin.so
auth     [user_unknown=ignore success=ok ignore=ignore auth_err=die
default=bad]pam_securetty.so
auth     include         common-auth
account  include         common-account
password include         common-password
session  required        pam_loginuid.so
session  include         common-session
session  required        pam_lastlog.so  nowtmp
session  optional        pam_mail.so standard
session  optional        pam_ck_connector.so
```

The line that reads auth requisite pam_nologin.so causes PAM to check whether a file named *nologin* exists in */etc*. If it does, PAM does not allow regular users to log in.

After the full, clean backup is completed by the administrator, logins can be re-enabled by deleting or renaming the *nologin* file. For example, renaming it by entering

```
[root@localhost ~]# mv /etc/nologin /etc/nologin.bak
```

at the shell prompt will still allow users to log in.

Let's next discuss how to audit files to locate files with the SUID or SGID permission set.

EXAM TIP Administrators can modify the "Message of the Day" file, or */etc/motd*, so that maintenance warning messages appear on the end users' terminal at every login.

Security Auditing Using find

In addition to disabling user logins, another user security-related issue you need be familiar with is auditing files that have SUID root permissions set. As you learned in Chapter 6, SUID stands for "set user ID." When an executable file with the SUID permission set is run, the process is granted access to the system as the user who owns the executable file, not on the user who actually ran the command. *This is a serious issue if the file is owned by root.* When the root user owns a file with the SUID permission set, it allows the process created by the file to perform actions as root, which the user who started it is probably not allowed to do. The same issue applies to files owned by the root group that have "set group ID" (SGID) permission set.

Be aware that a small number of files owned by root on a Linux system do need to have these permissions set. However, other files owned by root/root that have the SUID/SGID permission set represent a security vulnerability on the system. Many exploits are facilitated using files with this permission set. A file that has the SUID permission set appears as follows when listed with the ls command at the shell prompt:

```
-rwSr-xr-x
```

A file that has the SGID permission set appears as follows when listed with the ls command at the shell prompt:

```
-rw-r-Sr-x
```

Therefore, the administrator needs to consider running periodic audits to identify any files owned by root that have either of these permissions set. Any files beyond the minimal necessary files should be scrutinized carefully to make sure they are not part of some type of exploit. Administrators can search for files on Linux systems that have SUID permissions set using the following command at the shell prompt as the root user:

```
find / -type f -perm -u=s -ls
```

Here is an example:

```
[root@localhost ~]# find / -type f -perm -u=s -ls
36406    32 -rwsr-xr-x   1 root      root        31848 Sep  5  2019 /bin/su
30659    36 -rwsr-xr-x   1 root      root        35796 May  3  2017 /bin/ping
84596    20 -rwsr-xr-x   1 root      audio       20252 Jun 16  2016 /bin/eject
85643   324 -rwsr-xr-x   1 root      root       330420 Sep  5  2019 /bin/mount
30661    36 -rwsr-xr-x   1 root      root        35716 May  3  2017 /bin/ping6
85644   120 -rwsr-xr-x   1 root      root       121111 Sep  5  2019 /bin/umount
```

The -perm option tells find to match files that have the specified permission assigned to the mode; in this case, the S permission is assigned to user. You can also identify any files with the SGID permission set using the following command:

```
find / -type f -perm -g=s -ls
```

When you do, a list of all files with the SGID permission set is displayed. Here is an example:

```
[root@localhost ~]# find / -type f -perm -g=s -ls
94451    12 -rwxr-sr-x   1 root      tty         10588 May 18  2017 /opt/gnome/lib
85710    12 -rwxr-sr-x   1 root      tty         10404 Sep  5  2019 /usr/bin/wall
5867     12 -rwxr-sr-x   1 root      shadow       8800 Jun 16  2016 /usr/bin/vlock
85713    12 -rwxr-sr-x   1 root      tty          9024 Sep  5  2019 /usr/bin/write
93913    12 -rwxr-sr-x   1 root      maildrop    11300 Sep  5  2019 /usr/sbin/postdrop
93919    12 -rwxr-sr-x   1 root      maildrop    11668 Sep  5  2019 /usr/sbin/postqueue
26192     8 -rwxr-sr-x   1 root      tty          7288 Jun 16  2016 /usr/sbin/utempter
35720    24 -rwxr-sr-x   1 root      shadow      20672 Sep  5  2019 /sbin/unix_chkpwd
```

EXAM TIP Administrators can avoid disruptive server shutdowns by disabling CTRL-ALT-DEL as follows:

```
[root]#  systemctl mask ctrl-alt-del.target
[root]#  systemctl daemon-reload
```

Practice controlling user access to a Linux system in Exercise 16-1.

Exercise 16-1: Managing User Access

In this exercise, you practice setting age limits on user passwords. Also, you configure sudo to allow a standard user to kill processes on the system as the root user. Perform this exercise using the virtual machine that comes with this book.

VIDEO Watch the Exercise 16-1 video for a demonstration on how to perform this task.

Complete the following steps:

1. Boot your Linux system and log in as your **student1** user with a password of **student1**.
2. Open a terminal session.
3. Switch to your root user account by entering **su** - followed by a password of **password**.
4. Practice configuring age limits by completing the following steps:
   a. Use the cat or less utility to view the */etc/passwd* file. Identify a user on the system who you want to configure password age limits for.
   b. Set the minimum password age to three days, the maximum password age to 60 days, and the number of warning days before expiration to seven by entering **chage -m 3 -M 60 –W 7 <username>** at the shell prompt.
5. Configure sudo to allow a user on your system to kill processes as the root user by doing the following:
   a. Identify a user on your system to whom you want to grant the ability to kill processes as root.
   b. As your root user, enter visudo at the shell prompt. You should see the */etc/sudoers* file loaded in the vi text editor.
   c. Scroll down to the lines shown in the example that follows and comment them out by inserting a # character at the beginning of each one.

```
Defaults targetpw   # ask for the password of target user i.e. root
ALL   ALL=(ALL) ALL   # WARNING! Only use with 'Defaults targetpw'!
```

d. Add the following lines to the end of the sudoers file by pressing G and then O:

```
User_Alias PWRUSRS = your_user
Cmnd_Alias KILLPROCS = /bin/kill, /usr/bin/killall
Host_Alias MYHSTS = openSUSE
PWRUSRS MYHSTS = (root) KILLPROCS
```

e. Press ESC and then enter **:x** to save the changes to the *sudoers* file.

f. Run **top** at the shell prompt as your root user.

g. Open a new terminal session and (as your standard user) enter **ps -elf | grep top**. You should see a top process running that is owned by the root user.

h. Kill that process as your standard user by entering **sudo killall top** at the shell prompt.

i. When prompted, enter your user's password.

j. Enter **ps -elf | grep top** at the shell prompt again. You should see that the top process that was owned by the root user has been killed.

Managing System Logs

Log files are a gold mine of information for the system administrator. Log files are used to detect intruders into a system, troubleshoot problems, and determine performance issues within the system. Linux usually uses an audit trail system called auditd, but in this section, you will learn how to manage and use system log files with more advanced tools. We will discuss the following topics:

- Configuring log files
- Using log files to troubleshoot problems
- Using log files to detect intruders

Let's begin by discussing how to configure log files.

Configuring Log Files

System log files are stored in the */var/log* directory, shown in Figure 16-9.

Notice in this figure that there are a number of subdirectories in */var/log* where system daemons, such as mysql, apparmor, audit, and cups, store their log files. Some of these log files are simple text files that can be read with text manipulation utilities. Others are binary files that require the use of a special utility, such as lastlog, which displays the most recent logins of users. As you can see in Figure 16-9, there are quite a number of files within */var/log* and its subdirectories. As with most anything, some log files are much more useful than others. Table 16-2 contains a list of some of the more important log files.

```
root@openSUSE:/var/log
File  Edit  View  Search  Terminal  Help
openSUSE:/var/log # ls
NetworkManager     btmp            mail.err               pm-powersave.log
Xorg.0.log         cups            mail.info              samba
Xorg.0.log.old     faillog         mail.warn              speech-dispatcher
Xorg.1.log         firewall        messages               warn
YaST2              gdm             messages-20141222.xz   wpa_supplicant.log
acpid              hp              mysql                  wtmp
alternatives.log   krb5            news                   zypp
apparmor           lastlog         ntp
audit              localmessages   pbl.log
boot.log           mail            pk_backend_zypp
```

Figure 16-9 Contents of the */var/log* directory

NOTE The files shown in Table 16-2 are log files used on a SUSE Linux system. Other distributions may use different files by default. You can customize logging using the */etc/rsyslog.conf* file.

How logging is implemented on Linux depends on the Linux distribution. For the Linux+ exam, you need be familiar with the following logging implementations:

- rsyslogd
- journald

Log File	Description
faillog	Contains failed authentication attempts.
firewall	Contains firewall log entries.
kern.log	Contains detailed log messages from the Linux kernel.
lastlog	Contains the last login information for users.
mail	Contains messages generated by the postfix and sendmail daemons.
messages	Contains messages from most running processes. This is probably one of the most useful of all the log files. Administrators can use it to troubleshoot services that won't start, services that don't appear to work properly, and so on.
secure	Contains messages related to authentication and authorization. The sshd process logs messages here, including unsuccessful login attempts.
wtmp	Contains a list of users who have authenticated to the system.
xinetd.log	Contains log entries from the xinetd daemon.

Table 16-2 Useful Log Files

rsyslogd

Logging on a Linux system that uses init is usually handled by the rsyslogd daemon. Instead of each daemon maintaining its own individual log file, most of your Linux services are configured to write log entries to */dev/log* by default. This device file is maintained by the rsyslogd daemon. When a service writes to this socket, the input is captured by rsyslogd. The rsyslogd daemon then uses the entries in the */etc/rsyslog.conf* file, shown in Figure 16-10, to determine where the information should go.

NOTE Some Linux distributions use syslog-ng or syslogd instead of rsyslogd to manage logging.

The syntax for the */etc/rsyslog.conf* file is

```
<facility>.<priority>        <file>
```

A <facility> refers to a subsystem that provides a message. Each process on your Linux system that uses rsyslog for logging is assigned to one of the following facilities:

- **authpriv** Facility used by services associated with system security and authorization
- **cron** Facility that accepts log messages from cron and at
- **daemon** Facility that can be used by daemons that do not have their own facility

```
# Log all kernel messages to the console.
# Logging much else clutters up the screen.
#kern.*                                                 /dev/console

# Log anything (except mail) of level info or higher.
# Don't log private authentication messages!
*.info;mail.none;authpriv.none;cron.none                /var/log/messages

# The authpriv file has restricted access.
authpriv.*                                              /var/log/secure

# Log all the mail messages in one place.
mail.*                                                  -/var/log/maillog


# Log cron stuff
cron.*                                                  /var/log/cron

# Everybody gets emergency messages
*.emerg                                                 *

# Save news errors of level crit and higher in a special file.
uucp,news.crit                                          /var/log/spooler
./syslog.conf
```

Figure 16-10 The */etc/rsyslog.conf* file

- **kern** Facility used for all kernel log messages
- **lpr** Facility that handles messages from the printing system
- **mail** Facility for log messages from the mail MTA (for example, postfix or sendmail)
- **news** Facility for log messages from the news daemon
- **rsyslog** Facility for internal messages from the rsyslog daemon itself
- **user** Facility for user-related log messages (such as failed login attempts)
- **uucp** Facility for log messages from the uucp daemon
- **local0-7** Facilities used to capture log messages from user-created applications

In addition to facilities, the rsyslogd daemon also provides *priorities* to customize how logging occurs on the system. Prioritization is handled by the klogd daemon on most distributions, which runs as a client of rsyslogd. Use the following priorities with rsyslogd, listed from most to fewest messages:

- **debug** All information; normally used for debugging activities.
- **info** Informational and unremarkable messages.
- **notice** Issues of concern, but not yet a problem.
- **warn** Noncritical errors that can potentially cause harm.
- **err** Serious errors fatal to the daemon but not the system.
- **crit** Critical errors, but no need to take immediate action.
- **alert** Action must be taken immediately, but the system is still usable.
- **emerg** Fatal errors to the computer; system unusable.
- **none** Do not log any activity.

For example, review the */etc/rsyslog.conf* file shown in Figure 16-10 and go down about 15 lines, where you will see the following:

```
# Log cron stuff
cron.*                         /var/log/cron
```

Here, the rsyslogd daemon directs messages of all priority levels (*) from the cron facility to the */var/log/cron* file. If desired, an administrator could customize the */etc/rsyslog.conf* file to split messages of different priority levels to different files, as shown here:

```
user.info                      /var/log/messages
user.alert                     /var/log/secure
```

The preceding definitions in */etc/rsyslog.conf* will send all user-related info-level messages (and higher priorities) to the */var/log/messages* file, and */var/log/secure* will receive only user alert messages and higher.

Disk Space Management Using Log File Rotating

Linux distributions also include a utility named **logrotate**. The logrotate utility is run daily, by default, by the cron daemon. To customize how log files are rotated, modify the */etc/logrotate.conf* file, as shown in Figure 16-11.

The */etc/logrotate.conf* file contains default global parameters used by logrotate to determine how and when log files are rotated. However, these defaults can be overridden for specific daemons using the configuration files located in the */etc/logrotate.d/* directory. For example, in Figure 16-12, the */etc/logrotate.d/apache2* file is used to customize logging for the apache2 daemon.

Also, the first line shown in Figure 16-12 means the */var/log/apache2/access_log* file will be compressed. It can have a maximum age of 365 days, after which it will be removed (maxage 365). Old versions of the file will be archived using a date extension (dateext).

```
# see "man logrotate" for details
# rotate log files weekly
weekly

# keep 4 weeks worth of backlogs
rotate 4

# create new (empty) log files after rotating old ones
create

# use date as a suffix of the rotated file
dateext

# uncomment this if you want your log files compressed
#compress

# comment these to switch compression to use gzip or another
# compression scheme
compresscmd /usr/bin/bzip2
uncompresscmd /usr/bin/bunzip2

# former versions had to have the compressext set accordingly
#compressext .bz2

# RPM packages drop log rotation information into this directory
include /etc/logrotate.d

# no packages own wtmp and btmp -- we'll rotate them here
#/var/log/wtmp {
#    monthly
#    create 0664 root utmp
#       minsize 1M
#    rotate 1
#}
#
# /var/log/btmp {
#   missingok
#    monthly
#    create 0600 root utmp
#    rotate 1
#}
/etc/logrotate.conf lines 1-41/43 93%
```

Figure 16-11 Configuring log file rotation in /etc/logrotate.conf

Figure 16-12 Configuring Apache web server logging

```
/var/log/apache2/access_log {
    compress
    dateext
    maxage 365
    rotate 99
    size=+4096k
    notifempty
    missingok
    create 644 root root
    postrotate
     /etc/init.d/apache2 reload
    endscript
}

/var/log/apache2/error_log {
    compress
    dateext
    maxage 365
    rotate 99
    size=+1024k
    notifempty
    missingok
    create 644 root root
    postrotate
     /etc/init.d/apache2 reload
apache2 lines 1-25/69 38%
```

The log file will go through 99 rotations before being removed (rotate 99). If the file grows larger than 4096 KB, it will be rotated (size=+4096k). The file will not be rotated if it is empty (notifempty). No error message will be generated if the file is missing (missingok). The file will be created with 644 permissions, will have the root user as the owner, and will be owned by the root group (create 644 root root). After a log file is rotated, the */etc/init.d/apache2* reload command will be run (postrotate /etc/init.d/apache2 reload).

EXAM TIP You can test your logging configuration using the logger utility. This command-line tool allows you to manually make entries in your logging system. The syntax is as follows:
logger -p <facility>.<priority> "<log_message>"

journald

Linux distributions that use the systemd daemon use the journald daemon for logging instead of rsyslogd. The journald daemon maintains a system log called the journal, located in */run/log/journal/*. To view the journal, use the journalctl command. When you enter this command at the shell prompt with no parameters, the entire journal is displayed, as shown in Figure 16-13.

NOTE By default, journal log data is lost at reboot. To make persistent, do the following:

```
# mkdir -p /var/log/journal
# systemd-tmpfiles --create --prefix /var/log/journal
```

```
root@openSUSE:~
File  Edit  View  Search  Terminal  Help
-- Logs begin at Thu 2015-01-22 16:56:49 MST, end at Thu 2015-01-22 17:08:25 MST
Jan 22 16:56:49 openSUSE systemd-journal[227]: Runtime journal is using 276.0K (
Jan 22 16:56:49 openSUSE systemd-journal[227]: Runtime journal is using 280.0K (
Jan 22 16:56:49 openSUSE kernel: Initializing cgroup subsys cpuset
Jan 22 16:56:49 openSUSE kernel: Initializing cgroup subsys cpu
Jan 22 16:56:49 openSUSE kernel: Initializing cgroup subsys cpuacct
Jan 22 16:56:49 openSUSE kernel: Linux version 3.11.10-21-desktop (geeko@buildho
Jan 22 16:56:49 openSUSE kernel: Disabled fast string operations
Jan 22 16:56:49 openSUSE kernel: e820: BIOS-provided physical RAM map:
Jan 22 16:56:49 openSUSE kernel: BIOS-e820: [mem 0x0000000000000000-0x0000000000
Jan 22 16:56:49 openSUSE kernel: BIOS-e820: [mem 0x000000000009f800-0x0000000000
Jan 22 16:56:49 openSUSE kernel: BIOS-e820: [mem 0x00000000000ca000-0x0000000000
Jan 22 16:56:49 openSUSE kernel: BIOS-e820: [mem 0x00000000000dc000-0x0000000000
Jan 22 16:56:49 openSUSE kernel: BIOS-e820: [mem 0x0000000000100000-0x000000005f
Jan 22 16:56:49 openSUSE kernel: BIOS-e820: [mem 0x000000005fef0000-0x000000005f
Jan 22 16:56:49 openSUSE kernel: BIOS-e820: [mem 0x000000005feff000-0x000000005f
Jan 22 16:56:49 openSUSE kernel: BIOS-e820: [mem 0x000000005ff00000-0x000000005f
Jan 22 16:56:49 openSUSE kernel: BIOS-e820: [mem 0x00000000e0000000-0x00000000ef
Jan 22 16:56:49 openSUSE kernel: BIOS-e820: [mem 0x00000000fec00000-0x00000000fe
Jan 22 16:56:49 openSUSE kernel: BIOS-e820: [mem 0x00000000fee00000-0x00000000fe
Jan 22 16:56:49 openSUSE kernel: BIOS-e820: [mem 0x00000000fffe0000-0x00000000ff
Jan 22 16:56:49 openSUSE kernel: NX (Execute Disable) protection: active
Jan 22 16:56:49 openSUSE kernel: SMBIOS 2.4 present.
lines 1-23
```

Figure 16-13 Viewing the journal with journalctl

One of the neat features of the journald daemon is the fact that you can use it to view system boot messages as well. To do this, enter journalctl -b at the shell prompt. The messages from the most recent system boot are displayed. In addition, you can use journalctl to view messages from previous system boots. This can be done in two different ways:

- Specifying the -b flag with the command followed by a positive number will look up messages from the specified system boot, starting from the beginning of the journal. For example, entering **journalctl -b 1** will display messages created during the first boot found at the beginning of the journal.
- Specifying the -b flag with the command followed by a negative number will look up the messages from the specified system boot starting from the end of the journal. For example, entering **journalctl -b -2** will display system messages created two boots ago.

The journalctl command can also be used to display only log entries related to a specific service running on the system. The syntax is **journalctl -u <service_name>**. For example, to view all journal entries related to the SSH daemon running on the system, enter **journalctl -u sshd** at the shell prompt. An example is shown in Figure 16-14.

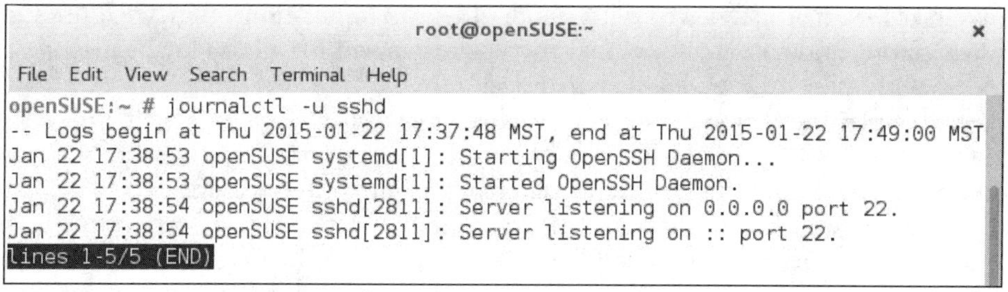

```
root@openSUSE:~
File Edit View Search Terminal Help
openSUSE:~ # journalctl -u sshd
-- Logs begin at Thu 2015-01-22 17:37:48 MST, end at Thu 2015-01-22 17:49:00 MST
Jan 22 17:38:53 openSUSE systemd[1]: Starting OpenSSH Daemon...
Jan 22 17:38:53 openSUSE systemd[1]: Started OpenSSH Daemon.
Jan 22 17:38:54 openSUSE sshd[2811]: Server listening on 0.0.0.0 port 22.
Jan 22 17:38:54 openSUSE sshd[2811]: Server listening on :: port 22.
lines 1-5/5 (END)
```

Figure 16-14 Viewing sshd journal events

The behavior of the journal daemon is configured using the */etc/systemd/journald.conf* file. This file has many configurable parameters. Here are some of the more useful ones:

- **ForwardToSyslog** Configures journald to forward its log messages to the traditional rsyslog daemon.
- **MaxLevelStore** Controls the maximum log level of messages stored in the journal file. All messages equal to or less than the log level specified are stored, whereas any messages above the specified level are dropped. This parameter can be set to one of the following values:
  - none
  - emerg (0)
  - alert (1)
  - crit (2)
  - err (3)
  - warning (4)
  - notice (5)
  - info (6)
  - debug (7)

With this background in mind, let's next discuss how to actually view and use your log files.

Using Log Files to Troubleshoot Problems

As mentioned earlier in this chapter, log files can be an invaluable resource when troubleshooting Linux problems. If the kernel or a service encounters a problem, it will be logged in a log file. Reviewing these log files can provide a wealth of information that may not necessarily be displayed on the screen.

Some log files are binary files that must be read with a special utility, like files in the */run/log/journal/* directory are binary files read by **journalctl**. However, most log files are simple text files that are viewed with standard text manipulation utilities. Utilities like cat, less, more, and so on can be used to view text-based log files. However, there is a problem with these utilities: log files are huge!

For example, the */var/log/messages* file, which logs generic system activity, may have 10,000 or more lines in it. That's a lot of text! The less utility displays only 24 lines at a time. You would have to press the spacebar a lot of times to get to the end of the file!

There are two strategies that can help. The first is to redirect the output of the cat command to the grep command to filter a specific term within a log file. For example, if you want to locate information within */var/log/messages* related to logins, you would enter

```
[root@localhost ~]# cat /var/log/messages | grep login | more
```

at the shell prompt. Then, only entries containing the term "login" would be displayed from the */var/log/messages* file. If the system uses systemd and a journal, the same could be done with the journalctl command:

```
[root@localhost ~]# journalctl | grep login | more
```

In addition to grep, you can also use the head and tail utilities to view log file entries. Understand that most log files record entries chronologically, usually oldest to newest. To view the beginning of a log file, enter **head <filename>** at the shell prompt to display the first lines of the file. For example, in Figure 16-15, the beginning of the */var/log/messages* file has been displayed with head.

```
root@openSUSE:~
File Edit View Search Terminal Help
openSUSE:~ # head /var/log/messages
2014-12-22T16:00:10.536035-07:00 openSUSE logrotate: ALERT exited abnormally wit
h [1]
2014-12-22T16:00:10.546737-07:00 openSUSE logrotate: error: skipping "/var/log/m
ysql/mysqld.log" because parent directory has insecure permissions (It's world w
ritable or writable by group which is not "root") Set "su" directive in config f
ile to tell logrotate which user/group should be used for rotation.
2014-12-22T16:00:10.549918-07:00 openSUSE logrotate: compress_ext is /usr/bin/xz
2014-12-22T16:00:10.551164-07:00 openSUSE logrotate: compress_ext was changed to
 .xz
2014-12-22T16:00:30.106794-07:00 openSUSE org.freedesktop.PackageKit[534]: Downl
oadProgressReportReceiver::start():http://download.opensuse.org/update/13.1/ --l
ibksba8;1.3.0-5.4.1;i586;repo-update
2014-12-22T16:00:33.767476-07:00 openSUSE org.freedesktop.PackageKit[534]: Downl
oadProgressReportReceiver::start():http://download.opensuse.org/update/13.1/ --n
tp;4.2.6p5-15.13.1;i586;repo-update
2014-12-22T16:00:58.500998-07:00 openSUSE /USR/SBIN/CRON[4257]: pam_unix(crond:s
ession): session closed for user root
2014-12-22T16:01:25.144933-07:00 openSUSE systemd[1]: Stopping Session 2 of user
 rtracy.
2014-12-22T16:01:25.157079-07:00 openSUSE systemd[1]: Stopped Session 2 of user
rtracy.
2014-12-22T16:01:25.213964-07:00 openSUSE systemd[1]: Stopping Stop Read-Ahead D
ata Collection 10s After Completed Startup.
```

Figure 16-15 Using head to view a log file

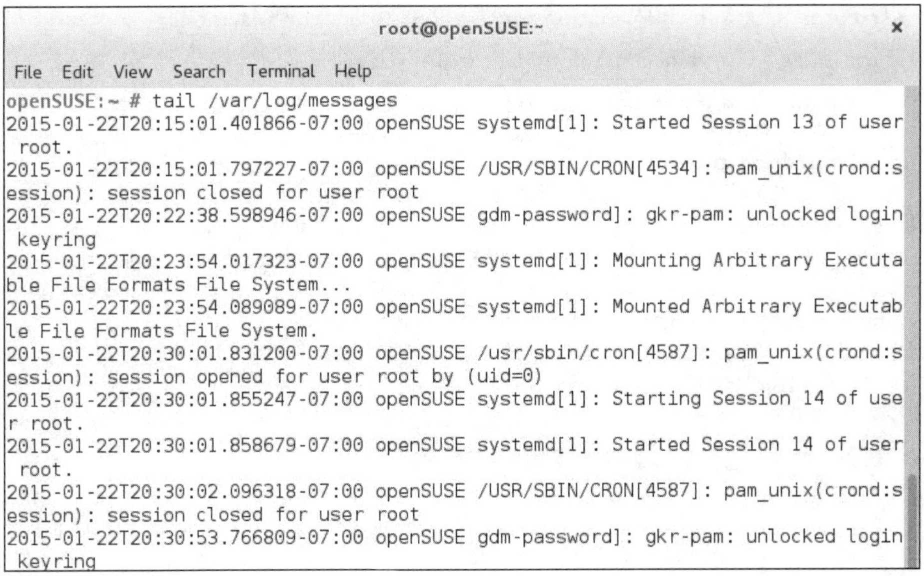

```
root@openSUSE:~
File Edit View Search Terminal Help
openSUSE:~ # tail /var/log/messages
2015-01-22T20:15:01.401866-07:00 openSUSE systemd[1]: Started Session 13 of user
 root.
2015-01-22T20:15:01.797227-07:00 openSUSE /USR/SBIN/CRON[4534]: pam_unix(crond:s
ession): session closed for user root
2015-01-22T20:22:38.598946-07:00 openSUSE gdm-password]: gkr-pam: unlocked login
 keyring
2015-01-22T20:23:54.017323-07:00 openSUSE systemd[1]: Mounting Arbitrary Executa
ble File Formats File System...
2015-01-22T20:23:54.089089-07:00 openSUSE systemd[1]: Mounted Arbitrary Executab
le File Formats File System.
2015-01-22T20:30:01.831200-07:00 openSUSE /usr/sbin/cron[4587]: pam_unix(crond:s
ession): session opened for user root by (uid=0)
2015-01-22T20:30:01.855247-07:00 openSUSE systemd[1]: Starting Session 14 of use
r root.
2015-01-22T20:30:01.858679-07:00 openSUSE systemd[1]: Started Session 14 of user
 root.
2015-01-22T20:30:02.096318-07:00 openSUSE /USR/SBIN/CRON[4587]: pam_unix(crond:s
ession): session closed for user root
2015-01-22T20:30:53.766809-07:00 openSUSE gdm-password]: gkr-pam: unlocked login
 keyring
```

Figure 16-16 Using tail to view a log file

The tail utility works in a manner opposite of head. Instead of displaying the first 10 lines of a file, it displays the last 10 lines. This is very useful because, when troubleshooting, you only need to see only the last few lines of a log file. To do this, enter **tail <filename>** at the shell prompt. In Figure 16-16, the */var/log/messages* file is being viewed using tail.

The tail utility provides the **-f** option, which is used often when troubleshooting. The -f option with tail will display the last lines of a log file as normal, but it monitors the file being displayed and displays new lines as they are added to the log file. For example, you could use the **tail -f /var/log/messages** command to monitor the system log file for error messages during the troubleshooting process. You can quit monitoring the file by pressing CTRL-C.

The "follow" feature is also available with systems that use the journald daemon to manage logging. Run **journalctl -f** at the shell prompt, and the last few entries in the journal are displayed. The journalctl command then monitors the journal and prints new entries as they are added. Again, you can quit monitoring by pressing CTRL-C.

You can check the system log files listed previously in Table 16-1 to troubleshoot problems, or other log files, including the following:

- cron Contains entries from the cron daemon
- dmesg Contains hardware detection information
- maillog Contains entries generated by the sendmail daemon

- secure Contains information about access to network daemons
- rpmpkgs Contains a list of installed rpm packages
- dpkg.log Contains a list of deb packages installed, upgraded, and removed

To troubleshoot problems associated with an application or service, check for a log file maintained specifically for that service. For example, check the *mail, mail.err, mail.info, mail.warn,* or the *maillog* file to troubleshoot problems with the postfix or sendmail daemon. If there is trouble with the mysqld daemon, check the *mysqld.log* file within the */var/log/mysql* directory. To troubleshoot problems with the Apache web server, investigate the various log files within the */var/log/apache2* directory.

In addition to using log files to troubleshoot problems on the Linux system, use them to detect unauthorized intrusion attempts.

Using Log Files to Detect Intruders

Detecting intruders involves looking for clues they left behind in the system. One of the best resources in this regard is the log files in the Linux system. Much like a CSI detective, practice and experience are best to develop an intuitive sense that informs you when something looks suspicious. The best way to develop this intuition is to spend a lot of time reviewing log files, because then you'll have a baseline of "normal" for your system. Once you know what is normal, you can spot what is *not* normal.

An important log file to review to identify suspicious activities is the */var/log/wtmp* file. This log file contains a list of all users who have authenticated to the system. The file is saved in binary format, so you cannot use cat, less, or a text editor such as vi to view it. Instead, you must use the last command at the shell prompt. Output from the last utility is shown in Figure 16-17.

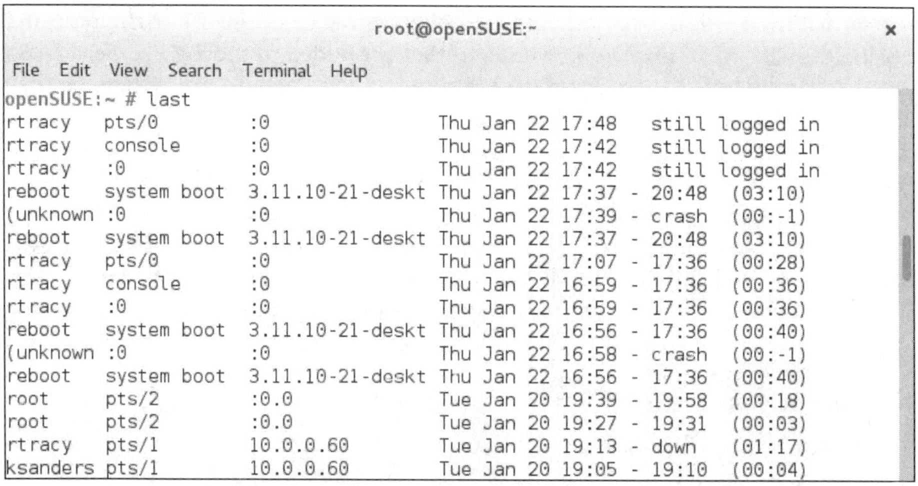

```
root@openSUSE:~
File  Edit  View  Search  Terminal  Help
openSUSE:~ # last
rtracy    pts/0        :0                Thu Jan 22 17:48   still logged in
rtracy    console      :0                Thu Jan 22 17:42   still logged in
rtracy    :0           :0                Thu Jan 22 17:42   still logged in
reboot    system boot  3.11.10-21-deskt Thu Jan 22 17:37 - 20:48  (03:10)
(unknown :0            :0                Thu Jan 22 17:39 - crash  (00:-1)
reboot    system boot  3.11.10-21-deskt Thu Jan 22 17:37 - 20:48  (03:10)
rtracy    pts/0        :0                Thu Jan 22 17:07 - 17:36  (00:28)
rtracy    console      :0                Thu Jan 22 16:59 - 17:36  (00:36)
rtracy    :0           :0                Thu Jan 22 16:59 - 17:36  (00:36)
reboot    system boot  3.11.10-21-deskt Thu Jan 22 16:56 - 17:36  (00:40)
(unknown :0            :0                Thu Jan 22 16:58 - crash  (00:-1)
reboot    system boot  3.11.10-21-deskt Thu Jan 22 16:56 - 17:36  (00:40)
root      pts/2        :0.0              Tue Jan 20 19:39 - 19:58  (00:18)
root      pts/2        :0.0              Tue Jan 20 19:27 - 19:31  (00:03)
rtracy    pts/1        10.0.0.60         Tue Jan 20 19:13 - down   (01:17)
ksanders  pts/1        10.0.0.60         Tue Jan 20 19:05 - 19:10  (00:04)
```

Figure 16-17 Using last to review login history

The last utility displays the user account, login time, logout time, and where users authenticated from. When reviewing this file, look for activity that appears unusual—for example, logins that occurred in the middle of the night when no one is at work should be considered suspicious.

Also view the */var/log/faillog* file. This log file contains a list of failed authentication attempts. This file is very effective at detecting dictionary attacks, which run through a list of dictionary terms, testing them as passwords for user accounts. Like *wtmp, faillog* is a binary file. To view it, use the faillog utility. This utility displays the user who tried to authenticate, how many times that user failed to log in, and when the last unsuccessful attempt occurred. Also, try the -u option to view login attempts for a specific user account—for example, **faillog -u hollis**.

EXAM TIP The **lastb** command also lists bad login attempts by reading the log file */var/log/btmp,* which contains all the bad login attempts.

The next log file to analyze is */var/log/lastlog*. This file contains a list of all the users in the system and when they last logged in. As with the other log files we have reviewed, you cannot view *lastlog* with less, cat, or a text editor. To view *lastlog,* use the lastlog utility from the shell prompt, as shown in Figure 16-18.

The last type of log file can help you detect intrusion attempts. These are */var/log/messages* and */var/log/journal* (if your distribution uses them). As mentioned earlier, these log files contain messages from all services running on the system. As such, they contain plenty of data that may or may not be related to intrusion attempts. You can use grep to isolate the relevant entries. For example, the **cat /var/log/messages | grep login | more** command will display login-related entries in the files. The same can be done with the **journalctl** command.

In addition to viewing log files, you can use a variety of command-line tools to see who is currently using the system, as discussed in Chapter 4. The first is the who command. Use who to see who is currently logged into your system. Also use the **w** utility to see who is currently logged in to the system, *and* what they are doing.

```
root            tty1                       Fri Jan  2 15:25:03 -0700 2015
rtkit                                      **Never logged in**
scard                                      **Never logged in**
srvGeoClue                                 **Never logged in**
sshd                                       **Never logged in**
statd                                      **Never logged in**
svn                                        **Never logged in**
tftp                                       **Never logged in**
usbmux                                     **Never logged in**
uucp                                       **Never logged in**
wwwrun                                     **Never logged in**
dtracy                                     **Never logged in**
ksanders        pts/1     10.0.0.60        Tue Jan 20 19:05:29 -0700 2015
rtracy          :0        console          Thu Jan 22 17:42:15 -0700 2015
student         pts/1     10.0.0.60        Tue Nov 25 17:27:58 -0700 2014
mysql                                      **Never logged in**
```

Figure 16-18 Using lastlog to view last login times

Enhancing Group and File Security

Security is considered a three-legged stool consisting of confidentiality, integrity, and availability. Linux systems are implemented with a priority of availability over confidentiality and integrity. This is called Discretionary Access Control (DAC). DAC systems allow users to set confidentiality rules at their own discretion. This is fine for most corporate environments where providing data as quickly as possible is important (for example, getting a sales quote out to a prospect).

Military environments demand confidentiality be the priority. These environments utilize a system known as Mandatory Access Control (MAC). Figure 16-19 shows how MAC works. If a user has Confidential access, they are allowed to access documents in Unclassified, and Confidential; however, they are not allowed to access documents in Secret or Top Secret because their clearance is too low.

To enable MAC on Linux systems, install a Linux Security Module. There are several, but the Linux+ exam focuses on the following:

- Implementing SELinux
- Implementing AppArmor

Implementing SELinux

The United States National Security Agency (NSA) developed SELinux to provide security mechanisms above user/group/other and read/write/execute, which provide only DAC. The SELinux design restricts operations to the least privilege possible; actions not explicitly allowed are denied by default. Red Hat 7, CentOS 7, and derivatives come with SELinux incorporated into the kernel.

SELinux Contexts

SELinux is based on a *subject* (that is, a user or application) that needs to access an *object* (that is, a file, socket, or some other application). A *reference monitor*, also simply known

Figure 16-19 The Mandatory Access Control model

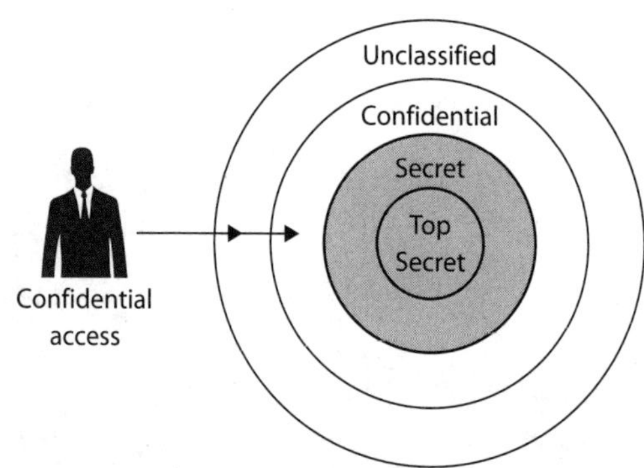

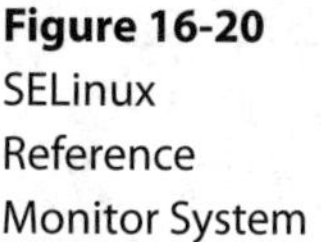

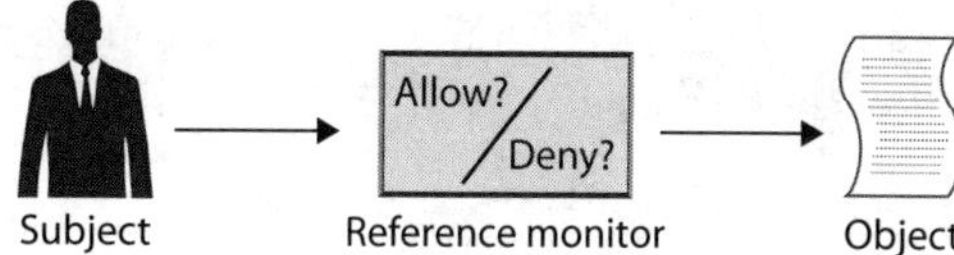

Figure 16-20 SELinux Reference Monitor System

as *monitor*, determines whether the subject has rights to the object depending on the *context*, or label defined onto the object, as shown in Figure 16-20. To view the contexts of files, run the command **ls -Z**.

```
[root@localhost ~]# ls -Z
drwxr-xr-x. root root unconfined_u:object_r:admin_home_t:s0 adir
-rw-------. root root system_u:object_r:admin_home_t:s0 anaconda-ks.cfg
-rw-r--r--. root root system_u:object_r:admin_home_t:s0 initial-setup-ks.cfg
-rwxr-xr-x. root root unconfined_u:object_r:admin_home_t:s0 runme
[root@localhost ~]#
```

The "dot" that appears at the end of the permissions means that SELinux is enabled, and the files have been defined a context. To view the contexts of commands, run **ps -Z**:

```
[cheryl@localhost ~]$ ps -Z
LABEL                              PID TTY          TIME CMD
user_u:user_r:user_t:s0          22706 pts/0    00:00:00 bash
user_u:user_r:user_t:s0          22764 pts/0    00:00:00 sleep
user_u:user_r:user_t:s0          22773 pts/0    00:00:00 ps
[cheryl@localhost ~]$
```

The contexts are defined as _u for user, _r for role, and _t for type, and s0 represents the sensitivity level. Rules of targeted policies are associated with _t contexts. Rules associated with MLS levels are associated with the s0 contexts. See Table 16-3 for a list of SELinux user context abilities.

User Context	Role Context	Type Context	GUI	sudo su	Execute in */home* and */tmp*	Network
unconfined_u	unconfined_r	unconfined_t	X	Both	X	X
sysadm_u	sysadm_r	sysadm_t	X	Both	X	X
staff_u	staff_r	staff_t	X	sudo	X	X
user_u	user_r	user_t	X		X	X
xguest_u	xguest_r	xguest_t	X			Firefox only
guest_u	guest_r	guest_t				

Table 16-3 SELinux User Context Abilities

File contexts can be modified using the chcon command. To recursively change files in subdirectories, use the -R flag:

```
[root@localhost ~]# setenforce 0
[root@localhost ~]# ls -Zd adir
drwxr-xr-x. root root unconfined_u:object_r:admin_home_t:s0 adir
[root@localhost ~]# ls -Z adir
-rw-r--r--. root root unconfined_u:object_r:admin_home_t:s0 file1
-rw-r--r--. root root unconfined_u:object_r:admin_home_t:s0 file2
-rw-r--r--. root root unconfined_u:object_r:admin_home_t:s0 file3
[root@localhost ~]# chcon -R -r unconfined_r -t unconfined_t ./adir
[root@localhost ~]# ls -Z adir
-rw-r--r--. root root unconfined_u:unconfined_r:unconfined_t:s0 file1
-rw-r--r--. root root unconfined_u:unconfined_r:unconfined_t:s0 file2
-rw-r--r--. root root unconfined_u:unconfined_r:unconfined_t:s0 file3
[root@localhost ~]# ls -Zd adir
drwxr-xr-x. root root unconfined_u:unconfined_r:unconfined_t:s0 adir
```

To return the filesystem to the default settings, either relabel the entire filesystem or use the restorecon command to change individual files and directories:

```
[root@localhost ~]# ls -Z adir
-rw-r--r--. root root unconfined_u:unconfined_r:unconfined_t:s0 file1
-rw-r--r--. root root unconfined_u:unconfined_r:unconfined_t:s0 file2
-rw-r--r--. root root unconfined_u:unconfined_r:unconfined_t:s0 file3
[root@localhost ~]# restorecon -R ./adir
[root@localhost ~]# ls -Z adir
-rw-r--r--. root root unconfined_u:unconfined_r:admin_home_t:s0 file1
-rw-r--r--. root root unconfined_u:unconfined_r:admin_home_t:s0 file2
-rw-r--r--. root root unconfined_u:unconfined_r:admin_home_t:s0 file3
```

The default contexts are defined in the file */etc/selinux/targeted/contexts/files/file_contexts*. To modify the SELinux contexts, use the **semanage** command.

EXAM TIP Per the announcement via the CompTIA Linux+ 2019 exam, semanage is *not* an exam requirement. It is still good to know that the following setting, where -s specifies the user and -a adds the constraining context to that user, provides more security in the real world because it forces users to comply with SELinux policies:

```
[root@localhost ~]# semanage login -a -s user_u gosia
```

Enabling SELinux

SELinux can be implemented in three modes:

- Enforcing
- Permissive
- Disabled

Where Enforcing mode denies access to users based on the defined SELinux policies. Permissive access simply logs actions that would have been denied under enforcing mode;

this is an excellent mode to use while tuning security policies. Disabled mode simply deactivates SELinux.

To see the current mode, use the getenforce command. To set the SELinux mode, use setenforce:

```
[root@localhost ~]# getenforce
Enforcing
[root@localhost ~]# senenforce Permissive
[root@localhost ~]# genenforce
Permissive
[root@localhost ~]#
```

SELinux enforcement modes are defined in either */etc/sysconfig/selinux* (on Red Hat, SUSE, and derivatives) or */etc/selinux/config* (on Debian, Ubuntu, and derivatives).

SELinux's default policy is called "targeted," which allows administrators to define contexts in a fine-grained manner to targeted processes. This allows, for example, for enforcing memory restrictions for all processes to minimize the vulnerability of buffer overflow attacks. For example, network services are targeted, but systemd, init, and user processes are not. The other policy mode is MLS, which uses the Bell-LaPadula model preferred at the United States Department of Defense.

NOTE To experience MLS, install the selinux-policy-mls package. MLS supports security levels from c0 to c1023, where c0 is the minimal level and c3 is Top Secret; the other levels are yet to be defined.

```
[root@localhost ~]# semanage login -l
Login Name     SELinux User     MLS/MCS Range          Service
__default__    unconfined_u     s0-s0:c0.c1023         *
```

The sestatus command provides detailed output of the SELinux settings:

```
[root@localhost ~]# sestatus
SELinux status:                 enabled
SELinuxfs mount:                /sys/fs/selinux
SELinux root directory:         /etc/selinux
Loaded policy name:             targeted
Current mode:                   enforcing
Mode from config file:          enforcing
Policy MLS status:              enabled
Policy deny_unknown status:     allowed
Max kernel policy version:      31
[root@localhost ~]#
```

The setenforce command allows SELinux modes to be set with booleans as well, where 0 equals permissive and 1 equals enforcing. To make the change permanent, change the SELINUX variable inside the */etc/selinux/config* file.

NOTE If the SELinux status is set to disabled, the setenforce command will not work. You will need to change the SELINUX variable to **enforcing** in the */etc/selinux/config* file and then reboot. After reboot, all files will be *relabeled* with SELinux contexts.

Using SELinux Booleans

To modify SELinux policies without reloading or rebooting, apply policy booleans. Currently there are about 300 boolean possibilities, and the list is growing. To list the available booleans, use semanage:

```
[root@localhost ~]# semanage boolean -l | egrep -e usb -e xguest -e cron -e Def
SELinux boolean                 State  Default Description
cron_userdomain_transition      (on   ,   on)  Allow cron to userdomain
transition
xguest_exec_content             (on   ,   on)  Allow xguest to exec content
xguest_connect_network          (on   ,   on)  Allow xguest to connect network
virt_use_usb                    (on   ,   on)  Allow virt to use usb
xguest_use_bluetooth            (on   ,   on)  Allow xguest to use bluetooth
xguest_mount_media              (on   ,   on)  Allow xguest to mount media
fcron_crond                     (off  ,  off)  Allow fcron to crond
cron_can_relabel                (off  ,  off)  Allow cron to can relabel
[root@localhost ~]#
```

From this listing, cron cannot relabel filesystems for restoring file contexts. Another way to display booleans is with getsebool:

```
[root@localhost ~]# getsebool cron_can_relabel
cron_can_relabel --> off
```

But However, getsebool does not display descriptions like semanage. Also, **getsebool -a** will display all booleans.

To configure booleans, use the setsebool command:

```
[root@localhost ~]# setsebool cron_can_relabel on
[root@localhost ~]# getsebool cron_can_relabel
cron_can_relabel --> on
```

This setting is lost when the system reboots. Run **setsebool -P** to make the setting permanent across reboots.

A few commonly used booleans are shown in Table 16-4. Booleans are stored in the */sys/fs/selinux* directory and can be listed with the following command:

```
[root@localhost ~]# ls /sys/fs/selinux/booleans
```

Boolean	Description
antivirus_can_scan_system	Allows antivirus to scan the system
cron_can_relabel	Allows cron jobs to provide SELinux context labels
ftpd_full_access	Allows FTP daemon full access
mozilla_read_content	Allows Mozilla web browser to read content
sysadm_exec_content	Allows sysadm_u users the right to execute scripts
xguest_exec_content	Allows xguest_u users the right to execute scripts

Table 16-4 Common SELinux Boolean Options

Auditing SELinux

Although SELinux *auditing* is not listed in the Linux+ 2019 exam requirements, it needs to be discussed for proper SELinux administration. First, install the setroubleshoot-server package to track SELinux notifications. Messages will be stored in */var/log/audit/audit.log*.

The */var/log/audit/audit.log* file can be read using sealert:

```
[root@localhost ~]# sealert -a /var/log/audit/audit.log
100% done
found 8 alerts in /var/log/audit/audit.log
------------------------------------------------------------------------------
SELinux is preventing /usr/bin/chcon from relabelto access on directory adir.
.
.
.
```

Implementing AppArmor

Like SELinux, AppArmor provides Mandatory Access Control (MAC) features to filesystem access. It also includes a "learning" mode that allows the system to observe application behaviors and set profiles so that applications run safely. The profiles limit how applications interconnect with processes and files.

Profiles are provided with Linux, but they also are supplied with applications or custom-built and tuned by administrators. These profiles are located in the */etc/apparmor.d/* directory and are simply text files that contain rules and capabilities. Profiles can be tuned using tunables, which reside in */etc/apparmor.d/tunables/*. These are simply global variable definitions that allow profiles to become portable to different environments.

Profiles can be run in either enforce mode or complain mode. Enforce mode runs at the minimum permission allowed them. Complain mode is similar to SELinux permissive mode, which simply logs events. This is a great way to test AppArmor before converting to enforce mode.

The status of AppArmor is displayed using apparmor_status:

```
[root@localhost ~]# apparmor_status
apparmor module is loaded.
5 profiles are loaded.
3 profiles are in enforce mode.
  /usr/bin/evince
  /usr/lib/cups/backend/cups-pdf
   /usr/sbin/cupsd
2 profiles are in complain mode.
  /usr/lib/dovecot/dovecot-auth
  /usr/sbin/dnsmasq
3 processes have profiles defined.
1 processes are in enforce mode.
  /usr/sbin/cupsd (524)
2 processes are in complain mode.
  /usr/sbin/avahi-daemon (521)
  /usr/sbin/avahi-daemon (559)
0 processes are unconfined but have a profile defined
```

If there is a profile in enforce mode and you want to switch the profile to complain mode, use the aa-complain command:

```
[root@localhost ~]# aa-complain /etc/apparmor.d/*
```

This places all profiles inside the */etc/apparmor.d* directory into complain mode. To revert all profiles to enforce mode, use aa-enforce:

```
[root@localhost ~]# aa-enforce /etc/apparmor.d/*
```

To disable a profile, use aa-disable. For example, to disable the CUPS printing profile, run the following:

```
[root@localhost ~]# aa-disable /etc/apparmor.d/usr.bin.cupsd
Disabling /etc/apparmor.d/usr.sbin.cupsd
```

Network security is a huge issue with hackers attacking systems from overseas to access a victim's computer or network. To view the PIDs and network processes not protected by AppArmor, run the command aa-unconfined and then determine whether *unconfined* processes need be protected with AppArmor:

```
[ root@localhost ~]# aa-unconfined
519 /usr/sbin/NetworkManager not confined
521 /usr/sbin/avahi-daemon confined by '/usr/sbin/avahi-daemon (complain)'
618 /usr/sbin/sshd not confined
891 /usr/sbin/minissdpd not confined
2087 /sbin/dhclient not confined
5501 /usr/sbin/cupsd not confined
5503 /usr/sbin/cups-browsed confined by '/usr/sbin/cups-browsed (complain)'
```

Exercise 16-2: Managing SELinux Contexts

In Exercise 16-2, you practice using SELinux contexts using the CentOS image. Install the Apache web server and configure the security using chcon. Perform this exercise using the virtual machine that comes with this book.

VIDEO Watch the Exercise 16-2 video for a demonstration on how to perform this task.

Complete the following steps:

1. Boot your Linux system and log in as your **student1** user with a password of **student1**.
2. Open a terminal session.
3. Switch to your root user account by entering **su -** followed by a password of **password**.

4. Verify SELinux is running in enforcing mode by using **getenforce** or **sestatus**.
   - If getenforce responds with "disabled," run **nano /etc/selinux/config** and modify the variable SELINUX from "disabled" to "enforcing." Save and exit from nano. Reboot. Return to step 1.
   - If SELinux is running in enforcing mode, proceed to step 5.
5. Install the Apache web server (if not already installed) by running **yum -y install httpd**. Start the web server by running **systemctl start httpd**.
6. Install the text-based web browser called Lynx by **running yum -y install lynx**.
7. Test your new webserver:

```
[ root@localhost ~]# echo "hello world" > /var/www/html/index.html
[ root@localhost ~]# lynx http://localhost
```

   a. View the new web page.

   b. Exit the browser by pressing Q to quit and Y to confirm.
8. Create another web page and attempt to view it:

```
[ root@localhost ~]# echo "page 2" > page2.html
[ root@localhost ~]# mv page2.html /var/www/html
[ root@localhost ~]# lynx http://localhost/page2.html
```

   The web page will show as "Forbidden" due to improper context settings.
9. Review the security SELinux context settings:

```
[ root@localhost ~]# cd /var/www/html
[ root@localhost ~]# ls -Z
```

10. Notice the type field for page2.html is not set to httpd_sys_content_t, so the web page is not allowed for viewing. Correct that here using chcon:

```
[ root@localhost ~]# chcon -t httpd_sys_content_t page2.html
[ root@localhost ~]# lynx http://localhost/page2.html
```

   a. View the new web page.

   b. Exit the browser by pressing Q to quit and Y to confirm.

Chapter Review

In this chapter, we introduced several security issues affecting Linux systems. It is important to physically secure the Linux system and take measures to secure the operating system itself.

Control user access to increase the security of your systems. The root user should be used only to complete root tasks. All other tasks should be completed using a standard user account. If users occasionally need to run commands as root, provide them access to sudo. Implement strong password policies, and lock accounts after failed authentications. Administrators can impose limits on how many times users may log in, how much CPU time they can consume, and how much memory they can use on a Linux system.

Administrators can configure system log files to troubleshoot Linux system issues and detect intruders. The chapter concluded with how to enable Mandatory Access Control by installing a Linux Security Module.

Make sure you understand the following points about increasing the security of Linux systems:

- Servers need the highest degree of physical security and should be locked in a server room. Access to the server room should be strictly controlled.
- Users should lock their workstations or log out completely before leaving their systems. To facilitate this, users can use the **nohup** command to run programs. This allows processes to continue running even if the user logs out.
- The root user should be used only to complete root tasks. All other tasks should be completed using a standard user account.
- Use the **su** command to switch to the root user account when you need to complete tasks that require root-level access, and the **exit** command to switch back when done.
- If users occasionally need to run commands as root, provide them access to sudo. Use the */etc/sudoers* file to specify which users can run as root with the **visudo** utility.
- Configure password aging with the **chage** command.
- Verify that Linux systems use shadow passwords. Storing passwords in */etc/passwd* is highly insecure. Use the **pwconv** command to migrate passwords from */etc/passwd* to */etc/shadow*.
- Administrators can impose limits on how many times users may log in, how much CPU time they can consume, and how much memory they can use on a Linux system. One way to do this is to use the pam_limits module with the Pluggable Authentication Modules (PAM) system.
- Limits are configured in the */etc/security/limits.conf* file.
- Administrators can also use the **ulimit** command to configure limits on system resources that are applied to programs launched from the shell prompt. The syntax for using ulimit is **ulimit <options> <limit>**.
- To temporarily disable user logins, first use the **w** command to view a list of all currently logged-in users. Warn them that the system is going down for service. After a few minutes, use the **pkill -KILL -u <username>** command to brute-force log out each non-cooperative user. Future logins are disabled by creating the */etc/nologin* file. As long as this file exists, no one but root is allowed to log in.
- Use the **find** command to audit files that have SUID or SGID root permissions set because this is a potential security risk that allows a hacker access without knowing the root password.

- Search for files on a Linux system that have SUID permissions set using the **find / -type f -perm -u=s -ls** command at the shell prompt as the root user.
- Identify any files with the SGID permission set using **find / -type f -perm -g=s -ls**.
- In addition to baselines, use system log files to troubleshoot Linux system issues. System log files are stored in */var/log*. Some of the more important log files include *kern.log*, *messages*, and *secure*.
- Logging is managed by the **rsyslogd** daemon and can be customized using the */etc/rsyslog.conf* file.
- On older distributions, logging is handled by the syslogd daemon, which can be customized using the */etc/syslog.conf* file.
- Most Linux distributions are configured to automatically rotate log files periodically, preventing them from growing too large. The cron daemon periodically runs the logrotate utility to do this.
- How logrotate specifies log files is configured using the */etc/logrotate.conf* file and the configuration files for individual services located in */etc/logrotate.d/*.
- For systemd systems, the journald daemon manages logging. The journald daemon maintains a system log called the journal (located in */var/log/journal/*).
- To view the journal, use the journalctl command. The behavior of the journal daemon is configured using the */etc/systemd/journald.conf* file.
- Use the **-f** option with **tail** or **journalctl** to monitor a log file for new entries.
- Periodically review the following log files, looking for anomalies that indicate intrusion attempts:
  - /var/log/wtmp
  - /var/log/faillog
  - /var/log/lastlog
  - /var/log/messages
- SELinux and AppArmor implement Mandatory Access Control on Linux systems.
- Use the **ls -Z** command to observe SELinux file context settings.
- Use the **ps -Z** command to view SELinux process context of currently running processes.
- Use the **chcon** command to change SELinux contexts on files. The **restorecon** command is used to return files to their default SELinux contexts.
- To view the current SELinux mode, use either the **sestatus** or **getenforce** command. The **setenforce** command can enable enforcing, permissive, or disabled SELinux mode, with a default policy of targeted. To make the mode permanent, modify the SELINUX variable in the */etc/selinux/config* file.

- SELinux policies settings are provided through booleans. To get the value of a boolean, use the **getsebool** command. To configure booleans, use the **setsebool** command.
- AppArmor uses a set of predefined profiles located in the */etc/apparmor.d* and */etc/apparmor.d/tunables* directories. Profile settings include the warn-only complain mode and the deny-unless-permitted enforce mode. To enable complain mode, use the **aa-complain** command. To enable enforcement mode, use the **aa-enforce** command. To disable AppArmor, run **aa-disable**.
- To view network applications unprotected by AppArmor, run the **aa-unconfined** command. This will list the unconfirmed processes and their process IDs.

Questions

1. Which of the following would be the most secure place to locate a Linux server?
   A. On the receptionist's front desk
   B. In the CIO's office
   C. In an unoccupied cubicle
   D. In a locked room
2. Which of the following can be used to secure users' workstations? (Choose two.)
   A. Screensaver password
   B. Session lock
   C. Long screensaver timeout period
   D. Passwords written on sticky notes and hidden in a drawer
   E. Easy-to-remember passwords
3. Which of the following commands will load the updatedb process and leave it running even if the user logs out of the shell?
   A. updatedb
   B. updatedb &
   C. updatedb -nohup
   D. nohup updatedb &
4. Which of the following commands can be used to switch to the root user account and load root's environment variables?
   A. su -
   B. su root
   C. su root -e
   D. su -env

5. Which of the following is a strong password?
   A. Bob3
   B. TuxP3nguin
   C. penguin
   D. Castle
6. You need to set password age limits for the ksanders user account. You want the minimum password age to be 1 day, the maximum password age to be 45 days, and the user to be warned 5 days prior to password expiration. Which command will do this?
   A. usermod –m 1 –M 45 –W 5 ksanders
   B. useradd –m 1 –M 45 –W 5 ksanders
   C. chage –M 1 –m 45 –W 5 ksanders
   D. chage –m 1 –M 45 –W 5 ksanders
7. Which log file contains a list of all users who have authenticated to the Linux system, when they logged in, when they logged out, and where they logged in from?
   A. /var/log/faillog
   B. /var/log/last
   C. /var/log/wtmp
   D. /var/log/login
8. Which log file contains a list of failed login attempts?
   A. /var/log/faillog
   B. /var/log/last
   C. /var/log/wtmp
   D. /var/log/login
9. Which log file contains messages from all services running on the system?
   A. /var/log/faillog
   B. /var/log/messages
   C. /var/log/wtmp
   D. /var/log/services
10. Which utility can you use to view your */var/log/lastlog* file?
   A. cat
   B. last
   C. grep
   D. lastlog

11. You need to view the first few lines of the really long */var/log/boot.msg* file. Which of the following commands will best do this? (Choose two.)
    A. head /var/log/boot.msg
    B. tail /var/log/boot.msg
    C. grep -l 10 /var/log/boot.msg
    D. less /var/log/boot.msg
    E. cat /var/log/boot.msg
12. You're configuring the */etc/logrotate.d/ntp* file to customize logging from the Network Time Protocol daemon on your system. You want old, archived logs to be saved using the current date in the filename extension. Which directive in the *ntp* file will do this?
    A. notifempty
    B. dateext
    C. rotate
    D. create
13. Which option, when used with the tail or journalctl command, will cause the tail or journalctl utility to monitor a log file for new entries?
    A. -
    B. -l
    C. -m
    D. -f
14. Which of the following commands can be used to change the SELinux context of a file?
    A. chcon
    B. conch
    C. contextchange
    D. context-change
15. You need to scan your Linux filesystem to locate all files that have either the SUID or SGID permission set. Which commands can you use to do this? (Choose two.)
    A. find / -type f -perm -u=s -ls
    B. find / -type f -perm -g=s -ls
    C. audit -p=SUID
    D. audit -p=SGID
    E. find / -p=s
    F. find / -p=g

16. The existence of which file prevents all users except root from logging in to a Linux system?
    - **A.** /root/nologin
    - **B.** /etc/nologin
    - **C.** /var/log/nologin
    - **D.** /tmp/nologin
17. You want to configure limits on the system resources your Linux users are allowed to consume using the pam_limits PAM module. Which file do you need to edit to set these limits?
    - **A.** /etc/limits.conf
    - **B.** /etc/pam_limits.conf
    - **C.** /etc/security/limits.conf
    - **D.** /etc/security/pam_limits.conf

Answers

1. **D.** A locked room would be the most secure place to locate a Linux server.
2. **A, B.** Screensaver passwords and the session lock function offered by KDE and GNOME can be used to secure users' workstations.
3. **D.** The **nohup updatedb &** command will load the updatedb process and leave it running, even if the user logs out of the shell.
4. **A.** The **su -** command switches to the root user account and loads root's environment variables.
5. **B.** The TuxP3nguin password meets the basic requirements for a strong password.
6. **D.** The **chage -m 1 -M 45 -W 5 ksanders** command will set the minimum password age to be 1 day, the maximum password age to be 45 days, and the user to be warned 5 days prior to password expiration.
7. **C.** The */var/log/wtmp* log file contains a list of all users who have authenticated to the Linux system, when they logged in, when they logged out, and where they logged in from.
8. **A.** The */var/log/faillog* log file contains a list of failed login attempts.
9. **B.** The */var/log/messages* log file contains messages from all services running on the system.
10. **D.** The lastlog command can be used to view your */var/log/lastlog* file.
11. **A, D.** The **head /var/log/boot.msg** and **less /var/log/boot.msg** commands will display the first few lines of a really long file onscreen.
12. **B.** The dateext directive will cause old, archived log files to be saved using the current date in the filename extension.

13. **D.** The -f option, when used with journalctl or tail, will cause the command to monitor a file for changes and display them on the screen.
14. **A.** The chcon command is used to change the SELinux context of a file.
15. **A, B.** The **find / -type f -perm -u=s -ls** command locates all files that have the SUID permission set. The **find / -type f -perm -g=s -ls** command locates all files that have the SGID permission set.
16. **B.** The existence of the */etc/nologin* file prevents all users except root from logging in to the Linux system.
17. **C.** User limits enforced by the pam_limits module are configured in the */etc/security/limits.conf* file.

CHAPTER 17

Applying DevOps: Automation and Orchestration

In this chapter, you will learn about

- Orchestration concepts
- Orchestration processes
- The Git revision control system

You have learned a great deal about Linux automation tools, such as using at, batch, crontab, and others. Automation is a magnitude more difficult, however, when Linux administrators manage thousands of computers for an organization. Orchestration tools such as Kubernetes, Ansible, Puppet, and Chef, among others, make it simpler to manage networked systems.

Let's begin this chapter by discussing how Linux handles processes.

Orchestration Concepts

The keys to launching an orchestration system capable of installing Linux onto hundreds of computers with a single keystroke are the tools behind the system. The foundation of orchestration includes Development teams that create new applications and tools, working together with Operation and Production teams that provide solutions for end users. Together this is called DevOps.

Without DevOps, Development teams work apart from Production teams, so what might be an ideal design for Development may not appeal to Operations. For example, consider a case of developers being tasked to design and implement a green line. Imagine developers deliver their solution, but the Operations team admits that although the solution meets the agreed-upon design, the green line is not as wide or long as expected.

With DevOps, Development and Operation teams work together during implementation and testing. The length and width of the green line is discussed and resolved well before the product is released, resulting in a product that better meets end-user expectations.

Program	Description
API Blueprint	Encourages dialog and communications with project stakeholders, designers, developers, and customers at any point in the application lifecycle
Flarum	Open source project under the MIT license that provides forum software for online discussions
github:pages	The system provides web pages to the public hosted from individual GitHub repositories
jekyll	Blog-aware, static site generator suitable on any web server
Markdown	Markup library that creates HTML output for formatting, linking, and imaging websites
OpenAPI Initiative	The Linux Foundation and OpenAPI Initiative's collaboration to describe REST APIs
Read the Docs	Automates building, versioning, and hosting of documentation for the open source community

Table 17-1 DevOps Collaboration Solutions

The widely used products for DevOps collaboration are described in Table 17-1.

Orchestration automates several tasks (in fact, the entire DevOps process). An example might be an online computer game design company that works with publishing content continuously. The company's deployment might include installing and configuring a gaming web server, designing and testing a computer application server, and developing and operating a virtual world engine. An orchestration system manages each step of the process. Orchestration even handles issues involved with the intermingling of operating systems and gaming architectures. Deployment systems can be cloud based or local.

Automation is a single task, and it builds infrastructures automatically. A series of these automated tasks is defined as orchestration, combining varied tasks such as installation, configuration, and patch updates. An example of this is having the game designer automate installations of the application onto gaming servers, while another automates deployment to users. These combined tasks and others deploying an application for thousands of worldwide users via servers and virtual machines can be simplified with orchestration.

Build automation tools focus on operating system installations to many computer machines. For example, SUSE Linux Enterprise Server performs build automation using its AutoYaST service, which performs multiple unattended mass deployments of SUSE across a network. AutoYaST contains installation and configuration data for consistent installations.

Automated configuration management forms uniform, orderly, and stable systems and maximizes productivity. Security and service level agreements (SLAs) are consistently measured, and change management and configuration management systems are significantly improved versus manual configurations and installations.

Orchestration Processes

Orchestration processes include tools that are agent or agentless. The difference between these tools depends on whether the application resides on the orchestration device (that is, *agent*) or does not (that is, *agentless*).

Orchestration steps involve designing a specific system configuration and developing and testing the solution based on the specifications. The systems administrators design the configuration(s) and create the definition files that build the systems. Finally, the systems are built and configured based on the definitions.

The widely used products for DevOps processes are described in Table 17-2.

NOTE Network orchestration occurs with YAML files contained in */etc/netplan/*. For example, *01-netcfg.yaml* can contain rules to set up dynamic networks.

The phrase "infrastructure as code" describes orchestration methods and tools that control configurations and deployments using mostly scripts, code, and libraries. Infrastructure as code means that one configuration design can deploy needed infrastructures (for example, the operating system) and other desired programs and services.

Orchestration tasks are defined by attributes, which are set by systems administrators to determine which applications should be installed based on hard drive size and operating system, for example. Canonical, which provides Ubuntu Linux, created Juju, an open source modeling tool, to facilitate fast deployment, and configuration uses attributes to support its "metal as a service" functions.

Orchestration tools are used to manage the inventory of virtual machines, networks, applications, hardware, hypervisors, operating systems, software licenses, and more. Inventory management is handled with various tools, such as SUSE Manager, which manages inventories, check compliance, and monitor containers running in Kubernetes for vulnerabilities.

Program	Description
Flynn	Open source platform-as-a-service solution for running applications in production environments
Mesos	Apache project that provides the ability to run containerized and non-containerized workloads in a distributed fashion
Rundeck	Provides tools that work with existing operations functions and systems that allow secure self-service to automation
Spinnaker	An open source continuous delivery platform that helps to release high-quality software changes quickly
Vagrant	Provides the configuration system that creates portable development environments

Table 17-2 DevOps Process Solutions

Program	Description
Ansible	Open source configuration management and application deployment
CF Engine	Automates complex, large-scale, mission-critical IT infrastructures
Chef	Designed to streamline server configurations and maintenance
puppet labs	Manages IT infrastructure lifecycle, such as patches and applications
Terraform	Defines and provisions data centers using JSON

Table 17-3 DevOps Inventory Solutions

The widely used products for DevOps inventories are described in Table 17-3.

EXAM TIP For your studies, focus on understanding the languages used in orchestration, such as JSON, XAML, and YAML.

The Git Revision Control System

Git is a robust revision control system designed to handle software programming changes and provide centralized storage for development teams. Software developers automate code management, enhance collaboration, and implement version control with this powerful system.

Git was created by the same individual who kicked off the Linux Project, Linus Torvalds, and it introduced features such as decentralization so that several revisions are allowed on several machines across the Internet. Git superseded such tools as RCS (Revision Control System) and CVS (Concurrent Versions System), which were popular development tools for UNIX but lacked the security requirements of today.

Version control is managed using the Git repository. One example of a centralized repository is the GitHub project at https://www.github.com, which manages millions of open source projects worldwide. But using GitHub is not a requirement; a development team can set up its own Git repository managed from a local computer or on a shared remote system across the Internet.

For the Linux+ exam, you must be familiar with the following concepts:

- Using Git
- Collaborating with Git

Using Git

Git is the "stupid content tracker" according to the Git man page, which later clarifies it as a "fast, scalable, distributed revision control system." Git's command set is divided into the high-level *porcelain* commands, which are the main revision control commands, and the low-level *plumbing* commands, which are designed for scripting. Some of the often-used Git commands are listed in Table 17-4.

Command	Description
add	Add files to the Git repository
branch	List, create, or delete branches from the Git repository
checkout	Check out files from the Git repository for development
clone	Duplicate a repository into a new directory
commit	Record changes into the repository, making a restore point
config	Set and get repository or user options, including global options
init	Create a new, empty Git repository or reinitializes an existing one
log	Show the commit logs (that is, repository changes)
merge	Join multiple development histories together
pull	Pull from and merge with another repository into a local branch
push	Update remote references from a working local copy
status	Show the status of the repository

Table 17-4 Git Commands and Descriptions

For administrators who prefer them, there are equivalent "git dash" commands located under */usr/libexec/git-core/*, such as git-config, git-init, and so on.

EXAM TIP The Linux+ exam Git requirements focus on the higher level porcelain commands listed in Table 17-4.

After installing Git using yum, zypper, or apt-get, depending on the professional version of Linux being used, administrators can quickly create a local project, as follows:

```
[heinrich@ebeth ~]$ mkdir gitting
[heinrich@ebeth ~]$ cd gitting/
[heinrich@ebeth gitting]$ git init
```

Initializing the new gitting project creates a *.git/* directory within the project, which contains the version control files required for the project. In this case, the directory is stored under */home/heinrich/gitting/.git/*. Listing the *.git/* directory displays the following files:

```
[heinrich@ebeth gitting]$ ls -l .git
total 20
drwxr-xr-x.  2 heinrich danny   6 May 26 14:12 branches
-rw-r--r--.  1 heinrich danny 158 May 26 18:42 config
-rw-r--r--.  1 heinrich danny  73 May 26 14:12 description
-rw-r--r--.  1 heinrich danny  23 May 26 14:12 HEAD
drwxr-xr-x.  2 heinrich danny 242 May 26 14:12 hooks
drwxr-xr-x.  2 heinrich danny  21 May 26 14:12 info
drwxr-xr-x. 10 heinrich danny  90 May 26 19:13 objects
drwxr-xr-x.  4 heinrich danny  31 May 26 14:12 refs
```

As the project is developed and modified over the coming days, a *.gitignore* file can be created that lists files to be ignored during any commit actions. This file is edited and maintained by the project developers and resides at the root of the repository (for example, *~/gitting/.gitignore*). To continue the example, a *project.txt* file is added to the project:

```
[heinrich@ebeth gitting]$ echo "my first project" > project.txt
[heinrich@ebeth gitting]$ git add project.txt
[heinrich@ebeth gitting]$ git status
# On branch master
#
# Initial commit
#
# Changes to be committed:
#   (use "git rm --cached <file>..." to unstage)
#
#     new file:   project.txt
#
```

At the moment the project is staged but not yet committed, as can be seen from the result of the status message.

Use git-config to define the individual in charge of this repository. Using the --global option defines the user for current and future repositories, as shown next:

```
[heinrich@ebeth gitting]$ git config --global user.name "Heinrich Username"
[heinrich@ebeth gitting]$ git config --global user.email "heinrich@ebeth.com"
```

After modifying the project, you can view differences with git-diff, as shown here:

```
[heinrich@ebeth gitting]$ echo "updating my first project" >> project.txt
[heinrich@ebeth gitting]$ git diff
diff --git a/project.txt b/project.txt
index 89e8713..6f4c457 100644
--- a/project.txt
+++ b/project.txt
@@ -1 +1,2 @@
my first project
+updating my first project
```

Again, the changes are only staged at this point. To finalize the changes, they must be committed with git-commit. Use the -m option to immediately apply a commit "message"; otherwise, an editor will open to apply the commit message:

```
[heinrich@ebeth gitting]$ git commit -m "the initial commitment"
[master (root-commit) 4dd2fb5] the initial commitment
1 file changed, 1 insertion(+)
create mode 100644 project.txt
```

To view the results of the recent interactions, run git-log. A 40-digit commit ID will list which git is used to track the project, as shown here:

```
[heinrich@ebeth gitting]$ git log
commit 4dd2fb576015462676ab74bd4533b24344821d64
Author: Heinrich Username <heinrich@ebeth.com>
Date:   Sun May 26 18:46:31 2019 -0400
   the initial commitment
```

Collaborating with Git

A new project can be downloaded, or pulled, from a remote repository such as github.com, gitlab.com, bitbucket.org, sourceforge.net, opendev.org, or launchpad.net, and further development can occur at the developer's local repository, as shown in Figure 17-1. Once the developer has completed changes for this phase, they can push the changes back to the remote repository.

To demonstrate how this works, suppose a fictional company named Trex Inc. decides to create a new software package that assists writers creating new science fiction works. The Trex project is called tribblers, an open source program hosted at www.sourceforge.net. Programming partners improve tribblers by writing code to enhance the project. Partners download the latest version of the tribblers source code by cloning the project onto their systems as follows:

```
$ git clone https://user@git.code.sf.net/p/tribblers/code tribblers
Cloning into 'tribblers'...
remote: Enumerating objects: 7, done.
remote: Counting objects: 100% (7/7), done.
remote: Compressing objects: 100% (7/7), done.
remote: Total 7 (delta 0), reused 0 (delta 0)
Unpacking objects: 100% (7/7), done.
```

Now that the tribblers project has been cloned, or pulled, from the remote repository, the developer can change directory to the local repository and view the files, as shown here:

```
$ cd tribblers
$ ls
mold.c  new.c  old.c
```

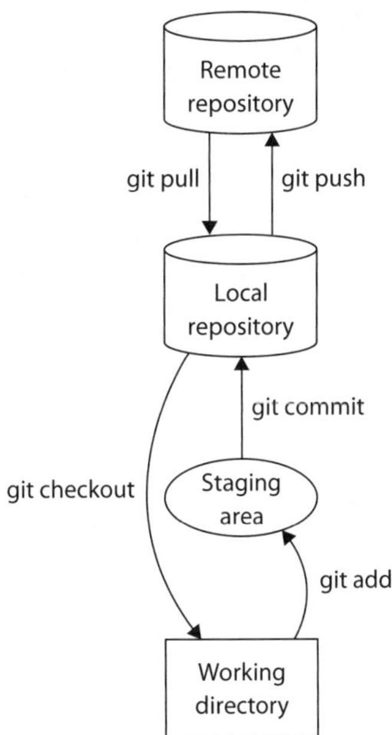

Figure 17-1 Git process flow example

EXAM TIP The developer could also use the git-pull function, as shown here:
$ git pull https://user@git.code.sf.net/p/tribblers/code

Work could continue from the current "master" branch, but in this case the developer would like to improve the tribblers code and test the changes before releasing them into the current version. To do this, the developer creates a new branch called alternate. Here they can perform updates and not affect the current project. They use the checkout function to switch branches, as shown here:

```
$ git branch alternate
$ git status
# On branch master
nothing to commit, working directory clean
$ git checkout alternate
Switched to branch 'alternate'
$ git status
# On branch alternate
nothing to commit, working directory clean
$ ls
mold.c  new.c  old.c
```

An example of updating the working project is shown next. A new file is created and added to the alternate branch. The tribbler developer then returns to the master branch, as no changes are made to the master branch, as shown here:

```
$ cp mold.c kold.c
$ sed -i s/howdy/goodbye/  kold.c
$ cat kold.c
/* this is my third c program */
main()
{
 printf("goodbye there");
}
$ git add .
$ git commit -m "added kold.c"
[alternate 46de219] added kold.c
1 file changed, 5 insertions(+)
create mode 100644 kold.c
$ git checkout master
Switched to branch 'master'
$ git status
# On branch master
nothing to commit, working directory clean
$ ls
mold.c  new.c  old.c
```

Work on the tribbler project could continue from the current "master" branch, but now the developer has found a bug and has developed a patch to repair the issue. To do this, the developer creates a new branch called patch. Here, they perform the changes without affecting the current project state. They use the checkout function, create the patch branch with -b, and switch branches, as shown here:

```
$ git checkout -b patch
Switched to a new branch 'patch'
```

An example of the patch file is the modification of *new.c*. The *new.c* file is updated and committed within the patch branch. No changes are made to the master branch, as shown here:

```
$ cat new.c
/* this is my first c program */
main()
{
 printf("hi there");
}
$ sed -i s/\"hi/'"howdy, hi'/  new.c
$ cat new.c
/* this is my first c program */
main()
{
 printf("howdy, hi there");
}
$ git add .
$ git commit -m "patched the new file"
[patch 576639d] patched the new file
1 file changed, 1 insertion(+), 1 deletion(-)
```

Now that the patch is complete, the developer returns to the master branch. Assuming the patch has been thoroughly tested and approved, the tribbler development team can now merge the fix in with the master branch, as shown here:

```
$ git checkout master
Switched to branch 'master'
$ git merge patch
Updating a56bda0..576639d
Fast-forward
new.c | 2 +-
1 file changed, 1 insertion(+), 1 deletion(-)
$ git status
# On branch master
# Your branch is ahead of 'origin/master' by 1 commit.
#   (use "git push" to publish your local commits)
#
nothing to commit, working directory clean
```

Now it is time for the developer to make the changes available to the entire tribbler worldwide team. The developer will create a shortcut name for the remote repository called "origin" using git-remote. Next, they push their changes back to the remote repository, as shown here:

```
$ git remote add origin ssh://user@git.code.sf.net/p/tribblers/code
$ git push -u origin master
Password for 'https://user@git.code.sf.net':
Counting objects: 5, done.
Delta compression using up to 2 threads.
Compressing objects: 100% (3/3), done.
Writing objects: 100% (3/3), 367 bytes | 0 bytes/s, done.
Total 3 (delta 0), reused 0 (delta 0)
remote: <Repository /git/p/tribblers/code.git> refresh queued.
To https://user@git.code.sf.net/p/tribblers/code
  a56bda0..576639d  master -> master
Branch master set up to track remote branch master from origin.
$
```

Let's practice working with a Git repository in Exercise 17-1.

Exercise 17-1: Working with a Git Repository

In this exercise, you practice using git commands to manage a local repository running on your system. Perform this exercise using the virtual machine that comes with this book.

VIDEO Please watch the Exercise 17-1 video for a demonstration on how to perform this task.

Complete the following steps:

1. Boot your Linux system and log in as a standard user.
2. Open a terminal session.
3. Create the directory for the repository to store the project, and then initialize Git:
```
$ mkdir project
$ cd project
$ git init
```
4. View the files created by the Git initialization process that are used for version control:
```
$ ls -alF .git
```
5. Create a file for the project and add it to the repository:
```
$ echo "my first git project" > file1
$ git add file1
```
6. View the status of the project and note that, at this point, it is staged but not yet committed:
```
$ git status
```
7. Define the user and e-mail for this repository, unless this is predefined in the global configuration file:
```
$ git config --global user.name "Hobson the Great"
$ git config --global user.email "hobson@magic.world"
```
8. Change the file and watch the modifications:
```
$ echo "updating my project" >> file1
$ git diff
```
9. Although *file1* has been modified, it is only staged at this point. Commit the changes to the repository here:
```
$ git commit -m "My first git commitment"
```
10. View the log file of the modifications. Git uses the commit numbers to track versions:
```
$ git log
```

Chapter Review

Orchestration tools allow Systems Administrators to install and configure hundreds of Linux systems from a single point of administration. Developers use applications and tools to create consistent results for operations and production. There are tools designed for collaboration, operations, inventory, scheduling, and deployment.

The key behind orchestration systems is automation, which is important for consistent deployments. Infrastructure automation ensures uniform deployments that are for specific applications. Build automation focuses on orderly and stable operating system installations on multiple servers or clients.

Tools that reside on the orchestration build system are considered agent tools; otherwise, they are considered agentless tools.

When code such as YAML, JSON, or XAML is used to control configurations and deployments, then the orchestration method is considered "infrastructure as code." Orchestration tasks are defined by attributes set by systems administrators that analyze systems to determine their needs.

Without inventory management, orchestration becomes hugely difficult because there is no knowledge of requirements for proper builds. Orchestration requires knowledge of the type of virtual machines, networks, hardware, and so on for accurate deployments.

Git is a revision control system designed to enhance collaboration and version control over a large network. The Git utility serves this purpose by allowing multiple developers to pull, clone, branch, add, and commit changes to projects while mitigating race conditions.

Be familiar with the following key concepts about orchestration:

- Orchestration systems use software languages such as YAML, XAML, XML, JSON, and others as a foundation for build automation.
- To initialize a local `git` repository, use the command **git init**.
- The *~/<projectname>/.git* directory has files and directories that track project revisions.
- The *~/<projectname>/.gitignore* file lists files to be ignored during commit actions.
- The **git add** command will stage a file.
- Running **git status** will display the current state of the repository.
- Use **git config** to set parameters of the repository, such as user.name and user.email.
- To visualize the project difference, run the **git diff** function.
- Changes are finalized using the **git commit** command sequence.
- To view a history of recent changes, run **git log**.
- Use **git clone** to download project source code from a remote repository.
- Developers can also use **git pull** to download a project from a remote repository.

- Use the **git branch** function to further development without affecting the current software version.
- To work in the new branch, run the **git checkout** command.
- To merge an alternate branch with a master, run **git merge**.

Questions

1. Select the software applications that are used in build automation. (Choose three.)
   A. YAML
   B. XAML
   C. JSON
   D. AutoC
2. In which orchestration process does the application not reside on the orchestration system?
   A. Agentless
   B. Agent
   C. Remote
   D. Local
3. What are orchestration systems that mostly use scripts, coding, and libraries called?
   A. Infrastructure automation
   B. Procedures
   C. Infrastructure as code
   D. Automated configuration
4. To download software source code from a remote repository to a local repository, which of the following commands do you use? (Choose two.)
   A. `git down`
   B. `git clone`
   C. `git push`
   D. `git pull`
   E. `git up`
5. When setting up a new Git project, the developer can create the *.git/* directory and related revision files with which command?
   A. `git commit`
   B. `git going`
   C. `git a2i`
   D. `git init`

6. Which of the following commands will stage software changes within Git?
   - **A.** `git commit`
   - **B.** `git init`
   - **C.** `git add`
   - **D.** `git branch`
7. Which command is used to view the Git branch the developer is working within?
   - **A.** `git status`
   - **B.** `git log`
   - **C.** `git init`
   - **D.** `git add`
8. Which of the following commands will show the current Git configuration?
   - **A.** `git commit`
   - **B.** `git log`
   - **C.** `git pull`
   - **D.** `git push`
9. Fill in the blank to complete the command to download a project from a remote repository:

   `$ git ________ https://user@git.code.sf.net/p/dr/code drivesim`
   - **A.** branch
   - **B.** merge
   - **C.** pull
   - **D.** clone
10. Fill in the blank to complete the command to download a project from a remote repository:

    `$ git ________ https://user@git.code.sf.net/p/dr/code`
    - **A.** branch
    - **B.** merge
    - **C.** pull
    - **D.** clone

Answers

1. **A, B, C.** YAML, XAML, and JSON are used for orchestration build automation.
2. **A.** Agentless systems do not reside on the orchestration system.
3. **C.** Infrastructure as code deploys systems primarily with scripts, code, and libraries.

4. **B, D.** Developers can use the **git clone** or **git pull** command to download the projects source code from the remote repository.
5. **D.** The developer can run **git init** to initiate a project. That will create the *.git/* directory and the related revision files.
6. **C.** Use the **git add** function to stage software changes within the git system.
7. **A.** Use the **git status** to view which branch the developer is working in.
8. **B.** Run **git log** to view the current repository configuration.
9. **D.** The clone function will download the drivesim project from the remote repository and place it in a directory called *drivesim*.
10. **C.** The pull function will download a software project from a remote repository into the current git project directory.

CHAPTER 18

Understanding Cloud and Virtualization

In this chapter, you will learn about

- Virtualization
- Containers
- Networking
- Automating installation with Kickstart

This chapter takes a look at cloud and virtualization configuration terms associated with virtual machines, hypervisors, storage, and networks.

Understanding Virtualization

Virtualization is a method of creating a logical operating system (guest) or operating systems inside a physical machine (host).

These logical operating systems (or guests) are managed by a hypervisor.

Hypervisors

Hypervisors were initially created by IBM to provide programmers a method of debugging an application without risking the integrity of the operating system.

Hypervisors, also called virtual machine managers (VMMs), create a boundary between the computer operating system and a logically isolated instance of a guest operating system contained in a virtual machine (VM).

Hypervisors come in several types: embedded, Type 1, and Type 2. Since a VM only accesses the hypervisor, it is unaware of the hypervisor's type.

Type 1

A Type 1 hypervisor, also called a bare-metal hypervisor, is installed as part of an operating system and has direct access to system hardware. This is illustrated in Figure 18-1.

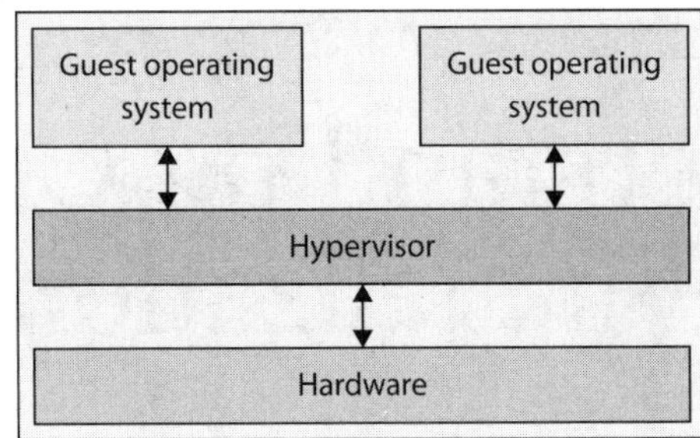

Figure 18-1 Type 1 (bare-metal) hypervisor

Each "guest" appears as a dedicated machine but in reality shares system resources with the "host" and other guest machines.

Examples of Type 1 hypervisors are KVM, Hyper-V, and Xen

Type 2

A Type 2 hypervisor, or hosted hypervisor, is an application installed on a host server, as illustrated in Figure 18-2. Guest machines use the installed hypervisor to access system resources via system calls.

Embedded Hypervisor

An embedded hypervisor is used in embedded systems. An embedded system is an independent or integrated device that contains a real-time operating system (RTOS), controller, and application software designed to perform a task. (Some embedded systems will not have an RTOS.) An alarm or car automation system is an example of an embedded system.

An embedded hypervisor is programmed directly into a processor.

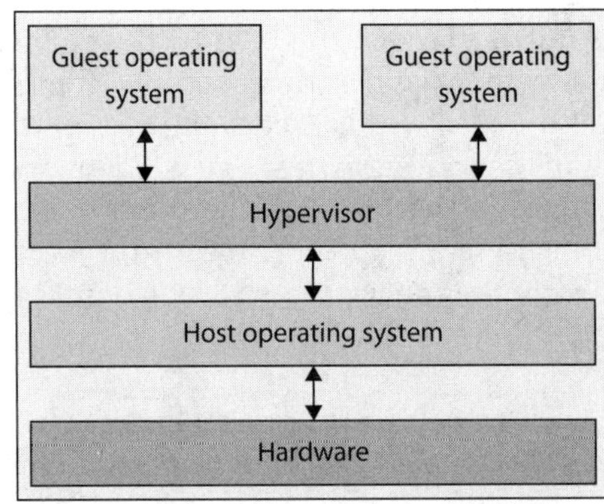

Figure 18-2 Type 2 (hosted) hypervisor

Thin vs. Thick Provisioning

Thick and thin provisioning define how storage space is allocated on a hard disk. When creating a virtual disk for a virtual machine, you have the choice of allocating the entire drive (thick provisioning) or dynamically allocating drive space as it is used (thin provisioning).

Thick provisioning is most efficient when the amount of storage allocated is close to the amount of space used.

Thin provisioning dynamically limits the size of a disk, but only allocates disk space as needed. Assume you have set a drive's size limit to 100MB and only used 20MB of storage. The drive size is only 20MB, but has the capability of growing to 100MB. Thin provisioning reduces the cost of storage space, but requires more monitoring.

Virtualization File Formats

The following formats are used to store virtual machine files.

Format	Description
HDD	HDD is a virtual hard disk file used with the Parallels para-virtualization application.
OVA	Open Virtual Application (OVA) files are an archive (tar file) of an OVF file. VMware and Oracle Virtual Box support OVA files.
OVF	Open Virtualization Format (OVF) is a design standard created by Distributed Management Task Force (DTMF) to provide a platform-independent method to archive and share virtual machines. An OVF file consists of a single directory that contains multiple configuration files. The directory includes a manifest file written in Extensible Markup Language (XML). The manifest file, or OVF descriptor file, contains network, storage, and other metadata used to configure a virtual machine.
QCOW	QCOW, or QEMU copy-on-write, is a disk image file used by QEMU. QCOW has been succeeded by QCOW2.
VDI	VDI files are default VirtualBox storage files.
VMDK	VMDK was designed by VMware but is also used by VirtualBox and QEMU.
VHD	VHD is a virtual hard disk format designed and used by Microsoft. VHD was succeeded by VHDX.

libvirt

Red Hat designed libvirt as a management utility for multiple hypervisors (KVM, LXC, Microsoft Hyper V, VirtualBox, VMware, and Xen). libvirt contains the command-line utility virsh and the libvirtd daemon, which are used to manage guest machines.

These management capabilities include the ability to stop, start, pause, save, and migrate virtual machines and manage system devices. libvirt also manages network interfaces, virtual networks, and storage devices.

Containers

A container is a runtime environment that consists of the files, libraries, other dependencies, and configuration requirements necessary to run a single instance of an application (see Figure 18-3).

The application is executed using the host operating system's resources, including local system libraries and binaries.

Containers are isolated at the application level rather than at the operating system level. This means an error at the application level does not affect the host.

Examples of containers include LXC, LXD, LXCFS, Docker, and LinuxKit.

In a cluster environment, a pod is one or more containers that share resources (e.g., network or storage). A cluster may manage multiple pods.

Persistent Volumes

In a container environment, a storage volume is a storage location (file) on the host system, which is removed when the container associated with the storage volume is removed. Persistent volume storage, which may be used by a container or pod, will remain after the container or pod is removed.

BLOB Storage

A BLOB (binary large object) is a collection of binary data that is transmitted via HTTP. BLOBs are grouped into containers assigned to a user account.

There are several BLOB types: block, append, and page. Each BLOB type is used for a specific type of data storage, identified by a unique tag called an ETag.

Block BLOBs

Block BLOBs are designed for data streaming and storage. Each block has a unique ID and may store up to 100MB. A block BLOB can contain up to 50,000 blocks.

Figure 18-3
Container

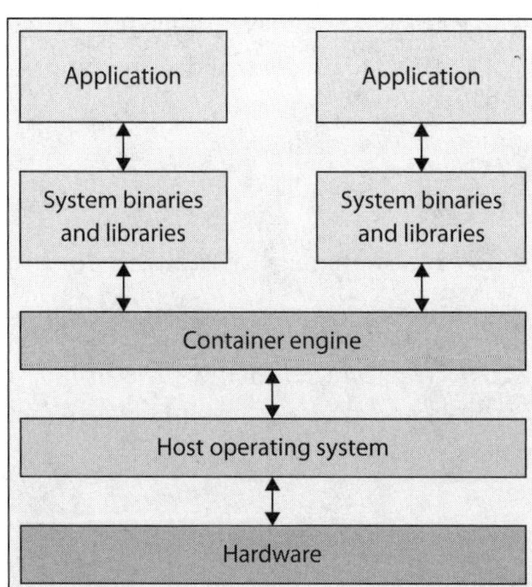

Block BLOBs may be updated by adding, replacing, or deleting data. In order for the changes to be made permanent, they must be committed. If the data has not been committed within a week, the data is removed.

Append BLOBs

Append BLOBs consist of a maximum of 50,000 4MB blocks and are used for logs. Existing blocks may not be deleted or modified. Data written to append BLOBs is always written to the end of the BLOB.

Page BLOBs

Page BLOBs consist of 512-byte pages and are used for random reads and writes. The maximum size of a page BLOB is 8TB.

Container Markup Languages

Configuration files for Docker, Docker Compose, and Kubernetes use either JSON (Docker) or YAML (Docker Compose and Kubernetes).

NOTE Kubernetes may use JSON, but best practices suggest the use of YAML.

JSON

JSON, or Java Script Object Notation, is a human-readable, text-based, data-serialization language designed to exchange data between a server and web applications. JSON files are stored as *<filename>.json*.

Data serialization converts data to a format that facilitates restoring data to its original structure. For example, JSON data may be converted into JavaScript objects.

An object is an independent structure that consists of a collection of related data. Although JSON is a subset of JavaScript, it may be used with other languages such as C, C++, Perl, Python, and Ruby. JSON does not support comments.

YAML

YAML, which stands for Yet Another Markup Language, is a human-readable data-serialization language that is a superset of JSON. An application that is a superset of another is an enhanced version of the "parent" application and contains all the features of the parent application.

YAML is found in programming languages such as Python and Ruby and is used to configure Docker and Kubernetes elements.

Cloud-init

A cloud instance is a single virtual server located in a cloud environment. Cloud-init is a bootstrap utility that configures the cloud instance using the configuration file */etc/cloud/cloud.cfg*.

Bootstrapping is the process used to load an operating system without user intervention.

Networking

This section describes various network configurations used with virtual machines.

NAT

A typical network consists of multiple host machines with unique IP addresses. Rather than make these IP address public, you can create a private network with world access using network address translation (NAT) or IP masquerading. Both NAT and IP masquerading present one public address for a network. When a host on the private network wishes to communicate with the world, the source address in the packet is changed to the public IP. The process is reversed when the packet returns.

NAT permits one connection to the public IP address at a time; IP masquerade permits multiple connections to the public IP address at a time.

Bridge

A bridge is used to connect multiple segments of a network. Network segments are used to split a network into subnetworks to improve security and performance.

A bridge differs from a router in that the bridge does not analyze, filter, or forward messages. Some routers also contain bridging functions.

Overlay

An overlay network is a computer network on top of another network using logical links.

Imagine a container pod in which the containers are hosts on the same virtual network, and a bridge attaches the virtual network to a physical. The virtual network is an overlay network.

Dual-Homed

A dual-homed network contains multiple network interface cards connected to the same network. Dual network cards are used to provide redundancy and therefore fault tolerance.

NOTE Redundancy is a method of using independent resources to achieve a goal if a primary resource fails. Fault tolerance is a result of creating redundancy.

The simplest form of redundancy on a dual-homed network is two network cards (master and slave) configured as failover devices for each other. At any time, only one network interface card is connected to the network. If one interface fails, traffic is rerouted to the second interface card.

Bonding Interfaces

Network interface redundancy is created by bonding two network interface cards.

For example, assume two network adapters, enp0s1 and etnp0s2, and the bonding module is available.

To set up the bonding interface, create a file in */etc/sysconfig/network-scripts* named *ifcfg-<bond#>* where # is the number of the bond interface. For this example, we will use bond0:

```
DEVICE=bond0                  #Name of physical device
NAME=bond0                    #Interface Name
TYPE=Bond                     #Interface Type
BONDING_MASTER=yes            #Master Bond configuration file
IP_ADDRESS=                   #IP Address of interface
PREFIX=24                     #First 24 bits are network number
ONBOOT=yes                    #Activated on boot
BOOTPROTO=none                #No boot protocol
BONDING_OPTIONS="mode 1"      #Space delimited list of bond options.
                             #Mode 1 is active e bonding
                                                   #
NM_CONTROLLED=no              #Network Manager will not configure
```

Edit the configuration files */etc/sysconfig/network-scripts/ifcfg- enp0s1* and */etc/sysconfig/network-scripts/ifcfg- enp0s2* to attach them to bond0 by adding or modifying the following entries:

```
BOOTPROTO=none
ONBOOT=yes
MASTER=bond0                  #Master
SLAVE=yes                     #Slave device to bond0
```

If you are using Network Manager, execute the command **nmcli con reload**. Restart the network by executing the command **systemctl restart network**. You can verify that the bond has been created by executing the command **cat /proc/net/bonding/bond#**.

Multi-homed networks have multiple network cards attached to different networks.

Virtual Switch

Network ports on virtual machines are associated with virtual network adapters, which are in turn associated with a virtual switch. The software-based virtual switch isolates and manages communications between virtual machines on the network.

Anaconda and Kickstart

Anaconda provides an open source distribution of both Python and R. Anaconda is also an installer (written in Python) for Red Hat and other Linux distributions.

Anaconda identifies the architecture of a computer system and configures an operating system (devices, filesystems, software, etc.) based on the choices made on multiple install menus.

As part of the installation process, Anaconda stores configuration choices to the file */root/anaconda-ks-cfg*. This file should be copied to the file */root/ks.cfg*.

ks.cfg may be used as is to perform an automatic install, or it can be modified via text mode (vi) or the GUI kickstart configurator, **system-config-kickstart**.

NOTE Use the command **yum -y install system-config-kickstart** to install the kickstart configurator.

The kickstart configuration file is made up of multiple sections that must be presented in a specific order. Most options within a section may be specified in any order.

The command **ksvalidator <config_file>** will validate the syntax of a kickstart file, and the command **ksverdiff <config_file_1> <config_file_2>** will display the differences between two configuration files.

NOTE The command **yum -y install pykickstart** will install ksvalidator, ksverdiff, and ksflatten.

Once the kickstart file is created and validated, it may be made available via a drive connected to an install process, DVD, or network (including PXE). The instruction **inst.ks=<ks_file_location>** will specify the kickstart location for the boot process. Network boots may require specifying the network address (ip option) or location of the repository (inst.repo=).

Chapter Review

This chapter described many of the configuration terms associated with virtual machines, hypervisors, storage, and networks. Here are some key takeaways from this chapter:

- Hypervisors were created by IBM as a debugging tool.
- Hypervisors are called virtual machine managers.
- Hypervisors isolate the host (resource provider) and guest machine.
- Embedded hypervisors are programmed into a processor.
- Type 1 (bare-metal) hypervisors have direct access to system hardware.
- Type 2 hypervisors are applications installed on the host.
- Thick provisioning allocates all the disk space when the disk is created.
- Thin provisioning dynamically allocates disk space.
- OVF is a file used to create virtual machines. It consists of a single directory that contains all the metadata needed to create a virtual machine.
- OVA is a tarred version of an OVF file.
- QCOW is a copy-on-write file.

- VDI is the default Oracle VirtualBox storage.
- VMDK was designed by VMware and is used by VirtualBox and QEMU.
- VHD is a virtual disk format designed by Microsoft. VHD was succeeded by VHDX.
- libvirt is an application designed by Red Hat to manage multiple hypervisors.
- libvirtd is the libvirt daemon.
- virsh is the CLI used to manage libvirt.
- Containers virtualize applications rather than machines.
- Persistent volumes are used for storing container data. Once the container is removed, data stored on persistent volumes will remain available.
- JSON and YAML are markup languages that may be used for data serialization.
- Cloud-init is a bootstrap utility for containers.
- NAT, or network address translation, uses a single IP to represent a private computer network.
- Bridging is a method of joining two networks as one.
- Overlay is a method of having one network sit on top of another network.
- A dual-homed network uses multiple interfaces to attach to one network.
- Bonding is a method of creating a dual-homed network.
- Kickstart is a method of creating an automated installation file.
- Kickstart uses Anaconda, an open source version of Python.

Questions

1. Which acronym is another name for a hypervisor?
   - **A.** HV
   - **B.** VM
   - **C.** VMM
   - **D.** HVV
2. Which method of storage provisioning allocates disk space dynamically?
   - **A.** Thin
   - **B.** Persistent
   - **C.** BLOB
   - **D.** Thick

3. Which virtualization file format is a single directory containing multiple configuration files?
   A. HDD
   B. OVA
   C. OVF
   D. VMDK
4. Which virtualization file format is a single directory containing an archive of an OVF file?
   A. HDD
   B. OVA
   C. OVF
   D. VMDK
5. Which command-line utility was developed by Red Hat as a management tool for the KVM hypervisor?
   A. libvirt
   B. vboxmanage
   C. virsh
   D. vmware-cmd
6. A container is an example of:
   A. Type 1 virtualization
   B. Type 2 virtualization
   C. Embedded virtualization
   D. None of the above
7. Persistent volumes are associated with which of the following?
   A. Pods
   B. Containers
   C. Thick provisioning
   D. Thin provisioning
8. Select all properties that apply to an append BLOB.
   A. New data must be appended.
   B. Existing data cannot be modified.
   C. Existing data can be modified.
   D. Existing data cannot be deleted.

9. Which BLOB type is used for random reads and writes?
   A. Append
   B. Page
   C. Block
   D. Bob Loblaw's Law Blog
10. Data serialization converts data to a format that facilitates restoring data to its original structure. Which tools provide data serialization? (Choose two.)
   A. vi
   B. YAML
   C. JSON
   D. nano
11. Cloud-init is a bootstrap facility whose configuration file is:
   A. */etc/cloud.cfg*
   B. */etc/cloud/cloud.config*
   C. */etc/cloud.config*
   D. */etc/cloud/cloud.cfg*
12. Bonding is associated with which network type?
   A. NAT
   B. Bridge
   C. Dual-homed
   D. Overlay
13. An overlay network would be associated with:
   A. Pods
   B. Dual-homed network
   C. NAT
   D. Bridge

Answers

1. **C.** Hypervisors are also called virtual machine managers (VMMs).
2. **A.** Thin provisioning allocates disk space as necessary. Thick provisioning allocates all disk space. Persistent volumes are used with pods to ensure data remains once a pod closes. BLOB storage is block data storage accessed via HTTP or HTTPS.
3. **C.** OVF files contain a single directory that consists of configuration files used to configure a virtual machine.

4. **B.** The OVA file is an archive of the OVF file.
5. **C.** virsh is the command-line utility used to manage KVM. virsh is a part of libvirt. libvert is a set of tools used to manage virtual machines.
6. **A.** A container is an example of Type 1, or bare-metal, virtualization.
7. **A.** Persistent volumes are associated with pods. Pod is the name for a container or group of containers within Kubernetes.
8. **A, B, D.** An append BLOB is used for logging data. Existing data in append BLOBs may not be modified or deleted, and any new entries are appended to the end of the BLOB.
9. **B.** The page BLOB is used for random read and write operations.
10. **B, C.** YAML and JSON are markup languages that facilitate data serialization.
11. **D.** */etc/cloud/cloud.cfg* is cloud-init's configuration file.
12. **C.** A dual-homed network is used to provide network card redundancy on a single network. This is accomplished by bonding multiple NIC cards.
13. **A.** An overlay network is a network which sits on top of another network. In the Kubernetes environment, each container in a pod is assigned an IP address on a local network assigned to the pod. This network may sit on top of a physical network.

CHAPTER 19

Troubleshooting and Diagnostics

In this chapter, you will learn about

- A standardized troubleshooting model
- Troubleshooting computer problems
- Troubleshooting network problems

When it comes to system security, one of the biggest issues companies face is insider threats. In this chapter, we tell the story of FOLDERMS Corp., a children's toy company. FOLDERMS plans to merge with EZPAGS, Inc., which offers excellent packaging solutions for toys, and executives see the merger as a great fit.

As is often the case with such ventures, staff get nervous about what is going to happen to them, so they plan to protect their jobs at FOLDERMS by any means necessary, thus making them *internal threats*.

A Standardized Troubleshooting Model

Mr. Mitchell Mugabe has experience with mergers and acquisitions (M&A) as a lead engineer and understands the issue of internal threats. His great patience, understanding of common vulnerabilities and exposures (CVEs), and real-world experience make him a great troubleshooter. Mitchell plans an eight-step approach to handling computer- and network-related issues similar to the approach mentioned in Chapter 14:

Step 1: **Identify the problem.** Mitchell determines what has happened by asking questions, detecting symptoms, and reviewing error messages.

Step 2: **Determine recent change.** Mitchell identifies the single change in the system, whether it's new software, new hardware, or a new configuration.

Step 3: **Create a causal theory.** Using information gathered from the previous steps, Mitchell develops a theory that could explain the problem.

Step 4: **Select the fix.** Mitchell usually works with a team of other engineers, including Ms. Jessica Yang and Mr. Carlos Gardner, to arrive at a solution and discuss if the fix will cause other problems.

Step 5: **Attempt the fix.** At this point, Jessica and Carlos work together to implement the fix, making sure the problem is solved and does not return.

Step 6: **Verify functionality.** Before unveiling the fix to customer, Mitchell verifies the repairs made by his team.

Step 7: **Ensure customer satisfaction.** Mitchell, Jessica, or Carlos verifies the client is happy. A final word is shared with their supervisor to let them know the problem is fixed.

Step 8: **Complete the paperwork.** Mitchell and his team document the solution within a ticketing database to quickly identify the issue if it occurs again.

EXAM TIP Knowledge of the 8-step troubleshooting steps is great for the CompTIA A+ exam, but is *not* a requirement for the Linux+ exam.

Troubleshooting Computer Problems

Mitchell starts by collecting an inventory of computer systems used by the FOLDERMS staff. Fortunately, like EZPAGS, FOLDERMS is a Linux-only environment, learning years earlier that Linux is a high-quality, well-supported operating system with fewer vulnerabilities than closed-sourced operating systems.

Ms. Tomika Jones, Mr. Davy Sullivan, Ms. Melanie Lopez, and other engineers at FOLDERMS are working to disrupt the merger, providing Mitchell with an inaccurate inventory. From past experience, Mitchell has learned to "trust, but verify." Therefore, Mitchell will verify and validate computer issues using the following approaches:

- Verify hardware configuration
- Verify CPU performance
- Verify memory performance
- Validate storage performance
- Validate other devices

NOTE The events, characters, and firms depicted in this scenario are fictitious. Any similarity to actual persons, living or dead, or to actual firms is purely coincidental.

Verify Hardware Configuration

Mitchell has a couple tools in his toolbox to verify the configuration of a computer without opening the system. These tools are the lshw and dmidecode commands.

The lshw command will "list hardware" installed on a Linux system, reporting an exact memory configuration, firmware version, motherboard configuration, CPU details, CPU cache details, bus speeds, and more. The report provided by Gary, another FOLDERMS team member unhappy about the coming merger, shows that each computer is configured with 2GB of RAM and no CD-ROM drive.

Mitchell runs the **lshw** command using the **-short** option, as shown next:

```
[root@cent71-5t buddy]# lshw -short
H/W path            Device      Class       Description
=====================================================
                                system      VirtualBox
/0                              bus         VirtualBox
/0/0                            memory      128KiB BIOS
/0/1                            memory      1GiB System memory
/0/2                            processor   Intel(R) Core(TM) i7-6500U CPU @ 2G
/0/100                          bridge      440FX - 82441FX PMC [Natoma]
/0/100/1                        bridge      82371SB PIIX3 ISA [Natoma/Triton I]
/0/100/1.1           scsi1      storage     82371AB/EB/MB PIIX4 IDE
/0/100/1.1/0.0.0    /dev/cdrom  disk        CD-ROM
/0/100/2                        display     VirtualBox Graphics Adapter
/0/100/3            enp0s3      network     82540EM Gigabit Ethernet Controller
/0/100/4                        generic     VirtualBox Guest Service
/0/100/5                        multimedia  82801AA AC'97 Audio Controller
/0/100/6                        bus         KeyLargo/Intrepid USB
/0/100/6/1          usb2        bus         OHCI PCI host controller
<...etc... >
```

The report shows that each system actually has 1GB of RAM and a CD-ROM installed. Later, Mitchell will complete a physical inspection to validate his findings.

The other command at Mitchell's disposal is **dmidecode**, which lists the computer's BIOS while in multi-user mode. The output shown next uses the **--quiet** option and shows that the mainboard supports ISA, PCI, and CD-ROM booting:

```
[root@cent71-5t buddy]# dmidecode --quiet
BIOS Information
      Vendor: innotek GmbH
      Version: VirtualBox
      Release Date: 12/01/2006
      Address: 0xE0000
      Runtime Size: 128 kB
      ROM Size: 128 kB
      Characteristics:
             ISA is supported
             PCI is supported
             Boot from CD is supported
             Selectable boot is supported
             8042 keyboard services are supported (int 9h)
             CGA/mono video services are supported (int 10h)
             ACPI is supported

System Information
      Manufacturer: innotek GmbH
      Product Name: VirtualBox

<...etc...>
```

To support his case for the merger, Mitchell gathered information, identified changes, and finally documented his findings into the ticketing system.

Verify CPU Performance

Davy at FOLDERMS is the kind of guy who never forgets anything, especially if it affects his job, so without any paperwork he assures Mitchell that the CPU load averages are greater than 50 percent! The load average defines how busy a CPU is; the more jobs that are ready to use the CPU (in other words, *runnable* jobs), the higher the load average.

To observe the CPU model, number of cores, and options, Mitchell reviews the contents of the */proc/cpuinfo* file to determine if it is underpowered, as follows:

```
[root@cent71-5t buddy]# more /proc/cpuinfo
processor    : 0
vendor_id    : GenuineIntel
cpu family   : 6
model        : 78
model name   : Intel(R) Core(TM) i7-6500U CPU @ 2.50GHz
stepping     : 3
cpu MHz      : 2592.002
cache size   : 4096 KB
physical id : 0
siblings     : 2
core id      : 0
cpu cores    : 2
apicid       : 0
initial apicid    : 0
fpu.         : yes
fpu_exception     : yes
cpuid level : 22
wp           : yes
flags        : fpu vme de pse tsc msr pae mce cx8 apic sep mtrr pge mca cmov
pat pse36 clflush mmx fxsr sse sse2 ht syscall nx rdtscp lm constant_tsc
rep_good nopl xtopology nonstop_tsc eagerfpu pni pclmulqdq ssse3 cx16 pcid
sse4_1 sse4_2 x2apic movbe popcnt aes xsave avx rdrand hypervisor lahf_lm
abm 3dnowprefetch fsgsbase avx2 invpcid rdseed clflush
opt flush_l1d
```

The CPU certainly looks capable enough for their applications, so to examine CPU load averages, Mitchell employs the uptime, w, and sar commands:

```
[root@cent71-5t buddy]# uptime
15:35:02 up  2:17,  2 users,  load average: 0.01, 0.04, 0.05
[root@cent71-5t buddy]# w
15:35:04 up  2:17,  2 users,  load average: 0.01, 0.04, 0.05
USER     TTY      FROM              LOGIN@   IDLE   JCPU   PCPU WHAT
buddy  :0       :0                13:21   ?xdm?   6:32   0.42s /usr/libexec/gn
buddy  pts/0    :0                13:21    0.00s 29.28s  9.29s /usr/libexec/gn
[root@cent71-5t buddy]# sar 2 5
Linux 3.10.0-957.10.1.el7.x86_64 (cent71-5t)     04/26/2019   x86_64_    (2 CPU)
03:35:11 PM     CPU     %user     %nice   %system   %iowait    %steal     %idle
03:35:13 PM     all      3.79      0.00      0.25      0.00      0.00     95.96
03:35:15 PM     all      4.31      0.00      0.51      0.00      0.00     95.18
03:35:17 PM     all      3.03      0.00      0.25      0.00      0.00     96.72
03:35:19 PM     all      3.79      0.00      0.51      0.00      0.00     95.71
03:35:21 PM     all      4.30      0.00      0.51      0.00      0.00     95.19
Average:        all      3.84      0.00      0.40      0.00      0.00     95.75
```

The **uptime** command shows how long a system has been running, and it outputs system load averages. In this example, the load average displays 1 percent over the past minute, 4 percent over the past 5 minutes, and 5 percent over the past 15 minutes—nowhere near the 50 percent load averages stated by Davy.

The **w** command shows who is logged in and what commands they are running. Mitchell uses this output to determine which programs are loading the system, and from which accounts.

Finally, **sar** is the "system activity reporter." This is an all-purpose tool that lists performance information for CPU, RAM, I/O, disk, communication ports, graphics, and so on. Running sar 2 5 will collect system activity data and display five lines of output, one for every two seconds. By default, the sar command lists CPU performance details, including idle states.

To support the case for the merger, Mitchell notes that system loads are less than 10 percent, nowhere near the 50 percent stated by the FOLDERMS representatives.

NOTE The **time** command is a useful tool. Simply run **time <program_name>** to determine how much CPU time is used by an individual program.

Verify Memory Performance

Melanie indicates from FOLDERMS reports that all their systems require memory upgrades. To review memory and swap performance, Mitchell examines the */proc/meminfo* file to observe how much memory is being used and how much is available, and then he runs **vmstat 2 5** to review memory performance, as shown here:

```
[root@cent71-5t buddy]#  more /proc/meminfo
MemTotal:          1014816 kB
MemFree:             98152 kB
MemAvailable:       154816 kB
Buffers:                52 kB
Cached:             207880 kB
SwapCached:          39000 kB
Active:             351388 kB
Inactive:           375428 kB
Active(anon):       269716 kB
Inactive(anon):     293084 kB
Active(file):        81672 kB
Inactive(file):      82344 kB
Unevictable:             0 kB
Mlocked:                 0 kB
SwapTotal:         1048572 kB
SwapFree:           740732 kB
Dirty:                  28 kB
Writeback:               0 kB
AnonPages:          499196 kB
Mapped:             113292 kB
Shmem:               43916 kB
Slab:                91300 kB
SReclaimable:        40868 kB
```

```
[root@cent71-5t buddy]# vmstat 2 5
procs ----------memory--------- --swap-- ----io---- -system-- ------cpu-----
r  b   swpd   free  buff  cache  si   so   bi    bo   in   cs us sy id wa st
2  0 307840 100952    52 299136   6   14  329    58  123  140  2  1 97  0  0
0  0 307840 101112    52 299168   0    0    0     0  457  641  6  1 93  0  0
0  0 307840 101000    52 299168   0    0    0     0  263  316  4  0 95  0  0
0  0 307840 100988    52 299168   0    0    0     0  288  334  4  1 95  0  0
0  0 307840 101004    52 299168   0    0    0     0  195  275  3  0 96  0  0
```

The first report shows averages since the system booted. Additional reports list activity for the two-second sampling period Mitchell defined. He notices from the output that there is ample free memory for their applications.

As with the sar command, **vmstat 2 5** reports virtual memory statistics five times, every two seconds. The vmstat command displays the amount of memory utilized in swap space, how much is idle, the amount used as buffers, and the volume saved as cache. The command also shows how much data is swapped to and from disk.

Out of Memory Killer

The OOM Killer, or *Out Of Memory Killer,* is employed by the Linux kernel when the system is critically low on memory. If enough processes begin to use memory, there will not be enough to support them all. So, the kernel invokes the OOM Killer to review the processes and kills one or more of them to free up memory and keep the system running.

The OOM Killer reviews all processes and assigns a severity score based on memory utilization and the number of child processes. The process with the highest score is killed. For security, the root, kernel, and important system processes are given much lower scores. If killing a process does not free enough memory, the server will soon crash.

To find whether the OOM Killer was the reason for why processes were killed, you would run the following command:

```
[root@cent71-5t buddy]# dmesg | grep -i "killed process"
host kernel: Out of Memory: Killed process 4121 (mysql).
```

In this case, mysql was killed, with a process identification number (PID) of 4121.

The OOM Killer only gets invoked when the system is critically low on memory. Consequently, to avoid it, you can either reduce memory requirements, increase the memory, or increase swap space.

Increasing Swap Space

Mitchell's years of experience in technology and management help him understand that there are quick ways to stop the OOM Killer, and he decides to mitigate the threat by increasing swap space. Swap space can be added using an additional new swap hard drive, additional swap partition, or by adding a swapfile using the swapon command, as shown in Figure 19-1.

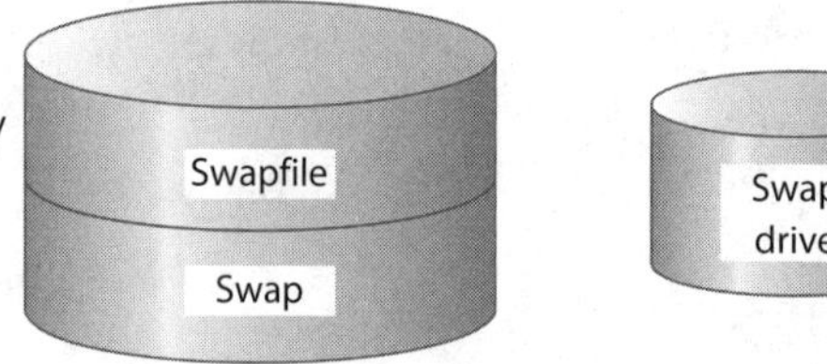

Figure 19-1 Additional swap space devices

To view the current swap space status, look at the contents of */proc/swaps* file, run the **swapon** command with the **-s** option, or even try the free command to view memory and swap utilization, as shown here:

```
[root@cent71-5t buddy]#  more /proc/swaps
Filename                Type            Size            Used            Priority
dev/sda8                partition       1048572         298880          -2
[root@cent71-5t buddy]# swapon -s
Filename                Type            Size            Used            Priority
/dev/sda8               partition       1048572         298880          -2
[root@cent71-5t buddy]# free
           total         used         free       shared  buff/cache   available
Mem:      1014816       665656        73860        44400      275300      109660
Swap:     1048572       298880       749692
```

After the new swap device is created, it can be enabled using swapon. Tomika of FOLDERMS intends to impede the merger by suggesting EZPAGS wait a month for new hard drives so they can be used as additional swap space. Mitchell decides that the simplest way to proceed is to add a swap file.

Adding a new swap disk would require purchasing and installing a new hard drive. Addition of a swap partition is even tougher, as data must be backed up from an existing drive and repartitioned to increase the swap partition, and then the data must be restored. Adding a swap file simply requires creating an empty file using dd, assuming there is space available in the filesystem, as shown next:

```
[root@cent71-5t buddy]# dd if=/dev/zero of=~/swapfile bs=1M count=1024
1024+0 records in
1024+0 records out
1073741824 bytes (1.1 GB) copied, 1.52779 s, 703 MB/s
[root@cent71-5t buddy]#
```

After adding the swap file, you can enable it using the swapon command, as shown here:

```
[root@cent71-5t buddy]# swapon /home/buddy/swapfile
swapon: /home/buddy/swapfile: insecure permissions 0644, 0600 suggested.
```

Mitchell is warned that the permissions are insecure. This is fixed with chmod and chown, as shown:

```
[root@cent71-5t buddy]# chown root:root /home/buddy/swapfile
[root@cent71-5t buddy]# chmod 600 /home/buddy/swapfile
```

Next, he ascertains that the swap file is added using the -s option to swapon. The Priority is set to -3, meaning it will be used after any Priority setting of -2 or -1 is filled. Once he has completed using the swap file, it can be disabled with **swapoff** and removed with rm, as shown here:

```
[root@cent71-5t buddy]# swapon -s
Filename                  Type            Size            Used            Priority
/dev/sda8                 partition       1048572         463708          -2
/home/buddy/swapfile      file            1048572         0               -3
[root@cent71-5t buddy]# swapoff /home/buddy/swapfile
[root@cent71-5t buddy]# rm /home/buddy/swapfile
```

Work with Mitchell to add a swapfile in Exercise 19-1.

Exercise 19-1: Working with Swap Space

In this exercise, you practice using swap space commands to manage and troubleshoot memory utilization. Use the virtual machine that comes with the book.

VIDEO Please watch the Exercise 19-1 video for a demonstration on how to perform this task.

Complete the following steps:

1. Boot your Linux system and log in as the student1 user.
2. Open a terminal session.
3. Switch to the root user account by entering **su -** followed by **student1** for the password.
4. Run **swapon -s** to review how much space there is currently.
5. Create a swapfile using the dd command by running the following:
   ```
   dd if=/dev/zero of=swapfile bs=1M count=250
   mkswap swapfile
   chown root:root swapfile
   chmod 600 swapfile
   ```
6. Run **swapon swapfile** to enable your new swap space.
7. Run **swapon -s** to verify the space was added.
8. Run **swapoff swapfile** to disable the swap space.
9. Run **rm swapfile** to return the computer to its previous state.

Validate Storage Performance

Melanie of FOLDERMS informs Mitchell that disk drive performance is subpar and that they need to budget for better and faster hard drives. Mitchell puts on his thinking cap and realizes that tuning some simple kernel parameters can help improve performance.

He looks at the result of the scheduler kernel variable found in the directories */sys/block/*<disk device>*/queue/*, which can be set to noop, deadline, or cfq:

```
[root@cent71-5t buddy]# cat /sys/block/sda/queue/scheduler
[noop] deadline cfq
```

Mitchell knows that hard drive I/O performance is application dependent and can improve depending on the setting, as shown in Table 19-1.

Completely Fair Queuing, or cfq, is in general best for single-user systems such as desktops. The noop scheduler is great for SAN or RAID systems because they provide their own scheduling. Finally, the deadline scheduler is good for multiuser environments.

Table 19-1 Disk Drive scheduler Settings

scheduler Setting	Description
noop	Handles requests in order of submission.
deadline	Each I/O request is on a timer and completes before it expires.
cfq	Higher priority processes are served first.

Mitchell analyzes I/O performance first using iostat, as shown next. For his analysis, he runs the corporate applications and uses the -z option to just observe drives that are in use. Also, measurements will take place over four seconds, and he only requires two outputs.

```
[root@cent71-5t buddy]# iostat -z 4 2 | tail -6
avg-cpu:  %user   %nice %system %iowait  %steal   %idle
          60.21    0.00   27.09    0.79    0.00   11.91

Device:            tps    kB_read/s    kB_wrtn/s    kB_read    kB_wrtn
sda             947.00     21978.00       776.50      87912       3106
```

The iostat output shows read and write activity per second, and total I/O over the entire eight-second period on drive */dev/sda*.

To test again and see performance results for deadline, he changes the scheduler setting by updating the kernel value, as shown:

```
[root@cent71-5t buddy]# echo deadline > /sys/block/sda/queue/scheduler
[root@cent71-5t buddy]# cat /sys/block/sda/queue/scheduler
noop [deadline] cfq
[root@cent71-5t buddy]# iostat -z 4 2 | tail -6
avg-cpu:  %user   %nice %system %iowait  %steal   %idle
          52.20    0.00   30.23    2.45    0.00   15.12

Device:            tps    kB_read/s    kB_wrtn/s    kB_read    kB_wrtn
sda             674.00      6889.00       281.12      27556       1124
```

Finally, he changes scheduler to cfq and then measures performance:

```
[root@cent71-5t buddy]# echo cfq > /sys/block/sda/queue/scheduler
[root@cent71-5t buddy]# cat /sys/block/sda/queue/scheduler
noop deadline [cfq]
[root@cent71-5t buddy]# iostat -z 4 2 | tail -6
avg-cpu:  %user   %nice %system %iowait  %steal   %idle
          49.10    0.00   25.77    0.00    0.00   25.13

Device:            tps    kB_read/s    kB_wrtn/s    kB_read    kB_wrtn
sda               1.75         0.00        20.00          0         80
```

Another tool in Mitchell's tool case is the **ioping** command, which measures disk I/O latency in real time. Here are some examples:

```
[root@cent71-5t buddy]# ioping /dev/sda
4 KiB <<< /dev/sda (block device 18 GiB): request=1 time=2.32 ms (warmup)
4 KiB <<< /dev/sda (block device 18 GiB): request=2 time=294.8 us
4 KiB <<< /dev/sda (block device 18 GiB): request=3 time=277.8 us
4 KiB <<< /dev/sda (block device 18 GiB): request=4 time=6.37 ms
4 KiB <<< /dev/sda (block device 18 GiB): request=5 time=280.8 us
^C
```

He uses the -c option to limit output so as not to use ^C to complete the session:

```
[root@cent71-5t buddy]# ioping -c 5 /dev/sda
4 KiB <<< /dev/sda (block device 18 GiB): request=1 time=10.3 ms (warmup)
4 KiB <<< /dev/sda (block device 18 GiB): request=2 time=325.8 us
4 KiB <<< /dev/sda (block device 18 GiB): request=3 time=248.3 us
4 KiB <<< /dev/sda (block device 18 GiB): request=4 time=47.2 ms
4 KiB <<< /dev/sda (block device 18 GiB): request=5 time=288.3 us
```

Finally, he uses ioping to measure disk latency for the current (or other) directory, as shown here:

```
[root@cent71-5t buddy]# ioping -c 5 .
4 KiB <<< . (xfs /dev/sda5): request=1 time=2.08 ms (warmup)
4 KiB <<< . (xfs /dev/sda5): request=2 time=1.43 ms
4 KiB <<< . (xfs /dev/sda5): request=3 time=657.0 us
4 KiB <<< . (xfs /dev/sda5): request=4 time=216.3 us
4 KiB <<< . (xfs /dev/sda5): request=5 time=5.51 ms
```

In the end, Mitchell finds that simply tuning the disk drive's scheduling parameter saves the firm millions of dollars in hard drive upgrades and labor expenses, making the merger more amenable. To make the changes permanent, he uses features of "tuned" to enable the new scheduling value at boot time, as shown next.

NOTE The tuned features are *not* a Linux+ exam requirement.

```
[root@cent71-5t buddy]# tuned-adm list
Available profiles:
- balanced                    - General non-specialized tuned profile
- desktop                     - Optimize for the desktop use-case
- latency-performance         - Optimize for performance but more power use
- network-latency             - Low latency network performance but power use
- network-throughput          - Optimize for streaming network throughput
- powersave                   - Optimize for low power consumption
- throughput-performance      - Broad tuning and performance over for workloads
- virtual-guest               - Optimize for running inside a virtual guest
- virtual-host                - Optimize for running KVM guests
Current active profile:
```

Since the "active profile" shows as virtual-guest, Mitchell modifies the *tuned.conf* file located in */usr/lib/tuned/virtual-guest/*. (Other tuned profiles are defined in the */usr/lib/tuned/* directory.) To make cfq the I/O scheduler at boot time, he uses

```
[root@cent71-5t buddy]# cat >> /usr/lib/tuned/virtual-guest/tuned.conf

[bootloader]
cmdline="elevator=cfq"

^D
```

where elevator is used to specify the desired I/O scheduler.

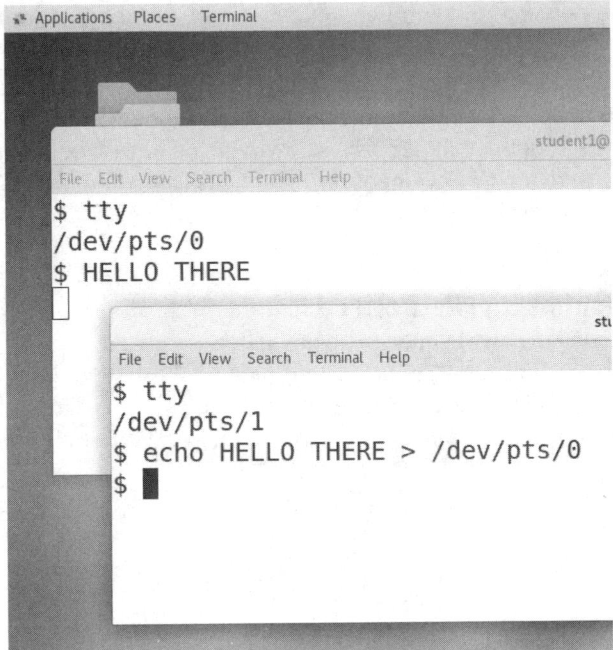

Figure 19-2 Working with pseudo-terminals

Validate Other Devices

Mitchell has several troubleshooting tools and tricks in his toolbox as well as several ways to run them. Most of the time he will run the commands within a pseudo-terminal, much like what is seen when logging in from a display manager (see Figure 19-2).

To see the pseudo-terminal value, he runs the tty command, as shown in Figure 19-2. In this case, Mitchell sends HELLO THERE from one pseudo-terminal to the other using the **echo HELLO THERE > /dev/pts/0** command from the */dev/pts/1* pseudo-terminal. This allows him to send error messages to different locations during troubleshooting.

There are also six alternative virtual consoles. These can be accessed with the key triad of CTRL-ALT-F{2,3,4,5,6,7}, where **ctrl-alt-f1** will return the user to the graphical desktop on Red Hat-class systems. On Debian-class systems, the key triad is CTRL-ALT-F{1,2,3,4,5,6} and **ctrl-alt-f7** returns the user to a graphical desktop. Figure 19-3 shows the result of using **ctrl-alt-f6**, and the result of the **tty** command, which shows Mitchell is using terminal */dev/tty6*.

Figure 19-3 Using the virtual console

```
CentOS Linux 7 (Core)
Kernel 3.10.0-957.10.1.el7.x86_64 on an x86_64

cent71-5t login: student1
Password:
Last login: Mon May  6 13:44:53 on tty6
[student1@cent71-5t ~]$ tty
/dev/tty6
[student1@cent71-5t ~]$
```

Virtual consoles are useful on systems when the display manager hangs due to a runaway process.

NOTE Many systems do not allow logging in as root, by default. This setting is defined in */etc/securetty*, which includes terminals where root is allowed to log in. Comment terminal lines using # to disallow logging in from that terminal.

Troubleshooting File-Related Issues

Robert of FOLDERMS informs Mitchell that they are out of disk space because of an error message that says "cannot create new files" or something similar. When Mitchell runs df, he can clearly see that there is plenty of disk space left. Using **df -i** on an ext4-type filesystem shows him the real problem, which is the system is out of inodes:

```
[root@cent71-5t buddy]# df /boot
Filesystem      1K-blocks   Used          Available Use% Mounted on
/dev/sda1          487634        221068    236870        49%  /boot
[root@cent71-5t buddy]# df -i /boot
Filesystem      Inodes  IUsed   IFree IUse% Mounted on
/dev/sda1       524288  524288 0      100%  /
[root@cent71-5t buddy]# dumpe2fs /dev/sda1 | grep -i 'inode count'
dumpe2fs 1.42.9 (28-Dec-2013)
Inode count:                524288
```

To increase the inode count, the filesystem will need to be re-created by backing up all the data and then using **mkfs.ext4 -N 1000000 /dev/sda1** to double the inode count. Once the data is restored, users will be able to create new files.

NOTE Administrators must externally label or banner backup tapes to know they are restoring the correct versions of files.

Changing Keyboard Maps

A few frustrated staffers (also known as *internal threats*) concerned about the merger have decided to alter the keyboard maps to work well, but not great. Mitchell uses **localectl** to fix this issue. He notices the keymap is set to "us-mac" instead of "us." He fixes this as follows:

```
[root@cent71-5t buddy]# localectl
  System Locale: LANG=en_US.UTF-8
      VC Keymap: us-mac
     X11 Layout: us-mac
[root@cent71-5t buddy]# localectl set-keymap us
[root@cent71-5t buddy]# localectl
  System Locale: LANG=en_US.UTF-8
      VC Keymap: us      X11 Layout: us
```

Troubleshooting Printers

The members of the staff at FOLDERMS have never set up printers on Linux because they always failed to work. Mitchell does some research and finds that the printing service, CUPS, is not enabled. He fixes the issue and verifies that CUPS port 631 is listening using netstat and lsof, as shown here:

```
[root@cent71-5t buddy]# systemctl status cups
● cups.service - CUPS Printing Service
  Loaded: loaded (/usr/lib/systemd/system/cups.service; disabled)
  Active: inactive (dead)
[root@cent71-5t buddy]# lsof -i tcp:631
[root@cent71-5t buddy]# netstat -a | grep ipp
[root@cent71-5t buddy]# systemctl start cups
[root@cent71-5t buddy]# lsof -i tcp:631
COMMAND  PID USER   FD   TYPE DEVICE SIZE/OFF NODE NAME
cupsd   8030 root   10u  IPv6  65928      0t0  TCP localhost:ipp (LISTEN)
cupsd   8030 root   11u  IPv4  65929      0t0  TCP localhost:ipp (LISTEN)
[root@cent71-5t buddy]# netstat -a | grep ipp
tcp        0      0 localhost:ipp          0.0.0.0:*               LISTEN
tcp6       0      0 localhost:ipp          [::]:*                  LISTEN
```

Finally, Mitchell ensures printing capability for future reboots by running **systemctl enable cups**, as shown next:

```
[root@cent71-5t buddy]# systemctl enable cups
Created symlink from /etc/systemd/system/multi-user.target.wants/cups.service to
/usr/lib/systemd/system/cups.service.
Created symlink from /etc/systemd/system/printer.target.wants/cups.service to
/usr/lib/systemd/system/cups.service.
Created symlink from /etc/systemd/system/sockets.target.wants/cups.socket to
/usr/lib/systemd/system/cups.socket.
Created symlink from /etc/systemd/system/multi-user.target.wants/cups.path to
/usr/lib/systemd/system/cups.path.
```

Verifying Graphics Cards

Several systems have NVIDIA graphics cards, but they are not functioning. Mitchell uses **lspci** and **lshw** to study the issue, as follows:

```
[root@cent71-5t buddy]# lspci -v | grep -i vga
00:02.0 VGA compatible controller: InnoTek Systemberatung GmbH VirtualBox
Graphics Adapter (prog-if 00 [VGA controller])
[root@cent71-5t buddy]# lshw -class display
 *-display
      description: VGA compatible controller
      product: VirtualBox Graphics Adapter
      vendor: InnoTek Systemberatung GmbH
      physical id: 2
      bus info: pci@0000:00:02.0
      version: 00
      width: 32 bits
      clock: 33MHz
      capabilities: vga_controller rom
      configuration: driver=vboxvideo latency=0
      resources: irq:18 memory:e0000000-e7ffffff
```

Since NVIDIA does not show in any of the output, it is clear to Mitchell what the issue is. The drivers have not been installed for the NVIDIA graphics cards. Once the GPU drivers are downloaded from NVIDIA and installed, the cards function.

Root Password Recovery

Invariably there are systems where administrators have changed jobs, or systems that get lost and are recovered, but the personnel who know the root password are no longer around. The root passwords on such systems can be recovered when the system is physically accessible, and the new administrator has access to GRUB, or a bootable image of Linux. For such cases, Mitchell keeps DVD and thumb drive versions of Linux.

To recover a system with an unknown root password, Mitchell has to first get into shell mode. Shell mode runs even fewer services than single-user mode and is used for emergency maintenance. First, he boots into GRUB and presses the ESC key so he can edit GRUB by selecting the "e" option, as shown in Figure 19-4.

Next, Mitchell alters the linux16 boot line that overrides booting into the multiuser graphical.target, and will now boot into the emergency level via shell mode. Here he replaces **ro** with **rw init=/sysroot/bin/sh**, as shown in Figure 19-5. This mounts "/" (the root directory) as read-write so that when the password is changed, the */etc/shadow* file will be altered. The **init=/sysroot/bin/sh** portion will substitute systemd with the */bin/sh* program at boot, allowing him to access the system before it requests the root password. To boot with the updates, he selects CTRL-X.

After the system boots, the shell prompt appears. His first step is to run **chroot /sysroot**, which makes */sysroot* the new / directory, which is where both */usr/bin/passwd* and */etc/shadow* reside (instead of */sysroot/usr/bin/passwd* or */sysroot/etc/shadow*). Then he can change

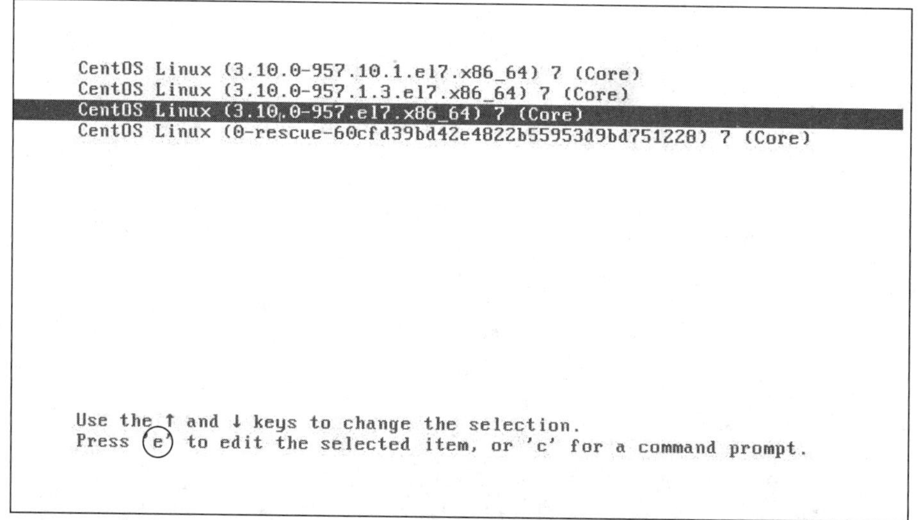

Figure 19-4 GRUB boot menu to access GRUB boot script

```
        insmod ext2
        set root='hd0,msdos1'
        if [ x$feature_platform_search_hint = xy ]; then
          search --no-floppy --fs-uuid --set=root --hint-bios=hd0,msdos1 --hin\
t-efi=hd0,msdos1 --hint-baremetal=ahci0,msdos1 --hint='hd0,msdos1'  87bcb08d-e\
8b2-4380-99a5-eaa23472c956
        else
          search --no-floppy --fs-uuid --set=root 87bcb08d-e8b2-4380-99a5-eaa2\
3472c956
        fi
        linux16 /vmlinuz-3.10.0-957.el7.x86_64 root=UUID=eb37c67d-25c0-4f24-bd\
d0-a8e0c9ed4870 rw init=/sysroot/bin/sh rd.lvm.lv=USR/usr rhgb quiet LANG=en_U\
S.UTF-8
        initrd16 /initramfs-3.10.0-957.el7.x86_64.img

      Press Ctrl-x to start, Ctrl-c for a command prompt or Escape to
      discard edits and return to the menu. Pressing Tab lists
      possible completions.
```

Figure 19-5 Altering GRUB boot script to access shell mode

```
Type "journalctl" to view system logs.
You might want to save "/run/initramfs/rdsosreport.txt" to a USB stick or /boot
after mounting them and attach it to a bug report.


:/# chroot /sysroot
:/# passwd root
Changing password for user root.
New password:
Retype new password:
passwd: all authentication tokens updated successfully.
:/# touch /.autorelabel
:/# exit
:/# logout
```

Figure 19-6 Changing the root user password

the root password by running **passwd root**, as shown in Figure 19-6. After making the update, he runs **touch /.autorelabel** to update the SELinux parameters after the system boots normally. Finally, he reboots the system and logs in as root using the new password.

Troubleshooting Network Problems

Getting the network interface installed is only half the battle. To enable communications, network administrators use a variety of testing and monitoring tools to make sure the network is working properly.

As Mitchell continues with his system and network analysis, he will verify and validate network issues using the following approaches:

- Verify network performance
- Validate user connections
- Validate the firewall

Verify Network Performance

Again, Mitchell has several software tools in his tool case to configure, monitor, and troubleshoot networks. To view network status, he uses the ip command. For example, by running **ip addr show**, he can see the current network devices and their status, as shown here:

```
[root@cent71-5t buddy]# ip addr show
1: lo: <LOOPBACK,UP,LOWER_UP> mtu 65536 qdisc noqueue state UNKNOWN group default
qlen 1000
    link/loopback 00:00:00:00:00:00 brd 00:00:00:00:00:00
    inet 127.0.0.1/8 scope host lo
       valid_lft forever preferred_lft forever
    inet6 ::1/128 scope host
       valid_lft forever preferred_lft forever
2: enp0s3: <BROADCAST,MULTICAST,UP,LOWER_UP> mtu 1500 qdisc pfifo_fast state UP
group default qlen 1000
    link/ether 08:00:27:2a:00:2b brd ff:ff:ff:ff:ff:ff
    inet 10.0.2.15/24 brd 10.0.2.255 scope global noprefixroute dynamic enp0s3
       valid_lft 62516sec preferred_lft 62516sec
    inet6 fe80::ab6d:48ca:f676:aacf/64 scope link noprefixroute
       valid_lft forever preferred_lft forever
3: enp0s8: <NO-CARRIER,BROADCAST,MULTICAST,UP> mtu 1500 qdisc pfifo_fast state
DOWN group default qlen 1000
    link/ether 08:00:27:be:b6:ee brd ff:ff:ff:ff:ff:ff
4: enp0s9: <BROADCAST,MULTICAST,UP,LOWER_UP> mtu 1500 qdisc pfifo_fast state UP
group default qlen 1000
    link/ether 08:00:27:79:dc:91 brd ff:ff:ff:ff:ff:ff
    inet 192.168.1.82/24 brd 192.168.1.255 scope global noprefixroute dynamic
enp0s9
       valid_lft 585297sec preferred_lft 585297sec
    inet6 2605:a000:1401:21e::973/128 scope global noprefixroute dynamic
       valid_lft 585306sec preferred_lft 585306sec
    inet6 2605:a000:1401:21e:a95c:b673:538e:b1da/64 scope global noprefixroute
dynamic
       valid_lft 604778sec preferred_lft 604778sec
    inet6 fe80::712c:f509:edbe:18d1/64 scope link noprefixroute
       valid_lft forever preferred_lft forever
```

The ip command can also configure networking, routing, and tunnels. The ip command has built-in features to configure IPv6 networks as well.

Mitchell can also use the ifconfig command is to configure networks. Like the ip command, the ifconfig command can assign IP addresses, netmasks addresses, broadcast addresses, and more. Plus, ifconfig provides performance information, as shown here:

```
[root@cent71-5t buddy]# ifconfig enp0s3
enp0s3: flags=4163<UP,BROADCAST,RUNNING,MULTICAST>  mtu 1500
        inet 10.0.2.15  netmask 255.255.255.0  broadcast 10.0.2.255
        inet6 fe80::ab6d:48ca:f676:aacf  prefixlen 64  scopeid 0x20<link>
        ether 08:00:27:2a:00:2b  txqueuelen 1000  (Ethernet)
        RX packets 35  bytes 6843 (6.6 KiB)
        RX errors 0  dropped 0  overruns 0  frame 0
        TX packets 66  bytes 8459 (8.2 KiB)
        TX errors 0  dropped 0 overruns 0  carrier 0  collisions 0
```

To determine which driver to use with network cards, Mitchell uses the **lspci** command with the **-v** option. This provides more details about the network card, including model and IRQ setting, as shown here:

```
[root@cent71-5t buddy]# lspci -v | head -33 | tail -10
00:03.0 Ethernet controller: Intel Corporation 82540EM Gigabit Ethernet Cont
roller (rev 02)
        Subsystem: Intel Corporation PRO/1000 MT Desktop Adapter
        Flags: bus master, 66MHz, medium devsel, latency 64, IRQ 19
        Memory at f0000000 (32-bit, non-prefetchable) [size=128K]
        I/O ports at d010 [size=8]
        Capabilities: [dc] Power Management version 2
        Capabilities: [e4] PCI-X non-bridge device
        Kernel driver in use: e1000
        Kernel modules: e1000
```

The lspci command can also be used to discover high-performance networking cards (for example, those that are RDMA capable). RDMA (Remote Direct Memory Access) over Ethernet allows direct access to the memory of one computer from the memory of another without using either systems' operating system, thus resulting in low latency and high throughput. If any of the network cards were RDMA capable, lspci would display the term "InfiniBand." Since this does not appear in the preceding result, the FOLDERMS computers do not support RDMA.

NOTE Performance can also be improved by using UNIX sockets. UNIX sockets are for interprocess communications to allow the exchange of processes on the same system, where IP sockets allow process communications over a network.

Troubleshooting a Local Area Network

Users complain to Mitchell of long delays when accessing computers on the network. Their systems are named after vegetables to remind staff that personal health is of the utmost importance. When users "ssh" or "ping" systems named tomato, cucumber, zucchini, and so on, it takes at least five minutes to get a response.

Mitchell first suspects the timeouts are due to network saturation. He runs iftop to monitor traffic bandwidth. The iftop command is similar to top in that it measures activity and automatically updates every two seconds. The results are shown in Figure 19-7 and indicate normal network activity.

EXAM TIP For command updates similar to top and iftop, try using the **watch** command. For example, try running **watch uptime** to visualize new uptime and load outputs every two seconds.

Another powerful network throughput measuring tool in Mitchell's tool case is iperf. The **iperf** command evaluates network throughput over a specific path, so a server and client are required for the command to function successfully. In the following example, Mitchell evaluates the bandwidth, loss, saturation, and latency between the client and the DNS server. On the DNS server, he starts the iperf server program by running **iperf -s**, as shown in Figure 19-8.

```
student1@cent71-5t:/home/student1                    student1@cent71-5t:~

              1.91Mb            3.81Mb            5.72Mb             7.63Mb     9.54Mb

cent71-5t                  => 192.168.1.3                       956Kb   960Kb   752Kb
                           <=                                   416b    416b    354b
cent71-5t                  => RAC2V1S                           240b    240b    96.9Kb
                           <=                                   160b    160b    60.0Kb
224.0.0.251                => 192.168.1.3                         0b      0b      0b
                           <=                                     0b    390b    171b
192.168.1.255              => 192.168.1.3                         0b      0b      0b
                           <=                                     0b    374b    220b
192.168.1.255              => Freezom                             0b      0b      0b
                           <=                                     0b    312b    142b
cent71-5t                  => Google-Home-Mini                    0b      0b    70.0Kb
                           <=                                     0b      0b    46.7Kb
cent71-5t                  => Chromecast                          0b      0b    36.7Kb
                           <=                                     0b      0b    24.5Kb
224.0.0.251                => Google-Home-Mini                    0b      0b      0b
                           <=                                     0b      0b    1.28Kb
224.0.0.251                => Chromecast                          0b      0b      0b
                           <=                                     0b      0b    1.20Kb

TX:            cum:   5.22MB   peak:   1.18Mb  rates:   956Kb   960Kb   956Kb
RX:                   910KB            488Kb            576b    1.61Kb  137Kb
TOTAL:                6.11MB           1.66Mb           956Kb   961Kb   1.07Mb
```

Figure 19-7 Output of iftop command

On the client machine, he runs iperf in client mode and lets it run for a few seconds to measure network activity, as shown in Figure 19-9. Again, Mitchell sees that network performance is acceptable.

Mitchell remembers a similar case while working as a summer intern with the U.S. government. The system is checking DNS tables first to resolve domain names, and after a five-minute timeout, it performs local domain name resolution. Mitchell therefore modifies the hosts line in */etc/nsswitch.conf*, changing it from

```
hosts:      dns   files
```

to

```
hosts:      files dns
```

```
student1@debian: ~
File  Edit  View  Search  Terminal  Help
root@debian:/home/student1# iperf -s
------------------------------------------------------------
Server listening on TCP port 5001
TCP window size: 85.3 KByte (default)
------------------------------------------------------------
```

Figure 19-8 Starting the iperf server

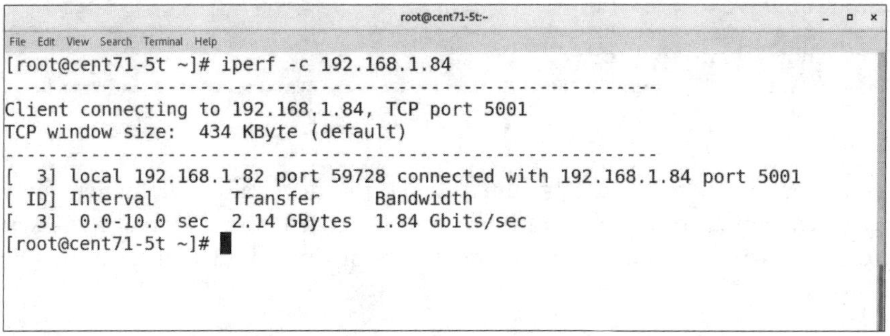

```
root@cent71-5t:~
File Edit View Search Terminal Help
[root@cent71-5t ~]# iperf -c 192.168.1.84
------------------------------------------------------------
Client connecting to 192.168.1.84, TCP port 5001
TCP window size:  434 KByte (default)
------------------------------------------------------------
[  3] local 192.168.1.82 port 59728 connected with 192.168.1.84 port 5001
[ ID] Interval       Transfer     Bandwidth
[  3]  0.0-10.0 sec  2.14 GBytes  1.84 Gbits/sec
[root@cent71-5t ~]#
```

Figure 19-9 Running the iperf client

so that the */etc/hosts* file is checked before */etc/resolv.conf* when resolving hostnames. Now users access their "salad ingredients" (that is, hosts named after vegetables) much faster. Mitchell uses tools like host, nslookup, and dig to verify name server status.

Troubleshooting Gateways with sysctl

As mentioned in Chapter 15, IP forwarding must be enabled for a Linux system to act as a network router or gateway. To verify whether IP forwarding has been enabled, run **cat /proc/sys/net/ipv{4,6}/ip_forward**, as shown here:

```
[root@cent71-5t buddy]# cat /proc/sys/net/ipv4/ip_forward
0
```

Alternatively, you can use the sysctl command (not to be confused with the systemctl command, which manages runlevels), as follows:

```
[root@cent71-5t buddy]# sysctl -a | grep ipv4.ip_forward
net.ipv4.ip_forward = 0
```

The sysctl command is used to configure kernel parameters that tune the computer. Tuning can help improve computer performance by up to 50 percent, depending on the application. To view all the kernel tunables, use the -a option, as shown here:

```
[root@cent71-5t buddy]# sysctl -a
abi.vsyscall32 = 1
crypto.fips_enabled = 0
debug.exception-trace = 1
debug.kprobes-optimization = 1
debug.panic_on_rcu_stall = 0
dev.cdrom.autoclose = 1
dev.cdrom.autoeject = 0
dev.cdrom.check_media = 0
dev.cdrom.debug = 0
dev.cdrom.info = CD-ROM information, Id: cdrom.c 3.20 2003/12/17
dev.cdrom.info =
dev.cdrom.info = drive name:           sr0
dev.cdrom.info = drive speed:          32
dev.cdrom.info = drive # of slots:     1
```

```
dev.cdrom.info = Can close tray:        1
dev.cdrom.info = Can open tray:         1
dev.cdrom.info = Can lock tray:         1
dev.cdrom.info = Can change speed:      1
dev.cdrom.info = Can select disk:       0
<...etc...>
```

Once the system is satisfactorily tuned, make the new values permanent by modifying */etc/sysctl.conf* or the */etc/sysctl.d/* directory. Mitchell wants to make the system a routable device as well as make it permanent at boot time. To accomplish, this he does the following:

```
[root@cent71-5t buddy]# cat >> /etc/sysctl.d/99-sysctl.conf
net.ipv4.ip_forward = 1
^D
[root@cent71-5t buddy]# reboot
```

Now the system can be used as a gateway device to other networks. (Updating */etc/sysctl.conf* with the cat command, as previously mentioned, would have worked as well.)

After reboot, the system reports that IP forwarding is automatically enabled at boot time, as shown next:

```
[root@cent71-5t buddy]# sysctl -a | grep ipv4.ip_forward
net.ipv4.ip_forward = 1
[root@cent71-5t buddy]# cat /proc/sys/net/ipv4/ip_forward
1
```

Validate User Connections

Gary reports to Mitchell that several users are locked out of their login accounts. This just started happening when the FOLDERMS systems merged with the EZPAGS network. Mitchell starts by testing whether users can log in locally without Kerberos or LDAP.

He scans the */etc/passwd* file and finds the usernames are there as they should be, and that there is an "x" in the second column so that the system knows to find passwords in */etc/shadow*. He also verifies that users are listed in */etc/shadow*. Next, he can attempts logging in as various users using su - <username> and is successful. Since he is able to access user accounts locally, there must be an issue with remote or external directory services.

He glances at the */etc/nsswitch.conf* file on the newer systems and notices that the passwd, shadow, and group fields only search files (*/etc/passwd, /etc/shadow,* and */etc/group*), as shown:

```
passwd:       files
shadow:       files
group:        files
```

Part of what will make the merger successful is that both companies, FOLDERMS and EZPAGS, use LDAP directory services for remote authentication. They also have identical password policies in that passwords should be at least eight characters long, with two uppercase characters and one special character that is defined in PAM. If this policy is violated, the account cannot be used.

So that users can access the LDAP server to be authenticated, Mitchell updates */etc/nsswitch.conf*, as follows:

```
passwd:         files   ldap
shadow:         files   ldap
group:          files   ldap
```

Users who are following the policy are now able to log in successfully.

NOTE To join the Linux system to a Windows Active Directory domain, use the winbind directive within */etc/nsswitch.conf*.

Validate the Firewall

Davy and Tomika of FOLDERMS notify Mitchell that he may have forgotten about the SSH issue users are having, but Davy has not forgotten about the issue and needs Mitchell to give this some attention, as their policy requires response times within 24 hours.

Mitchell's memory is not as good as Davy's, but he gets on the case because he wants a successful merger. He attempts using SSH as a FOLDERMS user and reproduces the issue. He cannot log in via SSH.

EXAM TIP Poor firewall settings cause most network-related issues, especially if a service is not available.

He next moves to the SSH server and verifies SSH is running with systemctl, as shown here:

```
[root@cent71-5t ~]# systemctl status sshd
• sshd.service - OpenSSH server daemon
  Loaded: loaded (/usr/lib/systemd/system/sshd.service; enabled; vendor preset:
enabled)
  Active: active (running) since Tue 2023-05-07 23:06:25 EDT; 10 day 15h ago
    Docs: man:sshd(8)
          man:sshd_config(5)
Main PID: 4084 (sshd)
   Tasks: 1
  CGroup: /system.slice/sshd.service
          └─4084 /usr/sbin/sshd -D
May 07 23:06:25 cent71-5t systemd[1]: Starting OpenSSH server daemon...
May 07 23:06:25 cent71-5t sshd[4084]: Server listening on 0.0.0.0 port 22.
May 07 23:06:25 cent71-5t sshd[4084]: Server listening on :: port 22.
May 07 23:06:25 cent71-5t systemd[1]: Started OpenSSH server daemon.
```

The results show that the **sshd** service is enabled.

Next, he investigates the firewall. He runs **firewall-cmd** to investigate whether port 22 is open, as shown here:

```
[root@cent71-5t ~]# firewall-cmd --list-services
mdns samba-client dhcpv6-client
```

The results show that port 22 using the TCP protocol for the SSH service is blocked. Apparently, the ACL allows features like Samba and DHCP, but not SSH. The ACL is too restrictive. Mitchell changes the rule using **firewall-cmd** to unblock port 22 and unblock the TCP protocol for this service, as follows:

```
[root@cent71-5t ~]# firewall-cmd --add-service ssh
success
[root@cent71-5t ~]# firewall-cmd --list-services
mdns samba-client dhcpv6-client ssh
[root@cent71-5t ~]# firewall-cmd --add-service ssh --permanent
success
[root@cent71-5t ~]# firewall-cmd --reload
success
[root@cent71-5t ~]# firewall-cmd --list-services
ssh mdns samba-client dhcpv6-client
```

Running **firewall-cmd --add-service ssh** opens port 22/TCP so that users can now access SSH. So that the port is open on following reboots, he runs the **firewall-cmd --add-service ssh --permanent** command string. SSH shows as one of the open ports when he runs the firewall-cmd --list-services command with options.

Finally, he tests whether users can log in to the system via SSH, and he finds that users from FOLDERMS and EZPAGS can now access the SSH server. Case closed—and even Tomika is impressed.

You practice working with network troubleshooting and performance commands in the Exercise 19-2.

Exercise 19-2: Troubleshooting Networking Issues

In this exercise, you practice using network and firewall commands to manage and troubleshoot a network connection. This exercise assumes two systems are connected, as follows:

- **sysA** IP address 10.1.1.2/24 (SSH server)
- **sysB** IP address 10.1.1.3/24

VIDEO Please watch the Exercise 19-2 video for a demonstration on how to perform this task.

Complete the following steps:

1. From sysB, test the network connection to sysA with the ping command:
   ```
   $ ping 10.1.1.3
   ```
2. From sysA, switch to the root user account by entering **su -** followed by **password** for the password.
3. Disable network activity at sysA:
   ```
   sysA # systemctl stop network
   ```

4. From sysB, test the network connection to sysA with the ping command:
```
sysB $ ping 10.1.1.3
```
5. Re-enable network activity at sysA:
```
sysA # systemctl start network
```
6. Verify the SSH server is running on sysA:
```
sysA # systemctl status sshd
```
If it is not running, start the SSH server with systemctl:
```
sysA # systemctl start sshd
```
7. Even though the SSH server is running, block access to the service by typing a **firewall-cmd** at sysA:
```
sysA # firewall-cmd --remove-service ssh
```
8. From sysB, attempt to log in via SSH. This should fail because the SSH service is blocked by the firewall.
```
sysB $ ssh student1@10.1.1.2
```
9. Re-enable access to the service by typing another **firewall-cmd** at sysA:
```
sysA # firewall-cmd -reload
```
10. From sysB, attempt to log in via SSH. This should succeed because the firewall port is now opened.
```
sysB $ ssh student1@10.1.1.2
```

Chapter Review

This chapter focused on troubleshooting, diagnostics, and performance tuning of hardware and networks. There are several software tools available to test CPU performance, RAM usage, and disk drive efficiency. Many of the tools read hardware states from the */proc* and */sys* pseudo-directories. Administrators can learn details of CPU, RAM, IRQ settings, and more, by reviewing files in */proc*.

With respect to RAM shortages, administrators can increase swap space to prevent the Out of Memory Killer (OOM Killer) from killing programs. If a swap partition is not available, a swap file can quickly be created and added as swap space.

Hard drives are tunable through a setting called scheduler. The possible disk drive scheduler settings are noop, deadline, and cfq. Each organization needs to evaluate which setting is best for its environment. Once the organization determines which is best for its applications, it can make the setting permanent using the tuned utility.

Administrators use the systemctl command to enable and disable services on a Linux server, such as SSH, FTP, Telnet, and shared printers.

Several familiar tools are available for troubleshooting networks, but most of them are not IPv6 friendly. However, the relatively new ip command replaces many networking commands that are normally used, and it handles IPv6 setup and troubleshooting as well.

Unfortunately, too often a service is running and available but users are unable to access it. Most of the time this is due to the firewall blocking the service. The fix is straightforward, of course (open the port for the service), but troubleshooting these types of issues can take hours to diagnose.

Review the following key points for exam preparation:

- The */proc/cpuinfo* file provides details of the CPU installed.
- The uptime command shows how long the system has been running and load averages.
- Run **watch uptime** to monitor uptime changes every two seconds.
- The w command shows who is logged in to the system and what they are doing.
- Running sar allows administrators to see performance info on CPU, disk, RAM, and so on. The */proc/meminfo* file provides details of the RAM installed.
- Use the dd command to create a swap file.
- Run mkswap to configure the new file as swap space.
- Enable the new swap space with the swapon command.
- Swap space can be disabled using swapoff.
- To access the second virtual console, run CTRL-ALT-F2.
- Where root users are allowed to log in is found in the */etc/securetty* file.
- Running **df -i** will display the number of inodes available on a filesystem.
- Use the **lsof -i** command to list listening network ports.
- Use the **lspci -v** command to verify graphic card installs.
- Use **ip addr show** to display network card settings.
- The **iftop** command measures network activity, updated every two seconds.
- Use **sysctl** to change kernel settings, such as */proc/sys/net/ipv4/ip_forward.*
- Modify */etc/sysctl.conf* so that ip_forward is enabled at boot time.
- Name server settings can be added within */etc/nsswitch.conf,* such as LDAP, Active Directory, and so on.

Questions

1. Which option to the lshw command will provide a hardware installation summary with device trees showing hardware paths?

   A. -X

   B. -summary

   C. -short

   D. -s

2. Which command lists the system's BIOS while in multi-user mode?
   A. dmidecode
   B. biosview
   C. bview
   D. lsbios
3. Commands like w and uptime only provide output once. Which command can be run with uptime or w to have the output automatically update every two seconds?
   A. look
   B. watch
   C. rerun
   D. repeat
4. Which system activity reporter function will list CPU, RAM, I/O, disk activity, and more, with five outputs displaying the result every two seconds?
   A. sar -A -s 2
   B. sar -A -s 2 -i 5
   C. sar -A 5 2
   D. sar -A 2 5
5. Which commands lists memory performance information? (Choose two.)
   A. vmstat
   B. memviewer
   C. perfmonitor
   D. lsram
   E. sar
6. Which command displays how much memory and swap are available on a Linux system?
   A. free
   B. swapon -s
   C. dd
   D. lsram
7. Which kernel variable can be changed to either noop, deadline, or cfq to change storage scheduling on drive */dev/sda*?
   A. /proc/block/sda/queue/scheduler
   B. /sysv/block/sda/queue/scheduler
   C. /sys/block/sda/queue/scheduler
   D. /sys/block/sda1/queue/scheduler

8. Which command will display disk I/O latency?
   A. pingio
   B. diskio
   C. lsdisk
   D. ioping
9. Which commands display disk I/O rates? (Choose two.)
   A. lssda
   B. sar
   C. iostat
   D. swapon
10. Which command will block access to the SSH server?
   A. firewall-cmd --del-service ssh
   B. firewall-cmd --remove-service ssh
   C. firewall-cmd --block-service ssh
   D. firewall-cmd --disable-service ssh

Answers

1. **C.** The command **lshw -short** outputs hardware information showing hardware paths with a device tree.
2. **A.** The dmidecode command lists the system's BIOS while in multi-user mode.
3. **B.** The watch command will execute a program periodically, showing output in full screen.
4. **D.** The sar command collects, reports, and saves system activity information, and the syntax is **sar <interval count>**.
5. **A, E.** Both sar and vmstat monitor memory performance.
6. **A.** The free command displays how much memory and swap space is available on a computer.
7. **A.** Modify the /proc/block/sda/queue/scheduler kernel variable to either noop, deadline, or cfq to change storage scheduling on drive */dev/sda*.
8. **D.** The ioping command will display disk drive latency performance output.
9. **B, C.** The sar and iostat commands are two commands that display disk I/O rates.
10. **B.** The command to close port 22 for SSH is **firewall-cmd --remove-service ssh** or **firewall-cmd --remove-service=ssh**.

CHAPTER 20

Installing and Configuring Linux

In this chapter, you will learn about

- Designing a Linux installation
- Installing Linux
- Configuring the X environment
- Configuring locale settings
- Configuring time zone settings
- Configuring printing with CUPS
- Configuring e-mail
- Configuring SQL databases

The new Linux+ exam *no longer requires* candidates to know how to perform a clean installation of a Linux distribution, or how to configure e-mail, printing, and databases. However, in order for you to practice the Linux features discussed in this chapter, we thought it important to explain how to set up and configure a Linux system. The exam covers the most common Linux distributions, but this chapter only instructs on how to install CentOS. CentOS was chosen because it similar to the version of Linux installed by most U.S. employers—Red Hat. Installing Debian and OpenSUSE is similar to installing CentOS as well.

Linux has become dramatically easier to install in the last few years. The distributions available in the mid-1990s were challenging to install, and hardware support was limited. Fortunately, modern Linux distributions employ an easy-to-use graphical installation wizard to facilitate the installation process. To install Linux properly, spend some time planning the installation *before* actually starting the installation process.

NOTE Although there are hundreds of Linux distributions, as listed at http://distrowatch.org, this discussion focuses on Linux distributions tested on the Linux+ exam.

Designing a Linux Installation

Linux installs on various types of hardware, and administrators need to consult the Linux vendors' system requirements to ensure their computers meet the required specifications. To validate hardware compatibility, visit http://www.tldp.org/HOWTO/Hardware-HOWTO/.

Linux Installers and the Linux+ Exam

When organizations deploy systems for their production environments, proper planning is critical. Mistakes will lead to system outages, and outages cost organizations time and money.

For example, suppose a major networking software vendor wanted to implement a new application that would make its employees' jobs easier. When reviewing the system requirements, it was found that the application required a specific version of the Windows server software—one not currently owned. Implementing the application would first require a new server be installed. Rather than develop a plan for the new server deployment, the design and installation team moved forward without a plan. They ordered a new server and set up the software without communicating with the employees.

In the end, all the employees' critical data was saved on this server. Thousands of human hours representing millions of dollars were never backed up. Good communications and change management would ensure this does not happen.

In this part of the chapter, we discuss how to go about planning a Linux installation. The following topics are addressed:

- Conducting a needs assessment
- Selecting a distribution
- Checking hardware compatibility
- Verifying system requirements
- Planning the filesystem
- Selecting software packages
- Identifying user accounts
- Gathering network information
- Selecting an installation source

The first step in any deployment plan is to conduct a needs assessment. Let's discuss this topic next.

Conducting a Needs Assessment

Conducting a needs assessment is one of the most important aspects of creating a Linux deployment plan. This is the process of determining *why* the Linux deployment is being undertaken, *what* outcomes are expected, and *when* it is expected to be complete.

Completing a needs assessment requires one to remove their technician hat and put on the project manager hat.

In this role, the project manager needs to meet with different individuals and understand their needs. This needs assessment should contain the following information (at a minimum):

- **What are the goals of the project?** What problem will this installation fix? What will be the final result of the implementation?
- **Who are the stakeholders in this project?** As a part of your needs assessment, identify all individuals who will be impacted by the project.
- **When is the system needed?** A key question to ask is, when should the project be completed? Begin with the "end in mind."

Once you have answers to these questions, do a reality check against the schedule. Remember that what looks good on paper might not work in real life.

With your project scope defined, move on to the next component in the project plan—the Linux distribution.

Selecting a Distribution

As discussed, Linux is available in a wide variety of flavors called *distributions* or *distros.* One of the key parts of the deployment plan is specifying which distribution to use. The best to use depends on your preferences. Most of the U.S. federal government prefers Red Hat or SUSE because they offer corporate support plans, and both provide Mandatory Access Control (MAC). Ethical hackers prefer Kali with the Tor browser because they provide the best auditing tools. Here are some guidelines to use to select the right distribution.

Determine if the system will function as a workstation or server. Most operating systems are designed to function as one or the other, but Linux can function as either a workstation or a server. This is unique among operating systems. Red Hat provides Red Hat Enterprise Linux distribution, designed to provide network services for medium to very large organizations with heavy server utilization. Red Hat also provides distributions designed specifically for use as desktops.

CentOS and Fedora are both open source versions of Red Hat. Fedora is designed for the casual user. CentOS is an enterprise-class operating system and is easily converted to Red Hat Enterprise by purchasing Red Hat's support plan. It is not recommended to use Fedora in an organization's production environment.

Likewise, Micro Focus International sells multiple versions of SUSE Linux and provides OpenSUSE for the open source community. Its distributions span offerings for the cloud and even embedded systems.

There are also purpose-specific distributions to create Linux-based appliances using standard PC hardware. For example, you can create a powerful network firewall using distributions such as Untangle.

Before selecting a specific distribution, evaluate whether the corporate applications will run and are supported by the operating system. Also, verify the distribution runs on the selected system hardware.

Checking Hardware Compatibility

Today, most vendors offer a Linux version of the drivers for their hardware. In addition, most of the drivers for common PC hardware are now included with the various Linux distributions, especially virtual machines.

Though rarely done, it is still a very good idea to check the distribution's website and verify that the system hardware is listed on the distribution's hardware compatibility list (HCL). Even though hardware support for Linux has become much better in the last decade, there are still some devices that are not supported. A good example is integrated wireless network interfaces used in many notebook systems. Check the distribution's HCL to verify that the system's devices are supported.

HCLs are usually available in two locations. First, Linux distributions include a list of supported hardware in a text file on the installation DVD. However, because it is a static document, it has not been updated since the disc image was created. If a device in the computer was released at some point after the disc image was created, the driver may be outdated.

Instead, use the HCL maintained on the distribution websites. This version of the HCL contains the most current data on supported hardware. For example, if you're installing the openSUSE distribution, access its HCL at https://en.opensuse.org/Hardware. Once there, search for the particular system hardware and see if it is supported. In Figure 20-1, the openSUSE HCL for video boards is displayed.

If you're choosing a Red Hat distribution, check the HCL on Red Hat's website (https://access.redhat.com/ecosystem/search/#/category/Server) to verify the system hardware is supported.

NOTE Driver availability is one reason organizations prefer to use big-name, well-supported Linux distributions when deploying in a production environment. Linux system administrators must protect data and ensure systems run at maximum efficiency. In production environments, it is critical to use Linux-supported hardware.

In addition to checking the HCL, also check the distribution's system requirements.

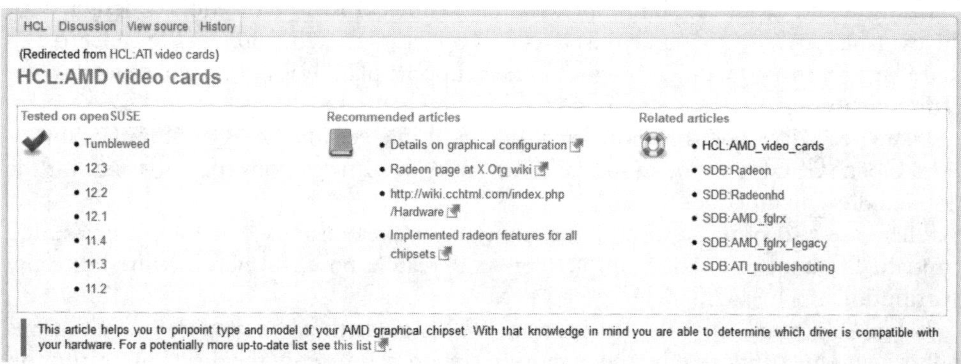

Figure 20-1 Using the openSUSE HCL

Verifying System Requirements

When formulating the deployment plan, be sure to specify the hardware needed by the distribution selected. A key aspect of the system requirements is the computer's CPU architecture. When downloading the Linux distribution, be sure to select the architecture that matches the system's CPU.

Today, there are many hardware options available to system administrators. There are still x86 and Alpha architectures, and the newer 64-bit x86 architecture. In addition, Intel produces the IA-64 architecture used by its Itanium CPUs. Each of these architectures requires a different version of Linux. In fact, many Linux distributions have even been ported to run on the Power PC (PPC) architecture from Apple. Other distributions are available for the iSeries, pSeries, and RS/6000 servers from IBM. There are now even versions of Linux that have been ported to run on the ARM architecture used by tablet devices.

Regardless of which distribution is chosen, make sure to download the correct version for the system's architecture. If you choose the wrong version, the Linux installers will generate an error and cancel the installation.

Planning the Filesystem

When planning a Linux implementation, include specifications for how the filesystem will be created and maintained on the system's hard disk drive.

With Linux, however, there are more choices. Administrators can customize how the disk will be partitioned and what filesystem will be used. In this part of the chapter, we will discuss the following:

- Choosing a filesystem
- Planning the partitions

Let's begin by discussing filesystems.

Choosing a Filesystem

The drive is made up of multiple aluminum platters, each with two read-write heads that are used to transfer data. When conducting disk I/O operations, the operating system needs to know where data is stored, how to access it, and where it is safe to write new information.

This is the job of the *filesystem,* which reliably stores data on the hard drive and organizes it in such a way that it is easily accessible. Choice of filesystems:

- ext3
- Reiser
- ext4
- btrfs
- xfs

NOTE Admins can also use many other filesystems with Linux, such as VFAT and NTFS filesystems. Avoid using ext2, however, because it is a non-journaling filesystem.

The best supported filesystems are reiser, ext4, btrfs, and xfs. These filesystems can handle larger file sizes of much greater than 2 terabytes, and filesystem partition sizes on the order of exabytes. Also, they manage system failures better because of journaling, being able to recover from system crashes in minutes instead of days with ext2.

Planning the Partitions

It is recommended to have at least two partitions (/ and swap), and it's best to define these during the initial installation of the system. Changing disk partitions after system installation is possible, but it is somewhat challenging and time consuming. Therefore, best practice is to plan the partition layout before starting the installation process.

By default, Linux distributions propose multiple partitions during the installation process (see Figure 20-2):

- **swap** The appropriate size for the swap partition is larger than the amount of installed RAM, because in the event of a system crash, the entire RAM image will fit the swap partition. The kernel dump can later be analyzed to determine why the system faulted.
- **/** The slash partition is mounted at the root directory (/) of the Linux filesystem.
- **/boot** Files important to booting reside here, such as the kernel and the initial RAM disk. Filesystem corruptions recover faster when this partition resides on its own.

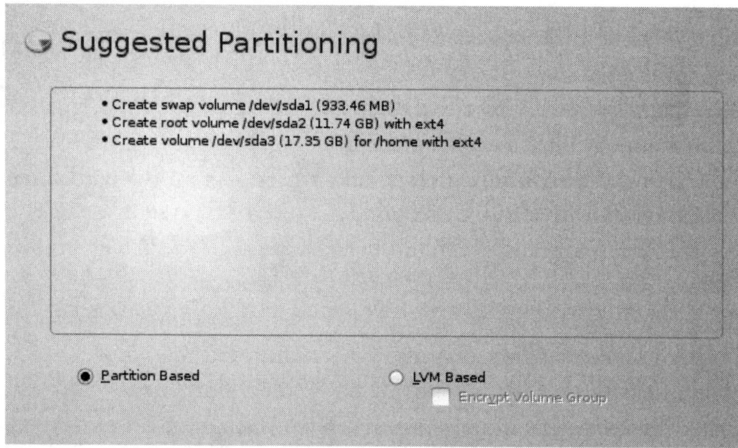

Figure 20-2 Default Linux partitioning

CAUTION The /boot partition must be created within the first 1,024 cylinders of the hard disk. A partition size of 250MB is plenty. To be safe, create this partition such that it begins with cylinder 0.

Using these recommended partitions will add stability to the system.

Selecting Software Packages

Linux includes a fairly extensive sampling of packages that administrators can choose to install with the operating system. Most distributions require multiple DVDs to store all the packages.

OpenSUSE offers many different packages, as shown in Figure 20-3.

Another feature of graphical Linux installers is they automatically manage *dependencies,* which are specific software packages that other software packages need in order to run. Most Linux packages installed will have many dependencies associated with them.

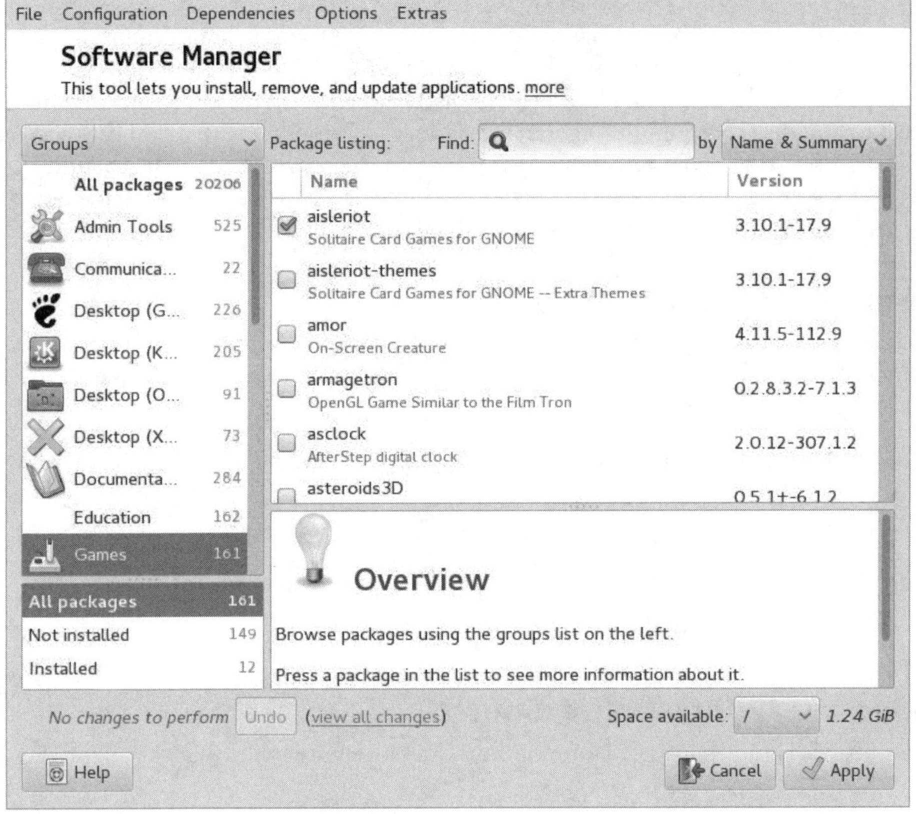

Figure 20-3 Installing software packages in openSUSE Linux

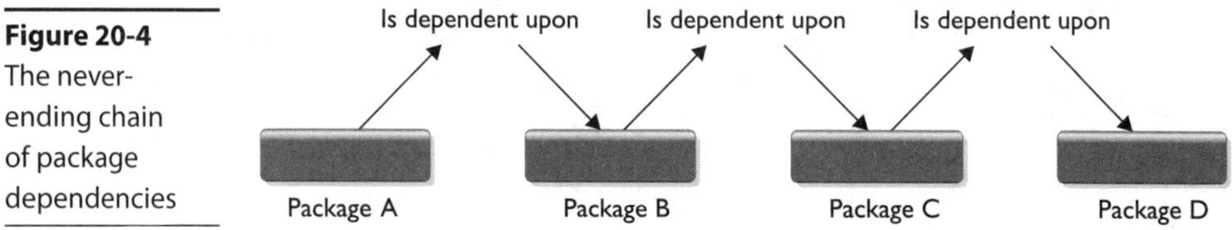

Figure 20-4 The never-ending chain of package dependencies

In the early days of Linux, administrators had to manually manage dependencies and include them in the installation. This was a tough job because of the layers of dependencies, as shown in Figure 20-4. The job was even tougher when dealing with "circular" dependencies, where package A depends on package B, but package B also depends on package A!

Today, the installers covered on the Linux+ exam automatically calculate package dependencies, include the necessary dependent packages in the installation, and manage circular dependencies.

Identifying User Accounts

When you're planning the installation, determine the user accounts needed on the system. The installation utilities used by Linux distributions provide the ability to create these accounts during the installation process. No matter what distribution you use, you need to create the root user account during the installation, along with one standard user account.

Part of the installation process requires passwords be provided for each account. Make sure to use strong passphrases with upper- and lowercase letters, special characters, and numbers. Also at this stage of the installation, select which users have sudo rights.

Gathering Network Information

You need to gather the information necessary to connect to the network before starting the installation and include it in the deployment plan. Here are some key items to consider:

- Will the system have its networking configuration dynamically assigned or will it need to be manually configured?
- What hostname will be assigned to the system?
- What is the name of the DNS domain the system will reside in?
- Will the system need a host firewall configured?

Selecting an Installation Source

Linux provides multiple installation options, including the following:

- Installing locally from an optical disc or thumb drive
- Installing remotely from a network server
- Completing a remote installation using Virtual Network Computing (VNC)

Installing Locally from an Optical Disc or Thumb Drive

One of the more common methods for installing Linux is locally from a set of installation discs. Using this method, you simply insert the appropriate disc into the system's optical drive and boot the system from the disc. Alternatively, you can upload the image to a thumb drive and install from there.

Simply download the disc image(s) from the vendor's website. For example, to install Fedora, navigate to http://getfedora.org and select the Download link. After you choose server or workstation, requests are forwarded to a mirror site for download.

Downloaded files have the extension .iso and are also known as *ISO images.* Once it is downloaded, burn the ISO image to a physical disc or thumb drive using Rufus, UNetbootin, or Universal USB Installer.

Installing Remotely from a Network Server

Another option for installing Linux is from a network server. This will work from installation sources using the SMB, NFS, HTTP, or FTP protocol. The key advantage of using a network is installing a large number of systems at once.

NOTE Not all Linux distributions support a network-based installation. To complete a network installation, copy the Linux installation files to a directory on the server or mount a DVD for remote access. Then select the protocol for network access.

Once the installation source server is set up, download a network boot installation image. For example, to complete a network installation of SUSE Linux, navigate to http://en.opensuse.org and select the Downloads link. In the page that is displayed, you can select a network boot image for download. Burn this image to disc and then boot the system from it. On the first installation screen, specify the installation source, as shown in Figure 20-5.

Completing a Remote Installation Using VNC

VNC stands for *Virtual Network Computing*, and it allows video output to be redirected from one system to another system. Using the VNC protocol, you can start the installation on a target system but then use a web browser or VNC client software on another system to view the installation screens.

On many distributions, such as openSUSE, you can enter **vnc=1** in the Boot Options field, as shown in Figure 20-6.

After you start the installation, prompts provide you with various network parameters needed to create a VNC connection. The installation system loads, and the IP address to access the system is displayed. The installation screens can be accessed remotely using either a web browser or VNC client software. For example, if the assigned IP address is 192.168.1.126 in the initial VNC configuration screen, a browser could access it by opening http://192.168.1.126:5801, as shown in Figure 20-7. Using this VNC connection, you can complete the installation process from the comfort of your home office.

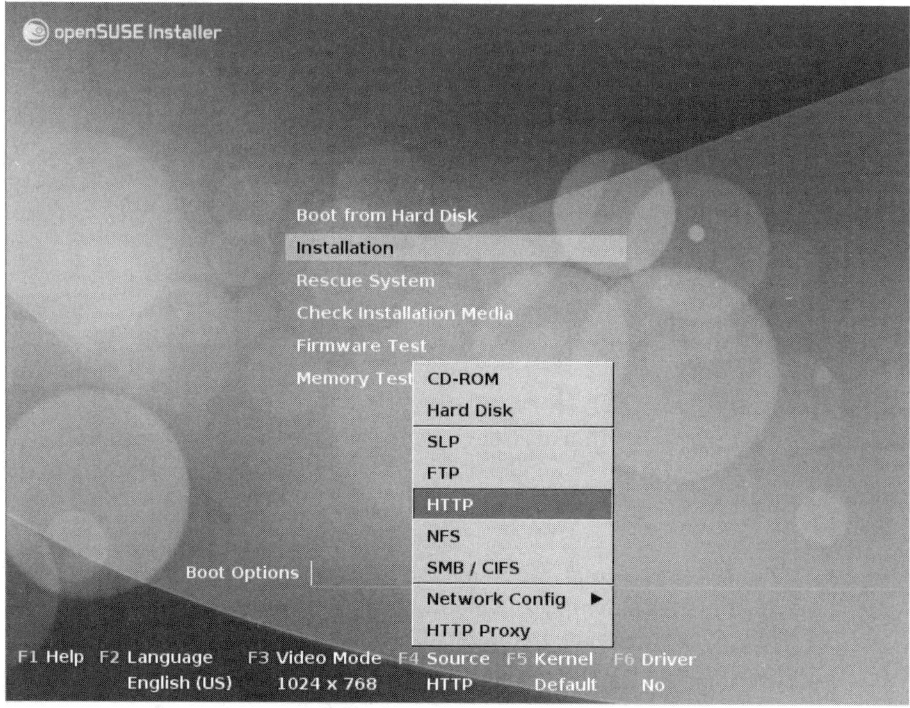

Figure 20-5 Selecting an installation source

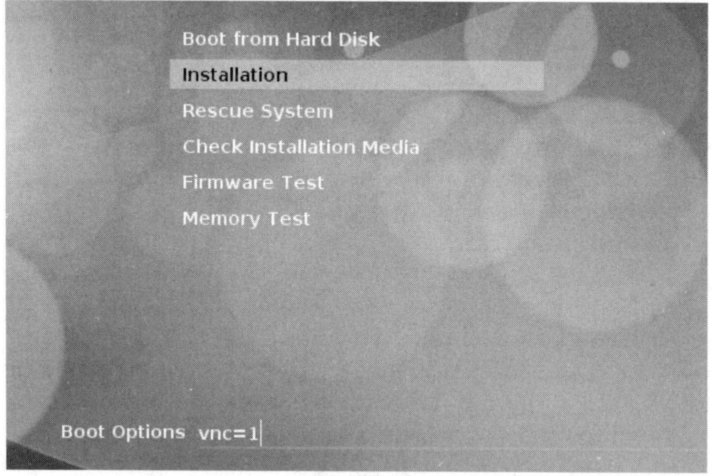

Figure 20-6 Configuring a VNC installation

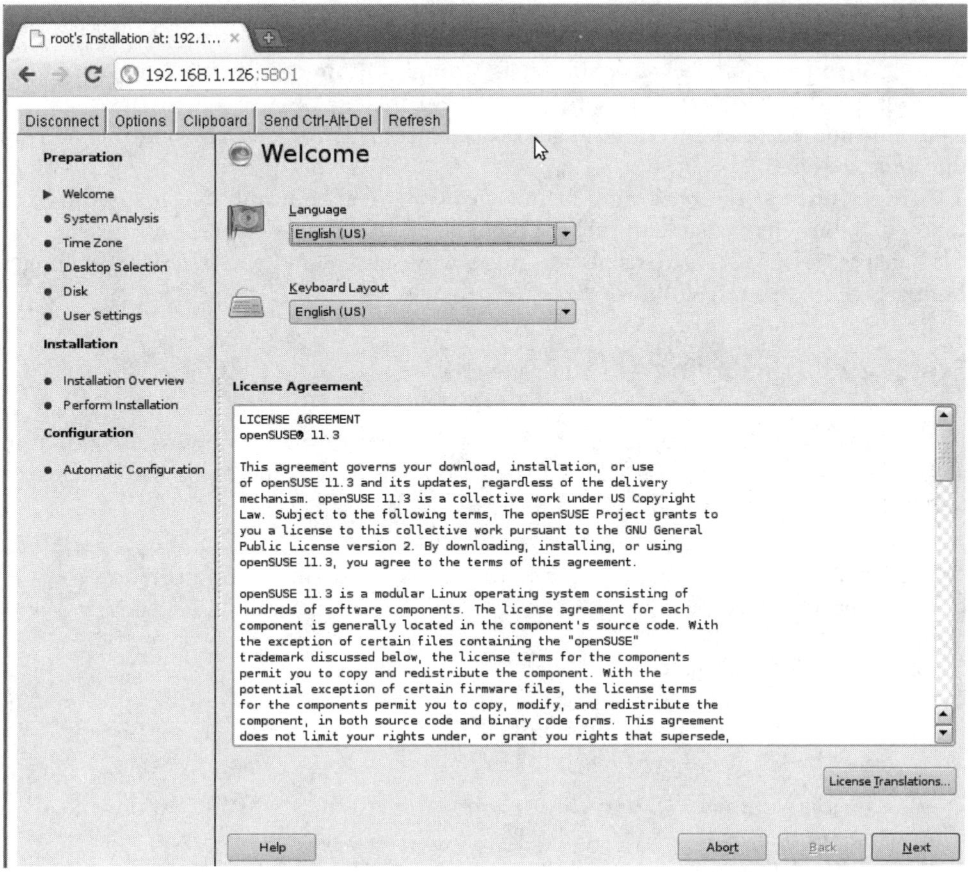

Figure 20-7 Completing the installation remotely in a browser

NOTE The VNC server can also be accessed using the vncviewer utility. Alternatively, on Windows systems you can use VNC Viewer from RealVNC.

For the deployment plan, you need to determine the installation method and prepare the prerequisite systems if necessary. Once you have done so, the Linux deployment plan is complete. Now the data necessary to complete the installation is all gathered in an organized, efficient, and measurable manner. File the deployment plan in a safe place once installation is complete. This information can be an invaluable help for other system administrators who may need to work on the systems at some point.

Installing Linux

When you're installing new systems, it is strongly recommended that you set them up an isolated lab environment and install them there. This will allow you to collect a baseline and ensure that everything is working properly before releasing the systems into production.

As mentioned at the beginning of this chapter, there are simply too many different Linux distributions available to include them all on the Linux+ exam or in this chapter. This chapter reviews how to install a CentOS workstation, and you practice installing a Linux system in Exercise 20-1.

Exercise 20-1: Installing a Linux System

In this exercise, we will first install the VirtualBox hypervisor and then CentOS Linux as a virtual machine. To follow along with the examples in the book, we will install CentOS 7 on top of VirtualBox 5.2.26.

VIDEO Please watch the Exercise 20-1 video for a demonstration on how to perform this task.

Complete the following steps:

1. On your computer, open a web browser and navigate to www.centos.org and select Get CentOS Now.
    a. Select Minimal ISO and choose a mirror that is near you for best download performance.
    b. After the download completes, continue to step 2.
2. On your computer, open a web browser, navigate to www.virtualbox.org, and select Downloads.
    a. Scroll down and select "VirtualBox older builds."
    b. Select VirtualBox 5.2 and then download VirtualBox 5.2.26 and initiate the installation.
    c. At the Welcome screen, click Next and then Next again at Custom Setup.
    d. Accept the defaults at the Options screen and click Yes for "Network Interfaces."
    e. Click Install at the "Ready to Install" screen, and then wait a few minutes for the software to install. If you're asked whether to install an Oracle device, choose Always Trust and then Install.
    f. Start VirtualBox by clicking Finish.

3. To install CentOS into the VirtualBox hypervisor, click New within VirtualBox.
   a. In the Name field, enter **CentOS-1**. The system should default to "Type: Linux" and "Version: Red Hat (64-bit)." If all checks out, click Next.

      If the version under "Type: Linux" shows as Red Hat (32-bit), you must select Cancel; then, shut down the host system, enter the *host* computer's BIOS, and enable virtualization.
   b. A memory size of 1024MB is fine. Click Next.
   c. Select "Create a virtual hard disk now" and click Create.
   d. VDI is fine for the "Hard disk file type" setting. Click Next.
   e. Choose "Dynamically allocated" and click Next.
   f. Set the hard drive size to 1.0TB and click Create.
   g. Click the down arrow next to Machine Tools and select Details. Then, click Display a few lines down and change Video Memory from 16MB to 128MB. Click OK.
4. Click the green Start button within VirtualBox.
   a. Under "Select start-up disk," click the yellow folder icon and under Downloads, select CentOS-7-x86_64-Minimal-1810 (or similar), and click Open.
   b. Click Start.
   c. After the CentOS 7 window appears, click the up arrow to select Install CentOS 7 and press ENTER; otherwise, the system will default to "Test this media."
   d. A couple of notification windows will appear at the top as the installation begins. Read the notices and then click the X to close them both.
   e. Press the right CTRL key and F to enter full-screen mode. Read the notification box, choose not to show the message again, and click Switch.
5. The system is ready to install CentOS at this point. Click the blue Continue button in the lower-right area of the screen.
   a. Read the notification, select "Do not show this message again," and click Capture.
   b. Click the Continue button again.
   c. Click Date & Time if you need to change your time zone. Then click the blue Done button in the upper-left corner.
   d. Click Network & Host Name. Enable Ethernet by switching the OFF button to ON in the upper-right area of the screen. In the upper left, select the Done button.
   e. Click Installation Destination and then click Done.
   f. Click Begin Installation.

6. The installation will start. In the meantime, let's set up the users.
   a. Click Root Password and define a password for yourself. Click Done when this is complete. (You may have to click Done twice.)
   b. Click Create User and create student1 with a password of student1.
   c. Click the option "Make this user administrator."
   d. Click Done twice.
7. Once the installation completes, click Reboot.
8. After the reboot process completes, login as student1.
   a. Type the following command to install a graphical desktop:
      ```
      sudo yum groupinstall "GNOME Desktop" "Graphical Administration Tools"
      ```
   b. After you enter the password for student1, the installation will begin.
   c. After a moment, enter **y** to install the software. Return in about 10 minutes.
   d. Enter **y** to install the keys. Return in about five minutes.
   e. Type the following command to convert the default runlevel to "graphics":
      ```
      sudo ln -sf /lib/systemd/system/runlevel5.target \
      /etc/systemd/system/default.target
      ```
      (A simpler method is to use **sudo systemctl set-default graphical.target**.)
   f. Type **sudo reboot** to reboot.
9. Log in as student1 to your new graphical desktop environment. Shortly, you will be asked to set up the language, keyboard, location, and so on. Select the appropriate options for you.

   Feel free to watch the "Getting Started" videos or close the window by clicking X in the upper-right corner.
10. Move the mouse to the upper right, hover over the speaker or battery icon, and click the "on/off" button in the applet. Select to install additional software updates and then select Power Off.

Congratulations! You now have a running CentOS Linux system. Installing other distributions, such as Debian, Ubuntu, Fedora, openSUSE, and others follows a very similar process. Feel free to install these as additional virtual machines—as many as your hardware supports.

Regarding the VirtualBox hypervisor, practice with it a bit to maneuver to and from the guest and host computers. The main tip is that pressing the right CTRL key will return you to the host machine. For the CentOS guest to take over, simply click into it with the mouse or enable "Mouse Pointer Integration" to switch systems by hovering the mouse pointer over them.

EXAM TIP Remote desktop tools available to Linux include VNC, XRDP, NX, and Spice.

Configuring the X Environment

Another great Linux topic to understand that is *not* part of the Linux+ exam requirements is understanding the X Window System. In practice, X configures itself pretty well as part of the installation process, so this section just explains how X Window works. In this part of the chapter, the following topics will be discussed:

- Configuring the X server
- Configuring the display manager
- Configuring accessibility

Configuring the X Server

Because the X server works directly with the video board and monitor, configuring it is critical. Use the correct settings; otherwise, the monitor could be damaged. Configuration can be done in two ways:

- By editing the X configuration file
- By using an X configuration utility

Let's look at the X configuration file first.

Editing the X Configuration File

Just like everything else in Linux, the X configuration is stored in a text file in the */etc* directory.

NOTE A good friend of mine coined an appropriate axiom: "Everything in Linux is a file." All of your system and service configurations are stored in files. You even access hardware devices through a file.

Configuration settings are saved in */etc/X11/xorg.conf*. Here is a portion of a sample *xorg.conf* file:

```
Section "InputDevice"
 Driver        "vmmouse"
 Identifier    "VMware Mouse"
 Option        "Buttons" "5"
 Option        "Device" "/dev/input/mice"
 Option        "Name" "ImPS/2 Generic Wheel Mouse"
 Option        "Protocol" "IMPS/2"
 Option        "Vendor" "Sysp"
 Option        "ZAxisMapping" "4 5"
 Option           "Emulate3Buttons"       "true"
EndSection

Section "Modes"
 Identifier    "Modes[0]"
 Modeline       "1024x768" 65.0 1024 1048 1184 1344 768 771 777 -hsync -vsync
 Modeline       "1024x768" 61.89 1024 1080 1184 1344 768 769 772
EndSection
```

NOTE Linux distributions that are based on systemd do not use the *xorg.conf* configuration file. Instead, the X11 configuration is stored in a series of configuration files located in */etc/X11/xorg.conf.d*.

Notice in this example that *xorg.conf* is broken into sections that begin with the **Section "<Name>"** directive and end with **EndSection**.

Let's look at commonly used sections in the *xorg.conf* file. First is the "Files" section. This section tells the X server where to find the files it needs to do its job, such as font files and input device files. Here is an abbreviated example of a "Files" section:

```
Section "Files"
 FontPath     "/usr/X11R6/lib/X11/fonts/misc:unscaled"
 FontPath     "/usr/X11R6/lib/X11/fonts/local"
 ...
 FontPath     "/usr/X11R6/lib/X11/fonts/xtest"
 InputDevices "/dev/input/mice"
EndSection
```

Next is the "InputDevice" section. This section configures the X server with the input devices it should use. You can use multiple "InputDevice" sections, such as one "InputDevice" section for the keyboard and another one for the mouse. Examples follow:

```
Section "InputDevice"
 Driver       "kbd"
 Identifier   "VMware Keyboard"
 Option       "Protocol" "Standard"
 Option       "XkbLayout" "us"
 Option       "XkbModel" "pc104"
 Option       "XkbRules" "xfree86"
EndSection

Section "InputDevice"
 Driver       "vmmouse"
 Identifier   "VMware Mouse"
 Option       "Buttons" "5"
 Option       "Device" "/dev/input/mice"
 Option       "Name" "ImPS/2 Generic Wheel Mouse"
 EndSection
```

The next section is the "Modes" section. The configuration file may have one or more of these sections. They define video modes the X server may use. Here is an example:

```
Section "Modes"
 Identifier   "Modes[0]"
 Modeline      "1024x768" 65.0 1024 1048 1184 1344 768 771 777 806 -hsync -vsync
 Modeline      "1024x768" 61.89 1024 1080 1184 1344 768 769 772 794
EndSection
```

The next section is the "Screen" section, which binds the video board to the monitor. Here is an example:

```
Section "Screen"
 Identifier    "Screen[0]"
   Device       "VMware SVGA"
   Monitor      "vmware"
   Subsection "Display"
       Depth        16
       Modes        "1024x768"
       ViewPort     0 0
   EndSubsection
   Subsection "Display"
       Depth        24
       Modes        "1024x768"
       ViewPort     0 0
   EndSubsection
EndSection
```

The last section we're going to look at is "ServerLayout." This section binds together one or more "Screen" sections and one or more "InputDevice" sections, as shown in the following example:

```
Section "ServerLayout"
 Identifier    "Layout[all]"
 Option        "Clone" "off"
 Option        "Xinerama" "off"
 Screen        "Screen[0]"
 InputDevice      "VMware Keyboard"        "CoreKeyboard"
 InputDevice "VMware Mouse"      "CorePointer"
EndSection
```

EXAM TIP Wayland is the newer, improved version of X11, currently the default for Fedora Linux

Using an X Configuration Utility

As with most Linux services, the X server configuration can be modified with a text editor such as vi. However, do not manually edit the file; instead, use the configuration utility under Settings | Displays, as shown in Figure 20-8. This applet allows you to configure screen resolution.

Enter **Xorg -configure** at the shell prompt to automatically detect all the hardware and create a configuration file named */root/xorg.conf.new*. Then test the configuration before committing it by entering **X -config /root/xorg.conf.new** at the shell prompt. If everything looks correct, rename the file to */etc/X11/xorg.conf* to start using the new configuration.

NOTE Use the xwininfo command to display information about open windows on your graphical desktop. The xdpyinfo command can be used to display the capabilities of a X server

Figure 20-8 The Displays applet

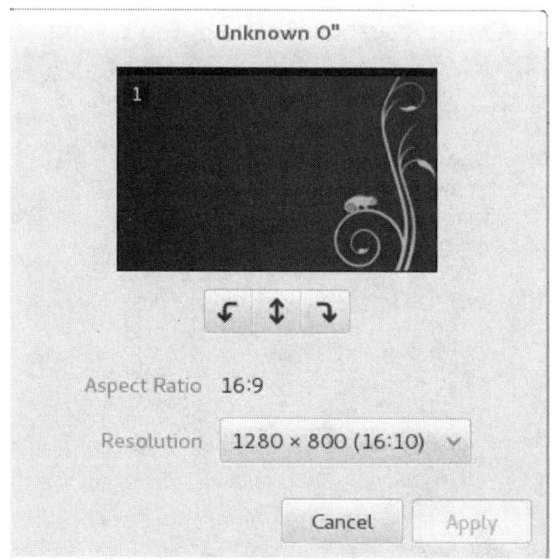

Configuring the Display Manager

This section covers the following topics:

- Enabling and disabling the display manager
- Configuring the display manager
- Configuring remote access to the display manager

Enabling and Disabling the Display Manager

On many Linux distributions, the display manager is managed by the xdm init script located in the */etc/init.d* directory. Other distributions may use the GNOME display manager (gdm) or the KDE display manager (kdm). To manually manage the display manager, enter **/etc/init.d/<init_script> stop** or **start** at the shell prompt.

EXAM TIP Graphical user interfaces (GUIs) available for Linux include Gnome, Unity, Cinnamon, MATE, and KDE.

Configuring the Display Manager

Configure the display manager by editing the appropriate configuration file:

- **xdm** /etc/X11/xdm/xdm-config
- **LightDM** The LightDM display manager is configured using several different files:
    - /usr/share/lightdm/lightdm.conf.d
    - /etc/lightdm/lightdm.conf.d
    - /etc/lightdm/lightdm.conf

- **kdm** The KDE display manager is actually based on xdm and usually uses the xdm configuration files. However, some distributions store your kdm settings in */etc/kde/kdm* or */etc/X11/ kdm* instead. In this situation, you will use the kdmrc file in either of these directories to make most configuration changes.
- **gdm** /etc/X11/gdm

Configuring Remote Access to the Display Manager

Many organizations use thin-client systems for their end users. This implementation allows organizations to provide a full graphical desktop to all its users using a larger number of inexpensive thin clients.

To configure remote access to listen on the network for inbound connection requests from the X server software on the thin clients, run the **xhost +** command on the X server.

The thin clients simply need to telnet to the X server, enter their login and password, and run any X client. The X client will display to the thin clients.

NOTE Secure console redirection can be enabled via X11 with **ssh -X**, and running **ssh -L** can further enhance security with port forwarding.

Configuring Accessibility

To support a diverse workforce, administrators must learn to configure accessibility settings for physically and visually impaired users using the following tools:

- Keyboard accessibility
- Mouse accessibility
- Screen readers

To access the Assistive Technologies Preferences application, search for and select Universal Access. The screen in Figure 20-9 is displayed.

Keyboard Accessibility

Universal Access allows you to configure the following:

- **StickyKeys** Allows users to lock keys such as CTRL and SHIFT to complete keyboard tasks with just one finger that would normally require two or more fingers.
- **SlowKeys** This helps the user avoid sending accidental keystrokes.
- **BounceKeys and DelayKeys** Inserts a slight delay between keystrokes to prevent the keyboard from sending unintentional keystrokes.

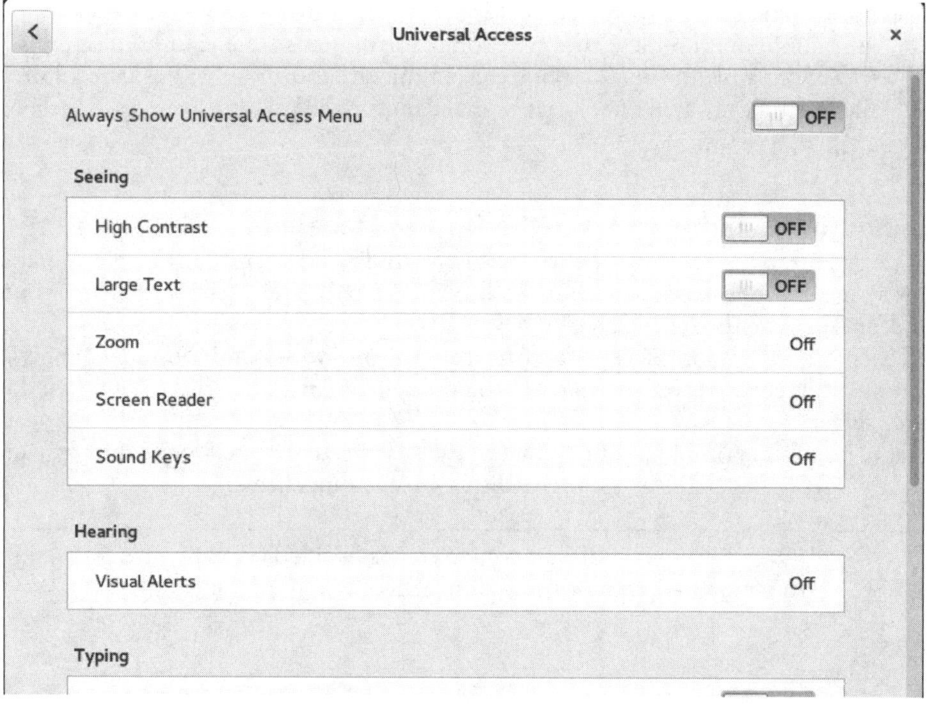

Figure 20-9 Enabling Assistive Technologies

For physically impaired users who are not able to use a traditional keyboard, Linux provides the option of using an onscreen keyboard, which allows users to use a mouse to select keys on a virtual keyboard. Commonly used onscreen keyboard applications include GOK (GNOME Onscreen Keyboard) and GTkeyboard.

Mouse Accessibility

In addition to keyboard accessibility, Assistive Technologies also provides mouse accessibility options for physically impaired users. For example, one can configure mouse options under Pointing and Clicking in the Universal Access panel. One such option is "Simulated Secondary Click," which sends a double-click after holding primary button down for a few seconds.

Screen Readers

One option available to visually impaired users is a screen reader, which "reads" the text displayed on the screen audibly for the user. The Orca application is probably the most commonly used screen reader. The other major screen reader is emacspeak.

Other accessibility utilities include screen magnifiers, braille devices, and high-contrast desktop themes.

Configuring Locale Settings

Administrators typically configure a system's *locale* during the installation process. They can also specify an encoding in the locale. For example, use en_US.UTF-8 to configure a default locale of U.S. English using UTF-8 character encoding (also known as *Unicode* encoding).

Not all of the LC_ variables have the same level of precedence. Linux uses the following rules:

- If the LC_ALL variable is defined, its value is used and the values assigned to all other LC_ variables are not checked.
- If LC_ALL is undefined, the specific LC_ variable in question is checked. If the specific LC_ variable has a value, it is used.
- If the LC_ variable in question has a null value, the LANG environment variable is used.

To define all of the LC_ variables to use the same value, set the LC_ALL variable.

NOTE Most distributions set the value of LC_CTYPE to define the default encoding and the value of LANG to provide a default value to all your other LC_ variables.

To view the current locale settings, enter the **/usr/bin/localectl** or **/usr/bin/locale** command at the shell prompt. Here is an example:

```
openSUSE:~ # locale
LANG=POSIX
LC_CTYPE=en_US.UTF-8
LC_NUMERIC="POSIX"
LC_TELEPHONE="POSIX"
LC_MEASUREMENT="POSIX"
LC_IDENTIFICATION="POSIX"
LC_ALL=
```

In this example, only the LANG and LC_CTYPE variables are actually defined. The other LC_ variables are automatically populated with the value assigned to LANG.

Use the -a option with locale to generate a list of all available locales. Use the -m option with the locale command to view a list of available encodings. An example follows:

```
openSUSE:~ # locale -a
C
POSIX
aa_DJ
aa_DJ.utf8
aa_ER
aa_ER.utf8
....
ws1:~ # locale -m
ANSI_X3.110-1983
ANSI_X3.4-1968
ARMSCII-8
....
```

Be aware that changing encodings may result in issues viewing other files created using a different encoding. To convert from using one encoding to a new one, use the iconv command at the shell prompt. The syntax is as follows:

```
iconv -f <source_encoding> -t <destination_encoding> -o <output_filename> \
<input_filename>
```

NOTE Commonly used text encodings include iso8859 (also called Latin-9 encoding), which is designed for Western European languages; ASCII, which uses an English-based character-encoding scheme; and Unicode, which is designed to handle character sets from languages around the world.

Configuring Time Zone Settings

During the initial installation of your Linux system, you are prompted to specify the time zone the system is located in. To view the current time zone, enter **timedatectl** or **date** at the shell prompt, like so:

```
openSUSE:~ # date
Wed Feb  9 11:40:05 MST 2021
openSUSE:~ #
```

To change time zones on a Debian system, change the value of the */etc/timezone* file. For other systems, modify the value of the TZ environment variable and then export it. This is useful in situations where you do not have the root password, or if you want to use a different time zone without changing the time zone used by other users. The syntax is **export TZ=<time_zone>**. A list of available time zones can be found in the */usr/share/zoneinfo/* directory, as shown here:

```
openSUSE:~ # ls /usr/share/zoneinfo/
Africa       Canada   Factory   Iceland     MST7MDT  Portugal   Zulu
Antarctica   Cuba     GB-Eire   Iran        Mideast  Singapore  posix
Asia         EST      GMT+0     Jamaica     NZ-CHAT  UCT        right
Australia    Egypt    GMT0      Kwajalein   PRC      UTC
CET          Etc      HST       MET         Pacific  W-SU
ws1:~ #
```

This change is not persistent. Upon reboot, the system returns to the default time zone. To make the time zone persistent, add the following to the *~<username>/.profile* file:

```
export TZ='America/Denver'
```

You can also change time zones by linking the */etc/localtime* file with a zone file under */usr/share/zoneinfo*. For example, to switch to the Mountain Standard Time zone, enter the following:

```
ws1:~ # ln -sf /usr/share/zoneinfo/MST /etc/localtime
```

Configuring Printing with CUPS

No matter what operating system you're using, one of the most important services it offers is the ability to send print jobs to a printer. Because of this, you need to be very familiar with Linux printing, even though it is *not* a requirement for the Linux+ exam. In this section, we cover the following topics related to printing in Linux:

- Configuring CUPS
- Using the Line Printer Daemon (lpd)

Let's begin by discussing how Linux printing works.

Configuring CUPS

All CUPS printers are defined in the */etc/cups/printers.conf* file. Although you can manually edit this file, you really should use the CUPS web-based administration utility instead. You can either configure CUPS to service a locally attached printer (and optionally make it available to other network users) or connect to a CUPS printer over the network. For example, to configure CUPS to use a locally attached printer, do the following:

1. On your Linux system, start a web browser and navigate to http://localhost:631.
2. Select Administration.
3. Under Printers, select Add Printer.
4. When prompted, log in as the administrative user you created previously.
5. Select a locally attached printer type under Local Printers and then select Continue.

TIP You could also select a network printer on this screen. All broadcasting CUPS printers on other network hosts are listed under Discovered Network Printers. To send print jobs to one of these printers, just select it.

6. In the Name field, enter a name for the printer.
7. In the Description field, enter a description of the printer.
8. In the Location field, enter a location for the printer.
9. If you want to share the printer with other network users, mark Share This Printer.
10. Select Continue.
11. Select the printer manufacturer; then select Continue.
12. In the Model field, select your printer model; then select Add Printer.
13. Configure your default options for the printer, such as paper size, color model, media source, print quality, two-sided printing, and so on. When complete, select Set Default Options.

At this point, a page is displayed indicating your printer has been added. The current status of your printer is displayed.

From the Printer Status page, you can manage your CUPS printer. You can send a test page, stop the printer, kill a print job, modify the printer configuration, or delete the printer altogether.

At this point, you can send print jobs to the printer. If you're using a graphical X application, you can simply select File | Print and then select the printer and click OK. You can also send print jobs from the command line to the printer. This is done using the lp command, which will send a specified file to the printer. The syntax for using lp is **lp -d <printer_name> <filename>**. For example, if I wanted to print the *myfiles* file in the current directory to the HPLJ2 printer I just created, I would enter **lp -d HPLJ2 ./myfiles** at the shell prompt, as shown here:

```
openSUSE:~ # lp -d HPLJ2 ./myfiles
request id is HPLJ2-2 (1 file(s))
```

As you can see in this example, the job is created and assigned an ID (in this case, HPLJ2-2). The job is added to the print queue and sent to the printer. The **lp** utility includes a variety of options besides **-d** that you can use to create print jobs, including the following:

- **-n *x*** Prints *x* number of copies
- **-m** E-mails a confirmation message to my local user account when the job is finished printing
- **-q *x*** Sets the priority of the print job to *x*
- **-o landscape** Prints the file landscape instead of portrait
- **-o sides=2** Prints the file double-sided on a printer that supports duplexing

You can also configure other Linux systems to print to the CUPS printer. Simply configure a new printer, but specify that it listen for CUPS announcements. The CUPS printer you configured should be displayed within 30 seconds. After you select it, all print jobs sent to that printer will be redirected over the network connection to your CUPS printer.

In addition, if you've installed Samba on your system, your CUPS printers are automatically shared. You can connect to them from Windows workstations and submit print jobs. Now that's cool!

In addition to the CUPS web-based administration utility, you can also use a variety of command-line tools to configure CUPS. To view CUPS printer information, you can use the lpstat utility. One of the most useful options you can use with lpstat is -t.

This will cause lpstat to display all information about all CUPS printers on the system, as this next example shows:

```
openSUSE:~ # lpstat -t
scheduler running
no system default destination
device for HPLJ2: parallel:/dev/lp0
HPLJ2 accepting requests since Fri 13 May 2011 10:57:13 AM MDT
printer HPLJ2 is idle.  enabled since Fri 13 May 2011 10:57:13 AM MDT
     Printer is now online.
```

This shows the default CUPS printer (HPLJ2), how it's connected (/dev/lp0), the print job currently being processed (if any), and a list of pending print jobs.

To cancel a pending print job, you can use the cancel command. The syntax is **cancel <job_ID>**. For example, suppose I sent a huge print job (a Linux user manual from */usr/share/doc/manual/*) and it was assigned a print ID of HPLJ2-4. While printing, I decided that this was a real waste of paper. I could kill the job and remove it from the print queue by entering **cancel HPLJ2-4** at the shell prompt. This can also be done from within the CUPS web-based administration utility. Just go to the Jobs tab and select Show Active Jobs. Locate the job that needs to be canceled and select Cancel Job.

If you have more than one CUPS printer connected, you can use the **lpoptions -d <printer>** command to specify the default printer. For example, to set the HPLJ5 printer as the default, I would enter **lpoptions -d HPLJ5**. This sets the default printer for all users on the system. Individual users can override this setting, however, by creating a file named *.lpoptions* in their home directory and adding the following directive:

```
default <printer_name>
```

If you want to view your printer's configuration settings, you can enter **lpoptions -l** at the shell prompt.

In addition to the lpoptions command, you can also use the **cupsaccept <printer_name>** or **cupsreject <printer_name>** command to enable or disable a printer's print queue. For example, I could enter **cupsreject HPLJ2** at the shell prompt to disable the printer's print queue, as shown in this example:

```
openSUSE:~ # cupsreject HPLJ2
openSUSE:~ # lpstat is -t
scheduler is running
system default destination: HPLJ2
device for HPLJ2: parallel:/dev/lp0
HPLJ2 not accepting requests since Fri 13 May 2011 11:03:07 AM MDT -
      Rejecting Jobs
printer HPLJ2 is idle.  enabled since Fri 13 May 2011 11:03:07 AM MDT
      Rejecting Jobs
```

The printer itself will continue processing queued print jobs, but cupsd will not allow any new jobs to enter the queue. The cupsdisable command also includes the --hold option, which stops printing after the current job is complete. To enable the queue again, I would enter **cupsaccept HPLJ2** at the shell prompt.

To disable the printer itself, not the queue, I could enter **cupsdisable HPLJ2** at the shell prompt, as this example shows:

```
openSUSE:~ # cupsdisable HPLJ2
openSUSE:~ # lpstat is -t
scheduler is running
system default destination: HPLJ2
device for HPLJ2: parallel:/dev/lp0
HPLJ2 accepting requests since Fri 13 May 2011 11:15:28 AM MDT
printer HPLJ2 disabled since Fri 13 May 2011 11:15:28 AM MDT -
     Paused
```

The print queue will continue to accept jobs, but none of them will be printed until I enter **cupsenable HPLJ2** at the shell prompt. The cupsenable command also includes the --release option to release pending jobs for printing.

Task	lpd Command-Line Utility
Print a document	lpr -P <printer_name> <filename>
View printer status	lpc status
View pending print jobs	lpq
Delete a pending print job from the queue	lprm <job_number>

Table 20-1 lpd Commands

By far, CUPS is the preferred printing system for modern Linux distributions. Years ago, the preferred printing system was the Line Printer Daemon (lpd). Most of the lpd commands have functionality similar to that offered by CUPS, as shown in Table 20-1.

As an interesting side note, these commands will also work with cupsd. For example, enter **lpc status** at the shell prompt and it will return the status of the CUPS printers.

Configuring E-mail

Although e-mail is important when using Linux systems, it is *not* a requirement for the Linux+ exam. Let's first look at reading messages stored in your local mail transfer agent (MTA). When you log in to a shell session, you will receive a notification if there are mail messages waiting for you. You can read messages for local users from the local MTA directly from the command line using the mail command at the shell prompt. When you do, a list of messages is displayed.

NOTE Some services running on Linux are configured to send notification messages to the root user.

These messages are stored in the user's mail queue, which is located in */var/spool/mail/*. The mail utility reads user's messages from the user's queue file. Because the mail utility is on the same system where the queue resides, there is no need that POP3 or IMAP support be configured. Enter the mail commands shown in Table 20-2 at the ? prompt.

Mail Command	Description
d	You can delete a message by entering **d <message_number>** at the ? prompt.
n	Enter **n** to display the next message in the queue.
r	You can reply to all recipients by entering **r <message_number>** at the ? prompt.
m	You can send a new message by entering **m <recipient>** at the ? prompt.
q	Enter **q** to quit mail.

Table 20-2 Mail Commands

To send a message, enter **mail <recipient_address>** at the shell prompt. Then enter a subject line and the text of the message. Press CTRL-D when done to actually send the message. Once done, the message is delivered to the other user's mail queue by the local MTA.

To view a list of unread messages in your mail queue, you can enter **mailq** at the shell prompt.

One can also configure aliases for the MTA running on a Linux system. Mail aliases redirect mail addressed to one user to another user's account. Use the */etc/aliases* file to configure aliases. This file defines one alias per line. The alias you define must point to an existing e-mail address. The syntax for this file follows:

```
<alias>:  <list of real e-mail addresses, separated by commas>
```

For example, the following two aliases must be present in this file on most Linux distributions:

```
postmaster:  root
mailer-daemon:      postmaster
```

These aliases cause any e-mail messages sent to the postmaster to be automatically redirected to the root user. Likewise, any e-mail messages sent to mailer-daemon will be redirected to postmaster (which will then be redirected to root). Depending on your distribution, you will probably find that many aliases are defined for you by default. Here is an example:

```
# General redirections for pseudo accounts in /etc/passwd.
administrator:      root
daemon:             root
lp:          root
news:        root
gnats:       root
nobody:      root
# "bin" used to be in /etc/passwd
bin:         root
```

Of course, you can enter your own custom aliases if needed. Just open the aliases file in a text editor and add the appropriate aliases, one per line. When done configuring aliases, you must run the newaliases command at the shell prompt as root to enable them.

Also use the *~/.forward* file to configure forwarding. Linux MTAs check for the existence of this file to configure forwarding of messages. Now email will automatically be forwarded to the email address in this file. To stop forwarding, delete this file.

NOTE The MTA will treat the addresses you enter in this file as an alias. This causes all e-mail to be forwarded to the forwarding e-mail address. Messages will *not* be delivered to the original user's mailbox.

Configuring SQL Databases

Another great Linux topic to understand that's *not* on the Linux+ exam requirements is SQL databases. A *database* is a collection of information organized so that data can be quickly selected and retrieved based on a search query created.

Database services run on a client/server model. Two database services are commonly implemented on Linux:

- MySQL
- PostgreSQL

By installing one of these database services, you install the software needed to run, operate, and manage the database using SQL (Structured Query Language), which is a standard language for accessing and manipulating databases.

Both of these database services are relational databases, which are hierarchical in nature. Relational databases are specialized to organize and store huge amounts of data. They are also designed to be highly scalable, allowing them to grow over time.

A relational database is organized using fields, records, and tables. A *field* is a single piece of information. A *record* is one complete set of fields, and a *table* is collection of records. Each table is identified by a name, such as Customers. Each table contains records (each one a single row) that contain one or more fields, which in turn contain the actual database data. For example, suppose you defined a table called Customers and create the following three records:

```
Last        First       Address                City        State       Zip
Tracy       Leah        1234 W. Longfellow     Bone        Idaho       83401
Morgan      Ken         3456 W. 100 S.         Rigby       Idaho       83442
```

Using the SQL language, you could create queries that select and retrieve specific data from the database. For example, suppose you were to compose the following query:

```
SELECT Last FROM Customers
```

The database would return the following data:

```
Last
Tracy
Morgan
```

You can use the following commands to manage data in an SQL database:

- **SELECT** Retrieves information from a table
- **UPDATE** Modifies information in a table
- **DELETE** Removes information from a table
- **INSERT INTO** Adds new data to a table
- **CREATE TABLE** Creates a new table
- **ALTER TABLE** Modifies an existing table
- **DROP TABLE** Deletes and existing table

A key feature of relational databases is the fact that you can create *relationships* between tables, which allows you to create interrelated data sets.

In order to manage data on the MySQL server, you must connect to it using some type of SQL client. You can choose from a plethora of different clients. If you can manipulate SQL Server data with this utility, all the other clients will be a piece of cake for you to use.

The command-line MySQL client is run by entering **mysql** at the shell prompt. The syntax is **mysql -h <hostname> -u <username> -p**. For example, to connect to the MySQL service running on the local Linux system as root, you would enter **mysql -h localhost -u root -p**. This is shown next:

```
openSUSE:/usr/bin # mysql -h localhost -u root -p
Enter password:
Welcome to the MySQL monitor.  Commands end with ; or \g.
Your MySQL connection id is 7
Server version: 5.6.12 openSUSE package
Copyright (c) 2000, 2013, Oracle and/or its affiliates. All rights reserved.
Oracle is a registered trademark of Oracle Corporation and/or its
affiliates. Other names may be trademarks of their respective owners.
Type 'help;' or '\h' for help. Type '\c' to clear the current input
statement.
mysql>
```

Questions

1. When conducting a needs assessment, what questions should you ask? (Choose two.)

   A. What problem will this installation fix?

   B. Which distribution should I use?

   C. Where can I get the best price on a new server?

   D. Who is requesting the new systems?

2. Which of the following is a properly stated goal in a needs assessment?

   A. Mike's boss wants a new server, so we're going to install it.

   B. We're going to install Linux on everyone's desktop.

   C. We need a new Linux server.

   D. The new Linux system will provide a network database to increase the documentation team's productivity by an anticipated 20 percent.

3. Suppose Karen from customer service approaches you and asks for a new Linux server for her team. Who else should you talk to as a part of your needs assessment? (Choose two.)

   A. Karen's boss

   B. Karen's coworkers

   C. The technical support supervisor

   D. Your hardware vendor

4. Which of the following are components of your project scope? (Choose two.)
   A. Customer demands
   B. Management decision-making
   C. Schedule
   D. Scale
5. You're responsible for implementing five new Linux servers in your organization's technical support department. The technical support supervisor has asked that four additional servers be added to the project. Due to time constraints, he won't allow you to adjust the original schedule. Which of the following is the most appropriate response?
   A. Ignore the request.
   B. Inform the supervisor that additional resources will have to be added to the project.
   C. Resign in protest.
   D. Cheerfully agree to the request and then miss the deadline.
6. You're installing new Linux systems that will be used by software engineers to develop advanced computer-aided design applications. Which distributions would be the best choices for this deployment? (Choose two.)
   A. Red Hat Enterprise Linux
   B. Red Hat Enterprise Desktop
   C. Red Hat Enterprise Linux Workstation
   D. SUSE Linux Enterprise Server
   E. SUSE Linux Enterprise Desktop
7. You're installing a new Linux system that will be used by an administrative assistant to type documents, create presentations, and manage e-mail. Which distributions would be the best choices for this deployment? (Choose two.)
   A. Red Hat Enterprise Linux
   B. Red Hat Enterprise Desktop
   C. Red Hat Enterprise Linux Workstation
   D. SUSE Linux Enterprise Server
   E. SUSE Linux Enterprise Desktop
8. You're installing a new Linux server that will be used to host mission-critical database applications. This server will be heavily utilized by a large number of users every day. Which distributions would be the best choices for this deployment? (Choose two.)
   A. Red Hat Enterprise Linux
   B. Red Hat Client

C. Red Hat Enterprise Linux Workstation

D. SUSE Linux Enterprise Server

E. SUSE Linux Enterprise Desktop

9. You're planning to install Linux on a system that you've built out of spare parts. Several components in the system aren't listed on your distribution's HCL. This system will be used by your team's administrative assistant to manage employee schedules, send and receive e-mail, and track employee hours. What should you do?

   A. Install the distribution anyway and hope for the best.

   B. Install the distribution and then install the latest product updates.

   C. Replace the incompatible parts with supported hardware.

   D. Spend three days scouring the Internet looking for drivers.

10. You're planning to install Fedora on a system that uses a 32-bit CPU. Which distribution architecture should you download?

    A. IA-64

    B. x86-Celeron

    C. x86-64

    D. x86

11. You're planning to install Fedora on a system that uses a 64-bit AMD multicore CPU. Which distribution architecture should you download?

    A. IA-64

    B. x86-AMD

    C. x86-64

    D. x86

12. You're installing a new Linux system. This system will be used by a civil engineer to model the behavior of buildings and bridges during an earthquake. This system must run as fast as possible. It must protect the integrity of the data if the system goes down unexpectedly. If it does go down, the system needs to be backed up and running as quickly as possible. Which filesystem would be the best choice?

    A. VFAT

    B. FAT32

    C. ext4

    D. ext3

13. Which partition is used for virtual memory by a Linux system?

    A. pagefile

    B. swap

    C. /swap

    D. /boot

14. If your system has 1GB of RAM installed, how big should your swap partition be?
    A. 256MB
    B. 1GB
    C. 512GB
    D. Depends on what the system will be used for
15. Which of the following directories should have their own partition? (Choose three.)
    A. /bin
    B. /boot
    C. /etc
    D. /usr
    E. /home
    F. /root
    G. /dev
16. You're installing a new Linux server. This system will function as an e-mail server for your organization. What ports should you open on its host firewall? (Choose three.)
    A. 110
    B. 80
    C. 25
    D. 143
    E. 443
17. You need to install Linux on a workstation. The hard drive has been wiped and is ready for the new operating system. You insert your Linux installation DVD in the optical drive and boot the system. Instead of the installation routine starting, the screen displays an error message indicating that an operating system couldn't be found. What's the most likely cause of the problem?
    A. Your Linux DVD is damaged.
    B. The hard drive is failing and needs to be replaced.
    C. The DVD drive is malfunctioning.
    D. The boot device order is set incorrectly in the BIOS.
18. Your Linux system uses two SATA hard disk drives. Which of the following refers to the second SATA drive in the system?
    A. /dev/sda
    B. /dev/sdc
    C. /dev/sdb
    D. /dev/sdd

19. Your Linux system uses a single SATA hard disk drive. Which of the following refers to the first partition on the drive?
   A. /dev/sda1
   B. /dev/sdb1
   C. /dev/sda2
   D. /dev/pdb2
20. Your Linux system uses a single SATA hard disk drive. Which of the following refers to the second partition on the drive?
   A. /dev/sda1
   B. /dev/hdb1
   C. /dev/sda2
   D. /dev/hdb2
21. Your Linux system uses two SCSI hard disk drives. The first drive is assigned SCSI ID 0; the second drive is assigned SCSI ID 1. Which of the following refers to the first partition on the second SCSI drive in the system?
   A. /dev/sda1
   B. /dev/sdc1
   C. /dev/sdb1
   D. /dev/sdd1
22. Which locale environment variable configures your default character encoding?
   A. LC_NUMERIC
   B. LC_CTYPE
   C. LC_MEASUREMENT
   D. LC_CHAR
23. Which locale value specifies French Canadian using Unicode encoding?
   A. en_US.UTF-8
   B. fr_CA.UTF-8
   C. fr_CA.ASCII
   D. en_CA.ASCII
24. Which locale variable overrides all other locale variables?
   A. LC_ALL
   B. LANG
   C. LANGUAGE
   D. LC_CTYPE–-d MIN2300W –-n 2 /home/tux/employees.txtlp –-d MIN2300W /home/tux/employees.txt–-d MIN2300Wlp default = MIN2300Wlpoptions

25. Which CUPS component handles IPP printing requests from CUPS clients?
    A. CUPS Scheduler
    B. PDLs
    C. CUPS Backends
    D. PPDs
26. Your Linux system has an IP address of 192.168.1.20. What URL should you use in a browser to access the CUPS web-based administration utility?
    A. http://192.168.1.20
    B. https://192.168.1.20
    C. http://192.168.1.20:631
    D. http://192.168.1.20/cups
27. Which directive in the */etc/cups/cupsd.conf* file specifies whether or not cupsd will announce its printers using broadcasts on the network?
    A. BrowseAddress
    B. BrowseAllow
    C. Broadcast
    D. Browsing
28. Which command can be used to set the hardware clock on a Linux system to the system time?
    A. hwclock -w
    B. hwclock -s
    C. hwclock -set
    D. hwclock -r
29. Which IP port does the NTP daemon use to synchronize time?
    A. 636
    B. 80
    C. 443
    D. 123

Answers

1. **A, D.** You should determine why the new systems are needed and who will be using them.
2. **D.** This response clearly states the goal of the project and is measurable.
3. **A, B.** Karen's boss and her coworkers are key stakeholders in the project.

4. **C, D.** The project scope is composed of schedule, scale, and resources.
5. **B.** The best response to this situation is to have a frank discussion with the stakeholder and point out the consequences of the decision. Either the scale will have to be reduced or more resources must be added to the project to complete it in the same time frame.
6. **C, E.** Technically, any Linux distribution could be used in this role. However, options C and E are specifically optimized for these kinds of tasks.
7. **B, E.** Red Hat Enterprise Desktop and SLED are optimized for basic workstation tasks such as word processing.
8. **A, D.** Red Hat Enterprise Linux and SUSE Linux Enterprise Server are designed for high-demand network servers.
9. **C.** The best approach is to use supported hardware.
10. **D.** A 32-bit CPU uses the x86 architecture.
11. **C.** The 64-bit AMD CPU uses a 64-bit x86 architecture.
12. **C.** The ext4 filesystem is the fastest, and it uses enhanced journaling to speed crash recovery while maintaining the overall integrity of the system.
13. **B.** Linux systems use a dedicated swap partition by default for virtual memory.
14. **D.** The optimal size of the swap partition depends on what the system will be used for. A workstation running lots of applications at once will need a large swap partition. A server providing network services may not need one as large.
15. **B, D, E.** You should consider creating separate partitions for /boot, /usr, and /home.
16. **A, C, D.** Port 110 is used by the POP3 e-mail protocol. Port 25 is used by the SMTP e-mail protocol. Port 143 is used by the IMAP e-mail protocol.
17. **D.** The most likely cause of this problem is that the system is set to boot off the hard drive first. When it can't find the operating system on the hard drive, the error message is displayed.
18. **C.** /dev/sdb points to the second hard drive installed in a system.
19. **A.** /dev/sda1 points to the first partition on the first hard drive in the system.
20. **C.** /dev/sda2 points to the second partition on the first hard drive in the system.
21. **C.** /dev/sdb1 points to the first partition on the second hard drive in the system.
22. **B.** The LC_CTYPE environment variable configures the default character encoding.
23. **B.** The fr_CA.UTF-8 locale value specifies French Canadian using Unicode encoding.
24. **A.** The LC_ALL locale variable overrides all other locale variables.
25. **A.** The CUPS Scheduler handles IPP printing requests from CUPS clients.

26. **C.** The http://192.168.1.20:631 URL can be used to access the CUPS administration utility on a Linux system with an IP address of 192.168.1.20.
27. **D.** The Browsing directive in the */etc/cups/cupsd.conf* file specifies whether cupsd will announce its printers using broadcasts on the network.
28. **A.** The **hwclock -w** command can be used to set the hardware clock on a Linux system to the system time.
29. **D.** Port 123 is used by the NTP daemon to synchronize time.

APPENDIX

About the Online Content

This book comes with TotalTester Online customizable practice exam software with 180 practice exam questions and other book resources, including video demonstrations of select chapter exercises and downloadable virtual machines.

System Requirements

The current and previous major versions of the following desktop browsers are recommended and supported: Chrome, Microsoft Edge, Firefox, and Safari. These browsers update frequently, and sometimes an update may cause compatibility issues with the TotalTester Online or other content hosted on the Training Hub. If you run into a problem using one of these browsers, please try using another until the problem is resolved.

Your Total Seminars Training Hub Account

To get access to the online content you will need to create an account on the Total Seminars Training Hub. Registration is free, and you will be able to track all your online content using your account. You may also opt in if you wish to receive marketing information from McGraw-Hill Education or Total Seminars, but this is not required for you to gain access to the online content.

Privacy Notice

McGraw-Hill Education values your privacy. Please be sure to read the Privacy Notice available during registration to see how the information you have provided will be used. You may view our Corporate Customer Privacy Policy by visiting the McGraw-Hill Education Privacy Center. Visit the **mheducation.com** site and click **Privacy** at the bottom of the page.

Single User License Terms and Conditions

Online access to the digital content included with this book is governed by the McGraw-Hill Education License Agreement outlined next. By using this digital content you agree to the terms of that license.

Access To register and activate your Total Seminars Training Hub account, simply follow these easy steps.

1. Go to **hub.totalsem.com/mheclaim**.
2. To Register and create a new Training Hub account, enter your e-mail address, name, and password. No further personal information (such as credit card number) is required to create an account.

NOTE If you already have a Total Seminars Training Hub account, select **Log in** and enter your e-mail and password. Otherwise, follow the remaining steps.

3. Enter your Product Key: `twwc-2d6p-2b4z`
4. Click to accept the user license terms.
5. Click **Register and Claim** to create your account. You will be taken to the Training Hub and have access to the content for this book.

Duration of License Access to your online content through the Total Seminars Training Hub will expire one year from the date the publisher declares the book out of print.

Your purchase of this McGraw-Hill Education product, including its access code, through a retail store is subject to the refund policy of that store.

Restrictions on Transfer The user is receiving only a limited right to use the Content for the user's own internal and personal use, dependent on purchase and continued ownership of this book. The user may not reproduce, forward, modify, create derivative works based upon, transmit, distribute, disseminate, sell, publish, or sublicense the Content or in any way commingle the Content with other third-party content without McGraw-Hill Education's consent.

Limited Warranty The McGraw-Hill Education Content is provided on an "as is" basis. Neither McGraw-Hill Education nor its licensors make any guarantees or warranties of any kind, either express or implied, including, but not limited to, implied warranties of merchantability or fitness for a particular purpose or use as to any McGraw-Hill Education Content or the information therein or any warranties as to the accuracy, completeness, correctness, or results to be obtained from, accessing or using the McGraw-Hill Education Content, or any material referenced in such Content or any information entered into licensee's product by users or other persons and/or any material available on or that can be accessed through the licensee's product (including via any hyperlink or otherwise) or as to non-infringement of third-party rights. Any warranties of any kind, whether express or implied, are disclaimed.

Any material or data obtained through use of the McGraw-Hill Education Content is at your own discretion and risk and user understands that it will be solely responsible for any resulting damage to its computer system or loss of data.

Neither McGraw-Hill Education nor its licensors shall be liable to any subscriber or to any user or anyone else for any inaccuracy, delay, interruption in service, error or omission, regardless of cause, or for any damage resulting therefrom.

In no event will McGraw-Hill Education or its licensors be liable for any indirect, special or consequential damages, including but not limited to, lost time, lost money, lost profits or good will, whether in contract, tort, strict liability or otherwise, and whether or not such damages are foreseen or unforeseen with respect to any use of the McGraw-Hill Education Content.

TotalTester Online

TotalTester Online provides you with a simulation of the CompTIA Linux+ exam. Exams can be taken in Practice Mode or Exam Mode. Practice Mode provides an assistance window with hints, references to the book, explanations of the correct and incorrect answers, and the option to check your answer as you take the test. Exam Mode provides a simulation of the actual exam. The number of questions, the types of questions, and the time allowed are intended to be an accurate representation of the exam environment. The option to customize your quiz allows you to create custom exams from selected domains or chapters, and you can further customize the number of questions and time allowed.

To take a test, follow the instructions provided in the previous section to register and activate your Total Seminars Training Hub account. When you register you will be taken to the Total Seminars Training Hub. From the Training Hub Home page, select **CompTIA Linux+ All-in-One Exam Guide (XK0-004) TotalTester** from the Study drop-down menu at the top of the page, or from the list of Your Topics on the Home page. You can then select the option to customize your quiz and begin testing yourself in Practice Mode or Exam Mode. All exams provide an overall grade and a grade broken down by domain.

Other Book Resources

The following sections detail the other resources available with your book. You can access these items by selecting the Resources tab, or by selecting **CompTIA Linux+ All-in-One Exam Guide (XK0-004) Resources** from the Study drop-down menu at the top of the page or from the list of Your Topics on the Home page. The menu on the right side of the screen outlines all of the available resources.

Virtual Machines

You can download the virtual machine files included with this book by navigating to the Resources tab and selecting Virtual Machines. Then select VM Setup Instructions to view detailed instructions on how to download and install the two virtual machine images provided.

Videos

Video MP4 clips from the authors of this book provide detailed demonstrations of select chapter exercises. You can access these videos by navigating to the Resources tab and selecting Videos.

Book Figures

Certain figures that were too wide to fit well in the format of the book are provided for reference. You can access these by navigating to the Resources tab and selecting Book Figures.

Technical Support

For questions regarding the TotalTester or operation of the Training Hub, visit **www.totalsem.com** or e-mail **support@totalsem.com**.

For questions regarding book content, visit **www.mheducation.com/customerservice**.

INDEX

A

B

C

D

E

F

H

I

M

O

Q

R

S

U

V

W

X

Y

Z